# OUR WORLD'S STORY

### Series Authors

**Dr. Richard G. Boehm**

**Claudia Hoone**

**Dr. Thomas M. McGowan**

**Dr. Mabel C. McKinney-Browning**

**Dr. Ofelia B. Miramontes**

### Series Consultants

**Dr. Alma Flor Ada**

**Dr. Phillip Bacon**

**Dr. W. Dorsey Hammond**

**Dr. Asa Grant Hilliard, III**

**HARCOURT BRACE & COMPANY**

Orlando  Atlanta  Austin  Boston  San Francisco  Chicago  Dallas

New York  Toronto  London

## SERIES AUTHORS

**Dr. Richard G. Boehm**
Professor
Department of Geography and Planning
Southwest Texas State University
San Marcos, Texas

**Claudia Hoone**
Teacher
Ralph Waldo Emerson School #58
Indianapolis, Indiana

**Dr. Thomas M. McGowan**
Associate Professor
Division of Curriculum and Instruction
Arizona State University
Tempe, Arizona

**Dr. Mabel C. McKinney-Browning**
Director
Division for Public Education
American Bar Association
Chicago, Illinois

**Dr. Ofelia B. Miramontes**
Associate Professor
School of Education
University of Colorado
Boulder, Colorado

## SERIES CONSULTANTS

**Dr. Alma Flor Ada**
Professor
School of Education
University of San Francisco
San Francisco, California

**Dr. Phillip Bacon**
Professor Emeritus of
   Geography and Anthropology
University of Houston
Houston, Texas

**Dr. W. Dorsey Hammond**
Professor of Education
Oakland University
Rochester, Michigan

**Dr. Asa Grant Hilliard, III**
Fuller E. Callaway Professor of Urban
   Education
Georgia State University
Atlanta, Georgia

## MEDIA AND LITERATURE SPECIALISTS

**Dr. Joseph A. Braun, Jr.**
Professor of Elementary Social Studies
Department of Curriculum and Instruction
Illinois State University
Normal, Illinois

**Meredith McGowan**
Youth Librarian
Tempe Public Library
Tempe, Arizona

## GRADE-LEVEL CONSULTANTS AND REVIEWERS

**Sandra Alfonsi**
Assistant Professor
Fordham University
Bronx, New York
Member, Academic Advisory Board
Hadassah Curriculum Watch
   (History Specialist)

**Dr. Penny S. Arnold**
Teacher
Springfield Local Schools
Akron, Ohio

**Alfred Bell**
Social Studies Supervisor
Knox County Schools
Knoxville, Tennessee

**Dr. Lois Harrison-Jones**
Former Superintendent of Boston,
   Massachusetts, Public Schools and
   Richmond, Virginia, Public Schools

**Shabbir Mansuri**
Founding Director
**Susan L. Douglass**
Affiliated Scholar
Council on Islamic Education
Fountain Valley, California

**Lawrence W. McBride**
Professor
Department of History
Illinois State University
Normal, Illinois

**Randy Milligan**
Teacher
Pampa Middle School
Pampa, Texas

**Ronald V. Sartor**
Social Studies Consultant
Warren Consolidated School District
Warren, Michigan

**Pat Shipman**
Adjunct Professor
Department of Anthropology
Pennsylvania State University
University Park, Pennsylvania

**Alan R. Standlee**
Teacher
Clute Intermediate School
Brazosport Independent School District
Clute, Texas

**Pat Steinbronn**
Teacher
St. Charles School
Fort Wayne, Indiana

Copyright © 1997 by Harcourt Brace & Company

Requests for permission to make copies of any part of the work should be mailed to: Permissions Department, Harcourt Brace & Company, 6277 Sea Harbor Drive, Orlando, Florida 32887-6777.

HARCOURT BRACE and Quill Design is a registered trademark of Harcourt Brace & Company.

Acknowledgments and other credits appear in the back of this book.

Printed in the United States of America

ISBN 0-15-302043-1

   4 5 6 7 8 9 10   032   99   98   97

# CONTENTS

25,000-year-old sculpture

Hammurabi

Tutankhamen

Olmec mask

Qin Chinese soldier

Young girl from India

Greek charioteer

Julius Caesar

Theodora

Genghis Khan

Egyptian trader

Viking wood carving

UNIT 7

Woman of the Renaissance

Benin sculpture

Ming dynasty empress

Queen Victoria

Faces of the Great Depression

United States marine in Vietnam

Woman from Peru

Muslim woman from North Africa

Young girl from Senegal

# F.Y.I.

## LITERATURE, PRIMARY SOURCES, AND DOCUMENTS

## LEARNING FROM VISUALS

### GEOGRAPHY SKILLS

### CHART AND GRAPH SKILLS

## BUILDING CITIZENSHIP

### READING AND WRITING SKILLS

# CHARTS, GRAPHS, DIAGRAMS, TABLES, AND TIME LINES

# ATLAS

## CONTENTS

ARCTIC OCEAN

180° 160° W 140° W 120° W 100° W 80° W 60° W

80° N

*Greenland*
**(DENMARK)**

ALASKA
(U.S.)

60° N

**CANADA**

**NORTH
AMERICA**

40° N

**UNITED STATES**

*Azores*
**(PORTUGAL)**

**ATLANTIC
OCEAN**

*Bermuda*
**(U.K.)**

Area of inset

Tropic of Cancer

20° N

*Midway
Islands*
**(U.S.)**

**MEXICO**

**CAPE VERDE**

HAWAII
**(U.S.)**

**PACIFIC**

**OCEAN**

**VENEZUELA**

**GUYANA**
**SURINAME**

**COLOMBIA**

**FRENCH GUIANA
(FRANCE)**

Equator

*Galápagos
Islands*
**(ECUADOR)**

**ECUADOR**

**BRAZIL**

*Tokelau*
**(N.Z.)**

**KIRIBATI**

**PERU**

**SOUTH
AMERICA**

*American
Samoa*
**(U.S.)**

**WESTERN
SAMOA**

*Cook
Islands*
**(N.Z.)**

*French
Polynesia*
**(FRANCE)**

**BOLIVIA**

**PARAGUAY**

20° S

**TONGA**

Tropic of Capricorn

*Pitcairn*
**(U.K.)**

**CHILE**

*Niue*
**(N.Z.)**

*Easter Island*
**(CHILE)**

**URUGUAY**

**ARGENTINA**

40° S

**PACIFIC**

**OCEAN**

*Falkland
Islands*
**(U.K.)**

*South
Georgia*
**(U.K.)**

60° S

Antarctic Circle

80° S

180° 160° W 140° W 120° W 100° W 80° W 60° W

**UNITED STATES**

30° N

100° W

*Gulf of Mexico*

**ATLANTIC**

**BAHAMAS**

OCEAN

Tropic of Cancer

**MEXICO**

20° N

20° N

**CUBA**

*Turks and
Caicos* **(U.K.)**

N

*Puerto
Rico*
**(U.S.)**

**Anguilla (U.K.)**

W E

*Cayman
Islands*
**(U.K.)**

**HAITI**

**DOMINICAN
REPUBLIC**

**St. Martin (FRANCE AND NETH.)**

S

**BELIZE**

**JAMAICA**

*Virgin Islands*
**(U.S. AND U.K.)**

**ANTIGUA AND BARBUDA**

*Montserrat* **(U.K.)**

**Guadeloupe (FRANCE)**

**GUATEMALA**

**HONDURAS**

*Caribbean Sea*

**ST. KITTS
AND NEVIS**

**DOMINICA**

**EL SALVADOR**

*Martinique* **(FRANCE)**

**NICARAGUA**

**ST. LUCIA**

**BARBADOS**

**PACIFIC OCEAN**

*Aruba*
**(NETH.)**

*Netherlands
Antilles*
**(NETH.)**

**ST. VINCENT AND
THE GRENADINES**

10° N

**GRENADA**

**TRINIDAD AND
TOBAGO**

10° N

*Panama
Canal*

**A2**

0     200     400 Miles

0   200   400 Kilometers

Azimuthal Equal-Area Projection

**COSTA
RICA**

**PANAMA**

**COLOMBIA**

90° W

80° W

70° W

**VENEZUELA**

**GUYANA**

60° W

ARCTIC OCEAN

Arctic Circle

RUSSIA

ASIA

EUROPE

ICELAND

KAZAKHSTAN

MONGOLIA

NORTH KOREA

JAPAN

PACIFIC OCEAN

GEORGIA
ARMENIA
AZERBAIJAN
TURKEY
UZBEKISTAN
KYRGYZSTAN
TAJIKISTAN
TURKMENISTAN
CYPRUS
SYRIA
LEBANON
ISRAEL
IRAQ
IRAN
AFGHANISTAN
SOUTH KOREA
CHINA

Canary Is. (SPAIN)
MOROCCO
TUNISIA
JORDAN
KUWAIT
BAHRAIN
QATAR
PAKISTAN
NEPAL
BHUTAN

WESTERN SAHARA (MOROCCO)
ALGERIA
LIBYA
EGYPT
SAUDI ARABIA
U.A.E.
OMAN
INDIA
BANGLADESH
BURMA (MYANMAR)
LAOS
TAIWAN

MAURITANIA
MALI
NIGER
CHAD
SUDAN
ERITREA
YEMEN
THAILAND
VIETNAM
PHILIPPINES

Northern Mariana Islands (U.S.)
Guam (U.S.)
MARSHALL ISLANDS

SENEGAL
BURKINA FASO
BENIN
NIGERIA
AFRICA
CENTRAL AFRICAN REPUBLIC
DJIBOUTI
CAMBODIA

GUINEA
SIERRA LEONE
CÔTE D'IVOIRE
LIBERIA
GHANA
TOGO
EQU. GUINEA
CAMEROON
ETHIOPIA
SOMALIA
MALDIVES
SRI LANKA
BRUNEI
MALAYSIA

PALAU
FEDERATED STATES OF MICRONESIA

GUINEA-BISSAU
GABON
CONGO
UGANDA
KENYA

THE GAMBIA
SÃO TOMÉ AND PRÍNCIPE
ZAIRE
RWANDA
BURUNDI
SINGAPORE
INDONESIA
PAPUA NEW GUINEA
NAURU
KIRIBATI

CABINDA (ANGOLA)
SEYCHELLES
INDIAN OCEAN
TUVALU

TANZANIA
COMOROS
SOLOMON ISLANDS

ANGOLA
MALAWI
ZAMBIA
MOZAMBIQUE
MADAGASCAR
VANUATU
FIJI

NAMIBIA
ZIMBABWE
MAURITIUS
New Caledonia (FRANCE)

BOTSWANA
Reunion (FRANCE)
AUSTRALIA

ATLANTIC OCEAN

SWAZILAND
SOUTH AFRICA
LESOTHO
NEW ZEALAND

N
W E
S

Kerguelen Archipelago (FRANCE)

0    1,000    2,000 Miles
0    1,000    2,000 Kilometers
Scale accurate at equator
Robinson Projection

ANTARCTICA

— National border

## Abbreviations

EQU. GUINEA — EQUATORIAL GUINEA
NETH. — NETHERLANDS
N.Z. — NEW ZEALAND
U.A.E. — UNITED ARAB EMIRATES
U.K. — UNITED KINGDOM
U.S. — UNITED STATES

EUROPE

FINLAND

NORWAY
SWEDEN
RUSSIA

ESTONIA
LATVIA
North Sea
Baltic Sea
LITHUANIA

UNITED KINGDOM
DENMARK
KALININGRAD (RUSSIA)
BELARUS

IRELAND
NETHERLANDS
GERMANY
POLAND
UKRAINE

BELGIUM
LUXEMBOURG
CZECH REPUBLIC
SLOVAKIA
MOLDOVA

LIECHTENSTEIN
AUSTRIA
HUNGARY
ROMANIA

FRANCE
SWITZERLAND
SLOVENIA
CROATIA
Black Sea

SAN MARINO
BOSNIA AND HERZEGOVINA
YUGOSLAVIA
BULGARIA

ANDORRA
MONACO
Corsica (FRANCE)
ITALY
MACEDONIA
Adriatic Sea
ALBANIA
TURKEY

PORTUGAL
SPAIN
Sardinia (ITALY)
VATICAN CITY
GREECE

Balearic Islands (SPAIN)
Sicily (ITALY)
Mediterranean Sea
MALTA
Crete (GREECE)

GIBRALTAR (U.K.)

0    200    400 Miles
0    200    400 Kilometers
Azimuthal Equal-Area Projection

ATLANTIC OCEAN

N
W E
S

# ATLAS

## THE WORLD: PHYSICAL

180°   160°W   140°W   120°W   100°W   80°W   60°W

80°N   ARCTIC   OCEAN

Beaufort Sea

Queen Elizabeth Islands

Baffin Island

Greenland

Mt. McKinley
20,320 ft.
(6,194 m)

Great Bear Lake

Bering
Sea

Yukon R.

Mt. Logan
19,524 ft.
(5,951 m)

Great Slave Lake

Hudson Bay

Gulf of Alaska

**NORTH AMERICA**

Aleutian Islands

Vancouver Island

Columbia R.

ROCKY MOUNTAINS

Mackenzie

Great Lakes

Newfoundland

40°N

GREAT PLAINS

Missouri R.

Mississippi R.

Ohio R.

APPALACHIAN MTS.

Azores

Mt. Whitney
14,494 ft.
(4,418 m)

Colorado R.

Bermuda

ATLANTIC OCEAN

Gulf of Mexico

Bahamas

Tropic of Cancer

20°N

Hawaiian Islands

Citlaltepetl
18,701 ft.
(5,700 m)

Yucatán Peninsula

Cuba

Hispaniola

West Indies

Cape Verde Islands

PACIFIC OCEAN

Caribbean Sea

Orinoco River

Guiana Highlands

Galápagos Islands

AMAZON

Amazon R.

Equator

Polynesia

BASIN

**SOUTH AMERICA**

ANDES MOUNTAINS

Atacama Desert

Brazilian Highlands

20°S

Gran Chaco

Paraná River

Tropic of Capricorn

Mt. Aconcagua
22,831 ft.
(6,959 m)

Pampa

40°S

Patagonia

Falkland Islands

Strait of Magellan

Tierra del Fuego

Cape Horn

60°S

Antarctic Circle

Antarctic Peninsula

80°S

Ross Sea

180°   160°W   140°W   120°W   100°W   80°W   60°W

### NORTHERN POLAR REGION

50°E   120°E   90°E   60°E   30°E

Sea of Okhotsk

150°E

**ASIA**

**EUROPE**

Kamchatka Peninsula

Severnaya Zemlya

Novaya Zemlya

Barents Sea

New Siberian Is.

70°N

Baltic Sea

0   400   800 Miles
0   400   800 Kilometers
Azimuthal Equidistant Projection

ARCTIC OCEAN

Svalbard

Norwegian Sea

North Sea

180°

Wrangel Island

North Pole

Bering Sea

Bering Strait

British Isles

Beaufort Sea

80°N

Iceland

BROOKS RANGE

North Magnetic Pole

Queen Elizabeth Islands

Greenland

ATLANTIC OCEAN

70°N

Baffin Bay

60°N   Arctic Circle   30°W

150°W

**A4**

**NORTH   AMERICA**

ARCTIC OCEAN

20° W  0°  20° E  40° E  60° E  80° E  100° E  120° E  140° E  160° E  180°

Svalbard
Severnaya Zemlya
Novaya Zemlya
New Siberian Islands
80° N

Arctic Circle
Iceland

Barents Sea

British Isles
North Sea
Baltic Sea
North European Plain

URAL MTS.
Volga R.
Yenisey River
Ob River
Irtysh River
Lena River
Amur R.
Kamchatka Peninsula
60° N

EUROPE
Mt. Elbrus 18,510 ft. (5,642 m)
SIBERIA
Sea of Okhotsk

ALPS
Mont Blanc 15,771 ft. (4,807 m)
Danube R.
Pyrenees
Balkan Peninsula
Black Sea
Caspian Sea
Aral Sea
ASIA
TIAN SHAN
GOBI (DESERT)
Kuril Is.
Hokkaido
40° N

Iberian Peninsula
Asia Minor
Caucasus Mts.
Tigris R.
Euphrates R.
HINDU KUSH
K2 28,250 ft. (8,611 m)
Plateau of Tibet
Huang He
Honshu
Sea of Japan
Shikoku
Kyushu

Madeira Islands
Atlas Mts.
Mediterranean Sea
Nile R.
Persian Gulf
Red Sea
HIMALAYAS
Mt. Everest 29,028 ft. (8,848 m)
Chang Jiang
East China Sea
PACIFIC OCEAN

Canary Islands
SAHARA
Arabian Peninsula
Thar Desert
Ganges R.
Taiwan
20° N

SAHEL
Lake Chad
Arabian Sea
Deccan Plateau
Bay of Bengal
Hainan
South China Sea
Philippine Islands
Micronesia

Niger River
AFRICA
Ethiopian Highlands
Sri Lanka
Maldives
Malay Peninsula
Sumatra
Borneo
0°

Congo River
CONGO BASIN
Mt. Kenya 17,058 ft. (5,199 m)
Lake Victoria
Mt. Kilimanjaro 19,340 ft. (5,895 m)
Seychelles
Celebes
New Guinea
Melanesia

Lake Tanganyika
Lake Nyasa
INDIAN OCEAN
Java
Fiji
20° S

ATLANTIC OCEAN
Madagascar
Kalahari Desert
AUSTRALIA
GREAT VICTORIA DESERT
GREAT DIVIDING RANGE

Cape of Good Hope
Cape Agulhas
Darling R.
Murray R.
Mt. Kosciusko 7,316 ft. (2,230 m)
40° S

N
W E
S

1,000  2,000 Miles
1,000  2,000 Kilometers
Robinson Projection
Scale accurate at equator

Tasmania

60° S

Ross Sea
80° S

ANTARCTICA

20° W  0°  20° E  40° E  60° E  80° E  100° E  120° E  140° E  160° E  180°

**SOUTHERN POLAR REGION**

South Shetland Islands
South Georgia
Bellingshausen Sea
Antarctic Peninsula
Alexander I.
ELLSWORTH LAND
Weddell Sea
60° W
30° W

PACIFIC OCEAN
150° W
120° W
MARIE BYRD LAND
Vinson Massif 16,860 ft. (5,139 m)
Ronne Ice Shelf
ATLANTIC OCEAN

70° S
Ross Sea
Ross Ice Shelf
TRANSANTARCTIC MOUNTAINS
POLAR PLATEAU
South Pole
80° S
ANTARCTICA
QUEEN MAUD LAND
0°

180°

WILKES LAND
ENDERBY LAND
Antarctic Circle
30° E
60° E

South Magnetic Pole
150° E
120° E
90° E

400  800 Miles
400  800 Kilometers
Azimuthal Equidistant Projection

# ATLAS
## AFRICA: POLITICAL

**EUROPE**

**ASIA**

ATLANTIC OCEAN

Mediterranean Sea

Madeira Islands (PORTUGAL)

Ceuta (SPAIN)
Algiers
Tunis
Tangier
Rabat
Oran
Constantine
Melilla (SPAIN)
Fès
Casablanca
Marrakech
**TUNISIA**
Sfax
Tripoli

**MOROCCO**

Canary Islands (SPAIN)

Banghazi
Alexandria
Port Said
Tanta
Al Jizah
Suez
Cairo

**ALGERIA**

**LIBYA**

**EGYPT**

WESTERN SAHARA (Occupied by Morocco)
El Aaiún

Tropic of Cancer

Aswan

Tropic of Cancer

**MAURITANIA**
Nouakchott

**NIGER**

**CHAD**

Port Sudan

Red Sea

Omdurman
**ERITREA**
Asmara

Dakar
Timbuktu
**MALI**
Gao
Khartoum
**SUDAN**

**SENEGAL**
Niamey
Kano
**GAMBIA**
Banjul
Bamako
**BURKINA FASO**
Ouagadougou
N'Djamena
**DJIBOUTI**
Djibouti

Gulf of Aden

**GUINEA-BISSAU**
Bissau
**BENIN**
**NIGERIA**
Abuja
Addis Ababa
Dire Dawa

**GUINEA**
**TOGO**
Ogbomosho
Ibadan
**ETHIOPIA**

Conakry
**SIERRA LEONE**
**CÔTE D'IVOIRE**
**GHANA**
Lomé
Lagos
Porto-Novo
**CENTRAL AFRICAN REPUBLIC**
Freetown
Monrovia
Yamoussoukro
Accra
Malabo
Douala
**SOMALIA**
**LIBERIA**
Abidjan
**CAMEROON**
Bangui
**EQUATORIAL GUINEA**
Yaoundé
Mogadishu
Gulf of Guinea

**SAO TOME AND PRINCIPE**
São Tomé
Libreville
**GABON**
**CONGO**
**UGANDA**
Kisangani
Kampala
**KENYA**
Kisumu
Kismaayo
Annobón (EQUATORIAL GUINEA)
**ZAIRE**
**RWANDA**
Kigali
Lake Victoria
Nairobi

**INDIAN OCEAN**
Ascension (UNITED KINGDOM)
Brazzaville
Kinshasa
Bujumbura
**BURUNDI**
Mwanza
Mombasa

Equator

Kananga
Lake Tanganyika
Dodoma
Mbuji-Mayi
**TANZANIA**
Dar es Salaam
Luanda

St. Helena (UNITED KINGDOM)
Kolwezi
Lake Malawi
**COMOROS**
Moroni

ATLANTIC OCEAN
Lobito
**ANGOLA**
Lubumbashi
Kitwe
**MALAWI**
Lilongwe
Huambo
**ZAMBIA**
Blantyre
Lusaka
Harare
**MOZAMBIQUE**
**ZIMBABWE**
Beira
Bulawayo
Antananarivo

**NAMIBIA**
**BOTSWANA**
**MADAGASCAR**
Windhoek

Tropic of Capricorn

Mozambique Channel

Gaborone
Pretoria
Maputo
Johannesburg
Mbabane
**SWAZILAND**
Kimberley
Bloemfontein
**LESOTHO**
Maseru
Durban

**SOUTH AFRICA**

Cape Town
Port Elizabeth

---

**Legend**

— National border
⬟ National capital
• Major city

A6

0 — 500 — 1,000 Miles
0 — 500 — 1,000 Kilometers
Azimuthal Equal-Area Projection

N
W E
S

ATLANTIC OCEAN

*Strait of Gibraltar*

*Madeira Islands*

*Canary Islands*

EUROPE

*Mediterranean Sea*

ASIA

Atlas Mountains

*Nile Delta*

*Qattara Depression*

*Suez Canal*

*Sinai Peninsula*

*Gulf of Suez*

S A H A R A

*Ahaggar Mountains*

*Libyan Desert*

Tropic of Cancer

*Tibesti Mountains*

*Lake Nasser*

*Nubian Desert*

*Aïr Massif*

*Red Sea*

*Nile River*

*Athara River*

S A H E L

*Senegal River*

*Cape Verde*

*Niger River*

*Lake Chad*

*White Volta*

*Black Volta R.*

*Chari River*

*Bah el Mandeb*

*Gulf of Aden*

*Fouta Djallon*

*Lake Volta*

*Niger River*

*Benue River*

*White Nile*

*Blue Nile*

*Lake Tana*

*Lake Assal –509 ft. (–155 m)*

*Cape Palmas*

▲ Mt. Cameroon 13,353 ft. (4,070 m)

*Gulf of Guinea*

*Bioko*

*Bah el Jabal*

*Ethiopian Highlands*

*Bomu River*

*Great Rift Valley*

*Lake Turkana*

*Príncipe*

*São Tomé*

*Sangha River*

*Ubangi River*

*Uele River*

*Lake Albert*

Margherita Peak ▲ 16,762 ft. (5,109 m)

▲ Mt. Kenya 17,058 ft. (5,199 m)

0° Equator

*Annobón*

*Zaire River*

Zaire Basin

*Lualaba River*

*Lake Victoria*

*Mitumba Mts.*

Serengeti Plain

▲ Mt. Kilimanjaro 19,340 ft. (5,895 m)

Equator 0°

INDIAN OCEAN

*Kasai River*

*Lake Tanganyika*

*Pemba Island*

*Zanzibar Island*

ATLANTIC

*Ascencion*

Katanga Plateau

*Great Rift Valley*

OCEAN

Bié Plateau

*Lake Malawi*

*Comoro Islands*

*St. Helena*

*Zambezi River*

*Mozambique Channel*

Madagascar

*Namib Desert*

*Victoria Falls*

*Kariba Lake*

Kalahari Desert

*Limpopo River*

Tropic of Capricorn

Tropic of Capricorn

*Vaal River*

*Orange River*

*Drakensberg Escarpment*

*Cape of Good Hope*

*Cape Agulhas*

N
W E
S

| | |
|---|---|
| —— | National border |
| ▲ | Mountain peak |
| ▼ | Below sea level |
| ⊢⊢⊢⊢ | Canal |
| ∥ | Falls |

0        500        1,000 Miles

0    500    1,000 Kilometers

Azimuthal Equal-Area Projection

# ATLAS

## EUROPE AND ASIA: POLITICAL

Legend:
- National border
- Disputed border
- ⊛ National capital
- • Major city

### Abbreviations

| | |
|---|---|
| **AUST.** | AUSTRIA |
| **BELG.** | BELGIUM |
| **BOS. & HERZ.** | BOSNIA AND HERZEGOVINA |
| **CRO.** | CROATIA |
| **LIECHT.** | LIECHTENSTEIN |
| **LUX.** | LUXEMBOURG |
| **MAC.** | MACEDONIA |
| **NETH.** | NETHERLANDS |
| **PORT.** | PORTUGAL |
| **SLOV.** | SLOVENIA |
| **SWITZ.** | SWITZERLAND |
| **U.K.** | UNITED KINGDOM |
| **U.S.** | UNITED STATES |
| **YUGO.** | YUGOSLAVIA |

A8

Robinson Projection

0 500 1,000 Miles
0 500 1,000 Kilometers

NORTH AMERICA

Arctic Circle

Iceland

Faeroe Islands

ATLANTIC OCEAN

Highlands

British Isles

Ireland

Great Britain

Celtic Sea

English Channel

North Sea

Jutland

Norwegian Sea

Kjølen Mountains  Lapland

Scandinavian Peninsula

Galdhøpiggen 8,100 ft. (2,469 m)

Gulf of Bothnia

Baltic Sea

Gulf of Finland

Kola Peninsula

White Sea

Lake Onega

Lake Ladoga

NORTHERN EUROPEAN PLAIN

Central Russian Upland

Volga River

Oka-Don Lowland

Kama River

Novaya Zemlya

Kara Sea

Gulf of Ob

Mt. Narodnaya 6,214 ft. (1,894 m)

U R A L   M O U N T A I N S

Ob River

West Siberian Plain

Irtysh River

Bay of Biscay

Mt. Blanc 15,771 ft. (4,807 m)

Rhine R.

A L P S

Massif Central (Plateau)

Pyrenees

Iberian Peninsula

Balearic Islands

Corsica

Sardinia

Apennines

Dinaric Alps

Carpathian Mountains

Danube River

Balkan Mts.

Balkan Peninsula

Pindus Mts.

Aegean Sea

Adriatic Sea

Tyrrhenian Sea

Sicily

Ionian Sea

Mediterranean Sea

Crete

Cyprus

Sea of Azov

Crimea

Black Sea

Bosporus

Dardanelles

Pontic Mountains

Plateau of Anatolia

Taurus Mts.

Don River

El'brus 18,510 ft. (5,642 m)

Caucasus Mts.

Mt. Ararat 16,946 ft. (5,165 m)

Tigris River

Mesopotamia

Euphrates R.

Syrian Desert

Dead Sea -1,319 ft. (-402 m)

Sinai Peninsula

Red Sea

Caspian Lowland

Volga Upland

Donets Basin

Caspian Sea

-92 ft. -28 m

Elburz Mts.

Mt. Damavand 18,934 ft. (5,771 m)

Dasht-e Kavir (Desert)

Zagros Mountains

Plateau of Iran

Strait of Hormuz

Persian Gulf

Gulf of Oman

Aral Sea

Turan Lowland

Kara Kum (Desert)

Amu Darya

The Steppes

Syr Darya

Kyzyl Kum (Desert)

Kazakh Upland

Lake Balkhash

Pamirs

HINDU KUSH

K2 28,250 ft. (8,611 m)

Takla Makan (Desert)

T I A N   S H A N

Kunlun

HIMALAYAS

Strait of Gibraltar

Ural River

Arabian Peninsula

Rub' al Khali

AFRICA

Tropic of Cancer

Gulf of Aden

Socotra

Arabian Sea

Indus River

Thar Desert

Narmada River

Deccan Plateau

Godavari River

Western Ghats

Eastern Ghats

Palk Strait

Sri Lanka

INDIAN OCEAN

### Legend

| | |
|---|---|
| ——— | National border |
| - - - | Disputed border |
| ▲ | Mountain peak |
| ▼ | Point below sea level |

N  W  E  S

0        500        1,000 Miles
0   500   1,000 Kilometers

Robinson Projection

ARCTIC OCEAN

Laptev
Sea

New Siberian Islands

East Siberian Sea

Wrangel
Island

Chukchi
Sea

Bering Strait

Taimyr Peninsula

90°E          105°E          120°E          135°E          150°E          165°E          180°          165°W

North Siberian Lowland

Kolyma
Lowland

75°N

Central
Siberian
Plateau

Verkhoyansk Range

Kolyma R.

Kolyma Mountains

Arctic Circle

Chukchi
Peninsula

Yenisey River

S I B E R I A

Lena River

Korya Range

60°N

Angara River

Stanovoy Range

Dzhugdzhur Range

Central Range

Bering Sea

Sayan Mountains

Yablonovyy Range

Kamchatka
Peninsula

Yenisey R.

Lake
Baikal

Sea
of
Okhotsk

Altai Mountains

Amur River

Sakhalin

Arctic Circle

Junggar
Basin

Plateau of
Mongolia

Greater Khingan Range

Manchurian Plain

Sikhote Alin Range

Kuril Islands

45°N

▼ Turpan Depression
-505 ft.
(-154 m)

Gobi (Desert)

Hokkaido

Tarim Basin

Qilian Shan

Korean
Peninsula

Sea of
Japan

Shan

North
China

Honshu

▲ Mt. Fuji
12,388 ft.
(3,776 m)

Plateau
of Tibet

Huang He

Plain

Yellow
Sea

Mt. Everest
29,028 ft.
(8,848 m)

Sichuan
Basin

Chang Jiang

Kyushu

Shikoku

▲
▲ Kanchenjunga
28,208 ft.
(8,598 m)

East
China
Sea

30°N

Ganges R.

Irrawaddy River

Ryukyu Islands

PACIFIC OCEAN

Taiwan

Philippine
Sea

Tropic of Cancer

Gulf
of
Tonkin

Mekong R.

Hainan

Bay
of
Bengal

Khorat
Plateau

South

Luzon

15°N

Indochina

China

Peninsula

Andaman
Islands

Sea

Philippine
Islands

Andaman
Sea

Gulf
of
Thailand

Palawan

Sulu
Sea

Mindanao

Nicobar
Islands

Malay

Celebes
Sea

Peninsula

Strait of Malacca

Halmahera

0° Equator

Sumatra

Borneo

Moluccas

Greater     Sunda

Celebes
▲ Rantekombola
11,335 ft.
(3,455 m)

Ceram

New   Guinea

Islands

Java
Sea

Banda Sea

Java

Bali

Sumbawa

Lesser

Lombok

Sumba

Sunda

Flores

Timor

Islands

Timor
Sea

Arafura Sea

15°S

90°E          105°E          120°E          135°E          150°E          165°E

**AUSTRALIA**

ARCTIC OCEAN

Beaufort Sea

Viscount Melville Sound

Baffin Bay

*Greenland*
**(DENMARK)**

Bering Strait

**ALASKA**
**(U.S.)**

Fairbanks

Anchorage

Whitehorse

Yukon River

Mackenzie River

Great Bear Lake

Davis Strait

Foxe Basin

Arctic Circle

60° N

Gulf of Alaska

Juneau

Liard River

Yellowknife

Great Slave Lake

**C A N A D A**

Hudson Strait

Bering Sea

Peace River

Athabasca R.

Saskatchewan R.

Lake Athabasca

James Bay

Hudson Bay

Labrador Sea

Edmonton

Calgary

Vancouver

Saskatoon

Regina

Lake Winnipeg

Winnipeg

Thunder Bay

St. John's

Puget Sound

Seattle

Portland

Columbia

**UNITED STATES**

Missouri R.

Great Lakes

Ottawa

Toronto

Detroit

Montreal

Québec

St. John

Gulf of St. Lawrence

St. Lawrence River

Boise

Snake R.

Great Salt Lake

Salt Lake City

Chicago

Cleveland

Albany

Boston

Halifax

Reno

Denver

St. Louis

Indianapolis

New York City

Philadelphia

Washington, D.C.

San Francisco

Las Vegas

Colorado R.

Memphis

Richmond

Norfolk

Los Angeles

Phoenix

Atlanta

Raleigh

San Diego

Tucson

El Paso

Dallas

Charleston

ATLANTIC OCEAN

Hermosillo

Rio Grande

Houston

New Orleans

Savannah

Jacksonville

30° N

Chihuahua

San Antonio

Tampa

Miami

Gulf of Mexico

**BAHAMAS**

Nassau

Honolulu

**HAWAII**
**(U.S.)**

Tropic of Cancer

**MEXICO**

Durango

Monterrey

Tampico

Havana

**CUBA**

**HAITI**

Port-au-Prince

Santo Domingo

León

**PACIFIC OCEAN**

Guadalajara

Mexico City

Veracruz

**JAMAICA**

Kingston

**PUERTO RICO (U.S.)**

**DOMINICAN REPUBLIC**

Acapulco

Puebla

**BELIZE**

Belmopan

Guatemala

**GUATEMALA**

San Salvador

**HONDURAS**

Tegucigalpa

Caribbean Sea

**EL SALVADOR**

Managua

**NICARAGUA**

San José

Maracaibo

**GUYANA**

**COSTA RICA**

Panama City

Caracas

**SURINAME**

**PANAMA**

Medellín

**VENEZUELA**

Georgetown

Paramaribo

Cayenne

Cali

Bogotá

**FRENCH GUIANA (FRANCE)**

Quito

**COLOMBIA**

Equator

0°

Galápagos Islands
**(ECUADOR)**

Guayaquil

**ECUADOR**

Rio Negro

Manaus

Amazon R.

Belém

Iquitos

Fortaleza

Trujillo

**PERU**

Tapajós River

Xingu R.

Recife

Lima

Cuzco

**BRAZIL**

Tocantins

São Francisco R.

Salvador

FRENCH POLYNESIA
**(FRANCE)**

Papeete

Lake Titicaca

La Paz

**BOLIVIA**

Arequipa

Brasília

Goiânia

Belo Horizonte

Rio de Janeiro

Sucre

Campo Grande

Tropic of Capricorn

Antofagasta

Paraguay R.

**PARAGUAY**

Asunción

São Paulo

Curitiba

San Miguel de Tucumán

Salta

Paraná R.

Pôrto Alegre

30° S

**CHILE**

Córdoba

Rosario

**URUGUAY**

Valparaíso

Santiago

Buenos Aires

La Plata

Montevideo

Mar del Plata

Concepción

Rio de la Plata

Bahía Blanca

Valdivia

0   1,000   2,000 Miles

0   1,000   2,000 Kilometers

Miller Cylindrical Projection

— National border

⊛ National capital

• City

N W E S

**ARGENTINA**

Falkland Islands
**(U.K.)**

South Georgia
**(U.K.)**

Punta Arenas

150° W      120° W      90° W      60° W      30° W

# ATLAS

## THE WESTERN HEMISPHERE: PHYSICAL

ARCTIC OCEAN

North Magnetic Pole
Queen Elizabeth Islands
Ellesmere Island

Melville Island
Devon Island

Banks Island
Viscount Melville Sound

Point Barrow
Beaufort Sea

Victoria Island

Baffin Bay

Greenland

Brooks Range

Great Bear Lake

CANADIAN

Baffin Island

Davis Strait

Mt. McKinley 20,320 ft. (6,194 m)
Yukon River
Mackenzie Mts.
Mackenzie River
Foxe Basin

Arctic Circle

Yukon Plateau
Liard River
Great Slave Lake

60° N

Cape Farewell

Mt. Logan 19,524 ft. (5,951 m)
Alaska Range
Gulf of Alaska
Peace River
Athabasca R.
Lake Athabasca

SHIELD

Labrador Sea

Kodiak Island
Alaska Peninsula

Coast Mountains

ROCKY

GREAT

Saskatchewan River
Lake Winnipeg

Hudson Bay

James Bay

Labrador

Aleutian Islands

Queen Charlotte Islands

MOUNTAINS

PLAINS

Missouri R.

Great Lakes
St. Lawrence R.

Newfoundland
Gulf of St. Lawrence

Vancouver Island
Puget Sound

Coast Ranges

Snake R.

Black Hills
Platte R.

Mississippi
Ohio R.

Nova Scotia
Bay of Fundy

Sierra Nevada

Great Salt Lake
GREAT BASIN

INTERIOR PLAINS

APPALACHIAN MTS.

Cape Cod
Long Island

Mt. Whitney 14,494 ft. (4,418 m)
Death Valley (lowest point in N.A.) -282 ft. (-86 m)

Colorado R.
Arkansas R.
Ozark Plateau

Cape Hatteras

ATLANTIC OCEAN

Sonoran Desert
Sierra Madre Occidental
Rio Grande

COASTAL PLAIN

30° N

Baja California
Gulf of California

Sierra Madre Oriental

Gulf of Mexico

Bahamas

Hawaiian Islands

Tropic of Cancer

Yucatán Peninsula

Cuba
Greater Antilles

Hispaniola
Puerto Rico

PACIFIC OCEAN

Citlaltépetl 18,701 ft. (5,700 m)

Lesser Antilles

Caribbean Sea

Lake Nicaragua

Isthmus of Panama

Lake Maracaibo
Orinoco R.
Llanos

Guiana Highlands

Chimborazo 20,561 ft. (6,267 m)

Galápagos Islands

Rio Negro
Amazon R.

Cape São Roque

Equator

ANDES

AMAZON BASIN

Line Islands

Marquesas Islands

Huascarán 22,205 ft. (6,768 m)

Tapajós River
Xingu River
Mato Grosso Plateau

Tocantins R.

Brazilian Highlands

São Francisco River

Cook Islands
Society Islands
Tuamotu Archipelago

Lake Titicaca

MOUNTAINS

Paraguay R.

Tropic of Capricorn

Atacama Desert

Gran Chaco

Paraná R.

Iguazú Falls

0    1,000    2,000 Miles
0    1,000    2,000 Kilometers
Miller Cylindrical Projection

Uruguay R.

30° S

Mt. Aconcagua 22,831 ft. (6,959 m)

Pampa

Rio de la Plata

▲ Mountain peak
▼ Point below sea level
— National border
≋ Waterfall

N
W E
S

Valdés Peninsula (lowest point in S.A.) -131 ft. (-40 m)

Patagonia

Falkland Islands

South Georgia

Strait of Magellan
Tierra del Fuego
Cape Horn

150° W          120° W          90° W          60° W          30° W

ARCTIC OCEAN

*Siberia*

Arctic Circle

Kolyma R.

**RUSSIA**

Lena River

60°N

Amur R.

*Sea of Okhotsk*

*Kamchatka Peninsula*

*Sakhalin*

*Kuril Islands*

Bering Strait

*Yukon River*

Brooks Range

**Alaska (U.S.)** ▲ Mt. McKinley 20,320 ft. 6,194 m)

Mt. Logan 19,524 ft. 5,951 m) ▲

*Bering Sea*

Aleutian Islands

*Alaska Peninsula*

*Gulf of Alaska*

Mackenzie R.

Coast Ranges

Peace R.

**CANADA**

• Edmonton

Saskatchewan R.

Vancouver •

Seattle •
Portland •

Columbia R.

Missouri River

R O C K Y   M O U N T A I N S

• Ottawa ✪

**UNITED STATES**

Washington D.C. •

Beijing •✪

P'yongyang •

**NORTH KOREA**

Seoul •✪ **SOUTH KOREA**

• Sapporo

*Sea of Japan*

**JAPAN**

✪ Tokyo

**CHINA**

Huang He

Shanghai •

*East China Sea*

PACIFIC OCEAN

Mt. Whitney 14,491 ft. (4,417 m)

San Francisco •
▲

Los Angeles •

Colorado R.

Missouri R.

Baja California

**MEXICO**

30°N

Chiang Jiang

Taipei •

**TAIWAN**

Hanoi •✪

Hong Kong • **(U.K.)**

*Philippine Sea*

Tropic of Cancer

*Northern Mariana Islands* **(U.S.)**

**Hawaii (U.S.)**

Honolulu •

Mexico City •✪

**THAILAND** **VIETNAM**

Bangkok •✪

**CAMBODIA**

Phnom Penh •✪

Manila •✪

*South China Sea*

**PHILIPPINES**

Ho Chi Minh City •

**GUATEMALA** **BELIZE**
**EL SALVADOR** **HONDURAS**
**NICARAGUA**

Kuala Lumpur •

**BRUNEI**

✪ Koror

Palikir •✪

**MARSHALL ISLANDS**

✪ Majuro

**COSTA RICA**
**PANAMA** **COLOMBIA**

Bogotá •✪

**MALAYSIA** •✪

Singapore •

**PALAU**

**FEDERATED STATES OF MICRONESIA**

✪ Tarawa

Equator

*Galápagos Islands* **(ECUADOR)**

Quito •✪

**ECUADOR**

I N D O N E S I A

Jakarta •

**PAPUA NEW GUINEA**

**NAURU**

Yaren ✪

**SOLOMON ISLANDS**

**TUVALU**

Funafuti ✪

**KIRIBATI**

**PERU**

Lima •

**INDIAN OCEAN**

Port Moresby •✪

Honiara •✪

**WESTERN SAMOA**

Apia •✪

*French Polynesia* **(FR.)**

*Coral Sea*

**VANUATU**

**FIJI**

**TONGA**

*Cook Islands* **(N.Z.)**

Papeete •
Tahiti

Portvila •✪

Suva •✪

Nuku'alofa •✪

*New Caledonia* **(FR.)**

Tropic of Capricorn

**AUSTRALIA**

GREAT DIVIDING RANGE

Brisbane •

*Pitcairn Island* **(U.K.)**

*Easter Island* **(CHILE)**

Aconcagua 22,831 ft. (6,959 m) ▲

30°S

Darling R.

Sydney •

Canberra ▲✪

Mt. Kosciusko 7,310 ft. (2,228 m)

Melbourne •

*Tasman Sea*

Auckland •

Santiago •✪

**CHILE**

A N D E S

*Tasmania*

**NEW ZEALAND**

Wellington •✪

Mt. Cook 12,349 ft. (3,764 m) ▲

PACIFIC OCEAN

Cape Horn

60°S

Antarctic Circle

N
W ✦ E
S

A N T A R C T I C A

**Legend:**

— National border

✪ National capital

• Major city

▲ Mountain Peak

0    1,000    2,000 Miles
0    1,000  2,000 Kilometers
Miller Cylindrical Projection

**Abbreviations**

| | |
|---|---|
| **FR.** | FRANCE |
| **N.Z.** | NEW ZEALAND |
| **U.K.** | UNITED KINGDOM |
| **U.S.** | UNITED STATES |

120°E    150°E    180°E    150°W    120°W    90°W

# ATLAS

## WORLD RELIGIONS

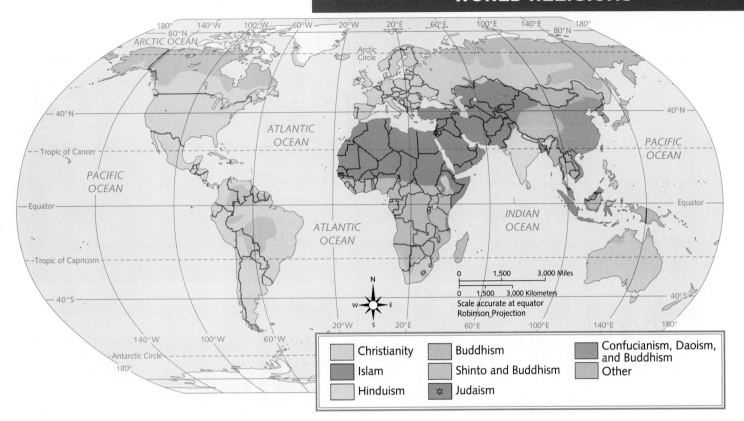

- Christianity
- Islam
- Hinduism
- Buddhism
- Shinto and Buddhism
- Judaism
- Confucianism, Daoism, and Buddhism
- Other

0 1,500 3,000 Miles
0 1,500 3,000 Kilometers
Scale accurate at equator
Robinson Projection

## WORLD LANGUAGES

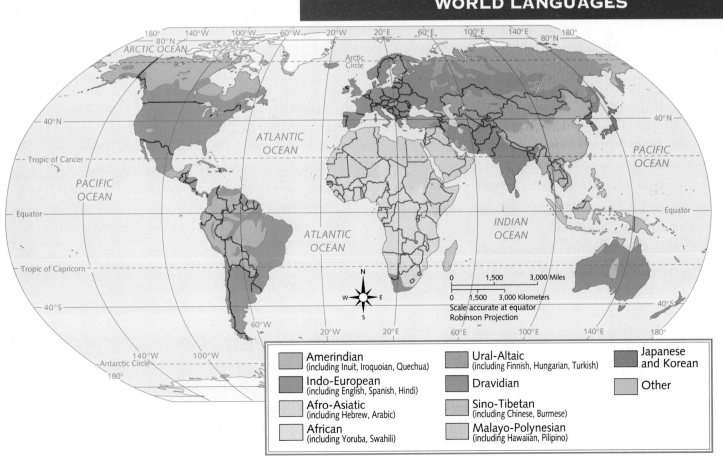

- Amerindian (including Inuit, Iroquoian, Quechua)
- Indo-European (including English, Spanish, Hindi)
- Afro-Asiatic (including Hebrew, Arabic)
- African (including Yoruba, Swahili)
- Ural-Altaic (including Finnish, Hungarian, Turkish)
- Dravidian
- Sino-Tibetan (including Chinese, Burmese)
- Malayo-Polynesian (including Hawaiian, Pilipino)
- Japanese and Korean
- Other

0 1,500 3,000 Miles
0 1,500 3,000 Kilometers
Scale accurate at equator
Robinson Projection

Timberline

MOUNTAIN RANGE

Sea level

Glacier

Fjord

PLATEAU

VALLEY

Canyon

Mesa

PLAIN

COASTAL PLAIN

Coast

Mouth of river

Sea level

Lake

Lagoon

Isthmus

Peninsula

Cape

OCEAN

**basin** bowl-shaped area of land surrounded by higher land

**bay** body of water that is part of a sea or ocean and is partly enclosed by land

**bluff** high, steep face of rock or earth

**canyon** deep, narrow valley with steep sides

**cape** a point of land that extends into water

**cataract** large waterfall

**cliff** high, steep face of rock or earth

**coast** land along a sea or ocean

**coastal plain** area of flat land along a sea or ocean

**delta** triangle-shaped area of land at the mouth of a river

**desert** dry land with few plants

**dune** hill of sand piled up by the wind

**fall line** area along which rivers form waterfalls or rapids as the rivers drop to lower land

**fjord** deep, narrow part of a sea or ocean, between high, steep banks

**floodplain** flat land that is near the edges of a river and is formed by the silt deposited by floods

**foothills** hilly area at the base of a mountain

**glacier** large ice mass that moves slowly down a mountain or across land

**gulf** body of water that is partly enclosed by land but is larger than a bay

**hill** land that rises above the land around it

**island** land that has water on all sides

**isthmus** narrow strip of land connecting two larger areas of land

**lagoon** body of shallow water

**lake** body of water with land on all sides

**marsh** lowland with moist soil and tall grasses

**mesa** flat-topped mountain with steep sides

Peak

Mountain pass

Mountain

Source of river

SAVANNA

Cataract

Tributary

Volcano

BASIN

FOOTHILLS

Dune

Fall line

Riverbank

Swamp

DESERT

River    FLOODPLAIN    Marsh    Delta    Gulf

Bay

Oasis

Hill

Island

Bluff or cliff

Strait

Reef

Sea

**mountain** highest kind of land

**mountain pass** gap between mountains

**mountain range** row of mountains

**mouth of river** place where a river empties into another body of water

**oasis** area of water and fertile land with desert on all sides

**ocean** body of salt water, larger than a sea

**peak** top of a mountain

**peninsula** land that is almost completely surrounded by water

**plain** flat land

**plateau** area of high, flat land with steep sides

**reef** ridge of sand, rock, or coral that lies at or near the surface of a sea or ocean

**river** large stream of water that flows across the land

**riverbank** land along a river

**savanna** large area of grassland containing scattered trees

**sea** body of salt water, smaller than an ocean

**sea level** the level that is even with the surface of an ocean or sea

**source of river** place where a river or stream begins

**strait** narrow channel of water connecting two larger bodies of water

**swamp** area of low, wet land with trees

**timberline** line on a mountain above which it is too cold for trees to grow

**tributary** stream or river that empties into a larger river

**valley** low land between hills or mountains

**volcano** opening in the Earth, often raised, through which lava, rock, ashes, and gases are forced out

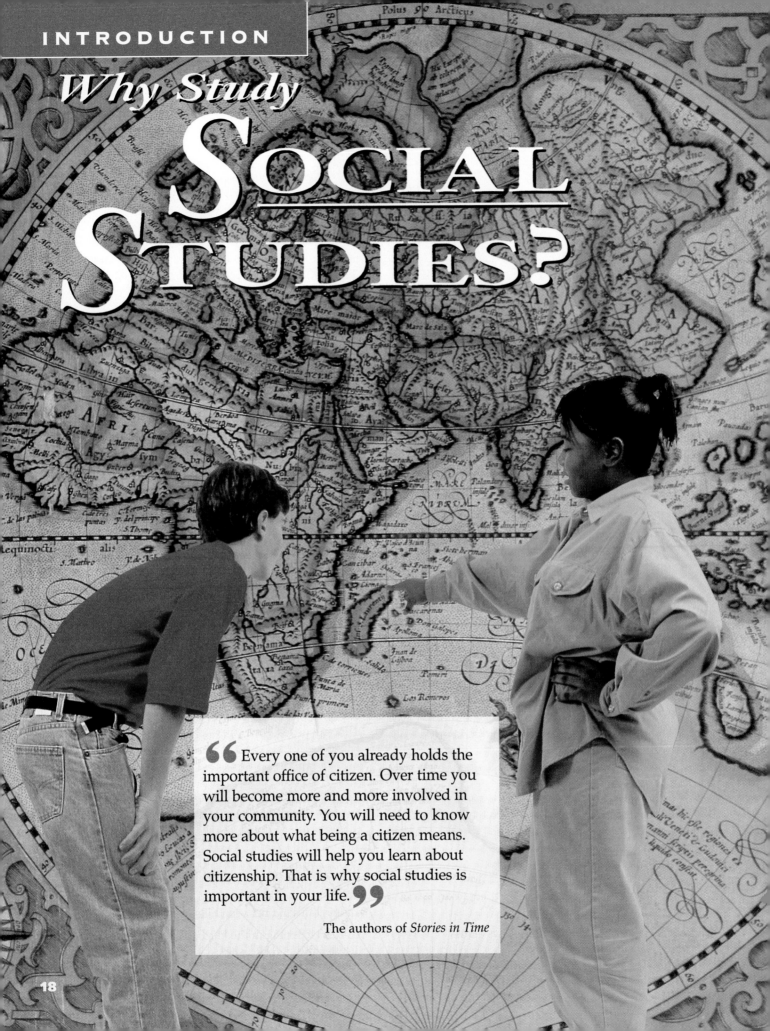

# Why Study SOCIAL STUDIES?

> 66 Every one of you already holds the important office of citizen. Over time you will become more and more involved in your community. You will need to know more about what being a citizen means. Social studies will help you learn about citizenship. That is why social studies is important in your life. 99
>
> The authors of *Stories in Time*

# THE POWERFUL IDEAS OF SOCIAL STUDIES

*T*hink about the many groups you are a part of. Your family, your class, and your community are each a different kind of group, and you are a member of each one. You are also a member—or **citizen**—of your town, your state, and your country. Citizens work to improve the many groups they belong to and to make the whole world a better place.

To help you think, feel, and act as a citizen, *Stories in Time* begins every lesson with a question. That question connects you with one or more of five powerful ideas that citizens need to understand in order to make decisions. Each question also links you to the lesson's story, helping you see how the story relates to your own life. The lesson helps you learn about being a citizen by letting you see how people from many places and times have thought, felt, and acted.

Each lesson will help you organize your thinking around one or more of the five powerful ideas of social studies.

## POWERFUL IDEA NUMBER *1*
## COMMONALITY AND DIVERSITY

In some ways people everywhere are alike. We all have basic needs for things like food, clothing, and shelter. We all laugh, get angry, and have our feelings hurt. These are examples of our commonality, or what we all share. At the same time, we need to understand that each person is different from everyone else. We each have our own ways of thinking, feeling, and acting. That is our diversity. An understanding of commonality and diversity can help you see that every person deserves respect.

In this painting the Roman orator Cicero delivers a speech in the Roman Senate. By taking part in government, Cicero and the Roman Senators were carrying out the office of citizen.

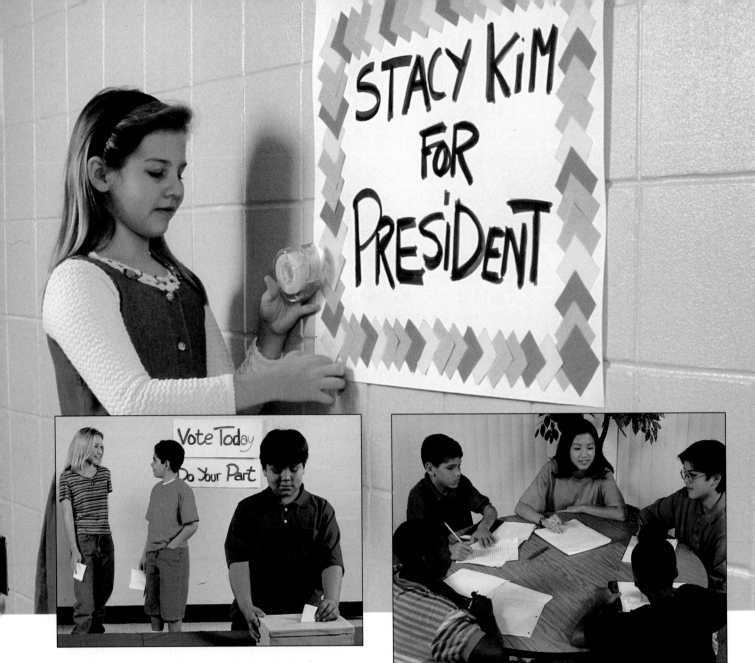

When you campaign in a school election, vote for class officers, or take part in a student government meeting, you are carrying out the office of citizen. Understanding each of the powerful ideas will help you make decisions as a citizen.

POWERFUL IDEA NUMBER **2**

## CONFLICT AND COOPERATION

Because people are not exactly alike, they may have conflicts, or disagreements. People can often overcome their conflicts by cooperating, or working together. In social studies you will learn about the disagreements people have had throughout time and about many of the ways people have found to settle their disagreements. You will also learn ways to cooperate and to resolve conflict in your own life.

## POWERFUL IDEA NUMBER *3*
## CONTINUITY AND CHANGE

While some things change over time, other things stay the same. Many things have stayed the same for years and will probably stay the same in the future. This means that they have continuity. Understanding continuity and change can help you see how things in the world came to be as they are. You will learn that past events have helped shape your life and that present events can help you make decisions about the future.

## POWERFUL IDEA NUMBER *4*
## INDIVIDUALISM AND INTERDEPENDENCE

Citizens can act by themselves to make a difference in the world. Their actions as individuals may be helpful or they may be harmful to other citizens. But much of the time, people do not act alone. They depend on others to help them. People depend on their families, their schools, their religious groups, their governments, and other groups and organizations. Such interdependence connects citizens with one another and affects their lives.

## POWERFUL IDEA NUMBER *5*
## INTERACTION WITHIN DIFFERENT ENVIRONMENTS

People's actions affect other people. People's actions also affect their surroundings, or environment. This is true of their physical environment as well as their home environment, their school environment, and other environments they may be a part of. Understanding such interactions is important to understanding why things happened in the past and why things happen today.

Understanding interaction is also key to understanding social studies. The subjects that make up social studies are all interconnected. You will learn, for example, that history—the study of people's past—is related to geography—the study of the Earth's surface and its people. Civics and government, or the study of how people live together in a community, is related to economics, or the study of how people use resources. And all of these subjects are related to the study of culture. Culture is the way of life of a group of people, including their customs, ideas, and practices. Together, all these subjects tell a story of how people have lived over time and how they have made contributions to the world. Understanding this story will help you learn how to hold the office of citizen.

 ***What are the five powerful ideas of social studies?***

# HISTORY

History helps you see the links between the past and the present. It also helps you better understand how what happens today can affect the future. History is about what happened last month and last year as well as in the ancient past.

As you read about the past, ask yourself the questions below. They will help you think more like a historian, a person who studies the past.

- **What happened?**
- **When did it happen?**
- **Who took part in it?**
- **How and why did it happen?**

## WHAT HAPPENED?

To find out what really happened in the past, you need proof. You can find proof by studying two kinds of sources—primary sources and secondary sources. Historians use these kinds of sources in writing about history.

**Primary sources** are the records made by people who saw or took part in an event, or something that happened. They might have etched a message in stone or written down their thoughts in a journal. They might have told their story in a letter or a poem. They might have taken a photograph, made a film, or painted a picture. Each of these records is a primary source, giving the people of today a direct link to a past event.

A **secondary source** is not a direct link to an event. It is a record of the event written by someone who was not there at the time. A magazine article, newspaper story, or book written at a later time by someone who did not take part in an event is a secondary source.

Arabic book, *Treatise on the Eye*, thirteenth century ⬇

When there are no written records of an event, historians gather proof with the help of archaeologists. Archaeologists study buildings, tools, and other objects people make or use. Based on their studies of these things, archaeologists form opinions about people and places in the past.

As you read this book, you will read many kinds of sources. The stories told in each lesson contain the words and pictures of people in the past—primary sources—as well as descriptions by historians—secondary sources. Maps, graphs, and pictures of objects made by people in the past also help tell the story.

Archaeologists study items made or used by peoples of the past. This archaeologist is looking at a tomb of the ancient Mayas in what is today Mexico.

## WHEN DID IT HAPPEN?

One way to build a story of the past is to put events related to that story in the order in which they happened. This order is the story's **chronology**. When you read this book, you will notice that it is organized by chronology. The events described at the beginning of the book happened before those described at the end of the book.

You will see many time lines in this book. They will help you understand each story's chronology. A time line is a diagram that shows the events that took place during a certain period of time in the order in which they happened. Some time lines show a period of a month or a year. Others show a period of a decade, a century, or a millennium—1,000 years. Time lines can help you understand how one event may have led to another.

People of the past often depended on the spoken word rather than the written word to tell of their past. At left is a nineteenth-century painting of a Native American storyteller. At right a present-day storyteller holds students' interest with a tale about the past.

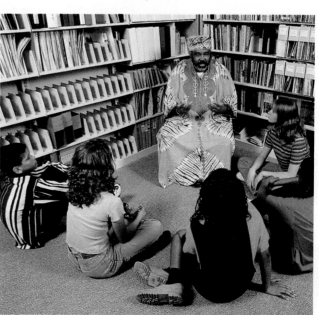

## WHO TOOK PART IN IT?

To understand the stories of the past, you need to know about the people in the stories and the times in which they lived. In this way you can understand the actions and feelings of people from other times and other places. This understanding is called historical empathy.

By reading the words of people of the past, you can come to understand their perspective, or point of view. A person's perspective is a set of beliefs that have been shaped by factors such as whether that person is old or young, a man or a woman, or rich or poor. A person's perspective is also shaped by culture and race. Your understanding of history will grow when you study the many perspectives of the people who took part in the story. This also will help you see that people living in other places and other times are a lot like you.

## HOW AND WHY DID IT HAPPEN?

Many events in history are linked to other events. To find the links between events, you will need to identify causes and effects. A cause is any action that makes something happen. What happens because of that action is an effect. Historians have found that some events have many causes and many effects.

To understand an event, you need to analyze its causes and effects. Analyzing is a thinking process in which you break something down into its parts and look closely at how those parts connect with one another. Once you have analyzed an event, you can summarize it or draw a conclusion about how or why it happened.

 *What questions can you ask yourself when you read about the past?*

History puts scenes of the past at your fingertips.

24

# HowTo

# Read Social Studies

## Why Is This Skill Important?

Social studies is made up of stories about people and places. Sometimes you read these stories in library books. Other times you read them in textbooks like this one. Knowing how to read social studies in a textbook can make it easier to study and to do your homework. It will help you identify main ideas and important people, places, and events.

## Understand the Process

Follow these steps to read any lesson in this book:

1. Preview the whole lesson.
   - Look at the title and headings to find out the topic of the lesson.
   - Look at the pictures, captions, and questions for clues to what is in the lesson.
   - Answer the Link to Our World question at the beginning of the lesson to find out how the lesson relates to life today.
   - Read the Focus on the Main Idea statement, which gives you the key idea that the lesson teaches.
   - Look at the Preview Vocabulary list to see what new terms will be introduced.

2. Read the lesson for information on the main idea. As you read, you will come to checkpoint questions. Find the answers to these questions before you continue reading.

3. When you finish reading the lesson, say in your own words what you have learned.

4. Look back over the lesson. Then answer the review questions, from memory if possible. The lesson review will help guide you in checking your understanding, thinking critically, and showing what you know.

## Think and Apply

Use the four steps in Understand the Process each time you are asked to read a lesson in *Stories in Time*.

# GEOGRAPHY

*T*he stories you will read in this book all have a setting. The setting of a story includes the place where it happens. Geography is the study of the many different settings around the world. Studying geography helps you answer these questions about a place:

- **Where is it?**
  **(location)**

- **What is it like there?**
  **(place)**

- **Who lives there, and what do they do?**
  **(human-environment interactions)**

- **How did they get there?**
  **(movement)**

- **How is the place like other places?**
  **How is it different?**
  **(regions)**

The answers to these questions tell you what you need to know in order to understand a setting. The five topics are so important that many people call them the five themes, or key topics, of geography.

## 1. LOCATION

Everything on the Earth has its own location. Knowing your location helps you tell other people where you are. It also helps you become aware of the world around you.

To tell exactly where you live in your town or city, you can use the names and numbers of your home address. To find your **absolute location**, or your exact location, on Earth, you can use the numbers of your "global address." These numbers appear on a pattern of imaginary lines drawn on globes and maps. You will read more about these lines on pages 28 and 29 when you review how to read a map.

The location of a place can also be described in relation to the location of other places. You describe the **relative location** of a place when you say what it is near or what is around it. You might say that the nearest bus stop is on the corner by the gas station. Or you might say that the city of New Orleans is south of the city of St. Louis.

## 2. PLACE

Every location on the Earth has a place identity made up of unique features that make it different from all other locations. A place can be described by its **physical features**—landforms, bodies of water, climate, soil, plant and animal life, and other natural resources. Many places also have **human features**—buildings, bridges, farms, roads, and the people themselves. People's cultures, or ways of life, also help make places different.

## 3. HUMAN-ENVIRONMENT INTERACTIONS

Humans and the environment interact, or behave in ways that affect each other. People interact with their environment in different ways. Sometimes they change it. They clear land to grow crops. They build cities and towns. Sometimes people pollute the environment. The environment can also cause people to change the way they act. People who live in cold places wear warm clothing. Sometimes things that happen in nature, such as hurricanes, tornadoes, and earthquakes, can cause great changes in people's lives.

## 4. MOVEMENT

Each day, people in different parts of the country and different parts of the world interact with one another. These kinds of interactions involve movement. People, products, and ideas move by transportation and communication. Geography helps you understand the causes and effects of this movement. It also helps you understand how people came to live where they do.

## 5. REGIONS

Areas on the Earth whose features make them different from other areas are called **regions**. A region can be described by physical features, such as mountains or dry climate, that exist all over the region. A region can also be described by its human features, such as the language most of its people speak or the way that people are governed.

Regions are sometimes divided into smaller regions that are easier to compare. Some geographers who study the Earth's surface and its people divide the United States into regions named for their relative locations—the Northeast, the Southeast, the Middle West, the Southwest, and the West. This division makes the geography of the United States easier to understand.

 **What are the five themes of geography?**

# How To
## Read a Map

### Why Is This Skill Important?

To answer questions you may have about the world around you, you need information. You can get this information by reading the stories in this book, by looking at its pictures and charts, and by studying its maps. Knowing how to read a map is an important skill both for learning social studies and for taking action as a citizen.

### Understand the Process

Maps are drawings of places on the Earth. Mapmakers include certain elements on most maps to help people read them. These are a title, a key, a compass rose, and a scale. Mapmakers often put a grid of numbered lines on their maps to help people locate places more easily.

1. The **map title** tells the subject of the map. The title may also help you understand what kind of map it is. Physical maps show landforms and bodies of water. Political maps show cities and national boundaries, or borders. Many of the maps in this book are historical maps that show parts of the world as they were in the past. Historical maps often

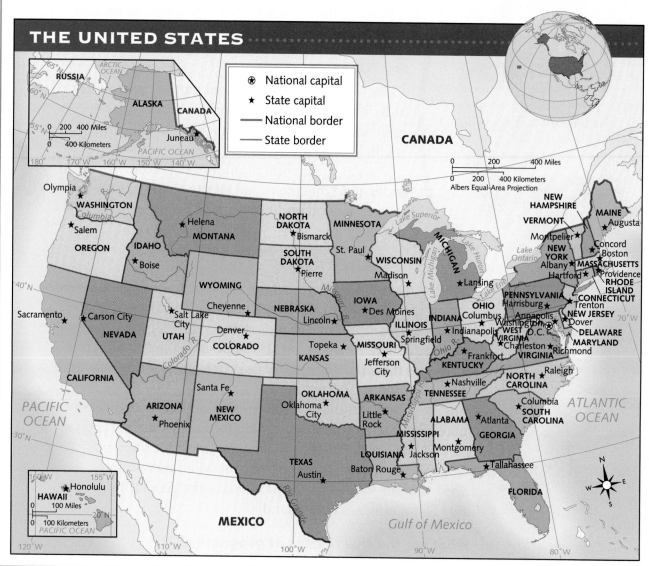

**THE UNITED STATES**

Key:
⊛ National capital
★ State capital
── National border
── State border

have dates in the title. When you look at any map, look for information in the title to find out what the map is about.

2. The **map key**, which is sometimes called a map legend, explains what the symbols on the map stand for. Symbols may be colors, patterns, lines, or other special marks, such as circles, triangles, or squares. The map key for the map on page 28 tells you that stars are used to show state capitals. A circle with a star inside it stands for a national capital.

3. The **compass rose**, or direction marker, on a map shows the main, or cardinal, directions—north, south, east, and west. A compass rose also helps you find the intermediate directions, which are between the cardinal directions. Intermediate directions are northeast, northwest, southeast, and southwest.

4. The **map scale** compares a distance on a map to a distance in the real world. A map scale helps you find the real distance between places on a map. Each map in this book has a scale that shows both miles and kilometers. Map scales are different depending on how much area is shown. On the map of the United States on page 28 are two smaller maps, one of Alaska and one of Hawaii. A small map within a larger map is called an **inset map**. Inset maps have their own scales. Inset maps make it possible to show places in greater detail or to show places that are outside the area shown on the main map.

5. The north-south and east-west lines on a map cross each other to form a pattern of squares called a **grid**. The east-west lines are lines of latitude. The north-south lines are lines of longitude. The global address, or absolute location, of a place can be found where a line of latitude and line of longitude cross.

## Think and Apply

Look at the map of Venezuela below. Identify the parts of the map. Discuss with a partner the information you find.

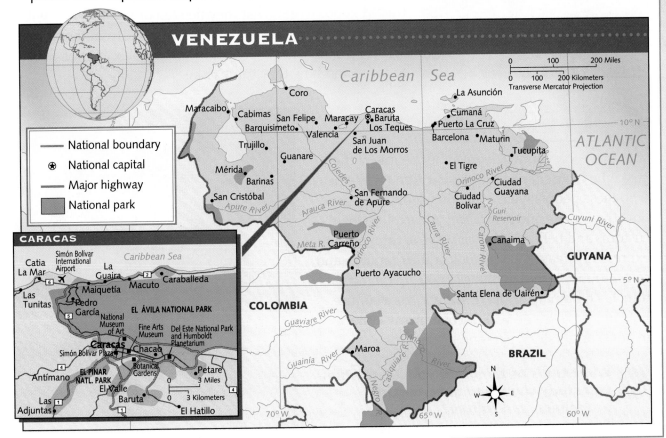

# CIVICS AND GOVERNMENT

Civics and government is the study of citizenship and the ways in which citizens govern themselves. A government is the system of leaders and laws that help people live together in their community, state, or country. In the United States, citizens have an important part in making the government work. The laws that guide the actions of people are written and carried out by citizens.

In *Stories in Time* you will learn about the different kinds of government in the world today. You will learn about the people and events that shaped governments in the past. You will also learn about citizenship and the rights and responsibilities of citizens in governments in both the past and the present.

# ECONOMICS

The **economy** of a country is the way its people use its resources to meet their needs. The study of how people do this is called economics. In *Stories in Time* you will read about how people in the past made, bought, sold, and traded goods to get what they needed or wanted. You will learn about different kinds of economies—from the simple ones of the ancient past to the more complex ones of today—and how they came to be.

# CULTURE

In this book you will learn about people of the past who have shaped the present. You will learn who these people were, what they looked like, and how they spoke and acted. You will explore their customs and beliefs and their ways of thinking and expressing ideas. You will look at their families and communities. All these things make up their culture. Each human group, or society, has a culture. In *Stories in Time* you will discover many cultures in our world's story, past and present.

 **What kinds of things do you learn when you study civics and government, economics, and culture?**

# Work Together in Groups

## Why Is This Skill Important?

Learning social studies is sometimes easier when you work with a partner or in a group. Many projects would be difficult for one person to do. If you work with other students, each of you can work on part of the project. For a group project to succeed, each member needs to cooperate with the others. Knowing how to work together is an important skill for everyone.

## Understand the Process

Suppose your group is asked to do a project, such as presenting a short play about everyday life long ago. You might find it helpful to follow a set of steps:

1. Organize and plan together.
   • Set your goal as a group.
   • Share your ideas.
   • Cooperate with your partner or other group members to plan your work.
   • Make sure everyone has a job.

2. Act on your plan together.
   • Take responsibility for your jobs.
   • Help one another.
   • If there are conflicts, take time to talk about them.
   • Show your group's finished work to the class.

3. Talk about your work.
   • Discuss what you learned by working together.

## Think and Apply

Follow these steps for working together as you take part in the activities in *Stories in Time*.

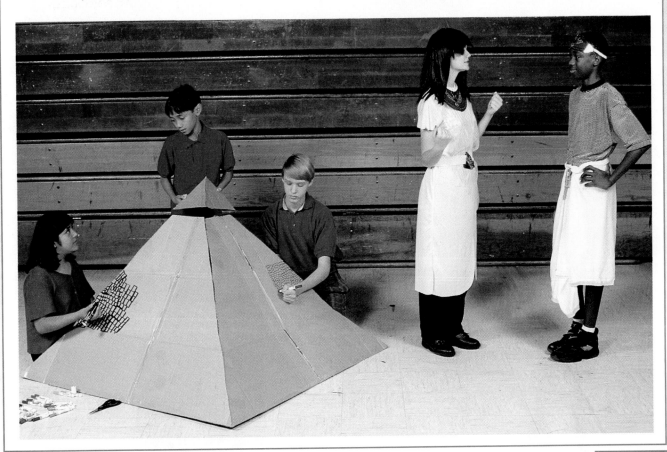

# UNIT 1

# EARLY PEOPLE and LIFEWAYS

**14,000 years ago**     **12,000 years ago**     **10,000 years ago**     **8,000 years ago**

**Before 12,000 years ago**
All people live as hunters and gatherers

**10,000 years ago**
First farming begins

*H*umans much like ourselves came on the scene about 200,000 years ago. For much of the time, humans lived in the same way. They wandered the world in small groups, hunting animals and gathering plants for food. Then, for reasons no one understands, some people started producing their own food and living in settlements. This development was among the most important in world history. From a similar way of life, groups of early people began to develop unique lifeways with their own customs, ideas, beliefs, languages, inventions, and tools.

◆ This scene by a present-day artist shows what life may have been like for early people about 15,000 years ago.

| 6,000 years ago | 4,000 years ago | 2,000 years ago | Present |
|---|---|---|---|

**5,500 years ago**
Earliest use of the wheel

**Cuneiform writing develops**

**5,000 years ago**
City-states rise in Sumer

**3,000 years ago**
First written alphabet

**2,600 years ago**
Earliest use of coined money

# BOY OF THE PAINTED CAVE

## *by Justin Denzel*

From rocky cliffs in Africa to caves in Europe and the Americas, early people left behind clear images of life thousands of years ago. The world's earliest artists covered the cave walls and rocks with beautiful paintings. Some of the earliest paintings were patterns of handprints. Other paintings showed magnificent scenes of the animals the early people hunted for food.

No one knows for sure why the early people of the world began painting. Perhaps they painted as part of their religious rituals. Or they may have wanted to leave a record of their times.

Tao and Graybeard are characters in the following story set in the Stone Age, a time more than 30,000 years ago when people made tools and weapons from stone. Tao is a young boy who is fascinated with the wild animals that his people depend on to meet their needs. He dreams of becoming a cave painter like Graybeard. Read now about Stone Age people who counted on the natural resources around them to survive.

Ancient artists used their own handprints to create this cave painting found in the South American country of Argentina.

Tao winced as he saw the worn face, the pinched cheekbones. He was worried, but he knew the old man would not want him to show concern. "The cave is ready," Tao said. "But first you must rest and eat." He took some dried meat and fish from his leather pouch and they sat with their backs against an old red oak and ate their meal. Tao wondered if Graybeard remembered his promise.

When they were finished, they started across the valley. Graybeard stopped many times, poking around the streambeds and gravel banks with the shaft of his spear, searching. Then he found what he was looking for. He picked up a stick and dug out a handful of bright red earth.

"Here," he said, as he poured it into an empty leather sack. "This will make good red paint. Now we must find yellows and whites."

"I have yellow clay," said Tao. The old man did remember.

"Good. We can dig up some limestone powder near the foot of the cliffs. That will mix well for the lighter colors."

When they had all the red, white and yellow earth they needed, they went up to the top of the cliff, using the easy path that Graybeard had found. They reached the tunnel to the Hidden Cave and removed the cover of branches to let in the sunlight.

In the cave Graybeard sat on the ground and Tao squatted beside him. The old man poured some of the red earth into one of the saucer-shaped rocks that Tao had collected. Then, using a smooth, round stone, he began grinding it into a fine powder. When it was to his liking, he added some of Tao's fish oil, mixing it into a dark red paint. He poured a small amount of this into three other shallow stone dishes. In the first one he added a lump of yellow clay, in the second he sprinkled limestone powder and in the third he added charcoal dust. Using a small, clean stick for each, he mixed them well, ending with three different colors: a bright orange, a salmon pink and a dark brown.

Tao was amazed. He sat quietly, watching. This too was magic, he thought. Graybeard spread out more saucers and began blending shades of yellows, browns, grays and blacks. Some he mixed with honey, and some with the boiled fat and clotted blood from the boar.

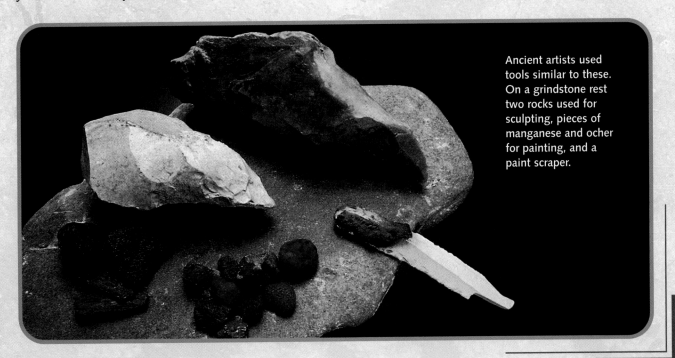

Ancient artists used tools similar to these. On a grindstone rest two rocks used for sculpting, pieces of manganese and ocher for painting, and a paint scraper.

Horses seem to come alive in this ancient cave painting from Lascaux, France.

"Next we must make our brushes," he said. He took a handful of twigs from his pouch and began mashing the ends with a stone until they were soft and ragged. He held one up in the shaft of sunlight beaming through the cave entrance. He turned it around for Tao to see. "These are small," he said, "for painting eyes and fine lines of hair and fur."

He made larger brushes by tying feathers and boar bristles around the ends of long sticks with strings of vegetable fiber.

When all the paints and brushes were made, the old man got to his feet. "Now," he said, "we are ready to paint."

Tao held out the shoulder blade of the horse, while Graybeard poured spots of the colored paints onto its broad white surface. He handed the boy one of the large brushes and pointed to Tao's pictures of the rhinos, bison and mammoths.

Cave painting from South America, near Perito Moreno, Argentina

The boy held his breath. He had never had a brush in his hand before. "Which one will I paint?"

Graybeard smiled. "You are the image maker. Paint the one you like the best."

"The mountain-that-walks," said Tao.

Graybeard nodded. "Then begin."

Tao hesitated, glancing at the paints on the shoulder blade, uncertain.

"You saw the mammoths," said Graybeard. "What color were they?"

"Reddish-brown."

"Good," said the old man. "Then mix a little black with the red until you have the color you wish."

Tao dipped his brush into the spot of black, then mixed it with the red. He lifted his hand and touched it to the drawing. It was still too light, so he dipped in another dab of black. Again his brush touched the drawing. He smiled. It was a deep reddish-brown, the color he wanted. He continued to dip and touch.

Graybeard watched as Tao repeated the motion again and again. He reached out and stopped the boy's hand. "You are not painting on an antler or a seashell," he said. "You are painting on a wall. Do not dab. Swing the brush with your whole arm."

Graybeard took the brush and began sweeping it across the drawing, following the lines of the mammoth's body.

Tao saw the old man's face brighten as he worked, laying on great swaths of color. He felt the excitement as the picture came alive.

"Do not be afraid," said Graybeard, his eyes glowing. "You can always go over what you do not like."

He gave the brush back to Tao and the boy tried again. This time he let his arm go free, swinging the brush across the wall. He mixed gray with yellow to fill in the light areas around the chest and stomach. He painted dark shadows on the shoulders and back to add shading. He saw his mammoth begin to breathe as he filled in the eye and the waving trunk.

When the painting was finished, Graybeard cracked open the duck eggs.

North American rock carving, found in Monument Valley, Utah

He separated the yolks and set them aside. He poured the whites into a clean cockleshell, stirred them with a stick and handed the shell to Tao.

The boy was puzzled. "What is this for?"

"Spread it over your painting and you will see."

With a feather brush Tao washed the egg white over the picture. This time the mammoth came alive with bright new colors. He stared at it in surprise. This had been done by his own hand. He smiled. Never had he felt so happy.

As you read more about early people in this unit, you will discover how people on different continents met their basic needs and developed unique ways of expressing how they lived.

# CHAPTER 1

# PEOPLE OF THE STONE AGE

> 66 The sudden emergence of full human creativity among the advanced hunters of this period . . . is surely one of the most astonishing chapters in all our history. 99
>
> Jacquetta Hawkes,
> *The Atlas of Early Man*

Found in France, this 25,000-year-old sculpture of a woman is one of the earliest images of a human face.

# HUNTERS *and* GATHERERS

**Why do people join groups today?**

**Focus on the Main Idea**
*As you read, look for reasons early people lived and worked in groups.*

**Preview Vocabulary**

| | |
|---|---|
| clan | culture |
| consequence | artifact |
| migration | society |
| Ice Age | division of labor |
| tundra | role |

The earliest humans, people like us, probably lived in Africa. Over tens of thousands of years, they slowly spread into Asia, Europe, Australia, and North and South America. Generation after generation of these early people moved in groups, hunting and gathering enough food to survive. As they wandered, they populated much of the Earth. They continued to follow the same way of life wherever they lived.

## GETTING FOOD

Most of the earliest people united in **clans**, groups of related families brought together for a common purpose. No more than 20 people lived and worked together in a clan. Members of a clan cooperated to meet their basic needs for food, clothing, and shelter. Clan members spent their days roaming the land, collecting wild fruits, nuts, roots, and seeds for the group to eat. Occasionally they captured fish, turtles, birds, or small rodents. Experience taught them which plants and animals could be eaten without causing unwelcome **consequences**, or effects, such as illness or death from poisoning.

Some clans hunted large animals that are now extinct, such as giant oxen and woolly rhinoceroses. These wild resources provided meat for food, bones for tools, and hides for clothing and shelter. A common prey of some early hunters was the mammoth, then the largest land animal on Earth. A mammoth was a kind of hairy elephant with huge, curling tusks. A fully grown mammoth stood 16 feet (4.9 m) at the shoulder—taller than a one-story house.

These blades from Southwest Asia (right) and this carved rock from North Africa (left) are examples of early tools used to hunt and kill prey.

To kill an animal as large as a mammoth, early hunters needed special tools. They sharpened stones, animal bones, antlers, or tusks to make spears and knives. Clan members also needed special skills and teamwork to hunt large game animals. Some early hunters, for example, killed these creatures by chasing them over a cliff. Others wrapped themselves in animal hides and crept close enough to make a kill.

Because early clans were always on the move to hunt animals and gather wild plants, they had no permanent year-round settlements. Rather, they set up seasonal camps in caves or rock shelters near places where plants and animals were plentiful. When food became scarce in one place, clans moved to other familiar places. There they knew they would find more food. Usually clans traveled around a particular area as they searched for food. By following a regular seasonal pattern of **migration**, or movement from one place to the next, clans found enough to eat.

✓ **What role did the clan play in the lives of early people?**

This ancient mammoth skeleton was found in Rancho La Brea, California.

## SPREADING THROUGH THE WORLD

As some clans grew in number, they had to roam farther from their usual hunting and gathering grounds to find enough food. Each new generation expanded the clan's migration pattern. Two or three miles (3.2 to 4.8 km) were added every 20 years—the average length of an early person's life. By this very slow process, humans began to spread throughout the world. It took hundreds of generations tens of thousands of years to accomplish this!

Archaeologists believe that the first clans of early people started in the Rift Valley of Africa about 200,000 years ago and crossed from Africa into southwestern Asia about 100,000 years ago. Today this land is a wide desert. At that time herds of gazelles and deer ranged over a grassy plain. Following these herds, generation after generation of early people slowly migrated farther in every direction.

Those who moved to the east about 60,000 years ago crossed land barriers of rugged mountains into the green valleys of what is now China. Later generations overcame the ocean barrier and crossed the deep, narrow passage east to what is now Indonesia.

**MOVEMENT** Early people probably began to migrate from Africa about 100,000 years ago.

■ On what continents had people arrived by about 60,000 years ago?

From there men, women, and children paddled log rafts across open sea, finally reaching Australia.

About 35,000 years ago some groups of people spread into Europe. Others migrated to the northeast, following herds of wild animals. They reached what is now Siberia in Russia about 25,000 years ago. This was during the time of the last **Ice Age**, a long cold-weather period when huge sheets of ice covered about one-third of the Earth's surface.

The world looked very different during the Ice Age. Because much of the ocean was ice, sea level was nearly 200 feet (61 m) lower than it is today. As a result, there was more land area than there is now. Land bridges connected some islands and continents. Large, moving ice sheets wore down the land into huge areas of **tundra**—large, treeless plains in Arctic regions.

"The hunters who inhabited these immense, frozen, and treeless expanses had to cover vast territories in pursuit of game and other food," says one archaeologist, describing early life on Siberia's tundra. "There were few caves and rock shelters for protection, so they had to build huts that could withstand the severe cold." These huts were built of sod—a layer of soil with grass growing from it—or mammoth bones.

Ice Age migrations did not stop in Siberia, however. Early clans moved east from Siberia over a land bridge that crossed the Bering Strait, a shallow sea between Asia and North America. At least 12,000 and perhaps 40,000 years ago or more, the first people moved into North America. In time, some clans reached South America.

✓ **How did the search for food result in populating the world?**

# EARLY CULTURES AND SOCIETIES

All early people, no matter where they lived, were hunters and gatherers. Eventually, however, the people in different parts of the world developed their own cultures. A **culture** is a unique way of life that sets a group apart from others.

Early people became known by the clothing they wore, the shelters they lived in, and the objects, or **artifacts**, they made. Art, beliefs, customs, and languages also set people apart.

Using spoken language, clan members shared their feelings and let each other know their needs. Older clan members used language to pass on customs to younger members. Language helped early people become a society. A **society** is an organized group of people living and working under an established set of rules and traditions.

As clans merged and grew in size, their society changed. In a clan with only 20 members, everyone did similar tasks. For example, they collected plants, hunted, made tools, built shelters, and prepared hides for clothing. In larger clans of 50 to 100 members, a **division of labor** began. Different members did different tasks based on their abilities and the clan's needs.

Each person in these larger clans took on a **role**, a part he or she played to help society. A person good at carving spent most of his or her time making tools for the group. An expert at preparing and sewing hides became the group's clothing maker. Because food gathering and hunting were important to early societies, the group's hunters and gatherers came to be viewed as its leaders.

In some early societies, women who were skilled at gathering plants became leaders. In other societies, men

↑ This horse carved from amber was found in Brandenburg, Germany.

↑ This carved bone found in Ishango, Zaire, may have been used as a counting device by early Africans about 8,500 years ago.

↑ The skill of ancient artists can be seen by studying this mammoth-tusk sculpture. Why do you think early people made such items?

## MAKING TOOLS WITH NATURAL RESOURCES

1.

2.

3.

**LEARNING FROM DIAGRAMS** Early people made needles by following these steps: (1) They used a flint tool to cut a triangle shape from an antler. (2) They then made the hole of the needle with a sharp piece of flint. (3) Next they sharpened the needle's point by rubbing it across a block of sandstone.

■ Why do you think early people decided to make needles?

who were successful at hunting were made leaders. With the division of labor, men's and women's roles in some societies most likely became different.

Leaders played a major role as the group's decision makers and the keepers of tradition. They decided how their society would handle danger from outside, and they kept

order within the society. One way leaders kept order was by controlling the sharing of scarce resources. In early societies this most often meant food—the most important resource for any people.

 ***What was the major advantage of a clan's getting larger?***

# *L*ESSON 1 REVIEW

## Check Understanding

1. **Recall the Facts**   How did early people get the food they needed to survive?
2. **Focus on the Main Idea**   How did living and working in groups help early people survive?

## Think Critically

3. **Think More About It**   For what purposes besides getting food might early people have worked together?
4. **Explore Viewpoints**   Leaders and other group members may have had different ideas

about how resources should be shared. Why might this have been so? What might have been the consequences of these differences?
5. **Past to Present**   How do people in our society cooperate in day-to-day living?

## Show What You Know

**Story Activity**   Imagine that you are a hunter-gatherer in a clan in central Asia. Make up a story you might tell your children about a time when the clan worked together to find food. Rehearse your story several times, and then tell it to a classmate.

# EARLY FARMERS

LESSON 2

## Link to Our World

**How does change affect your life today?**

**Focus on the Main Idea**
Consider the effects of change on the early people who became food producers instead of food collectors.

**Preview Vocabulary**

| | |
|---|---|
| domesticate | agriculture |
| economy | environment |
| livestock | maize |
| nomad | subsist |

As people began to raise their own crops, they needed new types of technology. Early people used this tool, called a quern, to grind grain. How do you think early people made this tool?

As early societies grew, many clans found that they could no longer depend on hunting and gathering for their basic needs. This method did not always bring in enough food. Because of this, some early societies began shifting from food collecting to food producing—growing crops and raising animals.

## CONTROLLING NATURE

About 10,000 years ago some early people in hunter-gatherer societies began to produce some of their food. This change was important because their food supply was no longer limited to what they could find or hunt. People learned to domesticate both plants and animals. To **domesticate** is to control nature for people's use.

Women did most of the food gathering in early societies and were probably the first to domesticate plants. Perhaps they saw that where they threw away seeds one year, new plants grew the next. Over time they learned to scatter plant seeds on purpose. They chose seeds from plants that were plentiful, grew fast, and tasted good.

Some societies soon came to depend less on wild plants and more on crops grown in small gardens by early farmers. Growing crops, however, meant that those societies had to stay in one place.

The process of planting, caring for, and harvesting crops takes many months of constant care. Early farming societies built year-round shelters, formed small villages, and grew crops on the surrounding land. These societies' **economy**, or the way people use resources to meet their needs, became based mainly on their crops.

REGIONS Early farming areas developed in different places around the world.
■ What does this map tell you about where early farming areas developed?

Even in farming societies animals were still an important resource. Some societies went on hunting wild animals for food, bones, and hides. Others began to domesticate animals as well as plants. The dog may have been the first animal domesticated to help hunters track wild animals. Later, people domesticated wild sheep and goats to provide a ready supply of meat, milk, and wool. Some early people came to depend less on raising crops and more on raising **livestock**, domesticated animals such as cattle, sheep, and pigs.

Many of the early people who cared for livestock were **nomads**. They moved from place to place with their herds of animals to find pasture and water. Like hunting and gathering nomads, those who herded livestock did not build villages or other year-round settlements. Instead, they lived in temporary shelters and traveled in clans.

Not all people adopted a new way of life as farmers or herders. Some went on hunting and gathering their food. In fact, a few groups of people still do.

✓ *What major change took place in the food supply of early people?*

## EFFECTS OF CHANGE

**Agriculture**, the raising of domesticated plants and animals, changed forever the societies that practiced it. Agriculture provided a reliable food source. Food production increased as people invented tools, such as the plow, and came up with refinements, such as domesticating cattle to pull plows and collecting water for crops.

Agriculture made more food available, but it also made living conditions more difficult in some ways. Instead of finding

## SETTLEMENTS IN SOUTHWEST ASIA

Black Sea

Caspian Sea

ASIA

Çatal Hüyük

Taurus Mts.

Mureybit

Nineveh

Tigris R.

Jarmo

Euphrates River

Zagros Mountains

Ali-Kosh

Mediterranean Sea

Syrian Desert

Jericho

al-Ubaid

Beidha

0      200      400 Miles

Eridu

0    200    400 Kilometers
Lambert Conformal Conic Projection

Nile River

Red Sea

AFRICA

• Early settlement
— Present-day border
----- Ancient coastline

**Map Skill HUMAN-ENVIRONMENT INTERACTIONS**
Early farming villages rose in Southwest Asia.
■ Near what type of natural feature did early people often build their farming villages?

deaths due to starvation and disease when drought and insect attacks killed crops and livestock. There were also deaths due to wars when people fought to protect farmland or to take land away from others.

People began to make weapons for war and to build walls around their farming villages for protection. One of the oldest known walled villages was built at a site known today as Jericho in Southwest Asia. The people lived in mud-brick huts grouped inside stone walls. The village walls were 20 feet (6.1 m) high and 6 feet (1.8 m) thick.

Some of the ways in which early farmers practiced agriculture had consequences for their surroundings, or **environment**. Farmers cleared land for crops by cutting and burning the wild plants that grew there. The ashes made good fertilizer. But the rich variety of wild plants that once supported herds of wild animals was lost when the land began to be used as fields and pastures.

**What were an advantage and a disadvantage of agriculture?**

food only for the clan, people also had to raise crops to feed their domesticated animals.

In some places agriculture increased the rate of population growth. Yet there were

## DIVERSITY IN EARLY AGRICULTURE

In the different places where agriculture developed, people domesticated a wide

**LEARNING FROM GRAPHS** The population of the world grew dramatically because of the introduction of agriculture.
■ What was the world's population in 10,000 B.C.? How many more people were there by 4000 B.C.?

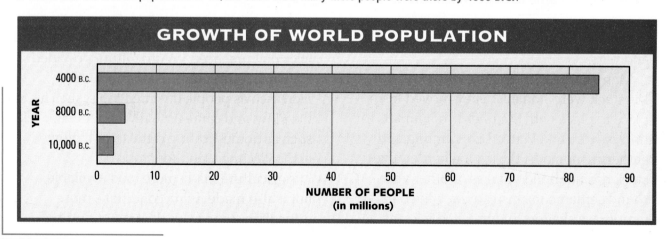

**GROWTH OF WORLD POPULATION**

YEAR

4000 B.C.

8000 B.C.

10,000 B.C.

0    10    20    30    40    50    60    70    80    90

**NUMBER OF PEOPLE**
(in millions)

Some cave paintings, like this one from Algeria, Africa, reflect everyday life. In this painting men, women, and children work alongside herds of cattle. At the far left is one main farm product of early people—wheat.

variety of plants and animals. Agriculture in the Tigris and Euphrates river valley of Southwest Asia was based on growing wheat and barley and on raising sheep, goats, and cattle. Throughout the Nile Valley in North Africa, agriculture produced wheat, barley, flax, sheep, goats, cattle, and pigs. Far to the east, people settling the river valleys of present-day Pakistan and China raised grains such as rice and millet and kept pigs, chickens, and water buffaloes.

Meanwhile, in the Americas, early farmers began growing beans and chili peppers in the mountain valleys of what is now Peru and potatoes in what is now Bolivia. Plants later

domesticated in the Americas included squash, gourds, guavas, and **maize**, or corn.

At its beginning, agriculture offered another way besides hunting and gathering for people to **subsist**, or survive. In many places agriculture led to year-round villages and more complex societies. People did not always stay in one place, however. Many groups went on migrating, searching for new land for their crops and fresh pastures for their herds.

 **What is meant by diversity of agriculture?**

# LESSON 2 REVIEW

## Check Understanding

1. **Recall the Facts**   What new way of getting food changed societies forever?
2. **Focus on the Main Idea**   How did early people become food producers? How did this change affect early societies?

## Think Critically

3. **Think More About It**   Why did ancient societies based on agriculture feel a need to control land while hunter-gatherer societies did not?

4. **Past to Present**   Clearing forest land today affects the environment just as clearing wild plants did long ago. What were the effects then? What are the effects now?

## Show What You Know

**Debate Activity**   Think about how domesticating plants and animals changed societies. Take the side either of a farmer or of a hunter-gatherer in a debate over the consequences of the change from hunting and gathering to agriculture among early people.

# HowTo

# Use a Parallel Time Line

## Why Is This Skill Important?

Just as maps help you understand *where* something happened, time lines help you understand *when* something happened. Time lines let you put events in sequence.

## Think About Time Lines

The time line you see on this page is called a **parallel time line**. It is really several time lines in one. This type of time line is useful if you want to show related events. You could use it to show when the same kinds of events happened in different areas. You could also show events that happened in different places during the same time. Or you might use a parallel time line to show different kinds of events that happened in one place during the same time.

The four parts of the time line below are divided into spans of 2,000 years, beginning at 8000 B.C. and ending at A.D. 2000. The abbreviation **B.C.** stands for "before Christ." **A.D.** stands for *anno Domini,* a Latin phrase meaning "in the year of the Lord." This abbreviation identifies how many years have passed since the birth of Jesus Christ.

## PARALLEL TIME LINE: EARLY AGRICULTURE

**AFRICA**

8000 B.C.　　6000 B.C.　　4000 B.C.　　2000 B.C.　　B.C. A.D.　　A.D. 2000

6000 B.C.
Northern Africa

2500 B.C.
Western Africa

A.D. 100
Southern Africa

**AMERICAS**

8000 B.C.　　6000 B.C.　　4000 B.C.　　2000 B.C.　　B.C. A.D.　　A.D. 2000

7800 B.C.
South America

3400 B.C.
Middle America

2000 B.C.
North America

**ASIA**

8000 B.C.　　6000 B.C.　　4000 B.C.　　2000 B.C.　　B.C. A.D.　　A.D. 2000

8000 B.C.
Southwestern
Asia

6000 B.C.
Western Asia

3000 B.C.
Southeastern
Asia

2500 B.C.
Southern Asia

**EUROPE**

8000 B.C.　　6000 B.C.　　4000 B.C.　　2000 B.C.　　B.C. A.D.　　A.D. 2000

6000 B.C.
Southeastern
Europe

5300 B.C.
Central Europe

4000 B.C.
Northern Europe

On this time line, years are numbered backward and forward from the time of Christ's birth. The larger the number of a year B.C., the longer ago it happened. The larger the number of a year A.D., the more recently it happened.

Other time lines may use different abbreviations. Some time lines are labeled using B.C.E. and C.E. rather than B.C. and A.D. On those time lines, **B.C.E.** stands for "before the Common Era," and **C.E.** stands for "Common Era." B.C.E. refers to the same years that B.C. does, while C.E. refers to the same years that A.D. does.

The dates of events in the very distant past are often approximate, or not exact, because no one knows just when these events happened. Sometimes a date on a time line does not mean that the event happened in that exact year. It means that the earliest **evidence**, or proof, is from about that time. These approximate times are often shown after the Latin term *circa* or its abbreviation *c. Circa* means "about."

The time line on page 48 shows when agriculture developed during the Stone Age in different geographic regions. The Stone Age was a time when early people developed the first societies. The Stone Age is divided into two parts. During the Paleolithic period, or the Old Stone Age (before 8000 B.C.), people were hunters and gatherers and lived in small clans. During the Neolithic period, or the New Stone Age (from 8000 B.C. to as late as A.D. 1000 in some parts of the world), people domesticated plants and animals. This led to the development of agriculture.

## Understand the Process

Look at each tier, or level, of the time line on page 48. Then answer the following questions.

1. Several geographic regions are shown on the time line. In which region did agriculture first appear?
2. Of the regions shown on the time line, which was the last to have agriculture?
3. In which regions of the world did people develop agriculture at about the same time?

4. The development of agriculture changed societies forever. Study the information on the time line. What conclusions can you draw about the development of agriculture and its effects on world history?

## Think and Apply

Make a parallel time line comparing important events in your life with those of family members or friends. Make sure that your time line has a bar for each person and a title. Write three questions for a classmate to answer using your time line.

The following steps will help you make your time line:

- Identify the events you want to show.
- Determine the length of time over which the events took place.
- Divide the time line into equal parts.
- Make the time line, and mark the years on it.
- Add the events you want to display. It is always a good idea to double-check the dates of events to be sure your information is accurate.
- Give your time line a title.

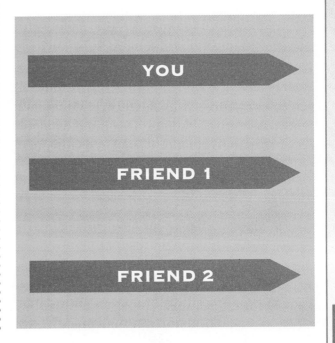

YOU

FRIEND 1

FRIEND 2

# Skara Brae

## THE STORY OF A PREHISTORIC VILLAGE

### by Olivier Dunrea

Skara Brae was an early farming village on an island off northern Scotland. Shortly before 2500 B.C. a sudden and intense storm covered the village in sand. It remained covered for more than 4,300 years. Then, in A.D. 1850, a powerful windstorm stripped the sand from the dunes and exposed the stone walls of the village. What archaeologists know about life in Skara Brae comes from studying the stone huts and the objects the early people left behind. Through careful study of this evidence, archaeologists were able to piece together the story of this village of long ago.

Read now about what life may have been like in Skara Brae and in other farming villages long ago. Think about how life in these early settlements compares with life in hunter-gatherer societies and with our lives today.

By 3500 B.C. farmers and herders had reached a group of islands to the north of Scotland—the Orkneys.

They found the Orkneys an ideal place to live. There were gently rolling hills, open grasslands for their sheep and cattle, and wide, sand-fringed bays. The islands had no predatory animals that would attack their livestock. It

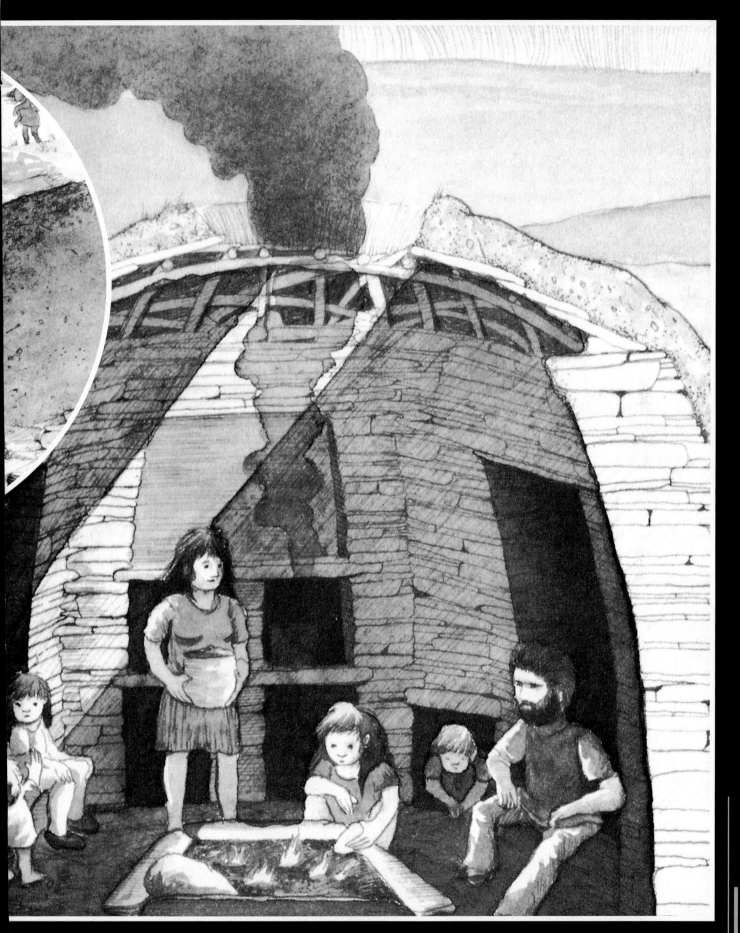

Writer/illustrator Olivier Dunrea pictures what life may have been like in Skara Brae.

Orkney was a strange place to these early settlers. They were accustomed to trees and forests. In Orkney there were far fewer trees.

But though there was very little wood, there was plenty of fuel. Mosses and other plants had decayed in bogs to form peat. The peat could be burned like coal. The settlers could keep warm and cook their meat around a peat fire.

Most of all, there was a great abundance of stone on the islands. Stones were everywhere—on the beaches, on the grasslands, and on the hills.

Pins made of bone in Skara Brae around 2500 B.C.

The herders and farmers chose these stones to build their permanent homes and monuments.

In time the Orkneys became more populated. New masses of migrating people reached their shores. Several generations of settlers came and went, and some ventured off to the smaller and less populated islands.

One band of settlers, seeking better grazing land for their animals, moved farther out on the main island. Making their way to the farthest west coast, they explored the land for a suitable place to live.

As they marched northward along the rugged cliffs and inlets, they came to a beautiful wide bay—the Bay of Skaill. There were sand dunes, open grassland, and no other settlers to compete for the land's resources. It was here the band decided to make their new home.

There were twenty people in the group: four small families. Together they owned a flock of sheep, a small herd of cattle, and a few pigs.

After surveying the land around the bay, they chose the southwest corner in which to erect their temporary shelters. The women and older children put up the tents, using wooden poles they had brought with them. These tents made of skins would protect them from rain and wind.

It was the task of the older children to tend the livestock, even though the animals mostly fended for themselves and found food wherever they could.

## ORKNEY ISLANDS

0     5     10 Miles
0     5     10 Kilometers
Lambert Conformal Conic Projection

ATLANTIC OCEAN

North Ronaldsay

Westray

Sanday

Rousay     Eday

North Sea

SKARA BRAE

Stronsay

Shapinsay

59°N

Mainland
Stromness     Kirkwall

UNITED KINGDOM

Hoy

FRANCE

EUROPE

South Ronaldsay

SPAIN

3°W

**PLACE** Study the map.
■ What do you think were some advantages and disadvantages of living in Skara Brae?

Example of building method used in Skara Brae home

SECTION THROUGH WALL

CORBELLING

HEARTH

During this period, settlers lived off their animals. To their diet of meat and milk they added wild foods foraged[1] from the land and sea—birds and eggs, fish, shellfish such as limpets,[2] and wild grains. The men sometimes brought in the meat of deer and other wild animals as well.

Through the summer, autumn, and winter the band continued to live in their tents. During the winter months they started construction of a new village that would have proper houses for all the families.

While they built the permanent stone houses, everyone worked. The men gathered the larger stones needed for the foundations and walls. The women and children also gathered stones to be used in the construction of the huts.

Everyone worked together on all the houses. One partly completed house was used as a shelter for the cattle, sheep, and pigs. The band continued to live off their animals as well as the land and sea.

There were plenty of stones on the beach around the bay, and collecting them went quickly. The stones could be easily split to make straight, uniform surfaces for building.

The stones were laid one on top of another without the use of mortar.[3] We now call this method of building drywall construction. The settlers might have used curved whalebones washed up on the beach to help support the roofs.

The houses were small when completed, measuring only twelve feet long by six to nine feet wide in the interior. The plan of each house was basically square, with rounded corners. In one of the corners, there was a small, beehive-shaped cell, used either for storage or as a latrine.[4]

The walls were built by piling stone upon stone. A few feet above the floor the stones began to project a little toward the inside of the hut. This overlapping construction is called corbelling.[5]

---

[1] **foraged:** hunted for food
[2] **limpets:** small shellfish

[3] **mortar:** mixture of lime, sand, and water
[4] **latrine:** toilet
[5] **corbelling:** stepping upward and outward

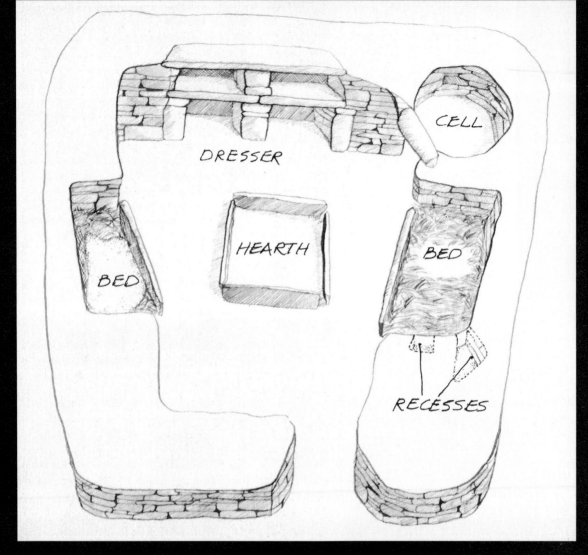

Layout of a typical Skara Brae home

Each hut was big enough to allow room for a central hearth,[6] a stone bed set into the wall on either side of the hearth, and a stone dresser built into the rear wall. The mother and small children slept in the bed to the left of the hearth; the father slept in the bed to the right.

The stone beds were filled with heather[7] and skins, making them comfortable and warm for sleeping. There were one or two small recesses for keeping personal possessions in the wall above each bed.

Within a few weeks the little huts were completed. And so began the occupation of the village. It was around 3100 B.C.

As they went about the routine of their daily life, the villagers allowed their refuse to pile up against the outside walls of their huts. Shells, broken bones, fragments of pottery, sand, and everything no longer used was heaped around the structures.

This refuse, called midden, helped to insulate the huts. It kept the cold winds from blowing through the chinks in the stones. Over the years these midden heaps mixed with sand and became a claylike covering from which grass grew.

Now the huts looked like the surrounding dunes of the Bay of Skaill. And thus came into existence the village we now call Skara Brae—the village of the hilly dunes.

As the generations came and went, so did the huts. The older huts were sometimes taken down stone by stone to build new huts.

The wind-blown sands constantly shifted around the dunes and the dwellings of Skara Brae. Sometimes one of the huts was overcome by the drifts and disappeared. Another hut was often built on top of it, and life continued as before.

The shifting sands and the ever-increasing midden heaps continually changed the appearance of the village. Other changes also took place. The new huts were built to be larger and more comfortable.

The beds had stone pillars at each corner supporting a canopy made of skins. The stone dresser was now built against the rear wall and was no longer set into it.

Inside, the hearth remained the focal point of the room. The stone beds, however, were no longer built into the walls but projected out into the room. Sometimes a third bed was added for the children.

The collecting of limpets, a kind of shellfish, had become increasingly important to the villagers. Limpet shells were heaped in great quantities around the huts along with

In the floor of the huts the villagers built stone boxes carefully sealed with clay to make them watertight. In these holding tanks they kept their limpets in the water for later use as bait or perhaps as food. Several tanks were built so that there could always be a ready supply of limpets.

At some point in their history the inhabitants of Skara Brae most likely began to cultivate small plots of grain. They remained an isolated group, living a quiet life off the land and sea and their stock of animals.

As the village grew, so did its population. The villagers were bound together by common need, common activity, and the beliefs and ceremonies that characterize all Stone Age peoples.

Evidence of one of these beliefs was found underneath a wall of one of the later huts. Two aged women of the village had died. Their bodies were buried beneath the wall in the hope and belief that their spirits would support the wall and help sustain the life of the village. This was the only time the villagers performed this rite. Henceforth the dead would be buried in communal burial mounds.

When the settlers were first building their permanent homes, there was little time for anything else. Several generations later, the village was well established and had settled into an ordered pattern of life. The villagers now attended to other matters. They were able to focus on the social and ceremonial life that

Comb made of bone from Skara Brae

For the Neolithic villagers of Skara Brae, one such activity might have been the construction of a communal burial mound, or cairn.

The construction of the cairn took longer than that of the huts because it was much larger. Once it was completed, it served generation after generation.

The exterior of the cairn was covered with earth, and in time grass grew over it. It looked like a hill in the landscape.

There was also time for the villagers to practice their various crafts. The women made pottery.

Necklace of bone and teeth made in Skara Brae about 2000 B.C.

Sometimes they made engraved or raised designs on their pots. But the people of Skara Brae, unlike many Neolithic peoples, were not especially skilled at this craft.

The men spent hours carving strange, intricate patterns on stone balls.

The teeth and bones from sheep, cattle, and whales were used to make beautiful beads and necklaces.

For a long time the life of Skara Brae continued uninterrupted. Then, around 2400 B.C., when the village had settled into its way of life, a terrible catastrophe occurred that caused it to be abandoned forever.

As the villagers went about their daily tasks of collecting food and tending their herds or practicing their crafts, a sudden and violent storm arose. The storm came so unexpectedly and with such severity that the inhabitants fled without being able to collect all their belongings.

In her haste to escape, one woman broke her string of beads as she squeezed through the narrow doorway of her hut.

The necklace fell to the floor of the passageway, and there it remained.

In another hut an old man was gnawing a choice bit of mutton when the storm took him by surprise. He dropped the bone by his bed and fled the hut in panic.

Then the wind-driven sands quickly filled all the stone huts, burying the necklace and the half-eaten bone for the ages.

The storm raged with a fury the villagers had never experienced before. They fled the village in blind terror.

The sea pounded in the bay, and to the prehistoric people of Skara Brae it must have seemed that the world was coming to an end.

The villagers abandoned their village in the hilly dunes. Several times a small number of them returned and camped under the remaining exposed walls of the huts. And then they never returned again. Over the centuries the sand continued to drift in, until nothing was visible.

Although the name Skara Brae remained, memory of the village itself vanished.

## Literature Review

1. In your own words, describe what life was like in Skara Brae.
2. In what ways was village life different from life in hunter-gatherer societies and from life today?
3. Make a diagram or model of what you think Skara Brae may have looked like. Use labels to identify and explain various features of your project.

# Make a Generalization

## Why Is This Skill Important?

Sometimes the same kind of event happens to you over and over and over. When this occurs, you can make a general statement about the cause of or the effect of the event. This kind of statement is called a generalization. A generalization is a general statement made about a group of people, events, or relationships. Generalizations explain things that are usually true. By making generalizations, you can describe events or relationships and how they are alike.

Suppose that you stayed up late and were too tired the next day to do your best on a test. Your friend, kept awake by noise, did poorly in math that same day. Another classmate did not sleep much because of a toothache and was too tired to do well on schoolwork.

How are these three examples alike? In each, a student didn't get enough sleep and didn't

Gathering fuel in Skara Brae

do his or her best work at school. You could say: *People don't do their best work when they haven't had enough sleep.* This is a generalization.

## Remember What You Have Read

You have read *Skara Brae: The Story of a Prehistoric Village.* Look at the following questions. Think of a generalization that explains how the people of Skara Brae met their basic needs.

1. What materials did the people of Skara Brae use to build houses? Where did they get those materials?
2. What did they eat at first? Where did they get that food?
3. What did they use as fuel? Where did they get that fuel?

To make a generalization, summarize the events and facts and determine how they are alike. You might say: *People in simple societies meet their basic needs by using materials from the environment around them.*

## Understand the Process

To formulate a generalization, use the following steps:

- List the facts or events.
- Think about how the facts or events are alike.
- Write a sentence that makes a general statement linking the facts or events.
- Test your generalization. Make sure it is true for most things that might happen.

## Think and Apply

How do people in society today meet their basic needs? How do they get housing materials, food, and fuel? Develop a generalization based on these questions. Test your generalization to be sure it is true.

BUILDING CITIZENSHIP

## CONNECT MAIN IDEAS

Use this organizer to show that you understand how the chapter's main ideas are connected. Copy the organizer onto a separate sheet of paper. Then complete it by writing three important details about hunters and gatherers and three important details about early farmers.

**Hunters and Gatherers**

Early people lived and worked in groups to collect food.

1. _____
   _____
2. _____
   _____
3. _____
   _____

**People of the Stone Age**

**Early Farmers**

Many early people became food producers instead of food collectors.

1. _____
   _____
2. _____
   _____
3. _____
   _____

## WRITE MORE ABOUT IT

1. **Write a Diary Entry**   Imagine that you are a young person in a clan. Write a diary entry about going on a mammoth hunt. What happened? Were you excited? scared? proud? Explain why. Could one hunter have killed a mammoth? How did hunters cooperate? Your entry should show how important cooperation was between clan members.

2. **Write a Magazine Article**   Describe a home in Skara Brae as if you were writing an article for a magazine about homes. Write as though you are giving a tour from one part of the home to another. Be sure to tell how the home fits into the environment. First write a rough draft. Then revise it. Your final article should look like it is part of a magazine.

## USE VOCABULARY

Write a term from this list to complete each of the sentences that follow.

agriculture     culture
artifact         domesticate
clan            migration

1. A group of families who band together in order to survive is called a ____.

2. The movement of clans from one place to another is called ____.

3. A ____ is a unique way of life that sets one group apart from others.

4. An ____ is an object made and used by people.

5. Raising plants and animals for the use of people is called ____.

6. People ____ plants and animals for food and other uses.

## CHECK UNDERSTANDING

1. Why did early people live and work in clans?

2. What plants and animals did early people domesticate?

3. What is a society?

4. What kinds of jobs did people have in large clans?

5. Why did the people of Skara Brae build stone houses?

## THINK CRITICALLY

1. **Personally Speaking**   Would you rather have been a hunter-gatherer or an early farmer? Give reasons to support your answer.

2. **Cause and Effect**   Some clans grew larger and larger. How did this affect the kinds of work their people did?

3. **Think More About It**   How do you think controlling the food supply might help a leader to keep order?

4. **Explore Viewpoints**   Why do you think some people prefer to live in large groups and others in small groups?

5. **Past to Present**   What are some of the objects, customs, and clothing that identify your culture?

## APPLY SKILLS

**How to Use a Parallel Time Line**   Look at the time line on page 48. Remember that complex societies—which have governments, social classes, and technologies—formed after the development of agriculture. After what date would you expect to find such a society in South America? in North America? in eastern Asia? Save your answers, and compare them with what you learn in Unit 2.

**How to Make a Generalization**   Make a generalization about the development of agriculture and complex societies. Use the development of the prehistoric village of Skara Brae to support your generalization.

## READ MORE ABOUT IT

*Digging Up the Past: The Story of an Archaeological Adventure* by Carollyn James. Franklin Watts. Damien, his mother, and a friend set up an archaeological dig to find out where the treasures and junk they have found in their neighborhood came from.

*Seth of the Lion People* by Bonnie Pryor. Morrow Junior Books. Seth, a young teenager with a twisted leg, is allowed to stay with his stone-age clan only because of his storytelling skills. Seth realizes that his people need to change from hunters to craftworkers and growers of food. Will they let him lead them and help them change their way of life?

# PEOPLE OF THE FERTILE CRESCENT

> 66 The scattered people I gathered; with pasturage and water I provided them; I pastured them with abundance, and settled them in peaceful dwellings. 99
>
> Hammurabi,
> King of Babylon
> 1792–1750 B.C.

Bronze statue of Hammurabi

# LESSON 1

# CIVILIZATION in MESOPOTAMIA

## Link to Our World

### Why do people today try new ways of doing things?

### Focus on the Main Idea
As you read, think about the new lifeways developed by societies living in ancient Mesopotamia.

### Preview Vocabulary

| | |
|---|---|
| civilization | authority |
| technology | surplus |
| ziggurat | merchant |
| government | social class |
| city-state | scribe |
| monarchy | innovation |

The Fertile Crescent starts on the eastern shore of the Mediterranean Sea in Southwest Asia. Like the shape of a quarter moon, it curves around the Syrian Desert, reaching south to the Persian Gulf. By about 4000 B.C. many farming villages dotted the rich land of the Fertile Crescent. In the valley of the Tigris and Euphrates rivers at the eastern end of the Fertile Crescent, some farming villages attracted thousands of new settlers. There in the region called Mesopotamia, "the land between the rivers," several villages grew into cities. The earliest cities rose up in a part of Mesopotamia called Sumer. As people began to live and work together in these cities, they formed a complex society, or civilization. A **civilization** is a culture with well-developed forms of government, religion, writing, and learning. City life brought new problems, however. The need arose to find creative ways to solve them.

## NEW INVENTIONS

Farmers living in the region of Sumer used the Tigris and Euphrates rivers to water their crops. Yet these rivers were unpredictable. At times they flooded the land without warning. They carried away crops and sometimes whole villages. For people who subsisted on agriculture, a flood was the worst possible natural disaster. The loss of crops when farmland was flooded meant starvation.

To control the water on which they depended, farmers in Sumer built dikes and dug canals. Dikes held the flooding rivers within their banks. Canals carried extra water back to the rivers after floods. Building dikes and canals took special knowledge of making and using tools. The use of tools and skills to make a product or achieve a goal is called **technology**. The early settlers of Sumer developed the technology to carry out successful agriculture and to build cities.

The technology of Sumer was greatly advanced by the invention of the wheel. Farmers in Sumer made wheels by attaching boards together and rounding them off. Later they covered the rims with pieces of copper.

Wheel technology made possible other inventions, including the wheeled cart. With a wheeled cart, a domesticated animal such as an ox or a donkey could pull a heavy load. Wheeled carts were important in moving construction materials for houses and other buildings in Sumer's growing cities.

✓ **What two inventions helped early farmers deal with flooding?**

## ARCHITECTURE AND RELIGIOUS BELIEFS

The largest building in most Sumerian cities was a huge mud-brick temple called a **ziggurat** (ZIH•guh•rat). Some ziggurats stood as tall as a seven-story building. They towered above the houses like skyscrapers.

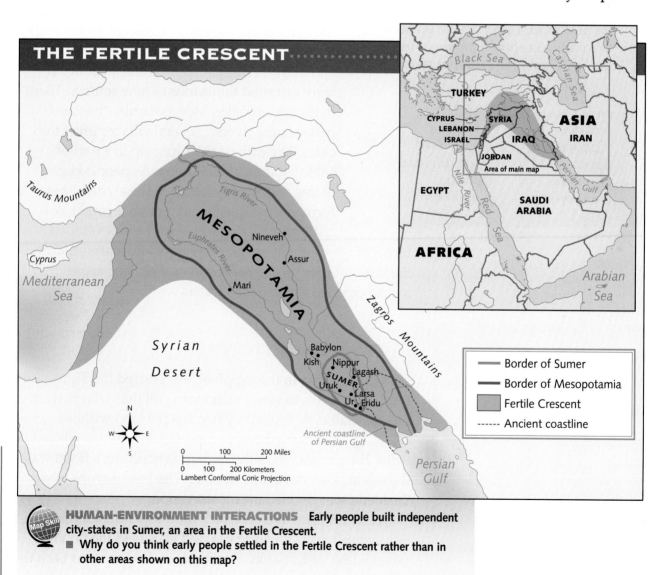

**THE FERTILE CRESCENT**

Taurus Mountains
Tigris River
MESOPOTAMIA
Nineveh
Assur
Euphrates River
Cyprus
Mediterranean Sea
Mari
Syrian Desert
Zagros Mountains
Babylon
Kish
Nippur
Lagash
SUMER
Uruk
Larsa
Ur
Eridu
Ancient coastline of Persian Gulf
Persian Gulf

N
W E
S

0   100   200 Miles
0   100   200 Kilometers
Lambert Conformal Conic Projection

Black Sea
Caspian Sea
TURKEY
CYPRUS
LEBANON
ISRAEL
SYRIA
IRAQ
ASIA
IRAN
JORDAN
Area of main map
EGYPT
Nile River
Red Sea
SAUDI ARABIA
Persian Gulf
AFRICA
Arabian Sea

— Border of Sumer
— Border of Mesopotamia
▨ Fertile Crescent
----- Ancient coastline

**HUMAN-ENVIRONMENT INTERACTIONS** Early people built independent city-states in Sumer, an area in the Fertile Crescent.
■ Why do you think early people settled in the Fertile Crescent rather than in other areas shown on this map?

Ancient ziggurats (left) towered above the land in ancient Mesopotamia about 5,000 years ago. Even after many years of erosion, the Ziggurat Assur (above) still stands in what is now Iraq.

Builders constructed a ziggurat in layers, each one smaller than the one below. On the highest level of each ziggurat stood a shrine for the city's special god.

The religious beliefs of the Sumerian people showed the importance of agriculture in their lives. They believed that by pleasing their gods, they would get large harvests in return. Floods and other natural disasters, they thought, were signs that the gods were angry at them. Chief among the gods of Sumer were Enlil, the god of winds, storm, and rain, and Ea, the god of the waters and wisdom.

In time a ziggurat became more than a shrine for a god. The people in Sumer built smaller buildings around the base of the ziggurat. Some of these buildings had different kinds of workshops where craft-workers, or skilled workers, made clothing and metal goods. Others were temples in which priests performed religious cere-monies. The ziggurat with all its buildings, enclosed within great walls, was the center of activity in each city.

 **How did religion in Sumer reflect the importance of agriculture?**

## THE ROLE OF GOVERNMENT

Constructing dikes, canals, ziggurats, and other city buildings took large numbers of people. When large numbers of people live and work together, laws are needed to keep order. In societies as large as those in Sumer, this could be done only with a government. A **government** is an organized system that groups use to make laws and decisions.

Sumer was made up of 12 independent city-states. A **city-state** included a city or village and the farmlands around it. Each city-state had its own leaders and its own government. In early days each government was run by a small group of leaders and a chief leader chosen by that group. Together they made laws and decided what work had to be done.

The city-states of Sumer often waged wars to enlarge their farmland or to protect it from others who wanted to take it. In times of peril, the group of leaders could not always agree on what to do. To provide stronger leadership, each Sumerian city-state formed a new government. The new government was a **monarchy**, in which one person had

## Gilgamesh

Gilgamesh was a real king who ruled over the Sumerian city-state of Uruk sometime between 2700 and 2500 B.C. Over time King Gilgamesh became a figure of legend. People described Gilgamesh as one-third man and two-thirds god. Stories of Gilgamesh and his adventures were probably passed on as oral tradition for centuries before being recorded in writing. Scribes in Mesopotamia put the stories of Gilgamesh into their most complete form by 1300 B.C.

complete **authority**, or right, to rule in peacetime and to lead soldiers in time of war.

Sumerians called the rulers of their city-states "big men," or kings, because the rulers were most often men. They were concerned with every part of Sumerian life. Because of the king's importance, the Sumerians believed their kings were almost like gods. One of the oldest stories in the world is a story poem from Sumerian times. It tells the adventures of Gilgamesh, a Sumerian "big man." The story praises Gilgamesh as "he who knew everything."

 **What type of government did Sumerian city-states form to provide stronger leadership?**

## CHANGING ECONOMY

By about 3000 B.C. some Sumerian city-states had large populations, while others remained small. The city-state of Ur grew to have more than 30,000 people. Such population growth was possible only because of the success of agriculture. Sumerian farms produced enough food to create a **surplus**, or extra supply, to feed the people who came to settle in Sumer.

Having a surplus meant that some people could spend their working hours doing things other than growing or finding food. As a result, a complex division of labor occurred. Some people became craftworkers in stone, clay, wool, leather, or metals such as copper. Others became managers, skilled at directing the work of others. Some became **merchants**, people who bought and sold goods for a living.

Sumerian merchants traded with merchants throughout the Fertile Crescent as far away as the Mediterranean Sea. The Sumerians traded what they had in surplus—wheat, barley, and copper tools such as axheads and plowheads. In return, they got what they wanted—wood, salt, precious stones, and raw copper.

 **What effect did a surplus of food have on life in Sumer?**

## DIVISIONS IN SOCIETY

Because the work of some people came to be valued more than the work of others, Sumerian society became divided. This division created **social classes**, or groups with different levels of importance.

The most important or highest social class in Sumer was made up of nobles—the king, priests, and other important leaders and their families. Nobles owned much of the land and were regarded as the privileged class. They had the most wealth and honor.

Next came the class of merchants, craftworkers, and managers. This middle class included carpenters, potters, bricklayers, doctors, and scribes. A **scribe** was a person who knew how to write. Writing was a valuable skill in Sumer, where most people—including kings and nobles—could neither read nor write. Scribes kept records, wrote letters for other people, and copied down stories and songs. Scribes and others in the middle social class of Sumer exchanged their services or the goods they made for the services and goods they needed.

Laborers, or unskilled workers, and slaves made up the lowest class in Sumerian society. Most slaves were prisoners of war. Others were enslaved as punishment for crimes or to pay off debts. Slaves in Sumerian society were not enslaved for life. For example, those who owed a debt could gain their freedom when the debt was paid.

In each Sumerian social class, a division existed between men and women. Men owned most of the property and held most leadership roles. Laws in Sumer allowed women to own property. However, most women did not. Women sometimes held positions of leadership, especially as priests. Ancient records also refer to women scribes and doctors. Most Sumerian women, however, did not hold positions of leadership in the community.

✓ *What were Sumer's social classes?*

These gypsum statues (left) show how one early artist pictured the Sumerians. Below is a model of a Sumerian house. What social class do you think the owners of this house belonged to?

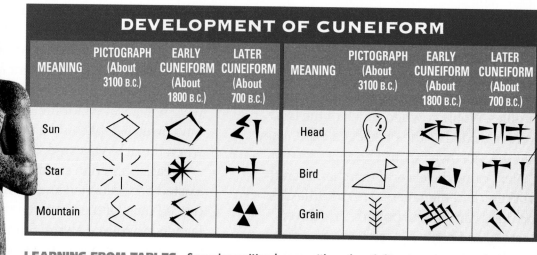

## DEVELOPMENT OF CUNEIFORM

| MEANING | PICTOGRAPH (About 3100 B.C.) | EARLY CUNEIFORM (About 1800 B.C.) | LATER CUNEIFORM (About 700 B.C.) | MEANING | PICTOGRAPH (About 3100 B.C.) | EARLY CUNEIFORM (About 1800 B.C.) | LATER CUNEIFORM (About 700 B.C.) |
|---|---|---|---|---|---|---|---|
| Sun | | | | Head | | | |
| Star | | | | Bird | | | |
| Mountain | | | | Grain | | | |

**LEARNING FROM TABLES** Sumerian writing began with scribes (left) using picture symbols.
■ In what columns do the symbols most often look like what they stand for?

## INNOVATIONS

The needs of a large complex society led to further **innovations**, or new ways of doing things. The need in Sumer to mark boundaries for farming led to a unit of land measurement the Sumerians called the *iqu*. Today we call it the *acre*.

The need to measure the wheat and barley harvests established the quart as a basic unit of measurement. The need to carry trade goods up the river led people to build cargo boats with sails. The need to keep a record of ownership and trade led to one of the Sumerians' greatest innovations—writing.

Scribes in Sumer marked picture symbols in pieces of wet clay. They attached these pieces to baskets as tags to identify the contents and the owner. Over time the Sumerians developed their symbols into a complete writing system. This system was based on *cuneiform*, (kyoo•NEE•uh•fawrm), or wedge-shaped, symbols.

To make the cuneiform marks in soft clay tablets, Sumerian scribes used a pointed reed, or stylus. The clay tablets were then baked to harden them. Cuneiform tablets that have been found give a record of

Sumer's growing economic activity, way of life, and history. With the invention of writing, people began to record their own stories.

 **What innovations did the Sumerians develop?**

# LESSON 1 REVIEW

## Check Understanding

1. **Recall the Facts**   What new type of government was formed in the Fertile Crescent?
2. **Focus on the Main Idea**   How did the need for organization affect the development of city-states in Sumer?

## Think Critically

3. **Cause and Effect**   What effect did a crop surplus have on early civilization?
4. **Past to Present**   Which of the problems faced by people in Sumer are similar to problems in the United States today?

## Show What You Know

 **News-Writing Activity**
Prepare a news story describing an important event that might have happened in Sumer when an innovation was introduced.

# WAR AND PEACE IN THE
# FERTILE CRESCENT

## *L*ink to Our World

**Why are laws important today?**

**Focus on the Main Idea**
*As you read, look for ways in which early civilizations protected themselves and kept order within their societies.*

**Preview Vocabulary**

| | |
|---|---|
| conquer | taxation |
| empire | Code of Hammurabi |
| emperor | equal justice |

As city-states all over the Fertile Crescent kept growing in area and population, conflict among them increased. City-states competed with one another to control fertile land and valuable water rights. As people began to **conquer**, or take over, the land of others, cries of war became a familiar sound.

## CAUSES AND EFFECTS OF CONFLICT

Most wars among early agricultural societies such as those in the Fertile Crescent were fought to protect farmland and water rights. A Sumerian saying warned of how unsure ownership was: "You can go and carry off the enemy's land; the enemy comes and carries off your land."

The land between the Tigris and Euphrates rivers was flat. No natural boundaries such as mountains separated one city-state from another. With no natural boundaries, city-states put up pillars to mark their borders. When one city-state moved or destroyed another city-state's pillars, it "violated both the decree of the gods, and the word given by man to man." Such acts often led to war.

As more disagreements about land and water arose, more wars were fought. With more wars, the need for weapons resulted in new technology. Craftworkers used what they had learned in making metal tools and improving the wheel to create such innovations as war chariots. A war chariot was a light, two-wheeled cart pulled by horses. From a fast-moving war chariot, a soldier could speed by and throw spears or shoot arrows at an enemy who was on foot. With

This Sumerian helmet was hammered from a single sheet of gold. About 4,500 years old, the helmet was uncovered in the royal cemetery of the ancient city of Ur.

Sumerian ruler,
possibly Sargon

As this ancient stone artwork shows, war was often a part of day-to-day living for the ancient Mesopotamians.

new technology for war, of course, more people died in battle.

> **What was the major cause of wars among the people of the Fertile Crescent?**

## SARGON THE CONQUEROR

The first known conqueror in the Fertile Crescent was a warrior named Sargon. He lived there in the city-state of Kish. As a young man he served as an official in the government of its king. Sargon later killed the king and took control of Kish. Gathering an army, Sargon then marched through Mesopotamia, establishing a vast empire. An **empire** is a conquered land of many

people and places governed by one ruler. Sargon became the region's first **emperor**, or ruler of an empire.

In the middle of his empire, Sargon built a capital city called Akkad. His empire and its people came to be known as Akkadian. As a sign of his conquest over the huge area, Sargon ordered every boundary pillar and city wall torn down.

For the next 55 years, Sargon of Akkad ruled over his empire. He maintained his rule both by force and by good organization. Sargon was the first king in the Fertile Crescent to set up a standing army. Before this time people became soldiers only in time of war. Sargon also appointed loyal nobles as governors to maintain control of conquered cities. Sargon organized his empire so well that it lasted long after his death. By about 2300 B.C. the Akkadian Empire stretched the entire length of the Fertile Crescent and included all the Sumerian city-states.

The Akkadian Empire, however, eventually weakened. When the Akkadian Empire ended, the city-states of the Fertile Crescent once again ruled themselves—until the next conqueror built another empire.

> **Why did Sargon tear down boundary pillars and city walls?**

# HAMMURABI THE LAWGIVER

Between 1792 and 1750 B.C. Hammurabi, king of the city-state of Babylon, conquered and reunited most of Mesopotamia and the upper valley of the Tigris and Euphrates rivers. Like Sargon, Hammurabi was more than a military leader. He improved each city-state under his rule by promoting trade and by building and keeping up dikes and canals.

To pay the expenses of his government, Hammurabi set up a system of **taxation**. That is, to support the government, people were required to pay taxes in crops or other goods they produced. Tax collectors went from house to house gathering money. If the tax collector could not get payment from a person, he had to pay it himself. In this way Hammurabi made certain that enough money would be collected for all his improvements.

Perhaps Hammurabi's most important contribution was a code, or collection, of laws that he wrote for all the people of his empire to follow. The **Code of Hammurabi** consisted of 282 laws that dealt with almost every aspect of life. The laws were divided into categories such as *family*, *trade*, and *work*.

In the years before the code, people who did wrong might or might not be convicted of crimes they had committed. Punishments might or might not be fair. People often took the law into their own hands,

punishing as they saw fit. So Hammurabi wrote laws about marriage and divorce, adoption, slaves, murder, stealing, military service, land and business practices, loans, prices, and wages.

Based on older codes of Sumerian and Akkadian laws, the Code of Hammurabi followed the law of "an eye for an eye." The code said that whoever caused an injury should be punished by being given that same injury. If a person broke someone's arm in a fight, that person was punished by having his or her arm broken.

In describing the purpose of his code, Hammurabi explained that he wrote it

66 To cause justice to prevail . . .
To destroy the wicked . . .
To enlighten the land and to further
the welfare of the people. 99

Besides writing a code of laws, Hammurabi introduced **equal justice**, or fair treatment under the law. His equal justice, however, was limited to equality within each social class. Under the Code of Hammurabi, nobles and priests were often favored over people in the middle class. Middle-class people were favored over laborers and slaves. And men were favored over women.

People believed that the Code of Hammurabi was a gift from the gods. According to them the sun god, Shamash, had given Hammurabi the authority to write down the laws. Backed by the authority of the gods and of the government, this code became a model for lawmaking in later civilizations in western Asia.

On this stela, or stone marker, Hammurabi stands before the Babylonian sun god. Hammurabi's laws are carved at the base of the stela.

# EVENTS IN MESOPOTAMIA

2500 B.C.    2250 B.C.    2000 B.C.    1750 B.C.    1500 B.C.    1250 B.C.    1000 B.C.    750 B.C.    500 B.C.

**About 2350 B.C.** Sargon establishes the Akkadian Empire

**About 2300 B.C.** The Akkadian Empire stretches the length of the Fertile Crescent

**About 1792 B.C.** Hammurabi becomes king of Babylon

Code of Hammurabi

**By about 1750 B.C.** Hammurabi conquers and reunites most of Mesopotamia

**About 689 B.C.** Sennacherib captures Babylon

**721 B.C.** Sennacherib captures the kingdom of Israel

**LEARNING FROM TIME LINES**   Many rulers fought for control of ancient Mesopotamia between 2500 B.C. and 500 B.C.
- Which of these rulers reigned longest ago?

Hammurabi's code lasted over the years, but his empire did not. By 1600 B.C. the Babylonians, too, had been conquered.

 **What is an "eye for an eye" law?**

## SENNACHERIB THE DESTROYER

After the collapse of Hammurabi's empire, Mesopotamia was ruled by several different peoples. First, the Hittites from the area now known as Turkey built an empire on the strength of their iron weapons. The Hittite weapons were the most advanced war technology of the time. Then another empire arose. This was Assyria.

Assyria was a region of rolling hills between the Tigris River and the Zagros Mountains in northern Mesopotamia. Most Assyrians lived in cities, of which the most important were Assur, Kalhu, and Nineveh. Surrounding each city were many small farming villages.

In need of more fertile land to farm, the Assyrians looked to the plains of the Fertile Crescent. The land there was perfect for growing crops. Advancing in war chariots, the Assyrians began conquering their

neighbors so they could gain this rich land. They went on taking land until their empire stretched across the Fertile Crescent.

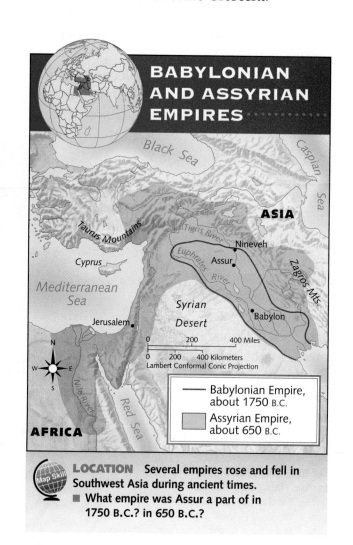

# BABYLONIAN AND ASSYRIAN EMPIRES

Babylonian Empire, about 1750 B.C.

Assyrian Empire, about 650 B.C.

**LOCATION**   Several empires rose and fell in Southwest Asia during ancient times.
- What empire was Assur a part of in 1750 B.C.? in 650 B.C.?

In 721 B.C. the Assyrian king Sennacherib (suh•NA•kuh•ruhb) stormed Israel, a kingdom in the western Fertile Crescent, near the Mediterranean Sea. Along the way his army attacked and destroyed 46 cities and forced more than 200,000 captives into slavery. In 689 B.C. he attacked and destroyed Babylon in Mesopotamia at the far-eastern end of the Fertile Crescent.

Sennacherib bragged, "The city and houses, from its foundation to its top, I destroyed, I devastated, I burned with fire." After destroying Babylon, he had canals dug from the Euphrates River and flooded the site. He wanted to turn the city, he said, into a meadow.

In time the mighty Assyrian Empire was brought down by other people. In 612 B.C. the Medes attacked Nineveh and killed its king.

........................................................................

This stela shows Assyrian warriors riding a chariot into battle.

A writer who may have lived near Nineveh described the fall of the city. The description shows how violent the age of conquest was in the Fertile Crescent.

> 66Woe to the bloody city! . . .
> The noise of a whip and the noise
>     of rattling wheels,
> And of the prancing horses, and
>     of leaping chariots.
> The horseman lifts up the bright sword
>     and glittering spear,
> And there is a multitude slain. . . .99

 **Why did the Assyrians attack their neighbors?**

# LESSON 2 REVIEW

## Check Understanding

1. **Recall the Facts**   What collection of "an eye for an eye" laws developed in Babylon?
2. **Focus on the Main Idea**   How did the people of the Fertile Crescent maintain order and protect themselves from outside threats?

## Think Critically

3. **Think More About It**   Some people today would consider Hammurabi's punishments to be cruel. Why would others support these punishments for crimes today?
4. **Past to Present**   What types of laws in your community do you consider the most important? Why?
5. **Cause and Effect**   What was the effect of empire building on the ancient peoples of the Fertile Crescent?

## Show What You Know

**List-Making Activity**
Hammurabi wrote a code of laws that seemed fair for his time. In a group, write a short code of rules for the students in your school with consequences that seem fair for your time.

# LESSON 3

# ISRAELITES, PHOENICIANS, and LYDIANS

## Link to Our World

**What changes have individuals and groups brought about in your community?**

**Focus on the Main Idea**
As you read, look for ways in which Israelites, Phoenicians, and Lydians contributed to change in the civilization of the Fertile Crescent.

**Preview Vocabulary**
monotheism
covenant
Ten Commandments
Judaism
Torah
colony
cultural diffusion
barter
money economy

The groups of people who lived in the western end of the Fertile Crescent did not create large empires. Yet they contributed to world history in important ways. Between about 2000 and 500 B.C., the Israelites, the Phoenicians, and the Lydians made important contributions in religion, language, and economics.

## ABRAHAM

Many people all over the world trace their identity as a people to a man named Abram. Abram was born in the Sumerian city of Ur and lived most of his life in the city of Haran in northern Mesopotamia. The Mesopotamians, like most early people, worshipped many gods. They prayed to one god for water, another god for rain, and still another god for good harvests. There were gods also for clouds, mists, and almost every part of nature important to an agricultural society.

Unlike their neighbors, Abram and his family worshipped one God. Belief in one supreme being is called **monotheism**. God, Abram believed, was all-powerful. According to Abram, God spoke to him one day, saying, "Leave your country, your people, and your father's house and go to the land I will show you."

Abram obeyed God without question. He soon left Mesopotamia and traveled west with his wife Sarah and other family members. By about 2000 B.C. they came to a region of hills, valleys, and coastal plains along the

Mediterranean Sea. This region was known as Canaan.

Abram and his family journeyed through Canaan until they reached a place called Shechem (SHEE•kuhm). It was there, according to the Bible, that Abram heard God say, "I will give this land to your children." Abram made a **covenant**, or agreement, with God. The covenant promised that in return for Abram's being faithful, God would give Abram's descendants the land of Canaan as a home country. As a sign of his promise, Abram changed his name to Abraham. The name means "father of many nations." Abraham became known as the father of the Jewish people through his son Isaac and the father of the Arab people through his son Ishmael.

**In what important way were Abraham's religious beliefs different from the beliefs of the people of Mesopotamia?**

## THE TEN COMMANDMENTS

Abraham's son Isaac had a son who was named Jacob. Later, Jacob also became known as Israel, and his descendants were called Israelites. When famine came to Canaan, many Israelites left for Egypt. The Israelites who left Canaan found food and work during their early years in Egypt. Later, however, they were enslaved by Egyptian rulers.

In about 1280 B.C. Moses, a leader of the Israelites, led his people back toward Canaan. The journey, which was filled with hardships, took many years. The Bible says that on a mountain in the Sinai desert, God gave Moses the **Ten Commandments**, a set of laws for responsible behavior. The First Commandment means that there is only one God and that God alone should be worshipped. The

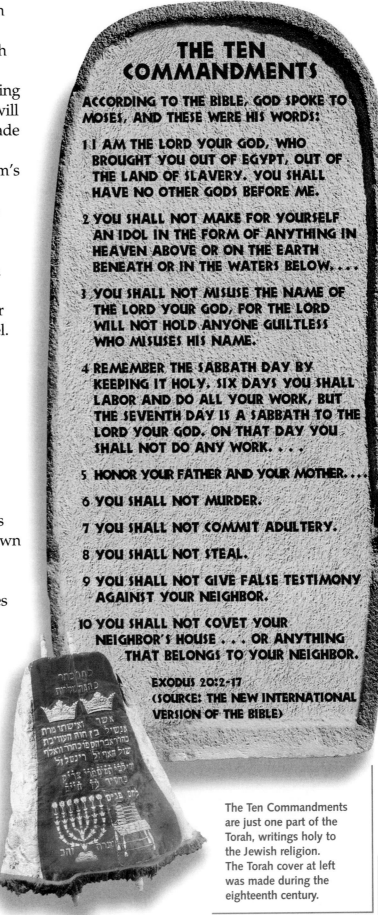

# THE TEN COMMANDMENTS

ACCORDING TO THE BIBLE, GOD SPOKE TO MOSES, AND THESE WERE HIS WORDS:

1. I AM THE LORD YOUR GOD, WHO BROUGHT YOU OUT OF EGYPT, OUT OF THE LAND OF SLAVERY. YOU SHALL HAVE NO OTHER GODS BEFORE ME.

2. YOU SHALL NOT MAKE FOR YOURSELF AN IDOL IN THE FORM OF ANYTHING IN HEAVEN ABOVE OR ON THE EARTH BENEATH OR IN THE WATERS BELOW. . . .

3. YOU SHALL NOT MISUSE THE NAME OF THE LORD YOUR GOD, FOR THE LORD WILL NOT HOLD ANYONE GUILTLESS WHO MISUSES HIS NAME.

4. REMEMBER THE SABBATH DAY BY KEEPING IT HOLY. SIX DAYS YOU SHALL LABOR AND DO ALL YOUR WORK, BUT THE SEVENTH DAY IS A SABBATH TO THE LORD YOUR GOD. ON THAT DAY YOU SHALL NOT DO ANY WORK. . . .

5. HONOR YOUR FATHER AND YOUR MOTHER. . . .

6. YOU SHALL NOT MURDER.

7. YOU SHALL NOT COMMIT ADULTERY.

8. YOU SHALL NOT STEAL.

9. YOU SHALL NOT GIVE FALSE TESTIMONY AGAINST YOUR NEIGHBOR.

10. YOU SHALL NOT COVET YOUR NEIGHBOR'S HOUSE . . . OR ANYTHING THAT BELONGS TO YOUR NEIGHBOR.

EXODUS 20:2-17
(SOURCE: THE NEW INTERNATIONAL VERSION OF THE BIBLE)

The Ten Commandments are just one part of the Torah, writings holy to the Jewish religion. The Torah cover at left was made during the eighteenth century.

other commandments set down rules for living and for keeping families strong.

The Ten Commandments helped Moses lead the Israelites during their long journey. These laws became an important part of **Judaism**—the religion of the Jewish people—and later of Christianity and of Islam. Judaism teaches belief in a God who cannot be pictured and whose qualities must be imitated. For example, God is fair, and people must deal fairly with their neighbors.

After their return to Canaan, the Israelites set up their own country, which they called the Land of Israel. The first king of Israel was Saul. Saul was followed as king by David, who built a capital city at Jerusalem. David's son, Solomon, became one of Israel's most famous kings, known for his ability to make good decisions. "Solomon's wisdom

# Who?

## Moses

According to the Bible, Moses was born in Egypt to Jewish parents who were enslaved there. At that time the Egyptian leader, the pharaoh, had ordered that all the sons of Jews be killed. Moses' mother placed her baby son in a basket at the edge of the Nile River. The pharaoh's daughter found the basket and decided to raise Moses as her own son. Moses' mother became his nurse and told him of his true identity. Moses never forgot that he was a Jew. Later, as the Bible recounts, he obeyed God's call to lead the enslaved Jewish people out of Egypt to Canaan, the Promised Land.

## ISRAEL AND JUDAH

- ☐ Israel at the beginning of Solomon's rule
- ▨ Kingdom of Israel
- ▨ Kingdom of Judah

0   25   50 Miles
0   25   50 Kilometers
Transverse Cylindrical Projection

N / W E / S

PHOENICIA

Sea of Galilee

Jordan R.

Nazareth

Samaria

Joppa

Bethel

Jericho

Jerusalem

*Mediterranean Sea*

PHILISTIA

Gaza

Hebron

*Dead Sea*

Beersheba

**PLACE** The land of Israel divided into two parts.
■ Which part was more likely to be invaded by sea?

excelled the wisdom of all the children of the east country," says the Bible. The stories of the Israelites are in the first five books of the Bible, or the Five Books of Moses. Jewish people refer to these five books as the **Torah**.

After Solomon's rule the Land of Israel was divided into two parts—the kingdom of Israel and the kingdom of Judah. The kingdom of Israel lasted until 721 B.C., when it was conquered by the Assyrians. Judah lasted until 587 B.C., when it was captured by the Babylonians. Much later the region of Judah became known as Judaea under the control of a people called the Romans. Around 130 B.C. the Jews were forced to leave Judaea. The Romans changed the region's name to Palestine to remove all connection of the land with the Jews.

**✓ What set of rules became an important part of three major religions?**

# THE ALPHABET

While Israel occupied the southern section of the narrow strip of the Fertile Crescent along the Mediterranean Sea, Phoenicia occupied the northern section. Phoenicia consisted of a loose union of city-states, each governed by a king. Phoenicia had little land to farm and few important natural resources. The nearby Lebanon Mountains did have cedar trees, however. So the people of Phoenicia traded cedar trees to get the food and materials they needed.

For hundreds of years the Phoenicians sailed the waters of the Mediterranean Sea in search of metals, ivory, and other goods they could not find at home. In the process, they developed the most advanced sailing technology among the ancient peoples.

Between 1000 and 700 B.C., the Phoenicians began to establish colonies all over the Mediterranean region. A **colony** is a settlement separated from, but under the control of, a home country. Phoenician colonies throughout the Mediterranean served as rest stops for sailors on long sea voyages and as trade links with other civilizations in Africa and Europe.

The Phoenicians modeled their civilization after those of the many different peoples with whom they came into contact. They borrowed ideas from the Egyptians, the Babylonians, and other trading partners. Basing their work on the writing systems of the Egyptians and others, the Phoenicians developed the earliest alphabet.

The Phoenician alphabet made writing easier. Earlier written language used wedge

## Wʜat?

### Phoenician Purple

The Phoenicians are remembered not only for their alphabet but also for a color. In the coastal waters of Phoenicia lived a certain kind of mollusk, a sea animal with a hard shell. The early Phoenicians used this mollusk to make a purple dye called Tyrian purple. Kings often wore clothes dyed this beautiful color. Soon Tyrian purple came to be thought of as a royal color. Some leaders even ruled that only they could wear it. The Phoenicians' sea trade grew as more and more rulers demanded Tyrian purple. Over time the dye became very closely connected with the land where it was made. In fact, the name *Phoenician* comes from a Greek word for red-purple.

## DEVELOPMENT OF THE ALPHABET

| EGYPTIAN (About 3000 B.C.) | PHOENICIAN (About 1000 B.C.) | GREEK (About 600 B.C.) | PRESENT-DAY |
|---|---|---|---|
| 🐟 | K | A | A |
| ⊐ | 9 | B | B |
| ⬚ | △ | △ | D |
| 👄 | ٦ | I | I, J |
| ⌐ | ( | Λ | L |
| ∿ | y | M | M |
| ⬯ | ) | Γ | P |
| X | + | T | T |
| Y | Y | Ƴ | Y |
| ⊶ | I | Z | Z |

**LEARNING FROM TABLES** The Phoenician alphabet was an important step in the development of many present-day alphabets.
■ Which Phoenician letters look most like letters in our alphabet today?

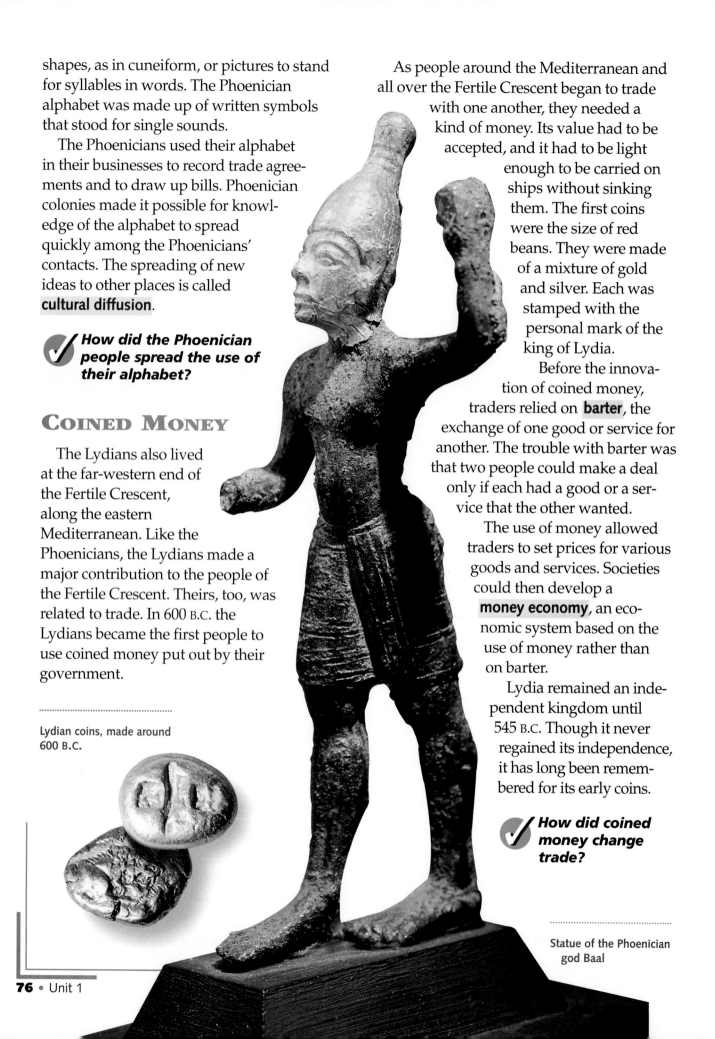

shapes, as in cuneiform, or pictures to stand for syllables in words. The Phoenician alphabet was made up of written symbols that stood for single sounds.

The Phoenicians used their alphabet in their businesses to record trade agreements and to draw up bills. Phoenician colonies made it possible for knowledge of the alphabet to spread quickly among the Phoenicians' contacts. The spreading of new ideas to other places is called **cultural diffusion**.

**How did the Phoenician people spread the use of their alphabet?**

## COINED MONEY

The Lydians also lived at the far-western end of the Fertile Crescent, along the eastern Mediterranean. Like the Phoenicians, the Lydians made a major contribution to the people of the Fertile Crescent. Theirs, too, was related to trade. In 600 B.C. the Lydians became the first people to use coined money put out by their government.

Lydian coins, made around 600 B.C.

As people around the Mediterranean and all over the Fertile Crescent began to trade with one another, they needed a kind of money. Its value had to be accepted, and it had to be light enough to be carried on ships without sinking them. The first coins were the size of red beans. They were made of a mixture of gold and silver. Each was stamped with the personal mark of the king of Lydia.

Before the innovation of coined money, traders relied on **barter**, the exchange of one good or service for another. The trouble with barter was that two people could make a deal only if each had a good or a service that the other wanted.

The use of money allowed traders to set prices for various goods and services. Societies could then develop a **money economy**, an economic system based on the use of money rather than on barter.

Lydia remained an independent kingdom until 545 B.C. Though it never regained its independence, it has long been remembered for its early coins.

**How did coined money change trade?**

Statue of the Phoenician god Baal

## THE EASTERN MEDITERRANEAN

Area of main map

EGYPT

ARABIA

Israel, about 1000 B.C.
Phoenicia, about 1200 B.C.
Lydia, about 600 B.C.

**MOVEMENT**  The ideas of the Israelites, Phoenicians, and Lydians influenced the peoples around them.
■ Why do you think ideas traveled freely among people of the eastern Mediterranean?

# LESSON 3 REVIEW

## Check Understanding

1. **Recall the Facts**  What did the Israelites, the Phoenicians, and the Lydians each give to the civilization of the Fertile Crescent?

2. **Focus on the Main idea**  How were the contributions of the Israelites, the Phoenicians, and the Lydians helpful to the people of the Fertile Crescent?

## Think Critically

3. **Think More About It**  What were some of the advantages and the disadvantages of

the use of a written alphabet and the use of coined money?

4. **Past to Present**  How do the contributions made by the Israelites, the Phoenicians, and the Lydians affect our lives today?

## Show What You Know

**Speech Activity**  With a partner, prepare a speech to persuade a person who has never heard of it to adopt either the Phoenician alphabet or Lydian coined money. If time allows, practice your speech aloud.

# Follow Routes on a Map

## Why Is This Skill Important?

Suppose you are camping with your family and you have gone on an early morning walk. Now you cannot find your way back to camp. You have a map with you, however, and you also know that the sun rises in the east. But which way is east on the map? If you knew, you would be able to find your way back to camp easily. Luckily, your map has a compass rose.

A compass rose is a symbol that shows directions on a map. The directions it shows are north, south, east, west, and points in between. The compass rose makes it possible to relate the map to the real world.

## Understand the Process

The map on this page shows the route that Abraham may have followed from Ur to Canaan. It also shows the route that Moses and his people may have followed when they traveled from Egypt to Canaan. Since Abraham and Moses did not leave maps, we are not sure of their exact routes.

Use the compass rose to answer the questions:

1. The migration of Abraham and his family began at Ur, in the Fertile Crescent. In which direction did the family travel to get from Ur to Haran?

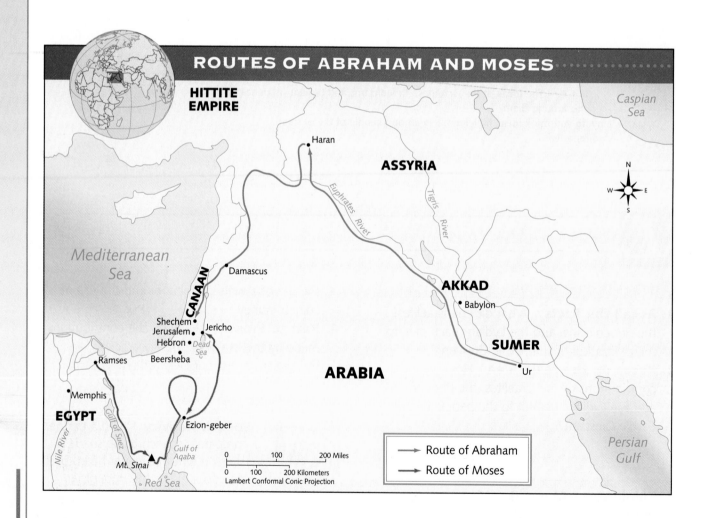

ROUTES OF ABRAHAM AND MOSES

2. Abraham and his family then moved to the land of Canaan. In what direction did the family travel on the way from Haran to Canaan?

3. When Moses and the Israelites fled from Egypt, they left from Ramses. Find that city on the map. In which direction did they travel from Ramses to Mt. Sinai?

4. From Mt. Sinai, Moses and his followers traveled to Ezion-geber, at the north end of the Gulf of Aqaba. From Mt. Sinai to Ezion-geber, the route curves and turns. If the Israelites had traveled in a straight line from Mt. Sinai to Ezion-geber, in what direction would they have gone?

5. On the last part of their journey, Moses and the ancient Israelites traveled from the Gulf of Aqaba to the Dead Sea and on to Jericho. In what direction did they turn when they left Ezion-geber?

6. If an ancient traveler had gone in a straight line from Hebron to Ur, in what direction would he or she have gone?

7. If an ancient traveler had traveled from Ur to Ezion-geber to Jericho in the straightest way possible, in what directions would he or she have gone?

## Think and Apply

Think about someone you would like to visit who lives in another city. Look at the map below to learn the best route to get to that city. Then draw your own map that shows the route you would take to get to the city you have chosen. Put a compass rose on your map. In which general direction would you travel to the place you have chosen? Does your route change directions along the way? Why or why not?

THE UNITED STATES: MAJOR ROUTES

CANADA

500 Miles
500 Kilometers
Albers Equal-Area Projection

PACIFIC OCEAN

MEXICO

Gulf of Mexico

ATLANTIC OCEAN

—— Interstate highway

# REVIEW

## CONNECT MAIN IDEAS

Use this organizer to show that you understand how the chapter's main ideas are connected. Copy the organizer onto a separate sheet of paper. Then complete it by writing three details to support each main idea.

**People of the Fertile Crescent**

**War and Peace in the Fertile Crescent**
Early civilizations protected themselves and kept order within their societies.

1. _____
2. _____
3. _____

**Civilization in Mesopotamia**
The people of ancient Sumer developed new ways of doing things.

1. _____
2. _____
3. _____

**Israelites, Phoenicians, and Lydians**
Cultures of the Fertile Crescent contributed to change.

1. _____
2. _____
3. _____

## WRITE MORE ABOUT IT

1. **Write a Character Sketch** Imagine a clan leader of long ago, and write a character sketch.

2. **Write a Short Short Story** To understand the importance of writing, imagine that you are a scribe in Sumer. Write a very short story telling how and why writing was invented.

3. **Write a Report** Explain the importance of agriculture by telling how a surplus of food affected life in Sumer.

4. **Write Your Opinion** Do you think that inventions always change life for the better? Or do they sometimes cause problems? List reasons for your opinion. Use examples from the Fertile Crescent and from today to see how much or how little things have changed.

5. **Write a Commercial** Design an advertisement for a new invention—the wheel. Be sure to tell how the wheel will affect life in Mesopotamia.

# USE VOCABULARY

Write the term that correctly matches each definition. Then use each term in a complete sentence.

| | | |
|---|---|---|
| city-state | equal justice | scribe |
| empire | innovation | technology |

1. a change in the usual way of doing things

2. the use of tools and skills to create or build things

3. a city that had its own government

4. a person whose job was to write down records, letters, and stories for others

5. conquered lands of many people in many places, governed by one ruler

6. fair treatment under the law

# CHECK UNDERSTANDING

1. How did a person's job affect his or her social class in Sumer?

2. What were some needs that led to innovations in Sumer? What were the innovations?

3. What were some of the causes of war in Mesopotamia?

4. Why did Hammurabi write his code of laws?

5. How did the worship of one God change religion in the area of Southwest Asia?

6. Why was the introduction of a written alphabet important?

# THINK CRITICALLY

1. **Cause and Effect** How did the waging of wars affect the government of Sumer?

2. **Personally Speaking** Do you think that Hammurabi's idea of equal justice was fair or unfair? Explain your answer.

3. **Think More About It** What were some ways in which the Code of Hammurabi and the Ten Commandments were the same? How were they different?

4. **Past to Present** How many things can you think of in today's world that would not work without the wheel? What would life be like without it? Can you think of an innovation of our time that seems as important as the wheel has been?

# APPLY SKILLS

**How to Follow Routes on a Map**
Look at the map on page 78. Then answer these questions.

1. In what direction was Abraham traveling when he entered Canaan? In what direction were the followers of Moses traveling when they entered Canaan?

2. When Moses and his followers traveled from Egypt to Jericho, in what main direction or directions did they go?

# READ MORE ABOUT IT

*Gilgamesh the King* by Ludmila Zeman. Tundra Books. This ancient tale retold from stone tablets over 5,000 years old is about the stern ruler Gilgamesh, who is taught to be kind to his people by the wild man Inkidu.

*Science in Ancient Mesopotamia* by Carol Moss. Franklin Watts. This book shows how the scientific achievements of the ancient Sumerians and Babylonians of ancient Mesopotamia affect our own everyday lives.

*Money* by Joe Cribb. Knopf. Using words and pictures, the author presents a complete history of money—from shells and beads to gold, silver, and credit cards. The book also includes hints for starting your own coin collection.

# MAKING SOCIAL STUDIES
# RELEVANT

## Will There Be Enough Food?

From the distant past to the present day, agriculture has made it possible for civilizations to feed their many people. Today, however, people wonder whether agriculture can produce enough food for a world population that grows by 90 million people each year.

Already, more than 700 million people are at risk of starving to death every day. The secretary-general of the United Nations says, "We have more hungry people than ever before in human history." Right here in the United States, 30 million people—12 million of them children—do not get enough food to stay in good health.

New technology is helping the farmers of today grow more food. On large commercial farms, machines plant, care for, and harvest crops faster and better than people can. New ways of breeding help produce larger and healthier plants and animals. Modern chemicals improve the soil, fight plant diseases, and kill pests.

Yet even with these new and better ways of farming, many people in the world go to bed hungry every night. In some cases political disorder and poor leadership prevent food from getting to hungry people. Most people realize that technology alone will not solve the problem of hunger.

Carrot harvesting in the United States

Raising plants without soil, or hydroponic farming, in Japan

Think about ways you might help people who do not get enough to eat each day. One way might be to collect food in your school for a community food bank. Make a list of ideas, and share your list with the class.

BUILDING CITIZENSHIP

A young child in India

Soybean harvesting in Zambia

# STORY CLOTH

Study the pictures shown in this story cloth to help you review the events you read about in Unit 1.

## Summarize the Main Ideas

**1.** Early people lived in groups and cooperated to hunt animals and gather plants.

**2.** Early people learned to domesticate plants and animals.

**3.** The domestication of plants and animals let people settle and caused great changes in their ways of life.

**4.** As populations increased, some farming villages grew into cities.

**5.** The ancient Sumerians of the Fertile Crescent developed creative ways to solve the problems of city life.

**6.** The use of coined money by the Lydians, the invention of the alphabet by the Phoenicians, and the Israelites' belief in one God brought change to the Fertile Crescent.

**Interpreting Pictures**   Look closely at the scenes in the story cloth. In a group, discuss how people's lives differed during the time periods illustrated.

**Write About the Story**   Write a caption or a descriptive sentence for each of the scenes shown in the story cloth.

# COOPERATIVE LEARNING WORKSHOP

## Remember

- Share your ideas.
- Cooperate with others to plan your work.
- Take responsibility for your work.
- Show your group's work to the class.
- Discuss what you learned by working together.

### Activity 1

## Make a Classroom Midden

One way in which archaeologists learned about Skara Brae was by studying its middens, or garbage piles. To see how people can learn from garbage, make a classroom midden. At home, choose some items that you will probably throw away or recycle soon, such as clean food wrappers, broken toys, old jewelry, or worn-out clothing. Make sure what you choose is clean and safe. Then bring the items to school in a bag.

At school, work with a group. All of you should put your items together in one pile. Then change places with another group and examine that group's pile carefully. What items are the most common? What items are the least common? What do the things found in the midden tell about the group that made it?

### Activity 2

## Draw a Map

Work with a group to draw an outline map of the world on a sheet of paper. Use a map in your textbook to guide you. Add pictures or symbols of the crops grown in the ancient world. Draw each picture or symbol as near as you can to the place in which the crop was grown. Make a generalization that explains why some areas have similar crops.

### Activity 3

## Draw Plans for a Model Home

Work with classmates to draw a picture of the outside of a home at Skara Brae. Make several drawings until your group is happy with one. On a separate sheet of paper, draw the inside of the home. Show your drawings to the class, and explain how the environment helped determine the way the home looked.

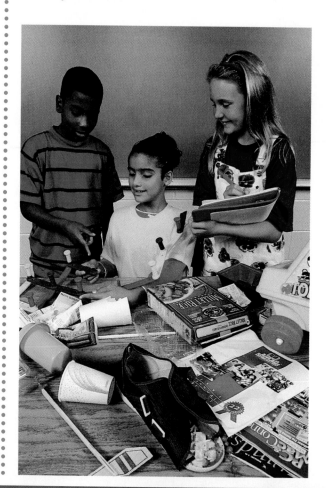

# USE VOCABULARY

To show that you know what these words mean, use each pair in a sentence.

1. clan, migration

2. agriculture, domesticate

3. nomads, livestock

4. technology, innovation

5. city-state, monarchy

# CHECK UNDERSTANDING

1. What were advantages of living in clans?

2. How did migration change the population of the world?

3. How did agriculture change early societies?

4. How did food surpluses lead to a division of labor in Sumer?

5. Why did early societies need governments?

# THINK CRITICALLY

1. **Cause and Effect** Agriculture changed society forever. In what ways were the effects of agriculture positive? In what ways were the effects negative?

2. **Explore Viewpoints** Why do some people dislike using new technology or inventions?

3. **Personally Speaking** A story about King Gilgamesh calls him "he who knew everything." Do you think it is wise to feel that a leader knows everything? Explain.

4. **Past to Present** How did the Israelites, the Phoenicians, and the Lydians change society?

5. **Think More About It** How would life be different if we bartered instead of using money? What would a trip to a store be like?

# APPLY GEOGRAPHY SKILLS

### How to Follow Routes on a Map

The map below shows the routes used by different armies as they conquered areas in Mesopotamia. Hammurabi's routes of conquest are shown in purple. Study the key to see other routes marked on the map. Use the map to answer the questions.

1. In what direction did Hammurabi travel to get from Babylon to

   **a.** Larsa?     **b.** Eshnunna?     **c.** Mari?

2. From what direction did the Hittites come to conquer Babylon?

3. From what direction did the Assyrians come to conquer Babylon?

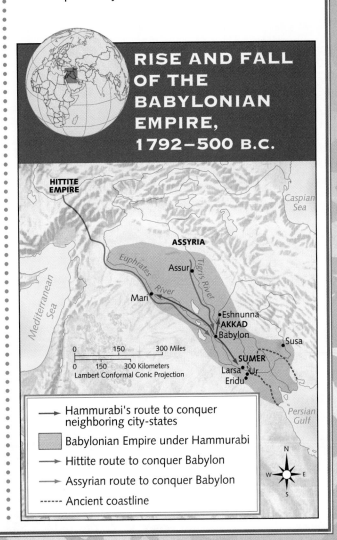

**RISE AND FALL OF THE BABYLONIAN EMPIRE, 1792–500 B.C.**

→ Hammurabi's route to conquer neighboring city-states

▨ Babylonian Empire under Hammurabi

→ Hittite route to conquer Babylon

→ Assyrian route to conquer Babylon

----- Ancient coastline

# UNIT 2

# CRADLES of CIVILIZATION

**3000 B.C.**

**2500 B.C.**

**2000 B.C.**

**3100 B.C.**
King Narmer unites Upper and Lower Egypt.

**2650 B.C.**
First Egyptian pyramid built

**About 2500 B.C.**
Cities rise in Indus Valley

**About 2300 B.C.**
Trade begins between merchants of Indus Valley and merchants of Fertile Crescent

**About 1800 B.C.**
Shang dynasty gains control of China

*I*n the same centuries in which the people of the Fertile Crescent formed their civilization, other people began forming civilizations in different regions of the world. Between 3100 B.C. and A.D. 250, people developed complex societies in northern Africa, eastern Asia, southern Asia, and the Americas. These were places where conditions were right for growing crops and raising livestock. In each place a unique set of challenges helped shape these early civilizations in different ways.

← **Wall painting from a tomb at the Valley of Queens, Egypt**

**1500 B.C.**

**1000 B.C.**

**500 B.C.**

**1500 B.C.**
Olmecs settle along Gulf of Mexico

**1465 B.C.**
Egyptian Empire expands to its largest size

**About 750 B.C.**
Kush conquers Upper Egypt

**500 B.C.**
Mayas begin building cities

# E·G·Y·P·T·I·A·N STORIES

### retold by Robert Hull

*People in early civilizations around the world looked for ways to explain the world and their place in it. Many people turned to religion for an explanation. In ancient Egypt, all life revolved around worship of the Egyptian gods. The Egyptians believed that one god, Osiris, gave life to the Earth. Ancient Egyptian stories told of the adventures of Osiris and other gods. This retelling of one ancient story describes how Osiris helped the early Egyptians survive on Earth.*

Osiris taught the people of the world when to expect the gentle wind from the north. He taught them how to make buildings and raise them up toward the stars, how to make words, how to write down memories with marks on stone, how to make laws. Osiris spoke a law to keep people from killing and eating each other.

Osiris wondered what else he could give to the people. One day, he was walking near the Nile, among the high barley grasses. A breeze swept through the grass, and Osiris watched the ripe grains being blown through the air and rolling along the earth. Then his sharp eyes noticed that though most of the ripe grains blew away in the wind, some of the heavier ones fell alongside the plant, and stayed there, undisturbed. "Next year," he thought, "those seeds will grow again here, in the same place. Most grains will be scattered and lost, but if a few fall where they have grown, men can gather the grains and keep them. In that way men can make barley grow always in the same place."

Agriculture was an important part of the lives of the ancient Egyptians. This painting from ancient times shows farmers planting seeds.

Osiris kept the grain that hadn't blown away and buried it in the earth. Next year, in the same place, the barley grass grew. He had found the way to make barley stay in one place. He told men to scrape at the earth with sticks and make a safe place to put the heavy barley grain, the grain that fell where it had grown.

Osiris had given the people fields.

Then Osiris saw something else. When the Nile came, and the soft wind blew from the north and the world shone with water, the barley grew more thickly. He told men and women to dig small channels to the fields and guide the waters out along these channels. So, with the guidance of the great god-king Osiris, the people learned to lead the waters to the barley and spread the waters there.

Gradually the people had learned to till and sow the earth and guide water to it from the Nile, and to gather the crops that grew from the fields. Osiris had taught them to be farmers. He had given them the harvest.

*As you read this unit, you will learn more about the ancient Egyptians and their lifeways. You will also learn about other civilizations around the world.*

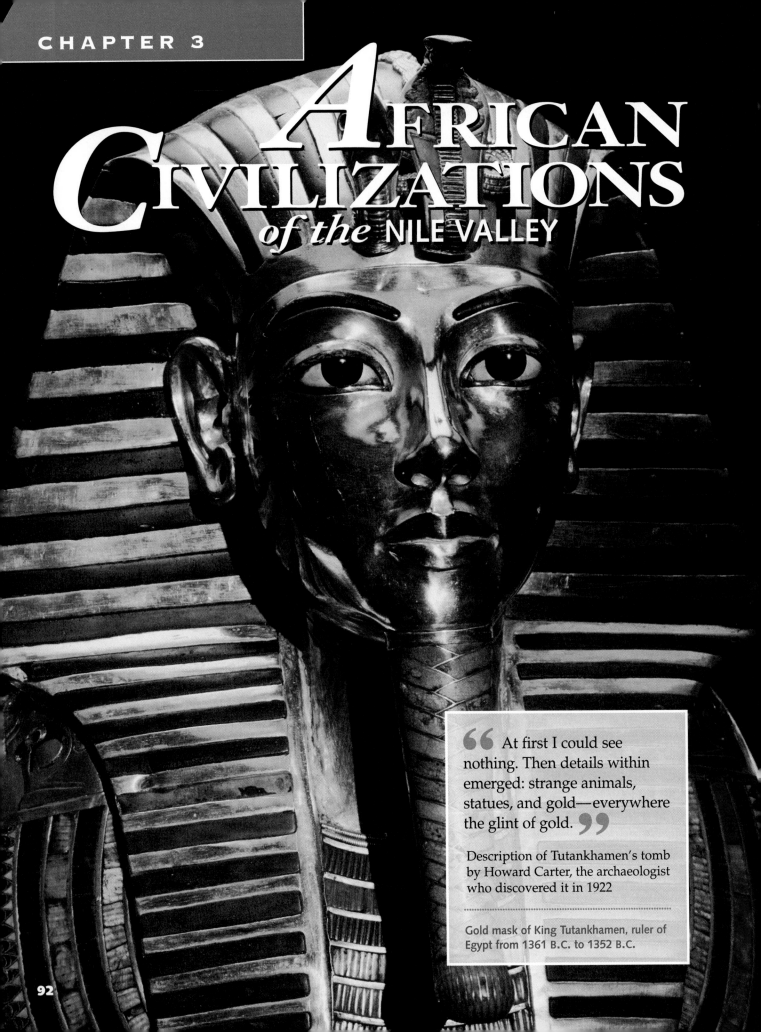

# AFRICAN CIVILIZATIONS of the NILE VALLEY

66 At first I could see nothing. Then details within emerged: strange animals, statues, and gold—everywhere the glint of gold. 99

Description of Tutankhamen's tomb by Howard Carter, the archaeologist who discovered it in 1922

Gold mask of King Tutankhamen, ruler of Egypt from 1361 B.C. to 1352 B.C.

# The IMPORTANCE of the NILE RIVER

## Link to Our World

**How might people today be affected by their physical environment?**

*Focus on the Main Idea*
**Read to discover how the physical setting of the Nile Valley affected the development of civilization in North Africa.**

*Preview Vocabulary*
**desertification       predict
delta             cataract
silt**

A narrow ribbon of fertile land cut by a single river divides the desert in the northeast corner of Africa. This river, the Nile, flows more than 4,000 miles (6,500 km) from its source in the mountains of eastern Africa downstream to its mouth at the Mediterranean Sea. The Nile is the world's longest river. Along its course developed the first great center of civilization in Africa and one of the world's longest-lasting civilizations.

## GIVER (AND TAKER) OF LIFE

During the Paleolithic period, or Old Stone Age, people in northeastern Africa subsisted just by hunting and gathering. At that time a grassy plain covered that part of Africa. The plain provided a ready supply of plants and wild animals for food. Then the climate slowly grew drier. The change in climate turned the land to desert. Any change of fertile land into desert, whether caused by climate or human actions, is called **desertification**. As the land became desert, plants died, and animals left to search for water. The people, who also needed water, moved into the valley of the Nile.

Near the Mediterranean Sea the Nile River divides into several branches and spreads out over a wide area. There it drops much of the soil it has carried from far upriver. Over time this soil has formed a huge, triangle-shaped **delta** of islands and marshes. By about 6000 B.C., Neolithic people began growing their own food on the delta and in the river valley leading to it. The rich soil helped these early farmers begin their agriculture. The people grew wheat and barley and raised sheep, goats, and cattle.

The Egyptians understood how important the Nile River was to their survival. Because of this the Nile played a role in their religion, their writing, and their art. This painting shows a ruler and his wife traveling to a life after death.

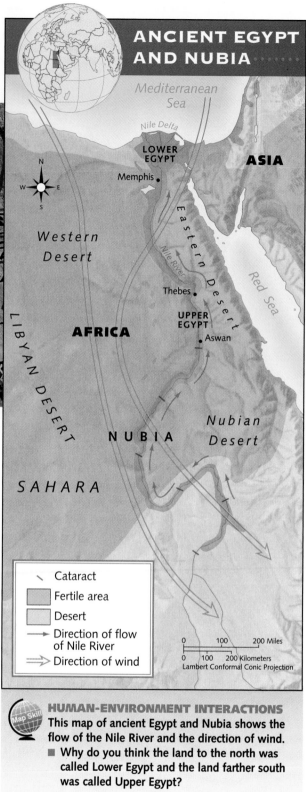

## ANCIENT EGYPT AND NUBIA

Mediterranean Sea

Nile Delta

LOWER EGYPT

ASIA

Memphis

Western Desert

Eastern Desert

Red Sea

Thebes

UPPER EGYPT

Aswan

LIBYAN DESERT

AFRICA

NUBIA

Nubian Desert

SAHARA

Nile River

| | Cataract |
| --- | --- |
| | Fertile area |
| | Desert |
| → | Direction of flow of Nile River |
| ⇒ | Direction of wind |

0     100     200 Miles
0   100   200 Kilometers
Lambert Conformal Conic Projection

**HUMAN-ENVIRONMENT INTERACTIONS**
This map of ancient Egypt and Nubia shows the flow of the Nile River and the direction of wind.
■ Why do you think the land to the north was called Lower Egypt and the land farther south was called Upper Egypt?

By 5000 B.C. small villages had grown up on the delta and along the valley. The people called this place Kemet, or the Black Land, because of the rich, dark mud found along the banks of the Nile. They called the dried-out desert that surrounded Kemet the Red Land. Kemet of ancient times is known today as ancient Egypt. *Egypt* was the name given to Kemet by the ancient Greeks. The people of Kemet are remembered as Egyptians.

"Hail to you, O Nile, that flows from the Earth and keeps Egypt alive!" an Egyptian prayer begins. Just as the Sumerians depended on the waters of the Tigris and Euphrates rivers, the early Egyptians depended on the Nile.

The great river gave not only water but also good farmland. When the Nile flowed over its banks each year, it spread **silt**, fine bits of rock and soil. After the river returned to its banks, early farmers plowed their fields and sprinkled seeds in the fertile silt. Then they led cattle and sheep through the fields to walk over the seeds and push them into the

ground. The sunny weather did the rest. Crops grew quickly, sometimes producing two or three harvests a year. "It is to be a beautiful year, free from want and rich in all herbs," an Egyptian farmer said in a year of plentiful crops. The Nile, it was said, was a "giver of life."

Some years the Nile took life away. When rains fell too lightly upriver, the Nile did not overflow. The land lay baked by the hot sun and crops dried up. Without a harvest, people starved. When too much rain fell, the Nile flooded wildly. It washed away crops and drowned people and animals. For a long time, the people could not **predict**, or tell ahead of time, what the river might do.

✓ **How did the Nile help the ancient Egyptians?**

## SOURCE OF INNOVATION

Over the centuries, the Egyptians worked out ways to predict when the Nile would flood. By studying the skies, they began to understand the weather and learned to predict times of heavy rain and the floods that followed. They kept track of the pattern of flooding by using a calendar with a 365-day year. This calendar is the oldest known calendar based on the sun.

The Egyptian calendar divided a year into three parts: Inundation, Emergence, and Drought. Each part lasted several months, and its name told what was happening to the land along the Nile.

Egyptians celebrated during the late spring when the floods began. The rising water spilled onto the land along the river. The Egyptians called this time Inundation. In late summer the waters reached their peak and then began to leave the fields. This time of returning waters became known as Emergence. At this time of the year, farmers plowed their fields and planted crops. Emergence lasted until the middle of winter and was followed by the dry time of Drought. At this time, farmers cared for and harvested their crops.

Little rain fell in Egypt. To solve the problem of keeping their land well watered during the growing season, the Egyptians developed irrigation methods. During

The season of Emergence was a time of great activity for Egyptian farmers. In this wooden model from 2000 B.C., an Egyptian farmer plows the land after it is no longer flooded. Why do you think the Egyptians made models like this?

Emergence people trapped water in ponds to use later for irrigation during Drought. Like the people of Mesopotamia, the Egyptians built dams and dikes to hold back the river in places during Inundation. They also built canals to carry unwanted water back to the river during Emergence.

 **How did the Egyptians try to control the Nile?**

## SOURCE OF RELIGION

Science and technology could not solve all the Egyptians' problems with the Nile River. Some years there was not enough water for the river to flood. Other years there was too much water, and floods destroyed the fields. Then the Egyptians turned to their gods for help.

The people of ancient Egypt used stories about their gods to explain nature. The sun, they said, was a god who was born each day and died each night. To the Egyptians, this story explained why the sun seemed to go away at night and return each morning. The sun became a symbol of the life cycle.

The Egyptians believed that the god Osiris taught their people about farming and made things grow. Horus—the son of Osiris and his wife, Isis—ruled the sky. Horus often took the form of a falcon.

To the Egyptians the sun god, Ra, later called Amon-Ra, was

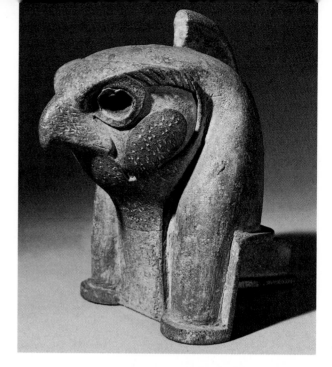

The Egyptians often thought of their gods as part animal and part human. This bronze statue shows the Egyptian sun god Ra in the form of a bird.

the most important god. According to Egyptian belief, Ra's eye left him and set out on its own. When the other gods tried to catch the eye, it began to cry. The tears became the first people of Egypt.

 **How did the Egyptians explain natural events?**

## UNITY FOR THE EGYPTIANS

Most of the small farming villages of Egypt rose up along the part of the Nile River far down-stream from the first of six cataracts to the delta. A **cataract** is a waterfall or a place where water runs fast over rocks. Villages in the northern region of Egypt, on

Many Egyptian myths were about the goddess Isis and her adventures. As this statue shows, Isis was often pictured with cow horns and a sun.

the Nile Delta were said to be in Lower Egypt. Villages in the river valley south of the delta were part of Upper Egypt.

At first the villages in the Two Lands, as they were called, were small. Most were made up of a few clans that subsisted on crops grown in fields around a group of mud-brick homes. As population increased, villages grew into towns with more buildings and more land. Some towns became capitals of huge city-states whose rulers competed for control of land.

The people of the Two Lands came into close contact throughout the years. Using reed boats, traders sailed up the Nile with the wind or drifted downstream with the current. Traders exchanged not only goods but ideas as well.

By about 3100 B.C. Upper and Lower Egypt had each become a single kingdom. The two kingdoms fought with each other for power and control over all Egypt. Upper Egypt eventually won, uniting the delta and the valley.

The ruler who made the Two Lands one was King Narmer of Upper Egypt. As an act of peace and unity, Narmer founded the capital city of Memphis near where the delta and the valley joined. The founding of Memphis marked the beginning of a single Egyptian country that would last for the next 3,000 years.

 **Why did King Narmer build Egypt's capital where the delta and the valley joined?**

## When?

### Egypt and Sumer in 3500 B.C. and 3100 B.C.

If you could have traveled from Sumer to Egypt in 3500 B.C., how might you have compared the two places? Sumer had large cities with many buildings and thousands of people. Egypt was mostly open country with groups of huts scattered in the Nile Valley. While the Sumerians built huge ziggurats as temples to their gods, the Egyptians had only small shrines. Only a few hundred years later all that changed. By 3100 B.C. Egypt began to pass Sumer both in population and in the splendor of its buildings.

# LESSON 1 REVIEW

## Check Understanding

1. **Recall the Facts**   What two things did the Nile River give to the land around it?
2. **Focus on the Main Idea**   How did the Nile River affect the development of Egyptian civilization?

## Think Critically

3. **Think More About It**   The Nile River cut through all of ancient Egypt. How do you think travel and trade up and down the Nile may have helped unite the Egyptians?
4. **Cause and Effect**   The Egyptians believed that they would have another life after death. What things in nature may have given them this idea?
5. **Past to Present**   How do natural features such as rivers, lakes, or mountains affect the way people live in your community today?

## Show What You Know

**Writing Activity**   The ancient Egyptians told stories to help explain acts of nature. Think of an act of nature, and imagine a story you might use to explain it. Write down your story, illustrate it, and share it with a classmate.

# The DYNASTIES of EGYPT

## Link to Our World

**What causes some societies to change over time and others to stay the same?**

### Focus on the Main Idea
*Read to find out how the ancient Egyptian people maintained their civilization for so long while making some changes.*

### Preview Vocabulary

| | |
|---|---|
| dynasty | papyrus |
| pharaoh | pyramid |
| edict | mummy |
| hieroglyphics | peasant |

The ancient Egyptians have left behind many examples of fine artwork and jewelry. This ring, made from solid gold, was worn by Pharaoh Ramses II.

Ancient Egyptians traced the beginning of their civilization to the rule of King Narmer. Narmer was the king of Upper Egypt who united the Two Lands in about 3100 B.C. When Narmer died, his son became ruler of Egypt. In turn, Narmer's son passed on leadership to his son. This continued for several generations, creating Egypt's first **dynasty**, or series of rulers from the same family. More than 30 dynasties ruled Egypt over the next 3,000 years, making the Egyptian civilization one of the longest-lasting in world history.

## THE EARLY PERIOD

The kings of Dynasties 1 and 2 went by names that showed a relationship with the gods. Later, Egyptians began to call their king **pharaoh**. The word means "great house" and referred to the ruler's magnificent palace.

Egyptians believed that their pharaoh was a god in human form. They honored the ruler as the son of Ra, the sun god. As a god in human form, the pharaoh held total authority over both the people and the land.

The strong rule of the pharaoh helped the Egyptians keep their civilization going for hundreds of years. The pharaoh decided almost everything about the people's lives and made sure that Egyptian lifeways and government did not change much over the years.

Many nobles and officials helped the pharaoh govern Egypt. These people collected taxes, planned building projects, and made sure the laws were obeyed. The most important government official was the vizier (vuh•ZIR), or adviser. The vizier carried out the pharaoh's **edicts**, or

In front, a royal scribe is hard at work. In the background appear sheets of papyrus with hieroglyphics, from the *Book of the Dead.* Why do you think the Egyptians used papyrus as a writing material?

# EGYPTIAN HIEROGLYPHICS

| HIEROGLYPH | ENGLISH WORD | HIEROGLYPH | ENGLISH WORD |
|---|---|---|---|
| | Female | | Male |
| | Life | | Live |
| | Water | | Mouth |
| | See | | Eyes |
| | You | | Peace |

**LEARNING FROM CHARTS**  This chart lists a few hieroglyphic symbols along with their meanings.
■ Which symbols most clearly show their meaning?

commands, and took care of the day-to-day running of the government.

We know about Egypt's earliest pharaohs and their governments because the Egyptians left written records. They developed a system of writing known as **hieroglyphics** (hy•ruh•GLIH•fiks). Egyptian hieroglyphic writing used more than 700 different symbols, mostly pictures of things or ideas. In time, hieroglyphic symbols came to stand for sounds, too.

The Egyptians wrote on stone, on walls, and on a paperlike material called **papyrus** (puh•PY•ruhs). Our word *paper* comes from *papyrus.* Papyrus, one of the great innovations of the Egyptians, helped make Egypt's central government possible. The Egyptians used papyrus for keeping all the important written records of their society.

To make this type of paper, the Egyptians cut strips of the stalk of the papyrus plant, a reed that grows in the marshes of the Nile Delta. They laid the strips close together, with the edges touching. Across the top of these strips, they placed another layer. Then they pressed the layers of papyrus with stones until the layers became a single sheet. To write, the Egyptian scribes sharpened other reeds to use as pens. The scribes then dipped the reeds into ink made of soot, ground-up plants, and water.

For the Egyptians a "book" was a scroll— a roll made of sheets of papyrus joined end to end. Some rolls were more than 100 feet

(30 m) long. On these rolls, or scrolls, scribes recorded the history of Egypt. This history is usually divided into three parts: the Old Kingdom, the Middle Kingdom, and the New Kingdom. Each kingdom lasted hundreds of years.

 **Who controlled the land and people of ancient Egypt?**

## THE OLD KINGDOM

The Old Kingdom, also known as the Age of the Pyramids, lasted from about 2686 B.C. to 2181 B.C. During this 500-year rule of Dynasties 3 through 6, the Egyptians developed the technology to construct the biggest stone buildings in the world—the pyramids. A **pyramid** is a tomb for the dead, often a ruler.

Before this time the kings of Egypt had been buried in flat-topped, mud-brick tombs called mastabas (MAS•tuh•buhz). The mastabas were built far from the Nile's banks so the floods would not wash them away. Egyptians built these strong tombs because they believed they would need their bodies in another life after death. For this reason also, the Egyptians developed ways to preserve dead bodies. They removed all the body organs except the heart. Then they rubbed the body with special oils and wrapped it in linen cloth. This process took about 70 days. Only then was the preserved

body, or **mummy**, ready to be placed in its tomb.

Besides the mummy itself, Egyptians placed in the tomb all the things a person might need in the life after death. They put in clothing, jewelry, furniture, and even games. Sometimes special prayers were carved into the walls of tombs to help the person in the afterlife. These prayers came from an ancient collection of prayers known as the Book of the Dead.

Not every person would have a life after death. The Egyptians believed that the soul of a dead person appeared before a group of judges. The judges placed the dead person's heart on one side of a scale. They placed a feather, the symbol of truth, on the other side. If the two balanced, the soul earned life forever. If not, the soul was eaten by an animal that was part crocodile, part lion, and part hippopotamus.

Thoughts about the afterlife caused rulers to care deeply about their tombs. Sometime about 2650 B.C. Pharaoh Zoser asked his royal architect, Imhotep, to build his tomb of stone, not mud brick. Imhotep started a stone tomb that looked much like a mastaba. Then he changed his mind. He had more mastabas built on top of the first one,

Egyptian mummy cases are usually covered with scenes showing various gods. Cases for mummies were usually made to look like the person they held. This mummy case was prepared for Paankhenamun, an Egyptian who lived sometime between 900 B.C. and 700 B.C.

each smaller than the one below. The result was a pyramid of mastabas, looking somewhat like a Sumerian ziggurat. This early pyramid looked so much like a set of steps that people today call it a step pyramid.

At about that time, a new idea came about in the Egyptian religion. The Egyptians began to believe that after death the pharaoh went to live with Amon-Ra, the sun god. One of their religious writings said, "A staircase to heaven is laid for him so that he may climb to heaven." This may have been the reason that Imhotep built a step pyramid.

Around 2600 B.C. pyramid builders tried still another idea. They made pyramids with slanting sides and a pointed peak instead of steps. This, too, may have had to do with the sun god. Possibly the slanting sides of the pyramids stood for the rays of the sun.

The best known of Egypt's pyramids is the Great Pyramid built at Giza (GEE•zuh). The pharaoh Khufu ordered this pyramid built for himself. He wanted his tomb to be better than any pyramid ever built. Workers spent 20 years building the Great Pyramid. During the times of Inundation, when no one was able to farm, the pharaoh ordered as many as 100,000 farmers to work on the Great Pyramid.

The workers cut and moved more than 2 million blocks of stone. Most blocks weighed about 5,000 pounds (about 2,300 kg). No one knows exactly how the Egyptians solved the problem of moving the large blocks from the ground to the top of the pyramid. Most archaeologists believe the Egyptians built ramps to move the blocks. Whatever solution they chose worked. When completed, the Great Pyramid stood about 480 feet (about 146 m) high and covered 13 acres. Its tip was covered with gold to reflect the sun's rays. It was the largest and most spectacular pyramid built in Egypt.

**How are pyramids and mastabas alike yet different?**

## Where?

### Giza

The city of Giza lies along the Nile River across from Cairo, the present-day capital of Egypt. Giza is the site of the two most famous monuments of ancient Egypt—the Great Pyramid and the Great Sphinx.

Mediterranean Sea

GIZA
Cairo
Great Pyramid and Great Sphinx

EGYPT

Nile River

Red Sea

N
W   E
S

0    100    200 Miles
0  100   200 Kilometers

Egyptian workers built more than 80 pyramids at Giza during the time of the Old Kingdom. Some of these pyramids still stand. These huge stone structures are proof of the Egyptians' understanding of mathematics, engineering, and architecture.

# THE MIDDLE KINGDOM

The 200-year rule of Dynasty 12 marks the period of the Middle Kingdom, which lasted from 1991 B.C. to 1786 B.C. It began when Amenemhet, a vizier in Lower Egypt, took over as pharaoh. He and those who ruled after him made Egypt an empire. They conquered much of Nubia, a land to the south, and led armies into the Fertile Crescent to protect trade routes.

Prisoners of war from both places were taken as slaves to Thebes and other large Egyptian cities. Unlike slaves in some societies, Egyptian slaves had some rights. They were allowed to own personal items and even hold government jobs. They were also allowed to earn their freedom.

During the Middle Kingdom, Egyptian society saw the rise of a middle class. Before this time, Egyptian society had been made up of two social classes—nobles, who governed the people, and **peasants**, who farmed the land. The new middle class was made up of craftworkers, merchants, scribes, and people who had jobs in the pharaoh's government. During the Middle Kingdom, members of the middle class gained the right to own land—a right that once only pharaohs had.

Middle-class merchants eager for wealth traded with merchants of the area that is now known as Lebanon, in Southwest Asia, for cedar and pine timber to use for boats and furniture. They traded with people in Nubia for animal tusks and hardwoods such as ebony. Back in Egypt, craftworkers used these materials, as well as copper and gold, to make jewelry and fine art.

Beginning with Dynasty 13 strong rule began to give way to weak rule and disorder. Egypt's prosperity came to an end by about 1670 B.C. when the Hyksos (HIK•sohs) gained control of Lower Egypt. The Hyksos were one of many groups that had been migrating with horses south from Europe and central Asia. These people migrated from Asia and settled near the Nile Delta. Using weapons that the Egyptians had never seen before, the Hyksos attacked in horse-drawn war chariots. They quickly captured land and property from the Egyptians and set up their own government in Egypt.

✓ *How did Egypt's social classes change during the Middle Kingdom?*

## EGYPT'S SOCIAL PYRAMID

PHARAOH

NOBLES

CRAFTWORKERS, MERCHANTS, SCRIBES

FARMERS

SLAVES

**LEARNING FROM CHARTS**
This pyramid-shaped drawing shows the different classes of Egyptian society.
- Why do you think artists often use the shape of a pyramid to show Egyptian social classes?

Akhenaton and the royal family offer gifts to the Egyptian god Aton, shown here as a sun disk.

## THE NEW KINGDOM

After about 100 years of Hyksos rule, the Egyptians took back their country by learning to use war chariots and other new weapons. To be safe from other wars, Dynasty 18 rulers formed Egypt's first full-time army. Pharaohs then sent armies to conquer lands beyond the Nile Valley.

Pharaoh Thutmose I led armies as far north as the Euphrates River. His son, Thutmose II, continued the Egyptian conquests. After Thutmose II died, his queen, Hatshepsut, (hat•SHEP•soot) became pharaoh. Hatshepsut sent armies into the western part of the Fertile Crescent and pushed trade routes farther south in Africa. Thutmose III continued Egypt's conquests by invading both Nubia

and the Fertile Crescent. By 1465 B.C. the Egyptian Empire had grown to its largest size.

Amenhotep IV (ah•muhn•HOH•tep) came to the throne in 1367 B.C. It was a time of peace in the empire, but Amenhotep wanted change. Amenhotep and his wife Nefertiti (nef•er•TEET•ee) urged the Egyptian people to worship only one god, the god Aton. Amenhotep was so devoted to Aton that he

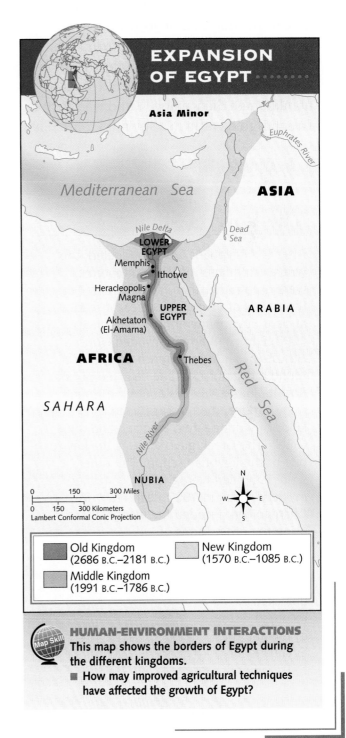

**EXPANSION OF EGYPT**

Asia Minor

Euphrates River

Mediterranean Sea

ASIA

Nile Delta

Dead Sea

LOWER EGYPT

Memphis

Ithotwe

Heracleopolis Magna

UPPER EGYPT

Akhetaton (El-Amarna)

ARABIA

AFRICA

Thebes

Red Sea

SAHARA

Nile River

0    150    300 Miles

0    150    300 Kilometers
Lambert Conformal Conic Projection

NUBIA

| Old Kingdom (2686 B.C.–2181 B.C.) | New Kingdom (1570 B.C.–1085 B.C.) |
| Middle Kingdom (1991 B.C.–1786 B.C.) | |

**HUMAN-ENVIRONMENT INTERACTIONS**
This map shows the borders of Egypt during the different kingdoms.
■ How may improved agricultural techniques have affected the growth of Egypt?

changed his own name to Akhenaton (ahk•NAH•tuhn), or "servant of Aton." The Egyptian people feared that such a change would bring an end to their civilization.

The attack on Amon-Ra and the other gods of Egypt's long-established religion angered the priests. When Akhenaton died, they picked a new pharaoh whom they could control. They chose a 9-year-old boy of the royal house and changed the young leader's name from Tutankhaton to Tutankhamen (too•tahng•KAH•muhn). Tutankhamen ruled Egypt for only nine years. During that time his ministers brought back the old gods. Tutankhamen died at age 18 and was buried in a solid-gold coffin in a splendid tomb filled with gold and jewelry. It was a very visible display of Egypt's great wealth.

Following Tutankhamen's death, Egypt's wealth and its hold on the empire began to slip away. By 1085 B.C., in Dynasty 21, the New Kingdom had ended. For the next 700 years, ten dynasties ruled the Egyptian people. Most of them were formed by conquerors from outside Egypt.

Rule by outsiders caused Egyptian civilization to weaken. However, the achievements of the ancient Egyptians were not forgotten.

 **What was the major source of conflict between Akhenaton and the people he ruled?**

# **What?**

## The Rosetta Stone

After the Egyptians were conquered, the written languages of their conquerors were used rather than hieroglyphics. For thousands of years, no one could read ancient Egyptian writings. Then, in A.D. 1798, European armies invaded North Africa. A year later a French army officer found a large black stone near the city of Rosetta in the Nile Delta. On the stone's shiny surface, the message appears in three kinds of writing—two Egyptian and one Greek. The Greek gave scholars the key to one of the Egyptian scripts. The other script, Egyptian hieroglyphics, remained a mystery. Then, in 1822, Jean-François Champollion decoded the hieroglyphics using the other forms of writing as a guide. The ability to read hieroglyphics unlocked all the recorded history of the ancient Egyptians for today's world.

# **LESSON 2 REVIEW**

## Check Understanding

1. **Recall the Facts**   Into what three periods is Egyptian civilization usually divided?
2. **Focus on the Main Idea**   What stayed the same about Egypt's government, religion, and way of life throughout the years? What changed?

## Think Critically

3. **Think More About It**   How did the pharaohs both keep Egyptian civilization the same and change it? What roles did different classes of Egyptian society play?
4. **Past to Present**   In what ways has the United States stayed the same in recent years? How has it changed?

## Show What You Know

 **Art Activity**   In the style of the ancient Egyptians, draw pictures of one or more events from each of these periods: the Old Kingdom, the Middle Kingdom, and the New Kingdom. You may want to draw your pictures on shelf paper that can be rolled to look like an Egyptian scroll.

# Solve a Problem

## Why Is This Skill Important?

You probably have to solve problems almost every day. Some problems are bigger than others, but most problems are easier to solve if you follow a set of steps. Knowing the steps to use will help you solve problems your whole life.

## Remember What You Have Read

The builders of the Great Pyramid at Giza had a *big* problem. The pharaoh Khufu had ordered the largest pyramid ever made to be built in ancient Egypt. It was to cover 13 acres and rise as high as a 36-story building of today. Mud bricks would not be strong enough, so the Great Pyramid was to be built of huge blocks cut from limestone. The builders of the Great Pyramid had to figure out a way to move the huge limestone blocks without pulleys or wheels, which were not in use in ancient Egypt.

## Understand the Process

No one knows what steps the Egyptian builders used to solve their problem. The fact that the Great Pyramid still stands proves that they did find a solution. Listed below are some steps you can use to solve problems, whether large or small. Under each step is a brief description of how archaeologists think the Egyptian builders may have solved their problem.

1. **Identify the problem.** The builders had to raise huge blocks of stone to the top of the pyramid without pulleys or wheels.

2. **Think of possible solutions.**
   a. Workers could lift the stone blocks up each step of the pyramid.
   b. Workers could pull the blocks up a ramp built on the side of the pyramid.

3. **Compare the solutions, and choose the best one.**
   a. Building the pyramid already took thousands of workers. Even more workers would be needed to lift each stone up one step at a time.
   b. Fewer workers would be needed to move the stones up a ramp. They could do this more easily and in less time.

4. **Plan a way to carry out the solution.** Several ramps could be built on the sides of the pyramid. By building more ramps, workers could put stones in place faster.

5. **Try your solution, and think about how well it solves the problem.** The Great Pyramid at Giza is still standing after 4,500 years.

## Think and Apply

What if the Great Pyramid had to be built today? How would you solve the problem the Egyptian builders faced? With a partner, brainstorm ways builders today might solve the problem. Use the steps you just learned, and share your solution with your class.

**LEARN** *with* **LITERATURE**

Focus on Roles of Individuals

# His Majesty Queen Hatshepsut

▲ ■ ■ ■ ■ ■ ■ ▲

*by Dorothy Sharp Carter*

Women in ancient Egyptian society shared with men the right to own property and businesses. Some women in ancient Egypt became government officials and trusted advisers to pharaohs. Historians believe that Queen Tiye, wife of Pharaoh Amenhotep III, ruled alongside her husband, making many important decisions. Few women, however, became pharaohs.

Queen Hatshepsut also ruled with her husband, Thutmose II. Hatshepsut had married her half-brother, a common custom among Egyptian royalty. After the death of her husband, Hatshepsut refused to give up her rule to young Thutmose III, the son of Thutmose II and another of his wives. Because he was male, Thutmose III stood next in line to the throne. However, Hatshepsut believed she deserved to rule because she was the daughter of Thutmose I.

Hatshepsut succeeded in her quest to rule as pharaoh. In doing so, she became the first important woman ruler in world history. Advised by her vizier Hapusoneb (ha•POO•sohn•eb), Hatshepsut ruled Egypt during the period of the New Kingdom. As pharaoh she helped bring strength and wealth to Egypt. Hatshepsut is remembered for her expansion of trade routes to the land of Punt, which is now part of Ethiopia.

You will now read a story about Hatshepsut's coronation, or crowning, as pharaoh. As you read, think about what it might be like for a person to take on a new role in a society.

And so arrangements for my coronation go forward. The sooner it takes place, the better. For plots of defiance to hatch, time is essential. We will dispense with time.

Throughout the Two Lands and abroad, the edict of my ascension to the throne is sent, only a few weeks before the ceremony. By tradition the event takes place on a major religious holiday, in this case the Feast of Opet. Hapusoneb insists this is a bit hurried but perfectly proper. But then anything Pharaoh-to-be decides is proper.

The edict reads:

*A letter of the King to cause thee to know that My Majesty is risen as King on the throne of Horus, without equal forever. My titles are: for my Horus name, Usert-Kau, mighty in kas; for Vulture-Cobra, Uadjit-Renpet, fresh in years; for Golden Horus, Netert-khau, divine in apparitions[1]; my royal and birth names, Makare Hatshepsut.*

*Cause thou that worship of the gods be made at the desire of the King of Upper and Lower Egypt, Hatshepsut. Cause thou that all oaths be taken in the*

name of My Majesty, born of the royal mother Ahmose. This is written that thou mayest bow thy head in obedience and knowest that the royal house is firm and strong.

*The third year, third month of Inundation, day 7. Day of Coronation.*

I worry over my dress. As ceremony demands that the king wear the royal braided beard strapped to his chin (no matter whether he has a beard of his own or not), I shall certainly do so. Ought I, then, to wear

[1] **apparitions:** religious spirits

This painted sandstone sculpture captures the beauty of Queen Hatshepsut. Hatshepsut ruled Egypt as pharaoh from 1504 B.C. to 1482 B.C.

the long dress of a queen or the short kilt of a king? With a question Hapusoneb supplies the answer.

He is preoccupied, poor man, at having to oversee so many elaborate arrangements in such a short period of time. At each succeeding audience with me he appears more harried, more bent with care, until his back curves like a strung bow.

"One of the problems, Majesty, is that the titles and coronation ceremonies are designed for men. How are we to change them?"

The solution strikes me, clear as Hapusoneb's harassed face.

"There is no need to change anything, Vizier. I mean to rule as a king, with the full powers of a king. And I shall dress as a king. The rituals, the titles, will remain the same as those initiated by Narmer, first King of the Two Lands."

Hapusoneb appears dubious, then relieved. After all, he can scarcely overrule Pharaoh-to-be, no matter what his misgivings.

And as I am resolved to be as resolute, as forceful as any king, I will begin by donning full regalia[2] for my coronation. Around my waist, over the short kilt, I fasten a broad belt adorned with a metal buckle in the form of my

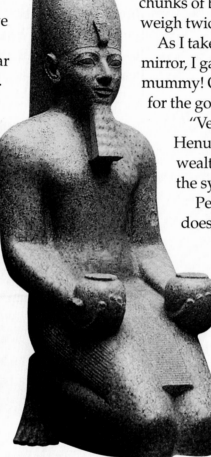

In this statue Queen Hatshepsut wears the traditional pharaoh's beard.

personal cartouche.[3] Tied to it in front is an apron of beads, in back a bull's tail. A girl attaches the beard to my chin. Over my wig is fitted the *nems,* the leather headcloth with the two striped lappets falling forward over my shoulders.

For the ceremony I have ordered a dazzling gold-and-jeweled pectoral[4] suspended from a double gold chain. On each of my arms a girl clasps a pair of wide bracelets, another on each wrist, a third pair on my ankles. On my fingers rings are strung like chunks of beef on skewers. Surely I must weigh twice as much as usual.

As I take a final peek in my silver mirror, I gasp to Henut,[5] "But I look a mummy! One can hardly see the flesh for the gold."

"Very appropriate, Highness." Henut nods approvingly. "Egypt is wealthy beyond measure. You are the symbol of that wealth."

Perhaps so, but wealth, I find, does not always signal comfort.

The ceremony goes off with fanfare. Although the coronation of my husband occurred fifteen years before, the rites are still clear in my memory.

I sit on a light throne borne by six slaves from the Great House to the royal barge, which carries us down the river. From the shore to the temple the procession is headed by heralds crying, "Earth, beware! Your god comes!" Rows of soldiers

---

[2] **regalia:** symbols of royalty

[3] **cartouche** (kahr•TOOSH): an Egyptian decoration with the name of a ruler written in hieroglyphics
[4] **pectoral:** an object worn on one's chest
[5] **Henut** (HEN•uht): Hatshepsut's servant

Pectoral, or chest plate, worn by a pharaoh of Dynasty 19.

pace before and behind my carrying chair, and in back of them hundreds of priests.

Behind my chair a servant supports a long-handled sunshade to provide me some relief from the sun, and beside me two young pages wave fans of ostrich plumes. (Vizier has promised boys with endurance and dedication enough not to whack off my headpiece.) The tail of the procession—a very long tail—is made up of government dignitaries,[6] the nobility, and foreign envoys.[7]

Most of the spectators sink to their knees, heads in the dust, although a few bewildered country folk stand gaping in amazement. A guard motions them sternly to bow, or even strikes one or two with his spear. As Hapusoneb says, "Manners grow more and more out of fashion." Still, the atmosphere is a happy mixture of reverence and rejoicing.

In the main hall of the temple my litter is lowered and I walk, accompanied by the High Priest, to the gleaming gilded throne set on a dais.[8] After prayers and hymns to Amon, the Priest makes an address in which he repeats my father's words uttered in the dream: "I have appointed her to be my successor upon my throne. She it is, assuredly, who shall sit upon my glorious throne; she shall order all matters for the people in every department of the state; she it is who shall lead you."

Finally he pronounces me Lord of the Two Lands, seated on the Horus-throne, and living forever and ever. Into my hands he puts the two scepters, emblems of Osiris: the golden crook, and the golden flail with its handle carved in the form of a lotus flower. And on my head he places one symbolic crown after another, ending with the double crown, combining the white crown of Upper Egypt and the red of Lower Egypt, with the golden uraeus, or cobra, attached to the front. The cobra has the reputation of spitting poisonous fire at anyone venturing too near to Pharaoh. (Someday for amusement I must persuade Vizier to test this.) The whole contraption is so heavy that my neck soon aches with the weight.

During the crowning I notice my daughter and the Prince standing beside each other. As Nefrure refused to ride in a carrying chair for fear of falling, the two march (when Nefrure is not being carried by a guard) in the procession, close behind my litter. Nefrure beams at me, proud and excited, while Thutmose's gaze is as blank as when he viewed the gems and vases at

---

[6] **dignitaries:** persons holding high office
[7] **envoys:** persons sent to another place or country as representatives

[8] **dais** (DAY•uhs): throne

the reception of ambassadors. Lost in his own world (perhaps a world where his stepmother is either feeble or dead), he seems oblivious of all movement about him.

The return journey to the palace is agonizing, so that I have to grit my teeth and lock my neck in position. What if suddenly my neck were to bend—or break—and the unwieldy crown bounce off onto the pavement and into the crowd? King Hatshepsut would have to fabricate a glib story; else all of Egypt would believe that Amon had sent a warning that I was unfit to be Pharaoh. I shudder and lock my neck even more tightly.

Finally it is over. I am home in my suite, resting, my head and neck painful but still intact. The reception and banquet lie ahead, but those I can manage easily. In the distance I hear the celebration of the people, with their eating and drinking, their singing and dancing, their roars of amusement at the acrobats and jugglers and clowns provided for their entertainment. Egypt's treasury will sink this day like the Nile during harvest, but then coronations do not happen every day, that of a queen practically never.

I, Makare Hatshepsut, am Pharaoh of all of Egypt! The thought is too stupendous to fit into my head just yet. First I must view it from all sides . . . and stroke it . . . and shape it . . . till it can slip naturally into place.

## Literature Review

**1.** In what ways did Hatshepsut both keep to and change Egyptian tradition by taking on her new role as ruler?

**2.** What do you think caused Hatshepsut to challenge tradition and seek to become pharaoh?

**3.** Use what you have learned about Hatshepsut to write a character sketch of the female pharaoh. Be sure to mention any leadership qualities you think she showed.

Thutmose III, who followed Hatshepsut as pharaoh, destroyed many statues of her. This sphinx, or statue of a creature half-human and half-animal, honoring Hatshepsut remained untouched.

# KUSH: EGYPT'S RIVAL

## Link to Our World

**How can contact between neighboring groups lead to both cooperation and conflict?**

### Focus on the Main Idea
*Look for ways that the people of Nubia and the people of Egypt influenced each other.*

### Preview Vocabulary
obelisk      independence
annex      trading network

Near the Temple of Karnak stands a stone pillar called an **obelisk** (OH•buh•lisk), an ancient monument, honoring Hatshepsut and her glorious reign. The single piece of granite rises almost 100 feet (about 30 m). Hieroglyphics on the sides describe gold, emeralds, ostrich feathers, and panthers. The obelisk tells of the sources of these prized goods—lands south of Egypt in Africa. One of these lands was Nubia.

## EARLY PEOPLE IN NUBIA

The land of Nubia extended along the Nile River from Egypt's southern border almost to where the city of Khartoum, Sudan, stands today. Some of the earliest settlers in Nubia built villages and farmed the Nile floodplain. Others lived as nomads, herding cattle in the nearby desert and hills.

The people of Nubia will long be remembered for their many achievements. Ancient artifacts such as these show their skill as craftworkers. These finely made pieces of pottery date from around 2000 B.C. (Detail from a photo grouping)

The people of Nubia lived just as the Egyptians had lived before the dynasties. In fact, some experts believe that the ancient Nubians provided some of the basic ideas of Egyptian culture. For example, some Egyptian gods may have been first worshipped in Nubia. Nubian culture almost certainly began at least 8,000 years ago.

As in Egypt, the clan was the basic social unit. Each clan lived independently of the others. No single king was powerful enough to unite the clans. There were no cities and probably few specialized craftworkers. Almost everyone either farmed crops or herded livestock.

Exactly when a civilization, or complex society, began to develop in Nubia is not known. Based on evidence of irrigation canals,

While under the rule of the Egyptians, ancient Nubians were often required to offer tribute to the Egyptian pharaoh. This wall painting shows a Nubian princess riding in a chariot and four Nubian princes on foot. The group is on its way to offer gold to the pharaoh.

archaeologists believe it may have been about 2000 B.C. The early people of Nubia must have developed an advanced technology to be able to build canals there.

During the Middle Kingdom some Nubians came into contact with neighboring Egyptians. Egyptian merchants traded their goods for gold, hardwoods, animal tusks, and even huge blocks of granite from Nubian cliffs. The granite was used to build temples and obelisks in Egypt.

Coming to depend on Nubia's natural resources, the Egyptians built trading centers there. Then, during the Middle Kingdom, Egyptian pharaohs moved to **annex**, or take over, northern Nubia, making it a part of Egypt. The Egyptians named the northern region Wawat. The southern region of Nubia became known as Kush.

 *Why did the Egyptians build trading centers in Nubia?*

## KUSH

By the time the Hyksos took over Egypt at the end of the Middle Kingdom, Nubia had regained its **independence**, or complete freedom, from Egypt. At about the same time, the city of Kerma became the capital of Kushite government. It also became an important trading center for Central and Southern Africa. Goods such as gold, salt, elephants, rhinoceros horns, and spices moved through Kerma to markets throughout Africa and across the Red Sea. Human beings were also offered there as slaves in exchange for trade goods. Kerma became the center for the Kush civilization. This civilization was known for its fine pottery and its use of metals.

In the 1500s B.C. the empire-building pharaohs of the New Kingdom invaded Nubia, taking back their control over its people. The Egyptians introduced their way of life into the Kushite way of life. Because they wanted to keep a government apart from Egypt, Kushite leaders fled Kerma and set up a new capital at Napata, farther south along the Nile River. Over the next centuries, Kush became an independent kingdom. The only ties it kept with Egypt were for trade.

 **How did the Kushites maintain their civilization after being conquered?**

## CONQUEST OF EGYPT

Several weak dynasties brought the Egyptian Empire into a time of disorder. King Kashta (KAHSH•tuh) of Kush saw this weakness and invaded Egypt. By about 750 B.C. Kashta's armies had taken over Upper Egypt. Twenty years later his son Piankhi (PYANG•kee) followed his father's successes and conquered Lower Egypt. After Piankhi's

death his brother Shabaka (SHA•buh•kuh) claimed the pharaoh's throne in Thebes, beginning a new dynasty in Egypt. Dynasty 25 is known as the Kushite dynasty.

**KINGDOM OF KUSH**

**CAPITALS OF KUSH**

3rd Cataract
Kerma 1991 B.C.
Napata 1465 B.C.
4th Cataract
5th Cataract
6th Cataract
Meroë 670 B.C.

0   50   100 Miles
0   50   100 Kilometers

Mediterranean Sea
ASIA
Red Sea
EGYPT
Nile River
AFRICA
KUSH
Area of inset

0   150   300 Miles
0   150   300 Kilometers
Lambert Conformal Conic Projection

⊛ Capital city

Cataract

1991 B.C. Year when capital was established

**MOVEMENT** Kush's capital city moved from Kerma to Napata and then to Meroë.
■ Why do you think the Kushites moved their capital farther and farther south?

.......................................................

The ancient Nubians were known for their skills as archers. Below is an army of wooden Nubian soldiers, complete with bows and arrows, made about 2100 B.C.

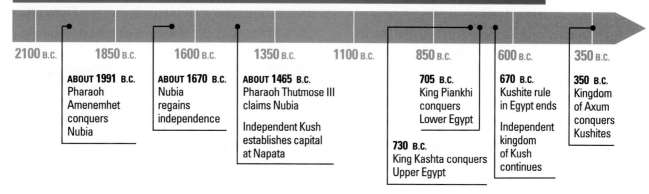

| 2100 B.C. | 1850 B.C. | 1600 B.C. | 1350 B.C. | 1100 B.C. | 850 B.C. | 600 B.C. | 350 B.C. |
|---|---|---|---|---|---|---|---|
| | **ABOUT 1991 B.C.** Pharaoh Amenemhet conquers Nubia | **ABOUT 1670 B.C.** Nubia regains independence | **ABOUT 1465 B.C.** Pharaoh Thutmose III claims Nubia  Independent Kush establishes capital at Napata | | **705 B.C.** King Piankhi conquers Lower Egypt  **730 B.C.** King Kashta conquers Upper Egypt | **670 B.C.** Kushite rule in Egypt ends  Independent kingdom of Kush continues | **350 B.C.** Kingdom of Axum conquers Kushites |

**LEARNING FROM TIME LINES** This time line shows that Egypt and Nubia often were in conflict with one another.
■ According to the time line, during what years was Kush in control of Egypt?

The Kushite pharaohs ruled less than 100 years. During that time they made Egypt stronger by setting up trade links with other peoples again. They rebuilt many temples that had been destroyed by earlier invasions of Egypt and built many new ones. They also created lasting records of their conquests on stone obelisks.

The writing on one stone column repeats Piankhi's orders to his soldiers in their final victory over Egypt:

66Delay not, day or night . . .
Fight at sight . . .
Yoke the war-horse!
Draw up the line of
battle!99

Piankhi had conquered a world power. In conquering Egypt, he made Kush a world power.

 **What two Kushite rulers conquered Egypt?**

## EARLY IRONWORKERS

Kushite rule of Egypt ended about 670 B.C., when invaders from the Fertile Crescent gained control of the Nile Valley. Chased but not defeated, Kushite leaders moved their capital south to Meroë (MAR•oh•ee), where Kushite civilization grew once again.

Free from Egyptian influence, the Kushite people built temples to their own gods and pyramids for their own leaders. They returned to their own customs and developed their own innovations. The Kushites invented their own writing, using an alphabet of 23 letters. They used their writing system to keep records of trade.

In Meroë, Kushite merchants once again set up their old **trading network**, or group of buyers and sellers. Traders from the Fertile Crescent and from all

This statue is of King Aspelta, ruler of Kush from 593 B.C. to 568 B.C. As in Egypt, the people of Kush saw their ruler as a direct link to the gods.

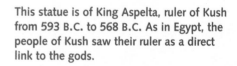

parts of Africa came to Meroë. Along with gold and spices, the Kushites began to offer well-made iron products, including spears, plows, and wheel rims.

The people of Kush discovered that under their new land lay much iron ore. In mining pits near Meroë, Kushite workers dug up pieces of the iron ore from beneath the rock and sand. Ironworkers melted the metal, removing the minerals and other materials that could not be used. The metal was then hauled to the city, where craftworkers used it to make iron tools and weapons.

Meroë was one of the earliest centers for ironworking in Africa. Today huge heaps of slag, the waste from melting iron ore, are evidence of this important economic activity of long ago.

Many experts believe that women often held positions of authority in Nubia. This silver and gold mask shows Queen Malaqaye of Kush. The mask was made about 2,500 years ago.

Meroë grew weaker as traders began to use new trade routes that bypassed the city. Then, around A.D. 350, the African kingdom of Axum defeated the Kushites. "I burned their towns, both those built of bricks and those built of reeds," the leader of Axum said as the Kushites suffered defeat.

 **What changes came about once the Kushites were free of Egyptian control?**

# LESSON 4 REVIEW

## Check Understanding

1. **Recall the Facts**   How did the people of Egypt and the people of Nubia come into close contact with each other?
2. **Focus on the Main Idea**   How did the people of Egypt and the people of Nubia influence each other?

## Think Critically

3. **Explore Viewpoints**   As a Nubian farmer, how might you have felt about Egypt's conquest of Nubia? As an Egyptian soldier in Nubia, how might you have felt about the conquest?
4. **Personally Speaking**   Why do you think Kashta of Kush wanted control of Egypt?
5. **Past to Present**   How has United States society been affected by other societies? How has the United States kept its own ways of life?

## Show What You Know

 **Brainstorming Activity**   In a group, brainstorm ways your community has cooperated with other communities. You may want to look in the newspaper for ideas. List all your ideas on a sheet of paper. Then, with your group, write several paragraphs about how cooperation with others has affected your community.

# WHICH CIVILIZATION CAME FIRST:
# *N*UBIA
## *or*
# *E*GYPT?

**T**he ancient African peoples of Nubia and Egypt were often in conflict with one another. Sometimes Egypt conquered Nubia, and other times Nubia conquered Egypt. The rivalry between the two civilizations began about 4,000 years ago and lasted more than 1,000 years. Today archaeologists debate which civilization was the first to have a unified government ruled by a single king.

For many years archaeologists and other scholars knew little about either civilization. Then in 1822 Jean-François Champollion used the Rosetta stone to decode the language of the ancient Egyptians, giving the world the key to understanding their written records. However, these writings told only the Egyptians' view of their rivalry with the Nubians. For more than 150 years, scholars believed that the Nubians were of little importance.

It was not until the 1960s that archaeologists and scholars began to learn more about ancient Nubia. Because they had no key for decoding the ancient Nubian language, archaeologists had to use other evidence. The archaeologists and scholars have uncovered and studied artifacts and monuments that show that Nubia had a highly developed civilization.

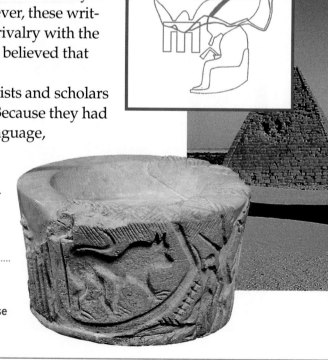

At near right is the incense burner that Bruce Williams speaks of. This artifact was found among the remains of ancient Nubia. The sketch shows the portion of the incense burner with an image of a falcon and a king.

Now some scholars wonder which civilization, Nubia or Egypt, affected the other more. As the Nubians and Egyptians did in their rivalry, scholars today are taking sides.

Bruce Williams, an archaeologist at the University of Chicago, believes that Nubian artifacts from 3300 B.C. show the world's earliest representations of kings. One of the artifacts Williams has studied is a stone incense burner that shows a falcon and a human figure.

66 The falcon means a god. . . . That [figure] is definitely a representation of a king, and he's wearing a crown. . . . The burner is definitely a typical Nubian, not an Egyptian, object. 99

David O'Connor of the University of Pennsylvania believes that the Nubians copied many Egyptian ideas, including that of a united government ruled by a king.

66 I think there may well have been an elite group in Nubia at the time, in charge of a complex chiefdom. But the artifacts Williams's argument depends on are almost certainly Egyptian, not Nubian—traded to Nubia in early . . . times. The kings he sees were Egyptian kings. 99

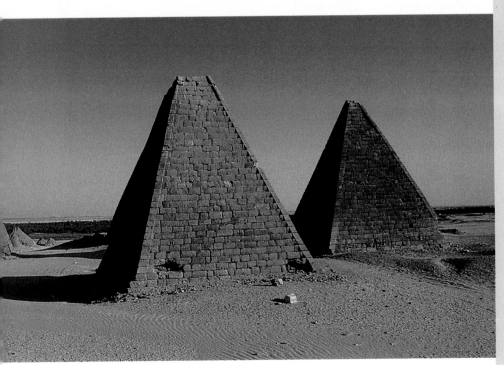
Pyramids built during the time of the kingdom of Kush are reminders of the civilizations that developed long ago in ancient Nubia.

# COMPARE
## VIEWPOINTS

1. Why does Bruce Williams believe that Nubia was the first civilization to have kings?

2. Why does David O'Connor disagree with Bruce Williams?

3. How would being able to translate the Nubian language help archaeologists settle this disagreement?

# THINK
## —AND—
# APPLY

BUILDING CITIZENSHIP

People often use evidence, or proof, to support their views. However, people do not always agree on what the evidence means. What situations today deal with the meaning of evidence? Does everyone agree on what that evidence means?

# REVIEW

## CONNECT MAIN IDEAS

Use this organizer to show that you understand how the chapter's main ideas are connected. Copy the organizer onto a separate sheet of paper. Then complete it by writing three details to support each main idea.

**The Importance of the Nile River**

The physical setting of the Nile Valley affected the development of civilization in North Africa.

1. _____
2. _____
3. _____

**The Dynasties of Egypt**

The ancient Egyptian people maintained their civilization for centuries while making some changes.

1. _____
2. _____
3. _____

**African Civilizations of the Nile Valley**

**Kush: Egypt's Rival**

The people of Nubia and the people of Egypt influenced each other.

1. _____
2. _____
3. _____

## WRITE MORE ABOUT IT

1. **Write a Description** Imagine that you are the son or daughter of an Egyptian farmer. You are living alongside the Nile in about the year 2000 B.C. Describe what your life is like. Use these questions to help you plan what you will write: How does the Nile River affect you? What do you do during the day? What is important to you and your family? What are your plans for the future?

2. **Write a News Report** Think about how the environment has affected people's lives throughout history. Then picture yourself as a reporter for the *Ancient Egyptian Times*. Write a news article about what happened in ancient Egypt when the Nile River flooded. Be sure to describe both the good and the bad results of the flooding. Then explain how the Egyptian calendar followed the actions of the Nile.

## USE VOCABULARY

For each group of terms, write at least one sentence that shows how the terms are related.

1. delta, cataract

2. dynasty, pharaoh, edict

3. papyrus, hieroglyphics

4. pyramid, mummy

5. annex, independence

## CHECK UNDERSTANDING

1. What is silt? Why was it important to early Egyptian farmers?

2. How did nature affect the religion of the ancient Egyptians?

3. Who united the upper and lower kingdoms of Egypt in 3100 B.C.?

4. In what ways did the pharaohs of Egypt give continuity to Egyptian life?

5. How did the Egyptian religion cause changes in the building of tombs of the pharaohs?

6. How did Egyptian society change during the Middle Kingdom?

7. Why was the reign of the Egyptian pharaoh Hatshepsut important?

8. How was King Kashta of Kush able to take control of Upper Egypt in 750 B.C.?

9. What was the result of the nearly 100 years of Kushite rule of Egypt?

10. What important activity was centered in the Kushite capital of Meroë?

## THINK CRITICALLY

1. **Cause and Effect**   What is the Rosetta stone, and how did its discovery help our understanding of ancient Egyptian history?

2. **Think More About It**   Why was the new religion of Amenhotep IV not popular among the Egyptian people?

3. **Explore Viewpoints**   Queen Hatshepsut of ancient Egypt chose to keep many of the traditions started by the male pharaohs who had ruled before her. What changes could she have made? How do you think the people of Hatshepsut's time would have reacted to those changes?

4. **Past to Present**   Heaps of very old iron scraps have been found in Sudan, Africa. These scraps prove that the ancient Kushites worked with iron. What might archaeologists find in the United States 2,000 years from now that could give them clues about the ways of life of our culture?

## APPLY SKILLS

**How to Address and Solve a Problem**
Ask an adult family member about a problem he or she has had to solve. What steps did that person take? Compare those steps with the ones listed on page 105.

## READ MORE ABOUT IT

*Aïda: A Picture Book for All Ages* as told by Leontyne Price. Harcourt Brace. An Ethiopian princess and a young Egyptian army captain fall in love while their nations are at war.

*Into the Mummy's Tomb: The Real-Life Discovery of Tutankhamun's Treasures* by Nicholas Reeves. Scholastic. This book tells about Howard Carter's discovery of the tomb of King Tut and the artifacts found inside.

*Pyramids of Ancient Egypt* by John D. Clare. Harcourt Brace. Included in this description of daily life in ancient Egypt during the time of the pharaohs is information about clothing, makeup, home life, religious practices, burial rituals, and the building of the pyramids.

# EARLY CIVILIZATIONS IN ASIA *and the* AMERICAS

> 66 Only a century ago, the Olmecs were entirely unknown, yet today they are regarded as the creators of the first civilization of America. 99

Henri Stierlin
*The World's Last Mysteries*

This wood and jade mask from the time of the Olmec culture of the Americas was found in what is now Mexico.

# CIVILIZATION in the INDUS VALLEY

LESSON 1

## Link to Our World

**Why do some civilizations last a long time, while others do not?**

**Focus on the Main Idea**
*As you read, consider how the physical setting of the Indus Valley civilization affected its development and survival.*

**Preview Vocabulary**
subcontinent          inscription
tributary

The present-day countries of Pakistan, Bangladesh, and India are located on a large peninsula that juts out from southern Asia. Geographers call the peninsula a **subcontinent** because of its size and its isolation from the rest of the continent of Asia. A long wall of rocky, snowy mountain peaks separates the subcontinent from the rest of Asia. High in these mountains, called the Himalayas (hih•muh•LAY•uhz), a river begins. That river is the Indus. In its valley the subcontinent's earliest civilization developed.

## SETTLING THE INDUS VALLEY

Fed by melting snows, the Indus River tumbles down from the high mountains, carrying rocks, gravel, and silt. It flows west and south onto a hot, dry plain in present-day Pakistan. Four **tributaries**, or smaller rivers that feed into a larger river, join the Indus as it flows over the low plain and out to the Arabian Sea.

Each spring, when the snow melts, the Indus swells and spills over its banks. Muddy water spreads across the floodplain, and old soil is made fertile by a new layer of silt.

Early farmers in the Indus Valley grew barley and other grains in the rich soil. These grains supplemented, or added to, the food people got by hunting animals and gathering wild plants.

The plain where the four tributaries flow into the Indus offered the best conditions for early agriculture. People settled there, piling mud and stones into large mounds so that they could live safely above the flooded land. People built small villages on the mounds and farmed

Children of the ancient Indus Valley played with toys like this pottery ram on wheels.

HINDU KUSH
AFGHANISTAN
IRAN
CHINA
PAKISTAN
Indus River
H I M A L A Y A S
NEPAL
BHUTAN
OMAN
Tropic of Cancer
Ganges River
BANGLADESH
20°N
Vindhya Range
BURMA (MYANMAR)
INDIA
20°N
Arabian Sea
60°E
70°E
Bay of Bengal
Western Ghats
Eastern Ghats
THAILAND
INDIAN OCEAN
N
W E
S
——— Present-day border
Feet        Meters
Above 13,120 — Above 4,000
6,560 — 2,000
1,640 — 500
655 — 200
0 — 0
Below sea level
10°N
10°N
0      200      400 Miles
0   200   400 Kilometers
Two-Point Equidistant Projection
SRI LANKA
90°E
100°E

**PLACE** This map shows the elevations of the Indian subcontinent.
■ In what ways could the natural barrier of the Himalayas have both helped and hurt the civilization of the Indus Valley?

the surrounding land. By about 2500 B.C., not long after people in the Fertile Crescent and in the Nile Valley had developed civilizations, the early people of the Indus Valley had built cities and formed a civilization of their own.

Two of the largest and most important cities in the Indus Valley of long ago were Harappa (huh•RA•puh) and Mohenjo-Daro (moh•HEN•joh•DAR•oh). Harappa became so important that this early civilization is often called the Harappan civilization. However, the remains of Mohenjo-Daro provide more complete evidence of city life in the early Indus Valley.

✓ **Why did early people in the Indus Valley build cities where they did?**

## THE CITY OF MOHENJO-DARO

In its time, Mohenjo-Daro was a model of city planning. Straight, wide streets, some as wide as 30 feet (about 9 m), crisscrossed the city. These streets were carefully laid out to form rectangular blocks for houses and other buildings.

On a hill at the end of the city nearest the Indus River, a walled fortress was built on a platform of bricks. The thick walls protected government buildings, a bathhouse, and a huge storage shed. The shed stood 30 feet (about 9 m) tall and 1,200 feet (about 366 m) long. It held more than enough grain to feed the city's population, which by 1500 B.C. was about 45,000.

Most of the buildings in Mohenjo-Daro, including the huge grain shed, were made of bricks. Instead of sun-drying their bricks, as people in the Fertile Crescent and in the Nile Valley did, people of the Indus Valley baked their bricks in ovens. These baked bricks became harder and lasted longer than sun-dried bricks.

Most people in the Indus Valley lived in small huts in villages surrounding Mohenjo-Daro. Only the civilization's wealthiest families lived in the city. Some city houses were two stories high and were large enough to have a courtyard and rooms for servants. The doors of most city houses opened onto alleys rather than onto the busy main streets. The fronts of the houses, which had no windows, looked much alike.

Even the smallest city houses had inside walls to make separate rooms for cooking, sleeping, and bathing. Almost every house in Mohenjo-Daro had a bathroom. Family members showered by pouring fresh water over themselves with jugs. The runoff water then flowed through brick pipes into a city drain system running along the main streets. Each house also had a chute through which trash could be emptied into a bin in the street. Then the garbage would be collected by city workers.

In what is today Pakistan, archaeologists are unearthing the remains of the ancient city of Mohenjo-Daro.

Near Mohenjo-Daro's fortress was a large bathhouse. The main tank was 40 feet (12 m) long and 8 feet (2.4 m) deep. The bathhouse may have been used by the people in the practice of their religion. It may also have been a gathering place where people exchanged news and conducted business.

✔ **What were streets like in Mohenjo-Daro?**

CITIES OF THE INDUS VALLEY

CHINA

HINDU KUSH

AFGHANISTAN

HIMALAYAS

Harappa

PAKISTAN

Indus River

Mohenjo-Daro

Thar Desert

INDIA

Arabian Sea

Lothal

Narmada River

0    150    300 Miles
0    150    300 Kilometers
Two-Point Equidistant Projection

Indus Valley civilization
● Ancient city
— Present-day border

N
W   E
S

**REGIONS** Excavations have revealed that three ancient cities shown on this map—Mohenjo-Daro, Harappa, and Lothal—looked almost identical.
■ Why is it interesting that these ancient cities were so much alike?

## City People

Most people in Mohenjo-Daro were craftworkers or merchants. Craftworkers wove cotton cloth, shaped clay pots, and made metal items such as silver jewelry. As early as 2300 B.C., Indus Valley merchants traded these goods as well as surplus grain for turquoise, gold, copper, and food from settlements in Asia as far away as the Fertile Crescent.

Many of the craftworkers and merchants in Mohenjo-Daro knew how to read and write. Picture signs marked their clay pots and other items. Trade goods had stone seals carved with pictures of animals such as elephants and tigers. These seals showed who owned the items.

Many seals also had an **inscription**, or written message. By putting a string through a hole at the back, a person could tie the seal to bales of grain and other trade goods.

An interesting fact about Harappan cities is that they were all very much alike. People in each city used the same standard weights and measures. Their street layouts were similar. So were their beads, jewelry, and copper and bronze tools.

✓ *What was interesting about Harappan cities?*

## The Mystery of Mohenjo-Daro

No one has lived in Mohenjo-Daro for more than 3,000 years. And no one knows how the city and all the rest of Harappan civilization ended. We do know that the end came quickly, probably sometime around 1500 B.C.

Looking for evidence of ancient life in the city of Mohenjo-Daro, archaeologists found signs of sudden death. They discovered many unburied human skeletons. The poses of the skeletons suggested the people had been running from something. Houses and other buildings appear to have been

To identify goods and crafts, Indus Valley merchants marked their property with seals. The seals were either stamped onto goods or tied to them with string. How do merchants identify their products today?

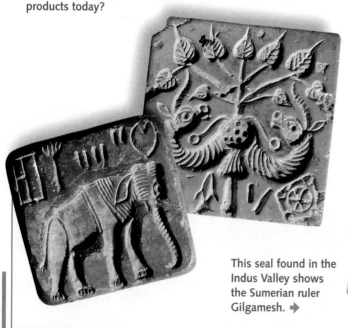

This seal found in the Indus Valley shows the Sumerian ruler Gilgamesh. ➔

# What?

## Trade Beyond the Indus Valley

Indus Valley seals have been uncovered in Ur and other Mesopotamian cities. Not only that, seals from Mesopotamia have been found in the ruins of the Indus Valley port city of Lothal. Seafaring Indus Valley traders may have made use of the strong monsoon winds to cross the Arabian Sea from Lothal. Their ships probably carried gems, sesame oil, and cotton. The Sumerians most likely sailed to Lothal bringing barley, wool, and silver.

Games and toys were just as popular in the Indus Valley long ago as they are today. At left is an ancient board game played with pegs and stones. At right is a two-wheeled toy cart.

abandoned suddenly. Perhaps the people of Mohenjo-Daro were victims of an earthquake or a flood.

Some skeletons showed evidence of sword cuts, however. This suggests that Mohenjo-Daro was attacked by invaders. No one knows exactly who the invaders might have been. If such an attack did come, perhaps the people were already weak. Floods had become more frequent, and this may have caused the people to suffer. There is also evidence that underground water in the Indus Valley had become salty, making the farmland salty too. If so, farmers would have had a hard time growing crops. Without food many people would have starved. The rest of the people of the Indus Valley probably deserted their cities and moved somewhere else. In time they may have become part of other cultures.

What we know today about Mohenjo-Daro, the Harappan people, and their lifeways comes from bits of evidence archaeologists have pieced together. Only parts of walls of buildings and small artifacts, human-made objects such as pots, jewelry, and toys, remain as proof of a civilization that no longer exists.

✔ *What are some possible reasons for the end of early civilization in the Indus Valley?*

# LESSON 1 REVIEW

## Check Understanding

1. **Recall the Facts**   Why is the early civilization of India called Harappan?
2. **Focus on the Main Idea**   In what ways did the physical setting of the Indus Valley civilization affect its development and its ability to survive?

## Think Critically

3. **Think More About It**   What does the great similarity among the Indus Valley cities tell you about the ancient Harappan civilization?
4. **Past to Present**   Why might large groups of people today leave their homelands and move elsewhere?
5. **Explore Viewpoints**   What are some concerns that people have about the environment today? Why do people disagree about the nature of these problems?

## Show What You Know

**Diary Activity**   Imagine that you are an archaeologist who is exploring the ruins of the ancient Indus Valley civilization. Write diary entries that record your work for one week. Describe what you are learning about how the people of the Indus Valley made use of natural resources.

# CIVILIZATION IN THE HUANG HE VALLEY

## Link to Our World

**How can people's beliefs affect the way a civilization forms and changes?**

**Focus on the Main Idea**
*Read to find out how the beliefs of the ancient Chinese people affected the development and growth of their civilization.*

**Preview Vocabulary**
legend
mandate
Mandate of Heaven
ancestor
oracle
pictograph

This metal ax head was made during the Shang dynasty in what is now China.

Of all the civilizations in the world, Chinese civilization has one of the longest continuous histories. The chain of Chinese history links present-day China back to China's earliest civilization. The roots of Chinese civilization go back thousands of years to the valley of the Huang He (HWAHNG HUH), the "Yellow River" of the North China Plain.

## LEGENDS AND FACTS ABOUT CHINA'S ORIGINS

Like many other people, the Chinese have often used **legends**, stories handed down from earlier times, to explain the distant past. One such legend tells of Pan Gu (PAHN GOO). According to this story, Pan Gu worked 18,000 years to create the universe in which all people live.

Another legend tells of Yu the Great, who is said to have ruled China in about 2000 B.C. This legend tells that Yu the Great made agriculture possible in China by building dikes and canals to keep the Huang He from flooding crops. Even today Chinese children say, "If it were not for Yu the Great, we would all be fishes."

There is no proof that Yu the Great built the first dikes and canals in China or even that he existed. There is evidence, however, that farmers in the Huang He Valley grew crops and raised livestock as early as 5000 B.C. Early farmers found the sandy, yellow soil in the valley fertile and easy to farm. In fact, it was so soft that a plow was not needed to dig into it.

CHINA

RUSSIA

KAZAKHSTAN

KYRGYZSTAN

TIAN SHAN

Altai Mountains

MONGOLIA

Takla Makan
(Desert)

GOBI (DESERT)

KUNLUN SHAN

Plateau of
Tibet

CHINA

HIMALAYAS

NEPAL

INDIA

BHUTAN

BURMA
(MYANMAR)

VIETNAM

LAOS

NORTH
KOREA

SOUTH
KOREA

Sea of
Japan

JAPAN

Yellow
Sea

East China
Sea

PACIFIC
OCEAN

Chang

TAIWAN

Tropic of Cancer

South
China Sea

*Present-day border*

| Feet | Meters |
|---|---|
| Above 13,120 | Above 4,000 |
| 6,560 | 2,000 |
| 1,640 | 500 |
| 655 | 200 |
| 0 | 0 |
| Below sea level | |

0   250   500 Miles
0   250   500 Kilometers
Two-Point Equidistant Projection

**PLACE**  The elevation of China varies greatly.
■ Why do you think early Chinese civilization developed in the eastern part of
what is now China rather than in the western part?

The early Chinese people soon built settlements and developed technology for irrigation and flood control. In doing so, they started a civilization not long after civilizations had begun in the Fertile Crescent, in the Nile Valley, and in the Indus Valley.

The early Chinese traded and exchanged ideas with other peoples living in lands that are now part of China and Thailand. Their trade reached rice-growing villages in the valley of the Chang Jiang (CHAHNG JYAHNG) and even took them to the South China Sea.

Unlike people in the Indus Valley, the early Chinese did not trade with Sumer or the other distant civilizations. Surrounded by mountains and deserts and located far from these other peoples, China had no contact with these civilizations.

Because they did not come into contact with people of other cultures, the ancient Chinese came to have a strong feeling of their importance in the world. They named their land Zhongguo (JOONG•GWAW), which means "Middle Kingdom." The Chinese believed they were at the center of the universe Pan Gu had created.

✔ *What caused the ancient Chinese to have a strong sense of their importance in the world?*

# THE SHANG DYNASTY

By about 2000 B.C. there were hundreds of settlements in the Huang He Valley. As in other civilizations some settlements grew into towns. Later these towns developed into powerful city-states ruled by kings. The city-states fought each other for farmland. One king, perhaps Yu the Great, gained control of a number of villages and city-states. His family members continued to rule after his death, starting the Xia (SYAH) dynasty.

In 1766 B.C. a different city-state came to be the most powerful. Its king established a new ruling dynasty, the Shang. Many different families would rule China, but the idea of dynasty—rule passed down through the

This pot was used for cooking food during the Shang dynasty. Its shape allowed it to stand easily over a small fire.

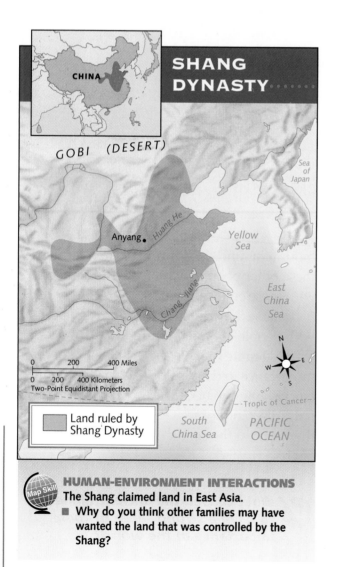

**HUMAN-ENVIRONMENT INTERACTIONS**
The Shang claimed land in East Asia.
■ Why do you think other families may have wanted the land that was controlled by the Shang?

generations of one family—continued for more than 3,500 years.

The Shang established their rule by conquering more than 1,800 city-states and villages in northern and central China. Shang warriors used war chariots and strong metal weapons to seize control by force.

To keep control of their lands, the Shang created a simple form of government. The Shang king gave land to his most important followers. In return the followers promised loyalty, performed certain services, and paid fees and taxes. A strong army helped the Shang gain more land.

The Chinese believed their rulers were a direct link between the people and heaven, where their gods lived. The gods gave the ruler a **mandate**, or order, to rule—an order known in China as the **Mandate of Heaven**. When a ruler's control was weak or when natural disasters occurred, the people said the ruler had lost the Mandate of Heaven.

## Loess

The enriched sandy soil of the Huang He Valley is called loess (LOH•uhs). Loess is different from other soils because it never stops collecting and then shifting in the howling winds. Loess can build up in the Huang He, causing the river to flood. The fast-moving flood swallows everything in its path. Mounds of loess in the river can even cause the river to change course, drowning people and destroying homes. Since earliest days, people have had good reason to call the Huang He "The River of Sorrows."

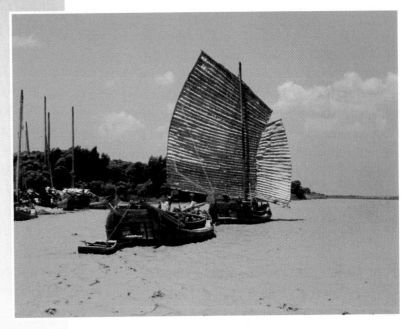

The yellow color of the Huang He comes from the loess that mixes with the river's water.

Then the mandate passed to a new ruler, and another dynasty began. Shang rulers kept their control of China until about 1122 B.C.

 **What was the Mandate of Heaven?**

## ORACLE BONES

Most people of the Shang period lived in small farming villages. The farmers grew a grain called millet, kept chickens and pigs, and raised silkworms for silk cloth. Craftworkers used bronze—a metal made by combining copper and tin—to form tools, weapons, and beautiful vessels.

The ancient Chinese looked to oracle bones for the answers to major and everyday problems. What sources do people today turn to for help in solving problems?

The people asked their ancestors and their gods for advice and for answers to their questions. They believed that their **ancestors**—dead relatives further back than grandparents—were wise and that they guided the lives of the living. They thought of their gods as very powerful. If the people pleased their gods, the gods would help them grow a good crop or defeat an enemy. If they angered their gods, the gods might send an enemy to kill them or a disease to make them ill. To get advice from their ancestors and the gods, ancient Chinese people used "dragon bones."

Archaeologists call the dragon bones by another name—oracle bones. An **oracle** is a person who gives wise advice. The bones uncovered by archaeologists had been marked by oracles with tiny symbols and pictures.

If early Chinese people wanted advice, they went to a temple, where the bones were kept. A person asked an oracle a question, and then the oracle selected a bone. Oracles usually selected the leg bone of an ox but they sometimes chose a piece of turtle shell. The oracle heated the bone or shell, causing the side near the fire to crack. The shape of the crack gave the oracle the answer to the question. The oracle then wrote the answer on the top of the bone or shell.

At first the people asked the oracles only very important questions, such as "Will the floods come?" or "Should the army attack?" After a while, they asked for advice on all sorts of everyday matters. Because of this, the writing on the oracle bones gives a clear idea of the problems the Chinese people faced and what their daily lives were like.

 **How were oracle bones used?**

## **W**hat?

### The Legend of Silk

Silk has long been used in China to weave beautiful clothing and fine ribbons. A legend tells that the Chinese discovered silk in 2700 B.C. when Xilingshi (SEE•LING•SHEE), a ruler's wife, noticed worms eating a prized mulberry tree. She dropped a cocoon into hot water and watched the thread unwind. Xilingshi then used the thread to weave a beautiful piece of cloth. No one knows whether this story is true or false, but silk has been produced throughout the Huang He Valley since 2700 B.C.

## SHANG WRITING

Ancient drawings on bones, bronze, and pottery formed the basis of the written language of the Shang period. The drawings, called **pictographs**, were combined to make thousands of words.

The people of the Shang period used writing to keep tax records and to record building plans. The Shang government sent its armies written orders and made written treaties with its enemies. At Shang funerals people carried silk banners with writing that told the name of the dead person and the details of his or her life. Legend says that people of the Shang period wrote in books of bamboo and wood, but none of these books have ever been found.

Silk cloth has long been a prized product of China. The earliest existing piece of Chinese silk is shown below at right. Below at left, eighteenth-century Chinese craftworkers weave silk on a large loom.

## CHINESE WRITING

| WRITING FROM SHANG PERIOD | ENGLISH WORD | CURRENT CHINESE WRITING |
|---|---|---|
| ⊙ | Sun | 日 |
| ☽ | Moon | 月 |
| ⋏ | Tree | 木 |
| ☔ | Rain | 雨 |
| ⊔ | Mountain | 山 |
| ≋ | Water | 水 |

**LEARNING FROM CHARTS** This chart shows the development of the Chinese language from ancient times to the present day.
■ What similarities can you see between the characters of the past and those of the present?

Writing had an important effect on the development of China's social classes. To read and write, a person had to learn as many as 5,000 different pictographs. Only the wealthy had the time to learn to read and write. Since all government officials had to be able to read and write, most farmers and laborers were unable to get these jobs. As a result, wealthy, educated Chinese were the ones in charge of the government. As government officials they passed laws to protect their wealth and to set themselves above other people. Social classes became separate and clearly defined over time.

Over thousands of years Chinese writing has seen some change. In some cases, new ways of writing characters have developed.

Yet present-day Chinese writing has strong roots in the characters used long ago in the Shang dynasty.

 *What were the advantages of being wealthy in ancient China?*

# LESSON 2 REVIEW

## Check Understanding

1. **Recall the Facts** According to the ancient Chinese, who gave a ruler the Mandate of Heaven?
2. **Focus on the Main Idea** How did the beliefs of the ancient Chinese affect the growth of their civilization?

## Think Critically

3. **Think More About It** How might modern Chinese civilization be different if the early Chinese had traded with people in Sumer or the Indus Valley?
4. **Personally Speaking** The ancient Chinese felt that the family was very important. How important do you think the family is in our society? Explain your answer.
5. **Past to Present** Oracle bones provide a source for learning about the types of problems the early Chinese faced. What sources might give clues to the everyday problems people experience today?

## Show What You Know

 **Role-Play Activity** With a partner, plan and act out a dramatic scene in which an early Chinese person visits an oracle in a temple. The visitor will ask questions, and the oracle will answer them. The questions should ask how Shang beliefs and customs might affect Chinese people of the future. For example, one question might be "Will our system of writing still be used after we are gone?" Talk over the questions and responses with your partner as you work on the scene.

# Use Elevation Maps

## Why Is This Skill Important?

Different kinds of maps provide different kinds of information. A road map, for example, shows which routes go from one place to another and how far it is between places. Sometimes, however, people need information that is not given on a road map. If you wanted to know how high or low the land is, you would need an elevation (eh•luh•VAY•shuhn) map. **Elevation** is the height of the land. Elevation maps help city planners decide where to lay water pipes or build a shopping center. Elevation maps can also help you choose a good place for skateboarding or riding your bike.

## Think About Contour Lines and Color

To find out how tall you are, you must measure the distance from your base (the bottom of your feet) to your top (the top of your head). Land is also measured from the base to the top. The base for all landforms is sea level, or 0 feet (0 m). Find sea level on Drawing A.

The lines on this drawing of a hill are contour lines. A **contour line** connects all points of equal elevation. Find the 400-foot (122 m) contour line on Drawing A. This line connects all the points that are exactly 400 feet above sea level.

Imagine you are flying in an airplane over the hill shown in the drawing. Picture the drawing as a rising hill. As you look down on it from above, you can see the contour lines as loops. If you flew over the hill in Drawing B, you would see each contour line labeled with its elevation. You would see that the contour lines are not evenly spaced. On the steeper side of the hill, the contour lines are closer together. On the gently sloping side, the contour lines are farther apart.

On some elevation maps, such as Drawing C, color is added between the contour lines. A key is used instead of labels. The key shows that everything dark green is between sea level and 100 feet (30 m). The line between dark green and light green on the map is a 100-foot (30-m) contour line. The lines bordering the other colors are also contour lines.

## READING CONTOUR LINES

**DRAWING A**

400 feet (122 m)
300 feet (91 m)
200 feet (61 m)
100 feet (30 m)
Contour lines
0 feet (0 m) (sea level)

⟷ Gentle slope
⟶ Steep slope

**DRAWING B**

0 feet (0 m)
100 feet (30 m)
200 feet (61 m)
300 feet (91 m)
400 feet (122 m)
Peak 450 feet (137 m)
Contour lines

**DRAWING C**

| Feet | | Meters |
|---|---|---|
| Above 400 | | Above 122 |
| 300 | | 91 |
| 200 | | 61 |
| 100 | | 30 |
| 0 | | 0 |
| Below sea level | | |

## ELEVATION MAP: SOUTHEAST ASIA

CHINA

Hanoi

BURMA (MYANMAR)

LAOS

Vientiane

Gulf of Tonkin

Rangoon

THAILAND

VIETNAM

INDIAN OCEAN

Andaman Sea

Bangkok

CAMBODIA

Phnom Penh

South China Sea

Gulf of Thailand

Irrawaddy River

Chao Phraya

0    150    300 Miles
0    150    300 Kilometers
Two-Point Equidistant Projection

⊛ National capital

— Present-day border

| Feet | Meters |
|---|---|
| Above 13,120 | Above 4,000 |
| 6,560 | 2,000 |
| 1,640 | 500 |
| 655 | 200 |
| 0 | 0 |
| Below sea level | |

Most elevation maps use a few important contour lines with colors added between the lines. Look at the elevation map of Southeast Asia. The map key shows the range of elevation that each color stands for. Land that is 13,120 feet (4,000 m) above sea level or higher is shown in dark brown. Dark green is used for the lowest land, in the range between sea level and 655 feet (200 m). When you study the map, you cannot tell whether land in the dark green areas is at sea level, at 655 feet (200 m) above sea level, or at some elevation in between.

### Understand the Process

Use these questions as a guide for better understanding elevation maps.

**1.** What is the difference between what a contour line shows on a map and what an area of color shows?

**2.** To find the exact elevation of a place, should you look for a contour line or a band of color? Why?

**3.** How high are the highest areas of Burma? How can you tell?

**4.** Where are the lowest areas in Vietnam? How can you tell?

**5.** Is most of the land in Cambodia high or low? Explain your answer.

### Think and Apply

Around 2000 B.C. people living in northeastern and central Thailand began making bronze objects. They made tools and weapons, ornaments, and drums. They traded these objects with people in nearby settlements. Imagine that you are a Thai trader traveling from central Thailand to the coast of the South China Sea. Use your finger to trace the route. Describe the land you pass along the way.

# ANCIENT CIVILIZATIONS of the AMERICAS

## Link to Our World

**What advantages are there to building on the achievements of past societies?**

**Focus on the Main Idea**
*As you read, think about how the Mayas both built on the achievements of the Olmec civilization and contributed their own.*

**Preview Vocabulary**
Middle America
protein
intercropping
reclaim

The earliest known civilization in the Americas was the Olmec (AHL•mek) civilization, which developed along the southern coast of the Gulf of Mexico. Later civilizations that developed in Middle America used many of the Olmecs' ideas. **Middle America** is the region between North and South America where southern Mexico, Belize, Guatemala, Honduras, El Salvador, Nicaragua, Costa Rica, and Panama are today. The Olmec civilization was the "mother civilization" to those of the Mayas and other Middle American groups that arose in later centuries.

## EARLY OLMEC FARMERS

The Olmec people first settled along the coast of the Gulf of Mexico in what are now the Mexican states of Veracruz and Tabasco. By 1500 B.C. the Olmecs were living along coastal rivers in clusters of small houses made of reed and straw. The people fished in the rivers and farmed land made fertile by river flooding.

Olmec farmers grew beans, squash, and maize, an early form of corn. These three crops fed most early agricultural societies in Middle America, as well as in North and South America. Eaten together, beans, squash, and maize provided a diet rich in protein. **Protein** is a substance in food that helps build the body and keep it healthy.

Farmers planted these important crops together in the same mound. The stalk, or stiff stem, of the maize was also used as a pole to support the bean vines. The squash vines spread out on the ground between the stalks. By such **intercropping**, or planting different crops together, Olmec

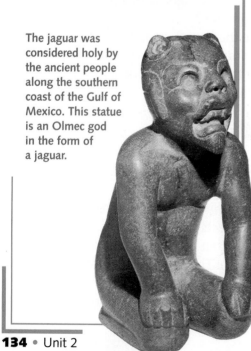

The jaguar was considered holy by the ancient people along the southern coast of the Gulf of Mexico. This statue is an Olmec god in the form of a jaguar.

## The Oldest Ball Game in the Americas

The word *Olmec* means "rubber people." The name was given to these people by later Middle American civilizations because the Olmecs found so many uses for the rubber they got from trees in the rain forest. For example, the Olmecs made a ball out of rubber and played a game in which two teams competed on a specially marked court. The game is still played today in Mexico. In the game, players cannot hit the ball with their hands or feet. Instead, they use other parts of their body such as their hips. Because the ball is very hard and travels at high speeds, all players must wear heavy protective clothing.

farmers made the best possible use of the small amount of fertile soil they had.

Like other agricultural societies the Olmecs came to depend on seasonal flooding to water their crops and make the soil rich. And like many early peoples in other parts of the world, the Olmecs developed a calendar to keep track of the flood season. The Olmecs also used hieroglyphic writing similar to that of the Egyptians to keep a record of events.

Also like early civilizations elsewhere, the Olmecs based their religion on the forces of nature that affected the growing of crops. The people worshipped many different gods, but the most important was the jaguar, the cat god, who sent the rain.

Olmec cities were centers for religion. In the middle of each city were great stone temples. Looking out over the city were huge faces of carved stone, 10 feet (about 3 m) high

and weighing 20 tons. The faces were carved to look like those of the Olmec rulers and priests. No one knows how the Olmec builders moved the giant stones. Their technology did not include the wheel. And some of these stones may have been hauled from more than 50 miles (about 80 km) away!

No one knows how or why the Olmec civilization came to an end. The last of its cities were left empty or destroyed about 300 B.C. Perhaps, like the Indus Valley civilization, the Olmec civilization ended with an enemy attack, with a natural disaster, or with crop failure. But the ideas of the Olmecs lived on in the cultures of later civilizations.

✓ **What ideas might the Olmecs have passed on to later peoples?**

This large head and others carved by the Olmecs long ago still amaze visitors to Mexico today. Some scientists think that the Olmecs may have moved the large heads by floating them downriver on rafts.

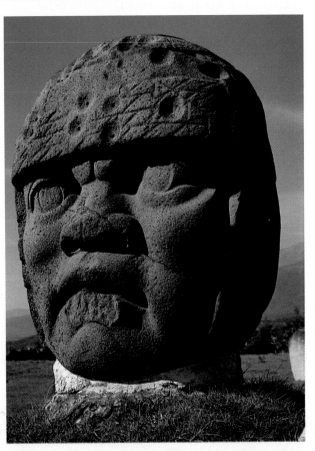

# THE MAYAS

At about the same time the Olmecs were building religious centers in Mexico, the Mayas had a simple farming culture. The people lived along the edges of the Middle American rain forests. By about 500 B.C. Mayan civilization began to take shape. Borrowing many Olmec ways, the Mayas cleared the forest to farm more land and to build cities. They built more than 100 cities in what is now Guatemala, Mexico, Belize, and Honduras. Chichén Itzá, (chee•IN it•SAH) Tikal, and Mayapán were just some of the many cities built by the Mayas.

Each city had its own ruler and its own government. Like the Olmecs, the Mayas never united to form a central government. Yet from time to time, one powerful ruler or another may have ruled many cities, building an empire.

The largest city of the Mayas was Tikal, with a population of more than 100,000. In the heart of Tikal, located in what is now Guatemala, six large temples surrounded the city center. Each was made of huge blocks of limestone and shaped like a pyramid. On top of the pyramids were roof combs, decorations that looked like a crown or the crest of a bird. A jaguar with sharp, curving claws is carved on one of the beams of Tikal's largest temple. This is the one sometimes called the Temple of the Giant Jaguar. It honors the

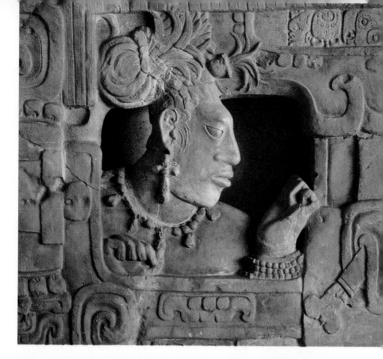

Carvings like this one of an ancient Maya help give people today a better understanding of the Mayan way of life.

rain god whom the Mayas borrowed from the Olmecs.

Religion was important in the lives of the Mayas, just as it was for the Olmecs. The Mayas had as many as 160 different gods. Each was believed to have control over some part of their daily lives.

As in other agricultural civilizations, the Mayas' innovations were based on farming needs. The Mayas had two calendars. One calendar had a 365-day year, used to keep track of planting, harvesting, and seasonal

Below are the ruins of the Mayan city Tikal, deep in the jungle of Guatemala. At right, a model shows Tikal as it may have looked during the time of Mayan civilization.

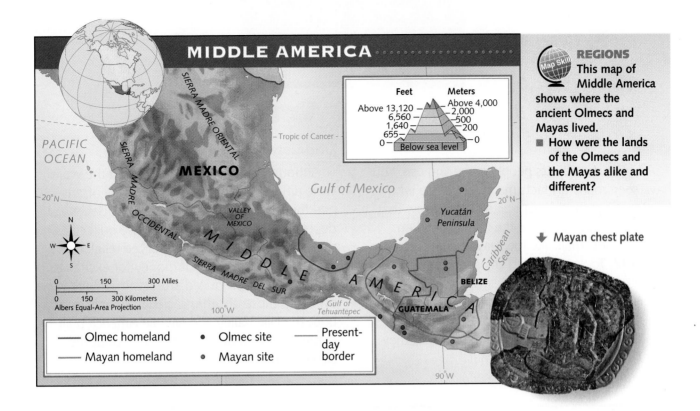

## MIDDLE AMERICA

PACIFIC OCEAN

SIERRA MADRE ORIENTAL

SIERRA MADRE OCCIDENTAL

MEXICO

VALLEY OF MEXICO

Gulf of Mexico

Tropic of Cancer

—20°N

MIDDLE AMERICA

SIERRA MADRE DEL SUR

100°W

Gulf of Tehuantepec

90°W

Yucatán Peninsula

20°N

Caribbean Sea

BELIZE

GUATEMALA

| Feet | Meters |
|---|---|
| Above 13,120 | Above 4,000 |
| 6,560 | 2,000 |
| 1,640 | 500 |
| 655 | 200 |
| 0 | 0 |
| Below sea level | |

0    150    300 Miles
0    150    300 Kilometers
Albers Equal-Area Projection

—— Olmec homeland      • Olmec site      —— Present-day border
—— Mayan homeland      • Mayan site

**REGIONS**
**Map Skill** This map of Middle America shows where the ancient Olmecs and Mayas lived.
■ How were the lands of the Olmecs and the Mayas alike and different?

⬇ Mayan chest plate

flooding. The Mayas also developed a number system based on the number 20 to keep track of their stored crops. Unlike other numbering systems, the Mayan system had a symbol for zero. Mathematicians today say that the zero is one of the greatest innovations of all time.

In addition to a number system, the Mayas created a system of hieroglyphic writing. They carved and painted picture messages on pillars, on bowls, on pots, and on walls. The Mayas also wrote in books. But archaeologists can read only a few Mayan pictographs, so they do not know what all the writing means.

Archaeologists do know that the great Mayan civilization lasted over 600 years. After A.D. 900, however, the Mayan cities were left empty and **reclaimed**, or taken back by the surrounding rain forests. The knowledge and skills of the Mayas, like those of the Olmecs, would become part of the culture of later civilizations in the Americas.

✔ *What ideas might the Mayas have passed on to later peoples?*

## *L*ESSON 3 REVIEW

### Check Understanding

1. **Recall the Facts** What did the Olmecs do to make the most of their limited soil?
2. **Focus on the Main Idea** How did the Mayas build on the Olmecs' achievements? What were their own innovations?

### Think Critically

3. **Cause and Effect** What influence did the Olmec civilization have on the later development of Mayan civilization?
4. **Past to Present** Why do archaeologists want to find out more about the Mayas? What else would you like to learn about the Mayas?

### Show What You Know

**Poster Activity** Think about ways the Olmecs and Mayas were similar to each other and to civilizations in other parts of the world. Make a poster that shows what these cultures had in common.

# How To

# Learn from Artifacts

## Why Is This Skill Important?

Artifacts are objects people make and use. You have seen many artifacts made by people who lived long ago in different places. You know that artifacts can be large, like the Olmec head on page 135, or small, like the Mayan chest plate on page 137. Tools, weapons, coins, and cooking pots are all artifacts. So are televisions, computers, automobiles, and watches. The artifacts of a society of long ago can tell us much about how its people lived and worked and what they may have thought was important.

## Understand the Process

Although early civilizations around the world were different from one another, they often had things in common. Most early societies depended on agriculture. They also built cities, set up governments, and practiced religions. Many used some form of money for exchange. Some societies produced artifacts that were very similar to those of other societies. People in both the Nile Valley and Middle America built pyramids. What does this tell you about the two cultures?

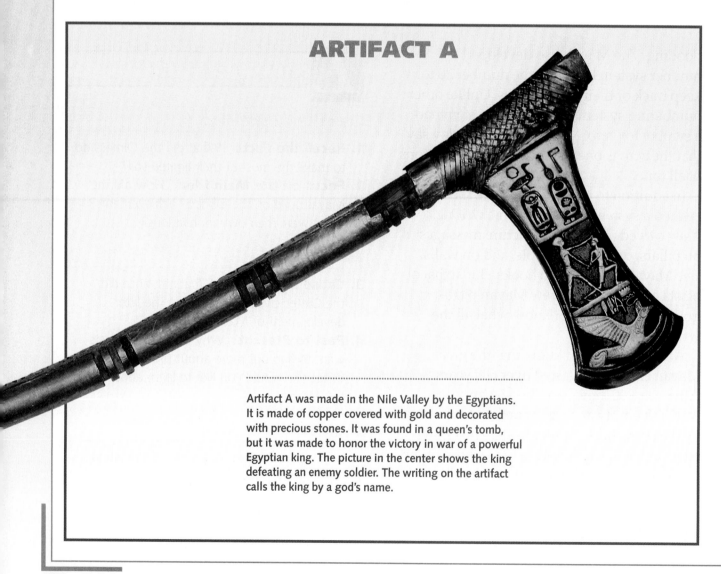

## ARTIFACT A

Artifact A was made in the Nile Valley by the Egyptians. It is made of copper covered with gold and decorated with precious stones. It was found in a queen's tomb, but it was made to honor the victory in war of a powerful Egyptian king. The picture in the center shows the king defeating an enemy soldier. The writing on the artifact calls the king by a god's name.

# ARTIFACT B

Artifact B was made in Middle America by the Olmecs. It is made of jade, a stone the Olmecs valued more than gold. The artifact is shaped like a creature part human and part jaguar. Such objects have been found in the tombs of kings and other leaders. The jaguar may have been a symbol of authority for the Olmecs.

# ARTIFACT C

Artifact C is from the Shang Dynasty in China. It is made of bronze, a metal with which the Shang formed objects used in public ceremonies. This artifact was found in the tomb of a Shang lord or king. To the Shang, it may have been a symbol of political strength.

Three artifacts are shown on pages 138–139. One was made in Egypt, one in the Americas, and one in China. They look different, yet they are alike in important ways. Study the pictures and their captions. Then use the questions as a guide in comparing these early civilizations.

1. How do you know what each artifact is?
2. How was each artifact used by the people who made it?
3. What tells you that each artifact was important to the people who made it?
4. How are the three artifacts alike? In what ways do you think the societies that made them may have been alike?

## Think and Apply

The Egyptian artifact gives information in hieroglyphics and pictures. The information provided by the writing and the pictures lets us know that a powerful king most likely owned the object. Look back at the illustrations in Chapter 3 and Chapter 4 of this unit. Find other ancient artifacts. Remember that ancient artifacts are items that people of long ago made and used. With a partner, make a list of the artifacts you have found. Then describe what these artifacts seem to tell you about the societies that made them. Share your findings with the class.

# REVIEW

## CONNECT MAIN IDEAS

Use this organizer to show that you understand how the chapter's main ideas are connected. Copy the organizer onto a separate sheet of paper. Then complete it by writing three details to support each main idea.

**Civilization in the Indus Valley**
The physical setting of the Indus Valley civilization affected its development and survival.
1. _____
2. _____
3. _____

**Civilization in the Huang He Valley**
The beliefs of the ancient Chinese people affected the development and growth of their civilization.
1. _____
2. _____
3. _____

**Early Civilizations in Asia and the Americas**

**Ancient Civilizations of the Americas**
The Mayas both built on earlier achievements of the Olmec civilization and contributed their own.
1. _____
2. _____
3. _____

## WRITE MORE ABOUT IT

1. **Write to Compare**   The ancient civilizations of the Indus Valley, the Huang He Valley, and the Nile Valley all depended on rivers for their survival. Think about how the different peoples made use of rivers. Then write a paragraph that compares the effects of the rivers on these people.

2. **Write a Letter**   Ancient Chinese people believed they could communicate with their ancestors through the use of oracle bones. Imagine that you can communicate with your ancestors. In the form of a personal letter to one of them, tell how life has changed since his or her time and how it has remained the same.

3. **Write an Inscription**   Imagine that you are a worker making an object for a time capsule that will be opened 1,000 years from now. To give the people of that time an understanding of how life has changed and how it has remained the same, write an inscription describing yourself and your culture.

## USE VOCABULARY

Write a word from this list to complete each of the sentences that follow.

**intercropping**
**mandate**
**oracle**
**protein**
**tributary**

1. A person who gives wise advice is called an _____.

2. _____ is a substance in food that helps build the body.

3. A _____ is a small river that flows into a larger river.

4. Planting combined crops, as the Olmecs did, is called _____.

5. The Chinese believed that the gods gave their leader an order, or a _____, to rule.

## CHECK UNDERSTANDING

1. What was life like in ancient Indus Valley cities?

2. What caused the fall of Mohenjo-Daro?

3. What proof do archaeologists have that Indus Valley civilizations existed?

4. What was the Mandate of Heaven? How did it affect Chinese rulers?

5. What are pictographs? How did the Shang people use pictographs?

6. The Olmec civilization developed in Middle America. What present-day countries are in Middle America?

7. Why did the Olmecs and the Mayas develop calendars?

8. What important ideas of the Mayas have been passed on to other cultures?

## THINK CRITICALLY

1. **Think More About It**   How was the city of Mohenjo-Daro similar to a small city of today?

2. **Personally Speaking**   The ancient Chinese felt a strong sense of their importance in the universe. Is this true of people in the United States today? Explain.

3. **Past to Present**   The Chinese used oracle bones to get advice. How do people in our society get advice?

4. **Cause and Effect**   How did flooding affect the development of early cultures in the Indus Valley and in China?

## APPLY SKILLS

**How to Use an Elevation Map**   Use the map of Middle America on page 137 to answer the questions:

1. Where in Mexico are the highest elevations?

2. What generalization can you make about the relationship between elevations and the locations of Olmec sites in Middle America?

**How to Learn from Artifacts**   Imagine that you are an archaeologist in the year A.D. 2999. You have just discovered an automobile that was used in the last years of the twentieth century. What information does this artifact give you about the society that used it?

## READ MORE ABOUT IT

*Ancient Indians: The First Americans* by Roy A. Gallant. Enslow. The author describes how the first Native Americans arrived from Asia and how their societies developed.

*Cities in the Sand: The Ancient Civilizations of the Southwest* by Scott S. Warren. Chronicle. This book offers information about the Anasazi, the Hohokam, and the Mogollon.

# Why Preserve the Past?

To some people in the United States, building a shopping mall on a Civil War battle site or knocking down an old school to put in a parking lot is making progress. To others, it is destroying a memory from a community's past.

Ancient buildings, monuments, and other structures link the world of today with history. They are reminders that people who lived long ago achieved important things. As long as the structures that they built remain, those people will not be forgotten.

One of the most remarkable of the world's monuments is the Sphinx of Egypt. It reminds people of the powerful Egyptian pharaohs who ruled more than 4,000 years ago. These pharaohs commanded that thousands of workers labor for years to build huge structures such as the pyramids and the Sphinx.

In recent years the Sphinx has shown much damage from pollution, weather, and age. The present-day Egyptian people might have lost this link with their past. To keep this from happening, they began a costly project to save the Sphinx. Adam Henein, an artist, explained his reason for giving long hours to restore and protect the Sphinx. "To me," said Henein, "[the Sphinx] is the soul of Egypt."

## THINK AND APPLY

Think about why it is important to preserve the memories of our past. What objects would you leave behind so that people in the future might remember what you achieved? Work with your class to prepare a time capsule that contains these objects. Find a safe place to keep the capsule so it can be opened by students in your school many years from now.

BUILDING CITIZENSHIP

Until recently, ropes and boards covered Egypt's Sphinx as workers made repairs (left). Farther south in Africa, workers uncover the ancient pyramids of Nubia (top). Across the Atlantic in Mexico City, the excavation of an Aztec temple is underway (bottom).

# STORY CLOTH

Study the pictures shown in this story cloth to help you review the events you read about in Unit 2.

## Summarize the Main Ideas

**1.** In the Americas the Mayas built on the achievements of the Olmec civilization and developed their own ideas.

**2.** The Nile River was important to the development of the Egyptian civilization in northern Africa.

**3.** The beliefs of the ancient Chinese people affected the growth of their civilization.

**4.** The people of Nubia influenced and were influenced by the ancient Egyptians as they built their civilization.

**5.** The physical setting of the Indus Valley civilization affected the development and survival of its well-planned cities.

**Compare and Contrast** As you look at the scenes in the story cloth, think about the way the environment affected the development of each civilization. Then make a table that compares and contrasts the environments of two or more of the civilizations shown in the scenes.

**Write a Description** Select one of the scenes in the story cloth. Write a description of the physical setting shown in the scene.

## COOPERATIVE LEARNING WORKSHOP

### Remember

- Share your ideas.
- Cooperate with others to plan your work.
- Take responsibility for your work.
- Show your group's work to the class.
- Discuss what you learned by working together.

### Activity 1
## Make an Egyptian Scroll

In a small group, make a scroll that describes parts of ancient Egyptian life. Building a pyramid, planning for the afterlife, making a mummy, or farming along the Nile River are just a few of the topics you could choose. To make your scroll, use a long piece of paper or several smaller sheets of paper taped end to end. Be sure to use only pictures on your scroll. When you have finished making your scroll, roll it and tie it. Trade scrolls with other groups, and try to figure out one another's picture stories.

### Activity 2
## Hold a Roundtable Discussion

With a group of four or five classmates, hold a roundtable discussion about similarities and differences between leaders of ancient Egypt and leaders today. Talk about the qualities needed to rule well as a pharaoh long ago and the qualities needed to rule well today. Then compare the qualities of effective leaders needed then with those needed now.

### Activity 3
## Make a Poster

Work with several classmates to create a poster that illustrates the seasons of the ancient Egyptian calendar. At the top of a sheet of posterboard, write the title *The Egyptian Calendar*. Next, draw a large circle, and divide it into three equal parts. Then, label each part with the name of one of the three seasons of the Egyptian calendar. Finally, take turns drawing pictures that show what took place during each season.

### Activity 4
## Make a Model of Mohenjo-Daro

Just as the ancient people of India cooperated to build their cities, work with your classmates to make a model of Mohenjo-Daro. Your model should have a bathhouse, a walled fortress protecting a palace, and a storage shed. Use cardboard and other easy-to-find materials to build your ancient city. Groups of classmates could each build a different part of the city. Then they could put the parts together to form the complete model.

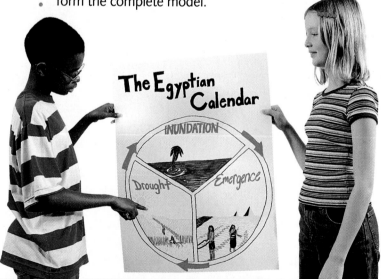

# USE VOCABULARY

Write the term that matches each meaning.

dynasty        legend        predict
intercropping    obelisk       protein

1. to tell what will happen in the future

2. planting different crops together

3. a substance in food that helps build the body

4. a story handed down from earlier times to explain the past

5. a series of rulers from the same family

6. a stone column often used to honor important people or events

# CHECK UNDERSTANDING

1. Why did Egyptians call the Nile River the "giver of life"? How was the Nile also a taker of life?

2. How did the pharaohs help continue Egyptian civilization throughout the centuries?

3. How did Kush's conquest of Egypt affect both Kush and Egypt?

4. How were Indus Valley settlers able to live safely on the floodplain at the place where the four tributaries flowed into the Indus River?

5. Why did the ancient Chinese not trade with outsiders?

6. How did writing affect the culture of China?

7. How do we know that religion played an important part in Mayan culture?

# THINK CRITICALLY

1. **Think More About It**   Why did the early Egyptians believe in an afterlife?

2. **Cause and Effect**   How did the problems caused by the Nile River lead to the development of Egyptian science and technology?

3. **Personally Speaking**   If you had been young Thutmose III, what would you have thought of Hatshepsut's becoming the first female pharaoh of Egypt?

4. **Past to Present**   Why do archaeologists want to learn the meaning of Mayan hieroglyphics?

# APPLY GEOGRAPHY SKILLS

**How to Read Elevation Maps**   Use the map shown below to answer the questions.

1. What country shown on the map has the highest areas?

2. Where are the highest areas of Egypt?

3. How would you describe Sudan's elevation?

4. Which is at a higher elevation, the mouth or the source of the Nile?

5. Can you use this map to find the exact height of land? Explain your answer.

ELEVATION MAP: NORTH AFRICA

# UNIT 3

# ASIA'S CLASSICAL AGE

**1500 B.C.**

**1200 B.C.**

**900 B.C.**

**About 1500 B.C.**
Aryan migrations begin

**1122 B.C.**
The Zhou claim the Mandate of Heaven in China

*B*etween 1500 B.C. and A.D. 100, the foundations of Asia's major civilizations were laid. Political, social, and economic changes created traditions that have lasted for thousands of years. Asia's Classical Age also saw the rise of new religions and new ideas about life. These continue to play a role in the way people live in Asia and in other parts of the world.

◀ The emperors of ancient China greatly affected the way of life of the people. In this miniature painting Emperor Mou of the Zhou dynasty travels in fine style.

600 B.C.

300 B.C.

B.C. A.D.

**551 B.C.**
Confucius born
in China

**About 320 B.C.**
Chandragupta
Maurya unites
northern India

**539 B.C.**
The Persians
conquer the
Babylonians

**221 B.C.**
Shi Huangdi
unites China

**About A.D.100**
Paper invented
in China

**About 106 B.C.**
China trade reaches
the Mediterranean
region

# 6 Chinese BROTHERS

## An Ancient Tale

retold by Cheng Hou-tien

............................................................................................

### illustrated by Jean Hirashima

Before people learned to write, storytellers held an honored place in most ancient civilizations. Storytellers guarded people's history and legends. They kept stories alive by passing them on by word of mouth.

Later, scribes wrote down some of the stories that had been passed down by storytellers. Through these stories we can learn about the values, customs, and traditions of ancient people.

Now read a retelling of an ancient tale from China. In this story six brothers show their loyalty to their father and to one another in spite of danger and the threat of death. Generation after generation of Chinese people learned the importance of loyalty from stories like this.

Long ago, in ancient China, lived an old farmer with his six sons.

The first son was clever.

The second son could stretch his arms to either end of the world.

The third son had a head so hard, steel bounced off it.

The fourth son had skin like iron.

The fifth son could withstand the greatest heat.

And the sixth son, why he was able to stretch his legs for inches and feet and yards—and for miles and miles.

One day the old farmer fell ill. None of the doctors could cure him.

"There is only one way to save your father," said one. "You must get the pearl from the king's palace, boil it in water, and give your father the water to drink."

First Son said, "Second Son, stretch out your arms and get the pearl."

Second Son reached out across the plains into the city, where the palace was, and into the king's window and drew out the pearl. The brothers boiled the pearl and gave their father the water to drink, and the old man got better.

When the king discovered that his precious pearl was missing, he was furious. He sent his soldiers to find it. They went from door to door. When First Son opened the door and the soldiers saw the pearl, they seized it.

And they arrested First Son and brought him before the king.

"Off with his head!" cried the king.

First Son could not stand the thought of dying without seeing his father one more time.

"Please let me see my father before I die," he begged. The king allowed him to go.

When the old farmer learned that his son was to be beheaded, he was very sad. "But wait," said Third Son. "Let me go and take my brother's place."

The next day, it was Third Son who put his head on the block. The executioner lowered the ax, but the head remained. The people laughed and jeered.

The king was angry. He ordered his soldiers to run him through with a knife. Third Son was frightened. "Please let me see my father before I die," he said.

The king allowed him to go. When the brothers heard the news, it was suggested that Fourth Son go back instead. This, Fourth Son did.

And the next day, when the soldiers brought the knife down on him, the blade snapped in two, like a bamboo stick.

"Throw him into boiling water," cried the king. "That will finish him off."

"Please let me go home and see my father before I die," Fourth Son pleaded.

The next day, when Fifth Son was thrown into boiling water, to the great surprise of all around, he merely called for more heat and began to sing.

The king sputtered and railed. "Throw him into the sea! No one escapes from its depth," he cried.

"I accept my fate," said Fifth Son. "But before I die, please let me go home and see my father."

Fifth Son hurried home and told what had happened.

"Never mind," said First Son. "Sixth Son will take your place. He can never drown."

Sixth Son returned to the palace in his brother's place. He was taken out to sea and dropped overboard. The soldiers watched him disappear. They saw bubbles form on the surface of the water and were sure he had drowned.

But Sixth Son was far from gone. He stretched and stretched his legs until he was standing on the ocean floor. There, he found many precious jewels. When he rose to the surface, the surprised soldiers brought him to the king.

Sixth Son presented the king with the jewels he had found. The jewels pleased the king and he decided to spare the boy's life.

"How is it that you have escaped sure death again and again?" asked the king. When the king heard the story, he sent for the other five brothers and said, "You boys are a fine example of devotion to family. China is proud of you."

And he held a banquet for the old farmer and his six sons at the palace, which hundreds of people attended.

· · · · · · · · · · · · · · · · · · · · · · · · · · · · · · · · · · · · · · · · · · · · · · · · ·

*As you read about the ancient peoples of Asia, you will learn more about loyalty. You will also learn about values, customs, and traditions that developed long ago in Asia and have continued through the centuries.*

# CHINA

> 66 China is a sea that salts all rivers that run into it. 99
>
> Traditional Chinese saying

Life-size statue of a Chinese soldier, carved around 210 B.C.

# The ZHOU DYNASTY

LESSON 1

## Link to Our World

**Can a set of ideas held in common help people work together?**

### Focus on the Main Idea
*As you read, think about how a set of virtues helped the Chinese maintain order and increase cooperation.*

### Preview Vocabulary
heritage    philosopher
militia    responsibility
virtue    Confucianism
public works

The sacred *bi*, or ring of heaven, was a symbol of the bond between the Chinese gods and the leaders chosen to carry out the Mandate of Heaven.

The Classical Age in China began with the conquest of the Huang He Valley in 1122 B.C. by the Zhou (JOH) dynasty. Under the Zhou and the dynasties that followed, China became large and powerful. These dynasties left a heritage that has lasted for thousands of years. A **heritage** is a set of ideas that has passed down from one generation to another.

## WINNING THE MANDATE OF HEAVEN

The ancestors of the founders of the Zhou dynasty were a nomadic people. They lived in the western mountains of a land that today is part of China, near the source of the Huang He. In time the Zhou settled on the edge of the Shang Kingdom. Soon they became known not only as skilled farmers but as expert fighters as well.

The Zhou had settled just as the use of iron was spreading. They began to hammer this strong metal into tools and plows. They also formed pieces of iron into weapons— weapons that could help them defeat their fiercest enemies. When the Shang tried to expand their borders, Zhou **militia**, or volunteer soldiers, fought back to protect their land. Shang weapons were no match for the Zhou's iron weapons.

In 1122 B.C. the Zhou king, Wu, claimed the Mandate of Heaven—the order from the gods to rule China. King Wu told the Chinese people that the last Shang king did not have the **virtues**, or good qualities, needed to lead the people. King Wu said that the Zhou would be better rulers. The Zhou ruled China for almost

900 years, until 256 B.C. This dynasty was the longest-lasting dynasty in all of China's history.

 **Who replaced the Shang as rulers of China?**

## DIVISION OF CLASSES

To help control the large kingdom, the Zhou created a new social structure. The king was at the top of Zhou society. Noble families were in the middle. Peasant farmers were at the bottom.

Everyone owed loyalty to the king. The king gave land to the nobles in return for military service. The nobles ruled their land as separate states, governing in whatever way they wanted. The king used the nobles' powerful armies to protect the kingdom.

The peasants lived on the land owned by the nobles and farmed it. In return for the right to farm a noble's land, the peasants had to serve in the noble's army.

The life of a peasant was filled with hardships. This poem from the *Book of Songs*, written sometime after 1000 B.C., offers a personal view of a peasant's life:

> ❝What plant is not faded?
> What day do we not march?
> What man is not taken
> To defend the four bounds?
> What plant is not wilting?
> What man is not taken from
> his wife?
> Alas for us soldiers,
> Treated as though we were
> not fellow-men!❞

Peasant farmers supplied the king with an almost endless number of workers. They constructed many huge public works. **Public works** are structures built by the government for everyone's use.

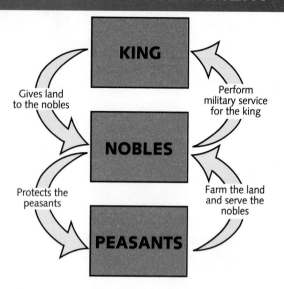

### SOCIAL STRUCTURE OF THE ZHOU GOVERNMENT

KING

Gives land to the nobles

Perform military service for the king

NOBLES

Protects the peasants

Farm the land and serve the nobles

PEASANTS

**LEARNING FROM CHARTS** Each of China's three social classes had responsibilities to the other classes.
■ What was the main responsibility of the nobles in relation to the peasants?

During the Zhou dynasty new dikes, dams, and canals helped improve agriculture and increase the food supply. New roads meant better transportation and communication.

Under the Zhou kings China's civilization grew. By the 700s B.C. more people lived in China than anywhere else in the world.

 **What were the advantages and disadvantages of China's system of government?**

This bronze and jade statue of a peasant child is from the time of the Zhou dynasty. Why do you think statues like these were made?

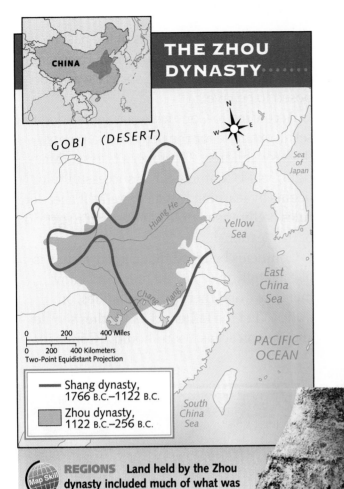

## THE ZHOU DYNASTY

CHINA

GOBI (DESERT)

Huang He

Yellow Sea

Sea of Japan

Chang Jiang

East China Sea

PACIFIC OCEAN

South China Sea

0      200      400 Miles
0      200      400 Kilometers
Two-Point Equidistant Projection

— Shang dynasty, 1766 B.C.–1122 B.C.
▨ Zhou dynasty, 1122 B.C.–256 B.C.

**REGIONS** Land held by the Zhou dynasty included much of what was once held by the Shang.
■ Why do you think the land controlled by the two dynasties was not exactly alike?

## THE WARRING STATES PERIOD

In the 700s B.C. nomadic peoples from central Asia invaded the Huang He Valley. Rather than unite to fight the invaders, China's nobles fought among themselves. The fighting weakened the Zhou authority, or power to rule, and threatened the dynasty. Without the loyalty of the nobles, China's ruling system broke down.

A Chinese artist may have been thinking of the legend of King Yoo when making this statue of a man holding a huge lamp. ➡

In 771 B.C. the people in the Zhou capital city of Hao (HOW) got ready for an attack by the invaders. A legend tells that the Chinese leader, King Yoo (YOO), ordered fires lighted on the nights before the attack. The fires would warn the nobles to gather their armies and defend the king. However, the disloyal nobles ignored the signals. King Yoo died in the attack.

As its ruling system crumbled, China began a time that historians call the Warring States Period. From around 600 B.C. China's many states were almost always at war with one another. Huge areas of farmland were burned, and many villages and public works were destroyed. The system that had kept order for hundreds of years was forgotten. Loyalty to a single powerful king was lost as well. This was a time of chaos. Finally, in 221 B.C., a strong leader claimed the Mandate of Heaven.

✓ **What was the Warring States Period?**

⬆ This bronze box, from the time of the Zhou dynasty, was used in religious ceremonies. Why do you think the person who created this box decorated it so beautifully?

# THE IDEAS OF CONFUCIUS

During the Warring States Period, Chinese people turned to their wisest philosophers to explain what had happened to their society. A **philosopher** is a person who studies the meaning of life. The most important of the Chinese philosophers was a teacher called Kung Fu Zi (KOONG FOO ZUH), or Master Kung. Kung Fu Zi later became known in the West as Confucius.

Confucius was born in 551 B.C. He compared his time with the time when the Zhou were strong. Confucius wondered why people then were loyal to their leaders.

He decided that the leaders of the past had given the people a sense of order. Everyone knew how each person in society was supposed to behave.

According to Confucius, a ruler needed to set an example for the people, as a parent does for children. "To govern is to set things right," said Confucius. The successful ruler begins by learning to act correctly. If a leader rules badly, the people have a right to get rid of that leader.

Confucius believed that a good society is like a family in which all members know their place and their **responsibilities**, or duties. "Let the father act as a father should and the son act as a son should," Confucius

## Who?

### Confucius
### 551–479 B.C.

Confucius grew up in the city-state of Lu in northeastern China. His father was a minor state official. Confucius also worked for the government. He began to think about how government could work for the good of all people. As a government worker, he had little chance to put his ideas into action. So he became a teacher of the sons of nobles. He hoped that when his students gained positions of authority they would govern by his ideas.

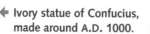
← Ivory statue of Confucius, made around A.D. 1000.

No one knows for sure what Confucius really looked like. The portrait above, made in A.D. 1734, and the one at left, from around A.D. 1000, provide two very different views.

# Proverbs of Confucius from the ANALECTS

## ON TRUTH

Those who know the truth are not up to those who love it; those who love the truth are not up to those who delight in it.

## ON EDUCATION

In education there are no class distinctions.

Learning without thinking is labor lost; thinking without learning is dangerous.

## ON GOVERNMENT

If a ruler himself is upright, all will go well without orders. But if he himself is not upright, even though he gives orders they will not be obeyed.

said. People must take part in society in the same way they take part in a family, Confucius thought. Comparing society to a family was important because family members worked together for the common good. The ancient Chinese especially honored older family members. Family decisions depended on their wisdom.

Confucius was ignored by the warring nobles. They were too busy fighting one another to listen to his teachings. Many people, however, respected Confucius. Long after his death in 479 B.C., Confucius's followers wrote down his teachings in a book called the *Analects*. In time his ideas, which came to be called **Confucianism**, spread among other people of eastern Asia, including the Japanese.

Confucianism became a guide for the way people lived. They were guided by the five virtues of Confucianism: charity, kindness, hard work, good faith, and courtesy.

**What were two important ideas of Confucianism?**

## LESSON 1 REVIEW

### Check Understanding

1. **Recall the Facts** What philosopher of ancient China developed an important system of ideas and values?
2. **Focus on the Main Idea** How did the Chinese people's shared belief in a set of ideas help them work together?

### Think Critically

3. **Think More About It** In what ways did Confucianism support the idea of the Mandate of Heaven?
4. **Personally Speaking** Zhou society was divided into three classes, each with different responsibilities. In your opinion, would such a system be more likely to lead to cooperation or to conflict? Explain.

### Show What You Know

**Creative Writing Activity**
Confucius often presented his ideas about society as proverbs, or short sayings. Some examples can be found in the Proverbs of Confucius from the *Analects*, on this page. Using these examples as models, write your own proverbs about the need for order and cooperation in your school or community.

# How To

# Identify Causes and Their Effects

## Why Is This Skill Important?

To find links between different events in history, you need to understand causes and their effects. A cause is something that makes something else happen. What happens is an effect. Knowing about causes and effects is important not only for understanding history but also for making personal decisions. It can help you think about the consequences of your actions. In that way you can make more thoughtful decisions.

## Remember What You Have Read

Before the Zhou lost the Mandate of Heaven, their rulers created a new social structure. The king was at the top, nobles were in the middle, and peasants were at the bottom. The whole structure depended on loyalty. For the structure to work successfully, the peasants had to remain loyal to the nobles, and the nobles had to remain loyal to the king. You read the legend of King Yoo. His story explains what caused the Zhou dynasty's social structure to crumble and the dynasty to fall.

## Understand the Process

Many events in history have more than one cause and more than one effect. Follow the arrows on the chart in the next column to help you understand the causes and effects of the fall of the Zhou dynasty.

1. What caused the Chinese nobles who lived during the time of the Zhou dynasty to fight among themselves? What was the effect of the fighting on the dynasty?
2. What caused King Yoo to signal the nobles by ordering fires lighted in the Zhou capital city of Hao?
3. What caused the death of King Yoo and the fall of the Zhou dynasty?
4. What were the effects of the fall of the Zhou dynasty?

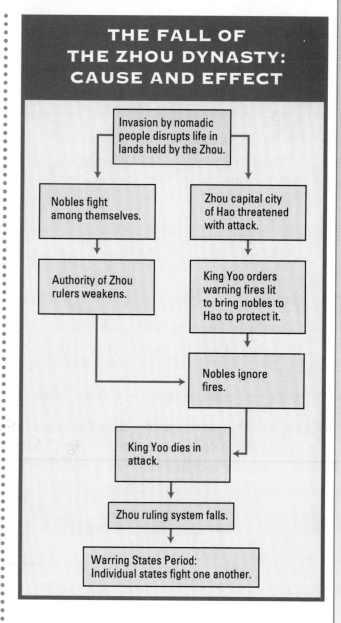

### THE FALL OF THE ZHOU DYNASTY: CAUSE AND EFFECT

- Invasion by nomadic people disrupts life in lands held by the Zhou.
  - Nobles fight among themselves.
    - Authority of Zhou rulers weakens.
  - Zhou capital city of Hao threatened with attack.
    - King Yoo orders warning fires lit to bring nobles to Hao to protect it.
      - Nobles ignore fires.
        - King Yoo dies in attack.
          - Zhou ruling system falls.
            - Warring States Period: Individual states fight one another.

## Think and Apply

Identify an event that took place in your community or one that was reported in the news. Perhaps there was a bad storm or a community clean-up day. Link the event's causes and effects on a chart like the one on this page. Use your chart to explain the event to a classmate or a family member.

BUILDING CITIZENSHIP

# United Rule IN THE QIN DYNASTY

LESSON 2

## Link to Our World

**How can a leader unite people?**

**Focus on the Main Idea**
*Read to discover how the first emperor of China united the people under his rule.*

**Preview Vocabulary**
Legalism
standardization
bureaucracy

Zhou rulers had no authority during the Warring States Period. Yet they continued to hold the Mandate of Heaven. Then the Qin (CHIN) claimed the Mandate in 221 B.C. and ruled until 207 B.C. During this short time the Qin dynasty united the warring city-states and created China's first great empire.

## RULE OF SHI HUANGDI

The person who brought the Qin to power was only 13 years old when he became their king. An enemy described the young king as having "the chest of a bird of prey, the voice of a jackal, and the heart of a tiger." The king wanted to do great things for himself. Even the name he took upon becoming king of the Qin showed his desire to succeed. The title *king* did not sound powerful enough for him, so he called himself Qin Shi Huangdi (CHIN SHEE HWAHNG•DEE), "First Emperor of Qin." And this was before he had an empire!

Shi Huangdi ruled with great cruelty. Those people foolish enough to challenge Shi Huangdi were executed along with their families. This warned others to obey.

Shi Huangdi based his cruel form of leadership on a set of teachings far different from those taught by Confucius. This set of teachings was called **Legalism**. Legalism taught that people obeyed their rulers out of fear, not out of respect. People who obeyed received rewards. Those who did not obey were punished. To the Legalists, harsh treatment of people was the only way to bring peace and wealth to China.

Shi Huangdi thought of the teachings of Confucius as a challenge to his authority. The ruler ordered all writings about Confucianism destroyed. If teachers refused to follow

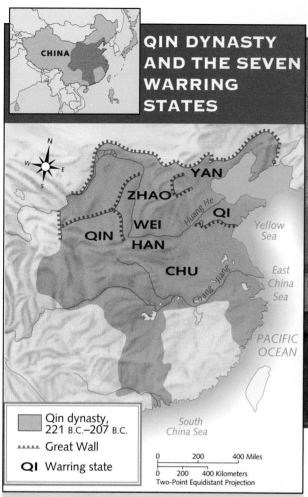

CHINA

YAN

ZHAO

QI

WEI

Huang He

QIN

HAN

CHU

Chang Jiang

Yellow Sea

East China Sea

PACIFIC OCEAN

South China Sea

Qin dynasty, 221 B.C.–207 B.C.

Great Wall

**QI** Warring state

0        200        400 Miles
0   200   400 Kilometers
Two-Point Equidistant Projection

**HUMAN-ENVIRONMENT INTERACTIONS**
Seven warring states joined together under the Qin dynasty.
■ In what directions would the Qin most likely have traveled to expand their empire?

To be sure that his subjects learned little of ideas other than his, Emperor Shi Huangdi ordered book burnings throughout his empire. This painting, by Hung Wu, from a later period, shows just one of the many book burnings.

his orders, they were killed. One person of the times noted that Shi Huangdi placed "violence above kindness and justice."

### Why was Legalism important to Shi Huangdi?

## UNITING CHINA

Shi Huangdi claimed the Mandate of Heaven in 221 B.C. He then quickly moved to unite the Chinese city-states under his rule. He knew he could unite China only by crushing the authority of every noble. To reach his goal, Shi Huangdi first attacked the city-states and seized all their weapons. He next divided China into military districts and named people he trusted to govern each one. In doing so, he created the empire he had longed for.

Once in control, Shi Huangdi ordered the noble families to leave their homelands and move to China's capital city. In this way he broke the ties of loyalty between nobles and peasants. Now the peasants owed their loyalty to no one but the emperor. Shi Huangdi created a strong army made up of hundreds of thousands of peasants. Using this fighting force, he pushed the borders of the empire farther south and east.

### Why did Shi Huangdi break ties of loyalty between nobles and peasants?

# THE GREAT WALL

Shi Huangdi had built a large empire. Now he faced another challenge. Communicating with and traveling to distant places in the empire was difficult. How could he control such a large empire? Immediately Shi Huangdi put plans into action to keep his empire together.

Like the Zhou rulers before him, Shi Huangdi used China's peasant farmers to build public works. His many workers built more than 4,000 miles (6,437 km) of roads. Even the distant parts of the empire were linked to the center of the Qin government. "For the first time he has united the world," one person said of Shi Huangdi.

Of all Shi Huangdi's building projects, one stands out as the largest and most costly. It was the Great Wall, a wall unlike any other in the world. Built to protect China from outsiders, the Great Wall stood 30 feet (9 m)

> ❝ *For the first time* *HE HAS UNITED THE* *WORLD.* ❞
>
> Said of Shi Huangdi

high, with 40-foot (12-m) towers. The wall was so thick that two wagons could pass each other while traveling on top of it.

The Great Wall stretched for almost 1,500 miles (2,414 km) across northern China, twisting and turning over mountains and through valleys, marshes, and deserts. Yet, in spite of its size, the Great Wall was built in just seven years. Only through the hard work of China's peasant farmers was this possible.

**LEARNING FROM DIAGRAMS** This cross-section diagram of the Great Wall shows how the wall was made.
■ Why do you think builders used a variety of materials to build different parts of the wall?

The Great Wall of China, though much of it has been rebuilt, still looks much as it did during Shi Huangdi's day. The wall is the world's longest human-made structure.

### THE GREAT WALL OF CHINA

BRICK

13 feet (4 m)

5 feet

15 feet

30 feet (9 m)

STONE OR BRICK

BROKEN ROCK AND POUNDED EARTH

STONE BASE 5 feet

STONE

25 feet (7.5 m)

40 feet (12 m)

The cost of building the wall was high in terms of human life. More than 500,000 workers died during the building of the wall. Some were buried between its stones. Nature gave China the Huang He, its "river of sorrows." Shi Huangdi gave China the Great Wall, its "wall of tears."

✓ **What was the purpose of the Great Wall of China? Why has it been called the "wall of tears"?**

## A PROGRAM OF STANDARDIZATION

Public works such as walls and roads helped protect and unite China. So, too, did Shi Huangdi's program of standardization. **Standardization** means making all things of a certain type alike. The use of standardized coins, weights, and writing throughout China helped make trade and communication easier. Use of the same standards helped the many peoples of the empire think of themselves as one.

To oversee his huge empire, Shi Huangdi created a bureaucracy. A **bureaucracy** is a network of appointed government officials. Each official was in charge of the day-to-day

# What?

## The Emperor's Clay Army

The tomb of Shi Huangdi is located near the present-day city of Xian (SEE•AHN), formerly Chang'an (CHANG•AHN), in the Wei He Valley. The lavish tomb originally stood 15 stories tall and covered about 3 acres. However, what makes it so unusual is not its size, but the army of clay soldiers that protects it. More than 6,000 life-size clay soldiers and 1,400 chariots surround the tomb. The warriors seem alive and ready for battle. No two soldiers look alike. Many hold real crossbows, spears, and swords. Shi Huangdi wanted his clay army to guard him in death, just as his real army had guarded him in life.

For centuries Shi Huangdi's clay army lay buried. Work is still being done to uncover more soldiers.

# When?

## 221–207 B.C.

While Shi Huangdi was bringing standardization to China, other civilizations around the world were changing as well. The long-lasting Egyptian Empire in northern Africa had lost its independence. The kingdom of Kush, however, was growing because of a successful iron-making industry. Europe had recently seen a time of empire building. Now it was in the midst of a time of scientific and mathematical advances. In the Americas, the Mayas were creating new hieroglyphics and experimenting with new ways of building.

Standard weights, like the one shown below, helped the Chinese be sure that goods such as pieces of jade were measured the same way. Why was it important that like goods be measured the same way?

governing of his part of the empire. In this way Shi Huangdi made sure that even the most distant places in the empire would not slip from his control.

The emperor believed that the bureaucracy he had formed would allow the Qin to rule for "ten thousand generations." However, unhappiness spread among the peasants. In time they began to fight back against their cruel rulers. The Qin dynasty ended not long after Shi Huangdi's death.

The Qin ruled for just a short time, but they had a great influence on China's civilization. Under Shi Huangdi, the Qin created the position of emperor. The Qin also united the Chinese states into a single empire under a strong central government. At the same time, they caused humans to suffer in ways few could have imagined.

✓ **What was an important result of standardization and the creation of a bureaucracy?**

# LESSON 2 REVIEW

## Check Understanding

1. **Recall the Facts**  What emotion did Legalists think brought leaders the loyalty of those they ruled?
2. **Focus on the Main Idea**  How did Shi Huangdi unify China?

## Think Critically

3. **Cause and Effect**  What effect do you think placing "violence above kindness and justice" had on the people Shi Huangdi ruled?
4. **Personally Speaking**  Do you think Shi Huangdi should be remembered more for uniting China or for causing human suffering? Explain your answer.
5. **Past to Present**  How can modern technology help leaders keep order in large countries?

## Show What You Know

**Poster Activity**  Divide a sheet of posterboard into two columns. In one column, list the qualities of Shi Huangdi that helped him unite China. In the other column, list those that made it more difficult. Some qualities may appear in both columns.

**PROGRESS UNDER THE**

# HAN DYNASTY

## Link to Our World

**Why are some periods in history remembered as times of achievement?**

*Focus on the Main Idea*
*Think about the achievements that made the years of Han rule an outstanding time in Chinese history.*

*Preview Vocabulary*

| | |
|---|---|
| civil war | export |
| ambassador | caravan |
| civil service | profit |
| Daoism | Silk Road |
| import | |

**Woman in traditional clothing of the Han period**

A time of disorder followed the fall of the Qin dynasty. Order finally returned when the Han dynasty gained control of China in 202 B.C. For the next 400 years, Han rulers advanced Chinese civilization. They led China into a golden age of peace, wealth, and progress. To this day the Chinese people proudly call themselves children of Han.

## THE HAN VIEW OF GOVERNMENT

After Shi Huangdi's death, China plunged into civil wars. In a **civil war** groups of people from the same place or country fight one another. During this time China's noble families regained their land. They fought one another for more land and authority. In the end the winner was a peasant, not a noble. His name was Liu Bang (LEE•OO BAHNG). Unlike the nobles, Liu Bang wanted China to be united.

In 202 B.C. Liu Bang claimed the Mandate of Heaven. Like other leaders, Liu Bang believed his name should tell of his accomplishments. He became Han Gao Zu (GOW ZOO), or the "Great Founder of the Han."

Gao Zu knew the importance of having the support of those he ruled. "The prince is the boat; the common people are the water. The water can support the boat, or the water can capsize the boat," he said. He thought out each of his decisions so that his ship of state—China—stayed afloat.

Gao Zu won the support of the nobles by giving them land and by allowing them to rule their lands as they wished. He won over the peasant farmers by lowering

# ANCIENT CHINESE DYNASTIES

| | | |
|---|---|---|
| ■ Shang dynasty | ■ Zhou dynasty | ····· Great Wall |
| ■ Qin dynasty | ■ Han dynasty | • Capital city |

0    500    1,000 Miles
0    500    1,000 Kilometers
Two-Point Equidistant Projection

**REGIONS** Ancient China grew under the various dynasties. Compare the size of China from the Shang dynasty to that from the Han dynasty.

■ In what directions did the empire expand during the Han dynasty?

taxes. The leaders of the Qin dynasty had taxed the peasants heavily to pay for the Great Wall and other public works. The peasants welcomed Gao Zu's new policy of lower taxes.

Gao Zu's view of government combined ideas from two conflicting philosophies— Legalism and Confucianism. Gao Zu accepted the Legalist idea of the need for a strong central government and an all-powerful ruler. But he rejected harsh laws and cruel treatment. Instead, Gao Zu believed in the Confucianist idea that a ruler should set an example for the people. He

believed that by setting a good example, he could win the respect of his people.

Gao Zu succeeded. He was as respected as Shi Huangdi had been feared. But just when Gao Zu had ended problems within China, trouble appeared on its borders. Invaders from the north attacked. One attack brought them to the city walls of Chang'an, the Han capital. Gao Zu was wounded while defending his city. He died from his wounds in 195 B.C.

 **What type of leader did Gao Zu think should rule China?**

## WU DI AND THE CIVIL SERVICE SYSTEM

In 140 B.C. Wu Di (WOO DEE) came to the Han throne. The name *Wu Di* means "Warlike Emperor." Wu Di created armies, some with as many as 300,000 soldiers, to conquer new lands. These armies pushed the borders of the empire north, south, and west.

To guard against attacks by nomads, Wu Di extended the Great Wall. Wu Di also took other actions. In some cases he paid nomads —with silk, rice, or money—not to attack. These payments gave outsiders their first taste of the riches of China.

Wu Di also sent out **ambassadors**, or representatives of the government, to make peace with his enemies. Wu Di's efforts helped bring about what historians later called the *Pax Sinica,* or "Chinese Peace."

Wu Di's changes in government brought peace within his empire. Wu Di set up China's first civil service system. A **civil service** oversees the day-to-day business of running a government.

In the bureaucracy created under the Qin, a job was a reward for loyalty. In contrast, Han civil service officials earned their jobs by scoring well on tests. Wu Di invited all people of the empire—peasants as well as nobles—to take the civil service tests.

Only those who made the highest grades earned government jobs. This examination system for government officials was used for centuries. The civil servants who ran the Han empire so well were proof that it worked.

**How did Wu Di protect his empire and run it?**

## A GOLDEN AGE

Under Wu Di's "Chinese Peace," China entered a Golden Age in both the arts and learning. Without the fear of war, the study of language, history, philosophy, and religion blossomed.

During Han rule, scholars improved the Chinese writing system. One scholar created the first Chinese dictionary, in 100 B.C. Other scholars, such as Sima Qian (SOO•MAH CHEN), recorded China's history. Sima's review of

**LEARNING FROM TIME LINES** The ancient Chinese made many advances in technology from prehistoric times to 220 A.D.
■ Which was invented first, an instrument for detecting earthquakes or the wheelbarrow?

## ANCIENT CHINESE TECHNOLOGY

**Prehistoric Times**
Silk obtained from silkworms

Prehistoric Times

2000 B.C.

**About 1200 B.C.**
Bronze casting developed; Chinese writing developed

1750

— 1700 B.C.

1500

Shang dynasty

**About 500 B.C.**
Canals, dikes, and reservoirs used for irrigation

1250

— 1122 B.C.

**About 210 B.C.**
Great Wall started

1000

Zhou dynasty

750

**About 200 B.C.**
Highways built

600 B.C.

500

Warring States Period

**A.D. 100**
Special instruments invented to observe sun; wheelbarrow, paper invented

250

221 B.C.
* 207 B.C.

B.C.
A.D.

Han dynasty

**A.D. 132**
Instruments invented for detecting earthquakes

— A.D. 200

A.D. 250

*Qin dynasty

Around A.D. 132 Chang Heng invented China's first seismograph. A modern seismograph tells the location and strength of earthquakes. The early Chinese seismograph at left worked in much the same way. A rod inside the seismograph fell toward the dragon nearest the earthquake, making a loud noise. A ball then dropped from the dragon's mouth into a bronze frog below. The noise let the Chinese emperor know that there had been an earthquake in his empire. The direction in which the ball fell told the relative location of the earthquake.

China's past from the earliest dynasties to the Han was not just a listing of dates and events. He connected causes and effects. This made it easier for people to understand *why* things happened.

Confucianism became the official teaching of the Han Empire. Wu Di and later Han rulers also supported the study of such teachings as **Daoism** (DOW•ih•zuhm). Daoism teaches that the key to long life and happiness is to accept life as it is.

The Han Golden Age also brought new ideas in technology. A Han general, for example, developed the wheelbarrow. This invention was of great use to the army because one soldier alone could now move more than 330 pounds (150 kg) of equipment. In A.D. 132 a Han inventor created an instrument to detect earthquakes.

The most important innovation of the Han dynasty was paper. Invented around A.D. 100, paper proved to be an ideal material for recording information. The use of paper led to advances in printing. Han workers soon began printing on paper by using designs etched on stone.

✓ **What was the most important innovation of the Han dynasty?**

## TRADE ON THE SILK ROAD

The early Chinese people had always depended upon their country's own resources. They did not **import**, or bring in, goods for

Wealthy Chinese during the Han dynasty lived in large houses like this. The poor usually lived in small, one-story houses.

sale from other lands. They also did not **export**, or send out, their own goods for sale in other places. But during the Han dynasty, Chinese goods began flowing out of the empire.

In 126 B.C. an ambassador sent west by Wu Di returned with incredible news. Beyond the deserts of central Asia lay other kingdoms of "civilized" people. These people wanted Chinese silk. In turn the Chinese emperor wanted their large and strong "heavenly horses."

In 106 B.C. the first camel **caravan**, or group of traders, headed west from China with a load of silk. Along the way nomadic tribes demanded payment for allowing others to pass through their lands. The journey was dangerous. However, the **profits**, or money gained, more than made up for the risks.

The Chinese easily found buyers for their silk. Those who received silk directly from the

Chinese traded it to others farther west. Chinese traders did not go all the way to Africa and Europe but their goods did. By the second century A.D., the trade route, now called the **Silk Road**, stretched 5,000 miles (8,047 km) to the Mediterranean Sea.

The arrival of silk in the West caused an even greater demand for goods. Caravans heading west carried apricots, iron and bronze goods, and silk. Caravans heading east to China carried such items as gold, ivory, wool, linen, grapevines, and new breeds of horses. Along with goods, news of China traveled to the continents of Africa and Europe. News of those places also made its way to China.

 **What was the Silk Road?**

This wooden model of a servant girl, placed in a tomb over 2,000 years ago, wears silk clothing that has been damaged little by time.

# LESSON 3 REVIEW

## Check Understanding

1. **Recall the Facts**   What advances were made during the time of Han rule?
2. **Focus on the Main Idea**   Why is the Han period thought to be an outstanding time in Chinese history?

## Think Critically

3. **Think More About It**   Why do you think the Han emperors were more successful than earlier emperors in keeping peace?
4. **Personally Speaking**   For centuries the Chinese people have proudly called themselves

children of Han. Why do you think they feel this way?
5. **Past to Present**   Do you live in an age of great achievement? Explain why or why not.

## Show What You Know

 **Collage Activity**   Some people say that the twentieth century has been a century of innovations. Using pictures and headlines from newspapers and magazines, create a collage that illustrates this idea.

# Use a Table to Classify Information

## Why Is This Skill Important?

Imagine looking through a pile of papers on your desk. Your math homework, book reports, and other assignments are mixed together in a big jumble. You cannot quickly find what you need. In the same way, it can be hard to search through jumbled information. Like a pile of papers, information is easier to use if it is **classified**, or sorted. Knowing how to classify information can make it easier for you to find the facts you need.

## Remember What You Have Read

When you read about the dynasties of the Classical Age in China, you were given a lot of information. You learned when the Zhou, Qin, and Han dynasties ruled China, when the Warring States Period occurred, who the important leaders were, and what contributions each dynasty made to Chinese civilization. These and other facts can be classified by using a table. A **table** is a chart that lists information in categories.

## Understand the Process

In the table on this page, China's early history is classified according to its dynasties and its Warring States Period. The years for each period appear in the first column. The years are arranged in order, with the earliest listed first.

Each row gives facts about a single period in Chinese history. Suppose you want to find information about the Qin dynasty. Move your finger down the second column, labeled *Name,* until you find *Qin*. Then move your finger across the row to the column labeled *Contributions*. What was a contribution of the Qin dynasty? Now go to the next column to find out who led the Qin.

## Think and Apply

Make your own table to show information about the Classical Age in China. Use the information in the table on this page, but classify it differently. Share your table with a partner as you review the chapter.

| CHINA'S EARLY HISTORY | | | |
|---|---|---|---|
| YEARS | NAME | CONTRIBUTIONS | IMPORTANT LEADERS |
| 1122 to 600 B.C. | Zhou dynasty | Use of iron<br>Improved ways of farming<br>Advances in irrigation | Wu |
| 600 to 221 B.C. | Warring States Period | Introduction of metal coins | |
| 221 to 207 B.C. | Qin dynasty | Building of Great Wall<br>Standardization of weights and measures<br>Creation of road system | Shi Huangdi |
| 202 B.C. to A.D. 200 | Han dynasty | Civil service examinations<br>Invention of paper<br>Invention of seismograph<br>Beginning of trade on the Silk Road | Gao Zu<br>Wu Di |

# REVIEW

## CONNECT MAIN IDEAS

Use this organizer to show that you understand how the chapter's main ideas are connected. Copy the organizer onto a separate sheet of paper. Then write a sentence or two describing each topic.

**Progress Under the Han Dynasty**

_____

_____

_____

**China**

**United Rule in the Qin Dynasty**

_____

_____

_____

**The Zhou Dynasty**

_____

_____

_____

**1122 B.C. to A.D. 220**

## WRITE MORE ABOUT IT

1. **Write Your Opinion** Zhou rulers ordered peasant farmers to build public works and serve as soldiers. Why did the farmers agree to this? Do you think the rulers were being fair? Have things changed in China or do they remain the same today?

2. **Write a Proverb** Write your own proverb about any one of the following: government, truth, or education.

3. **Write a Short Report** Compare and contrast the ruling methods of Shi Huangdi and Gao Zu. How did their different styles of leadership affect the Chinese people?

4. **Write a Description** Reread pages 163–164 about the Great Wall of China, and look at the picture on page 163. Then write your own description of the Great Wall. You may use other references.

## USE VOCABULARY

Write the term that correctly matches each definition. Then use each term in a complete sentence.

bureaucracy          philosopher
export               standardization
import               virtue

1. a person who studies the meaning of life

2. making all things of a certain kind alike

3. a good quality

4. to send out goods for sale in other countries

5. to bring in goods from other countries

6. a network of appointed government officials

## CHECK UNDERSTANDING

1. How did the Zhou king Wu support his claim to the Mandate of Heaven in 1122 B.C.?

2. What did Confucius say a ruler must do to be successful?

3. What was Legalism?

4. For what is Shi Huangdi of the Qin dynasty most remembered?

5. Why was standardization important to China?

6. How did Wu Di achieve the *Pax Sinica*, or the "Chinese Peace"?

7. What was the most important innovation of the Han dynasty? Why?

8. Why was the Silk Road important?

## THINK CRITICALLY

1. **Past to Present**  Confucius said that a good society is like a family in which each member knows his or her place. Would Confucius think our society is a good society? Explain your answer.

2. **Think More About It**  How did Wu Di's civil service program differ from Shi Huangdi's bureaucracy?

3. **Personally Speaking**  If you were a leader, would you prefer to be feared like Shi Huangdi or respected like Gao Zu? Explain.

4. **Cause and Effect**  What effects did Wu Di's Chinese Peace have on Chinese arts and sciences?

## APPLY SKILLS

**How to Classify Information**  Interview several classmates about the following: favorite foods, songs, books, and subjects in school. Then make a chart that classifies this information.

**How to Recognize Cause and Effect**  Look in a newspaper or magazine for an article that describes an event. List at least one cause mentioned in the article and the effect or effects of that cause.

## READ MORE ABOUT IT

*The Ancient Chinese* by Julia Waterlow. Thomson Learning. History, rulers, customs, ancient cities, inventions—these are just some of the topics included in this fascinating book.

*The Chinese Empire* by Marinella Terzi. Childrens Press. This picture-filled book offers a look at the culture of China over a 4,000-year period.

*The Great Wall of China* by Leonard Everett Fisher. Macmillan. The author provides a brief history of the Great Wall of China, which was built more than 2,000 years ago to keep out invaders.

*Science in Ancient China* by George Beshore. Franklin Watts. This book covers the science of the ancient Chinese and describes their inventions, such as the rocket, the compass, the waterwheel, and movable type.

# INDIA and PERSIA

> 66 An age like this one, which is golden while it lasts and proves a culture's greatness forever after, is never a sudden or rootless event. 99
>
> Lucille Schulberg, *Historic India*

Young girl from Madras, India, in traditional dress

174

# ARYANS
## BRING CHANGES TO
# INDIA

## *L**ink** to Our World*

**How does the movement of people into an area affect those already living there?**

*Focus on the Main Idea*
**As you read, consider how the arrival of the Aryans changed life for the people of India.**

*Preview Vocabulary*

| | |
|---|---|
| **Aryan** | **Hinduism** |
| **Sanskrit** | **caste** |
| **Vedas** | **untouchable** |
| **reincarnation** | **Buddhism** |

Around 1500 B.C. large numbers of people began to migrate into India. These migrations lasted for more than 3,000 years. They were important because they brought together people with different customs and ideas. The earliest immigrants called themselves **Aryans** (AIR•ee•uhnz). The Aryans were warriors and herders who came from central Asia near the Caspian Sea. Their arrival marked the beginning of the Classical Age in India.

## ARYAN IMMIGRANTS

The earliest Aryan migrations took place over hundreds of years. They were part of a larger southward movement of people called Indo-Europeans. Why the Aryans and others left their homeland is not known. Drought, famine, or disease may have forced them to leave their homes. Perhaps invaders drove them out.

Some Aryans moved west. Others pushed south. The Aryans who moved south crossed through the mountain passes of the Hindu Kush, the wall of mountains between the Indian subcontinent and the rest of Asia. These Aryans moved to the region of the Indus Valley now known as Pakistan. In time, however, the Aryans occupied much of the northern parts of India.

Each wave of migration brought more Aryans into the subcontinent. Soon the Aryans competed with the native people of India for farmland. The Aryans had one advantage in the fight for land: they had horses. Until the Aryans arrived, there were no horses in India.

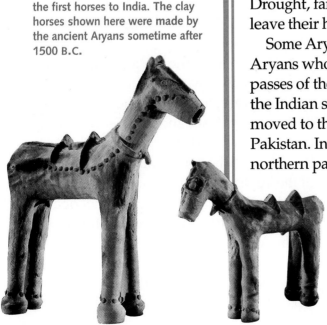

The Aryan migrations brought the first horses to India. The clay horses shown here were made by the ancient Aryans sometime after 1500 B.C.

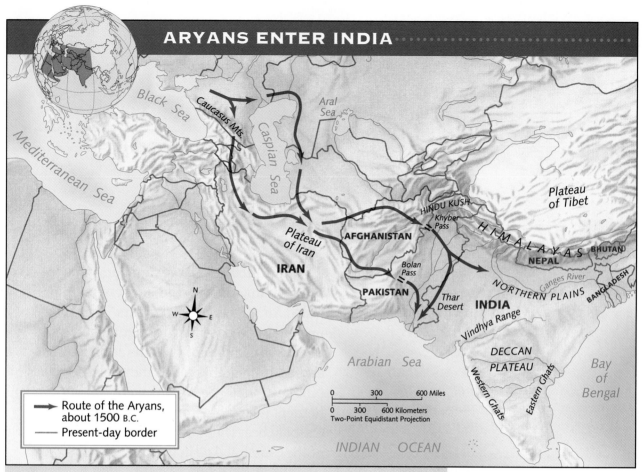

# ARYANS ENTER INDIA

MEDITERRANEAN Sea · Black Sea · Caucasus Mts. · Caspian Sea · Aral Sea · Plateau of Iran · IRAN · AFGHANISTAN · HINDU KUSH · Khyber Pass · Plateau of Tibet · HIMALAYAS · BHUTAN · NEPAL · Ganges River · Bolan Pass · PAKISTAN · NORTHERN PLAINS · BANGLADESH · Thar Desert · INDIA · Vindhya Range · DECCAN PLATEAU · Western Ghats · Eastern Ghats · Bay of Bengal · Arabian Sea · INDIAN OCEAN

→ Route of the Aryans, about 1500 B.C.
— Present-day border

0   300   600 Miles
0   300   600 Kilometers
Two-Point Equidistant Projection

**Map Skill** **MOVEMENT** **This map shows Aryan migration into India around 1500 B.C.**
■ Why do you suppose the Aryans stopped and settled in northern India?

Before coming to India the Aryans had lived as herders. They raised cattle, goats, horses, and sheep. In India they became farmers. Small villages rose up in the countryside. In the following centuries Indian life and work came to center on the villages. Even today, although India has huge cities, it remains a nation of villages.

✓ **Why did the Aryans leave their homeland?**

## HINDUISM

The ideas of the Aryans can be seen in present-day Indian culture and beliefs. For example, the Aryans brought their language, **Sanskrit**, to India. Many Indian languages of today are based on Sanskrit.

The Aryans believed that Sanskrit was a holy language, the language spoken by the gods. The Aryans' holiest books, the **Vedas** (VAY•duhz), are written in Sanskrit. These four books of sacred writings describe the Aryan religion.

A main belief of the Aryan religion was that people live many lives until they reach spiritual perfection. This belief that the soul lives on after death and returns to life in a new body is called **reincarnation**. The Aryans thought that those who obeyed the teachings of the Vedas would be reborn into higher social positions. Those who did not obey them would return as lower life-forms.

The Aryan religion developed into the religion of Hinduism. **Hinduism** is one of the oldest religions still practiced today. Believers in Hinduism worship three main gods: Brahma the Creator, Vishnu the Preserver, and Shiva the Destroyer. Below these gods are many other gods, who take the forms of plants and animals. Believers in Hinduism think that animals have souls and that cows are holy. For this reason, they do not eat beef.

 **What religion of today comes from the religion of the Aryans?**

## THE CASTE SYSTEM

For hundreds of years Aryan priests used the Vedas and the belief in reincarnation to give order to their society. Following the teachings of the Vedas, the Aryans divided their society into social classes: priests, warriors, farmers and merchants, and common people. In India the Aryans added a lower group for the conquered Indians.

The Aryan social classes led to India's caste system. A **caste** is an unchanging group within a society. A person born into one caste could never change caste or mix with members of other castes. Caste members lived, married, and worked within their own group.

To the Indian people the caste system was like the human body. The Brahmans (BRAH•muhnz), the priests and scholars, made up the head. The Kshatriyas (KSHAH•tree•uhz), the rulers and warriors, made up the arms. The Vaisyas (VYSH•yuhz), the farmers and merchants, made up the legs. The Sudras (SOO•druhz), the laborers, craftworkers, and servants, made up the feet.

The Hindu god Shiva, dancing

Below all the castes were the **untouchables**. These people did all the unpleasant jobs in Indian society. They picked up garbage, cleaned stables, and handled the dead. Untouchables were thought to be impure. They had to avoid all contact with the rest of society. An untouchable could not even let his or her shadow fall on a person of a higher caste.

Hinduism demanded that people accept the caste into which they were born. Each person had a place in society and a job to do. Life might be hard. But if people did the jobs of their caste, there was hope that the next life would be better.

For some Indian people belief in reincarnation was not enough to make life bearable. Around the sixth century B.C., a new religion challenged Hinduism.

 **What was the ancient Indian caste system?**

This statue (left) made in the second century A.D. shows a young female servant of the Sudra caste. At right are two Brahmans, or priests. Brahmans are often shown with the right hand raised as a sign of understanding.

# THE ORIGINS OF BUDDHISM

An Indian story tells that a traveling Brahman met a stranger one day. The Brahman asked the stranger's name and received this answer: "Although born in the world, grown up in the world, having overcome the world, I abide unsoiled by the world. Take it that I am Buddha."

We know little of this man who called himself Buddha, or the "Enlightened One." What we do know comes from information written many years after his death. These writings tell us that his given name was Siddhartha Gautama (sih•DAHR•tuh GOW•tuh•muh). Born in northern India in 563 B.C., Gautama lived a comfortable life as the son of an Indian prince. His father gave him everything he wanted and kept him from seeing the suffering of the common people.

At about age 30, Gautama went outside the walls of his palace for the first time. Outside the walls, he saw an old man bent over with age. Then, he came upon a man too sick to care for

> 66 **ALTHOUGH BORN IN THE WORLD,** *grown up in the world, having overcome the world, I abide unsoiled by the world.* 99
>
> Buddha, 563 B.C. to 483 B.C.

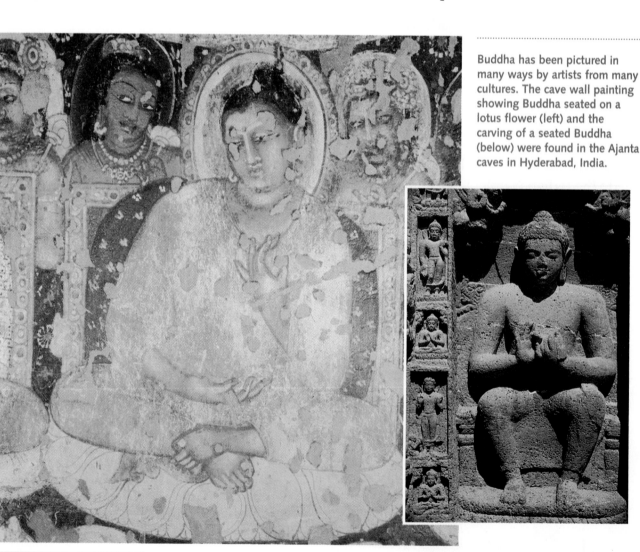

Buddha has been pictured in many ways by artists from many cultures. The cave wall painting showing Buddha seated on a lotus flower (left) and the carving of a seated Buddha (below) were found in the Ajanta caves in Hyderabad, India.

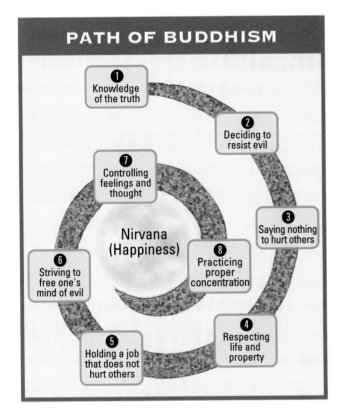

# PATH OF BUDDHISM

1. Knowledge of the truth
2. Deciding to resist evil
3. Saying nothing to hurt others
4. Respecting life and property
5. Holding a job that does not hurt others
6. Striving to free one's mind of evil
7. Controlling feelings and thought
8. Practicing proper concentration

Nirvana (Happiness)

**LEARNING FROM CHARTS** Buddhists follow these eight points, called the Noble Eightfold Path, in their search for *nirvana,* a feeling of happiness and peace.
■ Why would saying nothing to hurt others bring happiness?

himself. Finally, he saw a dead body. Gautama asked a servant to explain what he had seen. The servant said that age, sickness, and death come to us all. This answer was not enough for Gautama. Why, he asked, was there so much suffering? How might this suffering be ended? Gautama decided to spend the rest of his life finding the answers to his questions. He left his father's palace and lived the life of a wandering beggar.

For a few years Gautama studied with Brahman priests. Then he continued his search for knowledge by praying and fasting. Nothing helped him find answers. One day Gautama sat down to rest under a tree. He began once again to think about the problem. After hours of deep thought, Gautama suddenly felt that he understood the meaning of life. He decided that people should seek love, truth, the joy of knowledge, and a calm mind.

At that moment he became Buddha, the Enlightened One.

Gautama spent the rest of his life carrying his message to all who would listen. After his death his followers told of his teachings. **Buddhism**, the religion based on those teachings, eventually spread across Asia.

Neither Buddha nor his followers organized a central church. They did not write holy books like the Vedas. Their aim was to set an example for others. They did so through unselfish and peaceful behavior.

 **Why did Gautama begin a search for truth?**

# LESSON 1 REVIEW

## Check Understanding

1. **Recall the Facts**  Where did the Aryans come from? Where did they migrate to?
2. **Focus on the Main Idea**  How did the Aryan migrations affect civilization in India?

## Think Critically

3. **Past to Present**  Today India is an industrialized country. What effect do you think the development of industry has had on the caste system?
4. **Explore Viewpoints**  If you had been a Brahman in early Indian society, how might you have felt about the teachings of Buddha? How might you have felt about them if you had been an untouchable?

## Show What You Know

**Research Activity**  Use information from this textbook and from encyclopedias and almanacs to create a chart comparing Indian civilization before and after the arrival of the Aryans. Topics you might present in your chart include how people lived, where people lived, and what the social classes were.

# S·K·I·L·L·S

# HOW TO

# Use a Cultural Map

## Why Is This Skill Important?

Symbols on road signs give people information without using words. They show information in a way that lets people understand it quickly. If you see a road sign showing a picture of a leaping deer, for example, you know that deer cross the road there. On maps, too, symbols show information in a way that lets people understand it quickly. For example, map symbols may show you where certain products are made or where battles were fought.

Like other kinds of maps, cultural maps can give you a general picture of a region of the world. Cultural maps may use symbols that show places where most of the people speak a certain language or follow a certain religion. These maps can help you understand more about the people and cultures in those places.

## Think About Map Symbols

Notice that this map of the present-day Indian subcontinent has two map keys. The key on the left uses colors as symbols. The colors divide the subcontinent into regions based on language. The key tells you that there are five major language groups on the Indian subcontinent. One

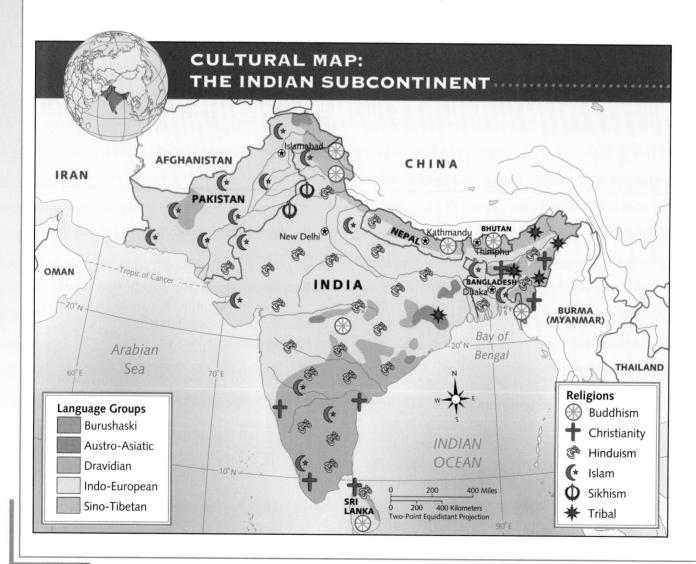

CULTURAL MAP:
THE INDIAN SUBCONTINENT

IRAN

AFGHANISTAN

Islamabad

CHINA

PAKISTAN

New Delhi

NEPAL   Kathmandu   BHUTAN
                     Thimphu

OMAN            Tropic of Cancer

20°N

INDIA

BANGLADESH
Dhaka

BURMA
(MYANMAR)

Arabian
Sea

20°N   Bay of
        Bengal

60°E        70°E

THAILAND

N
W    E
S

INDIAN
OCEAN

10°N

0        200        400 Miles

0     200     400 Kilometers
Two-Point Equidistant Projection

SRI
LANKA

90°E

**Language Groups**
- Burushaski
- Austro-Asiatic
- Dravidian
- Indo-European
- Sino-Tibetan

**Religions**
- ⊕ Buddhism
- ✝ Christianity
- 🕉 Hinduism
- ☪ Islam
- ☬ Sikhism
- ✸ Tribal

of these groups is the Indo-European group. One language within the Indo-European group is Hindi, the official language of India today. Other Indo-European languages, including English, are also spoken in India.

The map key on the right of the map uses pictures as symbols. Each picture symbol stands for a major religion and is shown in the middle of an area where that religion is practiced. Look at the symbol for Hinduism. It is the written form of *om*, a sacred Hindu word. The symbol for Buddhism is the Wheel of the Law. The spokes of the wheel stand for parts of the Noble Eightfold Path in Buddhist teachings.

## Understand the Process

Now that you know about the symbols in the map keys, use these questions as a guide for making generalizations about the present-day cultures of the Indian subcontinent.

1. Identify the color that covers most of the northern half of India. What generalizations can you make about the language of the people who live there?
2. What is the language group in southern India?
3. What is the main language group in Pakistan?

Sikh "Golden Temple" at Amritsar, India, near the India-Pakistan border

4. What do the symbols in Pakistan tell you?
5. In what country do most of the people practice Buddhism?
6. How is Sri Lanka divided according to language groups?
7. Do all the people in Bangladesh practice the same religion? Explain your answer.
8. Make a generalization about language and religion in each of the following countries:
   a. Bangladesh
   b. Bhutan
   c. India
   d. Nepal
   e. Pakistan

## Think and Apply

Draw a cultural map of all of Asia. Use an encyclopedia, atlas, or almanac to gather the information you will need. Use colors to show different language groups, and use picture symbols to show where different religions are practiced. Be sure to label the countries. What language groups and religions will appear on your map that do not appear on the map on page 180? Have a classmate use your map to make some generalizations about the cultures of present-day Asia.

# Two Fables

from *Jataka Tales*

edited by Nancy DeRoin

illustrated by Navin Patel

*When Buddha taught, he spoke in a way that all people could understand. Sometimes he used folktales to get his message across. A number of these folktales were fables, short stories that have animal characters and that teach a special lesson. Buddha's followers believed that he remembered these fables from past lives, when his soul was in the bodies of various animals. Many years after Buddha's death, some of these fables were collected and written down in a book called the **Jataka Tales,** or "Birth Stories." Although animals speak the words, the messages they have for humans are very clear.*

## The Wonders of Palace Life

Once upon a time when Brahmadatta ruled Benares, a young monkey lived with a troop of monkeys near the Himalaya

Mountains. A woodsman caught him and gave him to the king as a present.

During the winter months, the monkey lived as a palace pet. He charmed the king and the royal family with his ways. The monkey was allowed to run freely in the palace, and he learned a great deal about the ways of men.

When summer came, the king and his court prepared to move to the summer palace. The king called for the woodsman and said, "I have been very pleased with this little monkey. He has amused us very much. Here is a reward for you." And he gave the woodsman a sack of gold coins.

"Now, as a reward for this monkey, I want you to return him to the place where you captured him and set him free."

The woodsman was pleased to do as the king wished. The monkey, once free, returned to the Himalayas, and the monkey troop all gathered on a large rock to hear about his adventures.

"Friend," they asked, "where have you been all this time?"

"In the king's palace at Benares."

"How did you get free?"

"I amused the king and his court so well that the king felt kindly toward me and set me free."

"You must know all about palace life. How grand it must be! We would like to live in that grand style. Will you teach us the ways of men?"

At first the monkey refused. "No, you would not like to live that way."

But the monkeys insisted that he teach them the ways of men.

"Very well," he finally agreed. Then he picked the largest monkey and

The monkey was allowed to run freely in the palace, and he learned a great deal about the ways of men.

said, "Now, you are king. You must sit on this rock and order all the monkeys to bring you fruit."

The king monkey did as he was told. Each monkey brought him fruit.

"But I cannot eat all this fruit," the king monkey said.

"The fruit," said the monkey who had lived at the palace, "is not for you to eat. It is for you to keep in a big pile. To be king, you must be rich. To be rich, you must have a big pile of fruit."

So the monkeys, wishing to live like men, piled a mountain of fruit behind the king monkey.

"What next?" they all asked.

"Now all of you must approach the king and compliment him." The monkeys gladly agreed.

"Oh, King," one said, "your fur is very thick and shiny."

"Oh, King," said another, "your eyes are very bold and bright."

"Oh, King," said a third, "you are wise and very strong." And this went on until all the monkeys had spoken the king's praise.

"Now," said the monkey who had lived in the palace, "all you monkeys must go behind the king's back and say insulting things about him."

So the monkeys stood behind the king monkey and said in turn:

"His fur is thin. I think he must be getting bald."

"His eyes are dull. I don't think his eyesight is what it used to be."

"He is as weak as a worm and almost as stupid."

Finally, the king monkey became so angry that he left his throne and started chasing the monkeys who were insulting him. When he returned, all his fruit was gone.

"My fruit! My fruit! Someone has taken all my fruit!"

"Now," said the monkey who lived in the palace, "you must find the guilty monkey and put him to death."

"To death?" the king monkey cried. "Oh, what are you saying?" And he covered his ears with his hands and buried his head between his knees.

"Stop! Stop!" all the monkeys cried, covering their ears. "Teach us no more about palace life." And they ran away, crying:

Flattering, lying, stealing, killing,
The ways of men are really chilling!
If in a palace men do these,
We're safer here among our trees.

## Friends and Neighbors

One day while hunting deer, a big lion slipped down a steep hill and landed in a swamp. Due to his great weight,

he sank into the mud up to his neck. Try as he might, he could not get out. As soon as he lifted one foot, the other three sank in deeper. Finally, afraid to struggle any more for fear of sinking in above his head, he stood as still as a stone with only his huge head sticking out of the mud.

He stood there for seven days, his feet sunk like posts in the mud, without a bite to eat or a drop to drink.

Toward the end of the seventh day, a jackal, who was hunting for food, came upon him. Seeing a lion's head sticking out of the mud, the jackal ran away yelping in terror. But the lion called after him:

"I say, jackal, Stop! Don't run away. Here am I, caught fast in the mud. Please save me!"

The jackal came back slowly, looked at the lion, and said, "I could get you out I think, but I am afraid that once free you would eat me."

"Do not fear," the lion said. "If you save me, I will be your friend for life."

The jackal decided to trust him. He dug a hole around each of the lion's four feet. From these holes, he dug trenches out to the nearby pond. Water from the pond filled the trenches and ran into the holes at the lion's feet. It made the mud very soft, indeed. Then the jackal said:

"Now, make one great effort!"

The weakened lion strained every nerve, every muscle, every bone in his body. At last his feet broke loose from the mud

with a loud slurp! The lion crawled onto dry land.

After washing the mud from his golden body, the great lion killed a buffalo and said to the jackal, "Help yourself, friend."

As the jackal ate, the lion noticed that he saved part of the meat.

"Why do you not eat your fill?" the lion asked.

"I am saving some to take to my mate," the jackal replied.

"I, too, have a mate," said the lion. "I will go with you."

When they neared the jackal's den, his mate almost died of fright to see a huge lion heading straight toward her cave. But the jackal called out:

"Fear nothing. This lion is my friend." And the lion said to her, "Now, my lady, from this day on I am going to share my life with you and your family." He led the jackals to the place where he lived, and they moved into a cave next to his own.

After that, the jackal and the lion would go hunting together, leaving their mates at home. Soon, cubs were born to both families, and as they grew, they played together.

But one day, quite suddenly, the lioness thought, "My mate seems very fond of those jackals. It does not seem natural to me. They are different, after all." This thought stuck firmly in her mind, and she could think of nothing else. "We are lions and they are jackals," she thought. "I must get rid of them."

So, whenever the lion and the jackal were away on the hunt, the lioness began to frighten her neighbor. The lioness would spring from hiding and snarl, "Why do you stay where you are not wanted?" Or she would creep up on the sleeping jackal and hiss in her ear, "Do you not know when your life is in danger?" Then again, she would say under her breath, "Such darling little jackal cubs. Too bad their mother does not care about their safety."

Finally, the mother jackal told her mate all that had been happening. "It is clear," she said, "that the lion must have told his wife to do this. We have been here a long time, and he is tired of us. Let us leave, or those lions will be the death of us."

Hearing this, the jackal went to the lion and said:

"Friend lion, in this world the strong will always have their way. But, I must say, even if one does not like a neighbor, it is cruel to frighten his wife and children half to death."

"Why, what are you talking about?" the lion asked in surprise.

Then the jackal told him how the lioness had been scaring his wife and cubs. The lion listened very carefully; then he called his wife before him. In front of everyone he said:

"Wife, do you remember long ago when I was out hunting and did not come back for a week? After that, I brought this jackal and his wife back with me."

"Yes, I remember very well," the lioness replied.

"Do you know why I was gone for a week?"

"No, I do not," she answered.

"I was ashamed to tell you then," the lion said, "but I will now. I was trying to catch a deer, and I jumped too far, slipped down a hill, and got stuck fast in the mud. There I stayed for a week without food or water. Then along came this jackal and saved my life. This jackal is my friend."

From that day on, the lions and jackals lived in peace and friendship. Furthermore, after their parents died, the cubs did not part. They, too, lived together in friendship, always remembering the words of the great lion:

A friend who truly acts like one,
Whoever he may be,
Is my comrade and my kin,
He is flesh and blood to me.

## Literature Review

1. What lessons do you think people today might learn from these fables?
2. What message is Buddha teaching in the fable of the monkeys? in the fable of the lion and the jackal?
3. Consider a quality that is important to you—responsibility, honesty, friendship, cooperation, or respect for others, for example. Write your own fable that teaches a message about that quality. Be sure to end your fable with a verse, as in the *Jataka Tales*.

# UNITED RULE in INDIA

## Link to Our World

**What forces create and maintain unity among people?**

### Focus on the Main Idea
As you read, think about the methods used by Maurya and Gupta rulers to unite India.

### Preview Vocabulary
| | |
|---|---|
| rajah | missionary |
| assassination | Arabic numeral |
| turning point | inoculation |

This second-century Mauryan art was just one in a series of tablets describing ancient emperors.

During the time of Buddha, India was a divided land. Princes called **rajahs** ruled over large city-states rich in foods, jewels, and metals. This wealth attracted invaders such as the Persians from Asia and then the Greeks from Europe. For more than 200 years after the death of Buddha, parts of the Indian subcontinent were held by outsiders. Finally, a young Indian emperor drove the invaders out of India and conquered all the rajahs.

## INDIA'S FIRST EMPIRE

Around 320 B.C. the young emperor, Chandragupta Maurya (chuhn•druh•GUP•tuh MOW•ree•uh), united India and formed the Maurya Empire. India's first emperor was much like the Chinese emperor Shi Huangdi. Both were cruel rulers who backed up their authority with a variety of punishments for those who did not support them.

Like Shi Huangdi, Chandragupta forced peasants to work for and support his government. He forced the workers to chop down forests and drain swamps. He then made the peasants farm the newly cleared land. In addition, he taxed them on the crops they grew on the land.

Chandragupta's cruelty made him many enemies in the empire. He feared for his own safety. He had servants taste all his food before he ate it. To protect himself from assassination, Chandragupta slept in a different room every night. An **assassination** (uh•sa•suhn•AY•shun) is murder for a political reason. No attack came, however. In 297 B.C. Chandragupta quietly gave up the throne to his son.

Chandragupta and his son governed the empire according to a book called the *Arthashastra* (ar•thuh•SHAHS•truh). The *Arthashastra* said that rulers should govern with a firm hand. "Government is the science of punishment," it stated. It also said that war was an acceptable way for rulers to meet their goals.

 **How did Chandragupta rule India?**

This wall carving, from the Great Stupa at Sanchi, gives an idea of what life may have been like in India centuries ago.

# THE REIGN OF ASOKA

Chandragupta's grandson, Asoka (uh•SHOH•kuh), became Maurya emperor around 274 B.C. The new emperor ruled as firmly as his father and grandfather had. "Any power superior in might to another should launch into war," Asoka believed.

Around 262 B.C. Asoka's army marched into the kingdom of Kalinga on the empire's southern border. In a vicious war Maurya forces crushed the Kalingans. Asoka recorded that "150,000 people were deported, 100,000 were killed, and many times that number died."

The invasion of Kalinga was a turning point in Asoka's life. A **turning point** is a time of important change. The bloody invasion of Kalinga turned Asoka against

During the time of the Mauryas, Buddhists built large stupas, or religious shrines. The Great Stupa at Sanchi, India, still stands today. This stupa, like most, is filled with ancient drawings and carvings.

violence. He began to follow the teachings of Buddha. He refused to eat meat or to hunt and kill animals. His change led many of his people to adopt peaceful ways, too.

Asoka used his power to make the lives of his people better. At his command, people began to place less importance on the caste system.

To spread the message of Buddhism, Asoka issued a number of edicts. He had these edicts carved on rocks and stone pillars along main roads, where people might easily read them. One of Asoka's edicts called on people to show "obedience to mother and father." Asoka also sent **missionaries**, or religious teachers, to carry the ideas of Buddhism to other parts of Asia.

So fair was Asoka that he is known in history as "the greatest and noblest ruler India has known." Yet not long after his death in 232 B.C., his good works were forgotten for a time. The caste system returned. The ideas of Buddhism faded away in India. Today, however, the people of India again honor Asoka. The lion and the wheel, two designs Asoka used to decorate his edicts, are symbols of present-day India.

 **What principles guided the way Asoka governed India?**

**EARLY EMPIRES OF INDIA**

CHINA

HINDU KUSH

AFGHANISTAN

PAKISTAN

PLATEAU OF TIBET

HIMALAYAS

NEPAL

Indus River

Thar Desert

INDIA

Ganges River

Arabian Sea

DECCAN PLATEAU

Bay of Bengal

INDIAN OCEAN

SRI LANKA

0    300    600 Miles
0    300    600 Kilometers
Two-Point Equidistant Projection

☐ Maurya Empire under Asoka, about 250 B.C.

── Gupta Empire, about A.D. 400

···· Present-day border

**REGIONS** Both the Maurya Empire and the later Gupta Empire rose on the Indian subcontinent of Asia.
■ Why do you think neither empire expanded northeast into what is today China?

This sculpture of an armed soldier can be found on the Stupa of Babrut, in India.

## THE GUPTAS COME TO POWER

Only 50 years after Asoka's death, the Maurya Empire broke up into quarreling city-states. About 500 years passed before another great empire, the Gupta Empire, united India once again.

In A.D. 320 Chandragupta I became ruler of a small kingdom in the Ganges Valley. Chandragupta I soon controlled much of the valley. His son Samudra (suh•MUH•druh) Gupta and grandson Chandragupta II enlarged the empire. Even so, the Gupta Empire never grew as large as the Maurya

Chapter 6 • **189**

Empire had been. Gupta rule ended centuries of fighting. For 200 years India enjoyed peace and economic growth.

Much of what we know about Gupta society comes from the writings of Fa-xien (FAH•SHYUHN), a Chinese Buddhist monk. Around A.D. 400 he traveled through India and wrote down what he saw. The people, he observed, "are very well off." They had such freedom that "if they desire to go, they go; if they like to stop, they stop." Fa-xien marveled at the well-kept roads and the beautiful temples, monuments, and palaces. He also wrote of the free hospitals to which people went for treatment. The Gupta Empire, Fa-xien concluded, seemed to be a safe and happy place.

 **What was life like during Gupta times?**

# THE GOLDEN AGE OF INDIA

Fa-xien visited India during the rule of Chandragupta II. Historians call this period India's Golden Age. It was a time of peace, growth, and progress.

During the Golden Age, Chandragupta II supported many artists and writers. Perhaps the most famous of these was Kalidasa (kah•lih•DAH•suh), an author known for his poems and plays. Unknown writers collected and wrote down a series of folktales called the *Panchatantra* (pahn•chah•TAHN•truh). Over the centuries these popular tales traveled throughout the world. You may know some of the stories, such as "Sinbad the Sailor" and "Jack the Giant-Killer."

The most important advances came in mathematics and medicine. Indian

This coin (at right) shows Chandragupta II, who led ancient India during its Golden Age. The rulers of ancient India understood the importance of learning. These rulers began universities to help the Indian people gain knowledge. Below are the ruins of an ancient Buddhist university in what is now Nalanda, India.

The Ajanta Caves, in India, are actually Buddhist temples that were carved from solid rock sometime between 200 B.C. and A.D. 600. These caves have been the source of information for much of what we know about the ancient cultures of India.

mathematicians developed the base-ten number system: 1 through 9 and the zero. These so-called **Arabic numerals** were used in India as early as A.D. 595 before they were borrowed by Arab traders.

During the Golden Age, Indian doctors discovered ways to set broken bones and to help women give birth. Like surgeons today, they used skin from other parts of the body to mend ears and noses. Understanding the need for cleanliness in surgery, they sterilized their cutting tools. Indian doctors also used the technique of **inoculation**. This means giving a person a mild form of a disease so that he or she will not get sick with a more serious form. European and American doctors did not use inoculation until the 1700s.

Many of the ideas of India were carried to other lands by traders. Arab merchants took Indian spices, cloth, carpets, and jewelry west to the Mediterranean region. They carried Indian books and ideas to Europe and Africa. News of India's innovations reached many parts of the world.

✔ **What important advances in learning took place during the time of Gupta rule?**

# LESSON 3 REVIEW

## Check Understanding

1. **Recall the Facts**   Who created India's first empire? What ruler suddenly turned against violent ways?
2. **Focus on the Main Idea**   What methods did Maurya and Gupta rulers use to unite India? How were these methods similar? How were they different?

## Think Critically

3. **Personally Speaking**   Which ruler, Chandragupta Maurya or Asoka, do you think was more suited to be a leader? Why?
4. **Think More About It**   Why do historians refer to the period of the Gupta kings as India's Golden Age?

## Show What You Know

**Oral Presentation Activity**
Asoka tried to rule his empire by following Buddhist teachings. Imagine that you are a visitor to the India of Asoka's time. In your own words, describe the effect of Asoka's actions on the Indian people.

# The PERSIAN EMPIRE

## Link to Our World

**How do powerful leaders create change?**

**Focus on the Main Idea**
As you read, think about the ways strong leaders played a role in the development of the Persian Empire and its civilization.

**Preview Vocabulary**

| | |
|---|---|
| plateau | courier |
| cavalry | prophet |
| tribute | Zoroastrianism |

Some Aryans migrated to lands west of India and settled in what is now the country of Iran. The name *Iran* may come from the word *Aryan*. The Aryan people of Iran came to be known as Persians. They arrived around 900 B.C.

## CYRUS, THE EMPIRE BUILDER

The Persians of long ago lived on the Plateau of Iran, a large area stretching from India to the Zagros Mountains. From the **plateau**, a high, flat area of land, the Persians spread out in all directions. They began by conquering the Babylonians in the Fertile Crescent in 539 B.C. and Egypt in 525 B.C. Over the years, they formed the largest empire the world had seen.

The Persian army had huge numbers of soldiers, and this alone made most enemies tremble. Its war technology overwhelmed them all. Persian foot soldiers wore bronze helmets and carried shields. These weapons often made them the winners in hand-to-hand combat. The Persians also used **cavalry**, soldiers who rode horses and camels, to make swift attacks. In addition, they fought in war chariots with sharp knives attached to the wheels. The Persians fought well not only on land but also at sea. Within 20 years the Persian army had conquered lands from northern India to North Africa.

The leader who built the Persian Empire was Cyrus the Great. Cyrus never lost a battle—except his last. In that battle he led his army to fight people who lived near the Caspian Sea. Their ruler was Queen Tomyris (tuh•MY•ruhs). Angered at the Persian invasion of

The subject of this sculpture is possibly Cyrus the Great, who built the ancient Persian Empire.

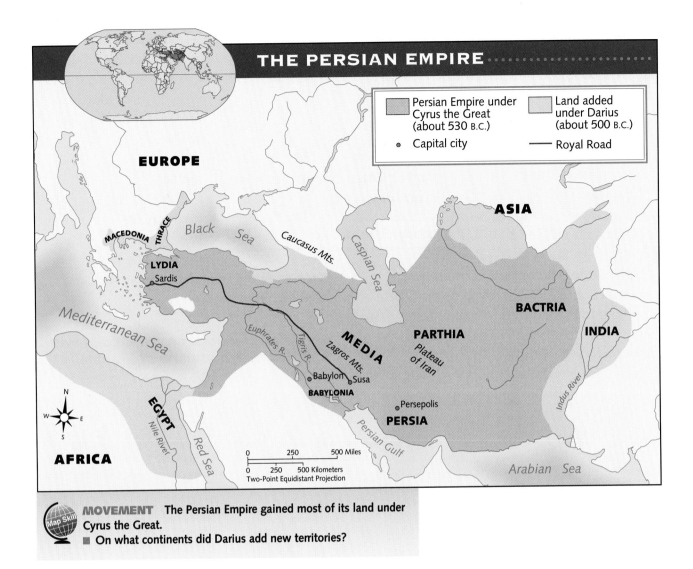

## THE PERSIAN EMPIRE

Persian Empire under Cyrus the Great (about 530 B.C.)

Land added under Darius (about 500 B.C.)

• Capital city

—— Royal Road

EUROPE

MACEDONIA
THRACE
Black Sea
Caucasus Mts.
Caspian Sea
ASIA
LYDIA
Sardis
Mediterranean Sea
Euphrates R.
Tigris R.
MEDIA
Zagros Mts.
Babylon Susa
BABYLONIA
PARTHIA
Plateau of Iran
BACTRIA
INDIA
Indus River
Persepolis
PERSIA
EGYPT
Nile River
Red Sea
Persian Gulf
Arabian Sea
AFRICA

0    250    500 Miles
0    250    500 Kilometers
Two-Point Equidistant Projection

**MOVEMENT** The Persian Empire gained most of its land under Cyrus the Great.
■ On what continents did Darius add new territories?

her land, Queen Tomyris led her smaller army against Cyrus's fighting force. One historian later described the bitter battle this way:

66 First the two armies stood apart and shot their arrows at each other. Then, when their quivers were empty, they closed and fought hand-to-hand with lances and daggers. And thus they continued fighting for a length of time, neither choosing to give ground. 99

In the end most of the Persians were killed, including Cyrus the Great. Persia's time of great growth had ended.

✓ **What leader created the Persian Empire?**

## DARIUS, THE ORGANIZER

Darius (duh•RY•uhs), a later Persian emperor, faced the task of organizing the large empire. Darius was successful because he let the different peoples in the empire keep their own customs. He also chose local leaders who would rule their own people fairly.

The people conquered by the Persians were expected to send **tribute**, or yearly payments, to the emperor. At Persepolis (per•SEH•puh•luhs), the capital built by Darius, artists left a record in stone of people paying tribute. Babylonians are shown bringing livestock and Assyrians bringing hides of tanned leather. Indians carry containers of gold dust. Other people offer fine cloth, pottery, horses, and camels.

Darius faced a great problem in ruling his widespread empire. How could he communicate with people a thousand miles from his capital? To solve this problem, Darius started a pony-express system for delivering messages. Riders called **couriers** galloped across the Persian Empire, changing horses at stations along the way.

With couriers, information could travel 1,677 miles (2,699 km) in seven days. "There is nothing in the world that travels faster than these Persian couriers," wrote the Greek historian Herodotus (hih•RAH•duh•tuhs).

> " **THERE IS NOTHING IN THE WORLD** *that travels faster than these Persian couriers.* "
>
> The Greek historian Herodotus, about 440 B.C.

"Nothing stops these couriers from covering their allotted stage in the quickest possible time—neither snow, rain, heat, nor darkness." Words like these are used today by the United States Postal Service to describe its mail carriers.

The Persians controlled their empire until it, too, was conquered by other people. These invaders came from the west in the region of the Mediterranean Sea.

✓ **How did Darius communicate with the different parts of his empire?**

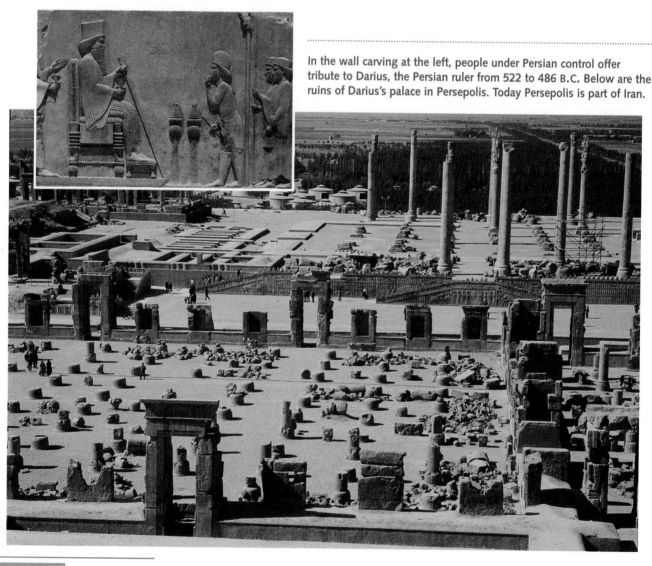

In the wall carving at the left, people under Persian control offer tribute to Darius, the Persian ruler from 522 to 486 B.C. Below are the ruins of Darius's palace in Persepolis. Today Persepolis is part of Iran.

## ZARATHUSTRA THE PROPHET

The earliest Persians worshipped many gods. But a prophet named Zarathustra (zar•uh•THOOS•trah) changed that. A **prophet** is a person who others believe speaks or writes with a divine message. Zarathustra began a religion called **Zoroastrianism** (zohr•uh•WASS•tree•uh•nih•zuhm), which taught the belief in two gods.

One god was the good and kind Ahura Mazda, or "Wise Lord." Ahura Mazda stood for truth. His enemy was Ahriman. Zoroastrians believed that good and evil fought each other but that one day good would win. "The Earth is a battleground, a struggle between forces of light and forces of darkness," said Zarathustra. People who followed this religion believed that they would live in Paradise after they died.

As the Persians built their empire, they spread the customs of their culture. As their

The stone carving above, from about 800 B.C., shows Ahura Mazda, the god of truth and kindness in the religion of Zoroastrianism. At left, a Zoroastrian priest carries twigs to light a sacred fire.

empire declined, they had to fight their conquerors to hold on to their Persian heritage. First they fought the Greeks and later the Byzantines. The fight continued until about A.D. 750. At that time the Arabs conquered the region. They brought with them their own religion, Islam.

 **What is Zoroastrianism?**

---

# LESSON 4 REVIEW

### Check Understanding

1. **Recall the Facts**   Who is credited with expanding the Persian Empire to its largest size?
2. **Focus on the Main Idea**   What was one accomplishment of each of these people: Cyrus, Darius, and Zarathustra?

### Think Critically

3. **Think More About It**   Why was it important for messages to reach all parts of the Persian Empire quickly?
4. **Cause and Effect**   What might have happened if Cyrus had won his battle against Queen Tomyris?

5. **Past to Present**   Think of a present-day leader you admire. In what way has that leader changed the government he or she represents?

### Show What You Know

**Simulation Activity**
Congratulations! You have been elected president of your class. Prepare a speech in which you describe the changes you plan to make as a strong but fair leader. Then say your speech aloud. If a tape recorder is available, you may want to record your speech and play it back to see how it sounds. Present your speech to your family or to your classmates.

# REVIEW

## CONNECT MAIN IDEAS

Use this organizer to show that you understand how the chapter's main ideas are connected. Copy the organizer onto a separate sheet of paper. Then complete it by writing two details to support each main idea.

**India and Persia**

**Aryans Bring Changes to India**
The arrival of the Aryans changed life for the early people of India.

1. _____

2. _____

**United Rule in India**
Maurya and Gupta rulers used different methods to unite India.

1. _____

2. _____

**The Persian Empire**
Strong leaders played an important role in the development of the Persian Empire and its civilization.

1. _____

2. _____

## WRITE MORE ABOUT IT

1. **Write Questions** Write five questions you would like to ask someone who practices the religion of Hinduism today.

2. **Write to Compare and Contrast** Write several paragraphs that tell ways Hinduism and Buddhism are similar and different.

3. **Write a Description** This quotation from the *Arthashastra* describes how some rulers govern: "Government is the science of punishment." Do you agree that punishing citizens is a good way for rulers to govern? Why or why not? Write your own brief description of a good government.

## USE VOCABULARY

For each group of terms, write a sentence or two that explain how the terms are related.

1. Sanskrit, Vedas

2. Hinduism, caste, untouchables

3. Arabic numerals, inoculation

4. prophet, Zoroastrianism

## CHECK UNDERSTANDING

1. What advantage did the Aryans have over the native people of India in the competition for farmland?

2. What were some of the things the Aryans brought to India?

3. Who are the three main gods of the Hindu religion?

4. How did the caste system affect early Indian society?

5. What caused Siddhartha Gautama to begin his search for knowledge?

6. What was the turning point of Asoka's life?

7. What important contributions were made during India's Golden Age?

8. How did Darius's "pony-express system" affect Persia?

## THINK CRITICALLY

1. **Think More About It**  How might a belief in reincarnation help people who live in the Indian subcontinent and are part of the Hindu caste system?

2. **Explore Viewpoints**  How would a Hindu priest probably view the Hindu caste system? How might someone thought of as an untouchable feel about it?

3. **Past to Present**  Buddhism has spread to many countries with very different cultures. Why do you think Buddhism is followed in so many different places?

4. **Personally Speaking**  Imagine that you are a member of the Sudra class—the laborers, craftworkers, and servants. Do you plan to willingly accept your place in society? Explain why or why not.

## APPLY SKILLS

**How to Use a Cultural Map**  Select a present-day country anywhere in the world. Use an encyclopedia to find out which religions and languages are most common in different parts of the country. Make a map that shows this information. Show different religions and different languages through the use of colors and symbols. Then exchange maps with a classmate. Write a paragraph that describes the information shown on your classmate's map.

## READ MORE ABOUT IT

*The Blue Jackal* by Rashmi Sharma. Vidya Books. Based on an ancient fable from India, this tale shows that skin color does not make some people better than others.

*The King's Chessboard* by David Birch. Dial. A king who is too proud to admit that he does not know everything learns a lesson when he grants a wise man's wish.

*The Red Lion: A Tale of Ancient Persia* by Diane Wolkstein. HarperCollins. In this story the future king of Persia must prove his courage by fighting the fierce Red Lion. Is he ready for the challenge or will he run?

*The Story of Wali Dad* by Kristinas Rodanas. Lothrop, Lee & Shepard. A poor grasscutter shares the little he has, setting off an amazing chain of events.

# MAKING SOCIAL STUDIES
# RELEVANT

## RELIGION in the WORLD TODAY

Religion has always played an important part in people's lives. Religion connects people who share beliefs. Many countries have a national religion or have one religion that most of its people follow. More than 80 percent of the people in India today are Hindus. In Japan most of the people are Buddhists and Shintos.

Unlike other countries in the world, the United States was founded on the idea of religious freedom. The Bill of Rights of the United States Constitution gives citizens the freedom to follow their own religious beliefs, whatever they may be. Members of religions that have been followed for centuries—Christianity, Islam, Hinduism, Buddhism, and Judaism—live together in the United States today. Followers of many newer religions live here, too. In fact, there are more than 1,000 different religious groups in our country!

**THINK AND APPLY**

Read a number of news sources to learn how differences in religious beliefs are affecting people's lives today—in schools, government, and other parts of society. Look for examples from our country and from other countries. Then, with a partner, make a visual display of your information and share it with classmates.

BUILDING CITIZENSHIP

# STORY CLOTH

Study the pictures shown in this story cloth to help you review the events you read about in Unit 3.

## Summarize the Main Ideas

1. The Chinese philosopher Confucius lived during a time of disorder known as the Warring States Period. Confucius taught that certain virtues were needed to bring order to society.

2. The emperor Shi Huangdi united many independent states to create China's first empire. Shi Huangdi is remembered most for his Great Wall and for bringing standardization to China.

3. The Han dynasty was a time of great achievement for the Chinese in government, writing, the recording of history, and trade.

4. The movement of Aryans into the Indian subcontinent caused many changes there.

5. The religions of Hinduism and Buddhism began in ancient India. These religions would affect Asia for centuries to come.

6. The Gupta dynasty in India brought about a time of growth in the arts, writing, mathematics, and medicine.

7. Strong leaders, such as King Darius, helped the Persian Empire grow.

**Examine the Scenes** Look closely at each scene. What details are shown for each period illustrated? After you have looked at every scene, write your own description for each.

# COOPERATIVE LEARNING WORKSHOP

## Remember
- Share your ideas.
- Cooperate with others to plan your work.
- Take responsibility for your work.
- Show your group's work to the class.
- Discuss what you learned by working together.

## Activity 1
### Create a Class Collage
As a class, make a collage that illustrates the five virtues of Confucianism. Cut out magazine and newspaper pictures of people doing things that show each virtue. Place pictures of the same virtue near each other in the collage. Then label each virtue. Display the collage outside your classroom.

## Activity 2
### Publish a Booklet
Innovations made during the Golden Ages of China and India changed the ways of life in these lands. With a small group of classmates, make a booklet that shows these innovations. The booklet should have two chapters. Title one chapter *The Golden Age of China* and the other chapter *The Golden Age of India*. Each group member should have a different job. For example, one member could be the researcher, another could be the artist, and still another could be the writer. Every member of the group should take a turn proofreading the booklet. Pass your booklet around the classroom for all to read.

## Activity 3
### Make a Travel Plan
Imagine that you have a chance to visit China. Make a list of the ancient Chinese sites you would most like to visit. Beside each entry, explain why you would want to visit that site.

## Activity 4
### Tell a Fable
With three or four classmates, think of a message you would like the world to know. Then with your group, write a fable that explains this message in an interesting way. Present your fable orally to the class.

# USE VOCABULARY

Write a term from this list to complete each of the sentences that follow.

civil service      missionary
courier           reincarnation
Legalism

1. A _____ oversees the day-to-day business of running a government.

2. A rider who delivered messages on horseback in the Persian Empire was called a _____.

3. The belief that the soul lives on after death and returns to life in a new body is called _____.

4. _____ taught that government should control people by fear based on harsh treatment.

5. A religious teacher sent to carry ideas to another land is known as a _____.

# CHECK UNDERSTANDING

1. What caused the breakdown of China's ruling system in the 700s B.C.?

2. What Chinese philosopher compared society to a family?

3. What were some of the innovations of the Han Golden Age?

4. Who were the untouchables?

5. Who was Zarathustra? What practice did he start?

# THINK CRITICALLY

1. **Personally Speaking** What do you think it would have been like to live during the time of the Zhou? the Qin? the Han?

2. **Cause and Effect** What effect did the conflicts of China's Warring States Period have on Chinese society?

3. **Past to Present** The arrival of Aryan immigrants changed life for the people of India. How does the arrival of immigrants in the United States change lives today?

# APPLY GEOGRAPHY SKILLS

**How to Interpret Cultural Maps** The labels on the map below show the locations of cultural groups in China. The colors show languages spoken. Use the map to answer the questions.

1. In what parts of China are languages other than Chinese spoken?

2. Why do you think different cultural groups live mainly on the edges of China?

3. Which groups live along the western and southern borders of China?

## PRESENT-DAY CHINA: POPULATION AND CULTURAL GROUPS

0   500   1,000 Miles
0   500   1,000 Kilometers
Two-Point Equidistant Projection

KAZAK
UIGUR
KIRGIZ
MONGOL
HUI
HAN
Harbin
Shenyang
Beijing
Tianjin
HAN
Nanjing   Shanghai
Chengdu   HAN   Wuhan
Chongqing
YI   MIAO   HAN
BAI   BOUVEI   YAO
HANI   ZHUANG
DAI
Guangzhou

| Chinese and Tibetan languages | Other languages |
|---|---|
| Mandarin | Tajik |
| Southern | Turkic |
| Tibetan | Mongolian |
| Kam-Tai | Manchu-Tungus |
| Miao-Yoa | Korean |

HAN Cultural group

# UNIT 4

# *The* MEDITERRANEAN

**2000 B.C.**

**1750 B.C.**

**About 1900 B.C.**
Minoans build
citylike palaces
on Crete

**1500 B.C.**

**1450 B.C.**
Minoan
civilization
weakens

Mycenaeans
invade Crete

**1250 B.C.**

**About
1240 B.C.**
Trojan War
begins

**1000 B.C.**

**1100 B.C.**
Mycenae
continues its
steady decline

*M*any civilizations developed in the Mediterranean region between 3000 B.C. and A.D. 500. Among these peoples were the ancient Greeks and Romans. The Greeks—and the Romans, who followed them—borrowed ideas from other societies that existed during their time. The Romans also built much of their civilization on the learning of the Greeks. Yet both peoples developed new ways of thinking and new ideas about science, politics, literature, language, and the arts. Many of the achievements that came to be called "Greek" and "Roman" have long since been admired.

← The ancient Minoan religious ceremony of leaping over bulls is shown in this painting made about 3,500 years ago.

**750 B.C.**
**About 800 B.C.**
Greek city-states begin to form

**500 B.C.**
**509 B.C.**
Roman Republic established

**250 B.C.**
**331 B.C.**
Alexander the Great's empire reaches greatest size

**B.C.  A.D.**
**27 B.C.**
Roman Empire established

**49 B.C.**
Julius Caesar leads army across the Rubicon

**A.D. 250**
**A.D. 313**
Christianity becomes the accepted religion in Roman Empire

# THE
# AVENGER

## *by Margaret Hodges*

*Like many people today, the people of the ancient Mediterranean civilizations enjoyed sports. They believed in "a sound mind in a sound body." The ancient Greeks, for example, included athletic contests in their religious festivals. The most famous contests in Greece were the Olympic Games.*

*The Greeks held the Olympic Games every four years to honor Zeus, the most powerful of the Greek gods. Cities and towns sent their finest young athletes to take part in the games. They came from many places such as Athens, Sparta, Asini, Elis, and Delphi, to run, throw, and wrestle. Like Olympic athletes today, they competed for the honor of their hometowns, their families, and themselves.*

*Read now about a 15-year-old athlete named Alexis, who competed in the Olympic Games in 492 B.C. for his hometown of Asini in Greece. As you read, imagine the sights, sounds, and feelings you would experience while watching or taking part in the Olympic Games long ago.*

---

### *Introducing the Characters:*

**Alexis:** a young athlete from Asini
**Lampis:** a rival athlete from Sparta
**Dion:** Alexis's brother
**Niki:** Alexis's sister
**Aristes:** Alexis's father
**Telamon:** Alexis's trainer

---

In the first light the athletes came again to the Altis[1] and gathered around the altar of Zeus at the center of the sacred olive grove. It towered high, filled with the ashes of sacrifices offered for more years than any living man could remember or even guess. A priest moved through the crowd, carrying a torch from the eternal fire that burned on the altar of Hestia, goddess of the hearth. He climbed the steps to the top of the altar of Zeus and set fire to the wood piled there. The smell of blazing poplar and of incense filled the grove. Then the Olympic flame burst through the smoke and the crowd gave a sigh like the sound of a wave breaking on a long beach. Officials were coming with this year's sacrifices for the Games, baskets of meat cut from the thighs of a hundred cattle that had been brought to the slaughter with their horns gilded[2] and with wreaths of flowers about their necks. At last the fire died down and was quenched with water from the Alpheus.[3] When the ashes were cold, they would be hard and smooth, and the altar of Zeus would have mounted even closer to heaven; earth, air, fire, and water mingled to praise him who ruled all things. On the last night of the Games, after the gods were satisfied, the crowds would feast.

Alexis remembered what followed as if it had been a dream. Somehow he got to the stadium for the boys' race. The slopes were filling, many of last night's revelers[4] having stretched out to sleep there.

Alexis drew his lot. Luckily, he was to run in the first heat[5] and would have time to rest while four other heats were run, supposing that he survived to run in the finals. There were fifteen boys in the first heat, but Lampis was not among them.

He remembered very little from the moment he toed the starting line and heard the trumpet until he reached the finish. He only knew that another runner had been ahead of him almost to the end. Then, with the blood beating in his ears and his lungs bursting, he had somehow closed the gap. But he did not know that he had won until he fell into the crowd at the finish line and felt himself being pounded on the back to shouts of "Asini! Asini has won the first heat! Alexis of Asini!"

His mouth was dry, his head throbbing. Then his father and Dion were breaking a path for him through the crowd to a stone water basin where he took a long drink and sank down on the grass. He could not believe that he had won. His legs were numb. Could he run again? He needed time, and it would not take much time to run off four more heats.

Telamon was rubbing him down and gently kneading the muscles of his legs. "There will be time enough. The managers will be announcing the name and town of each contestant, you know, and the umpires usually argue about who has won, and there may be

---

[1] **Altis:** name for the sacred olive grove
[2] **gilded:** coated with gold
[3] **Alpheus:** a river in Greece
[4] **revelers:** party-goers

[5] **heat:** a round or part of a contest

some false starts. It all takes time. You will be ready."

It was as Telamon had predicted. Twice the heats were delayed when runners made false starts and were punished by sharp blows from officials with long forked sticks. But Lampis won his heat easily, and all too soon they were announcing the final race for boys.

Aristes and Dion embraced Alexis. Above the noise of the crowd he could not hear what they were saying—something about Lampis, something about Asini—but he knew what they meant, and nodded as he went to the starting line.

"Eucles of Athens . . ." All over the stadium Athenians shouted encouragement to their runner. "Sotades of Elis . . . Lampis of Sparta . . . Alexis of Asini . . . Troilus of Delphi . . ." Each name was followed by cheers from some parts of the stadium and silence from others whose own champions had been beaten by one of the finalists or whose own city had been at war with one of these cities.

Alexis stared down the length of the stadium to the finish line. Lampis was the one to beat and he had to do it for Asini. But Lampis always went into the lead from the very start. If Alexis held himself back this time, tired as he was, he would never be able to close the gap at the end. He must start fast and stay even with Lampis all the way, then do even better in the last stretch. He drew a deep breath, let it out, and leaned forward, his toes gripping the starting stone. The trumpet blared and the runners shot forward.

Out of the corner of his eye Alexis saw to his left Lampis and the boy from Elis, running smoothly. On his right, no one. Athens and Delphi were somewhere behind. Another glance showed him that Lampis was going into the lead. Alexis felt his lungs and his legs laboring painfully. Then suddenly he heard, as if the words were spoken, "I belong to Zeus." He saw in his mind the beach at Asini, and he felt his breath coming easily and powerfully. His leg muscles were obeying his will and he was overtaking, passing Lampis. The crowd at the finish line loomed up and overwhelmed him.

It was over. Alexis had won. Sprays of flowers and olive branches flicked his shoulders. Arms pummeled him. And then, while faces were still a blur, he saw one familiar face that made him think he had gone mad. It happened in a flash. Slender arms were around his neck and a girl's voice spoke into his ear. "You won and I saw you win! Oh, you are excellent!"

It was Niki. Niki where no girl was allowed to be on pain of death, Niki with her hair cropped so like a boy's and wearing one of his old tunics that she must have brought from home, planning this trick all along. No one seemed to be giving her even a second glance, but his blood froze.

"You fool!" he said under his breath. "Quick! Leave, before it's too late. You know the penalty."

"I don't believe in the penalty." She gave him a flashing smile and slipped away into the crowd.

Telamon was wiping the sweat from Alexis's face, his father and brother lifted him shoulder-high, and his townsmen put a crown of flowers on his head. They tied a ribbon on his arm, another on his thigh, and so carried him to the stone seat of the judges to receive the palm branch that would serve as a token of victory until the final night when victors were crowned with wild olive. As Alexis looked down, dazed and smiling, from his high perch, he saw Lampis, his cheeks white and tear-stained, leaving the crowd, followed by his grim-faced trainer. Again, in the midst of his own triumph, Alexis felt pity. It was a weakness, one he must try to overcome. He did not allow himself to picture the arrival of Lampis in Sparta.

*As you read more about the ancient people of the Mediterranean, you will discover why Alexis felt pity for Lampis, the runner from Sparta. You also will learn that the ancient Greeks are remembered today for more than the Olympic Games.*

# CHAPTER 7

# ANCIENT GREECE

> 66 Here each individual is interested not only in his own affairs, but in the affairs of state as well. 99
>
> Pericles, leader of Athens, 450 B.C.

Statue of a young Greek charioteer, crafted about 470 B.C.

# EARLY PEOPLE of GREECE

## Link to Our World

**What could cause a culture to lose or gain control of an area?**

**Focus on the Main Idea**
*As you read, think about how different cultures came to control Greece as time passed.*

**Preview Vocabulary**
*isthmus*
*cultural borrowing*
*epic*

Over the centuries peoples of several cultures settled on the land now known as Greece. Directly or indirectly, each culture formed part of what would become the Greek civilization.

## MOUNTAINS AND THE SEA

Present-day Greece occupies a large peninsula on the southern edge of eastern Europe. This peninsula—the Balkan Peninsula—curves south and east into the Mediterranean Sea toward a part of the Asian continent called Asia Minor, or "Little Asia." Today the country of Turkey fills Asia Minor. Turkey and Greece are separated by an island-dotted arm of the Mediterranean called the Aegean (ih•JEE•uhn) Sea.

The surrounding sea reaches far into the southern part of the Balkan Peninsula. In fact, it nearly divides the peninsula in two. The southern part, called the Peloponnesus (peh•luh•puh•NEE•suhs), is connected to the rest of the mainland by a small strip of land, or **isthmus** (ISS•muhs).

Mountains cover nearly three-fourths of Greece. In the thin, rocky soil and dry climate, early farmers grew olives, grapes, and grain for food. They also raised sheep, goats, pigs, and cattle to get skins for clothing.

The rugged land made travel hard and trade nearly impossible. The people of each mountain village had to

The mountainous land of Greece made both travel and trade difficult.

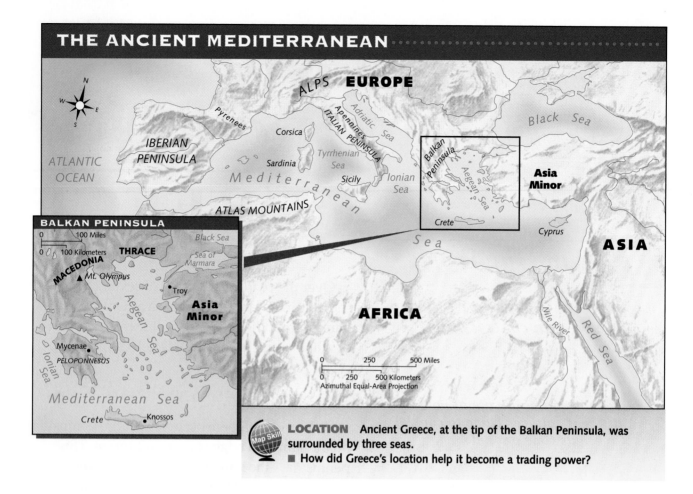

## THE ANCIENT MEDITERRANEAN

EUROPE

ALPS

Pyrenees

Corsica

Apennines

ITALIAN PENINSULA

Adriatic Sea

IBERIAN PENINSULA

ATLANTIC OCEAN

Sardinia

Tyrrhenian Sea

Sicily

Ionian Sea

Balkan Peninsula

Aegean Sea

Black Sea

Asia Minor

Mediterranean

Crete

ATLAS MOUNTAINS

Cyprus

ASIA

Sea

AFRICA

Nile River

Red Sea

0      250      500 Miles
0    250    500 Kilometers
Azimuthal Equal-Area Projection

### BALKAN PENINSULA

0      100 Miles
0    100 Kilometers

THRACE

Black Sea

Sea of Marmara

MACEDONIA

▲ Mt. Olympus

Troy

Asia Minor

Aegean Sea

Mycenae

PELOPONNESUS

Ionian Sea

Mediterranean Sea

Crete

Knossos

**LOCATION** Ancient Greece, at the tip of the Balkan Peninsula, was surrounded by three seas.
■ How did Greece's location help it become a trading power?

survive on only the food they raised. Since they had no contact with each other, each mountain village formed its own government and became fiercely independent.

Along the coast the sea connected Greeks with people in Asia and Africa. Greeks living near the Mediterranean became fishers, sailors, and merchants. The fact that Greece had only a few types of natural resources led the Greeks to look to the outside for trade.

Greece's location in the eastern Mediterranean made it a perfect trade center. Traders on the Mediterranean were eager to exchange their goods for Greek olive oil, wool, and wine. Between 3000 and 1550 B.C., the Mediterranean's first great trading center grew up on the island of Crete, to the south of Greece.

 *How did geography affect the way early people lived in ancient Greece?*

## THE MINOANS

The island of Crete lies 60 miles (97 km) south of the Peloponnesus. The Greek poet Homer described Crete as "a rich and lovely land, washed by the waves on every side."

Around 1900 B.C. the people of Crete began building huge buildings called palaces. These palaces were like small cities. They were centers for managing government and controlling the neighboring countryside. The palaces may also have been religious centers.

Archaeologists have uncovered the remains of four palaces. The largest, Knossos (NAHS•uhs), stood at

The Minoans will long be remembered for their beautiful wall paintings.

least three stories high. Knossos and two other palaces had large central courtyards and areas for storing food. Beautiful paintings showing peaceful scenes decorated the palace walls.

The people who built Knossos and the other cities of Crete are called Minoans (muh•NOH•uhnz). They were named for the legendary King Minos (MY•nuhs). If Minos existed, he probably ruled Crete in the years of its greatest success, sometime between 1750 and 1550 B.C.

The Minoans were seafaring traders. They traded with people in ancient Africa, Asia, and Europe. Egypt and Syria were just two of their many trading partners. Minoan trading ships carried olive oil, wine, wool, pottery, and other goods from Crete to overseas ports. The ships returned with such treasures as copper, tin, and gold. The Minoans were among the earliest people to mix copper and tin to form the metal bronze. Using bronze they crafted beautiful bowls and other objects.

To keep track of their trade, the Minoans developed a system of writing. Unfortunately, some of their writings may have been destroyed by a fire that swept through the Minoan kingdom in about 1450 B.C. Only

Dolphins were just one of the subjects of Minoan artists. This wall painting once decorated the Queen's Room in the Palace of Knossos.

records written on clay tablets remain. Some historians believe that fire may have brought an end to all Minoan civilization. Others believe a powerful earthquake struck the island. The way in which the Minoan kingdom ended may never be known.

 **What were Minoan palaces like?**

## THE MYCENAEANS

During the last years of their kingdom, Minoan merchants started trading with the city of Mycenae (my•SEE•nee), near the coast of the mountainous Peloponnesus. The Mycenaeans (my•suh•NEE•uhnz) seem to have been a warlike people who measured their wealth by the number of weapons they owned.

Through trade the Mycenaeans learned many Minoan customs. This **cultural borrowing** led the Mycenaeans to adapt Minoan art styles and pottery designs

Parts of the citylike palace of Knossos were restored in the beginning of the twentieth century. What can you tell about the ancient palace from the photograph?

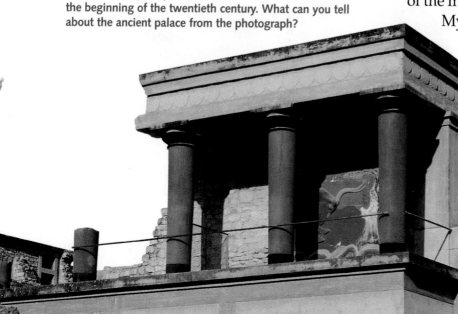

Mycenaean warriors wore bronze armor with helmets made from boars' tusks (top). Mycenaean vases (bottom) often showed warlike scenes.

to make them look more warlike. They changed Minoan writing to fit their language and also borrowed some religious beliefs.

In 1450 B.C., after the Minoan kingdom was destroyed, the warlike Mycenaeans invaded Crete. Mycenae controlled both Crete and much of the Peloponnesus from about 1450 to 1100 B.C. By 1100 B.C. the Mycenaeans had begun to lose their hold on Greece.

No one knows why Mycenaean control of Greece grew weaker. For centuries historians believed that warriors called Dorians marched south into the Peloponnesus and burned palaces and villages in their path. Now some experts believe that a seafaring people conquered the Mycenaeans. According to these experts, the Dorians simply moved into the area after this conquest. Others claim that disagreements among the Mycenaeans themselves weakened their civilization.

Some great change must have caused the Mycenaeans to give up their writing and art and stop trading. During the period from about 1100 to 800 B.C., much of Minoan and Mycenaean learning was lost. The ancient people of Greece returned to a simpler way of life.

 **From whom did the Mycenaeans borrow many ideas?**

## ANCIENT STORIES AND LEGENDS

Much of what we know about the Mycenaeans comes from the stories of Homer. Four centuries after the Mycenaean civilization had lost its strength, Homer created long story-poems, or **epics**, that kept its memory alive. The poems were based on old stories he had heard. Storytellers through the centuries had retold these epics.

# Who?

## Homer
## 700s B.C.

Historians know very little about Homer, the author of the *Iliad* and the *Odyssey*. Homer probably grew up in Ionia in Asia Minor sometime between 800 and 700 B.C. Tradition says that Homer was blind and that he recited from memory the 28,000 verses of his epic poems.

This gold mask, made by a Mycenaean artist, is a reminder of the early cultures that once lived in what is now Greece. What type of person do you think this mask shows?

One epic, the *Iliad*, tells about people's actions during a great war. Another epic, the *Odyssey*, describes the adventures of the hero Odysseus (oh•DIH•see•uhs) on his long journey home from the war described in the *Iliad*. During his ten-year journey, Odysseus has many strange adventures, such as a fight with a one-eyed giant. At the same time, his wife, Penelope (puh•NEH•luh•pee), deals with problems caused by his absence.

According to tradition, the war Homer described was fought between the Greeks and the people of Troy, a city in what is now northwestern Turkey. This war has become known as the Trojan War.

Legend says that the fighting began when a Trojan prince named Paris kidnapped Helen, the wife of a Greek king. The king's brother, Agamemnon, took soldiers to Troy to get Helen back. "Greece must defend its honor!" became their battle cry.

The conflict dragged on and on with no end in sight. Then the Greeks came up with a plan to trick the Trojans. They built a huge, hollow wooden horse, dragged it to the gates of Troy during the night, and left it there.

The curious Trojans pulled the large horse into the city the next morning, just as the Greeks had hoped they would. That night Greek soldiers hiding inside the hollow horse crawled out. They opened the city gates to other Greek soldiers waiting outside. By morning the Greeks had taken back Helen and set fire to the city of Troy.

The legend of the Trojan War, Homer's epics, and other stories left a lasting record of the early people of Greece. From this traditional beginning the Greek civilization continued to grow and change.

 **How did Homer keep alive the memory of Mycenae?**

# *L*SSON 1 REVIEW

## Check Understanding

1. **Recall the Facts** Who were the Minoans and the Mycenaeans?
2. **Focus on the Main Idea** What probably caused the Minoans to lose their strength? What may have caused the Mycenaeans to lose their strength?

## Think Critically

3. **Past to Present** What might cause a culture of today to gain and then lose its strength?
4. **Think More About It** Why did the Mycenaeans change the ideas of the Minoans rather than use them just as they were?

## Show What You Know

 **Art Activity** Make a wall painting that shows what you think may have caused the Minoans or the Mycenaeans to lose their power.

# CITY-STATES AND GREEK CULTURE

## Link to Our World

**What might cause people to develop very different ways of life?**

**Focus on the Main Idea**
*As you read, look for reasons the peoples of ancient Greece developed different ways of life.*

**Preview Vocabulary**

polis            oligarchy
acropolis        democracy
agora            majority rule
tyrant           cultural identity
aristocracy      myth
assembly

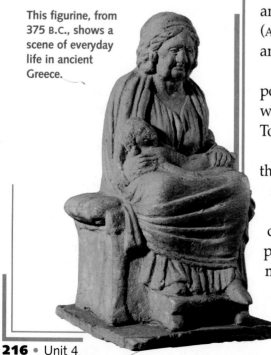

This figurine, from 375 B.C., shows a scene of everyday life in ancient Greece.

Around 800 B.C. the people of Greece again began to build settlements. At first most Greeks lived in small villages. The growth of trade in local products helped villages grow into towns. In time each town joined with nearby villages and farms to form a **polis**, or city-state.

## RISE OF CITY-STATES

To protect themselves from invaders, Greek communities built walled fortresses on the tops of hills. Farmers from the country-side moved inside the walls during enemy attacks. Later the walled fortress, or **acropolis** (uh•KRAH•puh•luhs), became the center for daily life in many city-states.

Outside the acropolis were houses, temples, and an open-air market and gathering place called an **agora** (AG•uh•ruh). People met in the agora to exchange goods and discuss the news of the day.

At first kings or tyrants ruled the city-states and made all political decisions. In ancient Greece a **tyrant** was someone who took control of a government by force and ruled alone. Today we think of a tyrant as a cruel ruler.

As time passed, the people in each city-state developed their own way of governing. In some city-states the richest men shared authority with a king. This wealthy ruling class, or **aristocracy**, was made up of landowners and mer-chants. In other city-states all free men, rich or poor, took part in government. These men met in an **assembly**, or law-making group, to make decisions for the whole community.

Most city-states had fewer than 5,000 people. As the number of people in a city-state grew, overcrowding

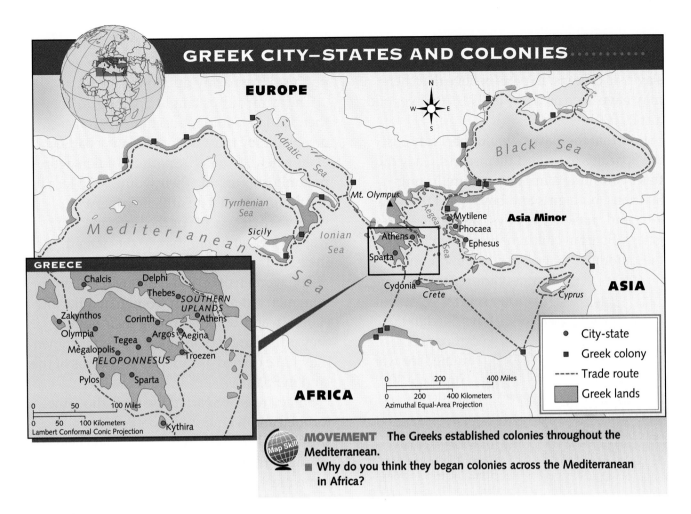

## GREEK CITY–STATES AND COLONIES

EUROPE

Adriatic Sea

Tyrrhenian Sea

Mediterranean Sea

Sicily

Ionian Sea

Mt. Olympus

Aegean Sea

Black Sea

Asia Minor

Mytilene
Phocaea
Ephesus

Athens

Sparta

Cydonia

Crete

Cyprus

ASIA

AFRICA

**GREECE**

Chalcis
Delphi
Thebes
Zakynthos
Corinth
Olympia
Tegea
Megalopolis
PELOPONNESUS
Pylos
Sparta
SOUTHERN UPLANDS
Athens
Argos
Aegina
Troezen
Kythira

0    50    100 Miles
0    50    100 Kilometers
Lambert Conformal Conic Projection

0    200    400 Miles
0    200    400 Kilometers
Azimuthal Equal-Area Projection

● City-state
■ Greek colony
---- Trade route
▨ Greek lands

**MOVEMENT** The Greeks established colonies throughout the Mediterranean.
■ Why do you think they began colonies across the Mediterranean in Africa?

occurred and some people had to look for new places to live. Several city-states set up colonies, creating new city-states in Asia Minor, southern Europe, and northern Africa.

Besides giving space for more people, the colonies brought the Greeks new natural resources and trade markets. As more and more colonies were set up, Greek ideas and customs spread through the Mediterranean region.

Rivalries grew as the city-states began to compete for land and colonies. The city-states of Sparta and Argos both wanted control of the Peloponnesus. Athens and Aegina fought to rule the southern uplands northeast of the Peloponnesus. While not rivals at first, Sparta and Athens had strikingly different ways of life.

✓ **What features did the city-states share? How were they different from one another?**

## SPARTA

Soldiers marching and young boys and girls exercising were common sights in ancient Sparta. A simple life filled with physical activity was typical for Spartan citizens.

The Spartans were descendants of Dorian settlers. Their slaves were descendants of the people who were there before the Dorians. Spartan leaders believed that

Physical training was an important part of the way of life of both women and men in ancient Sparta.

only through military strength could they control a city-state that had ten times as many slaves as citizens. Experts believe that there may have been as many as 250,000 slaves and just 25,000 citizens.

Fear that the slaves would rebel caused the Spartans to protect themselves. They did this by forming a military culture. Young Spartans, both girls and boys, went through long and challenging physical-training programs. Spartan children were taken from their mothers at age 7 and put in training camps. Girls returned home after several years, but boys lived in the camps and trained for war until age 30.

Spartan soldiers were fierce and disciplined. This bronze warrior still guards the tomb of King Leonidas, who lived during the 5th century B.C.

At age 30, men were allowed to become citizens, marry, and have families. They were not freed from army duty until age 60.

The army camps taught Spartans to obey their leaders without question. Spartans believed they must never give up a battle, even when wounded. Spartan soldiers wore red uniforms to hide their wounds. To lose in anything, whether an athletic contest or a war, was a disgrace. For the Spartans, there was no greater honor than to die defending their land.

The women of Sparta had fewer rights than men but more than women in other city-states. In addition to running their homes, they often handled business matters. Women may have owned as much as two-fifths of the land in Sparta.

Some areas of Spartan life were the same for men and women. All Spartans led a simple and sparse way of life. By law everyone ate "in common, of the same bread and same meat." Trading with outsiders was discouraged for fear that new ideas would bring unwanted change. For that reason, Spartan citizens were rarely allowed to travel outside their city-state. Therefore, Spartans had to depend on themselves and their own resources. Because the Spartans kept to themselves, their way of life changed little over time.

Sparta's way of governing also saw few changes over the years. Sparta had two kings, but they had little authority except in time of war. The city-state also had an assembly of citizens, but this, too, was fairly weak. Five wealthy landowners called *ephors* controlled the government. This **oligarchy**, or small ruling group, made all the decisions for Sparta. Although strict, Spartan government was among the most admired governments in all of Greece.

 **Why did Spartans feel they needed an army? How did this affect the children of Sparta?**

# ATHENS

Athens was the main city-state in Attica (AT•ih•kuh), the ancient name for land in the southern uplands. Unlike Sparta, Athens required its young men to serve in the army only in time of war. Athenian government encouraged the people to take part in community decisions. This civic participation grew into a system of **democracy**, or rule by the people. The Greek historian Thucydides (thoo•SIH•duh•deez) said about Athens, "Its administration favors the many instead of the few."

The Athenian leader Solon had helped bring democracy to Athens around 594 B.C. Under his leadership Athenians won more rights to take part in government. Later, around 508 B.C., a leader named Cleisthenes (KLYS•thuh•neez) changed the form of Athenian government so that individuals played even greater roles.

By the year 500 B.C., every free adult male over age 20 was considered a citizen in Athens. All citizens took part in the city-state's assembly, called the Ecclesia. Every member of the assembly had one vote. All decisions were made by **majority rule**. In other words, the idea that received the most votes became law.

The reforms of Cleisthenes kept any one person from taking control of Athens. To get rid of a troublesome person, citizens held a special meeting. Any citizen who received 6,000 ostraca (ahs•TRUH•kuh), or broken pieces of clay pots, marked against him was exiled from, or forced to leave, Athens for ten years. This

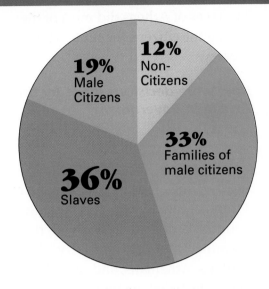

ancient practice gave us the English word *ostracism*, meaning "the act of shutting someone out."

The changes made by Cleisthenes let more people take part in government. But Athenian democracy did not include everyone. Women could not take part in government and did not count as citizens. However, as in Sparta, women managed the family budget and the household.

The people who gained the least from Athenian

> ❝ *ITS ADMINISTRATION FAVORS THE MANY instead of the few.* ❞
>
> Thucydides, Greek historian, born about 460 B.C.

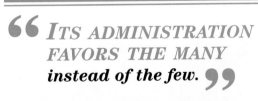

Paintings on Greek pottery illustrated stories of history and legend, religious ceremonies, or daily life.

democracy probably helped make that democracy possible. These were the slaves, who made up over one-third of the population. The slaves of Athens did most of the work, giving the citizens the time to take part in democracy.

 **How were decisions made by the Athenian government?**

## TO BE "GREEK"

During the time of the city-states, Greeks did not think of themselves as belonging to a single country. People identified with their city-state rather than with a country. They were Spartans, Athenians, and so on.

However, the Greek people did feel a cultural connection, or a **cultural identity**, with one another. All Greeks called themselves Hellenes because they believed they had a common ancestor, the hero Hellen. A Greek **myth**, or story passed down about an ancient

# **What?**

## The First Olympics

The first Olympic Games were held in the valley of Olympia near the city-state of Elis in 776 B.C. As many as 40,000 people watched athletes from city-states throughout Greece compete in one event—a footrace. Women were not allowed to enter the stadium at Olympia to compete or even to watch. Later, however, women in Elis held their own footraces to honor the goddess Hera.

**Early bronze discus**

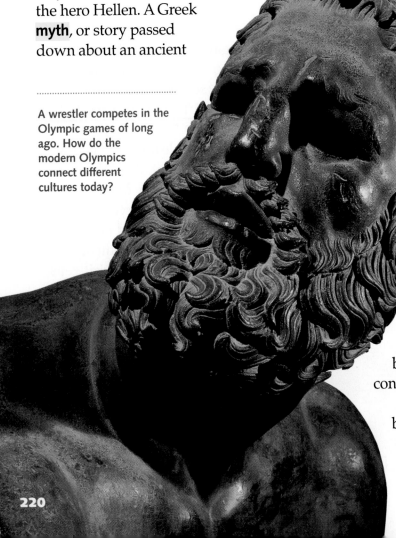

A wrestler competes in the Olympic games of long ago. How do the modern Olympics connect different cultures today?

god or hero, said that Hellen alone had survived a flood long ago. In addition, their shared religion set the Greeks apart, in their minds, from other peoples who lived alongside the Mediterranean, such as the Phoenicians and the Egyptians.

The Greek cultural identity was seen in various activities. The Olympic Games, for example, brought the city-states together in peace. Beginning about 776 B.C. Greeks met every four years to compete in athletic contests to honor the god Zeus. The Greeks believed that Zeus and their other gods controlled daily events in the world.

A common written language also helped bring the city-states closer together. In the 700s B.C. the Greeks developed an alphabet based on the alphabet of the

## THE GREEK ALPHABET

| GREEK LETTER | WRITTEN NAME | ENGLISH SOUND |
|---|---|---|
| A | alpha | a |
| B | beta | b |
| Γ | gamma | g |
| Δ | delta | d |
| E | epsilon | e |
| Z | zeta | z |
| H | eta | e |
| Θ | theta | th |
| I | iota | i |
| K | kappa | c, k |
| Λ | lambda | l |
| M | mu | m |
| N | nu | n |
| Ξ | xi | x |
| O | omicron | o |
| Π | pi | p |
| P | rho | r |
| Σ | sigma | s |
| T | tau | t |
| Y | upsilon | y, u |
| Φ | phi | ph |
| X | chi | ch |
| Ψ | psi | ps |
| Ω | omega | o |

**LEARNING FROM TABLES** The Greek alphabet borrowed many letters from the Phoenicians but added its own vowels to form a 24-letter alphabet.
■ In what ways is the ancient Greek alphabet similar to today's English alphabet?

Phoenicians. Like the Minoans long before them, the Phoenicians were traders and needed a writing system to keep track of their trade. Phoenician writing used symbols to stand for single sounds rather than whole ideas. In changing this system to fit their needs, the Greeks called the first letter *alpha*. The second letter was *beta*. Our word *alphabet* comes from the names of those Greek letters.

✔ *What helped the Greeks feel a cultural identity with one another?*

The painting decorating this bowl is of Zeus. The Greeks believed that many gods ruled both nature and people. According to the ancient Greeks, Zeus, the chief god, ruled the universe.

# LESSON 2 REVIEW

### Check Understanding

1. **Recall the Facts** Which Greek city-state was centered around its army? What Greek city-state had a democracy?
2. **Focus on the Main Idea** What caused the people in different parts of ancient Greece to develop different ways of life?

### Think Critically

3. **Think More About It** Why did the Athenians feel it was important for citizens to take part in government?
4. **Explore Viewpoints** Why do people around the world have different ideas about how to govern themselves?

### Show What You Know

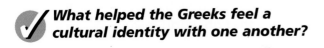

**Drawing Activity** The people of the different Greek city-states led very different ways of life. Imagine that you are an observer first in Sparta and then in Athens. Sketch what you see. Try to show differences in ways of life in the two city-states.

# LESSON 3

# The GOLDEN AGE of ATHENS

## Link to Our World

**How do times of war and times of peace affect societies today?**

*Focus on the Main Idea*
*Look for ways periods of war and peace affected the ways of life of the ancient Greeks.*

*Preview Vocabulary*
league            comedy
tragedy           demagogue

The Athenian leader Pericles lived from about 495 to 429 B.C.

For centuries the Greek city-states fought over land and differences in ways of life. Then, beginning in the early fifth century B.C., a common enemy brought the Greek people together.

## THE PERSIAN WARS

Around 499 B.C. armies from Persia set out to take over Egypt and other lands around the Mediterranean. Believing that more land meant more power, the Persians claimed northern Africa. Soon they also captured Greek colonies in Asia Minor. The people in the Greek colonies revolted, but they could not defeat the Persians.

In 490 Darius I, the Persian king, turned his soldiers toward Athens because Athens had helped the colonies fight the Persians. The Athenians met the Persians on the plain of Marathon, not far from Athens. Although the Persians had more soldiers, the Athenians managed to defeat them in just one day of fighting. A messenger ran to Athens from Marathon to tell of the victory. Athletes in today's Olympic Games re-create this act in the long-distance running event called the marathon.

Darius died in 486 B.C. In 480 B.C. his son Xerxes (ZERK•seez) sent 200,000 soldiers in 800 ships to attack Greece. This time the Persians met a united Greek army and navy made up of soldiers and sailors from Athens, Sparta, and other Greek city-states. The Persians still had more soldiers than all the city-states together had. Yet in a sea battle near the island of Salamis (SAL•uh•muhs), the Greeks defeated the Persians.

No one knew at the time that the war would have a lasting effect on world history. Because the

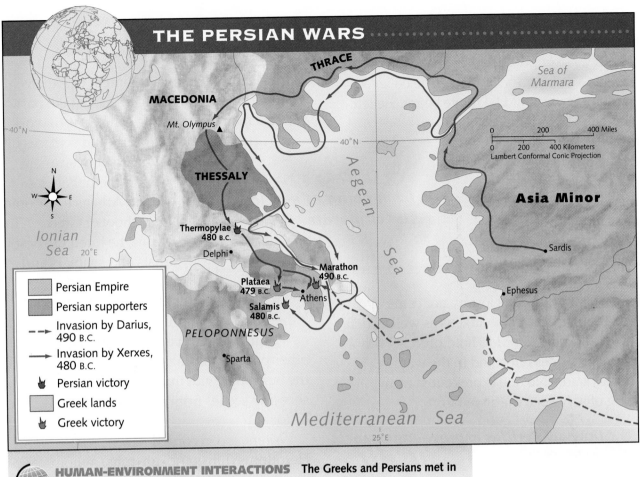

## THE PERSIAN WARS

Persian Empire

Persian supporters

– – – Invasion by Darius, 490 B.C.

—→ Invasion by Xerxes, 480 B.C.

Persian victory

Greek lands

Greek victory

**HUMAN-ENVIRONMENT INTERACTIONS** The Greeks and Persians met in battle on the Balkan Peninsula.

■ Who controlled the land on which the Greeks won victories?

Greeks won, it was their customs, language, and ideas and not those of the Persians that would shape many other cultures for centuries to come.

After the wars, the Greek city-states feared future attacks by invaders. They banded together to form **leagues,** or groups of allies, for protection. Sparta led a group of city-states in the Peloponnesian League. The city-states of Attica formed the Delian League, led by Athens.

### ✓ What caused the Greek city-states to band together?

## THE GOLDEN AGE

The Greeks, especially the Athenians, felt great pride after defeating Persia. From about 479 to 431 B.C., the Athenians turned their pride into a time of achievement that came to be known as the Golden Age.

A wealthy member of the aristocracy named Pericles (PAIR•uh•kleez) led Athens during much of this time. Pericles was a wise leader whose advice to those he ruled was "nothing to excess," meaning that they should not overdo anything.

Pericles ruled with the help of an assembly made up of thousands of men. Any member could speak to the assembly, and each had the right to vote. Members voted by raising their hands.

A group called the Council of 500 decided what would be discussed at each assembly meeting. Council members were chosen from the assembly each year by drawing names from a bowl. Most other government offices, as well as the juries for court cases, were also filled this way.

Pericles strongly supported the idea of Athenian democracy. However, he believed the democracy could be made better. He felt that every citizen had a right to take part in government, not just wealthy citizens.

Pericles also ordered that all public officials and jurors should be paid a salary for the days they served. This pay made up for the money citizens lost by not being at their regular jobs. Poor citizens as well as rich ones could now afford to hold office. "With us, poverty does not stand in the way," Pericles said. "No one is prevented from being of service to the city-state."

> 66 *NO ONE IS PREVENTED from being of service to the city-state.* 99
>
> Pericles, 495–429 B.C.

 **How did Pericles improve Athenian democracy?**

## ACHIEVEMENTS OF THE GOLDEN AGE

Pericles made the government of Athens stronger by allowing all citizens to take part. He also made it easier for Athenians to work in the arts and sciences by having the government support them. Pericles wanted Athens to become "the school of Greece." To do this, he hired the best artists and scholars and put them to work.

Architects and builders set about making Athens more beautiful. Architects designed new temples, gymnasiums, theaters, and other public buildings. Artists then decorated the buildings with murals, or wall paintings, showing scenes from Athens's glorious history.

Writers, too, recorded Athens's past. Herodotus (hih•RAHD•uh•tuhs), whom

## **W**hat?

### Direct Democracy

Unlike the democracy in the United States, ancient Athens had a direct democracy. Each citizen took a direct role in day-to-day government. Most countries today have too many people to have a direct democracy. The United States has a representative democracy. In this type of democracy, large numbers of citizens elect other citizens, or representatives, to make laws for them.

The most remarkable building of the Golden Age in Athens was the Parthenon, which was built on the city's acropolis. This marble temple celebrated Greek victories in the Persian Wars and honored the Greek goddess Athena. The Parthenon was completed in 432 B.C. Its ruins still stand in the present-day city of Athens, Greece.

some consider the first historian and one of the earliest geographers, wrote about the Persian Wars. Herodotus explained that he wrote this history to put on record "the astonishing achievements of our own and of other peoples."

Other great writers also contributed to the achievements of the Golden Age. Sophocles (SAHF•uh•kleez) wrote **tragedies**, or serious plays, in which the main character comes to an unhappy end. Aristophanes (air•uh•STAH•fuh•neez) wrote **comedies**, or humorous plays. His comedies usually made fun of political leaders or traditional ideas.

Pericles and the Athenian government also paid scholars to study nature and human life. Their findings changed forever the way people saw their world.

One of the greatest scientists of the Golden Age was Hippocrates (hip•AHK•ruh•teez). Hippocrates showed that illnesses came from natural causes. They were not punishment from the gods, as most people had believed.

To stay healthy, Hippocrates told the Athenians, "wheaten bread is to be preferred to barley cake, and roasted to boiled meats." While many of his suggestions made good sense, he also thought "vegetables should be reduced to a minimum." Hippocrates is perhaps best remembered for writing a code of conduct that doctors still follow today.

✓ **What kinds of people did Pericles support during the Golden Age?**

⬆ This mask was most likely worn by an actor in an ancient Greek comedy.

Greek amphitheaters, such as this one in Delphi, were designed so that even a whisper could reach the seats farthest from the stage. ⬇

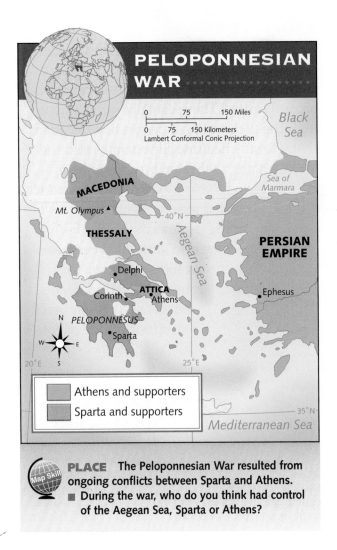

# PELOPONNESIAN WAR

0   75   150 Miles
0   75   150 Kilometers
Lambert Conformal Conic Projection

Black Sea

MACEDONIA
Mt. Olympus ▲

Sea of Marmara

40°N

THESSALY

Aegean Sea

PERSIAN EMPIRE

Delphi

ATTICA

Corinth
Athens

Ephesus

PELOPONNESUS

Sparta

N
W   E
S

20°E                    25°E

35°N

Mediterranean Sea

☐ Athens and supporters
☐ Sparta and supporters

**PLACE** The Peloponnesian War resulted from ongoing conflicts between Sparta and Athens.
■ During the war, who do you think had control of the Aegean Sea, Sparta or Athens?

# THE END OF THE GOLDEN AGE

During the time of the Golden Age, Athens and Sparta became the most powerful city-states in Greece. Yet neither was satisfied. Athens wanted more land. Sparta wanted to weaken the influence of Athens. The city-states of the Peloponnesian League supported Sparta, while those of the Delian League supported Athens. In 431 B.C. the Peloponnesian War broke out. The war lasted 27 years.

After Sparta attacked Attica, many people from the countryside moved into Athens. Because of the crowding, diseases swept through the city-state. One-fourth of the Athenian army died from diseases. Pericles, too, died at this time.

Without the wise leadership of Pericles, the members of the assembly began to follow bad leaders called **demagogues** (DEH•muh•gahgz). The demagogues made promises they could not keep and led the assembly into making foolish decisions. Faced with ruin, Athens surrendered to Sparta in 404 B.C. Sparta quickly replaced the Athenian assembly with an oligarchy like its own.

Great thinkers and teachers lived in Athens after the Peloponnesian War. However, the city-state no longer paid for their work as it had during the Golden Age. One famous teacher was Socrates (SAH•kruh•teez), who taught by asking questions and making his students think rather than by simply telling them information.

Socrates called himself Athens's "gadfly." As a fly bites a horse and makes it jump, Socrates used criticism to "sting" Athens into returning to its earlier greatness. Such criticism would have been welcome in Pericles' day. In 399 B.C., however, an Athenian court convicted Socrates of teaching dangerous ideas to the city's young people. The court sentenced Socrates to end his own life by drinking poison.

The ideas of Socrates are still studied today.

Aristotle, who lived from 384 to 322 B.C., loved all knowledge.

One of Socrates' students was Plato. Like Socrates, Plato was disappointed in the kinds of leaders who came after Pericles. Plato said that a ruler should be a good person, because good people are just and wise. He believed that it was possible to become a good person by studying hard and loving wisdom. He felt that philosophers, or "lovers of wisdom," would make the best rulers. In 385 B.C. Plato started a school called the Academy, where philosophers could learn the lessons they would need to govern well.

Plato also thought a lot about what it takes to be a good citizen. He pictured a good citizen as someone who thinks and feels and then takes action. Plato believed that every citizen had both the right and the responsibility to take part in public life. He felt it was important for people to be informed, to understand other viewpoints, and to be responsible for their own actions. This idea of citizenship is shared by many people today.

One of Plato's students, Aristotle (AIR•uh•stah•tuhl), was more interested in how things were rather than in how he would like them to be. His wide search for knowledge covered subjects as different as law, economics, astronomy, and sports.

**What brought an end to the Golden Age of Athens?**

# LESSON 3 REVIEW

## Check Understanding

1. **Recall the Facts**   What wars did the Athenians fight in the 400s B.C.?
2. **Focus on the Main Idea**   How did periods of war and peace affect life in Athens?

## Think Critically

3. **Past to Present**   Do people's ways of life change in time of war? Explain.
4. **Think More About It**   How did the Persian Wars help bring the Greeks together? How did the Peloponnesian War tear the Greeks apart?
5. **Personally Speaking**   Socrates taught by asking questions. Do you think asking or telling is a better way to teach? Why?

## Show What You Know

**Poster Activity**   After the defeat of the Persians, the Athenians showed pride in being Greek through great works in art and science. Think about the pride you feel in the United States. Make a poster that explains why you feel proud to be a citizen. Display your artwork in your classroom or somewhere else in your school.

At Plato's Academy, philosophers studied the responsibilities of citizens and leaders.

# HowTo

# Predict a Likely Outcome

## Why Is This Skill Important?

It is useful to be able to look at the way things are and decide what is likely to happen next. Making such predictions can help you make thoughtful decisions and useful plans. When you make predictions, you are not just guessing about what will happen in the future. Rather, you are using what you already know along with new information to predict a probable, or likely, outcome.

## Remember What You Have Read

After the Persian Wars, the Greek city-states feared future attacks by outside invaders. To protect themselves, some of the city-states banded together to form leagues, or groups of allies. The city-states in the southern part of Greece formed the Peloponnesian League, which was led by Sparta. Those in Attica formed the Delian League, led by Athens. The greater size, military strength, and influence of Sparta and Athens made them leaders. Suppose you had read Lesson 3 only up to this point. What prediction could you have made about what would happen between the two leagues? Why do you think events would turn out as you predicted?

## Understand the Process

To make a prediction about the leagues, you could have followed these steps:

- Think about what you already know. *Sparta and Athens had different ways of life.*
- Review any new information you have learned. *The rivalry between Sparta and Athens had grown by the end of the Golden Age. Athens wanted more land, and Sparta wanted to weaken the influence of Athens.*
- Make a prediction. *What do you think happened next between the two leagues?*
- As you read, ask yourself if your prediction still seems correct. You may revise your prediction as you find out additional information.

Following these steps might have helped you predict that the Peloponnesian and Delian leagues would go to war with each other.

## Think and Apply

The division that swept across Greece as a result of the Peloponnesian War led to a time of conflict and distrust among the city-states. Follow the steps listed above to predict how this conflict would affect Greece.

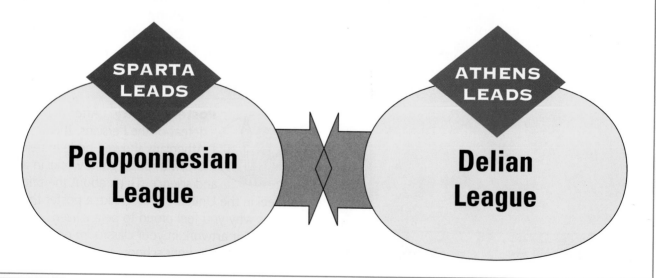

SPARTA LEADS

**Peloponnesian League**

ATHENS LEADS

**Delian League**

# LESSON 4

# ALEXANDER'S GREAT EMPIRE

## Link to Our World

**How can one person affect the course of history?**

*Focus on the Main Idea*
**As you read, look for ways in which Alexander the Great changed the Mediterranean region forever.**

*Preview Vocabulary*
**alliance**
**Hellenistic**
**multicultural**

Alexander the Great was only twenty when he became king of Macedonia. This marble sculpture is a Roman copy of the original, which was made in 320 B.C.

Greece needed a leader who could bring together people with different ideas and ways of life. In time such an individual came to power. He controlled lands that stretched from the Greek peninsula to northern India. This leader created the largest empire the world had known.

## CONQUEST OF GREECE

After the Peloponnesian War, Greece became a land of conflict and distrust. City-states formed **alliances**, or agreements to help each other. Most of these alliances did not last long. A friend in one conflict became an enemy in the next. Each city-state put its own interests above the common good of Greece.

Meanwhile, north of Greece in a land called Macedonia, a strong king named Philip II came to the throne. Philip had brought his own people together under one rule. He planned to do the same for Greece.

Philip had spent part of his boyhood in Greece and greatly admired Greek culture. Philip even hired the Greek philosopher Aristotle to teach his 13-year-old son, Alexander. From Aristotle, young Alexander learned to appreciate the cultures of other peoples. From his father, Alexander learned to be a fearless warrior. Stories say that Alexander slept with a dagger and a copy of Homer's *Iliad* under his pillow.

Even the Spartans could not stop Philip's well-trained Macedonian soldiers. Philip's armies moved south through northern Greece and on to the Peloponnesus. By 338 B.C. Philip controlled most of the Greek peninsula, including Athens.

The Macedonians did not take over Greece to destroy it. Philip knew that he could not make great changes in the lives of those he conquered. Under his rule the Greek city-states were free to manage themselves. Philip did make one important law, however. He forbade the Greeks to fight one another. Greece was at peace, united not by a Greek but by an outsider.

✓ **What ruler united Greece? Where was he from?**

## BUILDING AN EMPIRE

Alexander's mother, Olympias, had tried for years to convince Philip that Alexander should be the one to follow in his footsteps. When Philip died in 336 B.C., her dreams came true and 20-year-old Alexander became king.

Young Alexander wanted to rule not only Greece but all the world. The world known to Alexander was eastern Europe, northern Africa, and western Asia. Alexander began by conquering Greece's old enemies, the Persians.

In 334 B.C. Alexander led more than 35,000 soldiers from Greece to Asia Minor. One by one Alexander seized the region's Greek colonies, which were in Persian hands.

Alexander's soldiers moved forward easily. The people, who hated their Persian rulers, welcomed Alexander and the changes he brought.

Throughout his growing empire Alexander, or Alexander the Great as he came to be called, built new cities. The cities became centers of learning and helped spread Greek culture. Alexander named each city after himself, calling all of them Alexandria. In time Alexandria, Egypt,

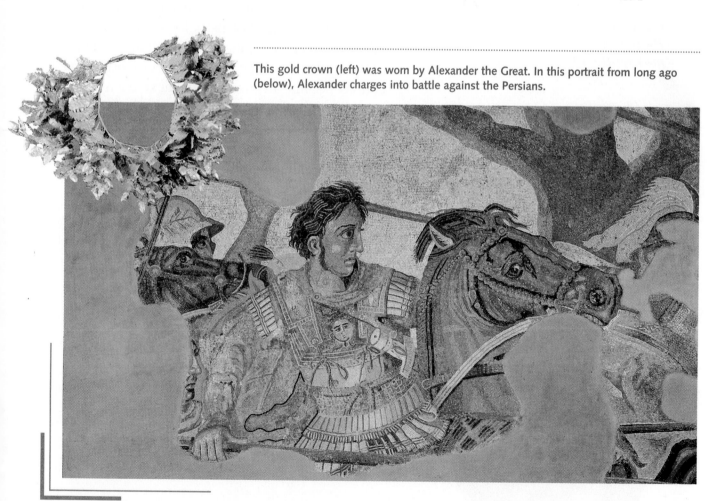

This gold crown (left) was worn by Alexander the Great. In this portrait from long ago (below), Alexander charges into battle against the Persians.

## EMPIRE OF ALEXANDER THE GREAT

Empire of Alexander the Great
Route of Alexander the Great

EUROPE

Danube R.

MACEDONIA  THRACE

Pella

Black Sea

Caucasus Mts.

Caspian Sea

ASIA

Alexandria

Athens  Asia Minor

Sparta  Sardis

Tigris R.

Alexandria

Alexandria

Alexandria

Mediterranean Sea

Crete

Antioch

SYRIA  MESOPOTAMIA

Euphrates River

Alexandria

Alexandria

Alexandria

Alexandria  EGYPT

Babylon

PERSIA

Indus River

AFRICA

Nile River

ARABIA

Alexandria

N  W  E  S

Red Sea

0  250  500 Miles
0  250  500 Kilometers
Two-Point Equidistant Projection

Persian Gulf

Arabian Sea

**REGIONS** In 13 years Alexander conquered much of the world known to him. He ruled over many people and cultures.
■ How many continents did Alexander's empire reach?

replaced Athens as the center of Greek culture.

The many different peoples throughout Alexander's empire learned to speak the Greek language and worship Greek gods. Greek influence became so strong that the period of Alexander's rule and the time shortly after his death became known as the **Hellenistic**, or "Greek-like," Age.

Alexander's conquests made him the ruler of a **multicultural** empire, or an empire of many cultures. As the ruler of many unique peoples, Alexander felt it was in his interest to adopt some of their customs as well as introduce them to Greek culture. Alexander hoped that if he adopted

some of their customs, the Persians and other conquered people would accept his rule. They did. By 331 B.C. Alexander's empire stretched from the Danube River in Europe to the Nile River in Africa and east beyond the Tigris and Euphrates rivers in Asia.

Alexander had conquered Asia Minor, Syria, Egypt, Mesopotamia, and the once-mighty Persian Empire—all without losing a single major battle!

✓ **How did Alexander build his empire? What were the boundaries of that empire?**

⬆ This silver coin made in Babylon honors Alexander's battle against soldiers on elephants in India.

This limestone coffin was created for Alexander the Great.

## THE BREAKUP OF THE EMPIRE

Alexander the Great now ruled a wide area, but still he wanted more lands. Beyond Persia lay India. Alexander led his soldiers east from Babylon to the Indus River. He planned to push on from there to the Ganges River. However, his conquest-weary soldiers refused to follow. Bitterly disappointed, Alexander turned back to Babylon in 326 B.C.

Shortly after he returned to Babylon, in 323 B.C., Alexander became ill with a fever. He died a few days later, just months before his thirty-third birthday. Legend says that before Alexander's death a soldier asked, "To whom will rule of the great empire go?" Alexander answered, "To the strongest!"

No one leader proved strong enough to replace Alexander. His empire broke up quickly after his death. His generals fought for control. In time the empire split into three parts: Macedonia, Syria, and Egypt. The three were often at war with one another. They destroyed much that Alexander had created.

✓ **Why did Alexander's empire break up after his death?**

## ALEXANDER'S LEGACY

The empire may not have lasted, but the Hellenistic culture that started with Alexander did. Like those in the time of Pericles, important thinkers of the Hellenistic Age shaped later cultures for centuries.

This stone artwork from India shows how far Hellenistic influences in art had reached.

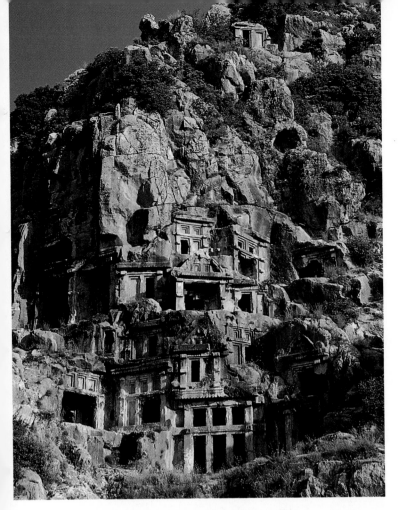

Hellenistic advances in architecture can be seen in these tombs, carved around the year 7 B.C. The tombs were cut out of rock in what is now Turkey.

Hellenistic Greek teachers worked out new ideas in mathematics. In Alexandria, Egypt, Euclid (YOO•kluhd) studied lines and angles and began the study of geometry. Archimedes (ar•kuh•MEE•deez), of Syracuse on the island of Sicily, used mathematics to build many useful machines.

Hellenistic geographers also used mathematics in their thinking about the Earth and the other planets. For example, Aristarchus (air•uh•STAHR•kuhs) used mathematics to discover that the Earth and the other planets move around the sun.

Hellenistic scientists built on the knowledge of medicine that Hippocrates had introduced. During the Hellenistic Age, Alexandria, Egypt, became the center for the study of medicine and surgery. Doctors there learned that the brain was the center of the nervous system.

By 146 B.C. another group of people, the Romans, had grown strong enough to gain control of the Mediterranean world. But the knowledge the Greeks had gained was not forgotten. The Romans borrowed from the religion, the art, the architecture, the philosophy, and the language of the Greeks to build their own civilization.

 ***In what subject areas did great thinkers of the Hellenistic Age make discoveries?***

# LESSON 4 REVIEW

## Check Understanding

1. **Recall the Facts**   Who was Alexander the Great?
2. **Focus on the Main Idea**   How did Alexander the Great affect the region around the Mediterranean?

## Think Critically

3. **Think More About It**   Why was Alexander able to create such a large empire?
4. **Explore Viewpoints**   Alexander believed that by taking up some of the ideas and customs of the people he conquered he could better control them. Many of his soldiers and generals did not share this view. Why do you think they disagreed on this issue?
5. **Past to Present**   Who are some individuals affecting events in the world today?

## Show What You Know

 **Leadership Activity**   In a group, choose one area of concern in your school, such as student attitudes, clothing, or behavior. Then, for one week, see how much impact your team can have in making changes in that area. When the week ends, conduct a survey and make a report to the class.

# CHAPTER 7

## CONNECT MAIN IDEAS

Use this organizer to show that you understand how the chapter's main ideas are connected. Copy the organizer onto a separate sheet of paper. Then complete it by writing two details to support each main idea.

**Early People of Greece**
Different cultures came to control ancient Greece.

1. _____
2. _____

**City-States and Greek Culture**
The people of ancient Greece developed different ways of life.

1. _____
2. _____

**Ancient Greece**

**The Golden Age of Athens**
Periods of war and peace affected the ways of life of ancient Greeks.

1. _____
2. _____

**Alexander's Great Empire**
Alexander the Great changed the Mediterranean region forever.

1. _____
2. _____

## WRITE MORE ABOUT IT

1. **Write a Journal Entry**  Imagine that you are a young Spartan living in a physical-training camp. Write a journal entry that tells about your way of life. Include descriptions of the physical-training programs you are experiencing and how you feel about them.

2. **Write a Letter**  Write a letter to the editor of a newspaper. Explain whether you think it is important for city governments to hire people to beautify, build, or write about their cities. Include examples from ancient Athens.

3. **Write a Compare-and-Contrast Report**  Write a report that compares and contrasts Athens and Sparta. Discuss lifeways, ways of governing, and achievements.

4. **Write a Description**  The poet Homer described Crete as "a rich and lovely land, washed by the waves on every side." Think about how the land of Greece is described in the text. You may also want to find books that show pictures of Greece's physical features. Then write your own poetic description of the physical setting of Greece.

## USE VOCABULARY

For each pair of terms, write at least one sentence that shows how the terms are different from each other.

1. epic, myth

2. polis, agora

3. aristocracy, oligarchy

4. league, alliance

## CHECK UNDERSTANDING

1. Why was Greece a good center for trade?

2. Who was Homer?

3. For what did the Minoans use their huge palaces?

4. Why did the Spartans form a military culture?

5. What is majority rule?

6. What people were not included in Athenian democracy?

7. What were three reasons the people in the different Greek city-states felt a cultural connection with one another?

8. How did winning the Persian Wars affect Athens?

9. Why is the period of Alexander's rule known as the Hellenistic Age?

10. What happened to Alexander's empire after his death? Why?

## THINK CRITICALLY

1. **Past to Present**   How is the present-day government of the United States similar to the Athenian government under Pericles? How is it different?

2. **Think More About It**   In the city-states of ancient Greece, people met in agoras to exchange goods and to discuss news of the day. How are present-day places for shopping and talking different from the agoras of long ago?

3. **Personally Speaking**   Why do you think Alexander wanted control of an empire?

4. **Cause and Effect**   What effect did the thinkers of the Hellenistic Age have on later cultures?

## APPLY SKILLS

**How to Predict Likely Outcomes**   During the time of Alexander the Great, Greek culture strongly affected the Mediterranean region. Before you read Chapter 8, predict how the death of Alexander the Great affected further Greek influence in that region. Be sure to use the four-step process listed on page 228. As you read Chapter 8, see whether the information you learn supports your prediction.

## READ MORE ABOUT IT

*Ancient Greece* by Rowena Loverance and Tim Wood. Viking. This unusual book offers not only descriptions of early Greek life but also see-through cutaways. The cutaways let readers look into a Greek home, a marketplace, a theater, and a warship.

*The Ancient Greeks: In the Land of the Gods* by Sophie Descamps-Lequime and Denise Vernerey. Millbrook. This book gives information about daily life in ancient Greece, including details about eating habits, clothing, and games.

*The Olympics* by Jane Duden. Macmillan. The author provides readers a look at the modern Olympic Games through facts, trivia, and time lines. Some history of the ancient Olympics held in Greece is included as well.

# CHAPTER 8

# ANCIENT ROME

> **" Veni, vidi, vici. "**
> ("I came, I saw, I conquered.")
>
> Julius Caesar, after a victory in
> war in 47 B.C.

# The ROMAN REPUBLIC

LESSON 1

## Link to Our World

### What causes change in government today?

### Focus on the Main Idea
*As you read, look for changes in the government of Rome and the reasons for these changes.*

### Preview Vocabulary

| | |
|---|---|
| republic | plebeian |
| Senate | tribune |
| consul | veto |
| dictator | province |
| patrician | |

In A.D. 79 the ancient city of Pompeii was covered by ashes and stone from a volcanic eruption of Mount Vesuvius. The ashes and stone helped protect artifacts and artwork, such as the portrait above.

After the death of Alexander in 323 B.C., influence in the Mediterranean slowly shifted from Greece to Rome. Beginning as a small village on the peninsula of Italy, Rome grew to control a great empire. As Rome grew larger, its government changed to help meet the changing needs of the Romans.

## THE PENINSULA OF ITALY

The peninsula of Italy lies just west of the Balkan Peninsula in southern Europe. It looks like a long, high-heeled boot. The "toe" of the boot seems ready to kick away the nearby island of Sicily. Less than 100 miles (about 160 km) across the Mediterranean Sea lies the northern coast of Africa. Halfway up the peninsula the Tiber River flows east to west. Surrounding Italy in every direction but north are seas—the Adriatic in the east, the Tyrrhenian (tuh•REE•nee•uhn) in the west, and the Mediterranean in the south.

Because the hills and mountains in Italy are less rugged than those in Greece, greater travel, trade, and communication within the peninsula were possible. Also, the peninsula's fertile soil let early farmers raise many different crops to meet their needs and wants. Italy, however, had few good harbors, so overseas travel and overseas trade were difficult. Because of this, the early people of Italy traded more with each other than with outsiders as the Greeks had done.

Mountains, not seas, line the northern part of the peninsula. Along the northern border of Italy rises a snow-capped mountain range called the Alps. Another mountain range, the Apennines (AP•uh•nynz), runs along Italy's northeast coast.

**How did geography affect early people of the Italian peninsula?**

## THE FOUNDING OF ROME

People have lived on the peninsula of Italy for thousands of years. Around 1000 B.C. people known as Latins migrated from central Europe to the peninsula. They built villages near the banks of the Tiber River. Among seven hills along the river rose a small Latin farming village known as Rome.

The rolling land around Rome offered good soil for farming. It also had natural resources such as wood and stone for building. The inland location and hilly country protected the settlers of Rome from enemies. "Not without good reason did gods and men choose this spot as the site of a city," a Roman historian wrote.

The early farmers of Rome told colorful legends to explain the beginnings of their city. One legend says that a cruel uncle left twin baby boys to die on the banks of the Tiber. A mother wolf saved the twins from almost certain death. Romulus and Remus grew up to be heroes. In 753 B.C., according to the legend, they founded a city near where they had grown up. Romulus became the first king of the new city. His followers named the city Rome in his honor. Romulus promised that the small city would rise to greatness. "My Rome shall be the capital of the world," Romulus said.

**Why was the area along the Tiber a good place to settle?**

## FROM MONARCHY TO REPUBLIC

In about 600 B.C. a neighboring people called the Etruscans took control of Rome.

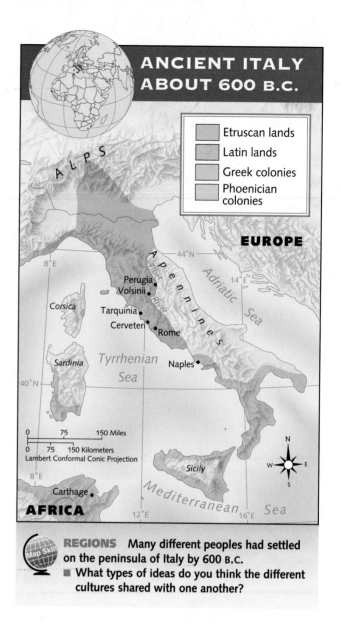

### ANCIENT ITALY ABOUT 600 B.C.

Etruscan lands
Latin lands
Greek colonies
Phoenician colonies

EUROPE

ALPS

Apennines

Adriatic Sea

44°N
14°E
8°E
Perugia
Volsinii
Corsica
Tarquinia
Cerveteri
Rome
Tyrrhenian Sea
Naples
Sardinia
40°N

0    75    150 Miles
0    75    150 Kilometers
Lambert Conformal Conic Projection
8°E

Sicily

Carthage
AFRICA
12°E
Mediterranean Sea
16°E

N
W    E
S

**REGIONS** Many different peoples had settled on the peninsula of Italy by 600 B.C.
■ What types of ideas do you think the different cultures shared with one another?

The Etruscans, who had frequently traded with the Greek colonies, introduced the Romans to Greek ideas and customs. Etruscan writing, which was based on the Greek alphabet, became the model for the Latin alphabet. After almost 100 years the Romans rebelled against a cruel Etruscan king called Tarquin the Proud. They ended the monarchy and started a new kind of government. Roman citizens now elected leaders to make all government decisions. They called their government a **republic**.

As in Athens, free males in the Roman Republic formed an assembly of citizens.

However, Roman citizens did not make all the decisions as citizens did in Athens. Instead, the Roman assembly elected representatives to make these decisions for them. The Romans called their council of representatives the **Senate**. From the Senate two members called **consuls** were then elected. The consuls ran the daily affairs of Rome and acted on the citizens' behalf.

To keep anyone from staying in power too long, the Roman Senate elected consuls every year. In an emergency Romans could appoint a dictator for a six-month term. A **dictator** is a ruler with absolute authority.

Some Roman citizens had more say in government than others. Roman society had long been divided into two social and economic classes. The **patricians** (puh•TRIH•shuhnz), the descendants of the city of Rome's earliest settlers, were one class. The **plebeians** (plih•BEE•uhnz)—the farmers, workers, merchants, and craftworkers, whose families came to Rome much later—made up the second class. The patricians had more rights than the plebeians. For example, patricians could be elected to the Senate, while plebeians could not.

In 494 B.C. the plebeians rebelled. They marched out of Rome to set up their own city. The patricians realized that Rome's economy would suffer without the plebeians. They agreed to let the plebeians elect ten special officials called **tribunes**. The tribunes could attend meetings of the Senate and **veto**, or refuse to approve, any laws they did not agree with.

In 451 and 450 B.C., the Roman government began recording its laws in a document called the Twelve Tables. Future Roman laws would build upon the Twelve Tables. In time the rights of plebeians and patricians would become more nearly equal.

Whether patrician or plebeian, men ruled all Roman households. A man could sell his family into slavery if he wanted to. But

The ancient Etruscans are particularly remembered for their fine art. This stone coffin, with the images of an Etruscan husband and wife, was made about 2,600 years ago. The Etruscans lived side by side with the Latins in ancient Italy. The people of Rome borrowed the Etruscan alphabet, technology, art, and customs as their own culture developed.

Because women were not allowed to have a say in the government, Roman senators were always men.

women did help make day-to-day decisions and often gave advice to their husbands. Women, though, took no direct part in governmental decision making.

**✓ What form of government replaced the Roman monarchy?**

## THE PATH OF ROMAN CONQUEST

Around 500 B.C. the Romans set out to conquer neighboring peoples. Better to attack than be attacked, they decided. By 274 B.C. the whole Italian peninsula belonged to Rome.

The Romans then looked across the Mediterranean Sea for rivals to conquer. Between 264 and 146 B.C., Rome fought three wars with Carthage, a city-state in northern Africa started by the Phoenicians. The wars are called the Punic (PYOO•nik) Wars, after the Roman name for Phoenician—*Punicus.*

The wars erupted because both Rome and Carthage wanted to control sea trade in the

Mediterranean. After a long fight Rome won the first of the Punic Wars. In the second war Carthage proved to be a serious threat to the city of Rome itself. Led by a general named Hannibal, Carthage's army marched on Rome. Starting from what is now Spain, Hannibal led his soldiers and war elephants over high, snow-covered mountains into Italy. A Roman historian later wrote about Hannibal:

66No work could tire his body or his spirit. Heat and cold were the same to him. . . . He was always the first into battle and the last to leave.99

Though tired, the soldiers of Carthage surprised the Romans with sudden and violent attacks. They fought so fiercely that they nearly defeated Rome. Then a Roman general named Scipio (SIH•pee•oh) made a surprising move. He left the Italian peninsula and attacked lands in northern Africa under the control of Carthage. Hannibal was forced to return and defend his home city. In 202 B.C.

Hannibal lost a key battle in the town of Zama near Carthage, and Carthage had to give up.

In 146 B.C. the third and final Punic War left Carthage in ruins. Many Carthaginians were sold as slaves.

By this time Greece, Macedonia, and parts of Southwest Asia were under Roman control. The Romans divided the land they now ruled into **provinces**, or self-governing regions. A Roman governor ruled each province. The people had to pay taxes to Rome, and many individuals were enslaved. For Rome the victory over Carthage meant a steady supply of grain to feed the growing number of people in the city.

✓ **What lands did Rome conquer between 500 and 146 B.C.?**

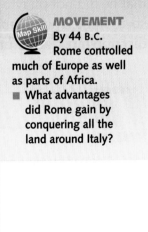

Hannibal's war methods are still studied by army leaders.

## FROM REPUBLIC TO DICTATORSHIP

The tax money from the provinces made the patricians richer, and the slaves made the plebeians poorer. Many plebeians lost their jobs to the enslaved workforce. Because of this, conflicts broke out between patricians and plebeians. Two brothers, Tiberius and Gaius Gracchus, tried to make changes in the laws to help the plebeians. However, the Senate rejected these changes. Both brothers were killed for their ideas.

For the next 50 years, many leaders tried to gain control of the republic. In 82 B.C., after a bloody civil war, Lucius Sulla became dictator. He ruled not just for six months, as Roman law allowed, but for three years. The Romans'

**LANDS CONTROLLED BY ROME, TO 44 B.C.**

ATLANTIC OCEAN

Rhine R.
EUROPE
ALPS
Po R.
Pyrenees
Apennines
Danube River
Black Sea
Byzantium
Tagus River
Rome
GREECE
Asia Minor
New Carthage (Cartagena)
Carthage
Zama
Athens
Antioch
Mediterranean Sea
Cyrene
Jerusalem
Alexandria
AFRICA
EGYPT
Nile R.
Red Sea

Roman lands, about 509 B.C.
New lands by 270 B.C.
New lands by 133 B.C.
New lands by 44 B.C.
→ Hannibal, 218–216 B.C.

N
W E
S

0     250     500 Miles
0   250   500 Kilometers
Azimuthal Equal-Area Projection

**MOVEMENT** By 44 B.C. Rome controlled much of Europe as well as parts of Africa.
■ What advantages did Rome gain by conquering all the land around Italy?

acceptance of absolute rule by one rather than many meant that the republic could not last much longer. Sulla retired in 79 B.C., and the office of consul was restored for a time. Such leaders as Pompey and Cicero (SIH•suh•roh) ruled as consuls after Sulla.

In 59 B.C. a Roman consul named Julius Caesar hungered to rule all Roman lands. Caesar put together a careful plan. His first move was to form an army and capture Gaul (today's France). His success in winning Gaul for the Romans proved his military genius. As governor of the new province of Gaul, Caesar kept close watch on Rome.

In 49 B.C. Caesar prepared to return to Rome. By this time the Senate feared that he would try to take over the Roman government. The Senate warned Caesar not to bring his soldiers past the Rubicon River, the border between Gaul and Italy. "The die is cast," Caesar shouted as he crossed the Rubicon with his army and declared war on the city of Rome. Civil war broke out as Caesar fought his enemies for power.

In 45 B.C. Julius Caesar was declared dictator of all Rome. By 44 B.C. it became clear that he did not plan to give up his rule after six months. The republic had become a dictatorship. Caesar proved to be a strong

## What?

### Roman Calendar

July, the seventh month of our modern calendar year, is named for Julius Caesar. Before Caesar's time, the calendar was not long enough to match the 365-day solar year. To solve this problem, Caesar added 67 days to the calendar. Then Caesar made the first year of the new calendar very long to get the new calendar back on track. The year 46 B.C. had 442 days! The Romans called this unusual year "the year of confusion."

Julius Caesar

leader. He immediately made changes, creating laws to help the poor. He also gave citizenship to more people.

Caesar's time of glory was short. He was stabbed to death in 44 B.C. on March 15, the Ides of March on the Roman calendar. Caesar's death led to a time of civil war.

✓ **What type of ruler was Julius Caesar?**

# LESSON 1 REVIEW

## Check Understanding

1. **Recall the Facts**   What three forms of government did Rome have between 600 and 44 B.C.?

2. **Focus on the Main Idea**   Why did Rome change its form of government?

## Think Critically

3. **Past to Present**   Has our country's government undergone changes? If so, describe the changes.

4. **Explore Viewpoints**   Only patricians could become senators and consuls in the early Roman Republic. How do you think a patrician would have felt about this? Why might a plebeian have felt differently?

## Show What You Know

**Writing Activity**   Imagine that you are a Roman politician trying to get people to vote for you. Write a speech promising good government for Rome.

# The ROMAN EMPIRE

LESSON 2

## Link to Our World

**What factors help unite many different peoples under one government today?**

**Focus on the Main Idea**
*As you read, look for reasons that many peoples united under the Roman Empire.*

**Preview Vocabulary**
forum         census
policy        legion
              basilica
              gladiator
              acid rain
              aqueduct

Julius Caesar's grandnephew, Octavian, later known as Augustus

After Julius Caesar's death a new leader rose up to rule the Roman lands. This new leader brought many different peoples into the Roman culture. Over the next few hundred years, more than 75 million people came to call themselves Romans.

## ROME BECOMES AN EMPIRE

Julius Caesar's death left Rome without a leader. Crowds gathered daily in Rome's **forum**, or public square. There they listened as people who wished to be leaders spoke for or against the **policies**, or plans, that Julius Caesar had wanted to carry out.

Meanwhile, Octavian (ahk•TAY•vee•uhn), Caesar's grandnephew, and Mark Antony, a general in the army, had gained control of all Roman lands. Octavian claimed the western part of the empire. Antony claimed the eastern part, made up of Asia Minor, Syria, and Egypt. However, Antony fell in love with Cleopatra, the Egyptian queen, and they planned to set up their own empire. Octavian declared war on Antony and Cleopatra when he learned of their plan.

In 31 B.C. Octavian and Antony met in a great sea battle near Actium in Greece. Octavian defeated Antony and Cleopatra and gained absolute leadership of all Roman lands.

In 27 B.C. the Roman Senate gave Octavian the title *Augustus.* The title means "respected one" or "holy one." Octavian has been known ever since as Augustus Caesar, or simply Augustus.

## THE ROMAN EMPIRE UNDER AUGUSTUS, 27 B.C. TO A.D. 14

EUROPE

ATLANTIC OCEAN

GAUL

Rhine R.

Danube River

SPAIN

Rome

Adriatic Sea

Tyrrhenian Sea

Ionian Sea

Black Sea

Byzantium

Asia Minor

Aegean Sea

GREECE    Athens

Antioch

Carthage

Mediterranean Sea

Cyrene

Alexandria

EGYPT

Nile R.

Red Sea

Thebes

AFRICA

0    250    500 Miles
0    250    500 Kilometers
Azimuthal Equal-Area Projection

Area of empire

N S E W

**PLACE**
Augustus's empire included lands in Europe, Asia, and Africa. The Roman Empire stretched for thousands of miles.
■ How do you think ancient Romans traveled to Carthage, by land or water?

Upon gaining control of Rome, Augustus boasted,

❝I freed the Roman Republic from the control of those who assassinated Julius Caesar. . . . The Roman Senate, the knights, and all the Roman people have called me 'Father of the Country.'❞

Augustus was Rome's first true emperor, but he never called himself by this title. The new leader believed that he was continuing the Roman Republic. Yet, unlike in a republic, Augustus ruled year after year after year.

The Roman people cherished the idea of a republic, so Augustus made sure his government seemed to be representative. But his rule signaled the end of the Roman Republic.

### ✓ Who became Rome's first emperor?

## THE AGE OF AUGUSTUS

Augustus turned out to be the strong leader the Romans wanted. Under Augustus a *Pax Romana*, or "Roman Peace," spread across the empire. This time of peace and unity for the Romans lasted for more than 200 years—from 27 B.C. to A.D. 180, long after Augustus's death. During this time, the empire grew to about 2½ million square miles (6.5 million sq km).

Augustus began his rule by making changes in the Roman government. He carefully chose the people for top government jobs, such as governors for the provinces. Like Julius Caesar, he passed laws that made more men eligible for citizenship. These policies helped create a government that was popular and strong enough to hold the empire together.

Over the years Roman laws were created so that people would be treated more fairly and equally. One law said that a person is innocent until proven guilty. Another law stated that people could not be forced to speak against themselves in a court of law. These principles are still important to our legal system today.

The Romans also created the idea of a **census**, or count of a country's people. The census helped the government make sure that all the people paid their taxes.

To help keep peace and unity, Augustus depended on the Roman army. The well-trained army was divided into large groups called **legions** (LEE•juhnz). A legion might have as many as 6,000 men. Augustus had legions stationed along the borders of the empire to keep invaders out.

The roads the army built and traveled on also helped unite the Roman people. The Roman road system was built to help legions move quickly from province to province. But traders and travelers used them, too. In time the roads connected almost all parts of the empire to Rome. The saying "All roads lead to Rome" came from this time. Roman roads brought together goods and ideas from all over the empire. The movement of ideas led to cultural borrowing between provinces.

 **How did the army and its road system unite the people of the Roman Empire?**

## PRIDE IN ROME

Augustus felt that the city of Rome did not look grand enough for the center of a great empire. He called for new government offices, libraries, temples, and public baths and ordered that existing buildings be rebuilt. "I found Rome a city of bricks and left it a city of marble," he said.

Around the Palatine hill in the center of Rome stood huge marble government buildings called **basilicas**. New temples and other buildings rose beside them. Around them merchants in small booths sold fresh meats and vegetables, cloth, and pottery. The rich could buy fine things from faraway parts of the empire such as Egypt and Spain. For those who could read, there were scrolls written by hand on Egyptian papyrus for sale.

The influence of Greek culture could be seen in every new building. Roman builders admired the beauty of the Greek building style. They used the straight Greek columns

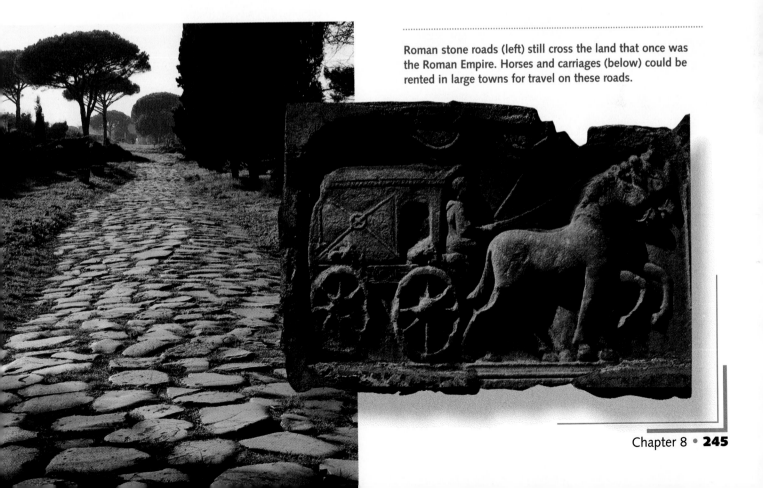

Roman stone roads (left) still cross the land that once was the Roman Empire. Horses and carriages (below) could be rented in large towns for travel on these roads.

and beams in their own buildings. Then the Romans added ideas of their own, such as domes. They also used arches, a structure they borrowed from the Etruscans.

The Romans enjoyed entertainment, so some of the new buildings were theaters and sports arenas. The largest arena, the Colosseum, was completed in A.D. 80, after Augustus's death. Here as many as 50,000 Romans watched battles between **gladiators**, who were slaves and prisoners forced to fight, often to their death.

The buildings in Rome gave leaders all over the empire the idea of rebuilding their cities in the same way. As far away as Britain and Syria, people built forums in the centers of their cities. Around the forums they built temples, baths, libraries, and arenas.

Some of Rome's ancient buildings still stand today. However, the survival of these buildings is in question. A type of pollution called acid rain is damaging the ancient ruins. **Acid rain** is water mixed with gases caused by the burning of fossil fuels, such as oil. The mixture forms acids that fall to earth with the rain.

All over the empire Romans built many aqueducts. An **aqueduct** uses bridges and canals to carry water from place to place. The stone aqueducts of the Roman Empire carried water from far-off rivers to the cities.

✓ **What types of buildings were put up in Rome?**

## LITERATURE, ARTS, AND LANGUAGE

Rome was the leader of the Mediterranean region, but Romans often looked to Greece for cultural ideas. Roman artists and sculptors copied Greek art. Roman writers copied

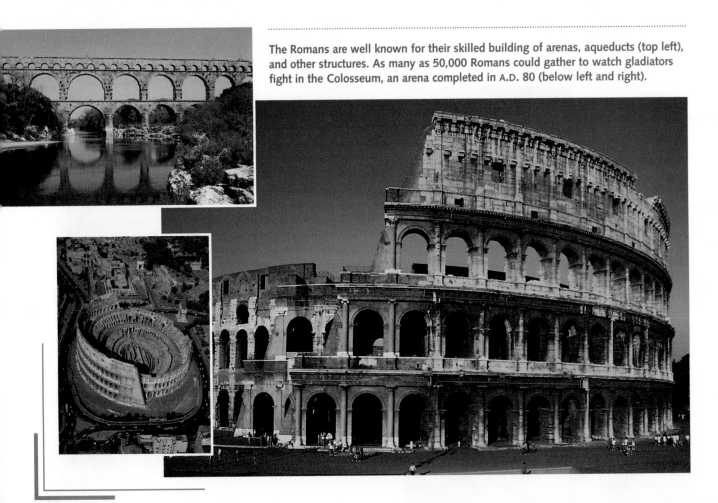

The Romans are well known for their skilled building of arenas, aqueducts (top left), and other structures. As many as 50,000 Romans could gather to watch gladiators fight in the Colosseum, an arena completed in A.D. 80 (below left and right).

# What?

## Public Baths

The Roman government built many large pools and baths. There people not only washed themselves but also met their friends or discussed business. Some Roman baths even contained libraries and shops. The Romans built baths all over the lands they had conquered. Ruins of Roman baths can be found in such places as Britain, France, Israel, Syria, Tunisia, and Algeria.

Greek writing styles. The ideas of the Greek philosophers Socrates, Plato, and Aristotle also spread to Rome. As the Roman poet Horace said, "Conquered Greece conquered its uncultured conqueror and brought the arts to Rome."

The Romans often borrowed the ideas of ➡ the Greeks. This statue of the Greek goddess Athena is a Roman copy of an early Greek statue.

Augustus asked Roman artists and writers to create works that would bring out patriotic feelings among the Roman people. Above all Augustus wanted an epic to glorify Rome as the *Iliad* and the *Odyssey* had glorified Greece. So a poet named Virgil (VER•juhl) wrote the *Aeneid* (ih•NEE•uhd), which gives the poet's view of early Roman history. As Augustus had hoped, the *Aeneid* stirred the feelings of Romans everywhere.

Language also helped bring together all parts of the Roman Empire. As Roman soldiers and traders traveled through the provinces, they carried the Latin language with them. Latin came to be used in government and education in all the Roman provinces. Latin became an important part of the Roman way of life that spread across the empire.

✔ **In what ways did the arts and literature help unify the Roman Empire?**

# LESSON 2 REVIEW

## Check Understanding

1. **Recall the Facts**   What improvements in government and the arts were made after Augustus became emperor of Rome?
2. **Focus on the Main Idea**   What helped unify the many different peoples of the Roman Empire?

## Think Critically

3. **Explore Viewpoints**   Why do you think Augustus liked to use peaceful ways to bring together the people of his empire?

4. **Past to Present**   Like the Roman Empire, the United States is a nation of many cultures. What unites this country's people?

## Show What You Know

**Map Activity**   Look at the map on page 244. Using this map as a guide, make a model or a relief map of the Roman Empire. Show the borders of the present-day countries that now occupy these lands, and write in their names. Use one color to shade all the lands that made up the Roman Empire.

# How To

# Compare Historical Maps

## Why Is This Skill Important?

One way to learn about history is to study historical maps. A **historical map** gives information about the past. Some historical maps show where events took place. Others show how the world looked at a certain time in the past. Knowing how to use historical maps can help you learn how boundaries have changed or what different names have been given to the same area at different times.

## MAP A: ROME IN 274 B.C.

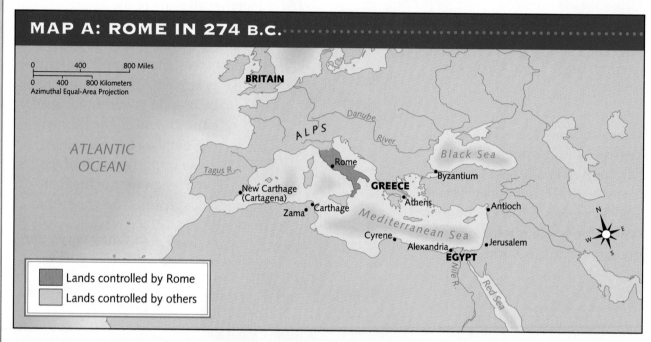

0   400   800 Miles
0   400   800 Kilometers
Azimuthal Equal-Area Projection

BRITAIN

ATLANTIC OCEAN

ALPS

Danube River

Rome

Black Sea

Byzantium

Tagus R.

New Carthage (Cartagena)

GREECE

Athens

Antioch

Zama   Carthage

Mediterranean Sea

Cyrene

Alexandria

Jerusalem

EGYPT

Nile R.

Red Sea

Lands controlled by Rome
Lands controlled by others

## MAP B: ROME IN A.D. 117

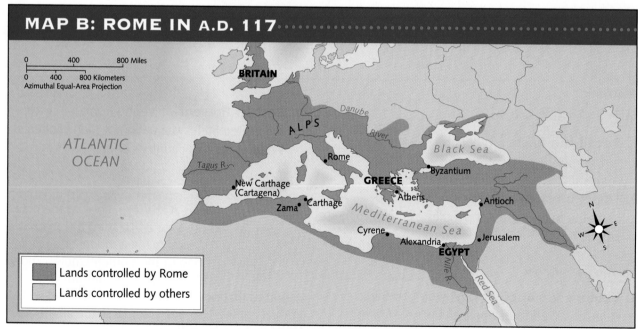

0   400   800 Miles
0   400   800 Kilometers
Azimuthal Equal-Area Projection

BRITAIN

ATLANTIC OCEAN

ALPS

Danube River

Rome

Black Sea

Byzantium

Tagus R.

New Carthage (Cartagena)

GREECE

Athens

Antioch

Zama   Carthage

Mediterranean Sea

Cyrene

Alexandria

Jerusalem

EGYPT

Nile R.

Red Sea

Lands controlled by Rome
Lands controlled by others

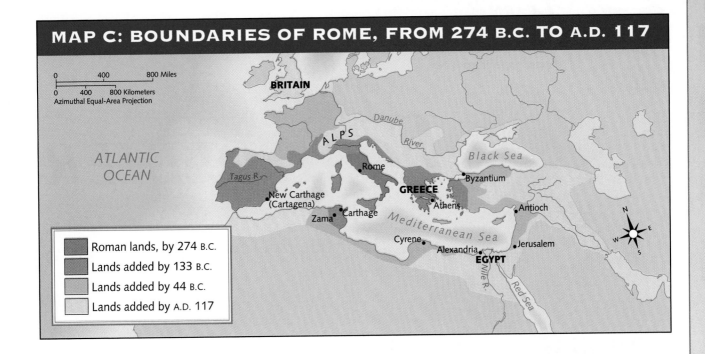

# MAP C: BOUNDARIES OF ROME, FROM 274 B.C. TO A.D. 117

0   400   800 Miles
0   400   800 Kilometers
Azimuthal Equal-Area Projection

ATLANTIC
OCEAN

BRITAIN

ALPS

Danube
River

Black Sea

Rome

Byzantium

GREECE
Athens

Antioch

Tagus R.

New Carthage
(Cartagena)

Zama   Carthage

Mediterranean Sea

Cyrene

Alexandria

Jerusalem

EGYPT

Nile R.

Red Sea

N E S W

Roman lands, by 274 B.C.
Lands added by 133 B.C.
Lands added by 44 B.C.
Lands added by A.D. 117

## Understand the Process

History books and many atlases contain historical maps. Often the title or key of a historical map tells what year or time period is shown on the map.

Map A shows ancient Roman lands in 274 B.C., when Rome controlled the whole Italian peninsula. The brown areas on the map show lands governed by Rome. The green areas show lands controlled by other groups.

The Roman Empire grew until it reached its greatest size under the emperor Trajan in A.D. 117. As on Map A, the brown areas on Map B show lands governed by Rome. The green areas show lands controlled by other groups.

Now look at Map C above. It combines information from Map A and Map B. It also shows how the boundaries of Rome changed from 274 B.C. to A.D. 117. Look at the map key to learn what each color means. Then use the questions to help you gather information about the growth of the Roman Empire.

1. What color is the land controlled by Rome in 274 B.C.?
2. What lands did Rome add to its empire by 133 B.C.?

3. By what year did Rome take control of Britain?
4. By what year did Rome take control of
   a. Alexandria?
   b. Athens?
   c. Byzantium?
   d. Carthage?
   e. Jerusalem?
5. Between what years did Roman lands grow the most? How can you tell?
6. By what year did Rome gain its first land in Africa?
7. Was Athens under Rome's control in 100 B.C.?

## Think and Apply

Use an atlas to find a historical map showing the territorial growth of the United States. Study how the map uses colors or symbols to show change over time. Using the map, write a paragraph that describes how and when your state became part of the United States. Then draw your own map to go with your paragraph. Using different colors, show how the United States looked before and after your state joined the Union. Share your paragraph and your map with a partner.

# The FOOTSOLDIER

*by Martin Windrow and Richard Hook*

Sextus Duratius, from the book *The Footsoldier*

*For centuries Rome's army consisted of volunteers, citizens who served only in times of need. As the Roman Empire grew, leaders discovered that a new type of soldier was necessary. This soldier was a trained fighter, paid by the Roman government to serve full-time. The following story tells about the life of a professional soldier, Sextus Duratius, 2nd Augusta Legion. As you read, think about what makes people willing to lead the life of a soldier.*

As a soldier, in what he considered the finest legion in the Empire, Sextus could hope for travel, adventure, and promotion: promotion, perhaps, to the unapproachable godlike status of a senior centurion, commanding a cohort of 500 men. In return for hard knocks and unquestioning obedience he would receive 337 ½ silver pennies a year, in three installments—less compulsory deductions for rations, boots, replacement of lost kit, burial insurance, and anything else the penny-pinching clerks could think up. He might get handsome bonuses from time to time—if he was in an important victory, or if a new Emperor came to power. Part of his pay would be safely banked for him, and if he survived his term of enlistment he would get a generous lump-sum pension, or a grant of land instead. It was not at all a bad deal—provided you lived to collect it.

During the first months Sextus often doubted that he would survive his first year. He learned the soldier's trade the hard way, harried about the parade ground and practice field by the brazen tongues and vinewood cudgels[1] of the instructing centurions. He learned how to keep his armor clean and bright, even if it meant sitting up half the night. He learned how to march twenty-five miles a day in full kit,[2] rain or shine, with hob-nailed sandals raising blisters on his blisters. As often as not he reeled back to barracks only to be herded straight off to the practice ground to dig ditches and build ramparts—and to see them filled in again, ready for tomorrow's session. He learned to handle javelin, sword and shield. He suffered more bruises and grazes than he could count from the double-weight wooden swords they practiced with before being trusted with Roman steel in their shaky hands. He learned to recognize the signals for the different battle formations—the "wedge," the "saw," and all the other tricks of combat. And he learned just who, when, and how much to bribe, in order to avoid the frequent appearance of his name on the centurion's little lists for latrine-cleaning, cookhouse-cleaning, camp-cleaning, and a dozen other traps for the unwary recruit. Before two years passed he was a thoroughly trained, disciplined, and dangerous professional soldier.

It had been eight years before Sextus and his comrades started their long journey by foot and barge and ship from the familiar surroundings of Strasbourg, with its stone barracks and

---

[1] **cudgels:** heavy clubs
[2] **in full kit:** with all supplies

....................................................

Roman soldiers fighting the Saxons for land in what is now Great Britain built this fort (below). Much later a castle was built within the walls of the fort.
(Michael Holford Photographs)

Roman soldiers protected themselves with helmets, leg armor, and body armor (right). The armor helped them advance against their enemies.
(Roma, Museo della Civilta Romana/Scala/Art Resource/NY)

Roman soldiers often faced hand-to-hand battles, charging horses, and incoming spears. The service of Roman soldiers is remembered on this stone carving. (Scala/Art Resource/NY)

lively civilian town, to the empty beaches and rolling, forested hills of Britain. In that time he had served on two or three short local expeditions on the German frontier—nothing serious, not much more than tax-gathering trips enlivened by the occasional brisk skirmish. He discovered that his training really worked, and that gave him confidence.

He had needed it, on this rather frightening expedition into the far northern mists. Only the gods knew what horrors awaited a man in these black woods and wind-haunted uplands, to say nothing of the dangers of drowning in the choppy grey seas or dying under the spears of the Britons. They were only savages, of course, but there had been a lot of them in some of the early battles of the invasion. But the magic of Roman arms and discipline worked again, and Sextus soon forgot his doubts and fears.

When the Augusta was detached from the other legions and marched westwards things improved even more. Away from the eyes of the generals and staff officers, the Legate Vespasian proved a fair and decent commander. He expected his legionaries to do their duty, and do it quickly and thoroughly; but he didn't nag at men who were fighting almost every day.

Tonight, for instance, when the battle was over—and to judge from the thickening smoke and the noise from beyond the gateway it wouldn't be long now—Sextus could hope for a good night's rest. Perhaps the auxiliary cohorts which hadn't been in action would be ordered to dig the ramparts and pitch the tents for the men who had fought today? At any rate, Sextus probably wouldn't have to stand guard.

## Literature Review

1. What led Sextus to join the army?
2. Why do you think people serve in the armed forces today?
3. Do you think Sextus would want his son to join the army? Make a list of the good points and bad points Sextus might mention about serving as a Roman soldier.

# LESSON 4

# BEGINNINGS of CHRISTIANITY

## Link to Our World

### How do religions begin, grow, and gain influence?

### Focus on the Main Idea
Look for ways the Christian religion spread through the Roman Empire and changed Roman life.

### Preview Vocabulary
messiah
crucifixion
apostle
Christianity

New Testament
Gospels
Old Testament
martyr

Belief in the many Roman gods was another bond for the people of the Roman Empire in its early days. As the empire grew, so did the number of religions. One religion—Christianity—began to spread across Roman lands. This new religion would have a lasting effect on the world.

## RELIGION AND THE ROMAN EMPIRE

Augustus was not only the ruler of the Roman Empire but also a leader of religion. He wanted all citizens to take part in religious ceremonies. He knew that this would help bring unity to the growing numbers of Romans.

Like many cultures of long ago, the Romans worshipped many gods. Saturn was the most ancient of all the Roman gods. Others included Mars, the god of war, and Ceres, the goddess of the harvest and agriculture. The month of January—the beginning of the new year—is named for Janus, the Roman god of doors, gates, and beginnings. In times of war the doors to the temple of Janus were opened. When peace came, the Romans closed the doors.

Although the Romans had their own religion, they often accepted the gods and the beliefs of the peoples whom they conquered. As a result, their religion included many Greek gods and Greek ideas. Often only the names of the gods were changed. For example, the Greek goddess Hera, who protected marriage and women, became the Roman goddess Juno. Zeus, the ruler of the Greek gods, became Jupiter, the main Roman god.

Belief in the gods was an important part of Roman life. The Romans believed harm would come to the empire if people did not respect the Roman gods. So Roman law punished those who refused to worship these gods. However, Roman control over religion was not always carried out. For example, the Romans allowed the Jewish people to follow their own religious leaders, laws, and teachings. This was what the Persians and others had done, too. Jews lived not only in the Roman province of Judaea but also throughout the Roman Empire.

 **Why did the Romans want everyone to respect the Roman gods?**

## THE RISE OF CHRISTIANITY

One belief of Judaism is that a messiah (muh•SY•uh) will come to bring world peace. The **messiah** would be a wise leader who would establish the kingdom of God on Earth. During the reign of a local ruler named Herod, news came that the Messiah had been born. It was reported that a child named Jesus had been born to a woman named Mary in the village of Bethlehem in Judaea. In later years there were reports about his teachings and performance of miracles.

Like other Jewish teachers Jesus taught the beliefs of Judaism. As he traveled through Judaea, Jesus taught belief in one God and in the Ten Commandments. His message of love

The Good Shepherd (left) and the *Chi-Rho* design (right), formed from the first two letters of the word *Christ* in Greek, were early symbols of Christianity.

for others and help for the poor was also based on Jewish ideas. Jesus, however, said that he was the Son of God and that he had been sent by God to redeem humankind for its sins. Followers believed he was the Messiah.

Roman and Jewish leaders in the province of Judaea became concerned as more and more people listened to the words of Jesus. Jewish leaders disliked the fact that Jesus did not strictly follow Jewish law. Roman leaders thought that Jesus might take over the empire and set up his own kingdom. In about A.D. 30 Pontius Pilate, the Roman governor of Judaea, ordered Jesus to be put to death by **crucifixion** (kroo•suh•FIK•shuhn). This type of execution meant that Jesus was to be nailed to a cross and left to die.

Twelve men, called the **apostles** (uh•PAH•suhlz), had become Jesus' most trusted followers. The apostles told of Jesus rising from the dead three days after his crucifixion. After the resurrection, the apostles began to spread Jesus' teachings.

The Roman roads that connected the empire soon also carried the message of Jesus. Wherever the followers of Jesus traveled, they gained new believers. Later followers preached in Greek, the language used in the eastern part of the Roman Empire. The Greek term for *messiah* was *christos*. Jesus came to be known as Jesus Christus, or Jesus Christ. His growing number of

Catacombs (left) were underground tunnels used as burial places for Christians persecuted and killed by the Romans. Many catacombs were decorated with paintings of early Christian scenes (above) or funeral writings (below left).

followers came to be known as Christians, and their religion as **Christianity**.

A convert, or new believer, named Paul was among the first to write down the teachings of Christianity. In many of the empire's largest cities, Paul started Christian churches. His letters to the members of these churches form a large part of the **New Testament**. This part of the Christian Bible tells about the life and teachings of Jesus and about his followers. The group of four books of the New Testament that describe Jesus' life and actions is called the **Gospels**. The Gospels, which means "good news," were written after Jesus' death by followers Matthew, Mark, Luke, and John. The first part of the Bible, the **Old Testament**, contains the same books as in the Jewish Bible.

 **What are some ways in which the message of Jesus spread through the Roman Empire?**

## ROME REACTS TO THE NEW RELIGION

Roman officials saw Christianity spreading across the empire and feared that the Christians might try to take over. To the Roman leaders, the growth of Christianity threatened the entire Roman Empire. So they arrested and persecuted, or mistreated, Christians who refused to worship Roman gods.

Around A.D. 112 Pliny (PLIH•nee) the Younger, a Roman government official in Asia Minor, explained his actions to Christians in this way:

66 With those who have been brought before me as Christians, I have acted as follows: I asked them whether they were Christians. If they answer yes twice, I threaten to punish them and ask a third time. Those who continue to say yes, I order executed. . . . I dismissed those who said they had never been Christians and those who offered sacrifices to our gods. 99

Roman emperor Trajan replied

66 You have acted rightly. . . . You must not seek out the Christians. But, if they are brought to you and refuse to honor our gods, then they must be punished. 99

Many early Christians became **martyrs** (MAR•terz), people who suffer or die for their beliefs. Some Christians faced hungry lions in the Colosseum and other arenas while Romans watched for entertainment.

The actions of the Romans made many Christians hold on to their beliefs even more strongly than before. Christians were willing to show their faith by dying for it.

Impressed by the power of this new religion, more Romans became Christians. The new religion flourished and grew throughout the Roman Empire.

 **How did the Romans' cruel treatment of Christians affect Christianity?**

## CONSTANTINE ACCEPTS CHRISTIANITY

As Christianity was growing stronger, the Roman government was growing weaker. The cost of running the empire was very high. Government workers had to be paid, and road work was costly. These were just a few of the empire's many expenses. The government increased taxes, but even this did

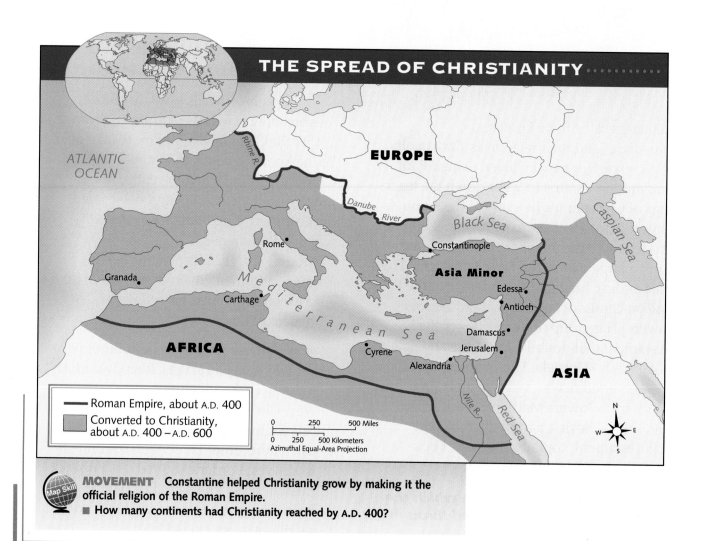

**THE SPREAD OF CHRISTIANITY**

- Roman Empire, about A.D. 400
- Converted to Christianity, about A.D. 400 – A.D. 600

0    250    500 Miles
0    250    500 Kilometers
Azimuthal Equal-Area Projection

**MOVEMENT** Constantine helped Christianity grow by making it the official religion of the Roman Empire.
■ How many continents had Christianity reached by A.D. 400?

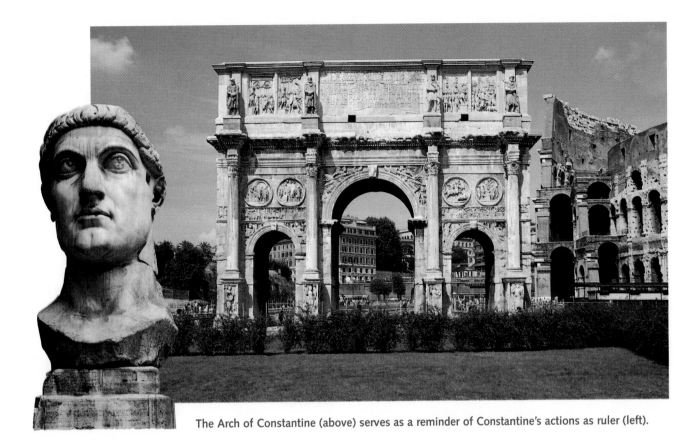

The Arch of Constantine (above) serves as a reminder of Constantine's actions as ruler (left).

not meet the empire's needs. It only caused great hardships for Roman citizens.

At the same time, the Roman Empire faced attack from every side. Outsiders frequently crossed the empire's borders and forced Romans into battle. Invaders from the north attacked Gaul and Spain. The Persians tried to seize Roman lands in Asia. An African people called the Berbers (BER•berz) raided Roman lands in North Africa.

In addition, many of the Roman emperors between A.D. 180 and 312 governed badly. They lost the respect of those they ruled. Also, the empire had grown so large that many of its citizens had never been to Rome. They did not care about being a part of the empire. Even the soldiers who fought to keep the empire together felt little loyalty to Rome. Instead, they gave their loyalty to their generals. Wars broke out within the empire as generals fought one another.

In A.D. 312 two Roman generals who wanted to be emperor faced each other at Rome's Milvian Bridge. One of them, named Constantine (KAHN•stuhn•teen), was not a Christian, but something had just happened that changed his life. According to Constantine the Greek letters for *christos* appeared in the sky above him. Over these letters were the Latin words *in hoc signo vinces*, meaning "In this sign you will conquer." So Constantine ordered his soldiers to paint crosses on their shields. The cross was a symbol of Christianity because Jesus had died on a cross.

Constantine won the battle and became emperor. Unlike Roman generals before him, Constantine did not thank the Roman gods. Instead, Constantine began to support Christianity. In A.D. 313 the Edict of Milan made Christianity an accepted religion. Later in that century Christianity became the official religion of the Roman Empire.

 **How did Constantine help Christianity grow?**

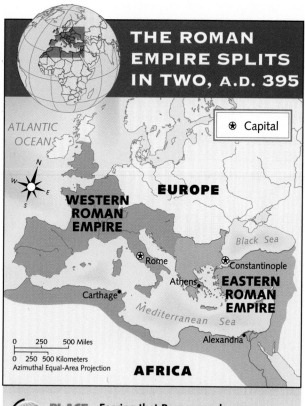

## THE ROMAN EMPIRE SPLITS IN TWO, A.D. 395

 Capital

ATLANTIC OCEAN

EUROPE

WESTERN ROMAN EMPIRE

Black Sea

Rome

Constantinople

Athens

Carthage

EASTERN ROMAN EMPIRE

Mediterranean Sea

Alexandria

AFRICA

0   250   500 Miles
0   250   500 Kilometers
Azimuthal Equal-Area Projection

 **PLACE** Fearing that Rome was dangerous, Constantine moved the Roman Empire's capital to Byzantium. Eventually, the empire began to decline and split in two.
■ Which city became the capital of the eastern part?

## THE DECLINE OF ROME

Constantine did not think Rome was a good place for the capital of the Roman Empire. He felt that Rome was too far from the center of things. He also feared that Rome was unsafe. Constantine chose the city of Byzantium (buh•ZAN•tee•uhm) on the shores of the Black Sea as the new capital. In A.D. 330 Byzantium was renamed Constantinople (kahn•stan•tuhn•OH•puhl), "the city of Constantine."

Rome's power declined after A.D. 330. Since the emperor no longer lived there, many other people left the city of Rome. Then in A.D. 410, Visigoths, led by their king, Alaric (AL•uh•rik), crossed the Alps and attacked the city of Rome.

Few Romans were ready to defend their city. The city of Rome lived on, but it no longer had much power. However, it was still important as the headquarters of the Christian Church.

The Roman Empire split apart. The eastern part of the former empire would keep Roman ways alive for centuries. The western part, which broke into small kingdoms, would see great changes.

The message of Jesus spread far beyond the Roman Empire. Christianity has brought together people of many races, languages, and cultures all over the world.

✓ **What made the city of Rome lose its importance in the Roman Empire?**

## LESSON 4 REVIEW

### Check Understanding

1. **Recall the Facts** Why did the Romans fear the growth of Christianity?
2. **Focus on the Main Idea** What are some ways Christianity spread through the Roman Empire?

### Think Critically

3. **Think More About It** Why did people help Christianity grow throughout the Roman Empire?
4. **Past to Present** How does religious freedom affect the United States today?
5. **Cause and Effect** What do you think caused the Roman Empire to split apart? What effects do you think the split had on the people of the Roman Empire?

### Show What You Know

**Speech Activity** Many early Christians risked their lives for their religion. Today, people still take stands for their beliefs. Look through magazines and newspapers for stories of people today who stand up for what they believe. Make a brief oral report about one person who took such a stand.

# Read a Telescoping Time Line

## Why Is This Skill Important?

Think of a time in your life that was very important to you. Maybe it was a vacation you took last summer. Perhaps it was when a favorite relative came for a visit. You probably want to remember every single detail of each day of that special time. In the same way, you may want to remember or take a closer look at a certain time in history. You may want to know more of the details about that time.

One way to look at the details of events in history is with a telescoping time line. Just as a telescope helps you take a closer look at a faraway object, a **telescoping time line** helps you take a closer look at a long-ago time. Knowing how to read a telescoping time line can help you learn the details of events in history.

## Understand the Process

The time line of early Christianity on this page shows the years between A.D. 1 and A.D. 350. Each date on the main part of the time line marks a period of 50 years. Like the inches or centimeters on a ruler, the dates on the time line are evenly spaced. The time line lists specific events that took place in A.D. 30, 64, 312, 313, 325, 330, and 337.

To show the events of A.D. 312, 313, 325, and 330, part of the time line was expanded, or enlarged. The second part of the time line gives a "telescope" view of that time period. The dates on the telescoping part of the time line are also evenly spaced. However, each of its dates marks a period of only 5 years.

Use the information on both parts of the time line to answer these questions:

1. Which event took place first, the issuing of the Edict of Milan or the death of Constantine? How do you know?
2. Was the Edict of Milan issued before or after Constantine became emperor? How do you know?
3. Did Constantinople become the capital of the Roman Empire before or after Constantine's death? How do you know?
4. What do you think the time line would look like if it had no telescoping part and all of the events were shown on the main time line?

## Think and Apply

Use events of your school year to make your own time line. Show one month in detail by including a telescoping section. Share your time line with a family member.

EARLY CHRISTIANITY

A.D. 1    A.D. 50    A.D. 100    A.D. 150    A.D. 200    A.D. 250    A.D. 300    A.D. 350

**A.D. 30**
Crucifixion of Jesus

**A.D. 64**
First persecution of Christians

A.D. 310    A.D. 315    A.D. 320    A.D. 325    A.D. 330

**A.D. 312**
Constantine becomes emperor

**A.D. 313**
Edict of Milan

Christians in Rome gain freedom to worship

**A.D. 325**
First world-wide council of the church meets at Nicaea to standardize Christian teachings

**A.D. 330**
Constantinople becomes capital of the Roman Empire

**A.D. 337**
Constantine dies

## CONNECT MAIN IDEAS

Use this organizer to show that you understand how the chapter's main ideas are connected. Copy the organizer onto a separate sheet of paper. Then complete it by writing two details to support each main idea.

**The Roman Republic**
Over the years the forms of government in Rome changed.

1. _____
   _____
2. _____
   _____

**Ancient Rome**

**The Roman Empire**
Many people were united under the Roman Empire.

1. _____
   _____
2. _____
   _____

**Beginnings of Christianity**
Christianity spread through the Roman Empire and changed Roman life.

1. _____
   _____
2. _____
   _____

## WRITE MORE ABOUT IT

1. **Write a History Lesson**   Describe in your own words how Rome conquered its neighbors.

2. **Write a Speech**   Write a speech that tells why you, a Roman emperor, think the Romans were able to unite many different peoples under one empire.

3. **Write a Diary Entry**   Imagine that you are a Roman soldier during the time of the Punic Wars. Write a diary entry that describes your thoughts about battle after seeing Hannibal and his soldiers on their war elephants.

4. **Write a Message That Explains**   Write a message that might have appeared in the ancient catacombs, the underground burial places for Christians in the Roman Empire. Explain in your message why the ancient Romans persecuted Christians.

USE VOCABULARY

For each pair of terms, write at least one sentence that shows how the terms are related.

1. patrician, plebeian

2. tribune, veto

3. forum, policy

4. Christianity, New Testament

## CHECK UNDERSTANDING

1. Who were Romulus and Remus?

2. What led the Romans to establish a republic?

3. How did Julius Caesar plan to rule Rome?

4. Why did Augustus call for new government offices, libraries, temples, and public baths?

5. What culture's influence was seen in every new Roman building?

6. Why did Virgil write the *Aeneid*?

7. Why did Roman leaders arrest, persecute, and mistreat Christians?

8. What made Constantine begin to support Christianity?

9. Why did Constantine make Byzantium his new capital?

## THINK CRITICALLY

1. **Cause and Effect**   How did Rome's conquest of land affect the lives of the patricians and plebeians?

2. **Personally Speaking**   Do you think that Julius Caesar was right to declare himself dictator of Rome? Explain your answer.

3. **Past to Present**   What Roman principles are still important to the United States legal system?

4. **Think More About It**   Why did the cruel actions of Roman leaders make many Christians hold on to their beliefs more strongly?

APPLY SKILLS

 **How to Compare Historical Maps**
Use Map C, on page 249, and the map titled "The Spread of Christianity," on page 256, to answer these questions.

1. Was the Roman Empire larger in A.D. 400 or in A.D. 117?

2. By A.D. 600 had Christianity come to all the lands that were parts of the Roman Empire in A.D. 117?

3. Why is a line used to show the borders of the Roman Empire on the map on page 256 rather than color as on the map on page 249?

**How to Read a Telescoping Time Line**   Use the information on the time line on page 259 to answer the questions.

1. Did Constantine become emperor nearer to the time of the crucifixion of Jesus or to the time of Constantinople becoming the capital of the Roman Empire? How do you know?

2. About how many years after the first persecution of Christians did Christians in Rome gain freedom to worship? How do you know?

3. Why is there a telescope view of the time period between A.D. 312 and A.D. 330?

READ MORE ABOUT IT

*Ancient Rome* by Simon James. Random House. Details about the ancient Roman people are revealed through the artifacts they left behind.

*The Roman Empire and the Dark Ages* by Giovanni Caselli. Bedrick. The author tells about the people of Rome of 50 B.C. to A.D. 1300.

# THE GIFTS OF CIVILIZATIONS LONG AGO

You can find many signs of earlier cultures in your life today. Look for the Latin words *e pluribus unum,* "out of many, one," on a coin. You might also find words written in Latin on government buildings. Look at such buildings in your town. They may look like those built by the Greeks and Romans long ago.

The ancient Greek and Roman cultures have affected present-day American life in many ways, especially in the areas of government and law. Many of our ideas about democracy came from the Greeks. And law students still study the ideas of Cicero, a Roman lawyer who lived from 106 to 43 B.C. United States citizens also elect national, state, and local representatives in much the same way that the Romans chose lawmakers during the Republic.

Just as Americans have built on the achievements of Greek and Roman civilizations, the Greeks and Romans built on the achievements of earlier civilizations in Africa and Asia. This cultural borrowing links us with the ancient past and explains how some of our ways of life came to be.

With a partner, make an illustrated booklet titled *Cultural Borrowing.* Show some ways in which different cultures from the past and present affect you. Include architecture, holidays, names, ideas, literature, clothing, art, music, and ways of daily life. Share your booklet with the class. Then take it home to discuss it with family members.

BUILDING CITIZENSHIP

# STORY CLOTH

Study the pictures shown in this story cloth to help you review the events you read about in Unit 4.

## Summarize the Main Ideas

**1.** The seafaring Minoans and the Mycenaeans were among the earliest people to live in the land now known as Greece.

**2.** Later, the peoples of ancient Greece developed different ways of life. The Spartans focused on the military. The Athenians developed ways for all male citizens to take part in governing.

**3.** Times of peace in the Greek city-state of Athens led to growth and the development of new ideas.

**4.** The conquests of Alexander the Great changed forever the way of life of the people of the Mediterranean.

**5.** The Roman form of government changed from a monarchy, to a republic, to an empire.

**6.** Augustus united many groups of people under the Roman Empire.

**7.** The Christian religion spread throughout the Roman Empire and changed Roman life.

**Illustrate the Story**   Draw your own story cloth for one of the following: 1) the development of democracy in Greece, 2) the growth of Rome, or 3) the beginning and growth of Christianity.

# REVIEW

## COOPERATIVE LEARNING WORKSHOP

### Remember

- Share your ideas.
- Cooperate with others to plan your work.
- Take responsibility for your work.
- Show your group's work to the class.
- Discuss what you learned by working together.

### Activity 1
## Paint a Mural

Work with a group of classmates to paint a mural that shows some of the people and the achievements of the Golden Age of Athens.

### Activity 2
## Build a Roman City

With your classmates, plan and build a model of a Roman city. Include in your model a forum, a temple, a bath, an arena, and an aqueduct system. The class might divide into several groups to complete this project. Each group could work on one part of the city, such as the arena or the aqueduct system.

### Activity 3
## Create a Chart

With a small group of classmates, prepare a chart that will appear in a book about Greece. The chart will feature Greek gods. Use this textbook, encyclopedias, and other library books to find the information that you need to complete the chart. Include in your chart the names of at least ten Greek gods. Tell what the Greeks thought each of the gods ruled, and give the Roman name for the god, if appropriate. Combine your chart with the charts of other groups. Be sure to eliminate any duplications.

### Activity 4
## Write an Outline

Form a group with three or four classmates. Imagine that your group has been asked to write a book about ancient civilizations of the Mediterranean. Your publisher says that you may include any topics you want. Write an outline that shows at least ten topics you plan to have in your book.

# USE VOCABULARY

Write the term that correctly matches each meaning.

| | | |
|---|---|---|
| gladiator | isthmus | messiah |
| Hellenistic | martyr | republic |

1. a small strip of land that connects two larger pieces of land

2. Greek-like

3. a form of government in which citizens elect leaders to make all governmental decisions

4. a slave or prisoner forced to fight, often to the death

5. a wise leader who would establish the kingdom of God on Earth

6. a person who suffers for his or her beliefs

# CHECK UNDERSTANDING

1. What do historians think brought an end to Minoan civilization?

2. Who was allowed to participate in Athenian democracy?

3. Why did all Greeks call themselves Hellenes?

4. Why did the early people of Italy trade more with one another than with outsiders?

5. What were the Punic Wars?

6. What effects did the teachings of Jesus have on the Roman Empire?

# THINK CRITICALLY

1. **Past to Present** Why might people today be interested in learning how the Minoan and Mycenaean civilizations ended?

2. **Think More About It** Do you think that it is a good idea for people to obey leaders without question, as citizens were taught to do in Sparta? Explain your answer.

3. **Personally Speaking** Write your opinion of the actions of Roman leaders during the time that Christians were persecuted for refusing to worship Roman gods.

# APPLY GEOGRAPHY SKILLS

**How to Compare Historical Maps**
Look closely at the two maps below. Then use them to answer the questions.

1. Why are there more colors on the second map than on the first map?

2. What kingdoms formed on the land once ruled by Alexander?

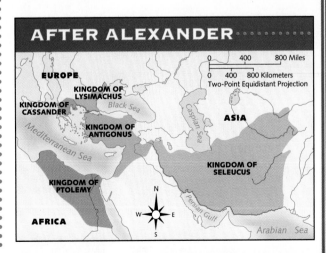

<br />

| UNIT 1 | UNIT 2 | UNIT 3 | UNIT 4 | UNIT 5 |
|---|---|---|---|---|
| Early People and Lifeways | Cradles of Civilization | Asia's Classical Age | The Mediterranean | Rise of New Empires |

## UNIT 5

# RISE of NEW EMPIRES

**500**

**527**
Justinian becomes Byzantine emperor

**618**
Tang dynasty founded in China

**622**
Muhammad's Hijra

**645**
Taika reforms begin in Japan

**700**

**800**
Charlemagne is crowned "Emperor of the Romans"

Feudalism takes hold in Europe

**900**

**900**
Feudalism in Japan

*T*he empires that rose between A.D. 500 and 1500 were vastly different from those of the past. The world had begun to change dramatically. People of different cultures came into closer contact than ever before. Goods, knowledge, and technology traveled longer distances. The pace of technology picked up as well. Civilizations developed new ideas to survive in a changing world. The effects of ideas and technologies, conquests, and religions of this time can still be seen in today's world.

← In this mural, or wall painting, Diego Rivera (1886–1957) shows the way of life of the Aztecs, who lived in what is now Mexico.

**1100**

**1095**
Pope Urban II calls for the crusades

**1215**
Signing of the Magna Carta

**1300**

**1271**
Mongols claim Chinese Mandate of Heaven

**1347**
Bubonic Plague hits Europe

**1500**

**1500**
Height of Aztec power in the Americas

# THE MOUNDS OF CAHOKIA

### by Marlene Smith-Baranzini & Howard Egger-Bovet
### illustrated by George Gaadt

Around the world, unique cultures and empires formed and grew between the years 500 and 1500. In Europe the fall of the Roman Empire brought changes in ways of life for the people in both the western and eastern parts of the continent. In Southwest Asia a growing belief in the religion of Islam brought many new ideas to the culture there. In Africa trade brought about strong, wealthy empires. In the Americas a variety of cultures tried out new ideas and new technologies.

One of these cultures was that of the Mississippians in North America. In what is today the state of Illinois arose the largest Mississippian city—Cahokia. The people who lived there and others of the same culture are perhaps best remembered for the huge mounds that they built in their cities.

First read the authors' introduction in the box at right. Then read the story that begins on the next page. The story is about a young man who travels to Cahokia and describes what he sees. Try to picture in your mind the city of Cahokia as it was about 1,000 years ago.

## A Society Comes and Goes

The city of Cahokia was part of a larger civilization that stretched from what is now the southeast of the United States, to Oklahoma in the west, and Wisconsin to the north. This society was called the Mississippian Society. It began in A.D. 800.

Cahokia was located near where the Illinois town of East St. Louis is today. Around A.D. 1200 the city declined. The reason is not clear.

Some experts believe the people of Cahokia moved to other nearby cities. Others believe Cahokia became so large it became impossible to grow enough food to feed the city's people. Whatever the reason, the great city of Cahokia was eventually abandoned.

he chief gazed out from his home atop a towering mound of earth. Before him was the city Cahokia with its broad plaza surrounded by many villages.

It was early morning. All across the flat, green land many of the thirty thousand residents had started fires in their homes. The smoke rose up through their dried grass roofs, creating miles of white ribbons in the sky.

By the only entrance to the city, traders, their paid bearers,[1] and city workers lined up waiting to be let in. A guard questioned each

person before allowing him to pass through the small gate shaped like an "L." The city designers created the gate this way to prevent large groups of people from rushing the guard and entering the city.

The wait was long. For those who had traveled to the city by canoe on Cahokia Creek, the wait was an annoyance, a test of their patience. For the bearers paid to carry a trader's supply of stone, it was a test of their strength. These men would get no rest till they reached the city marketplace.

One bearer was not thinking about the dark flintlike rocks he was carrying. He was thinking about Cahokia. As a boy, he had

_____

[1] **bearers:** people who carry objects for others

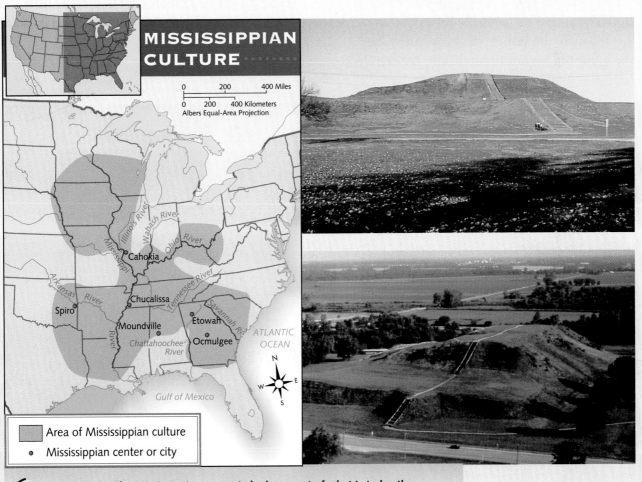

MISSISSIPPIAN CULTURE

0    200    400 Miles
0    200    400 Kilometers
Albers Equal-Area Projection

Illinois River
Wabash River
Ohio River
Mississippi
Cahokia
Akansas River
Tennessee River
Spiro
Chucalissa
Savannah River
Moundville
Etowah
Chattahoochee River
Ocmulgee
ATLANTIC OCEAN
N E S W
Gulf of Mexico

☐ Area of Mississippian culture
• Mississippian center or city

**REGIONS** The Mississippians occupied a large part of what is today the eastern half of the United States. At Cahokia Mounds Historic Site in Illinois, visitors can see some of the mounds (right) built by the Mississippians.
■ In which states might you find Mississippian artifacts?

watched the daily departure of farmers and traders to take their products to the city behind the walls. He had pestered the men, on their return, to tell him of Cahokia. He begged them to hire him as a bearer. They laughed and told him to stop asking and keep growing. He would see Cahokia in time. Now it was his time.

Passing through the gate, the bearer desperately wanted to stop and look around. He had no choice but to follow his trader. The bearer noticed mounds everywhere. He walked by open courts where children played. He passed hundreds of bare-backed men who were carrying baskets of dirt between villages. The bearer saw, among the clay and pole houses of the villages, that certain homes stood above the others upon high mounds.

These are the homes of the wealthy, he thought; the higher the mound the wealthier the person. He kept moving. Once again, he observed men who carried baskets of dirt.

The bearer stopped, even though his body ached to remove the enormous weight he was carrying. He couldn't believe the size of the mound he was standing next to. He squinted his eyes as he looked up, trying to see the flattened summit[2] 100 feet from the ground. All of Cahokia lived in this mound's shadow. It was the chief's mound, which was 700 feet wide and 1,000 feet long.

The bearer again saw bare-backed men who were carrying baskets of dirt. This time, though, he spotted them dumping the dirt from their baskets onto the ground. A new mound was being formed.

He realized what he had heard was true. These mounds were not created by nature. Workers, hired by the wealthy, carried basket

_____

[2] **summit:** top

after basket of dirt to form the earthworks. He wondered how long it would take to complete the mound. He had no idea that many of the men who were carrying the dirt would never live to see the mound completed. The chief's mound took over two hundred years to build.

The bearer raced to catch up with his trader. Fortunately, the trader hadn't noticed the bearer had been lagging[3] behind. The trader entered the bright, open plaza. It was a maze of traders and craftsmen, all urging the passersby to see their wares that rested beside them on the ground.

The bearer's employer maneuvered[4] his way through the crowd, talking to potential buyers. Craftsmen, who were making arrowheads, baskets, and pottery, discussed

business with wealthy men who wanted to buy their goods and sell them many miles away. A jeweler argued with a customer over the worth of his fresh-pearl jewelry.

The trader stopped. He ordered the bearer to put down his merchandise. The bearer released his heavy burden and looked out beyond the people-filled plaza at the burial mounds, and the mounds that held temples. The mounds mesmerized[5] him. Someday, he pondered,[6] I will live in Cahokia, even if I have to carry baskets of dirt.

**At the end of this unit, you will learn more about the Mississippians and other peoples of the Americas who lived between 500 and 1500. But first, read about the ways of life of others who lived at that time in Europe, Africa, and Asia.**

---

[3] **lagging:** moving slowly
[4] **maneuvered:** changed directions for a purpose

[5] **mesmerized:** fascinated
[6] **pondered:** thought

⬆ Statue of a Cahokia woman grinding corn

⬆ One artist's view of how Cahokia looked long ago

# HEIRS of ROME and PERSIA

> 66 Our kingdom is only an imitation of yours, a copy of the only true empire on earth. 99
>
> Theodoric, sixth-century king of the Ostrogoths, in a letter to Byzantine emperor Anastasius I

This picture, created in the sixth century A.D., shows the empress Theodora. She was the wife of Justinian I, an early emperor of the Byzantine Empire.

# The BYZANTINE EMPIRE

## Link to Our World

**How do people today keep the ways of the past while changing with the times?**

### Focus on the Main Idea
*As you read, look for ways the Byzantine emperors built on their Roman past while making needed changes.*

### Preview Vocabulary

| | |
|---|---|
| Justinian Code | icon |
| monopoly | patriarch |
| mosaic | catholic |
| orthodox | |

These armbands, which were worn by members of the Byzantine court, are made from two pieces of solid gold that are hinged together. The armbands were probably made in the early 900s.

Roman civilization lived on for centuries after invaders attacked the city of Rome. In the 400s Roman ways of life continued in the eastern region of the old empire. This thriving region became known as the Byzantine Empire. With its capital at Constantinople, the Byzantine Empire covered Greece, the Balkan lands, and Asia Minor (present-day Turkey). The Byzantine Empire lasted almost a thousand years. A strong army, good government, and a rich economy helped give it a long life.

## JUSTINIAN I LOOKS TO THE PAST

The people of the Byzantine Empire thought of themselves as Romans. They wanted the greatness of Rome to be remembered. They even built their homes and other buildings to be like those in Rome.

In 527 Emperor Justinian I began to plan ways to make his Byzantine Empire as mighty as the Roman Empire had been. He started conquering many of the lands that Rome had lost. With powerful armies Justinian pushed into North Africa and western Europe. By 565 much of the land along the Mediterranean Sea belonged to the Byzantine Empire. Once again people thought of the Mediterranean Sea as a "Roman lake." Such cities as Alexandria and Carthage in North Africa and Athens in Europe were all part of the Byzantine Empire.

Justinian did much more than conquer other lands. Early in his reign he ordered a code of laws written. This new code built on the old Roman codes and added to them. Laws were changed to fit the times and

# THE BYZANTINE EMPIRE

written in language that was easy to understand. As one sixth-century historian said, Justinian "purified" the laws, getting rid of "a mass of quibbles."

The new set of laws became known as the **Justinian Code**. It served as the law of the Byzantine Empire for hundreds of years. And it became the basis for many of the legal systems used in Europe today.

Justinian tried to make the Byzantine economy as strong as the Roman Empire's had been. He built up trade by making Constantinople a meeting place for merchants from Europe and Asia. He also developed new industries in Constantinople. For example, Justinian started the Byzantine silk

industry by ordering silkworm eggs smuggled out of China, along with mulberry trees to feed the silkworms. This action ended China's **monopoly**, or complete control, of the world silk trade.

Money from taxes on trade and industry paid for the building program Justinian began in order to make Constantinople a "New Rome." Many new churches, roads, bridges, and aqueducts were built in Constantinople. The greatest of the buildings still stands today—the church of Hagia Sophia (ah•YEE•uh soh•FEE•uh), or "Holy Wisdom." Artists filled it with magnificent paintings and **mosaics**, pictures made from bits of colored stone or glass. The base of the church's dome forms a circle of 40 windows. One visitor of long ago said that the dome seemed to be "suspended from heaven." In Justinian's time Hagia Sophia was the world's largest and most beautiful church.

As in the Roman Empire, the riches of the Byzantine Empire were enjoyed only by government leaders and merchants. Most people worked almost constantly and earned barely enough for food, clothing, and shelter—and for their taxes to the empire.

 **In what ways did Justinian look to the past to build his empire?**

## THEODORA, BRINGER OF CHANGE

Many laws in Justinian's new code showed the point of view of his wife, the empress Theodora. Theodora helped improve the lives of Byzantine women. She encouraged Justinian to make new laws that were more fair to women. One of these laws allowed parents to leave their property to daughters as well as to sons.

Theodora also took part in choosing government leaders. She believed that people should be given jobs because of their abilities, not because they were born into a high social class.

# Who?

**Theodora**
**About A.D. 500–548**

Most empresses of the Mediterranean region came from noble families. They grew up in fine palaces with everything they could want. Theodora's early life, however, was very different from this. Her father trained bears at the Hippodrome, a giant open-air theater in Constantinople. Theodora also became a circus performer. Then, in her early 20s, she left the circus. Not long after that, she met and married Justinian, becoming empress of the Byzantines.

The highest dome of Hagia Sophia (below) stands 200 feet high. The inside (far right) is decorated with gold, silver, marble, and ivory.

It was at her suggestion that Justinian chose Belisarius (beh•luh•SAR•ee•uhs) to head the Byzantine army. Belisarius was the son of a poor farmer and had little training as a soldier. However, he had shown skill as a leader during an important battle. With Belisarius in charge of the Byzantine army, Justinian was able to claim much of the old Roman Empire.

Theodora and Justinian were both Christians. However, they disagreed about religious ways. Justinian wanted all the Byzantine people to follow **orthodox**, or offically accepted, Christianity. Theodora worked to protect people who followed other forms of Christianity. Theodora's actions helped keep these Christians safe as well as loyal to the Byzantine government.

**How did Theodora help cause change in the Byzantine Empire?**

# THE CHRISTIAN CHURCH DIVIDES

Religion caused much disagreement throughout the Christian lands. People often quarreled bitterly about their beliefs. Many of their leaders felt that these matters were more important than trade, government, or the military.

One argument centered around **icons**, holy pictures of Jesus and the saints. Some people liked to look at the icons as they prayed at home and in churches. Others felt that using icons in this way was like worshipping idols, which is forbidden in the Ten Commandments.

This argument led to disagreement between Christians in western Europe and Christians in the Byzantine Empire. In western Europe few people could read or write. Church leaders there believed that the

Theodora worked to improve the lives of women, such as those shown here. How have women in our society tried to improve their lives?

278

Books for children who are still learning to read have many pictures and few words. Icons were a lot like these books. Icons allowed people who could not read to better understand their religion.

use of icons was a good way to teach about Christianity. The Byzantine **patriarchs**, or Church leaders, did not want people to use icons. They believed that the use of icons went against God's laws. In 726 the Byzantine emperor Leo ordered that all icons in the empire be destroyed. Later the Byzantine empress Irene, who ruled the empire from 780 to 802, declared that icons could be used as long as people prayed to God and not to the icons.

The quarrel over icons between Christians in western Europe and Christians in the Byzantine Empire helped pull the two groups apart. Over time other religious issues caused more conflict. Finally, in 1054, the Christian Church split. Eventually the Church in the Byzantine Empire became the Eastern Orthodox Church, based in Constantinople. The Church in western Europe became the Roman Catholic Church, based in Rome. The word **catholic** means "all-embracing."

Both churches continued to grow strong. However, the Byzantine Empire itself began to weaken. Eventually it lost both its strong army and its organized government. Its economic power weakened, as well. In 1453 the Byzantine Empire came to an end.

 **How did disagreements cause the Christian Church to change?**

# LESSON 1 REVIEW

## Check Understanding

1. **Recall the Facts**   Who were the leaders who brought change to the Byzantine Empire? What were their successes?
2. **Focus on the Main Idea**   How did the Byzantine Empire build on the ways of the Roman Empire? In what ways did the Byzantine Empire change with the times?

## Think Critically

3. **Think More About It**   One historian has called Justinian "the great simplifier." How else could you describe him?
4. **Past to Present**   What issues affecting women might Theodora have focused on if she were alive today?

## Show What You Know

 **Art Activity**   Byzantine mosaics were often displayed on the walls of government buildings and other public places. In this way everyone could see these images of Byzantine life. Make your own mosaic about our society. Where would you want to have your mosaic displayed?

# Understand Point of View

## Why Is This Skill Important?

By reading the words of people of the past, you can better understand their points of view. A person's point of view is the set of beliefs he or she holds. It may be shaped by such things as whether the person is old or young, a man or a woman, or rich or poor. Point of view can also be shaped by a person's culture and race or nationality. Studying the points of view of the different people who took part in an event will help your understanding of history grow. You will see that people of all places and all times are a lot like you.

## Remember What You Have Read

The empress Theodora of the Byzantine Empire helped the emperor Justinian make many decisions during his reign. Her point of view on the rights of women, government leadership, and freedom of religion affected the laws that ruled people's lives.

In 532, early in Justinian's reign, a terrible riot broke out in the city of Constantinople. The crowd burned much of the city and prepared to name a new emperor. Justinian and Theodora, hiding in the palace, debated what action they should take. Procopius (pruh•KOH•pee•uhs), a government official, wrote down what Theodora told Justinian:

66 As to the belief that a woman should not be daring among men or assert herself boldly, I consider the present crisis does not allow us to debate that. My opinion is that now is a poor time for flight, even though it bring safety. For any man who has seen the light of day will also die, but one who has been an emperor cannot endure to be a fugitive. If now you wish to go, Emperor, nothing prevents you. There is the sea, there are the steps to the boats. 99

Justinian decided to remain and defend his position.

## Understand the Process

Here are some steps to help you understand a speaker's or writer's point of view:

- Reread the quotation. Identify the person who is speaking or writing. Think about what you know about the person. This can help you see the reasons for his or her statements.
- Think about the situation in which the statements were made. Look for clues to what life was like in the time and place in which the person lived.
- Look for words that help you find a person's point of view. Often statements giving points of view contain words like *think, believe, probably,* and *in my opinion.*

## Think and Apply

Use the steps above as you answer these questions:

1. What reasons do you think Theodora had for making her statement?
2. What does Theodora's speech tell you about her point of view about women?
3. What words in Theodora's speech tell you that she is stating her point of view?

Empress Theodora

# The MUSLIM EMPIRE

## Link to Our World

*How can ideas about religion affect governments and their people's ways of life today?*

### Focus on the Main Idea
*Look for ways the religion of Islam affected people living in the lands into which it spread.*

### Preview Vocabulary

| | |
|---|---|
| steppe | mosque |
| Qur'an | minaret |
| Muslim | astrolabe |
| Islam | Sunni |
| caliph | Shiite |

At the end of the sixth century, the emperor of Persia wrote to the Byzantine emperor. He praised their two empires as the greatest of their day. The Persians and the Byzantines, he said, "are to the world what . . . two eyes are to a man." The Persian emperor did not know that this would soon change. Within 100 years a new empire—the Muslim Empire—would defeat the Persians and threaten the Byzantines.

## HERDERS AND TOWNSPEOPLE

Desert covers more than two-thirds of the peninsula of Arabia. Some parts of the desert are dunes of shifting sand. Other parts are semi-dry plains called **steppes**. Some grasses and plants grow on the steppes, but these provide only enough food for the camels, sheep, and goats of herders. In the 500s many tribes of Arab people lived as nomads on the steppes. A sheikh (SHAYK), or chief, led each tribe.

Towns formed on spots of fertile land with underground water supplies. The people who lived in these towns supported themselves by farming. Often the towns were stops for travelers on desert trading routes. As more and more traders visited, the towns grew.

One of the largest towns in Arabia was Mecca (MEH•kuh). There was no agriculture in the city, but other activities

The Arabian steppes (below) are part of the Arabian peninsula. The peninsula includes over 1,000,000 square miles of land.

281

supported its people. Mecca was an important stop on the caravan routes. Goods from Asia and Africa passed through on their way to Syria, Yemen, and the Mediterranean.

Mecca was also a religious center. Each year Arabs from across the Arabian peninsula came to worship at a cube-shaped building called the Ka'ba. The Ka'ba contained the statues of the gods that the Arabs had come to believe in. Having the Ka'ba in their town brought influence and income to the people of Mecca.

✓ **In what way did trade affect the Arab people?**

## MUHAMMAD AND ISLAM

In about 570 an Arab boy given the name of Muhammad was born into a poor but important family in Mecca. Muhammad's parents died when he was a child, and relatives cared for him. He grew up to be a man who was well respected by his tribe. Muhammad became a trader and married a wealthy widow named Khadija (kah•DEE•juh).

Muhammad became unhappy about his tribe's idol worship. He often spent time in deep thought in a cave outside the town. On one of these occasions, Muhammad had a vision—the angel Gabriel told him that he would become a messenger to humankind.

The message confirmed to Muhammad that there is no god but God, or *Allah* in Arabic. Over the next 23 years, Muhammad received more messages. Put together, they make up the **Qur'an** (kuh•RAN), the holy book of Islam. A **Muslim** (MUS•lim), or follower of Islam, believes that the Qur'an is God's word. **Islam** means "submitting to God's will." A Muslim tries to do that by following the Qur'an and Muhammad's example.

Muhammad's family and close friends became the first Muslims. As the number of Muslims grew, tribal leaders in Mecca became worried. They believed that they would lose their own religious influence. They also believed that if people accepted Islam, people would no longer come to worship at the Ka'ba. If this happened, Mecca's economy would suffer. The leaders of Mecca tried to force the Muslims to give up their

Early Muslim artists are remembered for their calligraphy, or beautiful handwriting.

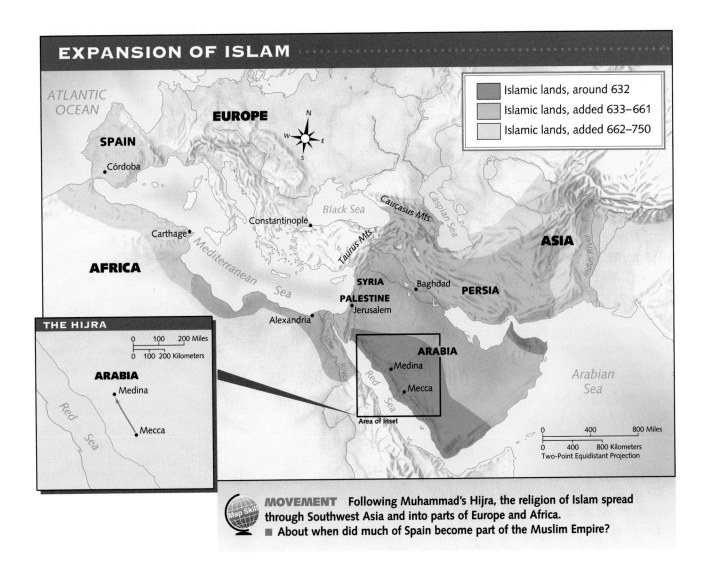

## EXPANSION OF ISLAM

Legend:
- Islamic lands, around 632
- Islamic lands, added 633–661
- Islamic lands, added 662–750

ATLANTIC OCEAN

EUROPE

SPAIN
• Córdoba

AFRICA

• Carthage

Mediterranean Sea

Constantinople

Black Sea

Caucasus Mts.

Caspian Sea

Taurus Mts.

ASIA

Indus River

SYRIA
PALESTINE
• Jerusalem

Baghdad

PERSIA

• Alexandria

Nile River

### THE HIJRA

0   100   200 Miles
0   100  200 Kilometers

ARABIA
• Medina
• Mecca

Red Sea

ARABIA
• Medina
• Mecca

Red Sea

Area of inset

Arabian Sea

0        400       800 Miles
0      400     800 Kilometers
Two-Point Equidistant Projection

**MOVEMENT** Following Muhammad's Hijra, the religion of Islam spread through Southwest Asia and into parts of Europe and Africa.
■ About when did much of Spain become part of the Muslim Empire?

beliefs. After ten years Muhammad left Mecca. His journey, called the Hijra (HIJ•rah), was the sign of a new beginning for Muslims. Its date—A.D. 622—marks the first year of the Muslim calendar.

Muhammad's journey took him to the town of Medina, where he was welcomed by Muslims already living there. As Islam spread to other Arab tribes, conflict with Mecca grew. Nine years after the Hijra, the Muslims defeated the Meccans. Muhammad destroyed all the idols in the Ka'ba. He then dedicated it to the worship of Allah only. Mecca is still a holy city for Muslims.

 *Why were tribal leaders in Mecca worried about the growth of Islam?*

## THE MUSLIM EMPIRE GROWS

Muhammad saw it as his duty to spread the message of Islam. He did this through teaching and by personal example. He also told his followers to spread the message to others.

After Muhammad's death Muslim leaders chose a **caliph** (KAY•luhf), or "successor" to Muhammad. The caliph's role was to govern the Muslim community according to the Qur'an and Muhammad's example.

Within a few years the first caliphs united Arabia under Muslim rule. Then they carried Islam to the peoples around them. Caliphs led their armies into Mesopotamia, Syria, and

Egypt. The Arabs met little resistance from people such as the Persians and the Byzantines. These peoples welcomed the invaders, believing that they would then be freed from the heavy taxes and religious persecution of their own rulers.

By about 750, less than 200 years after the death of Muhammad, the Muslim Empire reached from Spain and North Africa through Arabia and Persia into parts of China and the Indus River valley. Only the Byzantine Empire, much smaller than before, stood between the Muslim lands and eastern Europe.

✓ **What lands became part of the Muslim Empire?**

## ACHIEVEMENTS OF MUSLIM CIVILIZATION

The Muslim Empire united people of many languages and cultures. As Muslims grew in number in those lands, they created a civilization that has lasted since the seventh century.

From its beginnings the Muslim civilization took an interest in art and in science. Among the most beautiful works of

The style of a mosque and its minarets may differ from one region to another. This spiral minaret (right) is from a mosque in Iraq. The tall, slender minaret (left) is from one in Turkey.

284

**MAJOR DEVELOPMENTS IN THE MUSLIM EMPIRE, A.D. 570–800**

**RELIGION**

600 · 650 · 700 · 750 · 800

**622** Muhammad's Hijra
**570** Muhammad born
**632** Muhammad dies
**705** Great Mosque at Damascus built
**751** Muslim Empire divides

**SCIENCE AND MATHEMATICS**

600 · 650 · 700 · 750 · 800

**About 750** Astrolabe improved
**760** First known Arabic numbers in Arabia
**782** Advances in study of chemistry

**LITERATURE**

600 · 650 · 700 · 750 · 800

**640** Arabs discover library at Alexandria, Egypt
**700** Time of poet Omar ibn Abi Rabi'a
**800** Earliest known Persian poetry and literature

**ARTS**

600 · 650 · 700 · 750 · 800

**715** Islamic architecture in Spain begins
**785** Mosque at Córdoba built

**LEARNING FROM TIME LINES** The years 570 to 800 were times of great achievement for the Muslim Empire.
■ What important events happened between 700 and 750?

Islamic art are **mosques**, or houses of worship. The basic form of a mosque is simple, and the building has little furniture. A mosque might have one or more towers, called **minarets**, from which the call to prayer is heard five times a day. Mosques are often decorated with rich designs, using geometric shapes and verses from the Qur'an.

Muslims also made advances in science. Muslim scholars charted the movement of stars and planets. From their observations they improved the **astrolabe**, an instrument that helped sailors navigate using the positions of the stars. The astrolabe helped mapmakers prepare better maps.

Muslim scientists made contributions to medicine as well. As early as the 900s, a large teaching hospital was built as part of a mosque in Baghdad, in what is now Iraq. In this and other hospitals, doctors were trained to treat the sick. The work of these doctors became an important source of knowledge about diseases for centuries to come.

Trade within and outside of the empire helped bring Muslims new ideas. From the Chinese the Arabs learned how to make paper. From India, Muslims borrowed a system of numbers made up of nine digits and a zero. The Arabs called these Indian numerals, but we call them Arabic numerals, in honor of the traders who spread their use across the Muslim Empire and into the West. They are the numbers we use today.

> ✔ **What were some achievements of the Muslim culture?**

More than 800 marble columns line the Great Mosque of Córdoba, which was built in the late 700s.

# DIVISIONS WITHIN THE MUSLIM EMPIRE

As the Muslim Empire grew, powerful families argued over who should rule it. In 661 a member of the Umayyad (oo•MY•yuhd) family became caliph and moved the Muslim

## W**here?**

## Córdoba, Spain

In the ninth and tenth centuries, people from all over Europe and northern Africa went to Córdoba to study such subjects as philosophy, mathematics, medicine, poetry, astronomy, and theology (the study of religion). This center of Muslim learning had a huge library with more than 400,000 books. The city also had a university, more than 60 smaller libraries, and many bookshops. Visitors were amazed by the city's paved and lighted streets. Córdoba, as well as most of what is now Spain, was controlled by the Moors, Muslims who had left northern Africa to settle there.

EUROPE

SPAIN

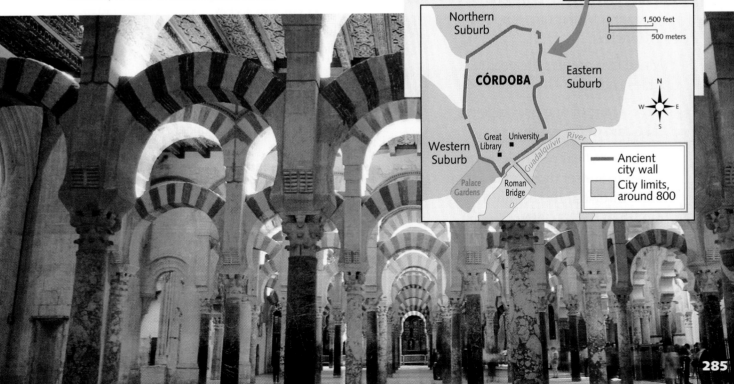

Northern Suburb

CÓRDOBA

Eastern Suburb

Western Suburb

Great Library    University

Guadalquivir River

Palace Gardens    Roman Bridge

0 ——— 1,500 feet
0 ——— 500 meters

Ancient city wall

City limits, around 800

capital from Medina to Damascus in Syria. The Umayyads ruled from the new capital until 750. In that year the Abbasid (uh•BA•suhd) family claimed the right to rule. The Abbasids moved their capital east and built the city of Baghdad on the Tigris River.

One member of the Umayyad family escaped the Abbasids and began his own government in Córdoba, Spain. Later, descendants of Muhammad's daughter Fatima formed still another government, with its capital in Cairo, Egypt. Now rival

A dinar, the gold coin issued by the Abbasid government

caliphs ruled different parts of the Muslim Empire.

As time passed, the Muslim community split into several groups. Perhaps the most important of these groups were the **Sunni** (SOON•nee) Muslims and the **Shiite** (SHEE•yt) Muslims. Shiite Muslims stayed loyal to the descendants of the fourth caliph, Ali. They did not want either the Umayyad or the Abbasid families as rulers. In contrast, Sunni Muslims accepted the changing dynasties. Sunni Muslims and Shiite Muslims still disagree on many issues today.

✔ **What caused divisions in Islam and the Muslim Empire?**

# The Five Pillars of Islam

The Qur'an says that the Islamic religion is based on five important ideas called the Five Pillars. More than just rituals, these acts help shape the lives of Muslims and their communities.

Believe that there is no god but God, and Muhammad is God's prophet.

Make five prayers at specific times each day.

Give a part of one's savings to take care of the needy.

Fast (do not eat or drink) from dawn to sunset during Ramadan (RAH•muh•dahn), the ninth month in the Muslim calendar.

Make a pilgrimage, or visit for religious reasons, to Mecca during one's lifetime.

# *L*SSON 2 REVIEW

## Check Understanding

1. **Recall the Facts**   What did Muhammad and his followers do to bring about the growth of Islam?
2. **Focus on the Main Idea**   How did Islam affect the lives of people living in the lands into which it spread?

## Think Critically

3. **Personally Speaking**   Do you think some people resisted coming under Arab rule? Explain.
4. **Past to Present**   What is the relationship between religion and government in the United States today?

## Show What You Know

**Map Activity**   Sketch a map of the world, showing all the continents. Then do research to find out where Muslims live today. Add this information to your map.

# LESSON 3

# EUROPE *in the* MIDDLE AGES

## Link to Our World

*How can the actions of both individuals and groups change governments today?*

### Focus on the Main Idea
*Read about how individuals and groups affected governments during the Middle Ages in Europe.*

### Preview Vocabulary
| | |
|---|---|
| *Middle Ages* | *feudal system* |
| *pope* | *Christendom* |
| *manor* | *crusader* |
| *serf* | *bubonic plague* |
| *tenant* | *nation-state* |
| *vassal* | *Magna Carta* |
| *contract* | |

During the early Middle Ages, Europe was a land of small kingdoms. This seventh-century horseman is from the kingdom of the Lombards.

At the time the Muslim Empire began expanding, the continent of Europe was divided into many small kingdoms. The Roman Empire's strong central government, which had once kept Europe together, was gone. Small, weak kingdoms had replaced Rome's strong central government. The small kingdoms were ruled by groups of people the Romans had called barbarians. Historians call the years from about 500 to about 1500 in Europe the medieval period, or **Middle Ages**.

## CHARLEMAGNE BUILDS AN EMPIRE

During the last years of the Roman Empire, groups of people from northern Europe—in or near what is now Germany—came to control much of western Europe. Together these groups were known as the Germanic tribes. The most powerful of these tribes was the Franks, from whom France got its name. Under their leader Charlemagne (SHAR•luh•mayn), the Franks brought new life to the lands of a dying Roman Empire.

The name Charlemagne means "Charles the Great." Great in size at 6 feet 4 inches (193 cm) tall, Charlemagne was also a great warrior. He led his armies to conquer large parts of Italy, Germany, and central Europe. He also won part of northern Spain. Soon he controlled land from the Pyrenees Mountains in the west to the Danube River in the east.

# CHARLEMAGNE'S EMPIRE

North Sea

Aachen

Paris

Tours

ATLANTIC OCEAN

Rhine River

Danube River

ALPS

Pyrenees

Corsica

Rome

Adriatic Sea

Balearic Islands

Mediterranean Sea

0    200    400 Miles
0    200    400 Kilometers
Azimuthal Equal-Area Projection

N W E S

Charlemagne's Empire, A.D. 768

New lands added to Charlemagne's Empire by A.D. 814

**PLACE** Charlemagne brought many people of western Europe together under one empire.
■ About how many miles across was Charlemagne's empire at its widest point?

Charlemagne had close ties with the **pope**, the leader of the Christian Church based in Rome. Both Charlemagne and his grandfather, Charles Martel, whose name means "Charles the Hammer," had helped popes by defending the city of Rome against other Germanic tribes. In the year 800 Pope Leo III rewarded Charlemagne by crowning him "Emperor of the Romans" on Christmas Day. Many people saw him as being like the Roman emperors of old.

The pope gave Charlemagne the title "Augustus," after the first Roman emperor. And Charlemagne tried to live up to the title. Like Augustus, Charlemagne wanted his government to be strong and his leaders to be wise. He saw it as his responsibility to teach his leaders how to govern. He often sent messages to his nobles about ruling fairly. In the

spring of each year, Charlemagne met with all of his nobles. These meetings, called the Fields of May, became famous. In meadows filled with flowers, Charlemagne set up tents and taught his nobles about law, religion, trade, and education.

Charlemagne truly respected learning. "Knowledge," he said, "must come before action." Charlemagne invited scholars from all over Europe to teach at the school he set up for his nobles' children. He also urged priests in all parts of the empire to teach "all those who with God's help are able to learn." While Charlemagne himself could not write, he read well. In fact, reading was one of his favorite activities.

Charlemagne's rule was a high point of the early Middle Ages. Even before his death in 814, however, Muslims from North Africa attacked the empire's Mediterranean coast. Then Slavs and Magyars from eastern Europe invaded from the east. Vikings came from the north, from what is now Norway, Sweden, and Denmark. The empire Charlemagne had built fell apart. Once again Europe became a land of small kingdoms.

**✓ How did Charlemagne strengthen his empire through cooperation?**

Here Pope Leo III crowns Charlemagne as Emperor of the Romans to thank him for protecting the city of Rome.

Peasants usually worked on the fields of wealthy landowners who lived in large manors (right). Few people, rich or poor, could read the illustrated manuscripts (above) that were made during this time.

## LIFE IN THE MIDDLE AGES

For much of the Middle Ages, most Europeans lived in small villages which were parts of a manor. The **manor** was a large block of land made up of forests, meadows, farmland, the village, a church, and the house or castle of the noble who owned it all.

The peasants, or **serfs**, who worked on the manor lived in the village. Each day they walked from the village to the fields to work. They grew the food and made the goods needed to support the noble's family. The serfs worked on the land, but they were not allowed to own it. They were the noble's tenants. A **tenant** is someone who pays rent to a landowner.

In return for being allowed to use the noble's land, the serfs paid the noble in services and goods. Each week they worked on his land. At harvest time, they gave him a part of their crops. In return, the noble protected the serfs from attacks by enemies from other villages.

The noble himself was a tenant of the king. Under the law of the time, the king owned all the land in his kingdom. He kept large parts of it for himself and divided the rest among the nobles who agreed to help him in times of war. These nobles were called **vassals**. A king's vassal agreed to perform services for the king in return for being given use of the land. The vassal also had to send soldiers to fight in the king's army, fight in battles himself, and collect the king's taxes.

A vassal's services were usually listed in a written agreement, or **contract**, with the king. (Unfortunately, most vassals could not read.) A typical contract started out like this:

> 66 As long as I shall live, I am bound to give you service and obedience. 99

The contract also listed the amount of land the vassal received, the buildings that went with it, and the number of peasants living on it. This system of trading protection for loyalty became known as the **feudal system**.

 **How did the feudal system work?**

## THE CHURCH AND THE CRUSADES

From about 800 to about 1300, almost everyone in Europe lived on a manor and was ruled by a king. Although Europe was divided into many separate kingdoms, Europeans united under the Christian Church of Rome. The idea of **Christendom**, or feeling that all Christians from all kingdoms formed a community, was very important to people.

## Jerusalem

The Dome of the Rock

Jews, Christians, and Muslims of today think of Jerusalem as a holy place, just as they did long ago. Jews gather daily to pray at Jerusalem's Western Wall— the last remaining wall of an ancient Jewish temple. Muslims visit the Dome of the Rock, honored as the site of Muhammad's journey to heaven. Christians visit sites such as the Church of the Holy Sepulchre, built on the site where Jesus was crucified and buried. Today Jerusalem is the capital of the country of Israel.

The Christian Church of the Middle Ages had more than just religious authority. It crowned emperors, as Pope Leo III crowned Charlemagne, and it sent soldiers to war.

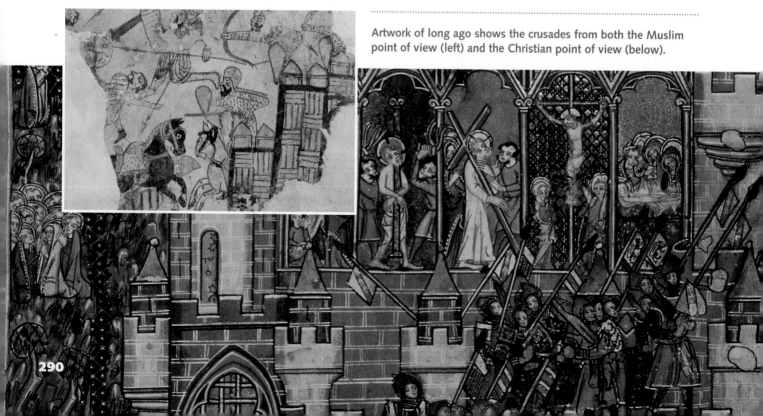

Artwork of long ago shows the crusades from both the Muslim point of view (left) and the Christian point of view (below).

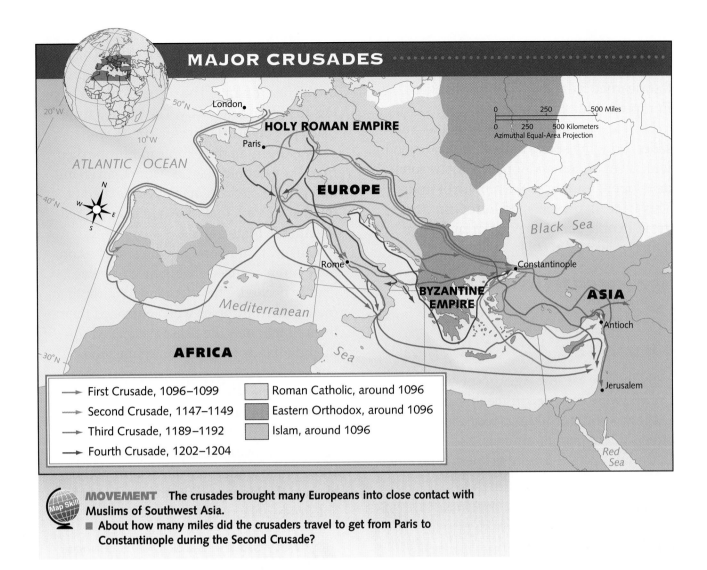

# MAJOR CRUSADES

ATLANTIC OCEAN

London

HOLY ROMAN EMPIRE

Paris

EUROPE

Rome

Black Sea

Constantinople

BYZANTINE EMPIRE

ASIA

Antioch

Mediterranean Sea

AFRICA

Jerusalem

Red Sea

0       250       500 Miles
0   250   500 Kilometers
Azimuthal Equal-Area Projection

→ First Crusade, 1096–1099
→ Second Crusade, 1147–1149
→ Third Crusade, 1189–1192
→ Fourth Crusade, 1202–1204

☐ Roman Catholic, around 1096
☐ Eastern Orthodox, around 1096
☐ Islam, around 1096

**MOVEMENT** The crusades brought many Europeans into close contact with Muslims of Southwest Asia.
■ About how many miles did the crusaders travel to get from Paris to Constantinople during the Second Crusade?

In 1095 Pope Urban II called on all of Christendom to help seize control of the holy city of Jerusalem back from the Seljuk Turks, who were Muslims. By this time the Seljuk Turks had gained control of the lands that were once part of the Muslim Empire, including the city of Jerusalem. Pope Urban said that the Turks would not let Christians visit Jerusalem and other places holy to Christians. The pope asked the people of Christendom to go to war for a holy cause. With cries of "God wills it! God wills it!," thousands of European Christians headed toward Jerusalem.

Excited volunteers tore cloth into strips, which they pinned to their clothes in the shape of a cross. Because these people took the cross as their sign, they were called **crusaders**. The wars these Christians fought were called crusades.

There were eight major crusades between 1095 and 1291. Some were called People's Crusades. Whole families left their homes and set out for Jerusalem. In every crusade people from across Europe marched together to battle. Even two armies of children marched off on what became known as the Children's Crusade. Most of them died of hunger on the long trip and never saw Jerusalem. In the wars for the Holy Land, thousands of Muslims and Christians died.

The crusaders were never able to gain control of Jerusalem. Yet the crusades did help the Europeans in another way. The crusades brought Europeans into close contact with Muslims and their way of life. The new ideas they learned from the Muslims changed European thinking forever.

Europeans returned home from the crusades, bringing spices and other Asian goods with them. A demand for such goods soon developed, leading to the growth of trade. This trade, in turn, helped European cities grow. People began moving from the manors to find new jobs in cities.

**✓ How did the crusades affect life in Europe?**

## DISASTER AND CHANGE

By the late Middle Ages, most cities in Europe were crowded, unhealthful places. Rickety wooden buildings rose above narrow streets full of people, animals, and garbage. In the late 1340s a deadly sickness called the **bubonic plague** hit European cities. The bubonic plague, or Black Death, was spread by the fleas on rats. The disease caused blisters to form on the body. The blisters turned black just before the person died.

One-fourth of the people in Europe died from the bubonic plague. More than 20 million people died. So many people died of the Black Death that they had to be buried together in huge graves.

The few farm workers who survived on the manors realized that their work was greatly needed. They demanded fairer treatment from the nobles who controlled their lives. Sometimes the peasants backed up their demands with revolts against the nobles.

During the late Middle Ages, many Europeans became unhappy with both the Church and the feudal system. The disagreements over authority between kings and Church leaders shocked some. Others blamed the kings and the popes for not being able to stop the plague.

**✓ How did the Black Death change Europe in the late 1340s?**

## THE RISE OF NATION-STATES

Beginning in the late Middle Ages, strong kings began to take authority away from the nobles and Church leaders. Nation-states formed in many parts of Europe, especially in England, France, and Spain. Each **nation-state** had a strong central government and a single ruler—the monarch, or king. Each also had its own laws, government leaders, and full-time army. Language, culture, and customs also brought people together in these nation-states.

Hoping to hold on to some of their authority, powerful nobles tried to find ways to stop the king from taking it all. In 1215 a

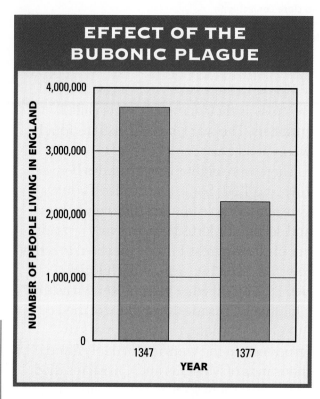

**EFFECT OF THE BUBONIC PLAGUE**

NUMBER OF PEOPLE LIVING IN ENGLAND

4,000,000

3,000,000

2,000,000

1,000,000

0

1347        1377

YEAR

**LEARNING FROM GRAPHS** In the 1340s many Europeans died from the bubonic plague.
■ About how many fewer people lived in England in 1377 than in 1347?

# Magna Carta

Copy of the original Magna Carta

**The following are 3 of the 63 demands the English nobles made in the Magna Carta.**

[30] No sheriff, or bailiff of ours, or anyone else shall take the horses or carts of any free man for transport work save [except] with the agreement of that free man.

[31] Neither we nor our bailiffs will take, for castles or other works of ours, timber which is not ours, except with the agreement of him whose timber it is.

[40] To no one will we sell, to no one will we refuse or delay right or justice.

group of English nobles presented King John, then the King of England, with a list of 63 demands in the form of a contract. This document came to be called the **Magna Carta**, or "Great Charter." King John was made to sign it. The Magna Carta forced the king to accept responsibility for his actions. In other words the king now had to follow laws like everyone else. For example, he could no longer take property without paying for it.

The Magna Carta was written by the nobles to protect themselves. However, parts of the charter later became the basis for laws in Europe that protected the freedoms of everyone. For example, the Magna Carta gave people the right to trial by jury.

Under the Magna Carta no one—not even the king—was above the law. The Magna Carta required the English monarch to have "the general consent of the realm [kingdom]" before ordering new taxes. The assembly of nobles who met to vote on taxes later became known as Parliament. In modern times the main lawmakers of Parliament are elected by the people.

The signing of the Magna Carta had long-lasting effects. For example, the Constitution of the United States has its roots in the ideas first expressed in the Magna Carta.

 **How did the nobles try to limit the authority of King John?**

## LESSON 3 REVIEW

### Check Understanding

1. **Recall the Facts**   What key factors shaped life in Europe during the Middle Ages?
2. **Focus on the Main Idea**   How did individuals and groups affect governments during the Middle Ages in Europe?

### Think Critically

3. **Personally Speaking**   If the plague had not happened, do you think people would still have tried to change the feudal system? Explain your answer.
4. **Past to Present**   How did the nobles' charter with King John help build the democracies of later times?

### Show What You Know

 **Simulation Activity**   Around the world there are many museums of living history where actors act, dress, and talk the way people did long ago. With several classmates, create a scene of "living history" that shows what life was like under the feudal system. Invite other classmates to ask questions about your "living history" scene.

# How To

# Understand National Symbols

## Why Is This Skill Important?

Since the forming of the first nation-states, flags have been used as symbols of national identity. A flag stands for a nation's land, its people, and its government. It also expresses ideas or qualities valued by the people of a nation. Knowing the kinds of things flags represent can help you better understand today's nations and their histories.

## Think About Flags

Flags were probably first used thousands of years ago. Egyptian soldiers went to battle carrying poles topped with streamers, hoping that they would persuade their gods to help them win. Later, Assyrians, Greeks, and Romans used flags in the same way. Their flags stood for their gods or their leaders.

During battles, generals often watched flags to follow the movement of the soldiers. Each side in a battle was represented by a flag. If their flag was captured, many soldiers would surrender. If the soldier carrying the flag was killed or wounded, others would pick it up and "rally around the flag" to prevent the enemy from capturing it.

In the Middle Ages, knights often decorated their shields with colors and other symbols to help their followers recognize them in their armor on the battlefield. Later, those symbols were used on flags, clothing, and other items. In the late Middle Ages, leaders of nation-states used those symbols on their national flags.

## Understand the Process

The designs on many flags were used in **heraldry**, the system of colors, patterns, and picture symbols that knights used during the Middle Ages in Europe. Today the flags of nations also use color, patterns, and picture symbols in their flags.

- **Colors**

  Most national flags today use one or more of seven colors: black, blue, green, orange, red, white, and yellow. These colors were used in heraldry to stand for different qualities: blue for loyalty, red for courage, and white for freedom.

  Several nations use the same colors in their flags. Black, green, red, and white stand for Arab unity. They are used in the flags of present-day Iraq, Jordan, Kuwait, Sudan, Syria, the United Arab Emirates, and Yemen.

- **Patterns**

  Patterns on many present-day national flags are similar to those used in heraldry. Some knights in the Middle Ages used a stripe of white or yellow to separate two colors. That pattern is used in many flags of today. The flag of Egypt has a white stripe between stripes of black and red. The Mexican flag has a stripe of white between stripes of green and red.

- **Picture Symbols**

  The picture symbols used on some flags stand for a religion practiced by its nation's people. The cross, a symbol for Christianity, has been used on some flags. The crescent and star, a symbol of Islam, is on the flags of many Muslim nations. The Star of David appears on the flag of Israel. Stars often stand for unity. The number of stars in a flag is often equal to the number of states or provinces united to form a country. The United States' flag has 50 stars.

  Picture symbols can also show an important element of a nation's past. On the Mexican flag, an eagle on a cactus holds a snake. This was the sign the Aztecs believed showed them where to build their capital city of Tenochtitlán. Argentina's flag shows a sun, which stands for the country's freedom from Spain.

## Think and Apply

Suppose you were asked to design a new flag for your school or class. What would it look like? Draw your flag, and write a paragraph to explain the symbols you used. Display your flag on a classroom bulletin board along with those of your classmates.

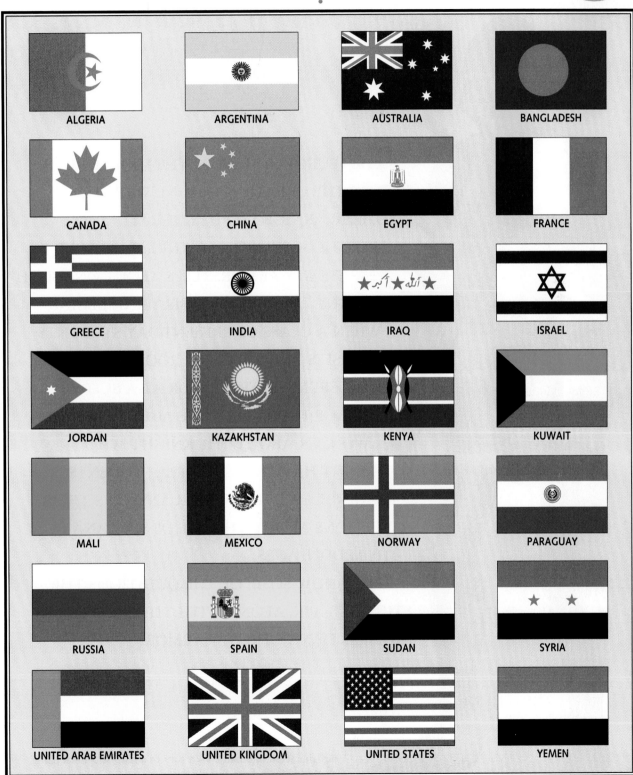

| | | | |
|---|---|---|---|
| ALGERIA | ARGENTINA | AUSTRALIA | BANGLADESH |
| CANADA | CHINA | EGYPT | FRANCE |
| GREECE | INDIA | IRAQ | ISRAEL |
| JORDAN | KAZAKHSTAN | KENYA | KUWAIT |
| MALI | MEXICO | NORWAY | PARAGUAY |
| RUSSIA | SPAIN | SUDAN | SYRIA |
| UNITED ARAB EMIRATES | UNITED KINGDOM | UNITED STATES | YEMEN |

# KNIGHTS
## *of the*
## MIDDLE AGES

THE FEUDAL SYSTEM OF THE MIDDLE AGES LED TO THE CREATION OF A NEW KIND OF SOLDIER—KNIGHTS. THE LITERATURE SELECTION, *SIR DANA: A KNIGHT, AS TOLD BY HIS TRUSTY ARMOR*, TELLS ABOUT ONE SUCH KNIGHT. THE STORY OF SIR DANA BEGINS WHEN A CLASS OF PRESENT-DAY STUDENTS VISITS THE MEDIEVAL ROOM OF A GREAT MUSEUM. AS THEY LOOK AT A SUIT OF ARMOR FROM 600 YEARS AGO, THEY WONDER ABOUT THE KNIGHT WHO MIGHT HAVE WORN IT. THE STUDENTS IMAGINE THAT THE ARMOR ANSWERS THEIR QUESTIONS ABOUT THE LIFE OF SIR DANA IN THE MIDDLE AGES.

READ NOW SOME OF THE QUESTIONS THE STUDENTS ASK, ALONG WITH THE ANSWERS FROM SIR DANA'S TRUSTY ARMOR.

Knights went into battle with suits of armor. The metal plates protected them from sword attacks.

# Sir Dana: A Knight

## As Told by His Trusty Armor
### Words and Pictures by Dana Fradon

 HY DID SIR DANA BECOME A KNIGHT?

"Truth to tell, as the son of a knight, no thought was ever given to his being anything else. From the day of his birth, he was prepared for this lifelong task. As a child, Sir Dana played games that developed his physical skills.

"Using toy wooden swords, he and his friends pretended they were knights.

"They walked on stilts.

"They played catch with a ball made of leather or cloth stuffed with almost anything. Wool was best. It was light and held its shape.

"Sometimes they would hit the ball over a net or a raised mound of earth with a gloved hand. . . ."

 HAT'S A SQUIRE?

"A squire was a knight's assistant, his apprentys,[1] you might say. A squire followed his knight on the way to battle, leading the knight's courser[2] and caring for his equipment. The knight rode his palfrey.[3]

"For the first few years, squires did not take part in battle. But as they grew older and stronger, many squires fought alongside their knights as equals, with much valor, and did great mischief[4] to the enemy. The great English knight Sir John Chandos met his death at the hands of a strong, experienced squire.

"Some men chose to remain squires their entire lives. Expensive it was to become a knight.[5] Living as an assistant to a rich lord or successful knight was often as good as being one."

---

[1] **apprentys:** medieval for *apprentice*
[2] **courser:** battle horse
[3] **palfrey:** regular riding horse
[4] **mischief:** damage
[5] A great lord needed to supply a new knight only with a horse, armor, and weapons. The new knight often had to pay for lavish feasting and ceremonies himself.

OW OLD WAS SIR DANA WHEN HE BECAME A KNIGHT?

"Sir Dana was twenty-one, the age most squires became knights. But many a squire was made a knight while still a teenager.

"On the other hand, the great French knight Sir Bertrand du Guesclin—the Tenth Worthy[6]—did not become a knight until he was thirty-five.

"Mind you this: A king could confer knighthood on almost anyone he wished—at any age. Many a rich merchant bought the honor of knighthood with money. Some poor but able foot soldiers earned it on the field of battle through their bravery. The nobles, of course, were exceedingly wroth[7] at this backward entry into their class, but they could not entirely halt it.

"Squire Dana became a knight, and received the title Sir, in a ceremony many centuries old. Having taken a purifying bath the night before to cleanse him of his sins, he dressed all in white to signify his purity. He vowed to serve and defend God, the king of Domania, his fellow knights, womanhood, and the weak. And at all times to act in a just, gentlemanly, and chivalrous manner.

"Then the king girded him—fastened a sword and belt around Squire Dana's waist. Riding spurs were attached to his boots.

"After that an odd, *very* odd, thing happened. The king delivered the buffet, an open-handed blow to the cheek. Sometimes it was merely symbolic, and sometimes it was powerful enough to send a knight reeling.

"The buffet ended the ceremony. Some say its purpose was to make sure the young knight never forgot his vows."

---

[6] **Tenth Worthy:** tenth greatest knight of all time, so deemed by his countrymen
[7] **wroth:** medieval for *upset*

OULD A GIRL BE A KNIGHT? WAS JOAN OF ARC A KNIGHT?

"No! Why, a knight was not even supposed to ride a mare! It was believed that females had no place on the battlefield. However, here and there, women did go to war—and as leaders, too. Queen Philippa of England was said to have urged her troops to fight manfully at the Battle of Neville's Cross. She prevented a Scottish invasion, while her husband, King Edward III, and most of his knights were across the English Channel fighting the French. And the countess of Montfort led the defense of her castle and lands when her husband was a prisoner of the French. She was said to possess the courage of a man and the heart of a lion!

"I know not directly of Joan of Arc. She died, burned at the stake, in 1431. Sir Dana would have been one hundred years old by then. A great leader, she wore full armor as she led her troops against the English. A saint she became, but not a knight. . . ."

# WHAT IS CHIVALRY?

"It was a code, the rules and values of knighthood, written and unwritten, going back at least to the ninth-century Anglo-Saxon king Alfred. It included a devotion to duty, fair play on the battlefield, honesty, good manners, and bravery. Also kindness toward the weak, respect for women, courtesy, generosity, and gentleness toward everyone. Above all, it pledged the knight to serve God. By Saint Denis! Not bad values, even for today, eh?

"Sad to say, these rules were much broken. Knights often killed needlessly. Ho! Is killing ever but needless? Chivalrous behavior was often forgotten in dealings with peasants, religious minorities, or anybody a knight disliked.

"If a captured knight promised to pay a ransom in exchange for being allowed to return home unharmed, he would almost always keep his word.

"If a king granted safe passage through his country to certain of the enemy—as during peace talks—his subjects were expected to honor his word.

"In a battle of the Hundred Years War, the blind king of Bohemia, showing much bravery and noble spirit, spoke to his several attendants. 'Gentlemen, friends, and

THERE MUST BE AN EASIER WAY TO GET TO BE A KNIGHT.

WHOOF!
WOUFF!
WUF!

brethren-at-arms—as I am blind, I request of you to lead me into battle that I may strike one stroke with my sword.' With their reins all tied together so they would not be separated, the king and his comrades rode into the fierce fray. The next morning they were found dead, still honorably tied together.

"If a knight broke a rule in a tournament, he dishonored himself and his comrades. For instance, on each charge of a joust, one or both knights could be violently unhelmed—at the least. It was an explosive shock to have a fully laced helmet ripped from your head. Sir Reginald de Roye, tilting[8] with Sir John Holland, attempted to soften this blow by fastening his helmet with but one slim thong. Thus his helmet flew off easily when struck.

_____

[8] **tilting:** charging on horseback with a lance to knock an opponent to the ground

Sir John's English comrades shouted, 'Ha! The French do not fight fair; why is not his helmet as well buckled on as Sir John Holland's? We say he is playing tricks.' They were sore put because they thought it was not chivalrous to seek clever, sneaky advantages.

"A friend of Sir Dana's, Sir Geoffrey de Charny, wrote three books on the meaning of chivalry, extending the code to include all men-at-arms, not just knights. His writings taught honor, compassion, moderation, cheerfulness, and above all the spirit of love. Sir Geoffrey was called the Perfect Knight, perhaps because he was not only a brave warrior but also a writer and philosopher. . . .'"

## Literature Review

1. What was it like to be a knight?
2. The time of knights is often thought of as a time of excitement and adventure. Do you think you would have enjoyed being a knight if you had lived in Europe during the Middle Ages? Why or why not? What might have prevented you from becoming a knight?
3. Write a poem or song that you think tells the most important information about knights.

Knights on horseback (right) were common sights during the Middle Ages in Europe. Most knights served as vassals to lords, who lived in castles such as this one (below)— Bodiam Castle in what is now the United Kingdom. Few knights were wealthy enough to own their own castles.

## CHAPTER 9
# REVIEW

## CONNECT MAIN IDEAS

Use this organizer to show that you understand how the chapter's main ideas are connected. Copy the organizer onto a separate sheet of paper. Then complete it by writing three examples to support each main idea.

### Heirs of Rome and Persia

**The Byzantine Empire**
Byzantine emperors built on their Roman past while making needed changes.

1. _____
   _____
2. _____
   _____
3. _____
   _____

**The Muslim Empire**
The religion of Islam affected people living in the lands into which it spread.

1. _____
   _____
2. _____
   _____
3. _____
   _____

**Europe in the Middle Ages**
Individuals and groups affected governments and ways of life during the Middle Ages in Europe.

1. _____
   _____
2. _____
   _____
3. _____
   _____

## WRITE MORE ABOUT IT

1. **Write a Letter**   Write a letter that might appear in your school newspaper about a school rule you think should be changed to keep up with the times. If you think your school should keep part of the old rule, tell which part and explain why that part should be kept.

2. **Write a Summary**   Tell in your own words how the religion of Islam grew.

3. **Write a Code of Conduct**   Write a code of conduct, like that of the medieval knights, for yourself and your friends. Decide whether or not you want to keep parts of the knights' code. Describe any parts you keep, and explain why you decided to keep them.

4. **Write a Schedule**   You are a European peasant-farmer during the Middle Ages. Write a schedule of your average day.

## USE VOCABULARY

Write a term from this list to complete each of the sentences that follow.

catholic          orthodox
Middle Ages    tenant
Muslim

1. Justinian wanted all the Byzantine people to follow _____, or officially accepted, Christianity.

2. The word _____ means "all-embracing."

3. A _____, or follower of Islam, believes that the Qur'an is God's word.

4. Historians call the years from about 500 to 1500 in Europe the medieval period, or the _____.

5. A _____ is someone who pays rent to a landowner.

## CHECK UNDERSTANDING

1. What was the Justinian Code? How did it relate to the old Roman codes?

2. How did Byzantine Empress Theodora influence Justinian?

3. What religious group considers Mecca to be a holy city? What religion is practiced by this group of people?

4. What were some of the advances made by the people of the Muslim Empire?

5. What new ideas did trade bring to people in the Muslim Empire?

6. What did Charlemagne do to strengthen his empire?

7. For what reason did people in Europe become crusaders?

8. The United States Constitution has its roots in the ideas first expressed in what English document?

## THINK CRITICALLY

1. **Past to Present**   How does Theodora's belief about why people should be given jobs compare with present-day beliefs?

2. **Explore Viewpoints**   How did different points of view about religion cause conflicts in Byzantine and Muslim civilizations?

3. **Think More About It**   Why do you think Europeans' views of Muslims changed when Europeans traveled to Muslim lands?

4. **Personally Speaking**   Do you think that children should ever fight in wars, as they did in the Children's Crusade? Explain your answer.

5. **Cause and Effect**   What effects did the bubonic plague have on Europe?

## APPLY SKILLS

**How to Understand National Symbols**
Reread the information on page 294 about symbols used on flags. Then create a flag to represent your family. If, for example, you consider physical strength an important quality of your family, you might include a strong animal in your design as a symbol of strength.

## READ MORE ABOUT IT

*The Middle Ages* by Fiona Macdonald. Facts on File. The history of the world from 500 to 1500 is explained through words and pictures.

*Science in Early Islamic Culture* by George W. Beshore. Franklin Watts. The author discusses the scientific discoveries and advances of the Islamic world.

*Walter Dragun's Town: Crafts and Trade in the Middle Ages* by Sheila Sancha. Crowell. This book follows a week's activities in the medieval town of Stanford (now Stamford), England, in 1275.

# EMPIRES IN ASIA *and the* AMERICAS

> 66 My descendants will wear gold, they will eat the choicest meats, they will ride the finest horses. 99
>
> Genghis Khan, founder of the Mongol Empire

Image of Mongol conqueror Genghis Khan, who lived from 1162 to 1227

# GROWTH for CHINA

## *L*ink to Our World

### In what ways can leaders of today help their countries develop rich cultures?

**Focus on the Main Idea**
*As you read, look for the ways that Chinese rulers helped China develop a rich culture.*

**Preview Vocabulary**
*draft*
*currency*
*porcelain*

Empress Wu, who lived in the late seventh century, was the first woman to rule China.

In the 1200s, while western Europe was still in the Middle Ages, China had a well-organized empire. Chinese cities, such as Beijing, bustled with trade. Boats and barges carrying people and goods crowded the Grand Canal, which linked Beijing (BAY•JING) with Hangzhou (HAHNG•JOH).

## BUILDING THE GRAND CANAL AND AN EMPIRE

The Chinese empire of the 1200s really began in A.D. 589. In that year the Sui (SWEE) dynasty brought China together after it had been divided for 400 years.

Sui emperors ruled for only 30 years. Yet in that short time they built one of the wonders of ancient times—the Grand Canal. By using existing waterways between the Huang He and the Chang Jiang and by digging new ones, they created a 1,000-mile (about 1,600-km) waterway. In this way they connected China's most important rivers. The Grand Canal linked northern and southern China for the first time.

Sui emperors made the peasants build the Grand Canal, just as earlier emperors had made peasants build the Great Wall. More than a million people worked on the job, and many died from the heavy work. The emperors also taxed the people heavily to pay for the project. In 610 the canal was opened. But in 618 the peasants rebelled against these cruel rulers, ending the Sui dynasty.

As the Sui dynasty ended, another ruling family, the Tang, claimed the Mandate of Heaven. Tang rulers added to China's lands by moving west into central Asia, south into what is now Vietnam, and east into Korea. To protect China's northern border, the Tang rebuilt parts of the Great Wall and made it longer.

Expanding China's empire required more soldiers, so Tang emperors made all male citizens serve in the army. Government officials used a **draft**, or system for choosing, to make sure China had enough soldiers whether the empire was at war or at peace. The Tang dynasty's powerful army kept China strong for 150 years.

 **In what ways did the Sui and Tang dynasties help build China's empire?**

The Tang gained control of China through military force. This clay figure represents a soldier in the Tang Imperial Guard. The job of the Imperial Guard was to protect the crown prince.

# A GOLDEN AGE

Under the Tang dynasty China entered a Golden Age that lasted from A.D. 618 to about 750. During this time the Chinese developed their civilization in many ways.

Much of the activity during the Golden Age took place in the Tang capital of Chang'an. A present-day historian has described ancient Chang'an as "the largest, wealthiest, and most cosmopolitan city in the world." Because the city stood at one end of the famous Silk Road, about 2 million people lived in and around Chang'an.

Many people in Chang'an worked for the government. During the Golden Age the Tang emperors improved the

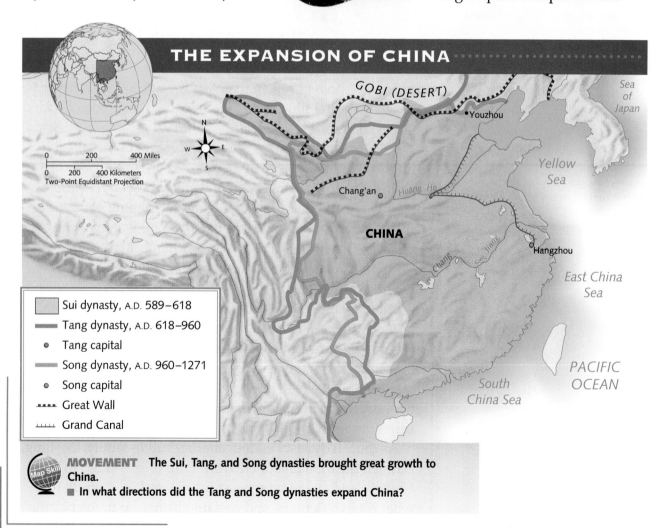

## THE EXPANSION OF CHINA

GOBI (DESERT)

Sea of Japan

•Youzhou

Yellow Sea

Chang'an ○ Huang He

CHINA

Chang     Jiang     ○Hangzhou

East China Sea

PACIFIC OCEAN

South China Sea

0   200   400 Miles
0   200   400 Kilometers
Two-Point Equidistant Projection

N W E S

Sui dynasty, A.D. 589–618
—— Tang dynasty, A.D. 618–960
● Tang capital
—— Song dynasty, A.D. 960–1271
● Song capital
▪▪▪▪ Great Wall
⊔⊔⊔⊔ Grand Canal

**MOVEMENT** The Sui, Tang, and Song dynasties brought great growth to China.
■ In what directions did the Tang and Song dynasties expand China?

This painting of court ladies and their servants (above) was found in a tomb near Chang'an. The Tang are remembered for both their paintings and their pottery (right).

government civil service examination system. More than ever, government jobs were filled on the basis of ability rather than on social class.

Books to help students pass the civil service examinations became popular. To print books faster, Tang craftworkers improved the use of block printing. The Chinese had long printed with blocks of stone that had words carved in them. Now they began to make wood or metal blocks to use as ink stamps. In later years Chinese printers invented movable type blocks for single characters. Better printing methods led to the invention of the first paper **currency**, or money. Paper currency was easier to carry around and exchange than heavy metal coins.

During the Tang dynasty the arts prospered. Potters made **porcelain**, a kind of clay pottery so thin that it looks almost clear. Chinese porcelain has been described as "so fine that the sparkle of water can be seen through it." The porcelain bowls and vases of the Tang were both beautiful and useful. Tang porcelain is still admired today.

Tang painters created beautiful landscapes and pictures of people and animals. The most famous Tang artist, Wu Dao-zu (WOO DOW•ZOO), worked with a "whirlwind brush," people said.

Poetry written during the Tang dynasty became as famous as Tang painting and porcelain. The work of one well-known poet, Li Bo (LEE BOH), reflects a pride in China's prosperity and cultural achievement. Li Bo, who lived from 705 to 762, wrote this of the Golden Age:

❝I desire to select and transmit the old, so that its splendor will last a thousand ages.❞

At this same time, the Chinese renewed their interest in religion. Tai Zung, the second Tang emperor, urged that people study Daoism and Buddhism. He also invited a priest to teach about Christianity. Under Tai Zung, Confucianism once again became China's official religion.

After about 750 the Tang dynasty grew weak because its emperors ruled poorly.

This Song painting shows the importance of both farming and the obedience of children to their parents in early China. In what way is each of these ideas shown?

By 900, leaders in some of China's distant lands began challenging Tang rule. In 960 one of them, Zhao Kuangyin (JOW KWAHNG•YIN), claimed the Mandate of Heaven and began the Song dynasty.

 **What new ideas developed during China's Golden Age?**

## CHINA UNDER THE SONG

By about 1050 China's population may have been more than 80 million. Most of these people were peasants, who lived in villages and worked on farms. Yet a large number of China's people also lived in cities and towns. Hangzhou, the capital of China after 1127, had a population of almost 1 million.

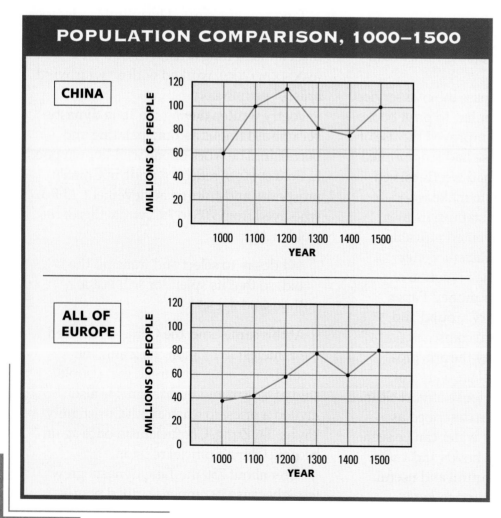

**POPULATION COMPARISON, 1000–1500**

CHINA

ALL OF EUROPE

**LEARNING FROM GRAPHS**
By the year 1000 China had a population of about 60 million.
■ In about what year did China have almost 60 million more people than in all of Europe?

The cities of Song China bustled with activity. Busy street traffic reflected the many kinds of people who lived in China's cities. Merchants moved their goods in carts and on bamboo poles. Servants carried wealthy people in sedan chairs, comfortable seats with poles attached so that they could be moved from place to place. Homeless people lived in the streets. And when floods came or crops failed, people who had lost their homes and farms crowded into the cities.

Changes were also taking place on the farms. A new, quick-growing rice let farmers raise two crops of rice each year instead of one. Water-control projects in southern China allowed more fields to be used. As more food was grown, the farmers sold their surplus, or extra amount, in the many small market towns.

Like the peasants in Europe, peasants in Song China were tenant farmers. They paid rent to a landlord. Sometimes the rent was half of their crops. Chinese landlords, like the nobles of the European manors, had much power over the peasants. Day after day, the landlords forced the peasants to work in the fields from morning until late at night to pay their rent. Few children had time to learn to read or write because they also worked in the fields.

# What?

## Rice

For the people of Song China, rice served as the main part of a meal, not a side dish. They ate huge amounts of the grain, perhaps as much as 2 pounds (about 1 kg) of cooked rice a day. They grew dozens of different kinds. Some had pretty colors. Others smelled like flowers when cooked. Rich families in Hangzhou even had their own kinds that they alone were allowed to eat.

The authority of the Song leaders did not last. By the early 1200s Mongol people from north of the Great Wall had conquered all of northern China. In 1271 Mongol leaders claimed the Mandate of Heaven and began the Yuan (yoo•AHN) dynasty.

**What was life like for Chinese peasants during the Song dynasty?**

# LESSON 1 REVIEW

## Check Understanding

1. **Recall the Facts**  How were Song China and western Europe both alike and different?
2. **Focus on the Main Idea**  How did the Sui, Tang, and Song leaders help China develop a rich culture?

## Think Critically

3. **Think More About It**  Why do you think the rule of the Tang dynasty is called the Golden Age of China?

4. **Cause and Effect**  What are possible causes for a time of great achievements in any country? What effect might a time of great achievements have on a country?

## Show What You Know

**Generalizing Activity**  On the basis of what you have read up to this point, write a generalization about leaders during the Golden Ages of civilizations.

# THE MONGOL EMPIRE

## Link to Our World

**What events today bring world cultures together?**

*Focus on the Main Idea*
*As you read, look for ways the Mongols brought the Chinese into closer contact with other cultures.*

*Preview Vocabulary*
khan
plunder

The Mongol people lived in a part of central Asia that today is called Mongolia. Like other people of the Asian steppe region, the Mongols were herders skilled as horse riders and warriors. Like nomads in most parts of the world, the Mongols lived in small clans. The Mongol clans often fought for grazing land and for water and firewood, which were scarce resources on the steppes.

From time to time a strong leader, or **khan**, brought some of these rival clans together. Because of their skills as riders and warriors, these united clans became an almost unstoppable fighting force. Under the leadership of the greatest of the khans, the Mongols conquered lands far and wide. The empire they created covered much of Asia.

## MONGOL CONQUESTS

Known for his cruelty, the khan Temujin (TEM•yug•juhn) struck fear in even the toughest Mongol warrior. At a meeting of clans in 1206, Temujin made himself leader over all the other khans. He took the title Genghis Khan, or "World Leader," and began to live up to his new name.

Genghis Khan and an army of about 130,000 riders swept down from Mongolia into northern China. Leaving behind a trail of destruction, the Mongols captured Beijing and renamed it Khanbalik (kahn•buh•LEEK). For the first time, China had been conquered by outsiders.

Before his death in 1227, Genghis Khan told his sons, "A deed is not glorious until it is finished." They knew he wanted the conquering to continue. The sons took their father's words as an order, and so did their sons after them.

The Mongol ruler Genghis Khan marched into China with his troops. What do you think was the outcome of the Mongol advances into China?

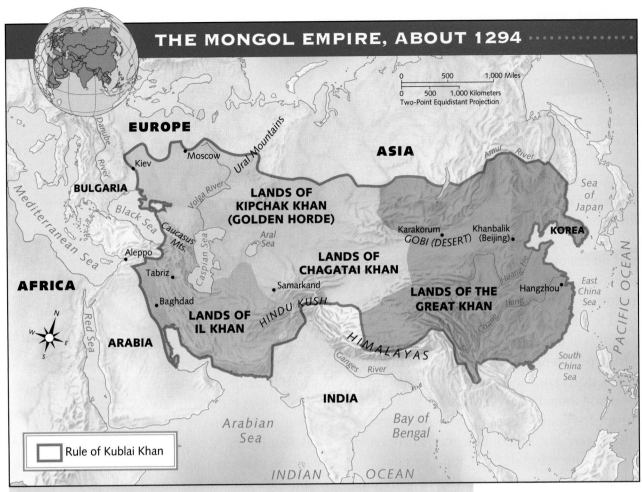

## THE MONGOL EMPIRE, ABOUT 1294

0 500 1,000 Miles
0 500 1,000 Kilometers
Two-Point Equidistant Projection

EUROPE

Danube River

Kiev · Moscow

Ural Mountains

ASIA

Amur River

BULGARIA

Volga River

Black Sea

Caucasus Mts.

Caspian Sea

Aral Sea

Mediterranean Sea

Aleppo

Tabriz

AFRICA

Baghdad

Red Sea

ARABIA

LANDS OF KIPCHAK KHAN (GOLDEN HORDE)

LANDS OF CHAGATAI KHAN

· Samarkand

HINDU KUSH

LANDS OF IL KHAN

Karakorum · GOBI (DESERT)

Khanbalik (Beijing) ·

KOREA

Sea of Japan

LANDS OF THE GREAT KHAN

Hangzhou

Huang He

East China Sea

PACIFIC OCEAN

Chang

HIMALAYAS

Ganges River

INDIA

South China Sea

Arabian Sea

Bay of Bengal

INDIAN OCEAN

☐ Rule of Kublai Khan

**REGIONS** The Mongol Empire, made up of several states called Khanates, grew to fill much of what is today the country of China.

■ Why do you think the Mongol Empire did not extend its borders farther?

The Mongols claimed Korea and tried unsuccessfully to invade Japan. They also captured central Asia and much of western Asia. Many of the lands once under Muslim control faced great destruction as the Mongols fought to claim them. Batu, one of Genghis Khan's grandsons, led armies into Europe, tearing through what is now Russia, Poland, and Hungary. They **plundered**, or took goods by force, everywhere they went. They also killed many people or took them as slaves. The frightened Europeans began to call the Mongol invaders the Golden Horde. "Golden" was for the riches they stole and "horde" meant "army on horses."

By about 1260 the Mongols had created the largest empire the world has ever known. It reached from the shores of the Black Sea to the Pacific Ocean. It covered central Asia, much of Persia, parts of eastern Europe, and all of China. In 1260 another grandson of Genghis Khan took the title Kublai Khan (KOO•bluh KAHN), or Great Khan, making himself head of the whole Mongol Empire.

Kublai Khan sent soldiers throughout the Mongol Empire to help bring about peace. With so much of Asia under Mongol control, merchants felt safe enough to travel the trade routes. They crossed Asia as they went to and from Europe and North Africa, carrying ideas as well as goods between East and West.

 *How did the Mongols bring both fear and safety to the lands they conquered?*

## AN EXCHANGE OF IDEAS AND GOODS

During the time of Mongol rule, Europeans and Chinese got to know one another better. In the late 1200s Marco Polo, his father Niccolò, and his uncle Maffeo were among the first Europeans to spend much time in China. They were amazed by what they saw.

Marco Polo marveled at Chinese inventions such as gunpowder and the compass. He also held paper currency for the first time. And on his visit to Kublai Khan's palace, he saw room after room filled with gold, jewels, and other riches. The Polos were also astonished to see Chinese cities with more than one million people.

Marco Polo returned to Europe with silks, jewels, porcelain, and stories about beautiful cities and amazing inventions. At first, few Europeans believed Polo's stories. When the stories were published, however, Europeans became very interested in China and its riches. European merchants began searching for the best trade routes to find their share of China's treasures.

The Mongols wanted to learn more about lands to the west that Marco Polo had described. Rabban Bar Sauma, a Christian who had been born in China, traveled to Europe to visit kingdoms there. All along the way, he gathered goods and tales of the West.

✓ **How did Marco Polo help bring Chinese ideas to the West?**

## THE MONGOL WAY OF LIFE

Chinese civilization dazzled Marco Polo and other visitors. The Chinese culture that had bloomed under the Tang and the Song continued to do so under the Mongols.

Although the Mongols conquered China, they took on many Chinese ways. The defeat by the Mongols seemed to change the Mongols more than it changed the Chinese. Chinese culture remained uniquely Chinese.

This early map (left) shows Marco Polo and his father and uncle with their caravan. The reports of their trip interested Europeans in Chinese products, such as this porcelain vase (below) from the Yuan dynasty.

Kublai Khan, grandson of the fierce Genghis Khan, was skilled both as a statesperson and as a warrior.

The Mongol leader Kublai Khan ruled well and did much for China. He extended the Grand Canal and had the main roads fixed.

His mail service, with more than 200,000 riders, reached the farthest parts of his empire. His strong armies kept the peace. Kublai Khan, however, is perhaps best known for bringing East and West together. Chinese cities became busy centers of trade as Westerners sought Chinese goods.

Although the Mongols had been cruel in their conquests, they tried to rule fairly. For example, the Mongols allowed people to practice their own religions. Even so, many Chinese did not like being ruled by the outsiders who had earlier destroyed so much.

The Mongols were better at fighting for more land than they were at governing it. Not long after Kublai Khan's death in 1294, the empire began to break up. It was too large for one person to rule. In addition, the peoples in the empire did not feel any connection with one another. Believing that the Mongols had lost the Mandate of Heaven, the people rebelled. In 1368 a rebel leader captured Khanbalik and formed a new dynasty, the Ming, which lasted almost 300 years.

 **For what is Kublai Khan most remembered?**

# LESSON 2 REVIEW

## Check Understanding

1. **Recall the Facts**  What was Genghis Khan's role in shaping the history of China?
2. **Focus on the Main Idea**  How did the actions of the Mongols bring Chinese people into closer contact with other cultures?

## Think Critically

3. **Personally Speaking**  Marco Polo praised the Mongol army for the sense of safety it brought to China. If you had been a Chinese citizen during this time, how would you have felt about the Mongol army?

4. **Past to Present**  How do people in the United States today learn about the customs of people around the world?

## Show What You Know

 **Research Activity**  Look through newspapers and magazines for something that has happened to bring together world cultures. Create a script for a television program that tells classmates how you think each culture was affected by this contact. Then act out the program as if you were on television.

# DID THE
# *M*ONGOLS
# HELP *or* HURT
# *C*HINA?

**U**nder the rule of Kublai Khan, China achieved many things. The Grand Canal was completed, an observatory was built, trade increased, and China became known everywhere for its wealth and greatness. One historian, speaking of the reign of Kublai Khan, said that it was "probably the most productive and beneficial of all the reigns of the Great Khans."

Not everyone living during the time of Kublai Khan, however, agreed that his rule was beneficial, or helpful, to the Chinese people. Some believed that the Chinese people suffered under the rule of the Mongol leader. Two people who held opposite views were Marco Polo, the European traveler who served in Kublai Khan's court for a number of years, and Cheng Sixiao (CHUHNG SOO•SHOO), a Chinese

painter and poet. Read the following quotation from Marco Polo and the poem by Cheng Sixiao to learn how each thought the rule of Kublai Khan affected the Chinese people.

The picture at right shows Mongol farmers peacefully at work, irrigating rice fields. The scene on page 315 shows a Mongol army attacking Persian forces.

## Marco Polo

“The great khan sends every year his commissioners to ascertain [find out] whether any of his subjects have suffered in their crops of grain from unfavorable weather, from storms of wind or violent rains, or by locusts, worms, or any other plague; and in such cases he . . . furnishes them from his granaries with so much grain as is necessary for their subsistence, as well as for sowing their land. . . . He provides in like manner for their clothing, which he has the means of doing from his tenths of wool, silk, and hemp. . . . By reason of this admirable and astonishing liberality which the grand khan exercises toward the poor, the people all adore him as a divinity [god].”

## Cheng Sixiao

“In the past, in the age of the former emperor,
Who faced the sun for forty years,
The bright light of learning and refinement flooded the
      world,
And superior and heroic men stood before their ruler.
But once the barbarian soldiers invaded,
With sudden shock, Han rule was toppled.
To this day the proper ways of men are in chaos.
To lonely mountain valleys have fled all the worthies of
      the former age.
In that age of peace, the ways of the superior man
      flourished,
Men of talent appeared who were models of human
      achievement.
With their open hearts they looked on the sun and moon,
From their mouths flowed words of lofty and noble
      import. . . .
Today the likes of it are not to be seen.
As I look about there is darkness on all sides.”

# COMPARE
## VIEWPOINTS

1. How did Marco Polo think the rule of Kublai Khan affected the Chinese people? How do you know?

2. How did Cheng Sixiao think the rule of Kublai Khan affected the Chinese people? How do you know?

3. Why might the viewpoint of a visitor to China during the time of Kublai Khan differ from that of a Chinese citizen?

# THINK
## –AND–
# APPLY

The people who live under the rule of a leader sometimes have a different view about their leader than people who view the leader from afar. What other leaders in history have given rise to these different views?

BUILDING CITIZENSHIP

# LESSON 3

# DEVELOPMENT OF JAPANESE CULTURE

## *Link to Our World*

### How can learning about other cultures affect societies?

### Focus on the Main Idea
*As you read, look for the ways in which the Japanese borrowed from and adapted Chinese culture.*

### Preview Vocabulary

| | |
|---|---|
| typhoon | daimyo |
| Shinto | samurai |
| kami | shogun |
| regent | |

The many islands that make up Japan lie close to the eastern edge of the Asian mainland. The Japanese call their island country Nippon, or "land of the rising sun." Many experts believe that the first Japanese migrated from the Asian mainland. When they reached the islands, they met the Ainu people who already lived there. Ancient Japanese legends say the first emperor of Japan was the descendant of the sun goddess. The Japanese thought their emperor was not just a human being with the right to rule but a Tenno, or "heavenly prince." Because of this, one family has inherited the emperor's authority in an unbroken chain.

The early Japanese believed that their emperor was a descendant of Amaterasu, the sun goddess. This picture, created in 1407, shows Amaterasu holding a globe with a rabbit inside.

## JAPAN'S EARLY DEVELOPMENT

Until the 400s the Japanese lived almost free from outside influence. Rough seas and fierce storms called **typhoons** kept other people away and stopped the Japanese from crossing the seas around them. Left alone, the Japanese developed strong feelings for their country. These feelings have shaped their culture for centuries.

The early Japanese were hunters and farmers, who had a great respect for nature. A central part of their culture was their religion, **Shinto**, or "the way of the gods." People who follow the Shinto religion believe that spirits called **kami** (KAH•mee) live in all natural things, such as stones, trees, and animals.

The Japanese believed that a different spirit protected each clan. Because of this belief, people felt great loyalty to their clans and clan leaders. The Japanese way of life, based on loyalty to clan leaders and respect for a godlike

# Where?

## Japan's Neighbor: Korea

The peninsula of Korea juts out from the Asian mainland, just 125 miles (200 km) away from the Japanese island of Kyushu. Like the ancient Japanese, the ancient Koreans felt the effects of Chinese civilization. For the Koreans, however, influences included not only the Chinese but the Japanese as well.

emperor, went on without change for hundreds of years.

> ✓ **What kept the early Japanese from contact with outsiders?**

## CHINA'S INFLUENCE ON JAPAN

Sometime during the first century A.D., the Japanese began to trade with people on the Asian mainland. Most likely, Korean merchants were the first to tell the Japanese about the Chinese civilization. The more the Japanese learned about China, the more interested they were.

In the mid-500s Chinese missionaries arrived in Japan. The missionaries brought not only Buddhism but also many Chinese customs. They introduced the Japanese to Chinese law, dress, architecture, art, and manners. The Japanese willingly accepted all these Chinese ways. In fact, for years they imitated the Chinese almost completely.

In 645, laws called the Taika (TY•kuh) reforms established a system of government for Japan based on Chinese government. But the Japanese changed some of the Chinese ways to meet their own needs. While the Chinese Mandate of Heaven passed from one dynasty to another, the Japanese rulers—the imperial family—claimed the right to rule for all time. And unlike the Chinese, the Japanese did not start a civil service. Instead, members of important clans held most of the government jobs.

As Japan began to use Chinese ideas about governing, the role of the emperor of Japan

| ORIGIN OF JAPANESE WRITING | | |
| --- | --- | --- |
| ENGLISH WORD | CHINESE WRITING | JAPANESE WRITING (KANSI) |
| Sun | 日 | 日 |
| Moon | 月 | 月 |
| Tree | 木 | 木 |
| Rain | 雨 | 雨 |
| Mountain | 山 | 山 |
| Water | 水 | 水 |

**LEARNING FROM CHARTS** The early Japanese based their way of writing on Chinese characters.
■ On the basis of these samples, do you think an ancient Chinese reader could have read Japanese writing?

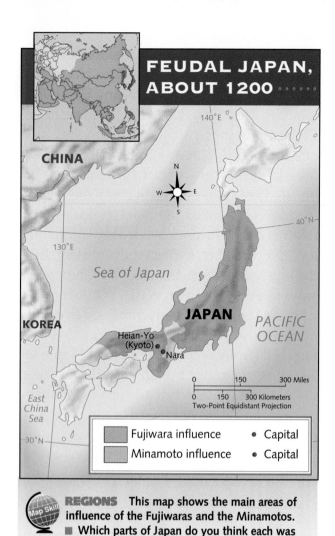

## FEUDAL JAPAN, ABOUT 1200

CHINA

KOREA

Sea of Japan

JAPAN

Heian-Yo
(Kyoto)
Nara

PACIFIC
OCEAN

East
China
Sea

140°E

40°N

130°E

30°N

0      150      300 Miles
0   150   300 Kilometers
Two-Point Equidistant Projection

Fujiwara influence  •  Capital
Minamoto influence  •  Capital

**REGIONS** This map shows the main areas of influence of the Fujiwaras and the Minamotos.
■ Which parts of Japan do you think each was less able to control?

changed. Once simply a religious leader, the emperor now also became a political leader, as Chinese emperors were. For the first time, the people of Japan united under the emperor. This unity lasted for about 300 years.

Like the Tang rulers of China, the Japanese imperial family supported the arts. They encouraged the people to create great works of art. For example, Lady Murasaki Shikibu (MUR•ah•SAHK•ee SHEE•KEE•boo) wrote the world's first novel, called *The Tale of Genji* (GEN•jee). It is filled with sensitive poems about nature and is considered one of Japan's finest pieces of literature.

✓ *How did the role of the Japanese emperor change in the 600s?*

## FEUDAL JAPAN

In the mid-800s the Japanese way of governing changed once more. About 858, a clan called the Fujiwara (FUJ•EE•WAH•rah) gained the right to rule in the emperor's name as regents. **Regents** are people who govern in place of a ruler. The Fujiwara, however, were unable to gain authority over Japan's most distant lands. The noble families who governed these provinces did not respect the regents as they respected the emperor. In these provinces nobles took control over the land and people.

As nobles claimed different parts of Japan, a system much like European feudalism began to form. The most powerful nobles, known as **daimyos** (DY•mee•ohz), or "great names," formed their own armies to defend and expand their lands. The soldiers, who became known as **samurai** (SA•muh•ry), vowed loyalty to their daimyo. The daimyo then gave them land won in battle. Peasants lived on and farmed the land owned by the samurai. They gave the samurai food and money to pay for his armor and weapons. In return, the samurai agreed to protect them.

Samurai were much like the knights of feudal Europe. Only the sons of nobles could become samurai, and their training was long and hard. As part of their training, they hiked barefoot in freezing weather. Sometimes they went for days without eating. This helped them accept pain

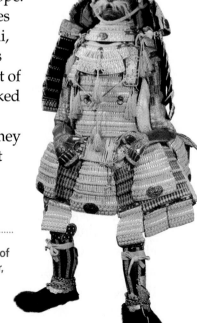

Samurai armor was made up of a helmet, a mask, body armor, and leg armor. Leather strips were laced together to make this easy-to-wear armor.

This woodblock print by Japanese artist Yoshitora shows Japanese samurai in battle. At the far left the shogun Minamoto Yoritomo rides a black horse. What mood does this artwork create?

and hunger without complaint. "When [a samurai's stomach] is empty," their teachers told them, "it is a disgrace to feel hungry." Their training also taught them to be ready at all times for battle and not to fear death.

As time went on, the daimyos took part in governing Japan. Late in the 1100s a daimyo named Minamoto Yoritomo (MEE•nah•MOH•toh YOH•rih•TOH•moh) set up a military government. In 1192 Minamoto Yoritomo convinced the emperor to give him the title of **shogun** (SHOH•guhn), or "leading general." The shogun was supposed to be the emperor's chief army officer. However, the shogun really held all the authority.

Minamoto Yoritomo and the shoguns who came after him built on the feudal system. They gave land to loyal daimyos. In return, the daimyos promised to send soldiers to the shoguns in times of war. This system lasted until the 1330s, when daimyos began to question the authority of the shoguns. Daimyos fought one another for control of land. By the late 1400s Japan was divided by civil war.

 **What was Japanese feudalism like?**

## Check Understanding

1. **Recall the Facts**   How did the Japanese learn about Chinese culture?
2. **Focus on the Main Idea**   How did the Japanese adapt Chinese culture to create their own civilization?

## Think Critically

3. **Personally Speaking**   Why do you think the Japanese took up many Chinese ways and ideas? Why did they change some of them?
4. **Think More About It**   Why do you think feudal systems developed in both Japan and Europe?

## Show What You Know

**Drama Activity**   In the early 1300s the Japanese developed a type of drama called the No play. The No play retells a historical event through the actors' hand and body movements. At the same time, key lines of the play are called out by a group of narrators. As a group, write your own No play about one event in the history of Japanese civilization. Assign parts, and then practice your play. Then perform the play for the rest of the class. You may want to add costumes and music to capture the attention of your audience.

# CIVILIZATIONS in the AMERICAS

LESSON 4

## Link to Our World

**How do people today change their environment, and how do these changes affect them?**

**Focus on the Main Idea**
*Think about the ways in which people living in the Americas between 1100 and 1500 adapted to and changed their environment.*

**Preview Vocabulary**
chinampa          pueblo
mesa          Mound Builders

In the 1400s the Japanese had plunged into "the time of the country at war." The Mongols had just lost the Mandate of Heaven. Europeans were recovering from the tragic Black Death. An ocean away, in the Americas, civilizations were reaching new heights.

In the late 1400s more than 45 million people lived in the Americas. From Alaska in the north to Tierra del Fuego in the south, the peoples of the Americas followed many different ways of life. Some groups of people lived as hunters and gatherers. Others settled in farming villages. Some of these villages grew into large cities with 150,000 to 250,000 people.

## THE AZTECS BUILD AN EMPIRE

The ancient Aztecs used this stone calendar, decorated with turquoise and shells, to keep track of the seasons.

Around 1150, groups of warlike nomads from the north invaded what is now central Mexico. The groups fought those who already lived there and one another for control of the region until one group, the Aztecs, won. With the land firmly under their control, the Aztecs settled it and became farmers.

According to legend, the Aztecs had moved south in search of a new homeland. Their war god, Huitzilopochtli (weet•see•loh•PAWCH•tlee), had promised they would find it where they saw an eagle fighting a snake on a cactus. Aztec warriors saw this sign on an island in Lake Texcoco (tes•KOH•koh) in central Mexico. There, in the mid-1300s, they built their capital city, which they called Tenochtitlán (tay•nohch•teet•LAHN).

The island had few natural resources, such as stone and wood, for building. Also, the land was marshy, and it

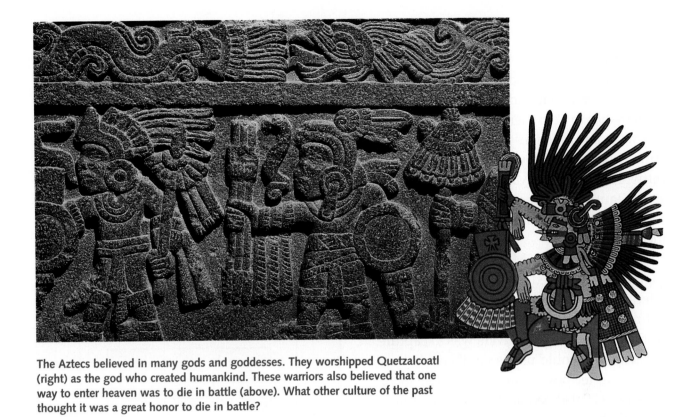

The Aztecs believed in many gods and goddesses. They worshipped Quetzalcoatl (right) as the god who created humankind. These warriors also believed that one way to enter heaven was to die in battle (above). What other culture of the past thought it was a great honor to die in battle?

flooded often. The Aztecs, however, found ways to solve these problems. They drove large posts deep into the ground and built reed houses on top of them. They also made bridges to connect the island capital to the mainland. They constructed a dike 9 miles (14.5 km) long to protect the city from floods. In addition, they built two brick aqueducts to bring drinking water from the mainland. Using wood and stone they had gotten through trade and as tribute, they built large palaces and flat-topped pyramid temples. By the 1400s Tenochtitlán had become a huge city of more than 300,000 people.

The Aztecs had another problem. The island on which Tenochtitlán was built did not have much good farmland. To solve this problem, the Aztecs built **chinampas** (chee•NAHM•pahz), islands made of platforms woven of reeds. They piled these platforms with mud taken from the lake bottom. On these "floating gardens" Aztec farmers grew corn, beans, peppers, and avocados.

Although the Aztecs settled as farmers, they continued their conquests. Armies of Aztec soldiers marched across central Mexico. The soldiers conquered one kingdom after another. By the 1500s the Aztecs controlled an empire that covered much of the land that is now present-day Mexico. The Aztec Empire grew to include as many as 5 million people. From every conquered people, the Aztecs demanded tribute in gold, silver, and cocao beans.

Like most early civilizations, Aztec society was divided into classes. The noble class made up the smallest part, while the farmers and slaves made up the largest. The slave class included people who had been taken as prisoners of war by the Aztecs. They had no rights. However, their children were born free rather than enslaved.

 **What did the Aztecs gain by adapting to and changing the environment?**

# THE AZTEC WAY OF LIFE

In many ways Aztec civilization was like the civilization of the Mayas. The Aztecs had an accurate calendar and made much use of mathematics to help them grow larger crops. They also developed a system of hieroglyphic writing, just as the Mayas had done. Their craftworkers, like the Mayan craftworkers, made beautiful jewelry and decorations. They also built many large, well-organized cities.

The Aztecs, like the Mayas, practiced a religion that included human sacrifice. The Aztecs believed that their gods needed the beating hearts of humans to survive. One reason the Aztecs fought wars was to capture prisoners they could use as sacrifices. At the height of Aztec power, around the year 1500, as many as 20,000 people died each year in Tenochtitlán's ceremonies.

The Aztec Empire lasted for fewer than 100 years. Peoples began to rebel against the Aztecs' harsh rule. Soon after, the Aztecs met their most fearsome enemy—the Spaniards who had come across the ocean from Europe.

 **How was Aztec civilization like Mayan civilization?**

### PLAN OF THE GREAT TEMPLE AT TENOCHTITLÁN

Wall
Temple of Huitzilopochtli
Main Temple
Street
Street
Ball court
Temple of Quetzalcoatl
Street
Pyramid of the Sun

**LEARNING FROM DIAGRAMS** This diagram shows a typical walled religious center for the Aztec people. This temple was an important part of the Aztec city of Tenochtitlán (below).
■ Why do you think a ball court was in the temple?

# What?

## Potatoes

The Incas grew more than 200 types of potatoes. They even knew how to freeze-dry their potato crop. First, they laid out potatoes in the chilly night air. The following morning they stamped out the water from the potatoes. Then they dried and stored them to be eaten during the winter when they were short of food.

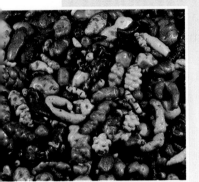

## THE INCA EMPIRE

The Incas in South America built their empire in much the same way the Aztecs built theirs. In time the Inca Empire covered more than 2,500 miles (about 4,000 km) along the Andes Mountains.

The Incas believed that they were descended from their sun god. Inca legends say that the Incas built their capital city of Cuzco (KOOS•koh) around 1200. In 1438, under a strong ruler named Pachacuti (pah•chah•KOO•tee), the Incas began to conquer many other kingdoms. By the 1500s Inca emperors ruled a wide area, which they called the Four Quarters of the World. In the empire lived 9 million people who spoke dozens of languages.

To hold the empire together, the Incas made the peoples they conquered follow the Inca way of life. The Incas believed that the many peoples of the empire would be less likely to rebel if everyone believed the same things and spoke the same language.

The Incas also brought unity to their empire by adapting to and changing their environment. They connected all regions of the empire with the capital city of Cuzco through a system of wide stone roads. They built bridges made of rope across deep mountain gorges, or narrow passes, where roads could not go. Runners passed messages to other runners along these roads and bridges.

Inca roads led to magnificent cities. The buildings in these cities were made of stones cut so carefully that they fit together perfectly. This way of building can still be seen in the ruins of the Inca city of Machu Picchu (mah•choo PEE•choo) in present-day Peru.

The Incas also changed their environment to make life easier. They used their engineering skills to make the land more suited to farming. They began by building terraces—flat ledges cut into hillsides and edged by stone walls. Then, using both irrigation and fertilizer, the Incas raised beans, corn, squash,

Ruins of the Inca city of Machu Picchu (right) and a gold knife (left) used in Inca religious ceremonies

tomatoes, and many kinds of potatoes on these terraces.

Most of the food grown on these terraces went to government storehouses. It was used to feed the Inca armies and was given to anyone who needed it. In return for this help, the Inca rulers expected the people to work for them on their many building projects.

✓ **In what ways did the Incas benefit from adapting to and changing their environment?**

# NORTH AMERICAN CULTURES

The peoples of what are now the United States and Canada were too few and lived too far apart to build empires like those of the Aztecs or the Incas. Even so, Native Americans in this region adapted to and changed their environment to form complex cultures.

Native peoples in the southwestern part of what is now the United States used irrigation

 **LOCATION** Throughout the Americas native peoples formed unique cultures. Each culture was influenced in some ways by its land and resources.

■ How do you think location affected the foods the first Americans ate? Which peoples do you think depended on fish and shellfish? Why?

**PEOPLES OF THE AMERICAS**

**TENOCHTITLÁN**

Valley of Mexico

Lake Texcoco

Tenochtitlán

Bridge

Lake Xochimilco

ARCTIC OCEAN

NORTH AMERICA

PACIFIC OCEAN

Gulf of Mexico

Tenochtitlán

MIDDLE AMERICA

Caribbean Sea

ATLANTIC OCEAN

Tropic of Cancer

SOUTH AMERICA

Machu Picchu
Cuzco

Equator

Tropic of Capricorn

**Indian Cultural Areas**
Arctic
Subarctic
Northwest Coast
Plateau
California
Great Basin
Southwest
Plains
Eastern Woodlands
Middle America
Caribbean
Andes
Tropical Forest
Marginal
Aztec
Inca

0   5   10 Miles
0   5   10 Kilometers

0   750   1,500 Miles
0   750   1,500 Kilometers
Azimuthal Equal-Area Projection

to make the dry land better for growing crops. They built systems of ditches—some of them 10 miles (16 km) long—to carry life-giving water to the fields.

Even though their environment was harsh, it did provide some natural resources. The people formed pots from clay and made baskets of grasses, woven tightly enough to hold water. They also built shelters several stories high on cliff ledges and on the tops of mesas. A **mesa** (MAY•sah) is a flat-topped hill with steep slopes. Some of these buildings, or **pueblos** (PWEH•blohs), had hundreds of rooms.

Across the continent of North America, life was quite different. In the Eastern Woodlands region lived people called the **Mound Builders**. Their civilization reached its peak between 1250 and 1400 with the Mississippian culture. This culture influenced the area from the Gulf of Mexico to the Great Lakes.

The Mound Builders got their name from the animal-shaped mounds of earth that they used to bury their dead or to build temples on. The largest settlement, Cahokia (kuh•HOH•kee•uh), near what is today St. Louis, Missouri, had 85 of these mounds.

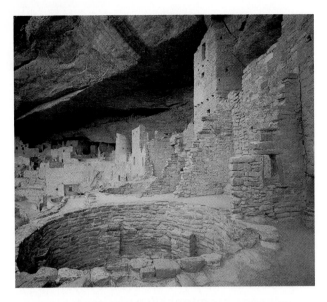
These pueblos were built into a wall of the Mesa Verde canyon in what is now southern Colorado.

The largest of them covered 16 acres and was 100 feet (30.5 m) high. Cahokia may have had a population of 75,000. At the time, few European cities were even close to this size.

 **How did the native peoples of North America change their environment?**

## LESSON 4 REVIEW

### Check Understanding

1. **Recall the Facts** Where in the Americas did the Aztecs and Incas live?
2. **Focus on the Main Idea** How did the native peoples of the Americas adapt to and change their environments?

### Think Critically

3. **Personally Speaking** Do you think the changes the Aztecs and Incas made hurt the environment in any way? Explain.
4. **Past to Present** What changes are being made to the environment in your community today? What effects have they had?

### Show What You Know

**Multimedia Activity** Work in a group to prepare and present a multimedia report to your class. Use library resources to find out which Native American groups lived in your state before 1500. Research their ways of life and how they adapted to and changed the environment to meet their needs. Also find out about family life, religion, government, education, and economy. Use any of the following as part of your report: posters, charts and graphs, slides, overhead transparencies, computers, music, dance, speeches, artwork, and models.

# Compare Maps with Different Scales

## Why Is This Skill Important?

Places are drawn larger or smaller on maps, depending on how much area is to be shown. Maps that show a large area must use a small scale—places must be drawn small to fit everything in. Maps that show only a small area can use a larger scale. Drawing places large allows details to be shown. Knowing about different map scales can help you choose the best map for gathering the information you need.

## Map Scales

The maps on these two pages show how scale can change depending on whether the map shows a close-up or faraway view of an area. Map A shows North America and highlights the Aztec Empire at the height of its power. Map B shows the Valley of Mexico, a high basin surrounded by mountains in central Mexico. Map C shows the Aztec capital city of Tenochtitlán.

Locate Tenochtitlán on all three maps. Map A shows it as a small dot. Map B shows the city and its surrounding area. Map C shows a close-up view of the area surrounding Tenochtitlán. Because Tenochtitlán is shown much larger on Map C than it is on Map A, the scale is said to be larger on Map C than on Map A. Like all large-scale maps, Map C shows a lot of detail about a small amount of land.

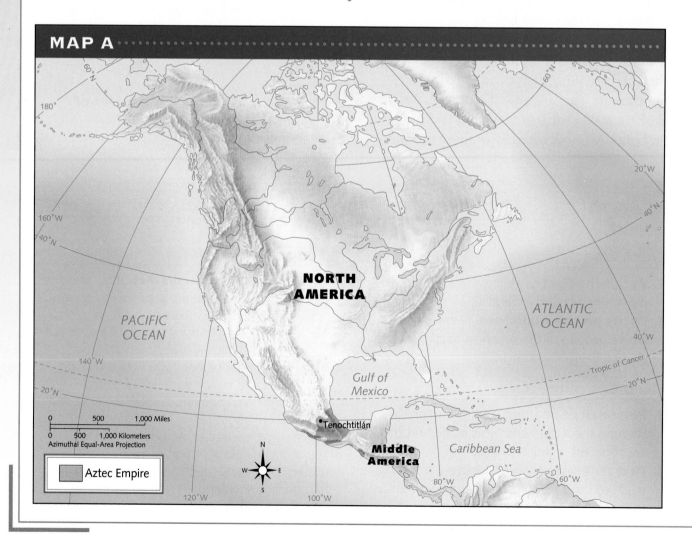

**MAP A**

180°
160°W
40°N
140°W
20°N
120°W
100°W
80°W
60°W
60°N
20°W
40°N
40°W
Tropic of Cancer
20°N

NORTH AMERICA
PACIFIC OCEAN
ATLANTIC OCEAN
Gulf of Mexico
•Tenochtitlán
Middle America
Caribbean Sea

0   500   1,000 Miles
0   500   1,000 Kilometers
Azimuthal Equal-Area Projection

N W E S

Aztec Empire

## MAP B

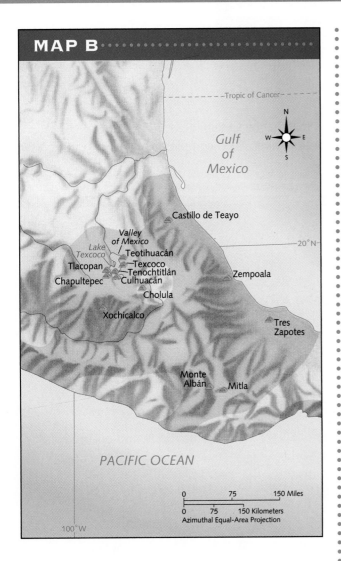

Tropic of Cancer

Gulf of Mexico

N
W   E
S

Castillo de Teayo

Valley of Mexico
Lake Texcoco
Tlacopan
Chapultepec
Teotihuacán
Texcoco
Tenochtitlán
Culhuacán
20°N
Zempoala

Cholula

Xochicalco

Tres Zapotes

Monte Albán    Mitla

PACIFIC OCEAN

0          75        150 Miles
0    75    150 Kilometers
Azimuthal Equal-Area Projection
100°W

## MAP C

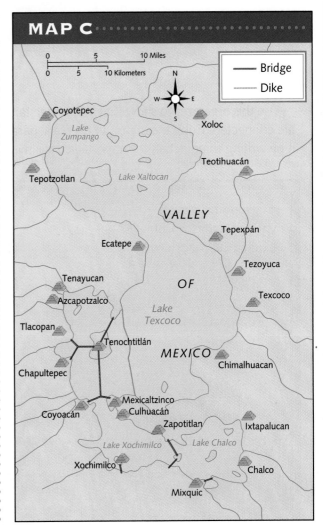

0          5          10 Miles
0      5      10 Kilometers

N
W   E
S

──── Bridge
──── Dike

Coyotepec
Lake Zumpango
Xoloc

Tepotzotlan
Lake Xaltocan
Teotihuacán

VALLEY

Tepexpán

Ecatepe

Tenayucan
Azcapotzalco

OF

Tezoyuca

Texcoco

Tlacopan
Lake Texcoco

Tenochtitlán

MEXICO

Chimalhuacan

Chapultepec

Coyoacán

Mexicaltzinco
Culhuacán

Zapotitlan

Ixtapalucan

Lake Xochimilco    Lake Chalco

Xochimilco

Chalco

Mixquic

## Understand the Process

Use the following questions as a guide to help you understand the best uses for small-scale and large-scale maps.

1. The Aztec capital was built on an island in Lake Texcoco. Find Tenochtitlán on all three maps. Also notice the other cities near the lake. Which map shows the most cities of the Aztec Empire?
2. Suppose that you wanted to travel from Tenochtitlán to the Gulf of Mexico. On which map can you best measure the distance between them? Tell why.
3. Suppose that you wanted to measure Lake Texcoco's length from its most northern point to its most southern point. Which map would you use?

4. You have read about the bridges that connected Tenochtitlán to the mainland. You have also read that the city's dike protected the city from floods. On which map can you find the bridges and the dike? Why do you think they appear on that map but not on the others?

## Think and Apply

Think about how you use maps when you travel. Find two road maps with different scales—perhaps a road map of your state and a road map of a large city within your state. When would it be more helpful to use the state map, with the smaller scale? When would it be more helpful to use the city map, with the larger scale?

# REVIEW

## CONNECT MAIN IDEAS

Use this organizer to show that you understand how the chapter's main ideas are connected. Copy the organizer onto a separate sheet of paper. Then complete it by writing three details to support each main idea.

### Growth for China
Under Sui, Tang, and Song rulers, China developed a rich culture.

1. _____
2. _____
3. _____

### Empires in Asia and the Americas

### The Mongol Empire
The Mongols brought the Chinese into closer contact with other cultures.

1. _____
2. _____
3. _____

### Development of Japanese Culture
The Japanese borrowed from and adapted Chinese culture.

1. _____
2. _____
3. _____

### Civilizations in the Americas
People living in the Americas between 1100 and 1500 adapted to and changed their environment.

1. _____
2. _____
3. _____

## WRITE MORE ABOUT IT

1. **Write a Poem** The Tang are remembered for their beautiful poetry and for many other cultural achievements. Write a brief poem that describes one cultural achievement of the Tang dynasty.

2. **Write a Character Sketch** Picture the life of Japanese samurai. Think of qualities that samurai had to have. Then write a character sketch describing one samurai who might have lived long ago.

3. **Write Journal Entries** Imagine first that you are Marco Polo. Write a journal entry that describes your impressions of China and of Kublai Khan's court. Then imagine that you are Kublai Khan. Write a journal entry about your impressions of Europe, based on what Marco Polo has said.

4. **Write a Description** In your own words, describe how the Aztecs both adapted to and changed their environment.

## USE VOCABULARY

Use each term in a complete sentence that helps explain its meaning.

| | |
|---|---|
| currency | plunder |
| daimyo | porcelain |
| khan | pueblo |
| mesa | samurai |

## CHECK UNDERSTANDING

1. Why was the Grand Canal important for China?

2. What role did Sui, Tang, and Song rulers play in helping China enter a Golden Age?

3. In what ways did Mongols hurt as well as help people in the lands they conquered?

4. Why did Europeans become interested in China?

5. How did the Mongols change Chinese policies toward outsiders?

6. From what culture did the early Japanese borrow ideas?

7. In what part of the Americas did the Aztecs live? In what part of the Americas did the Incas live?

8. Why did the Incas make the peoples they conquered follow the Inca way of life?

## THINK CRITICALLY

1. **Think More About It** Describe what you think your daily life would be like if you were a Chinese peasant living under the rule of the Sui dynasty.

2. **Personally Speaking** Write your opinion of leaders, such as Genghis Khan and Kublai Khan, who brought both destruction and positive change to the lands they conquered.

3. **Past to Present** Describe ways in which present-day peoples adapt to and change their environments to meet their needs. Tell which of these ways are useful and which you think are destructive.

4. **Cause and Effect** How does contact with people of different cultures affect people in the United States today?

## APPLY SKILLS

**How to Compare Maps with Different Scales** Use the maps on pages 326 and 327 to answer these questions.

1. Suppose you want to describe the location of Tenochtitlán to a friend. Which map would best show the city in relation to places your friend knows?

2. Suppose you want to find the distance between Texcoco and Chapultepec. Which map would you use? Why?

3. What might a map of Tenochtitlán look like at an even larger scale?

## READ MORE ABOUT IT

*Aztec, Inca and Maya* by Elizabeth Baquedano. Knopf. This book describes the history, beliefs, and everyday lives of the ancient Aztecs, Incas, and Mayas.

*The Aztecs* by Robert Nicholson and Claire Watts. Chelsea. The Aztec civilization of long ago is described through facts, illustrations, activities, and stories.

*Genghis Khan* by Judy Humphrey. Chelsea. The author shows how the Mongol leader built a large empire through both brutal force and careful planning.

*Journey into Civilization: The Mongols* by Robert Nicholson. Chelsea. Readers are introduced to the fascinating history of the Mongols and their ways of life.

# RELEVANT

## MAKE PEACE, NOT WAR!

During much of the world's history, war or the threat of war has been a way of life for many of the world's people. Leaders such as Charlemagne and Genghis Khan used war to build great empires in Europe and Asia. Few of these empires lasted long after the deaths of their builders, however.

Times of peace often followed the horrors of war. During peaceful times, cultural exchanges that promoted science, technology, literature, and art took place within and between empires. Also, different ways of governing were tried. All these developments changed people's lives. Soon rulers began to see that peace could be as useful as war for empire building. Genghis Khan, though known far and wide as a mighty warrior, once said that much trouble could be avoided if peaceful agreements could be reached.

Many world leaders today have come to agree with what Genghis Khan said long ago. More can be gained if we make peace, not war! In the 1990s, leaders of people in conflict—for example, leaders of the Israelis and the PLO in Southwest Asia and of the different ethnic groups in Bosnia in southeastern Europe— have finally decided to offer their hands in peace.

*World Peace,* by a 12-year-old artist from India

## THINK AND APPLY

Listen to the news on television and radio or look through newspapers and magazines to find out where war has been ended or avoided. What actions were taken by world leaders and world organizations to end these conflicts? Report your findings to the class in the form of a television news broadcast.

BUILDING CITIZENSHIP

THESE ARE THE COUNTRIES THAT HAVE RATIFIED (SIGNED) THE CONVENTION ON THE ... OF THE CHILD :

The painting in the background, called *Our Peaceful World,* is by an 11-year-old artist from the United States. The children shown in the foreground took part in a World Summit Children's Conference.

# STORY CLOTH

Study the pictures shown in this story cloth to help you review the events you read about in Unit 5.

## Summarize the Main Ideas

1. Roman civilization continued in the eastern region of the old Roman Empire. There the Byzantine Empire built on its Roman past while changing with the times.

2. Muhammad spread the message of Islam to people in the lands of Southwest Asia and beyond. Many of these people became Muslims. The people of the Muslim Empire are remembered for their achievements in science, geography, and mathematics.

3. In western Europe, many small independent kingdoms replaced the strong central government of the Roman Empire. During this time, many Europeans answered the call to join the Crusades.

4. Between 500 and 1300, China developed a rich culture.

5. The Mongols from Central Asia conquered the Chinese and brought them into closer contact with other cultures.

6. The Japanese borrowed ideas from Chinese culture as they developed their own civilization.

7. People in the Americas adapted to and changed their environment as they built civilizations.

**Making a Generalization**   Study the scenes in the story cloth. Then, based on what you see, make a generalization about life in different parts of the world between 500 and 1500.

## COOPERATIVE LEARNING WORKSHOP

### Remember

- Share your ideas.
- Cooperate with others to plan your work.
- Take responsibility for your work.
- Show your group's work to the class.
- Discuss what you learned by working together.

### Activity 1
## Present a Dramatization

Work with a partner to dramatize a reporter's interview with Marco Polo. One partner should be Marco Polo, and the other should be the reporter. Work together to write questions for the reporter to ask Marco Polo. Then write the answers Marco Polo will give. Practice the dramatization. Then act it out for your class.

### Activity 2
## Draw a Map

Work in a group to draw a map of North America. Then illustrate it with scenes from the lives of Native Americans who lived in North America between 500 and 1500. Be sure to include scenes showing Aztecs, Incas, and Mound Builders. Your group may also want to research and illustrate other Indian groups.

### Activity 3
## Make a Model

Work in a group to find out more about feudal life in Europe. Then work together to make a model of a manor. Label the parts of the model with small signs. Display your finished model in your classroom.

### Activity 4
## Write a Song

In a group, think about what your life would be like if you were one of the following: crusaders on the way to Jerusalem, Muslims defending their claim to the Holy Land, Japanese men and women living during the time of the shoguns, or early Aztecs. With group members, write the words of a song that describes your way of life.

Work with a partner. Use one of the groups of terms below to write a short story. Your story should help explain the meanings of the terms.

**Group A:** crusader, feudal system, manor, plague
**Group B:** mesa, Mound Builders, pueblo
**Group C:** Catholic, icon, mosaic, orthodox, patriarch

## HECK UNDERSTANDING

1. What were some of the achievements of the Byzantine emperor Justinian?

2. What is the Qur'an, and why is it important to the religion of Islam?

3. How did the defeat of China by the Mongols affect both Chinese and Mongol cultures?

4. In what ways did the Chinese influence Japanese civilization?

5. How did the Aztecs change their environment as they built Tenochtitlán?

6. How did Native Americans of the Southwest adapt to their dry environment?

## HINK CRITICALLY

1. **Past to Present** What present-day groups are fighting over differences in religion?

2. **Explore Viewpoints** Why do you think some groups of people, such as the samurai of Japan, have been willing to go through great difficulty to reach their goals?

3. **Personally Speaking** Which of the cultures you read about in this unit interests you the most? Why?

4. **Cause and Effect** How has American culture been influenced by the cultures of other countries?

## PPLY GEOGRAPHY SKILLS

 **How to Use Maps with Different Scales** Use Map A and Map B to answer the questions.

1. Which map would you use to identify ancient cities fewer than 100 miles (161 km) from Constantinople? Explain.

2. Which map would you use to find the distance from the western edge of Constantinople to its eastern edge? Explain.

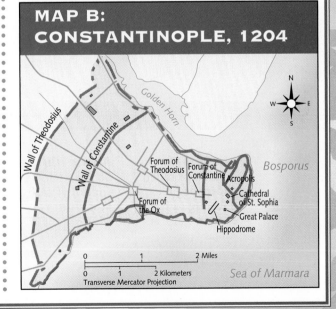

**MAP A: BYZANTINE EMPIRE, 1204**

**MAP B: CONSTANTINOPLE, 1204**

# UNIT 6

# GROWTH of TRADE

**500**

**About 600**
Arab ships called dhows begin traveling to the eastern coast of Africa

**700**

**About 700**
Soninke traders gain control of parts of West Africa

**762**
Baghdad rises as a Muslim trading center

**About 800**
Viking invasions begin in northern Europe

**900**

**About 900**
Muslims control Indian Ocean trade

*T*he empires that formed between 500 and 1500 came into closer contact than empires ever had before. Daring merchants traveled between these empires in search of new goods and trade markets. Over time, the thousands of miles of trails and waterways the merchants followed became trade routes. At first these routes just crossed land and followed rivers and coastal waters. Later, trade routes crossed oceans and linked continents. As trade grew, people of different lands learned more and more about one another.

◀ Scene of a Chinese port and market

**1100**

**About 1050**
African trading empire of Ghana flourishes

**1274**
Marco Polo travels to China

**1300**

**1324**
Mansa Musa, of Mali, makes his pilgrimage to Mecca

**About 1400**
Admiral Zheng He extends Chinese trade routes

**1500**

MARCVS POLVS

# THE ROYAL KINGDOMS OF
# Ghana, Mali, and Songhay
## LIFE IN MEDIEVAL AFRICA

by Patricia and
Fredrick McKissack

Muslim merchants traveling the north-south trade routes across the Sahara brought Arab culture and the religion of Islam to West Africa. In turn, the people of Africa shared their customs. Ideas moved back and forth as people traveled between Muslim and West African lands.

In 1324 Mansa Musa (MAN•sah MOO•sah), the ruler of the West African empire of Mali, made his hajj (HAJ), or pilgrimage, to the Muslim holy city of Mecca. Never before had the Muslims in such places as Egypt seen a visitor like Mansa Musa. Their ideas about the people of West Africa changed forever.

From 1307 to 1332 Mansa Musa ruled over the empire of Mali in West Africa.

# The Great Hajj

Months before Mansa[1] Musa's departure from Mali, officials and servants began preparing for the long trip. Five hundred slaves, each carrying a six-pound staff[2] of gold, arrived in Cairo, Egypt, in July of 1324. Next came Musa and his entourage,[3] followed by a caravan of one hundred camels, each carrying three hundred pounds of gold. A hundred more camels carried food, clothing, and other supplies. All together sixty thousand people accompanied the mansa to Mecca.

Mansa Musa reached Cairo after eight months of travel. His Arab guide suggested that he visit the local ruler or sultan. Musa rejected the idea, saying he wasn't interested in making a social call. The guide convinced him that his actions might be taken as an insult by an important Muslim brother. So Musa agreed to make the visit.

It was customary that a visitor kneel and kiss the ground before the sultan. Mansa Musa flatly refused. He was richer and controlled more territory than the sultan of Egypt, so why, he asked, should he kowtow[4] before a lesser king? Once again the guide explained the custom to Musa. "Very well," Musa agreed, choosing diplomacy. "I will prostrate[5] myself before Allah, who created me and brought me into the world." Having done this, the sultan compromised, too. He welcomed Musa to come sit beside him, a sign that they were equals.

Musa continued to Arabia, where he completed his hajj. Merchants and travelers had teased Middle Easterners with stories about

---

[1] **mansa:** ruler
[2] **staff:** stick or pole
[3] **entourage:** group of people who take care of the needs of an important person
[4] **kowtow:** kneel and touch forehead to the ground as a sign of respect
[5] **prostrate:** lie flat, face down

## MANSA MUSA'S HAJJ, 1324

- - - ➤ Possible route of Mansa Musa's hajj

ATLANTIC OCEAN
EUROPE
Mediterranean Sea
ASIA
Arabian Peninsula
Cairo
EGYPT
Medina
ARABIA
Mecca
Red Sea
Nile River
Walata
Timbuktu
Gao
MALI
Jenné
Niani
Niger River
AFRICA
Gulf of Guinea
INDIAN OCEAN

N W E S

0   500   1,000 Miles
0   500  1,000 Kilometers
Azimuthal Equal-Area Projection

**MOVEMENT** Muslims are expected to make a pilgrimage, if possible, to Mecca on the Arabian Peninsula.
■ How would you describe the route Mansa Musa took?

the gold-rich empires south of the Sahara. When news spread that the king of Mali was in the city, people lined the streets to see him.

Everywhere Mansa Musa went he graciously paid for every service in gold and gave lavish gifts to his hosts. Merchants scrambled to get his attention, for it was not uncommon for Musa to buy up everything that was presented to him. Beggars lined the streets as he passed, hoping to receive a gold nugget.

By the time Mansa Musa left the Middle East, he had put so much gold into circulation, its value fell sharply. A reporter in the service of the Egyptian sultan reported that the Cairo gold market had been so saturated that it still had not fully recovered twelve years after Mansa Musa's fabulous hajj.

*This unit tells more about Mansa Musa and his amazing trip. It also tells how people of different cultures learn more about one another through their trading contact.*

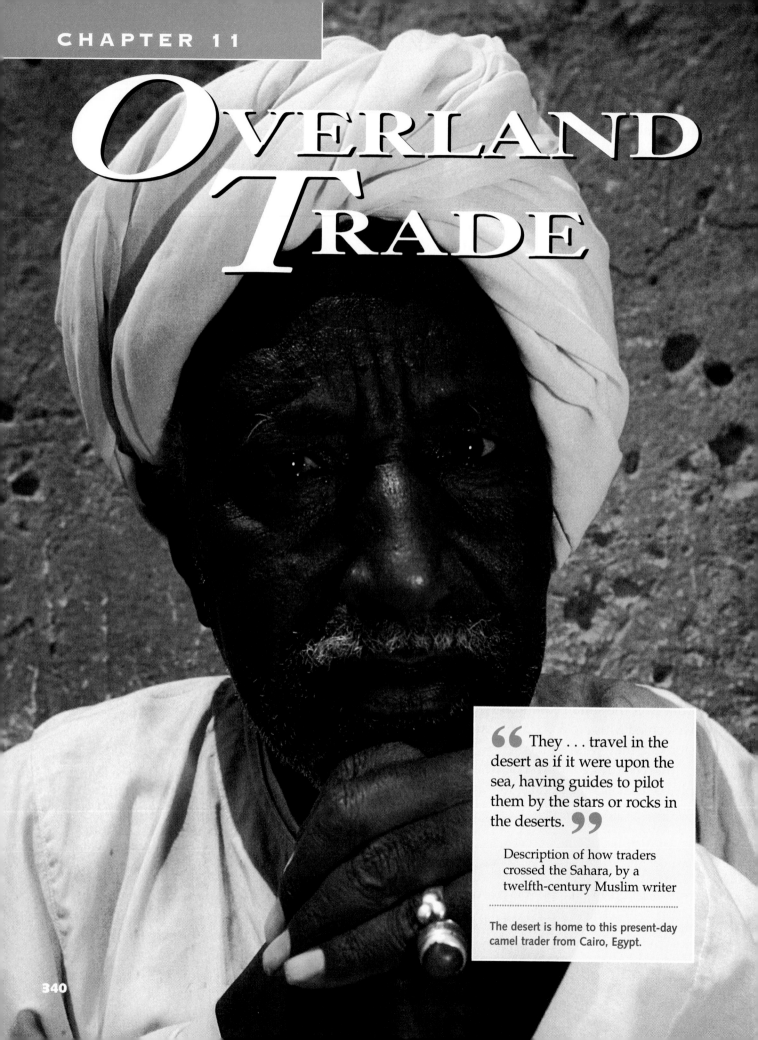

# CHAPTER 11

# OVERLAND TRADE

> 66 They . . . travel in the desert as if it were upon the sea, having guides to pilot them by the stars or rocks in the deserts. 99
>
> Description of how traders crossed the Sahara, by a twelfth-century Muslim writer
>
> The desert is home to this present-day camel trader from Cairo, Egypt.

# THE TRADING EMPIRES OF
# WEST AFRICA

LESSON 1

## Link to Our World

### Why do present-day countries seek trading partners?

### Focus on the Main Idea
*As you read, look for reasons the peoples of the West African empires traded with other peoples.*

### Preview Vocabulary
*savanna*
*tropical rain forest*
*tariff*
*mansa*

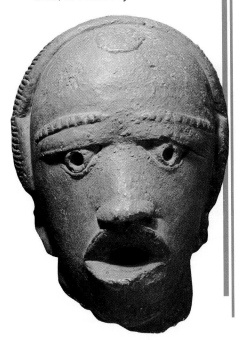

Found in 1943, this Nok sculpture is more than 2,000 years old. It is made of terra-cotta, or baked clay.

Trade has always been important to the peoples of Africa. Early peoples traded surplus resources for resources that were scarce where they lived. Over the years trade networks developed. Then, between the years 700 and 1500, powerful West African empires that were based on trade developed. The wealth of these empires attracted traders and travelers from many other lands.

## WEST AFRICAN BEGINNINGS

Africa is a giant among continents—the second largest in the world. Geographers usually describe the continent in terms of five regions—North Africa, West Africa, Central Africa, East Africa, and Southern Africa.

Much of Africa is a plateau broken in places by deep basins and valleys. The Great Rift Valley stretches about 3,500 miles (5,633 km) north and south through East Africa. It is one of the world's longest and deepest valley systems. Deserts also cover large parts of Africa. The Sahara, the world's largest desert, covers more than 3.5 million square miles (9 million sq km) of North Africa.

South of the Sahara lies West Africa. Much of West Africa is a grassy plain, or **savanna** (suh•VA•nuh). A tropical region covers West Africa's southern coast and much of Central Africa. This hot, wet land with trees so tall that they block the sunlight is a **tropical rain forest**.

Survival was easy for the early peoples of West Africa. The savanna was full of wild animals that could be hunted for food, and the fertile soil was perfect for growing crops. Because of this, West Africa's population grew quickly.

Africa offers much geographical diversity. The desert lands of the Sahara (top left) provide a sharp contrast to the jungle of the tropical rain forest (top right). South of the desert lie the grasslands of the savanna (bottom left).

About 300 B.C. people in the savanna learned how to shape iron by heating it. The earliest known iron users in West Africa were the Nok people. They lived from about 900 B.C. to A.D. 200 in the region that today is northern Nigeria (ny•JIR•ee•uh).

Iron changed the lives of the Nok people. It gave them stronger weapons for hunting and fighting. Iron tools also made it easier for them to clear land and grow crops. Because of these advantages, the Noks and other iron users grew powerful.

By the 700s iron users called the Soninkes had taken over much of the West African grassland. The land they lived on, alongside the Niger River, was fertile. The Soninkes made the most of their location by using water from the Niger to irrigate their land.

The Soninkes were not only skilled farmers but also good traders. Their location was ideal for a center of trade. The region lay between the forestlands south of the Niger and the desert lands of the Sahara in North Africa. North African merchants crossed the Sahara to trade with the Soninkes. As their main trade good, the Soninkes offered gold.

Gold, however, was a scarce resource in the grasslands where the Soninkes lived. To get gold to trade, they traded with the kingdom of Wangara, to the south. The Soninkes traded salt, which they had gotten from the Muslim merchants of North Africa, to the Wangaras for gold. Because the Wangaras had very little salt, they were willing to trade gold for it.

**LEARNING FROM DIAGRAMS** The Soninkes were at the center of the gold-and-salt trade.
■ Who ended up with the gold? Who ended up with the salt?

SONINKE TRADE CYCLE

Once the Soninkes got the gold from the Wangaras, they traded it to North African merchants for more salt. This cycle of trade in gold and salt went on through the years. The Soninkes also served as the go-betweens for the trade of other goods. In doing so, they took Mediterranean goods such as paper, woven cloth, and perfumes to the peoples farther south in Africa.

Because the Soninkes made a profit at both ends of their trade cycle, they grew powerful and rich. Their wealth led to the development of the first great empire in West Africa.

✓ **How did the Soninkes trade salt and gold? What was the result?**

## GHANA

The new West African empire soon became known by a title used by its rulers—*Ghana* (GAH•nuh), meaning "war chief." Ghana, which was located between the Senegal and upper Niger rivers, began its rise to power around 700. By the year 1000 the empire covered more than 100,000 square miles (258,980 sq km).

Much of what we know about early Ghana comes from the works of Muslim scholars. One of these scholars, al-Zuhri (al•ZUKH•ree), wrote about Ghana's rise to power. He said that the Ghanaians attacked peoples who were "ignorant of iron and who [fought] with

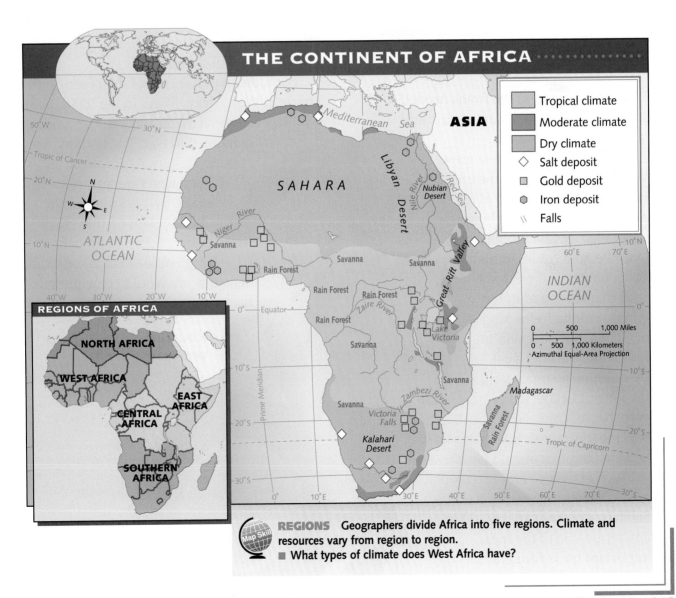

THE CONTINENT OF AFRICA

ASIA

- Tropical climate
- Moderate climate
- Dry climate
- ◇ Salt deposit
- □ Gold deposit
- ⬡ Iron deposit
- \\ Falls

Mediterranean Sea

SAHARA

Libyan Desert

Nubian Desert

Red Sea

Niger River

Savanna

ATLANTIC OCEAN

Rain Forest

Savanna

Savanna

Rain Forest

Rain Forest

Zaïre River

Great Rift Valley

INDIAN OCEAN

Lake Victoria

Savanna

Equator

Rain Forest

Savanna

Madagascar

Savanna Rain Forest

Zambezi River

Victoria Falls

Savanna

Prime Meridian

Kalahari Desert

0   500   1,000 Miles
0   500   1,000 Kilometers
Azimuthal Equal-Area Projection

Tropic of Capricorn

REGIONS OF AFRICA

NORTH AFRICA

WEST AFRICA

EAST AFRICA

CENTRAL AFRICA

SOUTHERN AFRICA

**REGIONS** Geographers divide Africa into five regions. Climate and resources vary from region to region.
■ What types of climate does West Africa have?

ebony clubs." The Ghanaians, with their iron spears, easily defeated these peoples.

As time passed, each Ghanaian king won authority over more kingdoms in West Africa. The kings ordered the Ghanaian army to keep trade routes across the savanna safe from enemy attacks. The kings then charged **tariffs**, or taxes, on all goods passing through the savanna. The eleventh-century Muslim geographer al-Bakri (al•BAHK•ree) explained how these tariffs worked:

> 66 The king exacts [demands] the right of one dinar [an Arab coin] of gold on each donkey-load of salt that enters his country, and two dinars of gold on each load of salt that goes out. 99

The tariffs provided the funds needed to feed the soldiers in Ghana's army and support its government.

As the empire of Ghana grew, lands rich with gold came under its control. The "master of the gold," as the Ghanaian king was called, held a monopoly over the gold trade. As al-Bakri wrote, "All pieces of gold that are found in the empire belong to the king of Ghana, but he leaves to his people the gold dust." By claiming so much gold, the king of Ghana made sure that this metal did not become too easy to get. In this way, he kept the price of gold high.

Much of the gold trade took place near Ghana's capital city, Kumbi-Saleh (KOOM•bee SAH•lay). This city lay on one of the most important trade routes across the western Sahara. North African merchants brought to Kumbi-Saleh their most important trade good—pure salt from mines in the Sahara. At that time salt was used not only to add more flavor to food but also to keep meat from rotting. Salt was worth a lot in West Africa because it was a scarce resource there. At times a trader might have to pay 1 pound (454 g) of gold to get an equal amount of salt!

Besides gold, the North Africans traded for ivory, cotton goods, and animal skins. They also bought slaves, whom they later sold to owners of salt mines or large farms. In return, the North Africans traded horses, swords, glass, and wool clothing.

For more than 300 years, Ghana controlled trade in West Africa. Then, in the 1000s, quarrels between Ghana and a Berber trading center led to war. The Berbers, from northwestern Africa, won, and Ghana never became powerful again. By 1203 the empire had broken up into small kingdoms. In time the people of the fallen Ghana Empire would come under the rule of other African empires.

**How did Ghana's kings get their wealth?**

66 *ALL PIECES OF GOLD that are found in the empire belong to the king of Ghana.* 99

Muslim geographer al-Bakri

Artifacts such as this bracelet and this sculpture of a bird called an ibis are evidence of metalworking skills in the empire of Ghana.

This section of a fourteenth-century map shows the great Mali Empire. The seated figure with a crown is the ruler Mansa Musa. Why has the mapmaker pictured Mansa Musa holding out a gold nugget to a trader?

## GROWTH OF ISLAM IN WEST AFRICA

The Ghanaians were not the only ones to trade with Muslim merchants. In the ninth century the kingdom of Kanem (KAHN•em), which had risen on the shores of Lake Chad, began to grow through trade. Around the same time trading centers formed along the Niger River at Jenné (jeh•NAY) and at Gao (GOW).

Contact with the Muslim North Africans through trade began to change the lives of the people in West Africa. The Muslim traders showed West African traders how to use money instead of bartering. They also brought with them the Arabic language.

Most important, West Africans began to accept the religion of Islam. The kings of Ghana, Kanem, and Gao became Muslims in the 1000s. Later the rulers of other kingdoms and many African traders also accepted Islam. The great empires that rose in Ghana's place were based not only on trade but also on Islam.

 **How did North African traders change life in the West African trading kingdoms?**

## MALI AND MANSA MUSA

About 25 years after the fall of Ghana, a new empire called Mali formed in West Africa. The people who founded Mali were called Malinkes (muh•LING•kayz). Under their Muslim leader Sundiata (sun•JAHT•ah), the Malinkes conquered many of the small kingdoms Ghana had once held, including those rich in gold. Mali's riches, like Ghana's, came from the gold-for-salt trade.

The **mansas**, or rulers, who followed Sundiata won more land for the Mali Empire. Mali grew to be nearly twice as large as the empire of Ghana had been. Mali's greatest growth came during the rule of Mansa Musa, from 1307 to 1332. During his rule Mansa Musa extended the empire to include the rich trading markets of Gao and Timbuktu (tim•buhk•TOO). The addition of lands brought even more wealth to the empire.

Mali became known for more than its wealth, however. Mansa Musa encouraged knowledge and study throughout his empire. A Muslim himself, Mansa Musa invited Arab scholars to come to Mali. Many did, and Mali became a center of learning. Students from as far away as Egypt and Arabia studied at the university at Timbuktu.

In 1324 Mansa Musa made his famous pilgrimage to Mecca, the Muslim holy city. All who saw him on his travels through North Africa and Southwest Asia were amazed. Mansa Musa's servants glittered in their fine clothing. His warriors carried golden spears. All along the way, Mansa Musa handed gifts to almost everyone he met.

The pilgrimage helped make Mansa Musa and the empire of Mali known far and wide. Mali's trading influence grew. Later rulers of Mali, however, were not as strong and wise as Mansa Musa had been. They could not hold on to the land that he had gained during his rule. Because of this, Mali's power began to slip away.

✓ **Why did people come to Mali during the rule of Mansa Musa?**

## SONGHAY

As Mali weakened, another West African empire began to grow. By the late 1400s much of what had been Mali had become part of the Songhay (SAWNG•hy) Empire. Like Ghana and Mali before it, the Songhay Empire grew rich from its control of trade routes across the Sahara. The Songhays also took control of the main trading centers along the Niger River—Jenné, Timbuktu, and Gao. War canoes along the Niger protected these trading cities from attacks by raiders.

The Muslim traveler and geographer Leo Africanus (LEE•oh af•rih•KAY•nuhs) visited Songhay in the early 1500s. In Gao he found "rich merchants who travel constantly about the region with their wares." The people of Gao, he saw, had more than enough gold to spend on goods imported from Europe and North Africa.

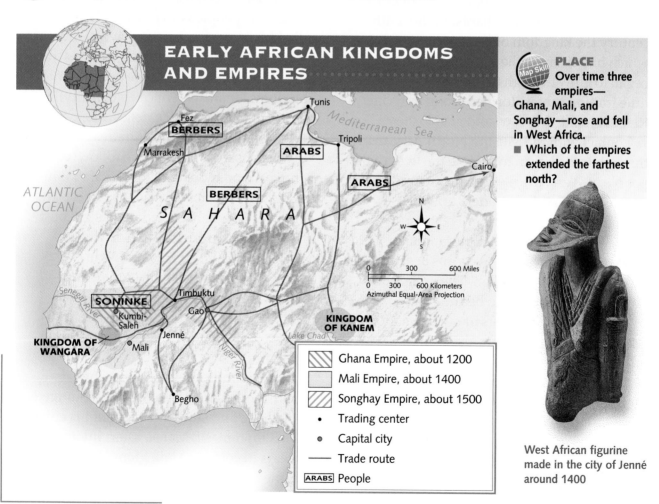

**EARLY AFRICAN KINGDOMS AND EMPIRES**

**PLACE** Over time three empires—Ghana, Mali, and Songhay—rose and fell in West Africa.
■ Which of the empires extended the farthest north?

Ghana Empire, about 1200
Mali Empire, about 1400
Songhay Empire, about 1500
• Trading center
• Capital city
— Trade route
ARABS People

West African figurine made in the city of Jenné around 1400

Rulers who wanted the wealth and power of Songhay waited for a chance to capture it. In 1591 the ruler of Morocco in North Africa sent an army of about 4,000 soldiers to attack Songhay. The Songhay soldiers fought with swords. Their attackers fought with weapons new to the Songhays—guns, which the

A sculpture made in the 1400s (left) and a tomb built in the 1500s are reminders of the Songhay Empire of long ago.

## What?

### Griots

Most West African societies had no system of writing. Their history, laws, religion, and customs were kept alive by people known as griots (GREE•ohz). The griots remembered all this information and passed it on to the next generation by word of mouth. This was such an important task that griots had to begin their training at a very early age. After the North Africans brought reading and writing to West Africa, West African scholars began to write down their history. Even so, the griots of West Africa continued to be the keepers of the people's history through the spoken word.

Moroccans had gotten from Southwest Asia. The Songhays could not hold off the Moroccan attacks. The Songhays' defeat led to the end of the Songhay Empire. The trade routes across the Sahara were still used, but they became less important. European ships sailing Africa's Atlantic coast created a new route for West African trade.

 **Why did other peoples want the lands of the Songhay Empire?**

## LESSON 1 REVIEW

### Check Understanding

1. **Recall the Facts**   What were three important West African empires?
2. **Focus on the Main Idea**   Why did the peoples of the West African empires trade with other peoples?

### Think Critically

3. **Think More About It**   Why did the North African traders want gold so much? Why were the Wangaras willing to trade it?
4. **Cause and Effect**   How did conquering kingdoms rich in gold help Ghana's economy?

5. **Past to Present**   What kinds of natural resources are scarce in your state? How do people in your state get products made from these natural resources?

### Show What You Know

 **Journal Activity**   Imagine that you are a North African merchant traveling with a caravan to one of the West African trading towns. Write journal entries about the trip across the Sahara, your arrival in West Africa, and the trading that takes place.

# Compare Maps with Different Projections

## Why Is This Skill Important?

Over the centuries Arab, Chinese, and European mapmakers have developed different ways to show the round Earth in the form of a flat map. These different representations of the Earth are called **projections**. Every map projection has **distortions**, or parts that are not accurate. This is because the shape of the round Earth needs to be split or stretched to make it flat. Identifying these distortions will help you understand how map projections can best be used.

## Map Projections and Their Uses

Different kinds of map projections have different kinds of distortions. Some map projections distort the shape or the size of the area shown. Some show distances to be greater or less than they actually are. One way that mapmakers classify map projections is by the properties that are distorted the least.

Map A is an equal-area projection. Notice that the prime meridian and the equator divide the hemispheres so that their areas are equal. An **equal-area projection** shows the sizes of regions in correct relation to one another, but it distorts shapes. Because an equal-area projection shows correct size relations of regions, it is useful for comparing information about different parts of the world. The projection on Map A below is just one of the many different kinds of equal-area projections.

Map B is a conformal projection. Notice that the lines of longitude are all an equal distance apart. On a globe the lines of longitude get closer together as they near the poles, where they meet. Also notice on Map B that the lines of latitude closer to the poles are farther apart. On

**MAP A: EQUAL-AREA PROJECTION**

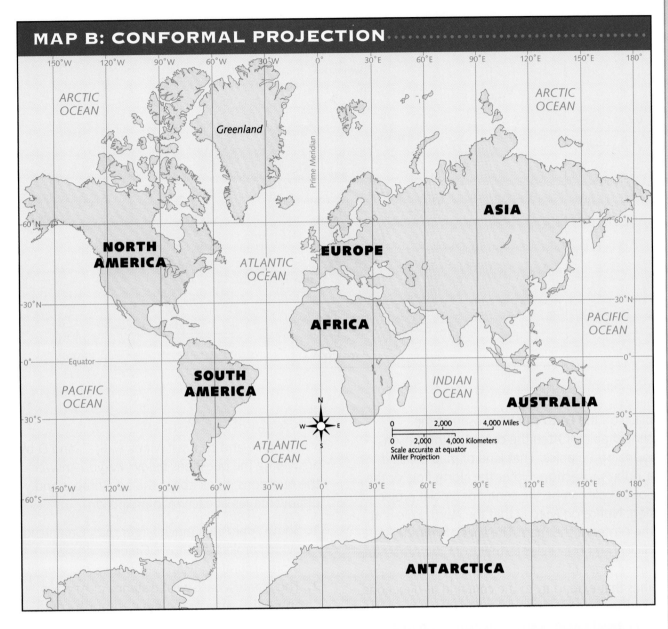

## MAP B: CONFORMAL PROJECTION

ARCTIC OCEAN

Greenland

Prime Meridian

ASIA

NORTH AMERICA

ATLANTIC OCEAN

EUROPE

AFRICA

PACIFIC OCEAN

SOUTH AMERICA

INDIAN OCEAN

AUSTRALIA

ATLANTIC OCEAN

0   2,000   4,000 Miles
0   2,000   4,000 Kilometers
Scale accurate at equator
Miller Projection

ANTARCTICA

a globe the lines of latitude are an equal distance apart. A **conformal projection** shows directions correctly, but it distorts sizes, especially of places near the poles. The Miller projection, shown above on Map B, is just one example of a conformal projection. Another that you may see is the Mercator (mer•KAY•ter) projection. Still another type of map, the Robinson projection, is a combination of equal-area and conformal projections. Map C is an example of a Robinson projection.

Map D is an **equidistant projection**. It shows accurate distances from a central point. Any

## MAP C: ROBINSON PROJECTION

## MAP D: EQUIDISTANT PROJECTION

ANTARCTICA

90°E

120°E

60°E

150°E

AUSTRALIA

INDIAN OCEAN

30°E

ASIA

AFRICA

180°

EUROPE

North Pole

0°

Greenland

PACIFIC OCEAN

NORTH AMERICA

ATLANTIC OCEAN

30°N

30°W

150°W

0°

30°S

60°S

SOUTH AMERICA

60°W

120°W

Equator

90°W

ANTARCTICA

0          2,000          4,000 Miles

0      2,000    4,000 Kilometers
Scale accurate at equator
Azimuthal Equidistant Projection

place on the Earth can be chosen as the central point. Often the central point chosen is one of the poles. That kind of map is called a **polar projection**. Either the North Pole or the South Pole can be the center of a polar projection. Notice on Map D that the North Pole is at the center of the map. The lines of latitude are circles, and the circles farther from the center are larger. Lines of longitude on Map D are straight lines that extend from the center in all directions, like the spokes of a wheel.

A **great circle** is any imaginary circle that divides the Earth into equal parts. The equator is a great circle. Lines of longitude are great circles, too. Because the Earth's surface is curved, the shortest distance between any two places is not really a straight line but part of a great circle. An equidistant projection is useful for finding the distance from the central point to other places on the map. Another projection, the gnomonic projection, is also important when studying great circle routes. In this projection all straight lines are great circle routes. Therefore, these lines show the shortest routes between two places. Distances on this projection are not accurate, however.

## Understand the Process

Compare and contrast Maps A, B, C, and D by answering the questions below. As you answer the questions, think about the advantages and disadvantages of each map projection.

1. South America is much larger than Greenland. Which projection shows Greenland's size more accurately, Map A or Map B?
2. The greatest east-west distance in Africa is about the same as the greatest north-south distance. Which projection shows Africa's shape more accurately, Map A or Map B?
3. The North Pole is a single point. Which projections show the North Pole accurately?
4. Which map can be called a polar projection?
5. On which map do the lines of longitude get closer together toward both poles?
6. On which map or maps are the lines of longitude parallel, or equally far apart?

## Think and Apply

 Write a paragraph about the advantages and disadvantages of using each kind of map.

# TRADE ROUTES LINKING ASIA and EUROPE

## Link to Our World

**How does trade change when countries grow?**

*Focus on the Main Idea*
*Look for ways in which the growth of unified empires led to trade among the peoples of Africa, Asia, and Europe.*

*Preview Vocabulary*
oasis
caravansary
cartographer

Painting of an Islamic pilgrimage, 1237

The caravan routes between the Sahara and West Africa were just one part of a trade network that linked Africa with Asia and Europe. This network of trade routes stretched over thousands of miles. It crossed deserts, went around forests, and climbed mountain ranges. Travel along the trade routes brought many cultures together. This led to the exchange of language and cultural ideas as well as goods.

## TRADE IN THE LANDS OF ISLAM

By the end of the 700s, Muslims controlled lands that reached east to the Indus River, west to what is now Spain and Portugal, and south to the Sahara. The empire included many peoples—Indians, Syrians, Persians, Egyptians, and Spaniards, among others. Little by little the different peoples under Muslim rule came together as one culture. Many of these people became Muslims, and peoples all over the Muslim lands began to speak Arabic. Muhammad is reported to have said, "Whoever speaks Arabic is an Arab."

The growing network of trade routes throughout Muslim lands also brought people together. This network included roads built by the Romans and the Persians as well as new roads. On the desert trade routes, the Arabian, or single-humped, camel was the main transportation. Well suited for desert trips, this "ship of the desert" can go for four days without water.

Desert travel was slow, however. On a good day camels could walk about 25 miles (40 km) in ten hours. Every two to three days, camel caravans needed to stop at an **oasis** (oh•AY•suhs), or water hole, to take on fresh water. Along the most-traveled routes, some of the watering places had **caravansaries** (kar•uh•VAN•suh•reez), inns where travelers could find food and shelter.

✓ **What helped connect the many peoples living in the lands controlled by the Muslims?**

## A TIME OF CULTURAL EXCHANGE

Trade brought wealth to the lands controlled by the Muslims. Merchants traveled far and wide, carrying new products to and from markets in Southwest Asia. The goods brought back to Muslim lands had an important effect on life there. For example, gold changed the way Muslims traded. Even in the early days of trade, the Muslims used gold from West Africa to make the coins called dinars. Over time the dinar became the standard coin for trade. Trade goods also changed the look of the land controlled by the Muslims. Muslim merchants brought fruit trees from Asia. Soon lemon and orange groves grew all along the Mediterranean.

Ideas traveled as freely as goods on the trade routes, and learning flourished in the Muslim Empire. Muslim scholars developed new ways to study medicine, mathematics, astronomy, and geography. For example, trade with India brought the Muslim world the number system that we know today as Arabic numerals.

**LEARNING FROM DIAGRAMS** The Muslims exchanged goods with peoples in Africa and Asia.
■ From where did Muslim traders get gold? spices? silk?

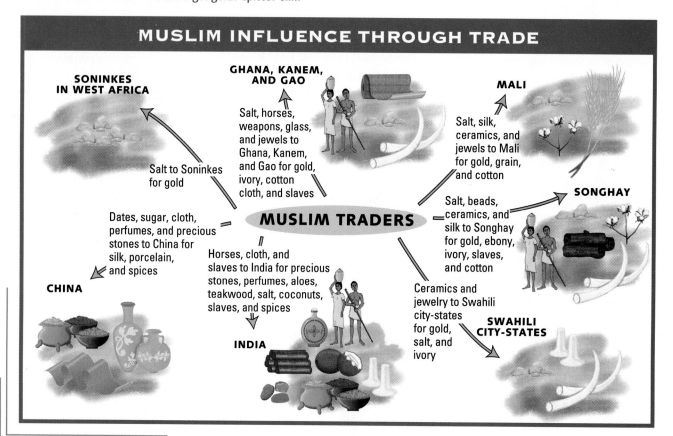

**MUSLIM INFLUENCE THROUGH TRADE**

**SONINKES IN WEST AFRICA**

**GHANA, KANEM, AND GAO**

**MALI**

Salt, horses, weapons, glass, and jewels to Ghana, Kanem, and Gao for gold, ivory, cotton cloth, and slaves

Salt, silk, ceramics, and jewels to Mali for gold, grain, and cotton

Salt to Soninkes for gold

**SONGHAY**

Dates, sugar, cloth, perfumes, and precious stones to China for silk, porcelain, and spices

**MUSLIM TRADERS**

Salt, beads, ceramics, and silk to Songhay for gold, ebony, ivory, slaves, and cotton

Horses, cloth, and slaves to India for precious stones, perfumes, aloes, teakwood, salt, coconuts, slaves, and spices

Ceramics and jewelry to Swahili city-states for gold, salt, and ivory

**CHINA**

**SWAHILI CITY-STATES**

**INDIA**

This painting from a fifteenth-century manuscript (left) illustrates the Muslims' skill in the practice of medicine. In Muslim pharmacies (below) scientists made medicines to treat many illnesses.

With this number system Muslim mathematicians advanced the study of algebra (*al-jabr* in Arabic). Algebra deals with relationships among numbers. Algebra problems use variables, such as $x$ and $y$. In ancient times the Egyptians had written about the idea of algebra. However, this branch of mathematics was fully developed only through the work of al-Khwarizmi (al•KWAR•uhz•mee) in Baghdad during the early 800s.

After hundreds of years of travel and trade, the Muslims had become expert geographers. Using the study of stars and the journals of travelers, Muslim **cartographers** (kar•TAH•gruh•ferz), or mapmakers, began to draw highly accurate maps. Their maps were used by European explorers of the 1400s and 1500s.

Literature, too, owed much to the flow of ideas along the trade routes. For example, many of the stories in

*The Arabian Nights* may have first been told in India and Persia. At the height of the Muslim Empire, however, the stories had become a part of Arabic literature.

Everywhere in the Muslim lands, people read Arabic poetry, essays, biographies, and tales. Through literature they also learned about Islamic history, law, and science.

Muslims kept control of the trade network even during invasions by Seljuk Turks from central Asia and by European crusaders. Then, in the mid-1200s, the Mongols destroyed the Muslim trade center of Baghdad. After that, control of the land trade routes fell from Muslim hands.

✓ **What achievements of the Muslim Empire resulted from the exchange of ideas?**

This twelfth-century map of the world was made by the Muslim geographer al-Idrisi. What continents are shown on this map?

# TRADE ON THE SILK ROAD CONTINUES

The Mongol invasions brought changes to Asia and Europe. The Mongols destroyed hundreds of cities and took thousands of lives. A Muslim poet who lived during the 1200s called the Mongols "an army as dense as the sands of the desert."

Yet when the Mongols set up governments in the lands they had taken, they also opened new trade opportunities. Like the Muslims, the Mongols brought many peoples together into one empire. From the Chinese in the southeast to the Russians in the northwest, the Mongols ruled over peoples of many cultures. Under Mongol rule warring peoples of the central Asian steppes came together in peace. A new wave of law and order made travel and trade much safer along the Silk Road.

The Silk Road, also called the Silk Route, was a way into Asia for European merchants and travelers. This was the route that Marco Polo had followed to and from China. As Europeans began to believe Marco Polo's reports of China's riches, more and more merchants set out for the East on the Silk Road. The trade centers of Italy made the most money from merchant travel on the Silk Road. In fact, the cities of Genoa, Venice, Florence, and Siena signed trade treaties with the Mongols. Merchants from these cities traveled deep into the Mongol Empire to buy spices, pearls, carpets, and silk.

**THE SILK ROAD**

Legend:
— Silk Road
→ Route of Marco Polo
- - - Trade route into Europe

**MOVEMENT** Marco Polo followed the general direction of the Silk Road in his travels to China.
■ How would you describe the route he followed back to Venice?

Then, in the 1300s, the Mongol Empire began to weaken. Civil war broke out in central Asia. Travel along the Silk Road became dangerous. Without safe land routes, Europeans depended more on sea routes to reach the treasures of China.

 **How did the Mongol Empire's control of the trade routes help Europeans?**

## TRADE IN SOUTH ASIA

Stories of the riches of India had traveled north along the Silk Road for centuries. One Muslim trader reported that "the Indian rivers are pearls, the mountains rubies, and trees perfumes." Such tales brought Muslim descendants of the Mongols from central Asia to India. Beginning in the early 1000s, they pushed south through the high mountain passes of the Hindu Kush range and conquered much of northern India.

The desire for gold, silver, precious jewels, and perfumes had brought the first Muslims to India. Now many other goods traveled north along the Silk Road. Coconuts, salt, and

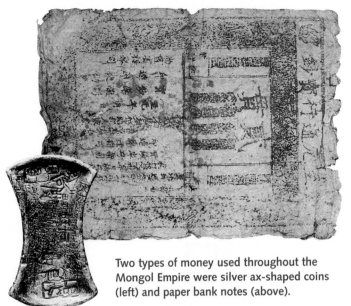

Two types of money used throughout the Mongol Empire were silver ax-shaped coins (left) and paper bank notes (above).

a scented wood called aloe were among the goods that left India. Horses and fine woven cloth traveled south into India. In addition to goods, slaves—often prisoners of war—were carried in caravans going in both directions.

 **What were some of the goods that flowed into India? What were some of the goods that flowed out?**

# LESSON 2 REVIEW

### Check Understanding

1. **Recall the Facts**   What bonds linked the many different peoples who lived in the Muslim Empire?
2. **Focus on the Main Idea**   How did the growth of the Muslim and Mongol empires lead to the trade of goods and ideas?

### Think Critically

3. **Think More About It**   How can the trade of goods lead to the trade of ideas?
4. **Past to Present**   What are some present-day examples of trade leading to cultural exchange?

5. **Personally Speaking**   What do you think was the most important idea traded during the period covered in this lesson? Explain.

### Show What You Know

 **Map Activity**   Using an atlas or another reference work, make your own physical map of Africa and the southern part of Asia. Be sure to show the physical features of the region. Then imagine that you have the job of choosing a trade route from India to West Africa. Thinking carefully about landforms, draw a route that you might take. Explain your choice.

# WHAT BROUGHT
# SUCCESS to
# MUSLIM
# TRADERS?

For hundreds of years Arab people controlled the world's major trade routes. Historian Veronica Wedgwood says, "The Arabs had long been known as adventurous traders by sea and land." Control over trade allowed the Arabs to spread the message of Islam far and wide. Trade also helped the spread of knowledge and ideas.

While most historians agree that the people of the Muslim Empire were successful traders, they have different opinions about the reasons for their success. Read the following quotations from James Simmons, Francis Robinson, and Fernand Braudel. Each has his own belief as to why the Muslim people were able to become successful traders.

## James Simmons

❝The domestication of the camel, not the invention of the wheel, liberated [freed] the early Arabs and allowed them to master the vast desert spaces and develop lucrative [profitable] trade routes. Great camel caravans, often numbering thousands of animals and their attendants, transported ivory, slaves, and exotic skins from . . . Africa, silks from India, and spices from southeastern Asia. Other caravans moved along the Incense Road from southern Arabia transporting myrrh, frankincense, and cinnamon northward through the deserts to the peoples beyond. Today we can hardly appreciate the enormous importance of incense in an ancient world where a general lack of sanitation required clouds of sweet-smelling smoke to cover noxious [disgusting] odors.❞

## Francis Robinson

❝Muslim traders, making good use of the fortunate geographical position of the Islamic heartlands, came in the years before 1500 to control much of the international traffic along the trade routes of the world. . . . These arteries of world economy formed natural channels along which Islamic influences flowed; as Muslims came to dominate key areas of the system, their non-Muslim trading partners often came to embrace Islam as well, in part because business was so much smoother if men shared a common culture and a common law.❞

## Fernand Braudel

❝Muslim merchants enjoyed from earliest times the consideration, at least from their political rulers, which was rarely forthcoming in Europe. The Prophet [Muhammad] himself is said to have said: 'The merchant enjoys the felicity [happiness] both of this world and the next'; 'he who makes money pleases God.' This is almost sufficient in itself to indicate the climate of respectability attaching to commercial life; and there are plenty of concrete examples.❞

# COMPARE
## VIEWPOINTS

1. What does James Simmons believe is the reason the Muslim people were able to become successful traders? How do you know?

2. What does Francis Robinson believe is the reason the Muslim people were able to become successful traders? How does Robinson's viewpoint differ from Fernand Braudel's?

3. In addition to the reasons given by these three historians, what else do you think may have been a reason for the trading success of the Muslim Empire?

# THINK
## –AND–
# APPLY

People often disagree about the reasons an event happened or a situation came about in history.
What are some examples of this type of disagreement today?

BUILDING CITIZENSHIP

---

← Muslim traders with their camel caravans (left on page 356) were common sights about 1,000 years ago. Muslim scribes, architects, scientists, and philosophers (right on page 356) received the support of their leaders.

LESSON 3

LEARN
with
LITERATURE

Focus on Interaction
Through Trade

# The Silk Route

## 7,000 MILES OF HISTORY

Written By
### JOHN S. MAJOR

Illustrated By
### STEPHEN FIESER

*The Silk Road, which connected empires in trade, was also referred to as the Silk Route. It was not actually a single road. Instead it was a general route traders followed to exchange goods over a wide area. On this route goods from China made their way to Central and Southern Asia and Europe, and goods from these places found their way to China.*

*Come along now with the merchants of long ago as they travel the Silk Route from Chang'an in China to the Byzantine Empire. On your journey, think about the ways in which trade linked the empires of the past.*

## THE JOURNEY BEGINS

The caravan includes many private merchants as well as Chinese government officials. Like the covered-wagon trains of the American West, members of the caravan travel together to help one another on the long, dangerous journey. Along the way they will face heat, hunger, thirst, and the ever-present possibility of bandit raids.

Few members of the original caravan will travel all the way to the Mediterranean. The silk and other goods that they are bringing from China will change hands several times along the way.

The caravan begins its journey, which will take many months. It is early spring. The caravan must get beyond the fierce western deserts before the heat of summer arrives. Leaving the city walls of Chang'an behind, it passes through rich farmland. A Buddhist temple is on a nearby hillside.

## DUNHUANG

The Buddhist religion came to China from India along the Silk Route around A.D. 100. The oasis town of Dunhuang, for centuries an important trading and supply center for caravans, soon grew into a great religious center as well. Hundreds of Buddhist cave-temples were cut into the soft rock of a nearby cliff. The cave-temples contain Buddhist statues; the walls are decorated with bright religious paintings.

Some of the merchants go to the cave-temples of Dunhuang to pray for a safe journey, while others buy supplies in the town market. Some Chinese officials take charge of a small herd of horses brought from the west by another caravan. They will escort the horses back to the capital; other officials will continue west to purchase still more of them.

---

The caravan faces rough travel across the dry desert sands of the Taklamakan.

## TAKLAMAKAN

The Taklamakan is one of the world's driest deserts. Its name means "if you go in, you won't come out" in Uighur Turkish, one of the main languages of Central Asia. The caravan skirts the northern edge of the desert, just south of the snow-capped peaks of the Tian Shan Mountains. The route is very rough, passing around sand dunes, across rocky flats, and through tangled willow thickets[1] along dry riverbeds. But the caravan's two-humped Bactrian camels are strong and hardy.[2] They are used to this difficult country.

Many of the camels and camel drivers that set out from Chang'an turned back at Dunhuang. The merchants hired new ones for this stage of the journey, along with extra animals to carry food and water for crossing

---

[1] **thickets:** thick growth of trees or bushes
[2] **hardy:** able to withstand bad conditions

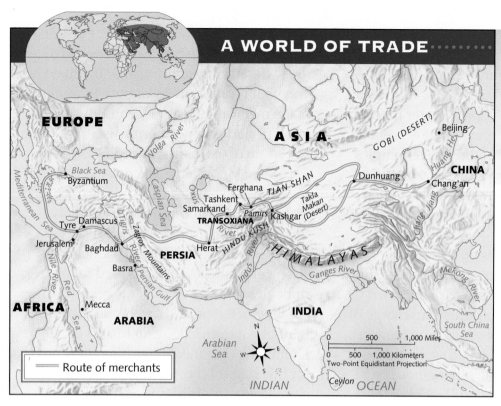

## A WORLD OF TRADE

EUROPE

ASIA

GOBI (DESERT)

Beijing

Volga River

Black Sea
Byzantium

Mediterranean Sea

Caspian Sea

Oxus River

Ferghana
Tashkent
Samarkand
Pamirs
TRANSOXIANA
Kashgar

TIAN SHAN

Takla Makan (Desert)

Dunhuang

Huang He

CHINA
Chang'an

Chang Jiang

Tyre
Damascus
Jerusalem
Baghdad
Basra

Tigris River
Zagros Mountains
Persian Gulf

PERSIA

Herat

HINDU KUSH

Indus River

HIMALAYAS

Ganges River

Mekong River

Nile River
Red Sea

AFRICA

Mecca

ARABIA

INDIA

South China Sea

Arabian Sea

N
W    E
S

0        500       1,000 Miles
0    500    1,000 Kilometers
Two-Point Equidistant Projection

INDIAN OCEAN

Ceylon

Route of merchants

**Map Skill PLACE** This map shows the route followed by the merchants in this story.
■ What places are stops on the "Silk Route"?

the desert. Such changes of men and animals will occur several times along the way from China to Damascus.

### KASHGAR

Hot and tired after their trip across the Taklamakan Desert, the men and animals hurry to reach the oasis city of Kashgar. The pastures near the city are dotted with grazing animals and the camps of herding peoples: Uighurs in round felt yurts,[3] Turkomans and Tibetans in black tents.

Kashgar is famous for its fruit. Dates, melons, and grapes are grown in irrigated fields and vineyards. Everyone in the caravan looks forward to fresh food and water.

Some of the Chinese members of the caravan will end their journey here. They trade silk for dried dates, raisins, jade, and other local products to bring back to China. Others will continue on toward the west, joined by new merchants, guards, and camel drivers with fresh animals from Kashgar.

[3] **yurts:** circle-shaped tents

### THE PAMIRS

The Pamirs are a range of high mountains in eastern Afghanistan. Here the route winds through narrow, high-walled valleys beside rushing rivers. The camel drivers call this section of the Silk Route the "Trail of Bones" because of the many men and animals that have died along the way from falls and from sudden storms in the high, cold passes. The westbound caravan meets a caravan heading for China with luxury goods from Western lands and a herd of fine horses from Ferghana.

### TASHKENT, KINGDOM OF FERGHANA

In the central market of Tashkent, the last remaining Chinese officials in the caravan trade bolts[4] of silk for horses that they will take back to China. The horses of Ferghana are considered by Chinese military leaders to be the strongest and toughest in the world.

Tashkent marks the eastern edge of the Persian cultural world. Some private

[4] **bolts:** rolls

merchants trade Chinese silk, porcelain, and other goods for Persian metalwork, glass, and musical instruments. They too will head back to China from here.

## TRANSOXIANA

After making another stop, in the city of Samarkand, the caravan enters the wild country east of the Oxus (Amu Darya) River. No government rules this land; the nomads who live here will rob caravans if they get a chance to.

Suddenly the caravan is attacked by a group of Turkoman bandits on horseback.

After a fierce fight with swords and bows and arrows, the bandits are driven off. But some members of the caravan have been killed or wounded, and the bandits escape with a few heavily laden[5] camels.

## HERAT

In this thriving Persian city, artisans produce fine metalwork, glassware, carpets, and other goods that can be sold for a high price in China. Herat is also, for the moment, on the eastern edge of the rapidly expanding Islamic world. A newly built mosque looms[6] over the city market.

----

Traders from many lands meet at the market of Herat, in Persia.

----

[5] **laden:** loaded
[6] **looms:** appears in great form

Merchants from the caravan mingle in the market with local merchants and Turkoman nomads, as well as with Arabs from Baghdad and Damascus. Traders from India are here too, selling spices and brightly dyed Indian cloth. Muslim imams,[7] Zoroastrian priests, Nestorian Christian priests, and Buddhist monks tend to the religious needs of the cosmopolitan city.

The caravan will leave its last Bactrian camels in Herat. For the rest of the journey they will use dromedaries, the one-humped camels of Western Asia.

## BAGHDAD

Baghdad is the greatest city of the Islamic world and a hub of world trade. Caravans crowd the roads leading to the city. An Arab merchant leads a group of African slaves bringing ivory, gold, and spices from Zanzibar. Ships coming upriver from the port at Basra bring spices and printed cotton cloth from India, pearls from the Persian Gulf, and precious stones from Ceylon (now Sri Lanka). Some of the goods will soon be heading east to China.

Only a handful of Chinese merchants remained with the caravan, and they will end their journey here. Most of the silk, porcelain, and other products from China have already changed hands several times along the way, increasing in value each time. The last remaining Chinese merchants will sell their goods for a fortune in Baghdad, but then they face a long, difficult, and dangerous trip home again.

---

[7] **imams:** prayer leaders at a mosque

A variety of goods from many parts of the world are exchanged in Baghdad.

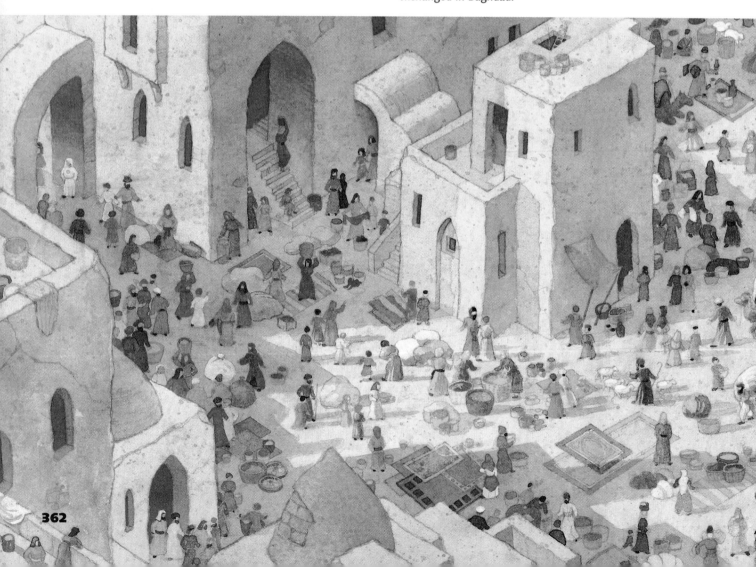

## DAMASCUS

Arab merchants have brought bolts of silk from Baghdad to Damascus. Only the finest silk cloth has traveled this far; it includes intricately[8] patterned brocades, brilliantly colored satins, and thin gauze to make nightgowns for aristocratic ladies. Wealthy Muslim women, heavily veiled, admire bolts of finished silk cloth in a shop.

## TYRE

In the port city of Tyre, on the Mediterranean coast of Lebanon, goods are loaded on ships bound for cities farther to the west. Some of the silk that was traded in the market at Damascus will be sent to Byzantium,[9] the capital of the Eastern Roman Empire.

---

[8] **intricately:** in a complicated manner
[9] **Byzantium:** Constantinople (now Istanbul)

## BYZANTIUM

In the main hall of a splendid palace, a Byzantine nobleman receives a visit from a bishop of the Orthodox Christian church. Both are dressed in rich garments of silk brocade. The palace women remain in an inner courtyard, out of sight of the men. A visiting prince from Russia, far to the north, awaits his turn to speak to the nobleman. Perhaps he will receive a small present of silk to take back home with him.

The garments worn by the wealthy people of Byzantium are made of silk cloth brought from China, more than 6,000 miles away. Few people in Byzantium have more than a vague idea of where China is or what its people are like, just as few Chinese know anything about the Eastern Roman Empire. Yet Chinese silk is sold in Byzantium, and Byzantine gold coins circulate in the markets of China. The two empires are linked together by trade, thanks to the brave and enterprising merchants of the Silk Route.

## Literature Review

1. How did the Silk Route link different groups of people?
2. In what ways could a trade good have given one group of people an idea of the way of life of another group of people?
3. Make your own map of Europe and Asia. Be sure to include present-day borders. Then look at the map on page 360. Copy the trade route onto your map. Make a list of the present-day countries that now occupy the land through which the trade route went.

## CONNECT MAIN IDEAS

Use this organizer to show that you understand how the chapter's main ideas are connected. Copy the organizer onto a separate sheet of paper. Then complete it by writing three details to support each main idea.

**Overland Trade**

**The Trading Empires of West Africa**
The peoples of West Africa grew strong through trade with others.

1. _____
2. _____
3. _____

**Trade Routes Linking Asia and Europe**
The growth of unified empires led to trade among the peoples of Africa, Asia, and Europe.

1. _____
2. _____
3. _____

## WRITE MORE ABOUT IT

1. **Write a Diary Entry**  Imagine that you are an innkeeper at Kumbi-Saleh in Africa. Write a diary entry in which you describe the traders who stay at your inn. Include your thoughts about how trade affects relationships among different peoples.

2. **Write a Personal History**  Describe a time when you traded with a friend. Perhaps you exchanged books, games, or sports cards. Explain why you decided to make the trade, and describe how the trade affected your relationship.

3. **Write a Story**  Imagine that you are one of these people: a mansa in Mali or a Muslim or Chinese trader on the Silk Road. Describe a day in your life.

## USE VOCABULARY

Write a definition for each of the terms.

1. cartographer
2. mansa
3. oasis
4. savanna
5. tariff
6. tropical rain forest

## CHECK UNDERSTANDING

1. How does Africa compare in size with the other continents?

2. How did learning to shape iron affect the lives of the Nok people of Africa?

3. What were the two main types of goods that the Soninkes traded?

4. What was the first great empire to rise in West Africa, and how did this empire grow in wealth?

5. How have we learned what we know about the ancient empire of Ghana?

6. How did contact with Muslim traders change the lives of people in West Africa?

7. Why was Mansa Musa's pilgrimage important?

8. What was the most common form of transportation on the desert routes used by Muslim traders?

9. How did trade influence life in the Muslim Empire?

10. How did the Mongol invasions affect Asia and Europe?

11. What brought the first Muslims to India?

## THINK CRITICALLY

1. **Personally Speaking** What do you think family life was like for early traders who were away from home for months or years at a time?

2. **Cause and Effect** What caused the collapse of the Mali Empire?

3. **Past to Present** In what ways are present-day countries affected by their trading relationships?

4. **Think More About It** Why do you think people began to search farther and farther away for trading partners in the years 500 to 1500?

5. **Explore Viewpoints** Mansa Musa of Mali visited Egypt during his pilgrimage to Mecca. What different viewpoints might Egyptians have formed about the African ruler from his visit?

## APPLY SKILLS

**Map Skill**

**How to Compare Maps with Different Projections** In your library, locate an atlas or another book containing many maps. Look through the maps to identify different projections. Make a list of the different types of projections that you find. Beside each projection name, describe the unusual features of that projection.

## READ MORE ABOUT IT

*The Kingdoms of Africa: The Making of the Past* by Peter Garlake. Bedrick. This book provides a record of Africa's past, based on archaeology and oral histories.

*Marco Polo and the Medieval Explorers* by Rebecca Stetoff. Chelsea. The author offers a close look at the life of Marco Polo and his travels to Asia. Information about other travelers, such as Ibn Battuta, is also included.

*Nadia the Willful* by Sue Alexander. Pantheon. When Nadia's brother is missing from the desert, their father rules that his name should never again be spoken. Nadia wants to remember her brother. What will she do?

# CHAPTER 12

# SEA and RIVER TRADE

> 66 The number of ships increases. The endless flood of Vikings never stops growing bigger. 99
>
> A French monk writing of the Vikings in the ninth century

Viking wood carving from about 1,100 years ago

# INDIAN OCEAN TRADE

**LESSON 1**

## Link to Our World

**How does trade link different cultures today?**

**Focus on the Main Idea**
Read about how trade around the Indian Ocean linked many peoples.

**Preview Vocabulary**

monsoon          junk
lateen sail      diplomat
dhow             Swahili

New knowledge about nature, improved ship design, and new navigation tools made traveling by sea easier than before. These Arab sailors (below) are setting out on a trading expedition.

Besides traveling over land routes, traders also went to sea. Far from home they found new sources of gold, fine cloth, ivory, glass, and porcelain. The trade of such goods at ports on the Indian Ocean brought many peoples together.

## FROM BAGHDAD TO GUANGZHOU

"This is the Tigris," the Muslim caliph al-Mansur (al•mon•SOOR) said in 762 when he chose Baghdad, in what is now Iraq, as his capital. "There is no obstacle between us and China. Everything on the sea can come to us on it." Baghdad did, indeed, become "the harbor of the world." Boats from Baghdad sailed down the Tigris to the deep harbor at Basra on the Persian Gulf. At Basra, merchants loaded their goods onto oceangoing ships. They then sailed out into the Indian Ocean and followed the sea routes to East Africa, India, and China.

Arab merchants set out for the East late in the year. When they planned their journeys, they took into account the climate of the region they were sailing to. Strong winds known as **monsoons** blow across the Indian Ocean. The winter monsoon blows from the northeast between November and March. The summer monsoon blows from the southwest between April and October.

Because of these steady winds, seagoing peoples in the Indian Ocean had developed the **lateen sail**. This triangle-shaped sail lets a ship travel into the wind. Arab ships, known as **dhows** (DOWZ), used lateen sails to travel east toward China when the northeast monsoon blew.

# What?

## The Dhow

The dhow was a wooden boat with one or two sails. The boards it was made of were not held together with nails or wooden pegs, as on European ships. Instead, they were "stitched together with cords made of coco[nut] husk." Arab shipbuilders then spread a coating of oil, such as shark oil, over the boards to keep water out.

The first stop for the merchants was Muscat, at the tip of the Arabian Peninsula. There the ships took on fresh water. Then a month's sailing took them to the Malabar Coast of southwestern India. By late winter their ships had reached the Nicobar Islands in the eastern Indian Ocean. From there they sailed into the China Sea. By this time the summer monsoon had begun. The southwest wind carried the ships to Guangzhou (GWAHNG•JOH), China's major port.

The ships arrived in China loaded with the products of Arabia—dates, sugar, linen cloth, perfumes, and jewels. After trading these goods for others in Guangzhou, the Arab merchants made use of the winter monsoon to sail home. They returned with Chinese silks and porcelain bowls, cotton and pepper from India, and spices from the East Indies.

The round trip took about 18 months. The Arab merchants spent 6 months at home gathering new goods that they could trade and were ready to set out again with the next winter monsoon.

 ***How did the people of Baghdad reach the people of Guangzhou for trading?***

## ARAB INFLUENCE ON THE INDIAN OCEAN

Arab dhows sailed across the Indian Ocean to China every year. However, Arab merchants did not have a monopoly on the east–west ocean trade routes. Jewish merchants from Southwest Asia traveled the sea routes from the Persian Gulf to China. Indian traders also sailed the seas, mostly in the eastern Indian Ocean.

Starting in the 800s, Chinese junks—wooden boats with four-sided sails—sailed to such places as the Malay Peninsula. In the early 1400s Chinese traders began to travel even farther. Under the command of Admiral Zheng He (JUHNG HUH), Chinese ships visited Siam, Indonesia, Ceylon, the Arabian Peninsula, and the eastern coast of Africa. Zheng He was not only a sailor but also a

In China, and in other parts of the world, women (left) often carried trade goods to markets and ports. Junks (below) are still used today to carry goods long distances.

Zheng He (seated) made many ocean voyages for the Chinese emperor. On his first trip, Zheng He commanded a fleet of more than 300 ships.

**diplomat**—a person skilled in developing treaties. Zheng got many of the peoples he visited interested in trading with China.

Even so, until the late 1400s Arab merchants were the leaders of trade on the Indian Ocean. Because their journeys were very long, Arab merchants set up communities in some of the larger trading ports they visited. Muslim settlements grew up in Sri Lanka, parts of Indonesia, and China.

The ways of the Muslim trading communities soon began to spread to the people living around them. Many of these people became Muslims. By the 1500s Arab merchants had taken their religion to southern India, Sri Lanka, and parts of Indonesia. Islam also spread to the lands along the western edges of the Indian Ocean.

 **How did Muslim ways and religion spread to countries bordering the Indian Ocean?**

# THE SWAHILI CITY-STATES

Arab dhows had been sailing to the east coast of Africa since the 600s. Arab traders wanted gold, ivory, animal skins, and—sometimes—slaves. They offered cloth, spices, pottery, and porcelain to the Africans.

Some of the Arab traders started communities in the trading ports of East Africa. They settled there, married African women, and raised families. By 900 a culture and a language that were part Arabian and part African had grown up along the coast. The people and the language they spoke were called **Swahili** (swah•HEE•lee). Most Swahilis became Muslims, but they also followed many African traditions and customs.

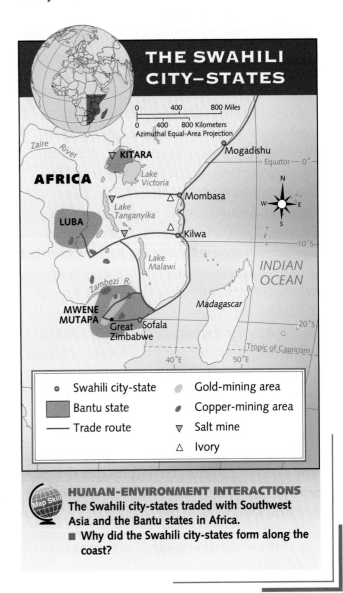

**THE SWAHILI CITY-STATES**

0    400    800 Miles
0    400    800 Kilometers
Azimuthal Equal-Area Projection

AFRICA

KITARA
LUBA
MWENE MUTAPA

Mogadishu
Mombasa
Kilwa
Sofala
Great Zimbabwe

Lake Victoria
Lake Tanganyika
Lake Malawi

Zaire River
Zambezi R.

Equator — 0°
10°S
20°S
Tropic of Capricorn
40°E    50°E

INDIAN OCEAN
Madagascar

- Swahili city-state
- Bantu state
- Trade route
- Gold-mining area
- Copper-mining area
- Salt mine
- Ivory

**HUMAN-ENVIRONMENT INTERACTIONS**
The Swahili city-states traded with Southwest Asia and the Bantu states in Africa.
■ Why did the Swahili city-states form along the coast?

This detail of a painting on silk by the artist Shen Tu is called *The Tribute Giraffe with Attendant*. It shows a giraffe brought to China from Africa in 1419 by Admiral Zheng He as a gift for the Chinese emperor.

Over the years the East African trading ports grew into independent city-states. By the 1300s there were as many as 40 trading cities along the eastern coast of Africa. The trade centers stretched from Mogadishu (mah•guh•DIH•shoo) in the north to Sofala (soh•FAHL•uh) in the south. A Muslim traveler who visited Sofala in the 1000s wrote that it had "gold in abundance and other marvels." Reports of this kind brought Chinese admiral Zheng He to East Africa in the early 1400s. Among the treasures he took back was something that amazed the Chinese: a giraffe.

One of the richest of the Swahili city-states was Kilwa (KIL•wah). Its wealth came from its trade in gold and could be seen everywhere. Kilwa's tall houses were made of coral stone, and its people wore fine clothing. The Muslim traveler Ibn Battuta called Kilwa "one of the most beautiful and best-constructed towns in the world."

✓ **How did the Swahili city-states develop?**

## GREAT ZIMBABWE

The people of the Swahili city-states did not produce the goods that they traded to the Arabs and others. Instead, they traded for these goods. The people of Sofala and Kilwa traded salt, tools, and cloth to people from Central Africa for gold. The ancestors of these Central Africans had migrated from West Africa hundreds of years before. These people, whom historians call Bantu speakers, settled in all parts of East Africa and Southern Africa.

Around 1200 a Bantu-speaking group called the Shonas (SHOH•nuhz) took control

## MIGRATION OF BANTU-SPEAKING PEOPLES

Migration paths of Bantu-speaking peoples

Original homeland of Bantu-speaking peoples

Area of Bantu-speaking peoples

**MOVEMENT** Bantu-speaking people began their migration from West Africa.
■ In what direction did these people move?

In what is today the African country of Zimbabwe stand the remains of the royal court walls of Great Zimbabwe (inset).

of the Central African mines from which Sofala's and Kilwa's gold came. This made the Shonas very wealthy. They also gained wealth from the large herds of cattle they kept. The Shonas came to rule a large empire in Central Africa. They built their capital at Great Zimbabwe. As a sign of their wealth, the Shona kings had a huge stone wall built around the royal court. More than 30 feet (about 9 m) tall, the wall closed in an area as long as a football field and about four times as wide.

The Shona Empire lasted for more than 200 years, trading gold to the Swahili city-states. Then, around 1450, the Shonas left Great Zimbabwe. Why they left is not known.

 **What part did the people of the Shona Empire play in trade across the Indian Ocean?**

## Check Understanding

1. **Recall the Facts**   Which people made the most use of the Indian Ocean for trade?
2. **Focus on the Main Idea**   How did trade around the Indian Ocean link the peoples of Asia and Africa?

## Think Critically

3. **Personally Speaking**   Why do you think African traders did not take to the seas in search of trade as Arab traders did?

4. **Cause and Effect**   Why might it be said that the cause of Great Zimbabwe's decline was its success?

## Show What You Know

**Letter-Writing Activity**
Imagine that you are a crew member on one of Admiral Zheng He's ships. Write a letter to a friend in China telling what you saw on your visit to one of the Swahili city-states.

# The MEDITERRANEAN and the BLACK SEA

## Link to Our World

**How do countries today become leaders in trade?**

*Focus on the Main Idea*
*Read about how some city-states became leaders of trade in the Mediterranean Sea and in the Black Sea.*

*Preview Vocabulary*
Greek fire
doge

The Byzantine Empire grew rich by controlling trade routes. These silver spoons and this ceiling painting from the Palace of Constantine and Helena show Byzantine wealth.

For many centuries the Mediterranean and Black seas both were "Roman lakes," controlled by the Roman Empire. Over these bodies of water, goods moved back and forth among the empire's many regions. When the Roman Empire broke up, problems developed over control of trade on these seas.

## BYZANTINE TRADE

During the sixth century Emperor Justinian I brought the Mediterranean and the Black seas under Byzantine rule. Constantinople, his capital, was between the two seas and served as a center of trade for both. "Into her harbors sailed expectantly the vessels of the world's trade," a poet of the times wrote.

Byzantine trade was carried on in many places besides the shores of these two seas. Byzantine merchant ships sailed through the Red Sea and across the Indian Ocean to India. Smaller boats crossed the Black Sea and journeyed up the Dnieper (NEE•per) River to trade with the Rus (ROOS) of Kiev (KEE•ef) in what is now Ukraine. Camel caravans followed land routes to China.

Traders on all these routes took many goods back to Constantinople. Furs, salt, wax, and honey came from Kiev. Ivory, porcelain, jewels, silk, and spices came from India and China. A tax on all trade goods that went through Constantinople made the empire very rich.

For hundreds of years the Byzantine navy kept the sea routes safe. The navy was able to control the seas by using a secret weapon called Greek fire. **Greek fire** was a chemical

## THE SHRINKING BYZANTINE EMPIRE

EUROPE

Byzantine Empire, about 1050
Byzantine Empire, about 1350

Crusaders conquer Constantinople, 1204

Ottoman Turks capture city from the Byzantines, 1453

Danube River

Adriatic Sea

Tyrrhenian Sea

•Rome

Black Sea

•Constantinople

ASIA

N W E S

Sicily

Mediterranean Sea

0    150    300 Miles
0    150    300 Kilometers
Azimuthal Equal-Area Projection

Crete

Cyprus

•Antioch

**LOCATION**
Map Skill

By 1350 the Byzantine Empire had lost much of its land.
- How would you describe the location of the Byzantine Empire in 1350?

mixture that caught fire when water hit it. One shot of Greek fire could set a ship on fire. The ships of Muslims and others who wished to take control of the Mediterranean became the targets of Greek fire.

 **How did trade make the Byzantine Empire wealthy?**

## MUSLIMS IN THE MEDITERRANEAN

From the earliest days of Mediterranean trade, the Muslims had tried to take control of it. In 649 Muslims took over the island of Cyprus in the eastern Mediterranean. About 150 years later, Muslims from Tunis, Morocco, and Spain took control of important Mediterranean islands, including Crete and Sicily. From these islands they were able to protect Muslim trade ships that sailed along the coast of North Africa. In this way the Muslims kept safe the western link of a Muslim trade network reaching all the way to China.

In the late 900s the Byzantines took back Cyprus and Crete. Then their government

ordered all merchants in the empire to stop sending wood and iron to Muslim lands. Byzantine leaders hoped that this action would keep the Muslims from building new boats to sail on the Mediterranean. But not all Byzantines obeyed the order. The Italian cities of Amalfi and Venice, which were far from the rest of the empire, paid no attention to it. For the most part, Amalfi and Venice acted as independent city-states, without ties to a larger government.

Amalfi's wealth came from trade with the Muslim Empire. Amalfi, located along the Tyrrhenian Sea, did not want to lose its trading partner just because of an order from the Byzantine government. Venice had also grown rich by trading with the Muslims. So the people of Venice, on the northern shores of the Adriatic Sea, felt the same way. As it turned out, it was the Venetians—not the Muslims of North Africa—who took control of Mediterranean trade from the Byzantines.

 **Why was gaining control of Mediterranean islands important to the Muslims of North Africa?**

# THE RISE OF THE ITALIAN CITY-STATES

Venice, as an eleventh-century document said, was a city-state "that does not plow, sow, or gather vintage." Instead, the Venetians "buy grain and wine in every port." Trade was certainly the most important activity in Venice. Its merchants bought wood, wool, and iron from western Europe. Then they sold these in the eastern Mediterranean ports of the Muslim Empire. The traders returned to Venice with silks, spices, and ivory, which they then sold in Europe.

Other Italian ports did much the same thing. In the western lands along the Mediterranean, the city-states of Pisa and Genoa formed strong ties with the Muslim ports of North Africa. Ships from Pisa and Genoa carried linen, cotton, jewels, perfumes, and spices south across the Mediterranean Sea. The ships returned with leather goods, animal skins, grain, and other items for further trade.

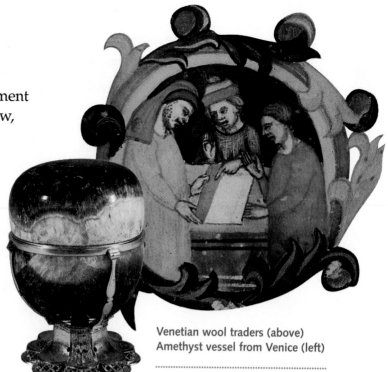

Venetian wool traders (above)
Amethyst vessel from Venice (left)

In the late 1000s, Normans, who controlled a small area of land in what is now France, sailed through the Strait of Gibraltar looking for new lands to conquer. Because Venice fought against the Normans, the Byzantines rewarded the city-state by letting Venetian traders pass through Constantinople without paying taxes.

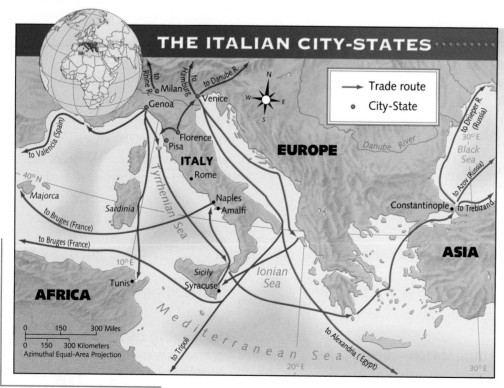

## THE ITALIAN CITY-STATES

Legend:
→ Trade route
• City-State

0 150 300 Miles
0 150 300 Kilometers
Azimuthal Equal-Area Projection

**MOVEMENT** Merchants from the Italian city-states traveled by land and sea to trade.

■ Why do you think Venetian merchants traveled in so many different directions?

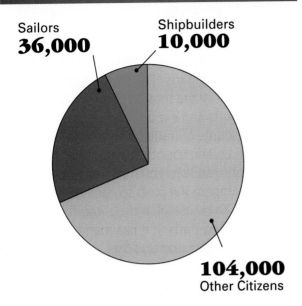

## IMPORTANCE OF THE SEA FOR VENICE, 1423

Sailors
**36,000**

Shipbuilders
**10,000**

**104,000**
Other Citizens

**LEARNING FROM GRAPHS** Venice's location on the Adriatic Sea made it an important sea-trade center.
■ About what percent of citizens were sailors or shipbuilders?

The Byzantines were sorry, however, when the Venetians helped the Normans drive the Byzantines from Italy. Then, in 1204, the **doge** (DOHJ), or leader, of Venice told crusaders on their way to the Holy Land to attack Constantinople. After three days of fighting, the city fell. Venice quickly took over most of the Byzantine lands along the eastern shores of the Mediterranean.

Venice now controlled the important trading routes in the eastern Mediterranean and in the Black Sea. Genoa controlled the western Mediterranean. As time passed, Venice won control of all Mediterranean trade.

At about this same time, inland city-states, such as Milan and Florence, started to trade as well. In 1252 Florence and other city-states began making gold coins. Florentine florins and Venetian ducats took the place of Arab dinars as coins used for trade in the Mediterranean lands.

The Italian city-states, with Venice in the lead, held a monopoly on trade in the Mediterranean for more than 200 years. Then, in 1453, Constantinople was taken by the Ottoman Turks. The Mediterranean and Black seas became Turkish waters. At about the same time, many European countries became jealous of the Italian city-states' control of trade. They began sailing out into the Atlantic in search of another route to Asia. This action set the stage for a time of exploration by Europeans.

✓ **What ended the Italian city-states' monopoly on Mediterranean trade?**

# LESSON 2 REVIEW

## Check Understanding

1. **Recall the Facts**   What groups wanted control of Mediterranean trade?
2. **Focus on the Main Idea**   How did the Italian city-states gain control of the trade routes in the Mediterranean and Black seas?

## Think Critically

3. **Past to Present**   How might countries today benefit from trading with the United States?

4. **Think More About It**   Study a map of the Mediterranean region. How did the geography of the region help Genoa and Venice become important in trade?

## Show What You Know

**Poetry Activity**   The people of Venice took great pride in their achievements. Imagine that you are a Venetian living in the early 1400s. Write a poem that describes your pride in being a citizen of this great city-state.

# Compare Information with Graphs

## Why Is This Skill Important?

Suppose you want to prepare a report on trade in the world today. You want to show a lot of information in a brief, clear way. One way you might do this is by making graphs. A **graph** is a diagram for showing relations between numbers. Knowing how to read and make graphs will help you see and compare large amounts of information.

## Bar, Circle, and Line Graphs and Their Uses

Different kinds of graphs show information in different ways. A **bar graph** uses bars and is especially useful for quick comparisons. Notice that the bars on the graphs of imports and exports are horizontal. On a horizontal bar graph, the bars go from left to right. Bar graphs can be vertical, too. On a vertical bar graph, the bars go from bottom to top.

A **circle graph**, often called a pie chart, divides information into parts. The circle graphs on the next page show the total amounts of the United States' imports and exports. The graphs' parts are the amounts of trade between the United States and certain countries. Like other graphs, circle graphs can help you make comparisons. You can compare the parts to each other or to the whole. To be useful, a circle graph should have only a few parts. If it has many parts, it becomes crowded and unclear.

A **line graph** shows change over time. The line graph on the next page shows how the amount of goods exported from the United States has changed between the years 1970 and 1995. Each dot shows how much trade took place in one year, and a line connects all the dots. Depending on the information, the line may go up or down or stay at the same level. Line graphs are most useful in showing a **trend**, or the way something changes over time.

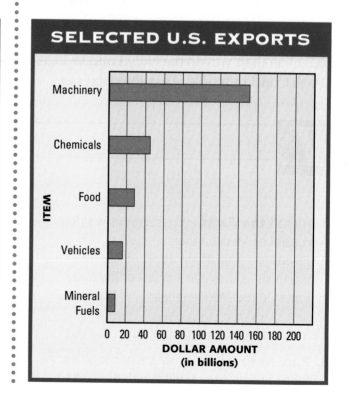

**SELECTED U.S. IMPORTS**

ITEM: Machinery, Vehicles, Mineral Fuels, Chemicals, Food

DOLLAR AMOUNT (in billions): 0 20 40 60 80 100 120 140 160 180 200

**SELECTED U.S. EXPORTS**

ITEM: Machinery, Chemicals, Food, Vehicles, Mineral Fuels

DOLLAR AMOUNT (in billions): 0 20 40 60 80 100 120 140 160 180 200

## TOP FIVE TRADING PARTNERS OF THE U.S.: IMPORTS

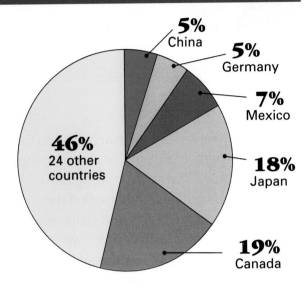

5% China
5% Germany
7% Mexico
18% Japan
19% Canada
46% 24 other countries

## TOP FIVE TRADING PARTNERS OF THE U.S.: EXPORTS

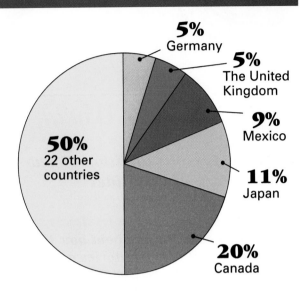

5% Germany
5% The United Kingdom
9% Mexico
11% Japan
20% Canada
50% 22 other countries

### Understand the Process

Compare and contrast the information in the bar, circle, and line graphs by answering the following questions. As you answer, think about the advantages and disadvantages of each kind of graph.

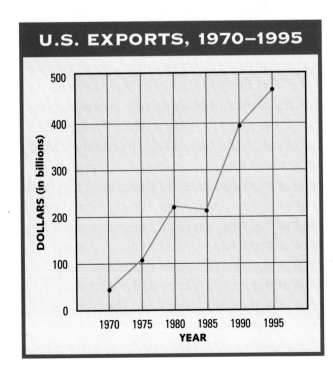

### U.S. EXPORTS, 1970–1995

DOLLARS (in billions): 0, 100, 200, 300, 400, 500
YEAR: 1970, 1975, 1980, 1985, 1990, 1995

1. Which graph or graphs would you use to find how much machinery the United States imports? Explain your choice.
2. Which graph or graphs would you use to find how much of the United States' international trade of products is with Japan? Explain your choice.
3. Which graph or graphs would you use to find how much change there was in the United States' exports between the years 1970 and 1980? Explain your choice.
4. Do you think the information on the bar graphs can be shown on circle graphs? Explain your answer.
5. Do you think the information on the line graphs can be shown on a circle graph? Explain your answer.

### Think and Apply

Using the graphs on these pages, write a paragraph summarizing information about the United States' international trade in recent years. Share your paragraph with a partner, and compare your summaries. Did you and your partner share like ideas?

# LESSON 3

# THE NORTHERN SEAS

## Link to Our World

**How does the addition of new territory affect trade?**

**Focus on the Main Idea**
*As you read, think about how the addition of new territories affected trade in northern Europe.*

**Preview Vocabulary**
*saga*
*territorial expansion*
*Hansa*
*embargo*

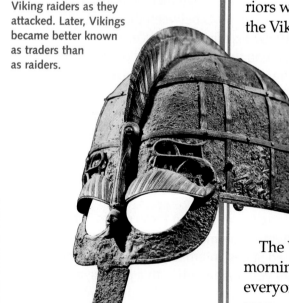

Designed to cover the head and face, this helmet protected early Viking raiders as they attacked. Later, Vikings became better known as traders than as raiders.

The silks and spices of Asia reached even the most northern parts of Europe. Seafaring people of the north formed their own trading networks to carry these goods. Their ships sailed the Atlantic Ocean and the North and Baltic seas and traveled up many rivers. Over time two great trading cultures developed—those of the Vikings and the members of the Hanseatic League.

## VIKING ADVENTURERS

In one Icelandic **saga**, or adventure story about the brave deeds of people, a young hero says to his father, "Give me a longship and crew therewith, and I go a-viking." The word *a-viking*, which meant "raiding overseas," soon came to describe the warriors who carried out the attacks—the Vikings. But why did the Vikings leave their northern lands to attack other people?

During the 700s the population of Scandinavia—the present-day countries of Denmark, Norway, and Sweden—grew quickly. After a while the land could not feed all the people who lived there. Many Scandinavians took to the seas each summer to search for food and items to steal. They traveled in their longships, or narrow, flat-bottomed boats. These fast-moving longboats were powered not only by a large, square sail but also by many strong rowers who served as fighters as well.

The Vikings often attacked at night or in the very early morning in order to take people by surprise. They killed everyone who tried to fight them. Often they carried off women and children to sell as slaves. What they could not steal, they set on fire.

# VIKING EXPANSION ROUTES, 800–1000

0 250 500 Miles
0 250 500 Kilometers
Azimuthal Equal-Area Projection

→ Viking expansion route

**MOVEMENT** From Scandinavia—the present-day countries of Denmark, Norway, and Sweden—the Vikings traveled in many directions.
■ How would you describe the route the Vikings took to get to Pisa in what is today Italy?

The people along the coasts of north-western Europe were the first to be attacked by Vikings. An English priest wrote, "Never has Britain known such terror." Later the Vikings began to sail inland along rivers and to attack cities such as Paris, Bordeaux, and Seville.

In time the Vikings began to settle on the lands they had attacked. This **territorial expansion**, or adding of new lands, gave the Vikings the room they believed they needed. To the east, Swedish Vikings pushed deep into what today is Russia. The Danes, from the land that is now called Denmark, took control of parts of England and France. In the west, Norwegians settled Iceland, Greenland, and parts of Scotland and Ireland. They even began a settlement in North America.

With settlement, a-viking became a thing of the past, remembered only in the sagas. Trading took the place of raiding as the Vikings' way of making a living.

> **Why did Scandinavians take up a-viking, and why did they stop their raids?**

Longships (far left) enabled the Vikings to travel easily and to capture riches. The Vikings traded the captured riches or used them to make items such as this gold brooch (near left).

## THE RUS

After a while many trade routes connected the lands of the Vikings. The most widely used routes were those in the east. Early in the Viking age, raiders from Sweden settled on the Baltic shores of present-day Latvia. They then traveled inland until they reached the Dnieper and Volga rivers. Some Vikings sailed downstream on the Dnieper and set up a trading center at Kiev. Others followed the Volga downstream from the trading center of Novgorod (NAHV•guh•rahd).

The people of this part of eastern Europe—the Slavs—called the Vikings the *Rus*. The word *Russia* may have come from this name. Stories of the Rus and their trading reached far and wide. Muslim geographer Ibn Rustah, writing in the 900s, noted that the only business of the Rus was "trade in sable and squirrel skins and other kinds of skins, selling them to those who will buy from them."

Goods were not the only things that traveled on the eastern trade routes, however. In

This "Great Crane of Danzig" helped people load and unload heavy cargo at the town of Bruges in northern Europe. What activities are taking place in this scene?

the late 900s Byzantine missionaries traveled north, taking Christianity to the Rus of Kiev.

The Rus and other descendants of the Vikings kept the lead in trade on the northern waterways until the 1200s. The people of western Europe grew to depend on these northern traders for furs and other luxuries. Later, however, other European traders began to follow the sea routes of the north in search of these goods.

 **What trade routes did the Rus control?**

## MERCHANTS IN EUROPE UNITE

European merchants faced many problems, such as bandits on land and pirates at sea. They also had to pay a tax at almost every port in which they stopped. In the early

## **W**hat?

### The Vikings in North America

Historians had long wondered if the Vikings had really gotten as far west as North America. Strong evidence was found in North America in the 1960s when a group of Viking-style houses was found in Newfoundland. One artifact dug up there was a stone weight similar to those used on Viking spindles for making yarn. Scholars knew that in Viking society, women did the spinning and weaving. They also knew that women did not go on voyages unless the Vikings planned to begin a settlement. From all these facts, historians concluded that the Vikings must have settled in North America.

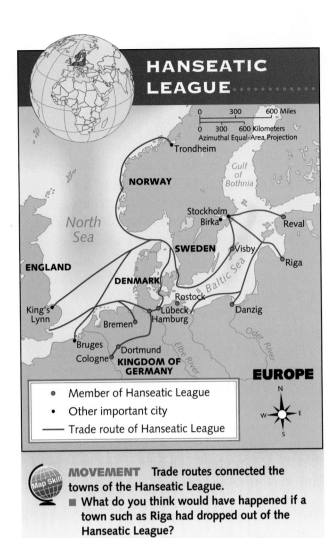

HANSEATIC LEAGUE

0    300    600 Miles
0    300    600 Kilometers
Azimuthal Equal-Area Projection

Trondheim

NORWAY

Gulf of Bothnia

North Sea

Stockholm
Birka

Reval

SWEDEN

Visby

Baltic Sea

Riga

ENGLAND

DENMARK

Rostock

King's Lynn

Lübeck
Hamburg

Danzig

Bremen

Bruges
Cologne

Dortmund

KINGDOM OF GERMANY

Oder River

Elbe River

EUROPE

N
W E
S

- Member of Hanseatic League
- Other important city
— Trade route of Hanseatic League

MOVEMENT  Trade routes connected the towns of the Hanseatic League.
■ What do you think would have happened if a town such as Riga had dropped out of the Hanseatic League?

1200s some merchants in northern European towns decided they could better protect themselves by working together. They formed groups called **Hansas** (HAN•suhz). Hansa members shared the costs of trading, such as renting ships and paying guards for trade caravans.

Around 1240 the Hansas of the German ports of Lübeck and Hamburg signed a treaty. They agreed to protect each other's merchants. Over the next hundred years, the merchants of about 200 northern European towns joined this Hanseatic (han•see•A•tik) League. The league was formed to protect the trading rights of its members. League members had to promise not to take one another's trade. Members who broke the rules were cut off from trade.

The league had its own navy. At times it used this navy to fight wars to protect its members and to gain new trade agreements. More often the league used economic power. **Embargoes**, or bans on trade, worked as well as war for getting the kind of trade agreements the league wanted. By the 1300s the Hanseatic League had almost a monopoly on the northern sea trade.

The Hanseatic League controlled the northern sea trade for more than 100 years. Then during the 1400s the center of European trade shifted to ports on the Atlantic Ocean. The Hanseatic League lasted into the 1600s, but it no longer had much power.

 **Why was the Hanseatic League formed?**

## LESSON 3 REVIEW

### Check Understanding

1. **Recall the Facts**  Where did the Vikings, and later the Hanseatic League, trade?
2. **Focus on the Main Idea**  How did Viking territorial expansion help the Vikings and the Hanseatic League become leaders of trade?

### Think Critically

3. **Past to Present**  Where is territorial expansion taking place today? How does it compare to expansion in earlier times?
4. **Think More About It**  When merchants work together, as the Hanseatic League merchants did, what happens to competition? How does this affect consumers?

### Show What You Know

**Simulation Activity**  Imagine that you are a leader of the Hanseatic League. You want to get more towns to join the league. Create a presentation that tells the advantages trade towns would gain by becoming league members.

# How To

# Form a Logical Conclusion

## Why Is This Skill Important?

A **logical conclusion** is a decision or an idea reached by thoughtful study of all the known facts. To form a logical conclusion, you must be able to put new facts and ideas together with those you already know. This will help you see why things happened as they did in the past, as well as why things happen in your own life today.

## Remember What You Have Read

By the 1960s historians had raised the question *Did the Vikings build settlements in North America?* There was evidence that the Vikings had traveled to North America, but no evidence proved that they had stayed there for any length of time. Then a discovery provided Norwegian scientists Helge Ingstad and Anne Stine the evidence that was needed.

The spindle part (bottom) uncovered by scientists Helge Ingstad and Anne Stine (top) proved to the world that the Vikings built settlements in North America.

Ingstad and Stine had studied the Viking sagas and had decided to look for traces of Viking settlement in Newfoundland, in present-day Canada. At the village of L'Anse aux Meadows, Ingstad, Stine, and their helpers uncovered eight homesites that looked like Viking homesites in Greenland and Iceland. They also found many artifacts that could have been made by the Vikings, but Ingstad and Stine were not completely sure.

Then one day Anne Stine found a ring made of stone. This was clearly a piece of a Viking spindle, a very important tool for spinning wool. This spindle was just like the ones found in other places where the Vikings had lived. With this evidence, Ingstad and Stine were able to conclude that the Vikings had built homes and lived for a time in North America.

## Understand the Process

There are many ways to form a conclusion. One way is to follow these steps:

- Form a question about the subject or the situation, such as *Did the Vikings build settlements in North America?*
- Think about evidence you already have that might help you answer the question.
- Gather new evidence that might give you the answer to your question.
- Think carefully about what the new evidence tells you.

## Think and Apply

Write as many as ten clues that lead to the identification of a place in your community, such as the library. Read the clues one by one to a partner. How many clues does it take before your partner can form a logical conclusion as to what the place is? Discuss with your partner how each clue led to the conclusion.

# LESSON 4

# CONQUERING the PACIFIC

## Link to Our World

**What problems do people face today as they begin to explore the universe?**

**Focus on the Main Idea**
Read to find out how people solved problems to explore and settle the islands in the Pacific Ocean.

**Preview Vocabulary**
atoll
lagoon
outrigger
star path
archipelago

A view from the volcanic island of Bora Bora in the Pacific Ocean

For hundreds of years merchants sailed up and down the coasts of the Pacific Ocean in search of trade. At first, few chose to risk their lives by sailing into the open ocean. Yet over time people did set out into the Pacific to explore and settle the islands there.

## THE PACIFIC ISLANDS

With Asia on its west side and the Americas on its east side, the Pacific Ocean is the world's largest body of water. At its widest point, the Pacific stretches 12,300 miles (19,794 km), or about halfway around the world. It is larger than all the world's land surfaces put together.

Although they take up little of its space, more than 20,000 islands dot the Pacific Ocean. Some of the Pacific islands were formed by volcanoes. Some of these volcanoes are still active. The volcanic islands are often made up mostly of mountains and hills. These types of islands are called the high islands. Other islands are **atolls**, islands formed from coral reefs. In the centers of these atolls are **lagoons**, or small bodies of water. Many of these islands are very beautiful. The islands formed from coral are called the low islands.

The Pacific islands are divided into three groups. To the northeast of Australia lies Melanesia (meh•luh•NEE•zhuh), or "dark islands." North of Melanesia lies Micronesia (my•kruh•NEE•zhuh), or "small islands." To the east of these two groups is Polynesia (pah•luh•NEE•zhuh), or "many islands." The Polynesian islands are small and very far apart. For example, Easter Island, which is only 50 square miles (129 sq km) in area, lies about 1,500 miles (2,414 km) from its nearest neighbor.

Fear of the unknown was the greatest barrier to travel in the Pacific. People on the rim of the ocean did not want to sail away into the unknown. A few did, but they rarely returned to tell what they had seen.

> **What was the greatest barrier to early travel in the Pacific Ocean?**

## TRADE ALONG THE PACIFIC COASTS

Chinese traders sailed the waters of the Pacific from earliest times. Chinese seafaring, however, almost came to an end when the Han emperors took up Confucianism. Confucianism said it was not right for people to take long voyages while their parents were

**HUMAN-ENVIRONMENT INTERACTIONS**
Chinese traders sailed the Pacific.
■ Why do you think Chinese sea traders stayed fairly close to the Chinese mainland?

The 1100s were a time of increased sea trade for China. Chinese ships traveled the Pacific and Indian oceans.

alive. It also taught that trade was not a worthwhile activity.

By the 800s ideas about sea travel began to change. The wealth of the Arab, Persian, and Indian merchants who visited the port of Guangzhou got many Chinese interested in trade. Soon Chinese merchant ships began sailing south to the Malay Peninsula and Sumatra, an island that is today part of Indonesia. Others sailed north to Korea and Japan.

By the 1100s the Chinese government knew that sea trade could help the country's economy. As Emperor Gao Zong (GOW ZAWNG) said:

> 66 Profits from maritime commerce [sea trade] are very great. If properly managed, they can amount to millions. Is this not better than taxing the people? 99

The government provided money to improve harbors and shipping. By mid-century, government profits from overseas trade had doubled. The government also offered rewards for new ship plans and ideas that would improve sea travel. By the start of the 1200s, the Chinese had the fastest ships in the South Seas. They controlled the waters

These statues were created by the early people of Easter Island in the southeastern Pacific Ocean. The statues, which weigh as much as 50 tons each, were carved from volcanic rock and placed on stone platforms. How the rock was moved and why the statues were created are still unknown.

from Guangzhou to Korea and Japan. Also, they had started to control the trade in the South China Sea westward toward the Indian Ocean. From this time on, the Indian Ocean—not the Pacific—became the center of Chinese sea travel.

Across the Pacific many peoples traveled along the coasts of North and South America. A rich trade route linked the regions that today are Mexico and Peru as early as the 700s. By the 1500s the Salangone—who lived near what is today Ecuador—controlled much of the trade along the coast. A Spanish document of the time described the water transportation of the Salangone as sailing rafts built of balsa wood. These rafts were large enough to carry a number of people and many goods.

 **Who controlled coastal trade at either end of the Pacific?**

## OUT INTO THE PACIFIC

The sturdy design of the balsa-wood rafts led some historians to wonder if Native Americans had ever traveled across the open ocean. Some even wondered if Native Americans could have sailed west with the winds to the Pacific islands. In the 1940s Thor Heyerdahl (THAWR HAY•er•dahl), a Norwegian explorer, proved that such a trip was possible. He built a balsa-wood raft and sailed it from Peru in South America to Polynesia. Even so, most archaeological evidence suggests that people settled the Pacific islands from Asia.

The people of almost every Pacific island have a legend about their earliest people.

## What?

### Passing on Knowledge

The Pacific islanders had different ways of passing on what they learned about navigation. The people of some islands passed on their learning in chants and songs that everyone learned. People of other islands chose certain families to keep the knowledge. These "navigator" families held an important place in their society. Still other islands had schools where young people were trained in navigation.

Scholars do not think all these old stories are true. However, they do feel that the legends give a picture of the interests of the people. One Polynesian tale praises a navigator as

66 The king of the black purple deep,
The king of the depths unknown. 99

The legends support the idea that settlement of the Pacific islands was not an accident. It happened because planned exploration and migration took place over a long period of time. It began as far back as 1500 B.C. when daring sailors set out from the larger islands off the Asian mainland. They arrived first in Melanesia. Later generations pushed north and east into Micronesia and Polynesia. By about A.D. 800, seafarers had settled every island in the Pacific that people

could live on. In doing so, said one scholar, they "achieved the greatest feats of maritime navigation in all human history."

Obviously, the Pacific islanders put great thought into their travels. Their boats were small but well suited to ocean travel. **Outriggers**, or wooden frames placed on each side, kept the boats from tipping over in rough seas. Large triangular sails called crab claws powered the boats. These sails, like lateen sails, allowed the boats to travel into the wind. To navigate, the Pacific islanders used the sun and the stars. They also studied **star paths**, the way the stars in the night sky seem to move because of the Earth's rotation.

When they migrated, the Pacific islanders took everything they would need in a new home. They loaded their boats with animals

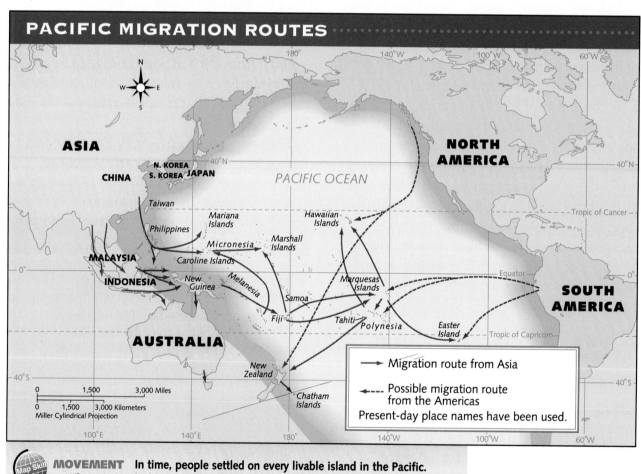

**PACIFIC MIGRATION ROUTES**

— Migration route from Asia

◄---- Possible migration route from the Americas

Present-day place names have been used.

**MOVEMENT** In time, people settled on every livable island in the Pacific.
■ What group of islands did the Asian explorers probably visit first?

Long ago, Micronesians made maps out of sticks (above). In Micronesia and elsewhere in the Pacific, outrigger canoes are still used (right).

and plants and took along people who knew how to farm and make tools.

After the age of exploration and migration, the Pacific islanders continued to make sea journeys. Some people sailed back and forth between their new and their old homes. Also, traders regularly sailed among all the islands in an archipelago. An **archipelago** (ar•kuh•PEH•luh•goh) is a group or chain of islands. Trade linked archipelagos that were far apart, such as Tahiti and Hawaii,

which are separated by nearly 2,400 miles (3,862 km) of ocean.

For the Pacific islanders the vast ocean was "a highway, not a barrier." They had this highway all to themselves for centuries. Then, in the 1500s, European seafarers entered the Pacific and took control of its waters.

 *How did the Pacific islanders make the ocean a "highway"?*

# LESSON 4 REVIEW

## Check Understanding

1. **Recall the Facts** Where did the earliest trade on the Pacific Ocean take place?
2. **Focus on the Main Idea** How were the Pacific islanders able to explore and settle the thousands of islands in the Pacific Ocean?

## Think Critically

3. **Past to Present** How was early exploration of the Pacific Ocean like present-day space or undersea exploration?
4. **Think More About It** A historian called the Pacific islanders "sea-attuned" people. *Attune* means "in touch with." What do you think the historian meant by "sea-attuned"?

5. **Explore Viewpoints** Some Chinese people believed that long trading voyages were wrong because older parents were left alone. Others believed that trading voyages were a good idea because wealth gained through trade reduced taxes. Which idea do you support? Give reasons for your decision.

## Show What You Know

 **Questioning Activity** Work in a group of five. List five questions you have about the early peoples of the Pacific Ocean. Each group member should use reference materials to find the answer to one question. Finally, the group members should share their findings.

## CONNECT MAIN IDEAS

Use this organizer to show that you understand how the chapter's main ideas are connected. Copy the organizer onto a separate sheet of paper. Then complete it by writing two details to support each main idea.

### Indian Ocean Trade
Trade around the Indian Ocean linked many peoples.

1. _____
2. _____

### The Mediterranean and the Black Sea
Some city-states became leaders of trade in the Mediterranean and the Black Sea.

1. _____
2. _____

**Sea and River Trade**

### The Northern Seas
Two important trading cultures developed in northern Europe.

1. _____
2. _____

### Conquering the Pacific
People solved problems to explore and settle the islands in the Pacific Ocean.

1. _____
2. _____

## WRITE MORE ABOUT IT

1. **Write a Report**   Write a one-page report that describes the different resources each member of a family can provide. Give examples of how family members can depend on one another, and explain how this can help the whole family.

2. **Write a Journal Entry**   Imagine that you are a Muslim sea trader who has just returned home from a voyage. Write a journal entry that describes how people at home react to the silk, porcelain, cotton, pepper, and other spices you brought from China, India, and the East Indies. Tell how these products affect your culture.

3. **Write a Story**   Write a very short story about a Viking adventurer who has gone "a-viking." Be sure to explain why he or she began the overseas raid.

## USE VOCABULARY

Write a sentence or two to explain the meaning of each of these terms.

1. atoll
2. dhow
3. Greek fire
4. lagoon
5. lateen sail
6. monsoon
7. outrigger

## CHECK UNDERSTANDING

1. Why was ancient Baghdad called the harbor of the world?

2. How did lateen sails improve sea trade?

3. How did Arab trade affect the communities in the trading ports of East Africa?

4. What types of goods did Byzantine traders bring back to Constantinople?

5. How were Muslim traders able to protect their trade ships along the coast of North Africa?

6. What led to the rise of Venice as a trading center?

7. Who were the Rus? Why did people in western Europe become dependent on their trade?

8. What kept the Chinese from exploring the Pacific Ocean for many years?

## THINK CRITICALLY

1. **Past to Present** What personal characteristics do you think present-day traders have in common with early sea traders?

2. **Think More About It** Why do you think early sea traders were most often men?

3. **Explore Viewpoints** What different views do you think people living in the 1200s may have had about sailing out onto the world's oceans?

4. **Personally Speaking** Imagine that you are a sea trader living in the 1200s. What made you decide to become a trader?

5. **Cause and Effect** The United States depends on resources from many different countries. What are the positive and negative effects of this dependence?

## APPLY SKILLS

**How to Compare Information with Graphs**
Use the graphs on pages 376 and 377 to answer these questions.

1. Which graph would you use to find the year in which United States exports totaled about $394 billion?

2. Which two graphs would you use to find out what rank Mexico holds as an export partner and as an import partner to the United States?

3. Imagine that you have been asked to prepare a graph showing how many automobiles the United States imported between 1970 and 1995. Which of the graphs shown might you use as a model? What type of graph is it?

**How to Form a Logical Conclusion** Use the steps on page 382 to support this conclusion: People from Asia settled the Pacific islands. Use this book and other books to gather evidence to support the conclusion. Make a list of the pieces of supporting evidence. Give the source for each piece of evidence.

## READ MORE ABOUT IT

*From Gibraltar to the Ganges* by Irene M. Franck and David M. Brownstone. Facts on File. In this book the authors describe trade routes, such as the Mediterranean–Black Sea Routes, the Great Desert Route, and the Persian Royal Road.

*The Vikings* by Robert Nicholson and Claire Watts. Chelsea. The culture and activities of the Vikings are described in this fascinating book.

## THE INTERNATIONAL MARKETPLACE

A thousand years ago the Chinese city of Chang'an (now Xian) lay at the eastern end of the Silk Road, the main world trade route of its day. In the city market, merchants sold goods from distant lands—sandalwood from Indonesia, cloves from India, and incense from eastern Africa. Some merchants offered Persian dates and pistachios. The smells of Burmese pepper and Tibetan mustard rose from the marketplace.

In the United States today, any shopping mall has more kinds of goods from more places in the world than the Chang'an marketplace offered. Present-day mall merchants might sell coffee and fruit grown in South America, cotton shirts from India, athletic shoes made in South Korea, compact disc players from Japan, and American products from nearly every state in the Union.

The international exchange of goods that is now a part of everyday life began hundreds of years ago with the traders who traveled the world. It was their idea to find new products and bring them to market. Thanks to these daring adventurers, you can choose from many kinds of basketball shoes—including those made in places as far away as South Korea!

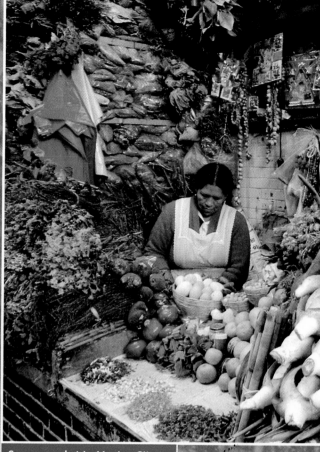
Sonora market in Mexico City

## THINK AND APPLY

Like an early trader, find products made in other parts of the world. Search your home for such products, and on a world map, mark the places where they were made. Where were most of your products made? Were certain kinds of goods more likely to come from certain areas? Work with a partner to write a short report that explains your findings.

BUILDING CITIZENSHIP

# STORY CLOTH

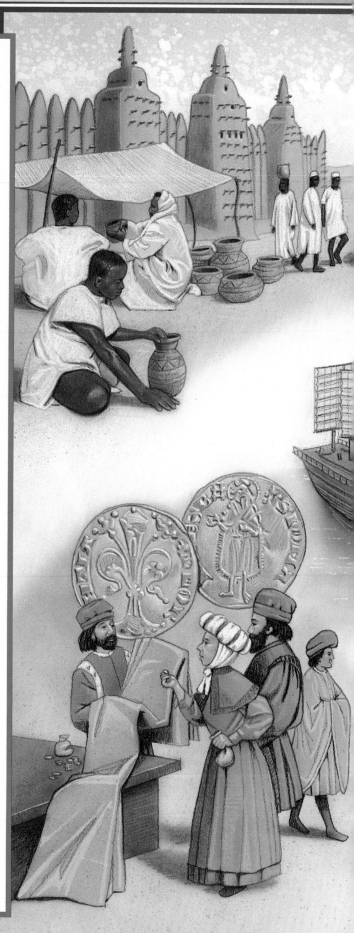

Study the pictures shown in this story cloth to help you review the events you read about in Unit 6.

## Summarize the Main Ideas

**1.** Between 500 and 1500, West Africans traded with many other peoples. Because of this trade, they were able to build wealthy empires.

**2.** As the Muslim Empire grew, it formed trade networks with the peoples of Asia, Africa, and Europe.

**3.** On the Silk Road both goods and ideas were carried back and forth between Europe and Asia.

**4.** Travel on the Indian Ocean brought together people in Asia and Africa, leading to the exchange of goods and ideas.

**5.** Venice and other Italian city-states came to control trade around the Mediterranean Sea and the Black Sea.

**6.** In northern Europe the Vikings took new territories, which brought them more trade. Northern European merchants joined together to expand their own trade.

**7.** People had to solve many problems as they explored the islands in the Pacific Ocean.

**Make a Map**   Sketch your own map of the world. Do not show borders of present-day countries. Label the continents, oceans, and major seas. Think about what you see on the story cloth and what you have read about trade in this unit. Add to your map written descriptions of trade activities in different parts of the world between 500 and 1500.

**Write About the Story**   Choose one scene in the story cloth. Write a paragraph that explains what you see.

## COOPERATIVE LEARNING WORKSHOP

### Remember

- Share your ideas.
- Cooperate with others to plan your work.
- Take responsibility for your work.
- Show your group's work to the class.
- Discuss what you learned by working together.

### Activity 1
## Make Flow Charts

Work with a partner to make a flow chart that shows how people depend on one another when they produce goods and services for export. Make another flow chart that shows how people depend on one another when they obtain imported goods and services. Include goods and services from businesses, factories, farms, and schools. Present the flow charts to your class when they are finished.

### Activity 2
## Make a Diorama

Review what you have learned about the African kingdoms of Ghana, Mali, and Songhay. Then work in a group to create a diorama that highlights one of these kingdoms.

### Activity 3
## Make a Guidebook

Imagine that the members of your group are geographers in the 1400s. The group has visited many different lands. Write a guidebook that tells about the places you visited and the types of trading you observed.

### Activity 4
## Draw a Map

Work with three or four classmates to create a map that shows world trade between the years 500 and 1500. On your map, identify each continent. Then show different trading cultures and the trading networks they formed. Compare your map with those of other groups.

# USE VOCABULARY

Write the word that correctly matches each definition. Then use each word in a sentence.

archipelago  oasis
dhow    savanna
embargo   tariff
hansa

1. a grassy plain

2. a tax on goods

3. a water hole

4. an Arab ship that used lateen sails

5. a ban on trade

6. a group whose members shared the costs of trading

7. a group or chain of islands

# CHECK UNDERSTANDING

1. Why did the population of early peoples in West Africa grow quickly?

2. How did the location of the Soninke people contribute to their success as traders?

3. How did the king of Ghana keep the price of gold high?

4. Why was salt worth a great deal in West Africa?

5. What factors helped bring people together in the ancient Muslim Empire?

6. Who controlled the gold mines of Central Africa?

7. Why was territorial expansion important to the Vikings?

8. How did membership in the Hanseatic League help merchants?

9. What was the greatest barrier to travel in the Pacific?

# THINK CRITICALLY

1. **Past to Present** How has technology changed the way peoples trade throughout the world today?

2. **Think More About It** Imagine that every country in the world could produce everything it needed. How do you think the lack of interdependence among countries would affect the world?

3. **Personally Speaking** Write your opinion of how the ancient Chinese government increased sea trade.

4. **Cause and Effect** Explain why trade between the years 500 and 1500 increased both understanding and conflict between cultures.

# APPLY GEOGRAPHY SKILLS

 **How to Compare Maps with Different Projections** Identify the projections of these maps as polar, conformal, or equal-area.

### MAP PROJECTIONS

1.

3.

2.

# UNIT 7

# *The* EARLY MODERN WORLD

1250      1300      1350      1400      1450

**1300**
Renaissance ideas begin to take hold in Italy

**1368**
Ming dynasty gains Mandate of Heaven in China

**About 1400**
Rise of Kingdom of Kongo in Africa

**1450**
Gutenberg develops movable type

*B*etween 1300 and 1700, the modern world began to take shape. In Europe people shook off traditions of the Middle Ages and tried new ideas. Through these ideas they began to understand their lives in different ways. As a result, government, industry, religion, philosophy, and art all took new forms. At the same time, Europeans set out to explore the world. In their search they found civilizations as great as their own—in Africa, the Americas, and Asia. These encounters, or meetings, caused more changes and helped to shape the world we live in today.

◀ Scene of port of Venice, oil painting by Antonio Canaletto

**1500**

**1492**
Columbus's first voyage to the Americas

**1550**

**About 1500**
Benin flourishes as trade center in West Africa

Slave trade across Atlantic begins

**1600**

**1588**
Defeat of the Spanish Armada

Queen

*Queen Eliz: visiting her Camp at Tilbury being mounted on Horseback w.th a Truntheon of an ordinary Captain in her hand*

**1650**

**1603**
First Tokugawa shogun in Japan

**1700**

**1687**
Newton publishes work on gravity

# I, Juan de Pareja

## by Elizabeth Borton de Treviño

The story I, Juan de Pareja (WAHN day pah•REH•hah) is based on the real life of the enslaved servant of Spanish artist Diego Velázquez (vah•LAHS•kays). Shown above is a self-portrait painted by Velázquez.

*The Middle Ages gave way to a period in which individuals examined their world more closely. Writers, scholars, scientists, and artists all took new directions in their work. Artists started to use new materials and new techniques to capture real life on the canvas on which they painted.*

*Read now about a Spanish artist who was swept up in the spirit of this age. His story is told by his enslaved servant, Juan (also called Juanico). Juan tells us about an artist living in a time of individualism and creativity.*

When Master was working intensely, he did not even glance at his palette, but put his brush unerringly[1] into the colors he wanted, taking the amounts he needed and blending them in the middle to the shades he required. I have seen him thus mix up the same shade time and time again, without glancing, and taking them straight to the canvas; they were always perfect.

His strokes on the canvas, too, sometimes seemed slapdash, rough and unintelligible, if one stood as close to the canvas as he. But a little distance away, and those spots and dashes of light cream or ivory would resolve themselves into a delicate frill of lace, or the daintiest of highlights on satin. Time after time I verified this, and it always seemed magical to me. Master never commented on my astonishment, but often I saw a slight smile curl the quiet mouth beneath the dark silky mustache.

---

[1] **unerringly:** without mistake

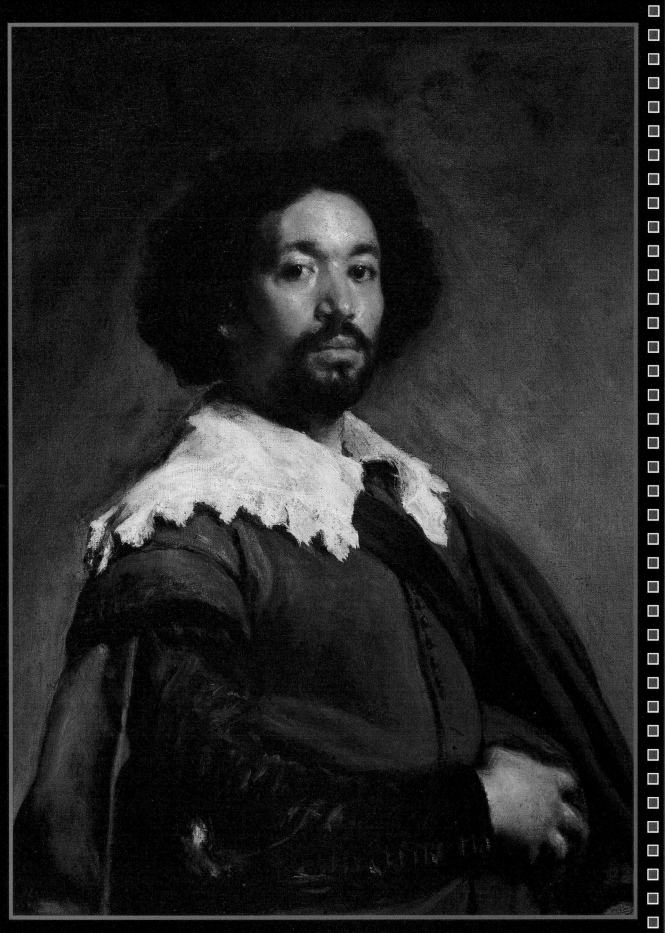

Oil painting of Juan de Pareja by Velázquez

This painting, *The Tapestry Weavers* by Velázquez, shows an artist's use of sitters.

And he never chatted while he worked. It was the sitter who spoke, and Master merely put in a word now and again, should there come an expectant silence. Then he would murmur, "Ah?" or "Possibly," or "Just so."

But he studied people. Once he said to me, when the sitter had gone home, and Master was working on a background, "I like to watch people when they talk about themselves, Juanico. Then they reveal to you what they really are. Women, for instance, love themselves; they speak of themselves as if they were talking about a beloved relative who is to be pardoned any foolishness. Men, on the other hand, seem to admire themselves. They speak of themselves like judges who have already brought in a verdict of 'Not guilty.'"

I ventured, "Isn't it difficult to show people their true selves when you paint them, Master?"

"No. Nobody ever knows what he really looks like. Bring me some more of the ochre."

And he was silent again.

Once in a while he would paint me, to keep his hand in, or would ask me to model some difficult fabric.

After he had taught the apprentices[2] to draw vases and fruits and cheeses and hams and all manner of objects, he began to let them sketch people. Then I was often told to pose for them. Then I had my revenge on Cristobal and I helped Alvaro, turning myself subtly so as to ruin Cristobal's drawing and holding myself very still when I noticed Alvaro's eyes on me. Master scolded me for this and watched me, but all the same I was sometimes mischievous.[3] I was always sorry

---

[2] **apprentices:** people who are in training
[3] **mischievous:** full of mischief

when Master criticized Alvaro's work and praised Cristobal's, and one day he answered the distress he saw that this caused me, by telling me his reason.

"Art must be true," he said. "It is the one thing in life that must rest on solid truth. Otherwise, it is worthless."

Then one day there was a knock at the door, and soon after, Mistress came running into the studio, pale with excitement. Behind her, pacing slowly, followed a messenger from the King. He handed a rolled parchment[4] to Master, bowed, and turned. Mistress ran ahead of him to open the door for his departure. The apprentices and I stood silent and respectful as Master unrolled the parchment and read it. He rolled it up again, and took up his palette and brush once more. I remember that he was painting a bronze vase, and I had been at great pains to keep moving it so the sunlight should continue to strike it at the same point every moment.

---

[4] **parchment:** animal skin used to write on

"Diego!" burst forth Mistress. "Tell me, please! Don't make me wait to know! What was in the King's message?"

"I am to paint his portrait," he answered at length, frowning.

"Oh, God be praised! How wonderful!"

"And I am to be given a studio in the palace."

Mistress collapsed onto a chair, which creaked ominously,[5] and she had to fan herself. Little black curls escaped from her pompadour[6] and fell down over her forehead. This meant she was to move in court circles. It meant a fortune, dignity, honors, position beyond anything she had dreamed of.

But Master was silent and pale as he continued to paint the vase. At last he murmured, under his breath, and only I heard, "I hope they haven't sent some courtier[7] to select and prepare a studio for me. It must have light. Light. Nothing else matters. . . ."

---

[5] **ominously:** in a way that threatens
[6] **pompadour:** a hair style
[7] **courtier:** royal attendant

In this oil painting by Velázquez, the family of Spanish King Philip IV visits the artist in his studio at the king's palace.

# NEW DIRECTIONS for EUROPE

> ❝ O, wonder!
> How many goodly creatures are there here!
> How beauteous mankind is! O brave new world
> That has such people in't! ❞
>
> Spoken by Miranda
> *The Tempest*
> William Shakespeare

Both the nonreligious subjects, such as this woman, and the religious subjects painted by sixteenth-century artist Michelangelo Merisi da Caravaggio look like real people.

# LESSON 1

# THE REBIRTH of IDEAS IN EUROPE

## *Link to Our World*

***How might greater freedom for the individual help bring about an age of creative ideas?***

*Focus on the Main Idea*
*As you read, think about how changes in European thought encouraged individualism and creativity.*

*Preview Vocabulary*

Renaissance
patron
perspective
movable type

telescope
gravity
scientific method

This portrait is typical of Renaissance painting, which captured everyday life.

As Europe emerged from the Middle Ages, people began to look at the world differently. They rejected old ways and started to explore new ideas. Yet some of their ideas were not really new. Many came from the learning of early Greece and Rome. Others came from cultures in Asia and Africa. Encounters with Muslims during the Crusades had given Europeans a better understanding of the importance of learning. Using all their new ideas, Europeans entered an age of thought, learning, art, and science. We call this time, which lasted from about 1400 to 1600, the **Renaissance** (REH•nuh•sahns), a French word meaning "rebirth."

## THE RENAISSANCE BEGINS IN ITALY

Renaissance ideas first took hold in Italy. During the Middle Ages, cities such as Venice, Naples, Milan, Florence, and Genoa served as important centers of trade between East and West. Merchants from the city-states brought back not only goods from the East but also ideas about philosophy, science, geography, and technology. These ideas inspired a new interest in learning in Italy.

The Italian merchants who sailed to the East and the bankers who paid for their trips became rich and powerful. The wealthy merchant and banking families soon took over as the government leaders of the city-states.

The new leaders placed high value on learning. They believed that it was important to study Greek and Roman classics. The Greeks' love of beauty and the Romans' practical ideas about government strongly appealed to them.

## ITALY DURING RENAISSANCE

0        50        100 Miles
0    50    100 Kilometers
Lambert Conformal Conic Projection

DUCHY OF SAVOY

DUCHY OF MILAN

ITALIAN ALPS

Milan

Po River

Verona

REPUBLIC OF VENICE

Venice

ASTI
MONTFERRAT

MANTUA

Genoa

MODENA

DUCHY OF FERRARA

Bologna

REPUBLIC OF GENOA

LUCCA

Lucca

Florence

REPUBLIC OF FLORENCE

Siena

Assisi

REPUBLIC OF SIENA

Elba

PAPAL STATES

Corsica

42°N

Rome

KINGDOM OF NAPLES (ARAGON)

Tyrrhenian Sea

Sardinia

8°E    10°E

Naples

40°N

12°E    14°E

Adriatic Sea

Apennines

Tiber R.

• Important cultural center
— Present-day border

**PLACE** During the Renaissance, Italy was controlled by powerful city-states.
■ Which city-states controlled land that is not part of present-day Italy?

For years the city-states had competed with one another for control of trade in the Mediterranean. Now they competed to become known as Europe's greatest center of learning. The wealthy merchants and bankers in the various city-states became **patrons**, or supporters, of the arts. They paid artists to create paintings and sculptures and promised to give scholars money if they would come to live in their city-state. The de' Medici (day MED•uh•chee) family of Florence gave much of their wealth to help the careers of artists and thinkers. Such encouragement helped make the Renaissance possible.

✓ **What contributed to the rebirth of ideas in Italy?**

## LEARNING ABOUT THE WORLD

The Italian patrons supported scholars who believed in an idea unheard of during the Middle Ages—the importance of the individual. In the Middle Ages, scholarly thinking had focused on God and religion. The ideas and actions of individuals were not considered worthy of study.

The scholars of the Renaissance studied all the old Greek and Roman works they could find. Many of the works came to them by way of Muslim scholars, who had saved the works when few Europeans were interested in them. Others had been stored in European monasteries.

The study of the Greek and Roman works led Renaissance scholars to a new way of thinking about the world. They believed that people needed to understand how things worked. Anything and everything had to be

Gaining knowledge was a focus of the Renaissance. This painting of a school in 1516 shows how important learning to read had become.

This painting (left) by the artist Raphael is a good example of the use of artistic perspective. Notice how all parts of the painting lead the eye to a center point (above).

looked at closely, not just religion. They felt that a person's life should be judged by the things he or she did, not just by faith.

This new way of thought first appeared in literature. Writers of the Renaissance borrowed many of their ideas from the Greek and Roman classics that had been written much earlier. However, the writers of this time chose to write in their own languages rather than in Latin or Greek.

 **What was the relationship between Greek and Roman culture and Renaissance thinking?**

## CHANGES IN ART

Renaissance ideas about the importance of the individual also changed art and artists. In the Middle Ages, artists used only religious subjects, and their works looked formal and stiff. Renaissance artists, however, studied Greek and Roman works and produced art that was far more lifelike and that showed both religious and nonreligious subjects.

People in Renaissance paintings and sculptures looked like real human beings, and their faces showed feelings. Even the backgrounds in these paintings looked real, because Renaissance painters used perspective. This technique allows an artist to show a difference between things that are close and things that are far away.

As art changed, the way people viewed artists also changed. In the Middle Ages, people thought of artists as craftworkers, much like carpenters or bricklayers. Groups of artists, called guilds, controlled where and for whom artists could work, and artists could not choose their subjects. During the Renaissance, however, patrons competed to attract the best artists of the time. As a result, artists could choose for whom they would work, and many were well paid.

Without a doubt, the greatest genius of the Renaissance was Leonardo da Vinci (lee•uh•NAR•doh duh VIN•chee). Leonardo lived from 1452 to 1519, but his accomplishments could have filled a dozen lifetimes. He was a scientist, an engineer, an inventor, a

Leonardo's creativity can be seen both in this self-portrait (left) and in the pages of his sketchbooks. This sketchbook drawing (above) is of a flying machine. What modern-day invention does it remind you of?

philosopher, and a writer as well as an artist. Leonardo filled notebook after notebook with his ideas and drawings. He sketched plants, animals, and the bones and muscles of the human body. He also filled his pages with "the imagining of things that are to be," such as a flying machine.

Leonardo's paintings stand as his greatest work. For centuries people have been trying to guess the secret behind the smile of his Mona Lisa. The attention to detail in his Last Supper still leaves people amazed.

Renaissance artist Michelangelo Buonarroti (my•kuh•LAN•juh•loh bwaw•naw•RAW•tee) also showed skill in many fields. His sculptures of David and Moses have the power of the greatest Greek sculptures. The magnificent dome of St. Peter's Church in Rome shows his ability as an architect. The glory of his painting can be seen in the scenes from the Bible that cover the ceiling of the Sistine (SIS•teen) Chapel. Pope Julius II, the patron who supported these paintings, once complained that Michelangelo worked too slowly. The artist's

answer showed the spirit of Renaissance artists: "It will be finished when I have done all that I believe is required to satisfy Art."

✓ **How did art change during the Renaissance?**

# **W**hat?

## The Mona Lisa

Leonardo da Vinci spent four years painting the world-famous portrait known as the Mona Lisa. The work shows the artist's skill in blending colors and using light and shadow. Everyone agrees that the Mona Lisa is a masterpiece. But no one knows the identity of the woman who inspired it. Some people say she was the wife of a Florentine merchant, Francesco del Giocondo (joh•KOHN•doh). Others think that she lived only in Leonardo da Vinci's mind.

# THE SPREAD OF IDEAS

Renaissance ideas spread through Europe with the help of an invention from Germany. During the fourteenth century, Europeans had printed books by carving words and pictures into a block of wood. The block was then inked and stamped onto paper. The whole block had to be recarved if anything on it needed to be changed.

Around 1450 a German printer named Johannes Gutenberg (yoh•HAHN•uhs GOO•tuhn•berg) became the first European to print with **movable type**. Gutenberg's printing press used many small pieces of metal, each with a single number or letter of the alphabet. These metal pieces could be arranged in trays to form rows of words and could be easily changed. The printing process became much faster and easier.

In 1455 Gutenberg printed a 1,200-page Bible, using a printing press with movable type. Soon after that, printing presses appeared in all the major cities of Europe. Because books could be printed in large numbers, they became cheaper. This meant that more people could buy them. Through the printed page the ideas of the Renaissance quickly spread to all parts of Europe.

Renaissance ideas reached into Spain, France, and England, bringing

> ❝ *HE WAS NOT OF AN AGE but for all time.* ❞
>
> Description of William Shakespeare

about some of the greatest writing of the time. English literature flourished during the time Elizabeth I ruled England. She loved poetry and drama and supported many English writers. The greatest writer of England's Golden Age—perhaps of all time—was William Shakespeare, who wrote poems and plays. Ordinary people, nobles, and royalty alike crowded London's Globe Theatre to see Shakespeare's plays. People still enjoy his works today. In fact, several of his plays have been made into movies. As English poet Ben Jonson noted, "He was not of an age but for all time."

✓ **How did the printing press affect the Renaissance?**

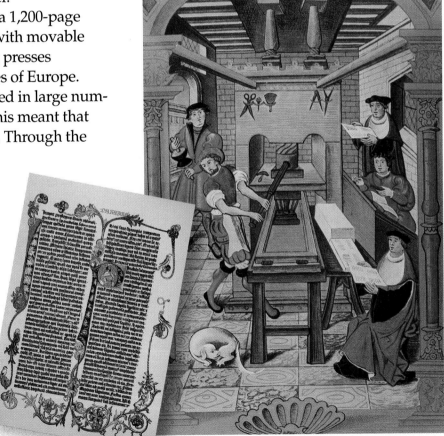

Each copy of the Gutenberg Bible (left) took six printing presses (right), many workers, and several months to make. As many as three million metal letters were also needed. Of the 200 copies made, fewer than 40 still exist.

# REVOLUTION IN SCIENCE

The questioning spirit of the Renaissance affected science as well as literature and the arts. More and more, scientists began to explore how the physical world works. One important Renaissance scientist was a Polish astronomer named Nicolaus Copernicus (nik•uh•LAY•uhs koh•PER•nih•kuhs). In the 1500s he presented calculations that showed the Earth revolves around the sun. This idea disputed beliefs that the Earth was the center of the solar system.

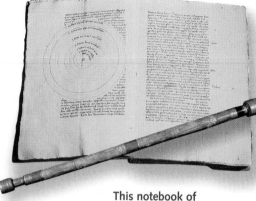

This notebook of Copernicus and this model of Galileo's telescope are both examples of the new ideas of Renaissance scientists.

In the early 1600s Galileo Galilei (ga•luh•LAY•oh ga•luh•LAY•ee), an Italian scientist, proved Copernicus's theory. Galileo had heard about an instrument that could make faraway objects seem close. He set out to make such an instrument. With the help of his telescope, he showed that the Earth did indeed move around the sun.

Galileo's work upset religious leaders. They felt that Galileo's ideas went against Church teachings, and they tried to make him say that he was wrong. Old and ill, Galileo gave in. However, legend says that as he lay dying, Galileo said, "And yet it [the Earth] *does* move!"

The work of Copernicus and Galileo interested an English mathematician named Isaac Newton. In 1687 Newton wrote a book explaining that objects are held to the Earth by a force called gravity. The same force, Newton said, keeps the planets circling the sun. In developing his theory, Isaac Newton followed a scientific method. Scientific methods require that ideas be tested through observing and experimenting. Scientists still work this way today.

✓ **What scientific contributions did Copernicus, Galileo, and Newton make?**

# *L*ESSON 1 REVIEW

## Check Understanding

1. **Recall the Facts**   Why is the Renaissance a good name for the age of learning?
2. **Focus on the Main Idea**   How did changes in European thought encourage individualism and creativity?

## Think Critically

3. **Think More About It**   Today we often call someone who is skilled in many fields a Renaissance man or a Renaissance woman. Do you think this is a good name? Explain your answer.

4. **Cause and Effect**   What helped the new learning spread so quickly throughout Europe? What changes did this spread of ideas bring?

## Show What You Know

**Art Appreciation Activity**
Work in a group to find Renaissance art in books or magazines. Identify the works and the artists. Your group should then take on the role of a panel of art experts. Discuss how each painting or piece of sculpture reflects the ideas of the Renaissance.

# CHANGES in EUROPE

## Link to Our World

**What can cause a society today to change over time?**

**Focus on the Main Idea**
As you read, look for reasons that European society gradually changed.

**Preview Vocabulary**

| | |
|---|---|
| Reconquista | heresy |
| clergy | Protestant |
| indulgence | Reformation |

By the mid-1500s the Renaissance in Italy had lost much of its force. Although its gift of learning and art remained, trade, wealth, and power began to shift to other parts of Europe—especially Spain, France, and England.

## NEW MONARCHIES

Since about 1100, Christian kings had been trying to drive the Moors out of Spain. The Moors were Muslims who had come from North Africa. In the 1400s King Ferdinand, who ruled the Spanish kingdom of Aragon (AR•ah•gohn), and Queen Isabella, who ruled the Spanish kingdom of Castile (ka•STEEL), led the effort to expel the Moors.

In 1469 Ferdinand and Isabella married. Several years later, they united their kingdoms and other parts of Spain under one rule. They believed, though, that true unity would come for Spain only if it were a completely Catholic country.

Their plan to make Spain all Catholic was called the **Reconquista** (ray•kohn•KEES•tah), or Reconquest. They immediately began driving the Muslims from Spain. By 1492 they had claimed all the land that the Moors once ruled. In the same year they drove more than 200,000 Jews from Spain. By the end of 1492, Ferdinand and Isabella had united Spain under one religion and one government.

The task of uniting France fell to Louis XI. In 1461 he became ruler of a divided kingdom. France had just won the Hundred Years' War with England. But the French people were tired of fighting and of special rights for the nobles.

King Ferdinand of Aragon and Queen Isabella of Castile ruled Spain from 1479 to 1516.

Powerful French nobles took care of their own needs first, treated others poorly, and refused to listen to their king. Louis XI saw the need to bring peace, order, and unity to France.

Louis immediately went to work. First he crushed the power of the nobles. Then he began to give special favors to the merchants in the growing towns and cities. He knew that they controlled business and finance and had the money to pay taxes. For the middle-class merchants, taxation was better than the disorder caused by warring nobles. Therefore, they supported Louis. By the time Louis died in 1483, he ruled all of France.

The uniting of England took much longer. After the Hundred Years' War, leading noble families quarreled about which one had the strongest claim to the English crown. In 1485 Henry Tudor, the Earl of Richmond, defeated Richard III at the Battle of Bosworth and became King Henry VII. Henry at once began to unite the country. He married a niece of Richard III to unite the warring families and make his claim to the throne stronger. Then he moved against the most powerful noble families who still opposed him. He seized

THE RECONQUISTA

PLACE By 1492 Spain had come under the control of Ferdinand and Isabella.
■ By what date had they conquered Granada?

their private armies and made them give up some of their lands. He chose lesser nobles and people from the middle class to help him govern. When Henry VII died in 1509, England was peaceful and united under a strong central government.

✔ **How did each of the new monarchies establish its authority?**

## LIFE IN EUROPE

Renaissance ideas and strong monarchs transformed Europe in many ways, but for most people life did not change much. At the beginning of the 1500s, most of the people of Europe lived in small villages. Poor families lived in huts of wood and straw, as people

Merchants lined this sixteenth-century Paris street. Why did Louis XI favor the merchants in the growing cities?

had during the Middle Ages. Tenant farmers, who worked long and hard, still had to hand over a part of their harvest to landowners.

By the mid-1500s life for peasant farmers had become worse than ever. The demand for wool was rising steadily. Landowners saw that they could make huge profits from raising sheep. To gain more pastures for sheep, they threw thousands of families off the land. The lucky ones found work on other farms. Some unlucky ones became beggars. Others became robbers. Still others headed for the towns and cities in search of jobs.

The arrival of large numbers of jobless people from the country made life harder for those already in the towns and cities. The newcomers were willing to work for any amount of pay. Employers hired them—and townspeople who had been working for years were suddenly out of jobs.

Europe's wealthy lived a life of leisure while its peasants lived a life of hardship.

In contrast to the poor, the wealthy nobles and merchants lived lives of luxury, dividing their time between palaces in the cities and manor houses in the country. They became patrons of the arts and spent a lot of money entertaining.

 **What caused life to change for European peasant farmers in the mid-1500s?**

## A WEAKENED CHURCH

In 1513 a member of the de' Medici family of Florence became the leader of the Catholic Church as Pope Leo X. It is said that he wrote to his brother, "God gave us the papacy [office of the Pope]—let us enjoy it." Leo X did indeed enjoy himself. He spent Church money freely on himself and as a patron of the arts. To replace the money, Leo sold positions in the Church to whoever could pay the most.

Most Christians in Europe never met the pope, but they did see their local priest. While many priests served the Church well, some behaved in less desirable ways. Some Europeans warned that poor judgment among members of the **clergy**, or church officers, would cause trouble.

**LEARNING FROM GRAPHS** In the 1500s many Europeans moved from the countryside to the cities.
■ How many times larger was the population of London in 1600 than in 1500?

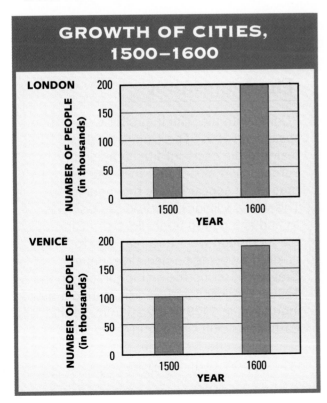

GROWTH OF CITIES,
1500–1600

LONDON

NUMBER OF PEOPLE (in thousands)
200
150
100
50
0
1500    1600
YEAR

VENICE

NUMBER OF PEOPLE (in thousands)
200
150
100
50
0
1500    1600
YEAR

This papal bull, or letter from the pope (left), demanded that Martin Luther (above) change his ideas.

Trouble came much sooner than most people expected. Leo X wanted to rebuild St. Peter's Church in Rome. To get the money for this work, he began to sell **indulgences**, or pardons for sins. Selling indulgences had been common in the Church. One church official stated, "The Lord desireth not the death of a sinner but that he live and pay." Leo X's new indulgences were different, however. They promised forgiveness for sins that people might commit in the future!

A priest named Martin Luther saw the sale of indulgences taking place in the public square of the German town of Wittenberg (WIH•tuhn•berg). The idea that forgiveness could be bought with money shocked Luther. That forgiveness for future sins could be bought shocked him even more. Luther wondered whether he should take independent action, since few other people seemed to care.

After much thought, he decided to challenge the practice of selling indulgences.

✓ **What were indulgences? Why did Martin Luther feel that they were wrong?**

## THE REFORMATION

At noon on October 31, 1517, Luther nailed his 95 Theses (THEE•seez), or statements of opinion, to the door of the castle church in Wittenberg. The papers listed Luther's complaints against his own church.

A Church court quickly put Luther on trial. It convicted him of **heresy**, or denying the beliefs of the Church. Charles V, the leader of the Holy Roman Empire—of which the German states were a part—also put Luther on trial. In both trials Luther explained that he did not intend to hurt the Church. He only wanted to identify and solve its problems. At the same time, however, he refused to deny or change any of his ideas. Luther was told, therefore, that he was no longer a member of the Church.

## **W**hat?

### The Inquisition

"Come with me. The Inquisitor wishes to speak with you." This command struck fear into the hearts of fifteenth-century Europeans. It meant that they had been ordered to appear before the Inquisition. This was a religious court whose task was to find and punish nonbelievers. Victims of the Inquisition were tortured, sent to prison, or killed by being burned alive. Pope Gregory IX set up the first Inquisition in the 1230s. Ferdinand and Isabella started a new Inquisition in 1478 as a way to make the Catholic religion stronger in Spain. The Spanish people lived under the Inquisitor's eye for more than 300 years.

## THE SPREAD OF PROTESTANTISM, 1618 ······

Protestant
Roman Catholic
Islamic
Eastern Orthodox

0    300    600 Miles
0  300  600 Kilometers
Azimuthal Equal-Area Projection

**MOVEMENT** The earliest Protestants lived in what is today known as Germany.
■ What was the major direction in which the Protestant religion spread?

Charles V declared Martin Luther an outlaw. No one in the empire was to help Luther. However, Frederick the Wise, a German prince, ignored the emperor's order and gave Luther a place to live.

By now Luther had begun to question the roles of priests and the pope. He came to believe that the Bible held all the religious teachings people needed to know. From his safe place Luther translated the Bible from Greek to German, the people's language. The improved printing press made it possible for many people to have Luther's translation of the Bible.

Over time, many Germans became followers of Luther, forming the Lutheran church. Catholic leaders tried to stamp out this new church. Some Germans strongly protested these actions and, as a result, became known as **Protestants**. The movement that gave rise to Protestant churches was

called the **Reformation** because its goal was to reform the Catholic Church.

The Protestant Reformation spread from Germany to other parts of Europe. Scandinavia, England, Scotland, and the Netherlands eventually became Protestant countries. Hundreds of new Christian churches were founded there. The Catholic Church remained strong in Spain, Portugal, Italy, France, Ireland, and parts of eastern Europe. However, the rise of Protestantism caused the Catholic Church to reform many of its practices.

✓ **How did the Reformation change Europe?**

# LESSON 2 REVIEW

## Check Understanding

1. **Recall the Facts** What was the Reformation? What effect did it have on Europe?
2. **Focus on the Main Idea** What factors caused great change during this time period?

## Think Critically

3. **Think More About It** How were trade and business linked to the rise of the new monarchies?
4. **Explore Viewpoints** Catholics viewed Protestants as heretics (people guilty of heresy). Protestants saw themselves as reformers. Give reasons why each side thought the way it did.
5. **Cause and Effect** How did Renaissance ideas and inventions contribute to the Reformation?

## Show What You Know

**Journal-Writing Activity**
Imagine that you are a student in Germany during the mid-1500s. Write journal entries describing the changes to life in your town caused by Martin Luther's actions.

# Act as a Responsible Citizen

## Why Is This Skill Important?

Nations, churches, and other large groups depend on their citizens or members to act responsibly. To be responsible, people must keep informed about what is happening in the group. They must choose thoughtful leaders and take part in the group's activities. When a large group such as a nation or church faces problems, its citizens or members may need to take action to solve those problems.

## Remember What You Have Read

You have read about the problems faced by the Catholic Church in the early 1500s. Many of its members took part in a movement called the Reformation. The movement's goal was to reform, or change, the actions of some church officials, such as those who were selling indulgences. Martin Luther, a leader of this movement, nailed his protest of 95 theses to the door of the Wittenberg castle church. This got the attention of church leaders and of Charles V, leader of the Holy Roman Empire. Luther was not the only person to make a difference in the Reformation. Hundreds of clergy and other local leaders, especially those in Germany, worked to solve the Church's problems.

Martin Luther posts his edicts.

## Understand the Process

Acting as a responsible citizen or group member is not always as difficult as it was for Martin Luther and his followers, who often risked their lives. It can be as simple as keeping informed or voting. However, it almost always needs some special thought and action.

Here are some steps that people today can follow to act as responsible citizens of the United States:

- They can inform themselves about the problems in their country.
- They can think about ways to solve these problems.
- They can decide how to bring about change in ways that would be good for the whole country.
- Each person can decide how he or she can help, acting either alone or with others.

## Think and Apply

Some acts of responsible citizenship, such as voting, can be done only by adults. Others can be done by citizens of any age. The four steps above can help anyone act as a responsible citizen. Use the four steps as you think of ways in which you and your classmates can act as responsible citizens of your community.

# EUROPEANS EXPLORE the GLOBE

## Link to Our World

**What leads people to explore the unknown?**

*Focus on the Main Idea*
*As you read, look for reasons European nations began to explore and claim lands overseas.*

*Preview Vocabulary*
*caravel*
*circumnavigation*
*Armada*

In mid-1453, the Ottoman Turks captured Constantinople from the Venetians.

As early as the fifteenth century, several European countries wanted to break the Italian and Muslim monopolies on trade with the East. To do this, they looked for new sea routes to Asia. The race to find these new routes began Europe's Age of Exploration.

## THE FALL OF CONSTANTINOPLE

In the early 1400s Venice was the leader in European trade with the East. A chain of Venetian trading posts reached from the eastern Mediterranean to the Black Sea. The routes beyond the Black Sea were controlled by Muslim traders, who took a share of the profits.

A threat to this trade arrangement arose when the Ottoman Turks began pushing west. In 1453 these Muslims captured the city of Constantinople. Constantinople had long served as the crossroads of the sea trade between Europe and Asia. The people of Venice saw the danger and fought to keep their trading empire. Yet by 1500 the Ottoman Empire controlled the trade routes to the East.

The capture of Constantinople by the Muslim Ottomans shocked Europeans, but they did not really feel sorry for Venice. Many European nations had already begun to look for new water routes to the East so that they would no longer have to pay Venetian traders. Such routes would allow them to trade directly with Asia and keep all the profits. The Europeans' search for a new route focused on the Atlantic Ocean.

 **How did the fall of Constantinople affect European trade with Asia?**

Sailors of the fifteenth century relied on tools of navigation such as this compass and this map showing sea monsters.

## EUROPEANS LOOK TOWARD THE ATLANTIC

Perhaps some word of the Viking explorations across the Atlantic had reached Spain and Portugal. That might explain why many people began to think that a huge piece of land was in the ocean to the west. Many Europeans also now believed that a sea route to Asia could be found by crossing the Atlantic.

Ships of the early 1400s were not strong enough to make a long ocean voyage. In the mid-1400s, though, shipbuilders in Portugal began to build a type of ship called a **caravel**. This ship used square or lateen sails to travel long distances swiftly and withstand heavy seas.

At the same time, European sailors became better navigators. They learned to use the compass and the astrolabe, and they had much better maps than before. Many of their maps came from Muslim geographers. With these tools European sailors were finally prepared to search for a sea route.

**What developments allowed sailors to sail out into the Atlantic Ocean?**

## PORTUGAL AND SPAIN LEAD THE WAY

Sailors from Portugal were the first to sail out into the Atlantic. Small and fairly poor, Portugal wanted a share of the trade with Asia. Its leaders felt sure that trade would bring wealth to Portugal.

The Portuguese expeditions into the Atlantic began mainly because of one man, Prince Henry the Navigator. He never went on a voyage of exploration himself, yet he turned Portugal into a world sea power. Around 1419 Henry began a school for navigators. There he brought together the best mapmakers, scientists, and ship designers from many lands. He put their ideas into use by paying for voyages of exploration along Africa's Atlantic coast.

Henry died in 1460, but the Portuguese continued their expeditions along Africa's western coast. In 1488 Bartholomeu Dias (DEE•ahsh) sailed around the southern tip of Africa and entered the Indian Ocean. Though Dias's crew made him turn back, he had opened a new way to the East. Ten years later, Vasco da Gama sailed as far as India. He returned to Portugal in 1499 with a cargo of Indian spices and jewels. The sale of the cargo brought 60 times what the trip had cost! The Portuguese quickly set up trading posts along the coasts of Africa and India. From there Portuguese ships pushed deeper into Asian waters. By the late 1500s a network of Portuguese trading posts reached from Africa's Atlantic coast to China.

Around the time of Dias's voyage, another sailor, named Christopher Columbus, met with the king of Portugal. Columbus, an Italian, felt sure that a ship could reach Asia by sailing west across the Atlantic. After being rejected by the king of

Vasco da Gama

Portugal, Columbus took his idea to Ferdinand and Isabella of Spain. He promised them great wealth and new lands. He also said he would take the Catholic faith to the people of Asia. Ferdinand and Isabella agreed to help.

On August 3, 1492, Columbus set sail with three ships. A little more than two months later, on October 12, he landed on a small island in the Caribbean Sea, which he named San Salvador ("Holy Savior"). Columbus was sure that he had reached the Indies, so he called the island's people Indians. When he returned to Spain in 1493, he received a hero's welcome. Columbus made three more voyages, but he never knew that he had found a new

## VOYAGES OF EXPLORATION

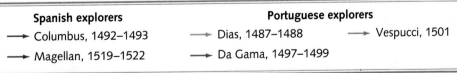

**Spanish explorers**
→ Columbus, 1492–1493
→ Magellan, 1519–1522

**Portuguese explorers**
→ Dias, 1487–1488
→ Da Gama, 1497–1499
→ Vespucci, 1501

**MOVEMENT** At the end of the fifteenth century, sailors from Spain and Portugal set off to explore the world.
■ Which explorer traveled mainly along the Tropic of Cancer?

Christopher Columbus is remembered for his voyages across the Atlantic, which forever changed ways of life in Europe and the Americas.

land. Others soon realized this, however. In 1501 Amerigo Vespucci (uh•MAIR•ih•goh veh•SPOO•chee), an Italian sailing for Portugal, explored the coast of what is now Brazil. He drew careful maps and wrote about what he saw. "It is lawful to call [the continent] a new world," he said, "because none of these countries were known to our ancestors." A mapmaker read Vespucci's observations and in 1507 named the "new" continent America in his honor.

At about this time Spain and Portugal signed a treaty that divided the undiscovered world between them. They drew an imaginary line north and south through the world as they knew it. Spain had the right to explore all lands west of the line. Portugal could explore all lands east of the line.

Under this treaty Spain was able to continue searching for a westward route to Asia. In 1519 five ships led by Ferdinand Magellan (mah•JEH•lahn) left Spain. Magellan sailed across the Atlantic, around the tip of South America, and into the Pacific Ocean. He then sailed on to Asia. Magellan was killed in a battle in the Philippines, but his sailors completed the trip around the world.

This **circumnavigation** of, or journey around, the world showed three important points. It proved that a ship could reach Asia by sailing west. It proved that there was a water route around the world. And it gave geographers a new way to calculate the size of the world.

✓ **Why were the voyages led by Portugal and Spain important?**

## ENGLISH EXPLORATION

The English began to search for new trade routes shortly after Columbus sailed across the Atlantic. King Henry VII paid for the voyages of the Italian explorer John Cabot, who also searched for a western route to Asia. In 1497 and 1498 Cabot sailed along the northeast coast of North America and claimed the land for England.

Henry VII's son, Henry VIII, concentrated on religious change and did not think much about exploration. Under his rule, England became a Protestant country. It was Henry VIII's daughter, Elizabeth I, who made England a sea power. After she came to the throne in 1558, she provided money to support a group of young sea captains, including Francis Drake, John Hawkins, and Walter Raleigh. Some of the sea captains were pirates as well as explorers. Elizabeth ignored their piracy because their attacks

This portrait of Elizabeth I shows her on the day she was crowned queen of England.

English warships defeated the Spanish Armada (left). England issued these playing cards (above) to celebrate its victory.

on Spanish and Portuguese ships filled her treasury with gold and silver.

The Spanish king, Philip II, became very angry about Queen Elizabeth's pirate-explorers. He also wanted to force Protestant England to return to the Catholic Church. In 1588 Philip put together a fleet of 130 warships, called the **Armada** (ar•MAH•dah), to attack England. The Spanish warships were

not as fast as England's, and the English drove the Spanish ships away. A fierce storm destroyed the Armada as it tried to return to Spain. This battle showed that Spain was declining as a world power and England was rising.

 **What event showed that England was becoming a world power?**

# LESSON 3 REVIEW

## Check Understanding

1. **Recall the Facts**  Where did Europeans look for a sea route to Asia?
2. **Focus on the Main Idea**  What led European nations to explore and claim lands on other continents?

## Think Critically

3. **Personally Speaking**  Imagine that you are about to start a voyage of exploration in the 1400s. How would you prepare yourself physically, mentally, and emotionally?
4. **Cause and Effect**  How did the Renaissance help bring about the age of European exploration?

5. **Past to Present**  Where do people go on today's great journeys of exploration? Why are people exploring these areas?

## Show What You Know

 **Letter-Writing Activity**
Explorers of long ago often had to persuade somebody, usually a monarch, to pay for their expeditions. Imagine that you want to set out on a voyage of exploration for Portugal, Spain, or England. Write a letter to the monarch of that country. Explain why conditions are right for your voyage and how helping you would help the monarch.

# REVIEW

## CONNECT MAIN IDEAS

Use this organizer to show that you understand how the chapter's main ideas are connected. Copy the organizer onto a separate sheet of paper. Then complete it by writing three details to support each main idea.

**Changes in Europe**
European government, society, and way of life changed.

1. _____
2. _____
3. _____

**New Directions for Europe**

**The Rebirth of Ideas in Europe**
Changes in European thought encouraged individualism and creativity.

1. _____
2. _____
3. _____

**Europeans Explore the Globe**
European nations began to explore and claim lands overseas.

1. _____
2. _____
3. _____

## WRITE MORE ABOUT IT

1. **Write Dialogue** William Shakespeare, perhaps the greatest playwright of all time, lived during the period described in this unit. Try your hand at playwriting. Select one of the following scenes: a European artist speaks to a patron; Galileo Galilei defends his ideas; King Ferdinand and Queen Isabella discuss plans for the Reconquista; an explorer tries to find a sponsor. Then write one page of dialogue for the scene you have chosen.

2. **Write a Ship's Log** Imagine that you are a crew member sailing with one of the European explorers, such as Vasco da Gama, Christopher Columbus, or Ferdinand Magellan. How did this explorer affect your life? What did you learn about the explorer? Write two log entries: one for the day you were most inspired by this explorer and one for the day you were most upset. Give details about each of the days you choose, and tell why you felt as you did.

## USE VOCABULARY

Write the term that matches each definition. Then use each term in a complete sentence.

Armada          caravel
indulgence      Reformation
Renaissance     scientific method

1. a French word meaning "rebirth"

2. a type of ship

3. a pardon for sins

4. the testing of ideas through observing and experimenting

5. a Spanish naval fleet

6. a sixteenth-century movement to change the Catholic Church

## CHECK UNDERSTANDING

1. In what part of Europe did the Renaissance begin?

2. How did Renaissance art differ from art of the Middle Ages?

3. What famous individual of the Renaissance was a scientist, a writer, a philosopher, an engineer, an inventor, and an artist?

4. Who was Johannes Gutenberg, and how did he help spread new learning in Europe?

5. How did Ferdinand and Isabella unite Spain?

6. What is the relationship between Martin Luther and Protestants?

7. Who was Prince Henry, and what effect did he have on exploration?

8. What two European nations were the first to begin overseas exploration?

9. Where did Columbus land in 1492?

10. Why was the ocean voyage of Magellan and his crew important?

## THINK CRITICALLY

1. **Explore Viewpoints** Talking about his work on the Sistine Chapel, Michelangelo said, "It will be finished when I have done all that I believe is required to satisfy Art." What do you think he meant by this statement?

2. **Past to Present** How different would the world be today if people such as Michelangelo, Leonardo da Vinci, and Isaac Newton had never lived?

3. **Think More About It** What were some benefits of the Reconquista to Spain? What were some ways the Reconquista may have hurt Spain?

4. **Personally Speaking** What changes in Europe between 1400 and 1700 do you think were most important? Why?

5. **Cause and Effect** What might have been the effect on world exploration if Italian and Muslim traders had not controlled the trade routes to the East?

## APPLY SKILLS

**How to Act as a Responsible Citizen** Look through recent newspapers and magazines to find an article that shows someone acting as a responsible citizen. Write a brief description of the action that person took and the results of that action.

## READ MORE ABOUT IT

*The Apprentice* by Pilar Molina Llorente, translated by Robin Longshaw. Farrar, Straus & Giroux. A young boy discovers the hard work that goes with being an apprentice in Renaissance Italy.

*The Renaissance and the New World* by Giovanni Caselli. Bedrick. The author looks at the culture of Europe after the Middle Ages and shows how it relates to everyday objects and luxuries.

# EUROPE, AFRICA, and the AMERICAS

## INTERACT

> 66 When the people of Malindi saw [the Portuguese], they knew they were bringers of war and corruption, and were troubled with very great fear. 99
>
> *The Chronicle of Kilwa,* describing the arrival of Vasco da Gama's fleet in East Africa

Brass sculpture of an oba (king) of Benin

# AFRICA and EUROPE

## Link to Our World

**What happens when people are forced to migrate against their will?**

**Focus on the Main Idea**
*As you read, consider how Europeans forced many Africans to leave their homeland.*

**Preview Vocabulary**
*plantation*
*triangle trade*
*Middle Passage*
*racism*

This bronze horn player is evidence that music was an important part of the culture of Benin, in Africa.

As the Middle Ages drew to a close in Europe, new kingdoms arose in Africa south of the Sahara. Like the ancient West African empires, these kingdoms grew mainly because of trade. For many of the African kingdoms, the arrival of Europeans in Africa seemed to mean more trade, wealth, and power. They would soon learn that they were mistaken.

## AFRICAN SOCIETIES

A military defeat in 1591 had led to the fall of the Songhay Empire. Soon another great empire, Kanem-Bornu (KAHN•em BAWR•noo), gained control of trade across the Sahara. The kingdom of Kanem had risen around Lake Chad in the 800s. Through trade with North Africa, Kanem grew wealthy and strong. Eventually, Kanem joined with the nearby kingdom of Bornu. By 1600 the soldiers of Kanem-Bornu had created a huge empire.

Kanem-Bornu's time of greatest growth came in the late 1500s under the rule of Idris Aloma (EE•drees al•OH•muh). Idris improved his army by importing the most up-to-date weapons and hiring military advisers to teach his soldiers the newest ways to fight. Idris was a devout Muslim who tried to spread his faith to the lands he governed. He also replaced Kanem-Bornu's old laws with ones based on Islamic law. But the rulers who followed Idris did not have his leadership abilities, and Kanem-Bornu slowly weakened.

To the southwest of Kanem-Bornu, in the West African forests, other trading kingdoms formed. By 1500 Benin (buh•NIN) was perhaps the most important. Benin grew rich by trading in spices, ivory, cloth, tools, and slaves. From a

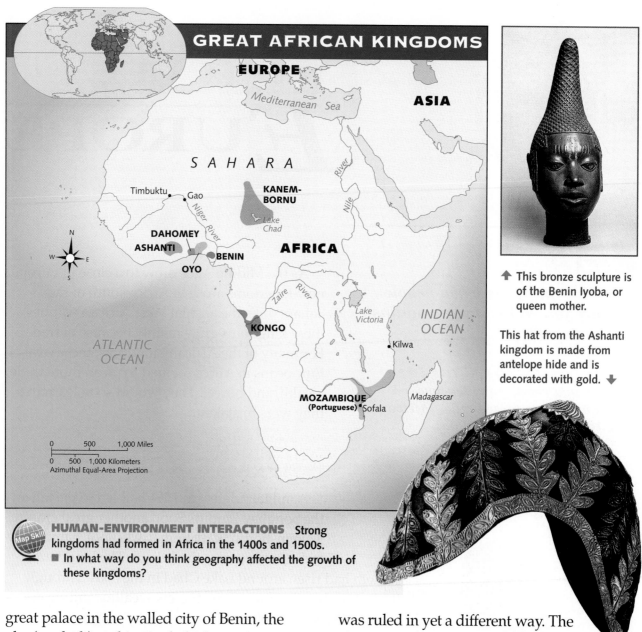

# GREAT AFRICAN KINGDOMS

EUROPE

ASIA

*Mediterranean Sea*

SAHARA

AFRICA

Timbuktu • Gao

KANEM-BORNU

*Lake Chad*

DAHOMEY
ASHANTI
OYO
BENIN

*Zaire River*

KONGO

ATLANTIC OCEAN

*Lake Victoria*

INDIAN OCEAN

• Kilwa

MOZAMBIQUE
(Portuguese) • Sofala

*Madagascar*

```
0        500     1,000 Miles
0    500   1,000 Kilometers
Azimuthal Equal-Area Projection
```

**Map Skill** **HUMAN-ENVIRONMENT INTERACTIONS** Strong kingdoms had formed in Africa in the 1400s and 1500s.
■ In what way do you think geography affected the growth of these kingdoms?

↑ This bronze sculpture is of the Benin Iyoba, or queen mother.

This hat from the Ashanti kingdom is made from antelope hide and is decorated with gold. ↓

great palace in the walled city of Benin, the oba (OH•buh), or king, ruled a huge empire. Its lands filled much of what is now south-central Nigeria.

To the west of Benin, other kingdoms arose. Benin's neighbor, Oyo (oh•YOH), grew rich in the late 1400s. A king, or alafin (ah•LAHF•in), ruled Oyo, but a council of advisers could remove him if they thought he was not a good leader. In Dahomey (duh•HOH•mee), which rose in the mid-1600s, government was very different. There the king controlled everything without any fear of being removed.

The kingdom of Ashanti (uh•SHAHN•tee), founded at about the same time as Dahomey,

was ruled in yet a different way. The king made decisions only after he had spoken with a council of local chiefs. Women, too, had a place in Ashanti's government. Female relatives of the king advised him and sometimes ruled in his place.

Far to the south, at the mouth of the Zaire River, the kingdom of the Kongo grew strong in the 1400s. The people thought of their king, the manikongo, as a god. As in the kingdoms to the north, the Kongo's economy was based on trade.

✓ **What did the African kingdoms have in common? How were they different?**

# EUROPEANS IN AFRICA

The arrival of Europeans in Africa brought many changes to these kingdoms. The Portuguese were the first Europeans to establish settlements. The Africans were willing to trade, and they allowed the Portuguese to set up stations all along the African coast. Local African rulers rented the stations to the Portuguese in return for a part of the profits and a promise of protection from their enemies in Africa. These stations were heavily armed, almost like forts. Most stations also had Catholic priests, who had come to teach the Africans about Christianity.

At first the Portuguese traded for spices, gold, and ivory. As time went on, however, slaves came to be the main export of African trade. Events across the Atlantic in the Americas brought about this change. Settlers had started colonies in all parts of North, Central, and South America. These settlers mined the mineral wealth of the Americas. They also started huge farms, called **plantations**, on which they grew sugarcane, pineapples, cotton, tobacco, and coffee. Work in the mines and fields was very hard. Few Europeans were willing to do it, so owners of mines and plantations used slave labor. Africa seemed to be a good source of slaves.

✓ **How did the Portuguese carry on trade in Africa?**

This ivory carving of a sailor in a ship's crow's nest (right) was created by a Benin carver. South, not north, is at the top of this European map (below) of West Africa. Why do you think the mapmaker drew the map in this way?

# THE SLAVE TRADE

Slavery was not new. It had existed since earliest times. Conquered people had been enslaved by the Sumerians, the Egyptians, the Greeks, and others. Slaves worked on building projects in the Roman Empire. Slavery had also been practiced in Africa for centuries. Up to that time, however, most African slaves were prisoners of war or criminals working off their punishment. Slaves were treated fairly well and might one day become free.

European slavery was different. African slaves were thought of as property, to be bought and sold as their owners saw fit. This type of slavery was for life. An enslaved person had little hope of ever becoming free. Children of a slave were born slaves and would remain enslaved all their lives.

First the Portuguese and then other Europeans took part in the transatlantic slave trade. Slave catchers went into the African countryside, capturing anyone they could. They then sold their captives to European traders at stations along the coast. The traders loaded the captured people on ships for the journey to the Americas. The traders showed no mercy. They separated "fathers from sons, husbands from wives, brothers from brothers," one Portuguese observer said.

Life on the slave ships was horrible. The more slaves aboard, the greater the traders' profits. So traders jammed people into every bit of space. For much of the long voyage across the Atlantic, the captured Africans were chained together in the cargo holds. A former slave named Olaudah Equiano

(oh•LOW•duh ek•wee•AHN•oh) said that the air "became unfit for respiration [breathing] from a variety of loathsome smells, and brought on a sickness among the slaves, of which many died. . . ."

Perhaps as many as one African in five died on this terrible trip. Those who lived to reach the Americas were sold at auction. The sale of human life was part of a system called the **triangle trade**. First, traders sailed from Europe to Africa with iron, cloth, guns, and liquor. In Africa the traders exchanged these goods for enslaved people. Next, during what is sometimes called the **Middle Passage**, the enslaved people were shipped across the

Atlantic to the Americas. There the traders sold the Africans for products from the plantations. The traders took these goods back to Europe, completing the triangle.

For more than 300 years, Africa was the focus of the slave trade. Eventually, many Europeans, especially religious leaders, began to feel that slavery was cruel and wrong. In 1807 the British government put a stop to Britain's part in the slave trade, and soon other countries did the same. Newly enslaved people were no longer taken to the United States. However, a cruel war would follow before slavery ended there in 1865.

✓ **How did the system of triangle trade operate?**

## EFFECTS OF THE SLAVE TRADE

As many as 12 million enslaved Africans were taken to the Americas during the time of the slave trade. In addition, many others died.

The slave trade had a terrible effect on the economy of Africa. In some places so many people were taken that the land was left almost empty. There were few people to work the fields or care for the herds. Also, the African kingdoms that took part in the slave trade made such large profits that they ignored all other economic activities. When the slave trade and its profits ended, the once-great African trading kingdoms were left with nothing.

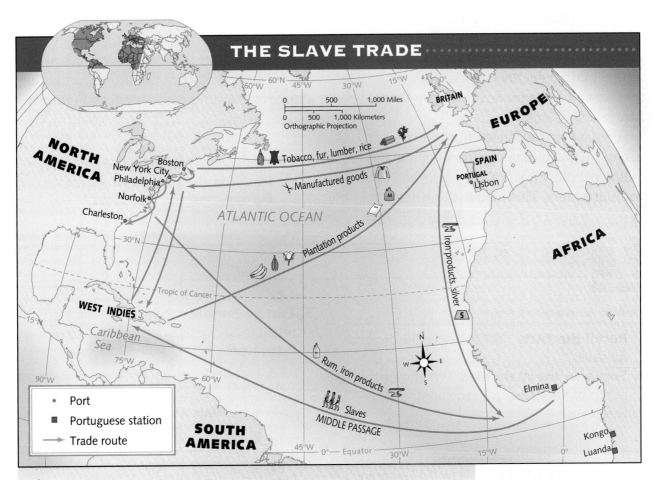

**THE SLAVE TRADE**

0   500   1,000 Miles
0   500   1,000 Kilometers
Orthographic Projection

NORTH AMERICA
Boston
New York City
Philadelphia
Norfolk
Charleston
30°N
ATLANTIC OCEAN
Tobacco, fur, lumber, rice
Manufactured goods
Plantation products
Tropic of Cancer
WEST INDIES
15°N
Caribbean Sea
75°W
90°W
60°W
SOUTH AMERICA
45°W  0°  Equator  30°W
Rum, iron products
Slaves
MIDDLE PASSAGE
BRITAIN
EUROPE
SPAIN
PORTUGAL Lisbon
AFRICA
Iron products, silver
Elmina
Kongo
Luanda
15°W

• Port
■ Portuguese station
→ Trade route

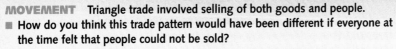

MOVEMENT  Triangle trade involved selling of both goods and people.
■ How do you think this trade pattern would have been different if everyone at the time felt that people could not be sold?

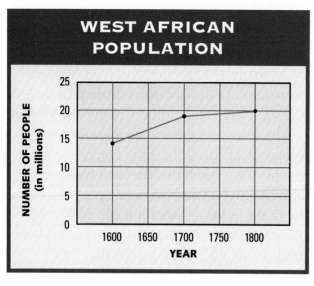

## WEST AFRICAN POPULATION

NUMBER OF PEOPLE (in millions)

25
20
15
10
5
0

1600 1650 1700 1750 1800
YEAR

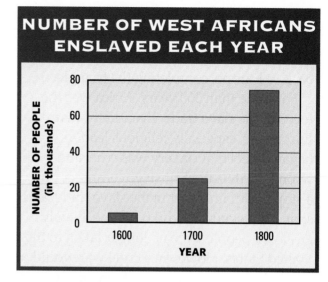

## NUMBER OF WEST AFRICANS ENSLAVED EACH YEAR

NUMBER OF PEOPLE (in thousands)

80
60
40
20
0

1600 1700 1800
YEAR

**LEARNING FROM GRAPHS** Between 1700 and 1800 the population of West Africa did not grow greatly.

■ Do you think the slave trade affected this slowing of population growth? Why or why not?

The slave trade also had a deep and lasting effect on African society. At first Africans sold mostly prisoners of war to Europeans. But as the demand for slaves grew, Africans started raiding nearby communities. As a result, many wars broke out among the African kingdoms.

The slave trade affected Europeans and Americans, too. To take part in buying and selling people, traders and owners had to act without feeling. They had to think of the Africans they had enslaved as inferior to them—as less than human. In lands affected by slavery, **racism**—a feeling of being better than other people because of their race or color—spread. Racism has been a continuing source of concern in the Americas, in Europe, and in Africa.

 ***What were the effects of the slave trade on the people of Africa, Europe, and the Americas?***

# LESSON 1 REVIEW

## Check Understanding

1. **Recall the Facts** What created the demand for slaves?
2. **Focus on the Main Idea** What were the effects of the forced migration of Africans by Europeans?

## Think Critically

3. **Think More About It** How did Europeans deny basic human rights to Africans?
4. **Cause and Effect** What effect did the slave trade have on African family life?

5. **Past to Present** In what ways do the results of slavery show themselves in life today in the United States?

## Show What You Know

 **Map Activity** Historians sometimes refer to the forced resettlement of Africans through the slave trade as the African *diaspora* (dy•AS•puh•ruh). Use resources in the library to make a map that shows the African diaspora. Be sure to show where Africans came from and where they were taken as slaves.

# A TIME OF ENCOUNTER

**What happens when different cultures come into contact?**

*Focus on the Main Idea*
*As you read, think about how the arrival of Europeans in the Americas affected life in both the Western and Eastern hemispheres.*

*Preview Vocabulary*
conquistador
immunity
Columbian exchange
encomienda
coureurs de bois

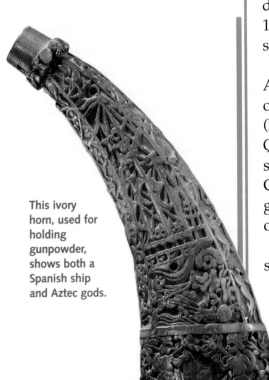

This ivory horn, used for holding gunpowder, shows both a Spanish ship and Aztec gods.

Across the Atlantic from Africa, the Americas also began to feel the effect of European political and economic activity. The cultures of the Americas and Europe would never be the same.

## SPAIN BUILDS AN EMPIRE

Columbus had promised Ferdinand and Isabella new lands and wealth. On his later voyages to the Americas, he tried to keep this promise. He started colonies on some Caribbean islands and looked for gold. Other people, also seeking treasure, soon followed Columbus.

The Spanish called these treasure seekers **conquistadors** (kahn•KEES•tah•doors), or "conquerors." One of the first of the conquistadors was Hernando Cortés (er•NAHN•doh kawr•TEZ). In 1519, attracted by stories of great wealth to be found, Cortés set out to explore Mexico.

When Motecuhzoma (maw•tay•kwah•SOH•mah), the Aztec emperor, heard of Cortés's arrival, he could think of only one explanation. Cortés must be the god Quetzalcoatl (khet•zahl•kuh•WAH•tahl). According to Aztec legend, Quetzalcoatl would one day appear as a bearded, light-skinned man, almost exactly the way Cortés looked. When Cortés arrived, Motecuhzoma ordered his people to give gifts to this "god." The golden jewelry that the Aztecs offered amazed Cortés. The conquistador wanted more.

Cortés's greed led the Aztecs to turn against him. In a surprise attack on June 30, 1520, they drove the Spaniards from their capital, Tenochtitlán. The following year, however, Cortés returned with a larger army. The Spaniards burned the Aztec city.

Cortés's gold gave other conquistadors the desire to search for riches. In 1526 Francisco Pizarro (fran•SIS•koh pee•ZAR•oh) led an expedition to the Inca Empire in South America. The Inca emperor, Atahuallpa (ah•tah•WAHL•pah), agreed to meet with Pizarro and was taken prisoner. In return for his freedom, Atahuallpa promised Pizarro a large room filled with gold. Atahuallpa kept his word, but Pizarro had him killed anyway. The Spaniards then conquered the Inca Empire easily.

The Aztecs honored their gods with temples, sculptures, and ceremonies. This bell is decorated with the image of an Aztec god.

Chasing dreams of gold, other conquistadors explored much of the Americas. Within 100 years of Columbus's first voyage, the Spanish ruled a large empire in the Americas. They did not control all of South America, however. In 1500 Pedro Cabral (kah•BRAHL) had claimed what is now the country of Brazil for Portugal.

✔ **Why did Spain create an empire in the Americas?**

## SPANISH ENCOUNTERS

Almost at once, ships began to carry gold, silver, and precious stones back to Spain. Spain became the richest, most powerful nation in the world during the 1500s.

As the Spanish moved through the Americas, they learned about many new foods. Corn, beans, squash, peppers, avocados, peanuts, tomatoes, and chocolate soon were added to the European diet. Some foods, such as the peanut, traveled beyond Europe to become important foods in Africa and Asia. Perhaps the food that caused the greatest change was the potato. Cheap and plentiful, the potato kept many poor people from starving. This caused a great population increase in Europe. One non-food crop—tobacco—also found its way to Europe.

The Spaniards who settled in the Americas brought European animals and plants with them. Cattle, chickens, pigs, sheep, chickpeas, sugarcane, and wheat changed the way the peoples of the Americas ate. The horse,

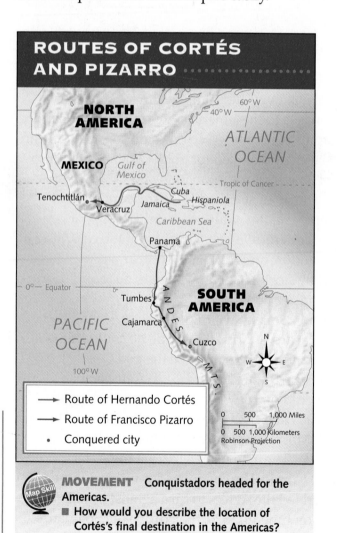

ROUTES OF CORTÉS AND PIZARRO

NORTH AMERICA
ATLANTIC OCEAN
MEXICO
Gulf of Mexico
Tenochtitlán
Veracruz
Cuba
Jamaica
Hispaniola
Caribbean Sea
Tropic of Cancer
Panama
0° — Equator
Tumbes
SOUTH AMERICA
Cajamarca
PACIFIC OCEAN
ANDES MTS.
Cuzco
100° W
60° W
40° W

→ Route of Hernando Cortés
→ Route of Francisco Pizarro
• Conquered city

0   500   1,000 Miles
0   500  1,000 Kilometers
Robinson Projection

**MOVEMENT** Conquistadors headed for the Americas.
■ How would you describe the location of Cortés's final destination in the Americas?

which had been unknown in the Western Hemisphere, changed transportation, hunting, and warfare.

At the same time, the Spanish brought deadly diseases such as influenza, smallpox, and measles to the Americas. The people of the Americas had never been exposed to many of these diseases. Therefore, they had not developed an **immunity**, or resistance, to them and usually died if they became ill with them. As many as 90 percent of the native peoples may have died from European diseases.

Historians refer to the movement of people, animals, plants, diseases, and ideas between Europe and the Americas as the **Columbian exchange**. People were certainly an important part of this exchange.

In Spanish America some European colonists established what was known as the **encomienda** (en•koh•mee•EN•dah) system. Under this system Native Americans had to work for the colonists and accept their religion. In return, the colonists were supposed to make certain that these people were well fed and were taught the Catholic faith. Many colonists, however, treated the people as slaves. When the Native Americans died from overwork and disease, the colonists replaced them with African slaves. They treated the Africans as poorly as they had the Native Americans.

Slowly the cultures of the Spanish, the Africans, and the Native Americans began to mix in Spanish America. For example, many Native Americans and slaves accepted the Catholic religion. The Spanish adopted the lifeways of the African slaves and the Native Americans that were suited to the American environment. This mixing of cultures created a new Latin American way of life.

**What exchanges took place between Europe and the Americas?**

# **W**ho?

## **Malintzin about 1501–1550**

When Hernando Cortés landed on the Yucatán Peninsula, he came into contact with the Mayas. As a peace offering, the Mayas gave him 20 slaves. Among them was a young Aztec princess named Malintzin (mah•LINT•chin). Cortés called the young woman Doña Marina and made her his interpreter. In time Malintzin became one of Cortés's most trusted advisers. He felt that the conquest of the Aztecs would have been almost impossible without her. For the same reason, many people in Mexico today think Malintzin was a traitor. In fact, some Mexicans call a person who betrays his or her own people a *Malinchista*.

Malintzin, at right

## FRENCH ENCOUNTERS

Meanwhile, far to the north, encounters between Native Americans and Europeans produced a very different American culture. The explorations of Jacques Cartier (ZHAHK kar•TYAY) in the 1530s gave France a claim to lands in what is now Canada. Cartier reported that the lands lying along the St. Lawrence River had many fur-bearing animals and that the Native Americans were willing to trade. French traders soon began bartering with the Indians for furs and skins, which brought high prices in Europe.

Trade grew as the French became friendly with both the Algonkin (al•GON•kin) and the Huron Indians. French trappers known as **coureurs de bois** (koo•RER duh BWAH), or "runners of the woods," trapped animals and traded with the Native Americans. They lived in Algonkin and Huron villages and adopted the peoples' languages and customs. As they traveled, they learned much about the geography of the area. Their reports gave the Europeans their first information about North America's interior lands.

French priests also journeyed into the interior to teach native peoples the Catholic faith. Many behaved like the *coureurs de bois.* People said that Father Jacques Marquette "could be a Huron with the Hurons, an Algonkin with the Algonkins, one with any among whom he lived and worked." Marquette traveled nearly the whole length of the Mississippi River. Those who followed Marquette claimed for France the lands around the Great Lakes and the Ohio River. There they found people making claims for another European country—England.

 **How did the coureurs de bois become accepted by the Native Americans?**

## ENGLISH ENCOUNTERS

The earliest English settlers arrived on the east coast of North America. For the most part, Native Americans were friendly to them. They taught the settlers how to grow corn, pumpkins, squash, and beans. They showed the settlers the best places to fish and to gather shellfish.

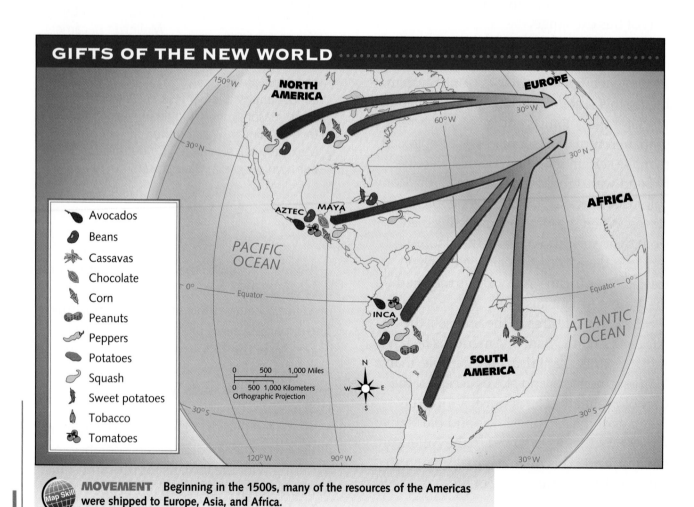

**GIFTS OF THE NEW WORLD**

Avocados
Beans
Cassavas
Chocolate
Corn
Peanuts
Peppers
Potatoes
Squash
Sweet potatoes
Tobacco
Tomatoes

NORTH AMERICA
EUROPE
AFRICA
SOUTH AMERICA
PACIFIC OCEAN
ATLANTIC OCEAN
AZTEC
MAYA
INCA
Equator

0   500   1,000 Miles
0   500  1,000 Kilometers
Orthographic Projection

**MOVEMENT** Beginning in the 1500s, many of the resources of the Americas were shipped to Europe, Asia, and Africa.
■ What products raised by the Incas moved across the Atlantic?

**IROQUOIS LEAGUE**

CANADA

Lake Champlain

Lake Ontario

Adirondack Mountains

ONEIDA

MOHAWK

ONONDAGA

CAYUGA

SENECA

Lake Erie

Allegheny River

Delaware River

Hudson River

0        50        100 Miles
0    50    100 Kilometers
Albers Equal-Area Projection

**HUMAN-ENVIRONMENT INTERACTIONS**
Five tribes united to form the Iroquois League.
■ What does this map tell you about why the tribes decided to work together?

With the help of the Native Americans, the English settlers survived their early years in North America. Soon they began to do well as farmers. Their success brought more settlers from England. To grow more food for the increasing population, the colonists started to feel the need for more land. Because of this, they began to drive the Native Americans off the lands on which they lived and hunted. As the number of new colonists grew, more and more Native Americans were pushed westward.

Several tribes who spoke the Iroquois language lived farther inland. These tribes united to form the Iroquois League. An unwritten constitution, or set of rules, kept peace among the members. Leaders from each tribe met in a Grand Council. The Grand Council declared war and made peace treaties, controlled trade, and protected

the members of the League. Recognizing the League's strength, the colonists made treaties with it. Peace lasted for a time, but later the League broke apart. However, a plan similar to the Iroquois idea of bringing together different groups in a league would be used by the writers of the Constitution of the United States more than 100 years later.

✓ **How did Native Americans help the English settlers?**

# LESSON 2 REVIEW

## Check Understanding

1. **Recall the Facts**   What is the name for the transfer of people, animals, plants, diseases, and ideas between the Eastern and the Western hemispheres?
2. **Focus on the Main Idea**   How did the arrival of Europeans in the Americas affect life in both the Western and Eastern hemispheres?

## Think Critically

3. **Think More About It**   Do you think conflict between the people of the Americas and the Europeans had to happen? Why or why not?
4. **Personally Speaking**   How would you react if people with a different language, religion, and way of life arrived in your community and claimed it for themselves?
5. **Cause and Effect**   What were the positive and negative effects of the Columbian exchange?

## Show What You Know

**Chart Activity**   Create an illustrated chart that identifies the people, animals, plants, diseases, and ideas that moved between Europe and the Americas in the Columbian exchange. Share and discuss your work with classmates.

# HowTo

# Compare Information on Maps

## Why Is This Skill Important?

Symbols, such as color, can have different meanings on different maps. On one map the color red may stand for a certain elevation. On another map it may stand for a certain number of people per square mile or square kilometer. But when symbols such as color have a similar meaning on two maps, they can help you compare information.

CENTRO HISTORICO

Spanish street sign, Puerto Rico

## Understand the Process

To compare information on different maps, you can follow these steps:

- Identify the subject and time period shown on each map.
- Find out from each map key what the symbols stand for.
- Think about what you can learn by comparing the maps that you could not learn from looking at one map alone.

## MAP A: EUROPEAN SETTLEMENT IN THE AMERICAS, 1750

0  800  1,600 Miles
0  800  1,600 Kilometers
Miller Cylindrical Projection

| England | Holland |
|---------|---------|
| Spain | Portugal |
| France | Present-day border |

Use the steps to compare Map A and Map B. Then answer the questions.

1. What does the title of Map A tell you?
2. What area is shown on Map A? What does the map show you about that area?
3. What time period is shown on Map A? What does the map show you about that time?
4. What does the title of Map B tell you?
5. What area is shown on Map B? What does the map show you about that area?
6. What time period is shown on Map B? What does the map show you about that time?
7. Compare Map A and Map B. Is there a connection between the European countries that settled certain areas and the languages spoken in those areas today? Explain.

8. What do the two maps show together that you could not learn from one map alone?

## Think and Apply

Use an atlas or an encyclopedia to find at least two kinds of maps of your state. They can be political, physical, economic, or cultural maps. Use the steps in Understand the Process to compare the maps. Then use what you learn from the two maps to write a paragraph describing your state.

Street sign in Canada, where English and French are spoken

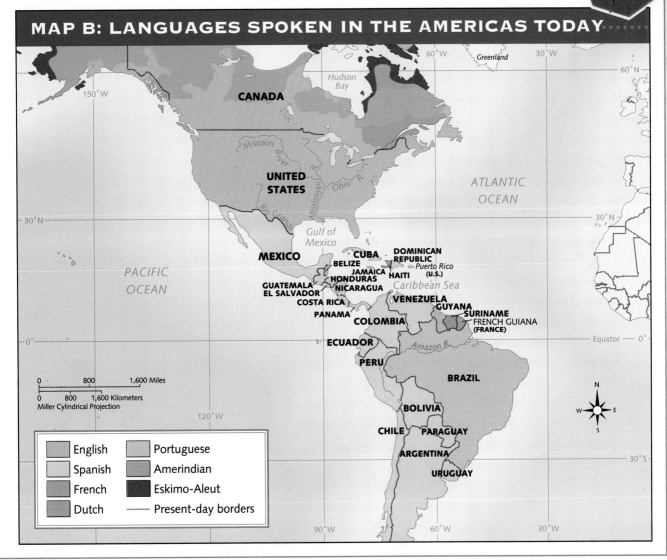

**MAP B: LANGUAGES SPOKEN IN THE AMERICAS TODAY**

Legend:
- English
- Spanish
- French
- Dutch
- Portuguese
- Amerindian
- Eskimo-Aleut
- ——— Present-day borders

0   800   1,600 Miles
0   800   1,600 Kilometers
Miller Cylindrical Projection

# MORNING GIRL

## BY MICHAEL DORRIS

### ILLUSTRATED BY DOROTHY SULLIVAN

*When Christopher Columbus landed on San Salvador Island in the Bahamas in 1492, he brought together very different cultures that had developed separately. In doing so, he set the world on a historic new course.*

*The first people Columbus met, the Tainos, had lived in the Bahamas for more than 1,500 years. In that time they had established a social system that did not accept violence. Columbus said, "There cannot be better or more gentle people than these anywhere in the world."*

*Now read an imaginary account of the Europeans' first meeting with the Tainos, from a Native American viewpoint. As you read, compare Morning Girl's reactions with those of the visitors. Think about how people from different cultures can hold very different ideas.*

I stepped over my mat very carefully and left the house. I set my feet into the hard-packed places, turned sideways to avoid the leaves of plants, ducked beneath low branches. From my quick dream I chose the idea of water, maybe because I was thirsty, maybe because the day was already hot and the thought of waves on my skin made me feel better, maybe because the sea promised me a story.

Smoke was not yet rising from cook fires, so I knew it was early. No wonder the sea called. It must be lonely, a feeling I could understand: today, I was in no one's good thoughts. Star Boy was unhappy with me, and now Mother and Father were, too, for their own reasons. They would be distant toward me until I helped them to forget my unsisterly words.

I wished there were someone I could complain to, someone who would easily forgive me either for being too nice, as I was to Star Boy at the feast, or too harsh, as I was last night. I missed the new sister who had never come home. I was sure I would never have argued with her. It seemed to me wrong that she had received no name. Grandmother said that we hadn't known her well enough . . . and yet I *did* know her. She was in my thoughts often, as she was this morning. Then I had an idea so surprising that I

stopped walking: *I* could give the new sister a name, just between her and me. I closed my eyes, held my breath, and found exactly the right one: She Listens. Now she was real.

I looked at the place where I was, to remember it. The island was all green and brown, the flowers red and yellow, the sky a deep and brilliant blue. At my feet, the tip of something white stuck from the sand. I stooped, dug with my fingers, and pried out a small, empty conch, washed so gently by the sea that not a single chip was missing— just the way Star Boy insisted for the shells he liked to keep. My gift would be the start of his new collection, replacing what the storm had borrowed. Things would be the way they had been, only better. I put the conch into a bowl of dried seaweed, where I could find it later, and ran into the water.

Dawn made a glare on the ocean, so I splashed through the shallow surf and dived without looking. I felt the hair lift from around my head, felt a school of tiny fish glide against my leg as I swam underwater. Then, far in the distance, I heard an unfamiliar and frightening sound. It was like the panting of some giant animal, a steady, slow rhythm, dangerous and hungry. And it was coming closer.

I forgot I was still beneath the surface until I needed air. But when I broke into sunlight, the water sparkling all around me, the noise turned out to be nothing! Only a canoe! The breathing was the dip of many paddles! It was only *people* coming to visit, and since I could see they hadn't painted themselves to appear fierce, they must be friendly or lost.

I swam closer to get a better look and had to stop myself from laughing. The strangers had wrapped every part of their bodies with colorful leaves and cotton. Some had decorated their faces with fur and wore shiny rocks on their heads. Compared to us, they were very round. Their canoe was short and square, and, in spite of all their dipping and pulling, it moved so slowly. What a backward, distant island they must have come from. But really, to laugh at guests, no matter how odd, would be impolite, especially since I was the first to meet them. If I was foolish, they would think they had arrived at a foolish place.

"I won't make a mistake," I told She Listens. "I won't be too good, and I won't say too much because I might choose the wrong words."

I kicked toward the canoe and called out the simplest thing.

"Hello!"

One of the people heard me, and he was so startled that he stood up, made his eyes small, as fearful as I had been a moment earlier. Then he spotted me, and I waved like I've seen adults do when visitors arrive, my fingers spread to show that my hand was empty.

The man stared at me as though he'd never seen a girl before, then shouted something to his relatives. They all stopped paddling and looked in my direction.

"Hello," I tried again. "Welcome to home. My name is Morning Girl. My mother is She Wins the Race. My father is Speaks to Birds. My brother is Star Boy. We will feed you and introduce you to everyone."

All the fat people in the canoe began pointing at me and talking at once. In their excitement they almost turned themselves over, and I allowed my body to sink beneath the waves for a moment in order to hide my smile. One must always treat guests with respect, I reminded She Listens, even when they are as brainless as gulls.

When I came up they were still watching, the way babies do: wide eyed and with their mouths uncovered. They had much to learn about how to behave.

"Bring your canoe to the beach," I shouted, saying each word slowly so that they might understand and calm themselves. "I will go to the village and bring back Mother and Father for you to talk to."

Finally one of them spoke to me, but I couldn't understand anything he said. Maybe he was talking Carib or some other impossible language. But I was sure that we would find ways to get along together. It never took that much time, and acting out your thoughts with your hands could be funny. You had to guess at everything and you made mistakes, but by midday I was certain we would all be seated in a circle, eating steamed fish and giving each other presents. It would be a special day, a memorable day, a day full and new.

I was close enough to shore now for my feet to touch bottom, and quickly I made my way to dry land. The air was warm against my shoulders, and there was a slight breeze that disturbed the palm fronds strewn on the ground. I squeezed my hair, ran my hands over my arms and legs to push off the water, and then stamped on the sand.

"Leave your canoe right here," I suggested in my most pleasant voice. "It will not wash away, because the tide is going out. I'll be back soon with the right people."

The strangers were drifting in the surf, arguing among themselves, not even paying attention to me any longer. They seemed very worried, very confused, very unsure what to do next. It was clear that they hadn't traveled much before.

I hurried up the path to our house, but not before She Listens reminded me to take the white conch shell from the seaweed where I had left it. As I dodged through the trees, I

hoped I hadn't done anything to make the visitors leave before I got back, before we learned their names. If they were gone, Star Boy would claim that they were just a story, just my last dream before daylight. But I didn't think that was true. I knew they were real.

## Literature Review

1. How did Morning Girl show she meant the strangers no harm? Do you think the strangers understood this? Explain why or why not.
2. What did Morning Girl think of the visitors? Based on what you have read, what do you think the visitors thought of Morning Girl?
3. With classmates, act out what you think happened the next time Morning Girl encountered the visitors.

# Compare Information on a Double-Line Graph

## Why Is This Skill Important?

As you have learned, a line graph shows changes over time. These changes are called trends. Some line graphs have one line. Others have two or more. Graphs with two or more lines allow you to compare trends. The double-line graph on page 441 compares trends in the populations of Native Americans and Europeans for a period of more than 250 years—from Columbus's first voyage until the year 1750.

## Remember What You Have Read

Beginning in the 1490s, Europeans caused many changes in the lives of the people they encountered in the Americas. The Europeans brought new weapons, animals, and crops that changed the way many Native Americans hunted as well as the foods they ate. The Europeans also brought new diseases that killed as many as 90 percent of the native peoples in North America and South America.

In the period from the 1490s to 1650, the Native American population became much smaller. Besides the deaths caused by disease, there were many deaths in battle as Native Americans defended their lands from soldiers and settlers.

## Understand the Process

The graph on page 441 is a double-line graph. The number scale on the left-hand side of the graph shows the population in millions. The number 100, near the top of the graph, stands for 100 million. The numbers along the bottom are years. The dots above these years show the estimated population of each group in the Americas for three different times.

You read a double-line graph the same way you read a single-line graph. Find the line marked 1492 at the bottom of the graph. Put your finger on the line and notice the first dot. The dot is part of the line that shows the

For centuries Native Americans lived alone in the Americas. Different groups of Native Americans developed different ways of life. In the painting titled *Ju-ah-kis-gaw* (left), artist George Catlin shows a mother and child of one of the many groups. The arrival of the Europeans brought many changes to the ways of life in the Americas. The embroidered cloth (above) shows the Spanish conquistador Cortés and his Native American interpreter, Malintzin.

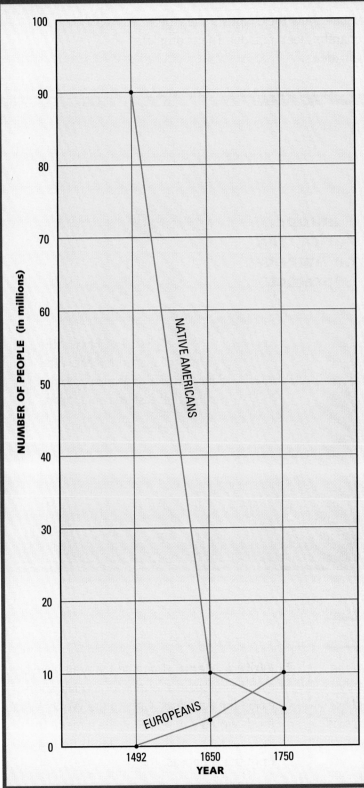

## POPULATION OF NATIVE AMERICANS AND EUROPEANS, 1492–1750

NATIVE AMERICANS

EUROPEANS

NUMBER OF PEOPLE (in millions)

YEAR

European population in the Americas. It is on the population scale at 0. This means there were almost no Europeans living in the Americas in 1492.

Now move your finger up to the second dot, which is part of the line that shows the Native American population. This dot is on the population scale at 90, meaning that about 90 million people lived in the Americas around the time Europeans arrived.

Next, find the dots for the European and Native American populations for 1650 and 1750. Then answer the questions.

1. What were the Native American and European populations in 1650? in 1750?
2. During which time period did the population of Native Americans drop more sharply? How large was the drop?
3. In about what year were the estimated populations of Native Americans and Europeans the same?
4. In 1750 about how much larger was the population of Europeans than that of Native Americans?
5. What prediction can you make about the direction in which the line for European population would go if it were continued to 1850?
6. What prediction can you make about the direction in which the line for Native American population would go if it were continued to 1850?

## Think and Apply

Think about what you have learned about line graphs with two or more lines. With a partner, brainstorm kinds of information that can be shown on this type of graph. Then write a paragraph summarizing the best uses for line graphs.

# REVIEW

## CONNECT MAIN IDEAS

Use this organizer to show that you understand how the chapter's main ideas are connected. Copy the organizer onto a separate sheet of paper. Then complete it by writing three details to support each main idea.

**Europe, Africa, and the Americas Interact**

**Africa and Europe**
Europeans forced many Africans to leave their homelands.

1. _____
2. _____
3. _____

**A Time of Encounter**
The arrival of Europeans in the Americas affected life in both the Western and Eastern hemispheres.

1. _____
2. _____
3. _____

## WRITE MORE ABOUT IT

1. **Write a Story**   Write a story about a young African who has heard that people in nearby communities have been captured and sold as slaves. Describe the young person's feelings on hearing this news. Will this news affect your character's life? If so, how?

2. **Write a Menu**   Imagine that you have been asked to prepare a dinner for a celebration called the Americas' Gifts to the World. What foods would you serve? Write a menu that includes some of the many foods that came from the Americas.

## USE VOCABULARY

Use each term in a complete sentence that helps explain its meaning.

1. conquistador
2. encomienda
3. immunity
4. Middle Passage
5. plantation
6. triangle trade

## CHECK UNDERSTANDING

1. What did the newer African kingdoms of the 1500s have in common with the older West African empires?

2. What did Idris Aloma do to bring about growth for Kanem-Bornu?

3. What role did women play in the government of Ashanti?

4. What was the triangle trade?

5. What effect did the slave trade have on African society?

6. What led the conquistadors to explore the Americas?

7. What happened as the English in the Americas needed more land for settlers and crops?

8. What was the Iroquois League?

## THINK CRITICALLY

1. **Think More About It** How did the Portuguese who rented stations along the African coast change the history of Africa?

2. **Past to Present** In what ways are people in the United States still battling racism? What is being done to overcome this problem?

3. **Cause and Effect** What effect do you think Cortés had on Aztec culture?

4. **Explore Viewpoints** Why was the Aztec ruler Motecuhzoma not suspicious of Hernando Cortés? What do you think Cortés thought of Motecuhzoma and the Aztecs? Why do you think he felt this way?

## APPLY SKILLS

**How to Compare Information on Maps** Use the maps on pages 434 and 435 to answer these questions.

1. What countries had settlements in South America by 1750?

2. What languages are spoken in South America today?

3. What relation does there seem to be between European claims in South America and the languages spoken there today?

**How to Compare Information on a Double-Line Graph** Look in a reference book for the average monthly high and low temperatures for two cities in your state. Use this information to create a double-line graph, with a set of lines for each city. Use your line graph to answer these questions.

1. Which city has the coldest month?

2. Which city has the hottest month?

3. During which month or months is the temperature difference between the two cities greatest?

## READ MORE ABOUT IT

*Pyramid of the Sun, Pyramid of the Moon* by Leonard Everett Fisher. Macmillan. This book discusses the history of the pyramids of Teotihuacan. It also tells about the way of life of the Aztecs.

*The World in 1492* by Jean Fritz, Katherine Paterson, Patricia and Fredrick McKissack, Margaret Mahy, and Jamake Highwater. Henry Holt. This book tells about the history, customs, and beliefs of people living throughout the world in the 1400s.

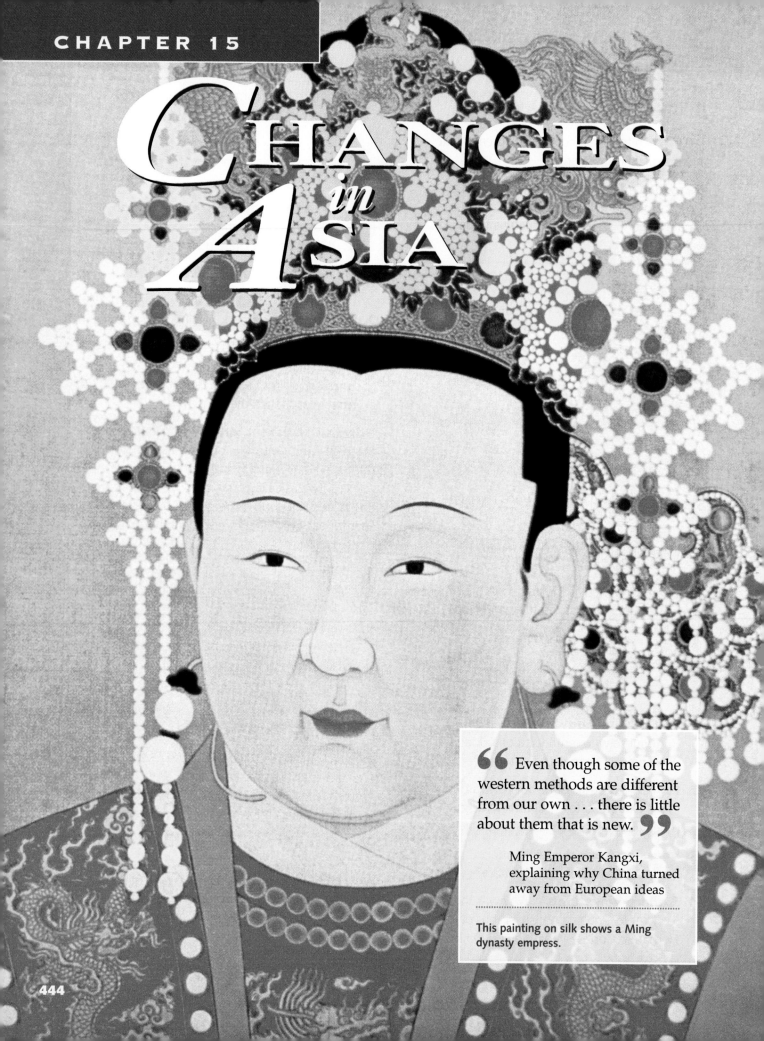

# CHAPTER 15

# CHANGES in ASIA

66 Even though some of the western methods are different from our own . . . there is little about them that is new. 99

Ming Emperor Kangxi, explaining why China turned away from European ideas

This painting on silk shows a Ming dynasty empress.

# CHINA and JAPAN
## IN EARLY MODERN TIMES

## Link to Our World

**How do peoples' views of their role in the world change over time?**

**Focus on the Main Idea**
*As you read, look for changes in the ways the people of China and Japan saw themselves in relation to the rest of the world.*

**Preview Vocabulary**
isolation
calligraphy
Bushido
haiku

A traditionally dressed Ming official of the 1600s

While Europe was going through the Renaissance and the Age of Exploration, the societies of China and Japan were also changing. For a time, China renewed contact with the outside world, but this did not go on for long. Soon it closed its borders to outsiders. Japan, too, tried to keep outsiders away. At this time, both countries counted on history and tradition to bring order and keep peace.

## RENEWED GROWTH FOR CHINA

During the mid-1300s the Mongols' dynasty weakened. Convinced that the Mongols had lost the Mandate of Heaven, the Chinese people rebelled. One of the rebel leaders, a former Buddhist monk, took power in 1368. Taking the name Hong Wu, he began the Ming dynasty.

On taking power, Hong Wu said, "I intend to reign like the Tang and Song." True to his word, Hong Wu set up a government based on Confucian ideas. He then started to rebuild the war-torn land. He restored fields, irrigation systems, canals, and roads. Under his program China's economy improved and the population grew. During his later years, however, Hong Wu became very cruel. He had thousands of people thrown into prison or killed. When he died in 1398, few people were sad.

Yong Le (YUHNG LEH), Hong Wu's son, wanted to make China a major force in Asia. He entered into an alliance with Korea and conquered parts of what is now Vietnam. Yong Le also paid for the great ocean voyages of Admiral Zheng He. Through these voyages the Chinese learned

During the Ming dynasty, artworks such as this painting and this porcelain vase were created in a distinctly Chinese style. What Ming policies helped to create such a unique style?

much about the rest of the world. At the same time, the fleets showed China's strength and wealth. Everywhere the fleets visited, people learned of the splendor of the Ming dynasty.

**How did China grow under Hong Wu and Yong Le?**

## CHINA LOOKS INWARD

Yong Le died in 1424, and China's interest in seafaring ended soon after. In 1433 government officials stopped all oceangoing voyages and destroyed Zheng He's records.

Why did this happen? Perhaps the voyages became too costly. Or perhaps Ming officials agreed with what an earlier emperor had said: "China's territory produces all goods in abundance, so why should we buy useless trifles from abroad?"

Whatever the reason, the Ming rulers would not let merchants trade outside of China. China turned to a policy of **isolation**, or separation from others. For centuries China had been physically separated from most of the world's people. Now the Chinese purposely tried to keep themselves apart from others.

Ming emperors now set about building China's strength from within. They made the Great Wall stronger and repaired the Grand Canal. The Ming rulers also helped farmers.

While Chinese merchants could not trade with the outside world, they did very well within lands controlled by China. Merchants moved farm products, cloth, iron, and precious metals along China's waterways. Some villages on the waterways became market towns, and many cities grew.

The Ming period was a time of growth for Chinese culture. Ming emperors encouraged learning. Some scholars wrote histories of earlier dynasties. Ming artists took styles of earlier times and improved on them. Two examples are the Chinese art of **calligraphy** (kuh•LIH•gruh•fee), or beautiful handwriting, and the making of porcelain.

Other Ming artists painted beautiful landscapes. Their paintings, however, did not look real. When told that European artists could show perspective, Ming painters were not interested. The Ming wanted to preserve traditional ideas, not adopt new ones.

**What important developments took place under Yong Le's successors?**

# PRESSURE FROM THE OUTSIDE

The Ming dynasty had turned its back on the outside world, but the outside world still had an interest in China. Foreign traders wanted China's fine porcelain and silks. In 1513 the Portuguese arrived in Guangzhou, hoping to trade with China. The Chinese thought the Portuguese acted more like robbers than like merchants. They wanted nothing to do with such "barbarians."

The Portuguese would not give up easily. In 1557 the Chinese allowed them to set up a trading post on an island near Macao (muh•KOW). Later, Spanish, Dutch, and English traders joined the Portuguese. The Ming government, however, kept tight control on contact between the Europeans and the Chinese people.

Surprisingly, the Ming allowed Catholic missionaries into China. These missionaries went there mainly to win converts. Yet they had respect for knowledge and showed interest in Chinese learning. In turn, Ming scholars wanted to learn European ideas on astronomy, mathematics, and technology. For the most part, though, the Chinese seemed to care little about European knowledge.

In the end, conflicts from within brought down the Ming dynasty. While the people of the Ming period fought one another, invaders from Manchuria in the north swept into China. In the mid-1600s the Manchus set up

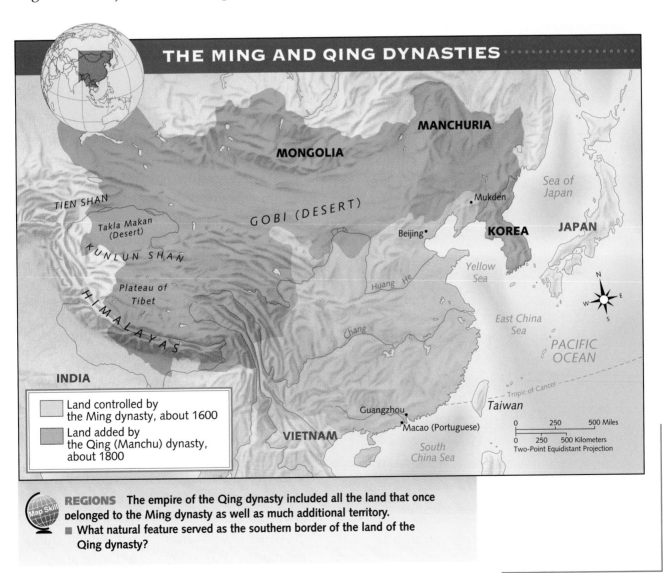

## THE MING AND QING DYNASTIES

MANCHURIA

MONGOLIA

Sea of Japan

TIEN SHAN

Takla Makan (Desert)

GOBI (DESERT)

Mukden

KUNLUN SHAN

Beijing

KOREA

JAPAN

Plateau of Tibet

Huang He

Yellow Sea

HIMALAYAS

Chang

East China Sea

PACIFIC OCEAN

INDIA

Tropic of Cancer

Guangzhou

Taiwan

Land controlled by the Ming dynasty, about 1600

Land added by the Qing (Manchu) dynasty, about 1800

Macao (Portuguese)

VIETNAM

South China Sea

0    250    500 Miles

0    250    500 Kilometers

Two-Point Equidistant Projection

**REGIONS** The empire of the Qing dynasty included all the land that once belonged to the Ming dynasty as well as much additional territory.
■ What natural feature served as the southern border of the land of the Qing dynasty?

the Qing (CHING) dynasty. After 300 years the Mandate of Heaven had once again fallen into foreign hands.

✓ **What caused the Ming dynasty to fall?**

## TOKUGAWA JAPAN

The Japanese also came face to face with Europeans. During the mid-1500s Portuguese merchants arrived at Japanese ports. Some daimyos eagerly traded with the Portuguese. They also welcomed the Christian missionaries who followed the traders.

In the year 1603, when Tokugawa Ieyasu (toh•ku•GAH•wah ee•uh•YAH•soo) became shogun, Japan's attitude toward Europeans

Unlike the samurai, Japanese ninjas, as shown in this woodblock print, were trained as spies.

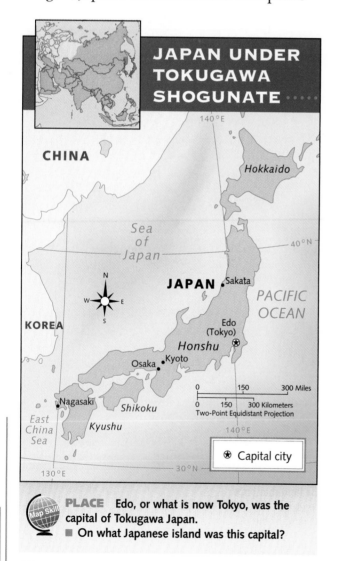

**JAPAN UNDER TOKUGAWA SHOGUNATE**

CHINA

Hokkaido

Sea of Japan

40°N

JAPAN · Sakata

PACIFIC OCEAN

KOREA

Edo (Tokyo) ✪

Honshu

Osaka · Kyoto

0       150       300 Miles
0   150   300 Kilometers
Two-Point Equidistant Projection

· Nagasaki  Shikoku

East China Sea  Kyushu

140°E

130°E   30°N

✪ Capital city

🌐 **PLACE**  Edo, or what is now Tokyo, was the capital of Tokugawa Japan.
■ On what Japanese island was this capital?

changed. The new shogun feared that Christianity would threaten Japan's unity. He drove Christian missionaries out of Japan and allowed European traders to land only at the port of Nagasaki (nah•guh•SAH•kee). A later shogun stopped even this contact. He prevented the Japanese from leaving their islands or having any dealings with foreigners. By 1639 Japan was closed to the rest of the world.

This "closed country" policy was one step the Tokugawa shoguns took to unify Japan. They also reformed the feudal system by limiting the authority of the daimyos.

In addition, the Tokugawa shoguns began a rigid class system. They adapted the Confucian idea of classes to Japanese society. At the top were the samurai, or soldiers. Filled with pride, the samurai paraded about the towns and villages. However, they did not lead easy lives. They had to live by a harsh code called **Bushido** (BU•shih•doh), or "the way of the warrior." Above all, Bushido demanded samurai loyalty to the daimyo.

Farmers, who were next in the social rank, had difficult lives as well. Government leaders took part of their crops in taxes. Landlords took their share, too. This left many farmers with barely enough to live on.

In contrast, those at the bottom of the social ladder—craftworkers and merchants—often did well economically. Cities were noisy with the sounds of people working at dozens of trades. Merchants grew rich by buying and selling goods and by lending money to samurai and tenant farmers.

As the merchants grew richer, they became patrons of the arts and literature. Perhaps the most popular writing form of Tokugawa times was the **haiku** (HY•koo), a 17-syllable poem. Without a doubt, the best haiku poet was Matsuo Basho (maht•SOO•oh BAH•shoh). Most of Basho's poems were about nature

..................................................

Craftspeople in Tokugawa Japan had a low social standing but many economic opportunities. These workers were probably paid well for the armor they made.

and had hidden meanings. Some, like this one translated by poet Harry Behn, were humorous:

66 There goes my best hat
as down comes rain on my bald
pate, plop! plop! Oh, well . . . 99

The Tokugawa shoguns' focus on traditional ways brought peaceful times. The Japanese made little progress in science and technology, however. Dutch traders, who were allowed to visit Japan once a year, brought news of exciting changes in the West. Soon some Japanese began to call for an end to the "closed country" policy.

 **What was Bushido?**

## Check Understanding

1. **Recall the Facts**   What was the "closed country" policy?
2. **Focus on the Main Idea**   What changes took place in the way China and Japan saw themselves in relation to the rest of the world?

## Think Critically

3. **Think More About It**   How did the Ming emperors and the Tokugawa shoguns unite their nations and keep order and peace?
4. **Personally Speaking**   Do you think that a policy of isolation was wise or unwise for China and Japan? Explain your answer.
5. **Past to Present**   In what ways might cultures today try to protect themselves from the influence of others?

## Show What You Know

**Poetry Activity**   Find out more about the haiku form of poetry. Practice writing one or two haiku about nature. Then write a haiku that describes the effect of isolation on Tokugawa Japan.

# THE OTTOMAN and MOGUL EMPIRES

## *Link to Our World*

*How can moving to a new place affect both the culture of the newcomers and the culture of the people they meet there?*

### Focus on the Main Idea
*Look for ways the policies of the Ottoman and Mogul empires affected the people they conquered.*

### Preview Vocabulary
Janissary       sultan
grand vizier

The capture of Constantinople strengthened the Ottoman Empire. Sultan Mehmed II began calling the city Istanbul.

During early modern times, two major Muslim empires grew to rival the greatness of the empires of Europe and the Americas. By the mid-1500s these two Muslim powers controlled lands that reached from southeastern Europe to Tibet. United by a common religion—Islam— the two empires developed cultures that were similar in many ways, including their treatment of the people they conquered.

## THE OTTOMAN EMPIRE

The empire of the Ottomans formed gradually. Migrating to Southwest Asia from central Asia, the Ottomans began claiming new lands around 1300. In 1453 the Ottomans, who were Muslim, moved into Asia Minor and captured the city of Constantinople.

When Sultan Mehmed (meh•MET) II captured the city of Constantinople, he believed he had made a prediction come true. The Muslim prophet Muhammad had foretold the rebirth of Constantinople as a great Islamic city. Mehmed made the city, now called Istanbul (is•tuhn•BOOL), the capital of the Ottoman Empire. Under Mehmed, Istanbul again became the greatest city in the Mediterranean region.

A learned man himself, Mehmed valued education. He started colleges and built a magnificent library, hoping to return Istanbul to its former glory as a center of learning. He even invited Christian and Jewish scholars to come to Istanbul. Non-Muslims were allowed to follow the laws of their own religions and their own religious leaders. They paid a special tax called *jizya* to the Ottoman government.

At the same time, Mehmed was a warlike ruler who dreamed of re-creating the Eastern Roman Empire under

Janissaries were soldiers who had been captured by the Ottomans or recruited as young boys and trained for years as fierce warriors.

Islamic rule. To make this dream true, Mehmed built a large and powerful army and an efficient government.

The Ottoman army got its soldiers from every corner of the empire. The best-trained, however, were the soldiers known as **Janissaries** (JA•nuh•sair•eez). Most were former Christians who had been captured or recruited as young boys and then became Muslims. Years of hard training prepared them for one thing—war—and taught them unquestioning loyalty to the sultan. With the Janissaries at its head, Mehmed's army pushed the boundaries of the empire deep into southeastern Europe.

Mehmed often chose non-Turks to govern parts of the empire. The Ottomans picked the most promising from among their enslaved youths to train for government service. After converting to Islam, these boys were sent to special schools. After they finished their training, they were given jobs as officials and advisers. This bureaucracy of slaves made Mehmed's empire run smoothly.

Later sultans built on the foundations laid by Mehmed II. The greatest of these sultans was Süleyman (soo•lay•mahn) I, who came to power in 1520.

 **What steps did Mehmed II take to achieve his dream of building a great empire?**

## SÜLEYMAN THE MAGNIFICENT

The people of the Ottoman Empire called Süleyman the Lawgiver, but Europeans knew him as Süleyman the Magnificent. Süleyman led his armies into central Europe, capturing the city of Belgrade in 1521. The following year his navy conquered the island of Rhodes. This victory gave the Ottomans control of much of the eastern Mediterranean. Over the next few years, Süleyman seized much of Hungary.

This miniature painting by an Ottoman artist shows a master philosopher and his students.

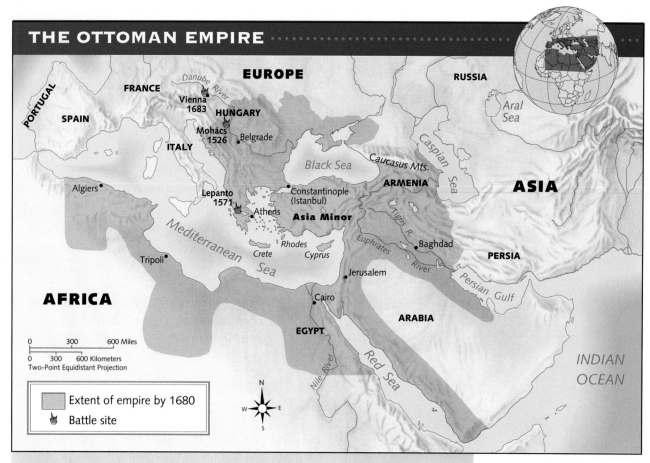

# THE OTTOMAN EMPIRE

EUROPE

FRANCE
Danube River
Vienna 1683
HUNGARY
Mohács 1526
Belgrade

PORTUGAL
SPAIN
ITALY

RUSSIA
Aral Sea

Black Sea
Caucasus Mts.
Caspian Sea

ARMENIA

ASIA

Algiers
Lepanto 1571
Constantinople (Istanbul)
Athens
Asia Minor

Tigris R.
Euphrates River
Baghdad

PERSIA

Mediterranean Sea
Rhodes
Crete
Cyprus
Jerusalem
Persian Gulf

Tripoli

Cairo

AFRICA
ARABIA

0    300    600 Miles
0    300    600 Kilometers
Two-Point Equidistant Projection

EGYPT

Nile River
Red Sea

INDIAN OCEAN

N W E S

**Extent of empire by 1680**
**Battle site**

**REGIONS** After the Ottomans captured Constantinople, they continued to conquer land in Europe.
■ How would conquering southwestern Europe have benefited the Ottomans?

Besides being a military leader, Süleyman was a patron of the arts. He encouraged poetry and painting and had the architect Sinan (suh•NAHN) plan new buildings for Istanbul.

Süleyman was called the Lawgiver because he made sure that all the people he ruled were treated fairly. He showed by his own example that officials could behave honestly. For advice Süleyman depended on Ibrahim Pasha (ih•brah•HEEM PAH•shah), his **grand vizier** (vuh•ZIR), or chief minister. Europeans who met Ibrahim were surprised to discover that he had once been a slave. Süleyman also asked for the advice of his favorite wife, Roxelana (rahk•suh•LAHN•uh). Like Ibrahim, she had also been a slave.

Süleyman often started wars to gain territory. Yet he brought peace to the lands he conquered. A Venetian ambassador reported in 1525:

66 I know of no State which is happier than this one. It . . . is rich in gold, in people, in ships, and in obedience; no state can be compared with it. 99

In 1566 Süleyman led his last invasion of Europe. Old and ill, he died on the plains of Hungary. The Ottoman soldiers could not go on without their leader. Their spirits shattered, they returned to Istanbul.

With Süleyman's death, the empire slowly began to fade. It lasted until the twentieth century, but it never regained the strength it had under Süleyman.

**Why was Süleyman called the Lawgiver?**

# INDIA'S MOGUL EMPIRE

Farther southeast, in India, another Muslim empire took shape in the 1500s. Much earlier Muslim Turks had gained control of almost all of India. This began a period of unified rule in India that historians call the Delhi sultanate. Under the Muslim **sultans**, or rulers, many Hindus became Muslims. By 1500 the Delhi sultans had begun to lose their hold in India. Central Asian Muslims swept through the Khyber Pass in 1526 and claimed northern India. Their leader, Babur (BAH•ber), founded the Mogul (MOH•guhl) Empire.

The greatest of the Mogul emperors was Babur's grandson, Akbar (AK•ber), who ruled from 1556 to 1605. Akbar, unlike the Delhi sultans, allowed Hindus to freely practice their own religion. He also got rid of the tax

Babur (the top left figure in this miniature) founded the Mogul Empire. This detailed work of gold (right) belonged to the ruler Akbar.

### MOGUL EMPIRE

HINDU KUSH
Khyber Pass
HIMALAYAS
Brahmaputra River
Indus River
Delhi
Agra
Ganges River
Calcutta
Arabian Sea
Bombay
Bay of Bengal
Goa
INDIAN OCEAN
Calicut
Ceylon (Sri Lanka)

0    300    600 Miles
0    300    600 Kilometers
Two-Point Equidistant Projection

N
W   E
S

- Mogul Empire by 1526
- Land added by 1605
- Land added by 1707
- — Trade route

 **MOVEMENT** By 1707 most of India had been united by the Moguls.
- By about what year had the Moguls gained control of Khyber Pass?

that had been placed on Hindus. Under Akbar, Hindus and other non-Muslims were allowed to become government officials.

Akbar also worked to improve India's economy. He lowered the farmers' taxes and made land reforms. These changes brought about a huge increase in agricultural production. Akbar encouraged merchants to trade with both China and Europe.

Akbar was a man of learning who supported the arts. Among his interests were architecture, painting, and literature. Mogul artists of his time painted in an original style, capturing the smallest of details.

In addition to the arts, religion interested Akbar. He studied not only Islam but also Hinduism, Buddhism, and Christianity. He welcomed priests of all religions in India and eagerly debated them about their beliefs.

A daring military leader, Akbar kept pushing the boundaries of the Mogul Empire south. By 1605, he had united nearly all of India under Mogul rule.

✓ **What impact did Akbar have on the Hindus in his empire?**

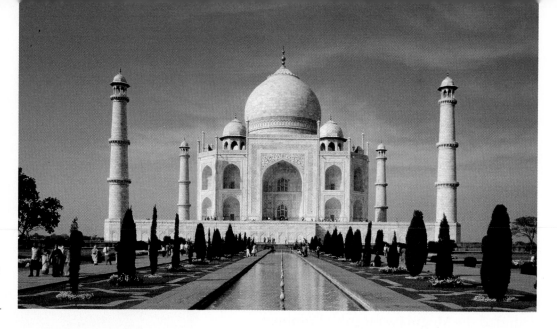

The Taj Mahal was built as a monument to Mumtaz, Shah Jahan's wife. She died in 1631, only three years after Shah Jahan became emperor. He is buried by her side beneath the floor of the Taj Mahal.

## INDIA AFTER AKBAR

Those who ruled after Akbar did not have his ability. His son Jahangir (juh•HAHN•gir) liked hunting more than governing. He left the running of the empire to his wife, Nur Jahan (NOOR juh•HAHN), who ruled well and fairly.

The next Mogul ruler, Shah Jahan (SHAH juh•HAHN), came to power in 1628. He was a cruel man with a surprising love of beauty. He personally directed the construction of some of the world's most beautiful buildings. The Taj Mahal (TAHZH muh•HAHL) stands today as Shah Jahan's greatest cultural contribution. Made of white marble inlaid with gold and precious stones, the Taj Mahal took 22 years to build.

In 1658 Shah Jahan's son Aurangzeb (ow•ruhng•ZEB) seized power. He ended the policy of treating Hindus as equals. Also, to pay for his military campaigns, he taxed the people heavily. Because of his actions Hindus and Muslims alike rebelled. The Mogul Empire became much smaller. The loss of central control in India made it easier for Europeans to gain land there.

 **How did later Mogul emperors help make it easy for Europeans to take over much of the Indian subcontinent?**

# LESSON 2 REVIEW

### Check Understanding

1. **Recall the Facts**   What did the Ottomans and the Moguls have in common?
2. **Focus on the Main Idea**   How did Ottoman and Mogul policies affect the peoples they governed?

### Think Critically

3. **Think More About It**   Would Süleyman be a successful world leader today? Explain your answer.

4. **Cause and Effect**   How did Akbar's treatment of Hindus help unify the Mogul Empire?

### Show What You Know

 **Speech Activity**   Imagine that you are a historian living in the Ottoman Empire or the Mogul Empire in the 1600s. Give an oral report on how life has changed in the empire from the early 1500s up to your time.

# Read a Population Pyramid

## Why Is This Skill Important?

A **population pyramid** is a graph that shows how a country's population is divided by age. It also shows what part of each age group is made up of males and of females. A pyramid's shape depends on the country's birth rate (the number of births each year for every 1,000 people) and death rate (the number of deaths each year for every 1,000 people). The shape also depends on the amount of immigration to and from the country. Knowing how to read a country's population pyramid can tell you a lot of information about that country.

## Understand the Process

The population pyramids below show the present-day populations of the United States and India by age groups.

The pyramids are made up of several bars. Each bar extends left and right from the center line. The bars show the percentage of males and of females in each age group.

Look at the shapes of the two pyramids. The shape of the United States' pyramid shows that its population is growing very slowly. The United States has a higher percentage of people over the age of 50 than India has. Less than 8 percent of the United States' population is under age 5. The shape of India's pyramid is quite different. Its rows get much shorter as the pyramid gets higher. This shows that the population of India is very young.

## Think and Apply

Use the graphs to answer the questions.

1. What percentage of the population of the United States is in your age group?
2. Are there more males or more females in this group?
3. Which of the two countries has a larger percentage of people under 15 years old?
4. What generalizations can you make about the populations of the United States and India?

**POPULATION PYRAMID: UNITED STATES**

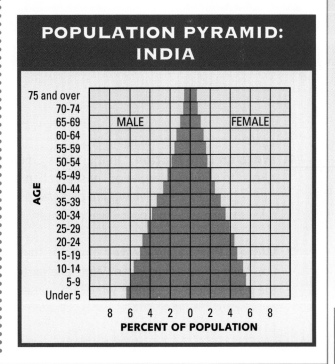

**POPULATION PYRAMID: INDIA**

## CONNECT MAIN IDEAS

Use this organizer to show that you understand how the chapter's main ideas are connected. Copy the organizer onto a separate sheet of paper. Then complete it by writing two details to support each main idea.

**Changes In Asia**

**China and Japan in Early Modern Times**
The people of China and Japan changed their view of themselves in relation to the rest of the world.

1. _____
2. _____

**The Ottoman and Mogul Empires**
The policies of the Ottoman and Mogul empires affected the people conquered.

1. _____
2. _____

## WRITE MORE ABOUT IT

**1. Write an Explanation** In the 1400s China turned to a policy of isolation, or separation from others. From the viewpoint of a Ming ruler, explain why this policy was necessary.

**2. Write a Persuasive Letter** Imagine that you are a merchant in Japan. Write a letter to the government explaining why Portuguese merchants should or should not be allowed to enter Japanese ports.

**3. Write a Speech** Imagine that you are living in the Ottoman Empire in the year 1560, under the rule of Süleyman the Magnificent. You have been asked to give a speech to honor the leader. Write notes about the information you plan to include in your speech. Be sure to describe Süleyman's achievements. Then organize your ideas, and practice your speech. Finally, present it in a dramatic way to a group of classmates.

## USE VOCABULARY

Write a term from this list to complete each of the sentences that follow.

Bushido          haiku
calligraphy      Janissary
grand vizier     sultan

1. _____ was "the way of the warrior."

2. Süleyman's chief minister was the _____.

3. _____ is beautiful handwriting.

4. A _____ was a well-trained Ottoman soldier.

5. A _____ is a 17-syllable poem.

6. A _____ is a Muslim ruler.

## CHECK UNDERSTANDING

1. How did the Ming feel about interacting with outsiders?

2. In what ways did Chinese culture grow during the Ming period?

3. What was the first European nation to set up a trading post in China?

4. What brought an end to China's Ming dynasty? What dynasty followed the Ming? How did this dynasty gain control?

5. Why did Tokugawa Ieyasu drive Christian missionaries from Japan?

6. What groups were at the top and at the bottom of the Japanese class system?

7. What is the present-day name of the city of Constantinople?

8. How did the Ottoman leader Mehmed treat people of other religions?

9. What made Akbar such a good ruler for the Moguls?

10. For what cultural contribution is Shah Jahan best known?

## THINK CRITICALLY

1. **Cause and Effect**   Suppose China had continued to explore the world in the late 1400s. What effect might this have had on today's world?

2. **Personally Speaking**   Japanese poets of the 1600s began to express their feelings about nature in haikus. How do you express your own feelings about nature?

3. **Think More About It**   Some boys volunteered to be Janissaries in the Ottoman army. Why do you think they did this?

4. **Explore Viewpoints**   At some times in history, United States citizens have wanted a policy of isolation. What are some of the good points of isolation? What is good about not being isolated?

## APPLY SKILLS

**How to Read a Population Pyramid**   Use the population pyramids on page 455 to answer these questions.

1. In India, what age group has the most people? What age group has the fewest people?

2. In the United States, what age group has the most people? What age group has the fewest people?

3. Why do you think the shapes of the population pyramids for India and the United States are so different?

## READ MORE ABOUT IT

*The Boy and the Samurai*  by Erik Christian Haugaard. Houghton Mifflin. Saru, an orphan, helps a samurai flee to a more peaceful life.

*Samurai Warriors* by Jenny Roberts. Gloucester. This book explains Japan's feudal system and discusses the roles and duties of samurai warriors.

# MAKING SOCIAL STUDIES
# RELEVANT

Spaghetti with tomato sauce    Stir-fry

## THE GREAT FOOD EXCHANGE

Deciding what to have for dinner can take some time. Will you have rice and beans? Perhaps stir-fried chicken with peanuts? Maybe a plate of spaghetti with tomato sauce? Or a meal spiced with curry? These choices, along with dozens of others you might make, show one part of the great exchange among Europe, Africa, Asia, and the Americas that began in the late 1400s.

Africans had grown rice for thousands of years. Enslaved Africans who had been brought to the Americas showed their masters how to raise this crop. If the Africans had not shared what they knew about farming, colonies such as South Carolina might have failed.

Native peoples of the Caribbean islands gave peanuts to Spanish explorers in the late 1400s. Later, Spanish ships carried peanuts to Europe and other parts of the world. Peanuts reached China sometime before 1600. Today the peanut is an important part of the Chinese diet.

What could be more Italian than spaghetti with tomato sauce? The tomato, however, is an American plant. It did not arrive in Italy until the sixteenth century. The chili pepper that gives Indian curry its spicy taste is also from the Americas. European ships took it to India during the 1500s.

It is hard to imagine Italian food without tomato sauce or Indian food without curry. The foods people now eat around the world show how past exchanges among cultures have affected what we find on our dinner tables today.

**Black beans with rice**

**Ghana jollof rice**

## THINK AND APPLY

Think about the different foods you eat during one week. Then use library resources to find out where some of these foods first came from. Using this information, create a quiz about the origins of foods. Then see how well friends and family members score on the quiz.

BUILDING CITIZENSHIP

# STORY CLOTH

Study the pictures shown in this story cloth to help you review the events you read about in Unit 7.

## Summarize the Main Ideas

1. Changes in European ways of thinking encouraged individualism and creativity, bringing about a period now known as the Renaissance.

2. European nations began to explore and claim land overseas.

3. Europeans changed life in Africa by enslaving many people there and forcing them to leave their homelands.

4. The arrival of Europeans affected life in the Americas in many ways.

5. China and Japan tried to keep from being changed by other cultures.

6. The growth of the Ottoman and Mogul empires affected the ways of life of the peoples they conquered.

**Telling Fact from Opinion** Study the scenes in the story cloth. Then practice telling fact from opinion. For each scene, write one fact and one opinion. Then exchange papers with a classmate. Identify as *fact* or *opinion* each statement on the paper you receive.

**Dramatize the Story** This story cloth shows the meeting of different cultures. Select one such meeting and act out this encounter.

## COOPERATIVE LEARNING WORKSHOP

### Remember

- Share your ideas.
- Cooperate with others to plan your work.
- Take responsibility for your work.
- Show your group's work to the class.
- Discuss what you learned by working together.

### Activity 1
## Hold a Renaissance Fair

Work in a small group to make a booth for a Renaissance Fair. Choose a topic related to the Renaissance, such as art, music, science, crafts, education, home life, foods, or roles of men and women. Find out about your topic so you can give a presentation at the fair. Use cardboard, paint, ribbons, flowers, and other items to decorate your booth. Your group may want to dress in Renaissance costumes.

### Activity 2
## Write a Letter

Imagine you are part of the group that traveled with Jacques Cartier on his explorations of Canada. Write a letter to a friend in your homeland of France, describing how you bartered with the Indians for furs and skins.

### Activity 3
## Tell a Story

Imagine you are an Aztec storyteller. It is your responsibility to remember and retell the history of the Aztecs. Retell the story of the encounter between Motecuhzoma and Cortés.

### Activity 4
## Design a Scene

Draw a scene that could be painted on a porcelain vase. The scene should show one of the following:

- Chinese reaction to outsiders during the Ming dynasty
- the growth of Chinese culture during the time of the Ming dynasty
- the rigid class system of the Tokugawas of Japan

# USE VOCABULARY

Use each term in a sentence that will help explain its meaning.

1. patron
2. perspective
3. movable type
4. telescope
5. clergy

6. heresy
7. Columbian exchange
8. circumnavigation
9. racism
10. Bushido

# CHECK UNDERSTANDING

1. What change took place in European art during the Renaissance?

2. What effect did Martin Luther's actions have on religion in Europe?

3. What led Europeans to explore overseas?

4. How did Spain and Portugal divide the undiscovered world between them?

5. How was the life of an African slave in 1700 different from the life of a slave who lived centuries earlier?

6. What was life like aboard a slave ship?

# THINK CRITICALLY

1. **Think More About It** Why did the Renaissance scholars think it was important to understand how things worked?

2. **Personally Speaking** Suppose you were asked to rename this unit. What name would you choose? Why?

3. **Explore Viewpoints** What viewpoint did Ferdinand and Isabella hold about religion in Spain? What viewpoint do you think the Moors held? What viewpoint do you think Jews living in Spain held?

4. **Past to Present** How is the world today affected by the encounters of Europeans and Native Americans?

5. **Cause and Effect** How did China's isolation preserve traditional ideas about art?

# APPLY GEOGRAPHY SKILLS

**How to Compare Information on Maps** Use the map below and the one on page 413 to answer the questions.

1. Which countries were mostly Protestant in 1618? Which are mostly Protestant today?

2. Are there any countries in this region today where almost all the people have the same religion? If so, which countries are they, and what is the religion for each?

3. What generalization can you make about religions in Europe today compared to religions in Europe in 1618?

MAJOR RELIGIONS IN EUROPE TODAY

# UNIT 8

# TIMES *of* RAPID CHANGE

1720

**1732**
Crop rotation introduced

**1733**
Flying shuttle invented

**1769**
James Watt builds working steam engine

1740

1760

**1776**
American colonies declare independence

1780

**1789**
French Revolution begins

**1799**
Napoleon gains control of France

1800

*E*xciting changes took place around the world during the 1700s and 1800s. The spread of new ideas about government and rights brought about political revolutions. Advances in technology led to another type of revolution, as machines began to take the place of human effort in Europe. Industrial might led Europe to dominate much of the world by the end of the 1800s.

◀ The Industrial Revolution changed the look of towns and cities in many parts of the world. This painting shows a starch factory in Oswego, New York, in the mid-1800s.

1820          1840          1860          1880          1900

**1815**
French Emperor Napoleon is defeated

**1839**
Opium War between China and Britain begins

**1862**
Otto von Bismarck becomes chancellor of Prussia

**1870**
European "scramble for Africa" begins

**1868**
Meiji Restoration in Japan

# THE RIGHTS OF MAN, THE REIGN OF TERROR

## THE STORY OF THE FRENCH REVOLUTION

### by Susan Banfield

*IN THE 1700s POWERFUL MONARCHS RULED THE NATIONS OF EUROPE. MOST LIVED IN LUXURY IN THEIR PALACES, COMPLETELY ISOLATED FROM THE PEOPLE THEY RULED. THESE MONARCHS DID NOT KNOW WHAT THE LIVES OF THEIR PEOPLE WERE LIKE—NOR DID THEY SEEM TO CARE.*

*READ NOW HOW THE RICH—IN THIS CASE, KING LOUIS THE XVI—AND THE POOR IN FRANCE BEGAN THE DAY. THINK ABOUT THE CONTRAST BETWEEN THE WAYS OF LIFE OF THE TWO FAMILIES DESCRIBED IN THE STORY.*

This portrait of French king Louis XVI by Francois Callet shows the wealth of the royal family before the French Revolution.

The King yawned as one of his valets[1] threw back the heavy brocade[2] curtains that surrounded the royal bed on four sides. The light that streamed through the tall casement windows now flooded the entire room. The King rose at once. After he had said his morning prayers, the elaborate process of dressing him began. First, one of his valets shaved him. Then, one at a time, each nobleman who had earned the privilege of waiting on the King handed him the article that was officially his to present. One might hand him his stockings, another his satin breeches,[3] yet another his garters.[4] Once he had been dressed, the King's hair was carefully curled and powdered.

Meanwhile, a similar little drama was being enacted[5] in the bedroom of the Queen. There, at the center of a circle of softly swishing silks, stood Queen Marie Antoinette. She shivered in the chill morning air as she waited for the appointed lady-in-waiting to hand her her undergarments. Several others then helped her into her dress—one of the three new ones she had bought for that week.

The royal husband and wife would not see each other until noon Mass.[6] They would then take the midday meal together, seated side by side at a small table. Dinner was far from an intimate meal for two, however. The women of the royal family and other noblewomen of the court sat on stools encircling the royal table. Beyond them was a crowd of spectators eager for the chance at a glimpse of their rulers. Servants brought out one heavy silver serving dish after another. The King, conscious of the dozens of pairs of eyes that followed his every move, might help his wife to the dishes she fancied[7] that day, but it was unlikely that there would be any further conversation between them. That would have been too informal.

Meanwhile, the sun was also rising on a crude mud cottage in Picardy.[8] Jean Flavier and his family could not see it, as windows were a luxury way beyond their means. But the light creeping in under the door let them know it was time to be up and about. Jean's wife Marie shivered as she quickly pulled on her tattered old linen dress and wooden shoes.

She ripped off a piece of bread for herself and her youngest son. The bread was made of grain so coarsely ground that pieces of straw still stuck in the loaf. Marie wrapped another hunk of the bread for her husband to take out to the fields, sticking in a few small apples along with it.

In sullen silence Jean Flavier took the small parcel that his wife pressed into his hand. Feelings of rage and hopelessness swirled inside him. The bailiff[9] was due to come any day to inquire about the grain they had borrowed from the lord last winter. After the Church took its due from their small garden, what was left would scarcely last them till Christmas. Surely their house would be stripped.

The sun was rising up above the trees now. Jean knew he was late again in setting out for the fields. But he could not seem to care.

*As you read more about Europe in the 1700s, you will discover that this contrast between the lives of the rich and the poor helped bring about a revolution in France.*

[1] **valets:** (va•LAYS) male servants
[2] **brocade:** heavy cloth with raised designs
[3] **breeches:** short pants reaching to just below the knees
[4] **garters:** straps for holding up long stockings
[5] **enacted:** acted out
[6] **Mass:** a Roman Catholic religious service

[7] **fancied:** liked; had a fondness for
[8] **Picardy:** (PI•ker•dee) region in northern France
[9] **bailiff:** official who makes arrests

This painting, *The Delivery Woman* by Jean Baptiste Chardin, shows what life was like for the poor of France.

# The GROWTH of DEMOCRACY

> 66 Hear, O mortals, the sacred cry of Liberty. 99
>
> Beginning of Argentina's national anthem, *Himno Nacional*

Portrait of José de San Martín

# DEMOCRATIC REVOLUTIONS

LESSON 1

## Link to Our World

**Why do leaders of today take different types of actions?**

**Focus on the Main Idea**
**Look for ways different leaders affected history during the 1700s.**

**Preview Vocabulary**

Declaration of
    Independence
English Bill of
    Rights
Enlightenment
confederation
Constitution
    of the United
    States of
    America

Bill of Rights
Declaration of
    the Rights of
    Man and of
    the Citizen
Reign of Terror
Napoleonic
    Code

Minutemen, volunteers who could be ready with a minute's notice, fought for American independence.

By the 1700s strong monarchs ruled most European countries. Many of them held absolute authority and gave few rights to those they ruled. In some countries people began to call for greater freedom and a greater voice in the running of the government. In time determined individuals stepped forward to lead the fight for independence and freedom.

## THE AMERICAN REVOLUTION

During the summer of 1776, American colonists took to the streets to celebrate. "Church bells rang," an observer said. "Cannons were discharged, and every face appeared joyful." The colonists had just heard readings of the **Declaration of Independence**. This document proclaimed the colonies' freedom from Great Britain. Great Britain was the name given to the Kingdom of England and Wales and the Kingdom of Scotland when they united.

For Thomas Jefferson, the main author of the Declaration, the reason for declaring independence was simple. The British, he said, did not care about the rights of the American colonists. Yet the rights of individuals had roots deep in the history of Britain. The Magna Carta, signed in 1215, became the base of laws that protected the rights of everyone in Britain. More than 470 years later, in 1689, the **English Bill of Rights** granted even more individual rights.

In the Declaration, Jefferson told what these British laws were supposed to protect. He explained that

George Washington knew that the key to an American victory was to keep his soldiers in the field and ready to fight. This painting by Louis Charles Auguste Couder shows General Washington at the Siege of Yorktown, October 17, 1781.

people have certain rights and that "among these are Life, Liberty, and the pursuit of Happiness." He said that when a government violates, or fails to protect, these rights, the people have a responsibility to change the government or end it. In the case of the American colonists, the change was a very great one—a revolution.

### English Bill of Rights

*Below are some of the important points of the English Bill of Rights of 1689:*

Suspending of laws . . . by [royal] authority without consent of parliament is illegal.

The freedom of speech and debates . . . in Parliament [should not be] questioned in any court. . . .

### United States Bill of Rights

*Amendment 1*
Congress shall make no law respecting an establishment of religion, or prohibiting the free exercise thereof; or abridging the freedom of speech, or of the press; or the right of the people peaceably to assemble, and to petition the government for a redress of grievances.

The ideas that inspired the American Revolution came from thinkers of the **Enlightenment**. This movement, which began in France in the early 1700s, focused on ways to create a government that would protect the rights of individuals. Leaders of the Enlightenment believed that reason—the act of thinking things through—would lead the way to a more nearly perfect society. Among the most important thinkers of the Enlightenment were the French *philosophes*, or philosophers, Voltaire (vohl•TAIR) and Jean-Jacques Rousseau (ZHAHN•ZHAK roo•SOH).

Jefferson's writings, which reflected Enlightenment ideas, made him the voice of the American Revolution. It was George Washington, however, who led the colonists to victory in their Revolutionary War with Britain. Washington took command of the American forces in 1775. With tattered clothing, few supplies, and no idea of the source of their next meal, the American farmer-soldiers were an unusual army. Washington knew that he had to keep their hopes high even if he believed they had little chance of winning. With this in mind, Washington treated his soldiers with respect. They repaid him with loyalty.

In 1781, after six years of fighting, the colonists won their independence. Now they needed to continue the work of forming a government. Because the former colonists disliked the idea of strong government, the United States became a **confederation**, or loose group of governments. The central government had little authority.

Under this government, the states did not always cooperate. Many state leaders agreed that a change was needed. In 1787 Washington led a meeting that drew up a new plan for government—the **Constitution of the United States of America**.

The Constitution established a democratic republic, in which citizens select people to represent them in government. In some ways the republic of the United States was like the Roman government of long ago. However, the writers of the Constitution made sure that they balanced the freedoms of the citizens with the need for a strong government. Under the Constitution the states and the central government shared authority.

The central, or national, government was divided into three branches—one to make the laws, one to interpret them, and one to enforce them. Each of these branches was designed to check and balance the authority of the others. A **Bill of Rights** was added to the Constitution in 1789. It protected individual rights—including freedom of speech and freedom of religion.

One important difference between this new democratic government and those of the past was that its highest leaders were responsible to the people who elected them. In the United States of the

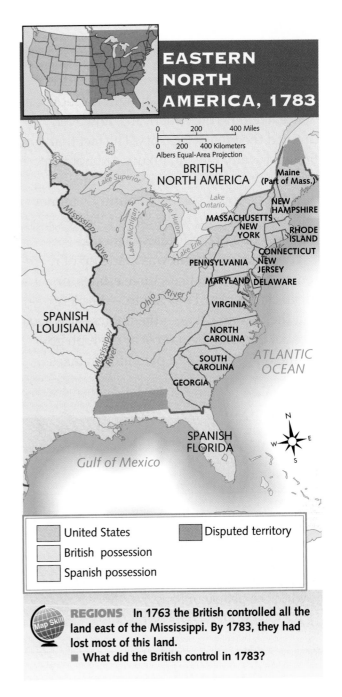

0        200        400 Miles
0    200    400 Kilometers
Albers Equal-Area Projection

BRITISH NORTH AMERICA

Lake Superior
Lake Ontario
Lake Michigan
Lake Huron
Lake Erie
Mississippi River
Ohio River
Mississippi River

Maine (Part of Mass.)
NEW HAMPSHIRE
MASSACHUSETTS
NEW YORK
RHODE ISLAND
CONNECTICUT
PENNSYLVANIA
NEW JERSEY
MARYLAND DELAWARE
VIRGINIA
NORTH CAROLINA
SOUTH CAROLINA
GEORGIA

SPANISH LOUISIANA

ATLANTIC OCEAN

SPANISH FLORIDA

Gulf of Mexico

N W E S

| | United States | | Disputed territory |
| | British possession | | |
| | Spanish possession | | |

**REGIONS** In 1763 the British controlled all the land east of the Mississippi. By 1783, they had lost most of this land.
■ What did the British control in 1783?

late 1700s, though, only white male property owners could vote. The Constitution gave women few rights. It also did little for Africans in the United States, whether free or enslaved. Even so, the Constitution stated a very important idea—that the government belonged to the people. This idea would soon echo around the world.

**What roles did Thomas Jefferson and George Washington play in the American Revolution?**

Abigail Adams, wife of the second U.S. President, John Adams, believed that women should take part in making laws.

## THE FRENCH REVOLUTION

France, long an enemy of Britain, sided with the Americans in their fight for independence. Helping the Americans, however, drained the French treasury. The fact that French royalty lived in luxury did not help. Louis (LOO•ee) XVI, the king of France, decided he could solve his country's money problem by raising taxes. So in 1788 he called for a meeting of the Estates-General.

The Estates-General was made up of representatives from France's three estates, or social classes. The First Estate—the clergy—and the Second Estate—the nobles—owned most of the land, held most of the high government positions, and paid little in taxes.

The storming of the Bastille, shown in this painting by artist Claude Cholat, began the French Revolution.

The Third Estate included everyone else, from doctors to merchants to peasants. Its members had little say in the government but paid nearly all the taxes.

The members of the Third Estate resented paying the most taxes when the rich lived in luxury and paid little. To make matters worse a poor wheat harvest made bread hard to get and very expensive. Many people were forced to spend money on taxes instead of on the food they needed to survive.

Every time the Third Estate tried to set up a fairer way of taxing, the votes of the other Estates stopped it. In June 1789 the Third Estate broke away from the Estates-General. It called itself the National Assembly and claimed the right to make laws.

Shocked by this action, Louis XVI brought soldiers into Paris. The people of France decided they would need weapons if the soldiers attacked. On July 14, 1789, an angry crowd marched through the streets of Paris, shouting, "To the Bastille! To the Bastille!" The Bastille (bas•TEEL) was a prison where Louis XVI's army also kept weapons. The crowd stormed the Bastille, killed many guards, and took the weapons. They then destroyed the Bastille, freeing the prisoners. The French Revolution had begun!

 **How did Louis XVI's actions help start the French Revolution?**

## Paris

In 1789, Paris was the main setting for the French Revolution. In nearby Versailles, King Louis XVI lived in luxury while the people of Paris faced food shortages and many other hardships.

Paris

**FRANCE**

Champs Elysées
Rue du Roule
Rue Neuve des Petits Champs
Place Vendôme
Place de Louis XV
Rue St. Honoré
Rue St. Denis
Rue St. Martin
Rue du Temple
Seine
Tuileries
Louvre
Palais Bourbon
River
N W E S
Hôtel Royal des Invalides
Nouveau Cours
Conciergerie
Hôtel de Ville
Cathédral du Nôtre Dame
Bastille
Rue de Sèvres
Rue de Vaugirard
Palais du Luxembourg
Pantheon
Seine River
Rue St. Victor
TO VERSAILLES 11 MILES
Rue d'Enfer
Rue St. Jacques

0   3,000 Feet
0   915 Meters

# A TIME OF TERROR

To keep violence from spreading, the National Assembly quickly passed new laws. It ended the special rights held by the First and Second Estates. It also approved the **Declaration of the Rights of Man and of the Citizen**. The document promised freedom of speech and religion and equal treatment of all citizens under the law.

These rights were not given to women, even though some women had been leaders of the attack on the Bastille. Later, in 1789, women led a march all the way from Paris to Louis XVI's palace at Versailles (ver•SY). The purpose of the march was to protest the lack of bread to feed their families.

Many women were angry that they received so little respect for what they had done. One woman, Olympe de Gouges (oh•LAMP duh GOOZH), wrote a paper titled *The Rights of Woman*, calling for fair treatment for all people. Still the National Assembly did nothing about women's rights.

The National Assembly did take other action. In 1791 it adopted a new constitution for France. The king would remain on the throne, but an elected assembly would make the laws.

Louis XVI publicly agreed to the new constitution. Secretly, however, he asked the monarchs of other countries to invade France with their armies and overthrow the revolutionaries. Learning of this, an angry crowd put the king and his wife, Marie Antoinette (an•twuh•NET), in prison. Soon after that, a new assembly met to write another constitution. The new constitution stripped Louis of all his authority and made France a republic.

At the same time, a group of young revolutionaries took over the government. They wanted to break with the past and build a new society for France. They began in January 1793 by ordering Louis XVI executed. The executioners used a machine called a guillotine (gih•luh•TEEN), which beheaded its victims with a swift drop of a heavy blade. The executions of Marie Antoinette and hundreds of nobles followed.

Shocked by this violence, a number of European countries formed an alliance to fight the French Republic. In addition, rebellions against the revolution sprang up across France. The revolutionaries reacted with a **Reign of Terror**, or a period of violence and rule by fear, against their political enemies. Anyone who questioned the revolution was killed. In 1794 the National Assembly

This engraving shows women marching to Versailles to protest a bread shortage. A poor harvest had made bread expensive and hard to get. Because members of the Third Estate had to pay high taxes, they could not afford to buy the bread. Why do you think the marchers shown in this picture carried weapons?

ordered the arrest and execution of the revolutionaries. The next year the Directory, a group of five people, took over the French government.

 **Why did the focus of the French Revolution change from human rights to terror?**

## NAPOLEON BONAPARTE

Throughout the Reign of Terror, France fought the armies of the European alliance who were shocked by the violence of the revolutionaries. A French officer named Napoleon Bonaparte (nuh•POH•lee•uhn BOH•nuh•part) won great fame in this fight.

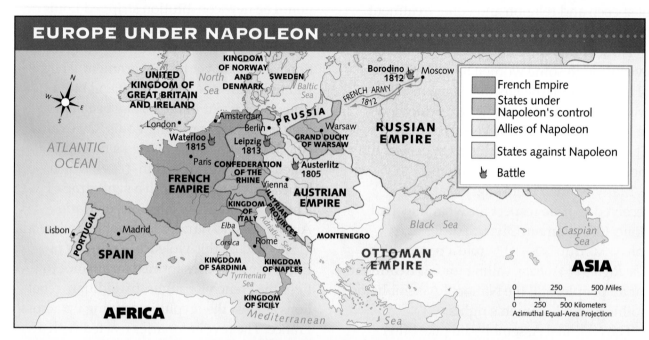

**EUROPE UNDER NAPOLEON**

KINGDOM OF NORWAY AND DENMARK
SWEDEN
North Sea
Baltic Sea
UNITED KINGDOM OF GREAT BRITAIN AND IRELAND
Borodino 1812
Moscow
FRENCH ARMY 1812
PRUSSIA
Amsterdam
London
Berlin
Warsaw
RUSSIAN EMPIRE
ATLANTIC OCEAN
Waterloo 1815
Leipzig 1813
GRAND DUCHY OF WARSAW
Paris
CONFEDERATION OF THE RHINE
Austerlitz 1805
FRENCH EMPIRE
Vienna
ILLYRIAN PROVINCES
AUSTRIAN EMPIRE
Lisbon
Madrid
Elba
KINGDOM OF ITALY
Black Sea
Caspian Sea
Corsica
Rome
Adriatic Sea
MONTENEGRO
PORTUGAL
SPAIN
KINGDOM OF SARDINIA
KINGDOM OF NAPLES
Tyrrhenian Sea
OTTOMAN EMPIRE
ASIA
AFRICA
KINGDOM OF SICILY
Mediterranean Sea

French Empire
States under Napoleon's control
Allies of Napoleon
States against Napoleon
Battle

0      250      500 Miles
0   250   500 Kilometers
Azimuthal Equal-Area Projection

**EUROPE AFTER NAPOLEON, 1815**

KINGDOM OF SWEDEN AND NORWAY
North Sea
UNITED KINGDOM OF GREAT BRITAIN AND IRELAND
DENMARK
Baltic Sea
Moscow
Amsterdam
Berlin
London
NETHERLANDS
PRUSSIA
RUSSIAN EMPIRE
ATLANTIC OCEAN
Paris
GERMAN STATES
AUSTRIAN EMPIRE
SWITZERLAND
Vienna
FRANCE
PARMA
MODENA
Caspian Sea
TUSCANY
Corsica
PAPAL STATES
Lisbon
Madrid
KINGDOM OF SARDINIA
Rome
Adriatic Sea
MONTENEGRO
Black Sea
PORTUGAL
SPAIN
Sardinia
KINGDOM OF THE TWO SICILIES
Tyrrhenian Sea
OTTOMAN EMPIRE
ASIA
Sicily
AFRICA
Mediterranean Sea

— Boundary of the German Confederation

0      250      500 Miles
0   250   500 Kilometers
Azimuthal Equal-Area Projection

 **REGIONS** After Napoleon's defeat, France lost control of much of the territory it had gained.

■ In what ways was the shape of the French Empire under Napoleon different from the shape of France after 1815 following the leader's defeat?

Napoleon (inset) brought his code of law to every country he conquered. His last stand was the Battle of Waterloo (left).

Napoleon supported the ideas of the revolution but also had a hunger for power. In November 1799 he overthrew the Directory and took control of the French government.

Napoleon soon changed the French way of governing. Perhaps his most important action was to oversee the writing of a set of laws known as the **Napoleonic Code**. This code guaranteed some of the freedoms people had fought for in the revolution. French law is still based on it today.

Despite his interest in law and rights, Napoleon ruled with an iron hand. In 1804 Napoleon went so far as to crown himself Emperor of France. He then led his army on a campaign to spread the ideas of the revolution. By 1812 the empire reached from Spain to the Russian border.

Napoleon's ambition eventually led to his downfall. In the summer of 1812, he marched into Russia with an army of 600,000 soldiers. Unexpectedly, his supplies ran out as the harsh winter weather set in. French soldiers died by the thousands. At the end, only 100,000 ragged soldiers were left.

Other defeats followed the disaster in Russia. Napoleon's empire began to crumble. Armies from Britain and its European allies finally defeated Napoleon at the Battle of Waterloo in 1815.

**How did Napoleon affect Europe?**

# LESSON 1 REVIEW

## Check Understanding

1. **Recall the Facts** How were Louis XVI and Napoleon alike? How were they different?
2. **Focus on the Main Idea** How did different types of leaders affect the revolutions in America and France during the late 1700s?

## Think Critically

3. **Past to Present** Can you think of a recent political happening in which one person, for better or worse, changed the outcome of events? Explain your answer.
4. **Cause and Effect** How did the American Revolution help bring about the French Revolution?
5. **Think More About It** If bread had been plentiful in France, do you think the Third Estate still would have sought greater individual rights?

## Show What You Know

**News-Writing Activity**
Imagine that you are a reporter working for a weekly newspaper in the late 1700s. Write a brief article describing one of the leaders mentioned in the lesson. Focus on how that individual's qualities helped him or her influence the way events developed. Post your article on a bulletin board for classmates to read.

# How To

# Read a Political Cartoon

## Why Is This Skill Important?

A cartoon is a drawing or series of drawings that expresses a message or opinion. Sometimes the messages are just for fun. Often, however, cartoons have a serious message purposely planned to make you think. A cartoon on the editorial page of a newspaper presents the artist's point of view about people and current events in politics and government. This kind of cartoon is called a **political cartoon**. Knowing how to read a political cartoon can help you understand its meaning and the artist's point of view.

## Early Political Cartoons

In 1754 Benjamin Franklin drew one of the first political cartoons. In his cartoon Franklin urged the 13 British colonies in North America to unite for protection against the French and the American Indians. Franklin's cartoon showed each colony as part of a cut-up snake, with the caption *Join, or Die*. Later, during the time of the American Revolution, Paul Revere engraved the cartoon to urge colonists to unite against Britain.

By the middle 1800s drawing cartoons had become a popular way for artists to express their ideas and opinions about current events. Honoré Daumier (ah•nuh•RAY dohm•YAY) became the leading cartoonist in France in the years after

*You are free to speak* by Honoré Daumier

Napoleon's rule. In 1835 the French artist drew a cartoon in which he attacked the French government for not allowing free speech. Daumier's cartoon carried the caption *You are free to speak*.

## Understand the Process

To understand the meaning of a political cartoon, you first need to identify its details. Look for a caption or any writing on the drawing that can help you identify the people or the setting. Many cartoonists use symbols, like Franklin's snake. You will need to identify the ideas the symbols stand for. In Daumier's cartoon, unbalanced scales on the judge's desk stand for injustice.

Cartoonists often use exaggeration when drawing people. The way the people look can help you know the artist's opinion of these people. What tells you that Daumier did not like the government officials he drew?

## Think and Apply

Choose a current event, and begin collecting political cartoons about it. Make a booklet of the cartoons, and write a short description explaining each one. Draw your own political cartoon to add to the booklet.

*Join, or Die* by Benjamin Franklin (Note: The colonies of Delaware and Georgia are not represented.)

# DEMOCRATIC IDEAS IN
# LATIN AMERICA

## *Link to Our World*

### *Why do people seek to change their government?*

#### *Focus on the Main Idea*
*As you read, look for reasons the peoples of Latin America wanted to change their governments.*

#### *Preview Vocabulary*
peninsular          mestizo
Creole              mulatto
hacienda            junta

Across the Atlantic Ocean, in what is often called Latin America, Spain and Portugal had created huge empires. Latin America consists of Mexico, Central America, South America, and nearby islands. The region got its name because most of its people speak languages that come from Latin, such as Spanish and Portuguese. In the 1700s the colonies in Latin America were under the complete control of Spain or Portugal. People who lived in those colonies had little say in the government. However, the spirit of revolution soon spread to Latin America from North America and France. Before long the Latin American colonies wanted independence.

## COLONIAL SOCIETY AND RELIGION

Society in colonial Latin America was divided into several social classes. Family and place of birth decided a person's social rank. Members of the highest class were called **peninsulars**. These were people born in Spain and Portugal, on Europe's Iberian Peninsula. Peninsulars held the important jobs in the government, the army, and the Catholic Church. They usually did not live permanently in Latin America.

**Creoles** (KREE•ohlz), people who had Spanish or Portuguese parents but had been born in Latin America, made up the next class. Many Creoles owned mines, ranches, or **haciendas** (ah•see•EN•dahs)—huge farms or plantations—and were very wealthy. Some Creoles held positions in local government, yet they were not respected by the peninsulars. As a German traveler said, "The lowest,

The owner and the manager of a Mexican hacienda

This painting, by an unknown eighteenth-century artist, shows a Mexican mestizo shoemaker and his family.

least educated, and uncultured European believes himself superior to the white born in the New World."

Far below the peninsulars and the Creoles came people of mixed blood. **Mestizos** (mes•TEE•zohs), people of both European and American Indian descent, lived mainly in the Spanish colonies. **Mulattoes** (moo•LAH•tohs), people of both African and European descent, were the most common mix in Portuguese America. Over the years millions of enslaved Africans had been brought to Latin America.

Some mestizos and mulattoes owned small farms. Most, however, were poor. Even so, people of mixed blood had a better life than Africans and Indians.

Africans and Indians were at the bottom of the social ladder in Latin America. Some free Africans lived in the towns and cities. Most Africans, however, were slaves on sugarcane, coffee, or tobacco plantations. Indians were free, but they were looked upon as little more than slaves. Most worked on haciendas and ranches for very low pay.

The Catholic Church was important to people of all classes in Latin America.

Catholic priests, who came to the Americas with the early explorers and conquistadors, converted millions of Indians to the Catholic faith. The missionaries did not treat the Indians as equals, but most felt a duty to help them. Often the missionaries alone protected the Indians against bad treatment by colonial landowners.

Religion was the center of life for both rich and poor. The largest building in a Latin American town was always its church. Every important religious holiday brought crowds to the towns for parades and carnivals. Also, for many people in Latin America, the church was the only place where they could get an education.

### ✓ How was society in colonial Latin America organized?

The church was an important part of every Latin American town. Below is an early Latin American church, Santa Prisca Cathedral in Taxco, Mexico, built around 1750. The inset shows an inside view of another Latin American church from about this same time.

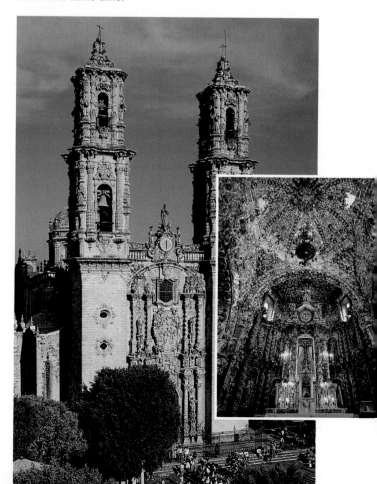

# MOVES TOWARD LATIN AMERICAN INDEPENDENCE

Many people were unhappy with colonial Latin American society and government, especially the Creoles. The Creoles had blood ties to Europe, but they did not think of themselves as Spanish or Portuguese. They resented being told what to do by a government across the sea. The representatives of that government, the peninsulars, behaved as if they thought they were better than the Creoles. This angered the Creoles. They wanted to be free of the peninsulars' rule and to control their own lives.

## Who?

### Tupac Amarú 1742–1781

A revolt against Spanish rule in Latin America took place in Peru in 1780 before the successful revolt in Haiti. It was led by Tupac Amarú (too•PAHK ahm•ar•OO), a descendant of the last Inca ruler. For years Tupac Amarú had tried to get rights for the Inca people through the courts. Nobody listened, however. In 1780 Tupac Amarú led an uprising. "From this day forth," he told his people, "no longer shall the Spaniard feast on your poverty." Tupac Amarú was taken prisoner and executed in 1781. Although the uprising lasted for two more years, the Inca people were unable to free themselves from Spanish rule.

REGIONS  By 1830 most Latin American countries had gained independence.
■ Which colonies in South America had not gained their independence by 1830?

Many Creoles had traveled and studied in Europe and knew about the ideas of the Enlightenment. They knew that their neighbor to the north, the United States, had thrown off its colonial ruler. They also were aware of the democratic revolution going on in France. These two revolutions showed them that people could fight for freedom and win.

The Creoles, however, did not lead the first successful revolt in Latin America. People in the French colony of St. Domingue (SAN duh•MANG) in the Caribbean fought the first war for independence.

In 1793 the French government abolished slavery in all its colonies. The freed slaves in St. Domingue, however, wanted more than an end to slavery. They wanted independence. Led by Toussaint-Louverture (TOO•san LOO•vair•tyoor), who had been a slave, they fought the French army for control of the colony and won. In 1804 they founded the independent country of Haiti. Others, including the dissatisfied Creoles, would soon follow Haiti's lead.

✓ **Why did the Creoles dislike being ruled by distant governments?**

## INDEPENDENCE FOR LATIN AMERICA

Events in France had provided the spark for the revolution in Haiti. These same events lit the fires of revolution throughout Latin America. In 1808 Napoleon conquered Spain and put his brother Joseph on the throne. The Creoles did not accept Joseph as the rightful king. With him on the throne, the Creoles saw no reason to stay loyal to Spain.

In 1810 Creoles in the city of Buenos Aires (BWAY•nahs IRE•ees) in Argentina formed an independent governing council, or **junta** (HUN•tah). This council replaced Spanish rule in the southern part of South America. Then in 1816 Argentina's Creoles declared total independence from Spain.

Creoles in the northern city of Caracas (kah•RAH•kahs), Venezuela, also set up a junta in 1810. Their leader, Simón Bolívar (see•MOHN boh•LEE•var), wanted to break with Spain and to create a United States of South America. It was not easy to meet those goals, however. Creoles and peninsulars loyal to Spain fought against Bolívar. Then in 1814 the rightful Spanish king won back his throne and sent soldiers to South America to take back the land controlled by Bolívar.

Bolívar proved to be a skilled military leader. His soldiers were loyal to him and showed confidence in him. By 1822 Bolívar and his soldiers had freed New Granada (now Colombia), Venezuela, and Ecuador from Spanish rule. Because of this success, Bolívar became known as the Liberator.

Another leader, José de San Martín (sahn mar•TEEN), led the fight for independence in southern South America. In 1817 San Martín started a daring and dangerous campaign. He led an army of 5,000 soldiers from Argentina across the snowcapped Andes Mountains to attack Spanish soldiers

Simón Bolívar, shown on a military campaign (left), freed many South American countries. General José de San Martín announced the independence of Peru at Plaza de Armas (below) in 1821.

Prince Pedro freed Brazil from the rule of Portugal and of his father, King John VI.

in Chile. Soldiers of African heritage made up more than one-fourth of his army. They had been promised their freedom in return for military service. As one of San Martín's generals said, "They were distinguished throughout the war for their valor, constancy, and patriotism."

San Martín's army took the Spanish by surprise and drove them out of Chile. San Martín moved into Peru, where he encountered Bolívar and his freedom fighters. San Martín soon withdrew. He did not want any disagreements over who would lead the fight. Bolívar went on to free Peru from Spanish rule. By 1825 almost all of Spanish South America had gained independence.

In Mexico the revolution took a different route. In 1810 a Creole priest named Miguel Hidalgo (ee•DAHL•goh) led a rebellion of Indians and mestizos. He called for independence, the return of Indian lands to the Indians, and an end to slavery. In less than two months, 80,000 people joined him. However, Hidalgo could not control this huge, angry army. Soldiers who were loyal to Spain stopped the rebels at the gates of Mexico City. Hidalgo was executed, but the revolution did not end. Independence for Mexico finally came in 1821, when Creoles, army officers, and the clergy united to demand a break with Spain.

Brazil, a Portuguese colony, gained independence peacefully. Prince Pedro, the son of the king of Portugal, ruled the huge colony. He listened to the Brazilians' demands for freedom. In 1822 Pedro said, "I proclaim Brazil forevermore separated from Portugal." Then he tore the symbol of Portugal from his hat and tossed it to the ground. Three years later, Portugal agreed to grant Brazil its independence.

 **How were the pathways to independence different in Brazil, Mexico, and Spanish South America?**

## LESSON 2 REVIEW

### Check Understanding

1. **Recall the Facts**   What two European countries controlled the Latin American colonies?
2. **Focus on the Main Idea**   Why did people in the Latin American colonies seek to change their governments?

### Think Critically

3. **Past to Present**   In which countries today are people trying to bring about changes in their governments? Why do they want to make these changes?
4. **Think More About It**   Would the Latin American countries have rebelled against Spain and Portugal if the American and French revolutions had not taken place? Explain your answer.
5. **Cause and Effect**   How did events in Europe help start revolutions in Latin America?

### Show What You Know

**Speech-Writing Activity**
Imagine that you are a Creole leader in the early 1800s. You want your friends to join the independence movement. Write a brief speech that explains why you think your colony should break away from Spanish rule.

# REVIEW

## CONNECT MAIN IDEAS

Use this organizer to show that you understand how the chapter's main ideas are connected. Copy the organizer onto a separate sheet of paper. Then complete it by writing three details to support each main idea.

**The Growth of Democracy**

**Democratic Revolutions**
Different types of leaders affected history in France and in what is now the United States during the late 1700s.

1. _____
2. _____
3. _____

**Democratic Ideas in Latin America**
The peoples of Latin America wanted changes in their governments.

1. _____
2. _____
3. _____

## WRITE MORE ABOUT IT

1. **Write a News Story** Write a news story about an event of the 1700s that changed history. You might write about the storming of the Bastille in France, George Washington leading his army into battle, or one of the Latin American revolutions. Present your story to the class as though you were a news reporter at the scene.

2. **Write a Biographical Sketch** Research and then write a biographical sketch about one of these people: Thomas Jefferson, George Washington, Napoleon, Abigail Adams, or Simón Bolívar. Include information on how this individual tried to bring change to the world.

3. **Write Your Opinion** Write several paragraphs about whether you think people have the right to rebel against those who rule them. Think about the following questions as you write. During the late 1700s, did the people of Latin America act fairly in doing what they did to gain their freedom? How do those conflicts compare with the fights for freedom going on around the world today?

# USE VOCABULARY

Write the term that correctly matches each meaning.

Enlightenment          peninsular
mestizo                Reign of Terror
Napoleonic Code

1. a person who was born in Spain or Portugal but lived in Latin America

2. a movement to create a perfect society that would protect individual rights

3. a period of rule by fear

4. laws that guaranteed freedoms that people fought for in the French Revolution

5. a person of European and native South American heritage

# CHECK UNDERSTANDING

1. According to Thomas Jefferson, why were the American colonists fighting for independence?

2. How did King Louis XVI decide to solve his country's money problems?

3. What role did the Bastille play in the fight for rights in France during the late 1700s?

4. What was the result of the Reign of Terror?

5. What lands did Napoleon bring under his control?

6. Where was Napoleon finally defeated?

7. Who were the Creoles?

8. What type of building was important to all classes of people in Latin America? Why?

9. Which was the first Latin American country to gain independence?

10. Who was Miguel Hidalgo?

11. How did Brazil gain independence?

# THINK CRITICALLY

1. **Past to Present**   How would life in the United States be different if the Declaration of Independence had never been written?

2. **Think More About It**   Do you think followers of the Enlightenment would be satisfied with the democratic societies of today? Explain your answer.

3. **Personally Speaking**   Many people thought of Napoleon as a great military and political leader. Others thought of him as a cruel dictator. What is your opinion?

4. **Explore Viewpoints**   Why do you think the First Estate and the Second Estate in France did not share the Third Estate's thoughts about taxes?

5. **Cause and Effect**   What effect do you think the American Revolution had on many people in Latin America?

# APPLY SKILLS

**How to Read a Political Cartoon**   Create a political cartoon that shows an opinion for or against an event in this chapter. Do you think your cartoon would have been popular or unpopular at the time of the event? Explain. Exchange your cartoon with that of a classmate. See if you understand the message of the cartoon you receive.

# READ MORE ABOUT IT

*The King's Day: Louis XIV of France* by Aliki. HarperCollins. This book tells about a day in the life of France's King Louis XIV, beginning when he dresses in the morning and ending when he prepares for bed at night.

*Napoleon Bonaparte* by Bob Carroll. Lucent. Details of Napoleon Bonaparte's life are examined.

# THE BEGINNING OF THE INDUSTRIAL AGE

> 66 It is the Age of Machinery, in every outward and inward sense of the word. 99
>
> Thomas Carlyle, nineteenth-century British historian

# The INDUSTRIAL REVOLUTION

## Link to Our World

### How can technology change people's ways of life?

### Focus on the Main Idea
*As you read, look for ways the new technology of the Industrial Revolution changed life in Britain.*

### Preview Vocabulary
**Industrial Revolution**
**crop rotation**
**textile**
**cottage industry**
**factory**
**patent**
**raw material**
**entrepreneur**

A seed drill, modeled after Jethro Tull's original

New ideas about government brought about political revolutions in the late 1700s. New technology brought about another great change, the **Industrial Revolution**. This revolution, which began in Britain, forever changed the way people lived and worked.

## CHANGES IN AGRICULTURE

Around the mid-1700s some British farmers began to use new technology in agriculture. Instead of wooden plows, they used iron ones. Instead of scattering seeds on top of the soil, they used the seed drill invented by a farmer named Jethro Tull. This invention planted seeds in neat rows. A farming method called crop rotation was also developed during this time. **Crop rotation** means alternating crops planted in a field from year to year. Because the crops use different nutrients, the soil remains fertile. Crop rotation made it possible to plant farmland for a longer period of time.

More than technology brought changes to agriculture during this time. A growing demand for wool created the need for more land on which to graze sheep. Wealthy farmers bought up many small plots of land and then fenced in large areas to use as private pastures. Up to this point farmers had been able to use some of this land for raising crops and as pasture land to feed their animals. They could no longer do this now that the land was enclosed, or fenced. They either had to rent land from the owners of large farms or stop farming altogether. Many of these farmers soon left the countryside to look for work in towns and

This 1834 engraving (left) shows calico cloth being made in a British factory. Before the mid-1700s textile-making was a cottage industry (above).

cities. They arrived just as the Industrial Revolution was beginning.

✓ **What new ways of farming did British farmers introduce?**

## THE AGE OF MACHINES

The Industrial Revolution started quietly with people tinkering in back rooms and workplaces all over Britain. The result was an explosion of technology that improved the way products were made.

During the early days of the Industrial Revolution, most of the new technology was developed for the **textile**, or cloth, industry. Until the mid-1700s textile making was a **cottage industry**. Families worked in their small homes, or cottages, to make cloth from cotton and wool supplied to them by a merchant. First, they spun the cotton and wool into thread by hand. Then they wove the thread into cloth on wooden looms. They returned the finished cloth to the merchant, who paid them for their work.

Soon people looked for ways to speed up production. The invention of the flying shuttle in 1733 made it possible to weave cloth twice as fast as on the old looms. Flying shuttles worked so well that it was hard to

get enough thread for them. As many as five people had to spin thread to make enough to use with just one flying shuttle.

In 1764 James Hargreaves, a weaver, solved this problem with the invention of the spinning jenny. With the jenny, one worker could spin eight threads at the same time.

Two other inventions, the spinning frame and the power loom, not only increased cloth production but also changed where the work was done. Families could not afford to buy these machines. Besides, the machines were too big to fit into a house. So rich textile merchants would buy a number of the machines and put them in **factories**—large buildings where goods are made. Workers were forced to move near these locations.

Because the large spinning and weaving machines depended on the power of running water, early factories were built near fast-flowing rivers. This changed in 1769, when James Watt built an efficient steam engine.

By 1800 about 1,200 steam engines were in use across Britain. They powered machines that spun thread or wove cloth, and later even powered locomotives. Steam became the power of the Industrial Revolution.

✓ **How did the new technology change the textile industry?**

## BRITAIN LEADS THE WAY

The Industrial Revolution began in Britain partly because of the inventions of people like James Watt and James Hargreaves. Experimenting was encouraged throughout Britain. Business owners ran contests and offered prizes for the best new ideas. Almost every large city had a science club, where inventors could meet and talk about their projects. All of this led to a rush of inventions. More than 1,000 new machines received patents in Britain between 1760 and 1789. A **patent** is a legal document guaranteeing that only the inventor has the right to make and sell the new idea or product.

Several other factors helped the British lead the Industrial Revolution. First, Britain had many natural resources, such as iron and coal. Iron was used to make machine parts.

James Watt showed that steam engines could produce large amounts of power. This steam engine was based on Watt's design.

Coal was burned to run steam engines. Second, Britain's colonies supplied industries with low-cost cotton, lumber, wool, and other **raw materials** used to manufacture goods. Also, growing numbers of people in Britain and its colonies meant that more manufactured goods were needed. British factory owners looked for ways to meet this growing demand.

Through trade Britain had become a very wealthy country. British banks had large amounts of money to lend to entrepreneurs (ahn•truh•pruh•NERZ). An **entrepreneur** is a person who takes a financial risk by putting up money to start a business. Of course, there is always some risk that the business will fail and that the owner will lose the money. Some British entrepreneurs failed, but many did very well.

✓ **Why did Britain lead the way in the Industrial Revolution?**

**LEARNING FROM TIME LINES** The period from the late 1700s through the 1800s is remembered as a time of invention.
■ Why did the invention of different types of machines increase after 1769?

## INNOVATIONS DURING THE INDUSTRIAL REVOLUTION

| 1725 | | 1750 | | 1775 | | 1800 | | 1825 | | 1850 |
|---|---|---|---|---|---|---|---|---|---|---|

**1732** Crop rotation

**1733** Flying shuttle

**1764** Spinning jenny

**1769** Spinning frame

James Watt perfects steam engine

**1785** Power loom

**1793** Cotton gin

**1807** Steamboat

**1814** Steam locomotive

**1834** Reaping machine

**1837** Steel plow

**1846** Sewing machine

# NEW WAYS OF WORKING AND LIVING

By the mid-1800s the Industrial Revolution was in full swing in Britain. Huge factories turned out more and more goods every day, greatly affecting workers' lives. Cities became crowded because many families came from the country in search of work. They jammed into poorly built houses. Streets were filthy, and the air was full of smoke from the factory chimneys. Unhealthful living conditions led to the spread of disease. Illnesses claimed the lives of many, especially young children.

People faced difficult working conditions as well. Most men worked at least 12 hours a day 6 days a week for very low pay. Women and children worked just as long and just as hard but for even less pay. As one textile worker said in 1832,

> 66 Whilst the engine runs the people must work—men, women, and children are yoked together with iron and steam. 99

Children often had the most dangerous jobs. For example, children were made to climb on the spinning and weaving machines to repair broken threads—while the machines were running! Many died or were injured.

Over time the Industrial Revolution did improve the lives of workers. Although wages were low, they were steady. Workers could buy meat and vegetables once in a while to go with their daily bread and cheese. They also had enough money to buy better clothes.

✓ **What was life like for working people during the Industrial Revolution?**

## WORLDWIDE IMPACT

In 1851 Britain hosted a show called the Great Exhibition in the Crystal Palace in London. People came from all over Europe and the United States to get a good look at Britain's technological wonders. There were steam hammers, power looms, farm machinery, and more. The Industrial Revolution, the visitors agreed, had made Britain the "workshop of the world." By 1851 Britain had more factories, more miles of railroad, and more oceangoing ships than any other country.

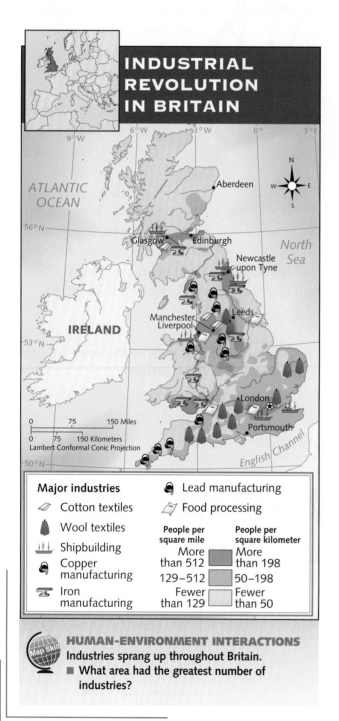

**INDUSTRIAL REVOLUTION IN BRITAIN**

ATLANTIC OCEAN

Aberdeen

Glasgow  Edinburgh

Newcastle upon Tyne

North Sea

Manchester Liverpool  Leeds

IRELAND

London

Portsmouth

English Channel

0   75   150 Miles
0   75   150 Kilometers
Lambert Conformal Conic Projection

| Major industries | |
|---|---|
| 〰 Cotton textiles | 🜂 Lead manufacturing |
| 🌰 Wool textiles | 🜂 Food processing |
| ⚓ Shipbuilding | |
| 🜍 Copper manufacturing | |
| 🜨 Iron manufacturing | |

| | People per square mile | People per square kilometer |
|---|---|---|
| ◼ | More than 512 | More than 198 |
| ◼ | 129–512 | 50–198 |
| ◻ | Fewer than 129 | Fewer than 50 |

**HUMAN-ENVIRONMENT INTERACTIONS**
Industries sprang up throughout Britain.
■ What area had the greatest number of industries?

The smoke from factories made cities grim places to live in (left). Nineteenth-century factories often relied on child labor (above).

By 1851 the United States, Germany, Belgium, and France had also started to industrialize. These countries used Britain as a model for their own industrial revolutions.

Economic success gave Britain and the other industrial nations new strength in dealing with other nations and peoples. In search of new markets—places to sell their goods—they expanded their colonies in Asia. They also forced China and Japan into signing new trade agreements. Next, the European industrial countries turned to Africa. This huge continent had plenty of inexpensive raw materials for Europe's factories and possible markets for its goods.

The strength of the industrial nations sent a clear message to the world: industrial countries would be the winners. Japan listened to this message and quickly passed laws that helped make it easier to build new industries. By 1900 Japan, too, was having an industrial revolution.

 **What steps did the industrial countries take to find new markets and new sources of raw materials?**

# LESSON 1 REVIEW

## Check Understanding

1. **Recall the Facts** What were some of the machines that changed the textile industry?
2. **Focus on the Main Idea** How did the new technology of the Industrial Revolution change life in Britain?

## Think Critically

3. **Past to Present** Name one recent development in technology. How has it changed everyday life in the United States?
4. **Think More About It** Which invention developed during the Industrial Revolution has changed everyday life the most? Why?

## Show What You Know

 **Simulation Activity** With a small group, hold a meeting of a science club similar to the ones in Britain in the late 1700s. At the meeting, discuss the latest technology of the period. Be sure to talk about how it affects people's everyday lives.

# Read and Compare Population Maps

## Why Is This Skill Important?

Like most other geographic information, population growth can be shown on maps. The two maps on these pages show the population of cities in Europe and the Mediterranean region in 1715 and 1815. Map A shows the area before the impact of the Industrial Revolution. Map B shows the area after it changes because of the industrialization that began in Britain. Knowing how to read and compare population maps of cities can help you see patterns in the way cities grow during times of great economic progress.

## Understand the Process

Look at the keys of both population maps. The map keys tell you that the different sizes of the dots stand for different ranges of population. The smallest dot on both maps stands for a city with a population of 30,000 to 50,000 people. The dot that is one size larger stands for a city of 50,000 to 80,000 people. The dots continue to get larger and larger to show more and more people. The largest dot appears on Map B only. This dot stands for a city of more than 500,000 people. These symbols do not give exact populations, but they do help you compare the sizes of cities.

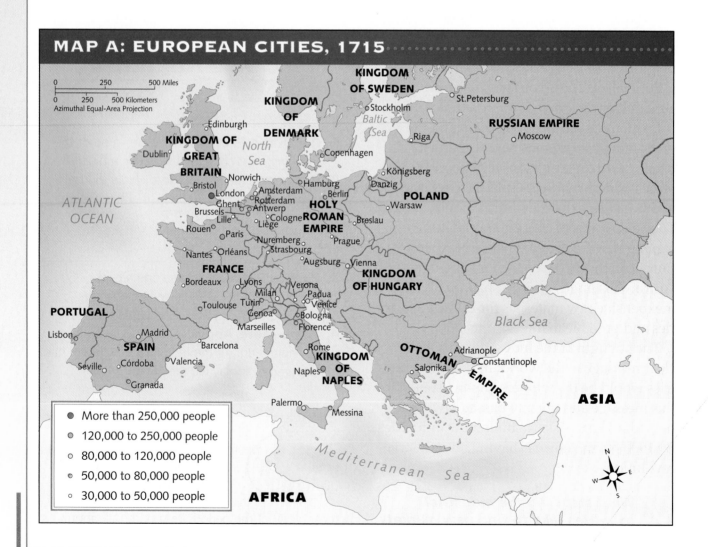

**MAP A: EUROPEAN CITIES, 1715**

- More than 250,000 people
- 120,000 to 250,000 people
- 80,000 to 120,000 people
- 50,000 to 80,000 people
- 30,000 to 50,000 people

Now use the information on both maps to answer the questions that follow.

1. Which city, London or Paris, had more people in 1715?
2. Did London or Paris have more people in 1815? Explain your choice.
3. What other cities in Europe were about the size of Paris in 1815?
4. What city or cities had more than 120,000 people in 1715?
5. What cities had more than 120,000 people in 1815?
6. What are five cities on Map B that had fewer than 50,000 people living in them in 1715?
7. In what part of Europe did the number of cities with more than 30,000 people increase the most? Why do you think that happened?
8. What generalization can you make about the population growth of cities between 1715 and 1815?
9. What generalization can you make about the population growth of cities in countries where the Industrial Revolution took place?

## Think and Apply

Study the population information given on the maps. Then use charts, graphs, or tables to show the same information for some of the cities. You might make a table comparing the ten largest cities in 1715 with the ten largest in 1815. You might make a bar graph comparing the numbers of cities in Britain, France, Italy, Germany, and Russia. Display your charts, graphs, and tables on a classroom bulletin board.

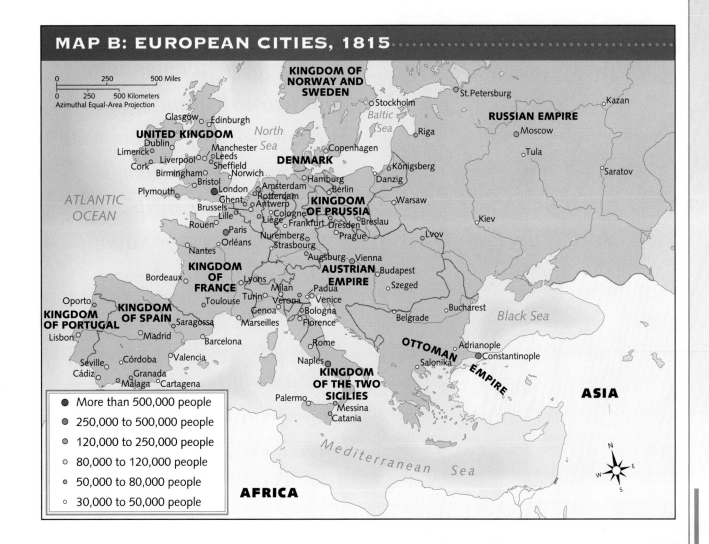

**MAP B: EUROPEAN CITIES, 1815**

Legend:
- More than 500,000 people
- 250,000 to 500,000 people
- 120,000 to 250,000 people
- 80,000 to 120,000 people
- 50,000 to 80,000 people
- 30,000 to 50,000 people

# The Clock

by James Lincoln Collier and Christopher Collier

*By the early 1800s the Industrial Revolution had begun to take hold in the northeastern United States. Many young women who had learned spinning and weaving at home were now working in huge New England textile mills.*

*Read now a story about a fictional character named Annie Steele. As you read, think about how the Industrial Revolution affected textile workers like Annie.*

← Scene at an American textile mill in the 1800s

ON Monday I started to work at the mill. There were eight of us girls, and we were put up on the second story in a room of our own to keep us from distracting the boys. I was glad about that in one way, for it made me blush when the boys winked at me like that; but in another way I was disappointed, for I was mighty curious about those New York boys, and wanted to hear their stories and find out what New York was like.

But still, it was nice to be with some girls. I knew most of them from church, anyway, although not as well as I knew Hetty Brown. Hetty's ma was an old friend of my ma, going way back to when Ma first came to Humphreysville with Pa. Naturally, we visited back and forth with them, especially during the winter, at times when things on the farm were slow. Hetty was short and plump, and always looked on the bright side of things. If you told Hetty you weren't feeling good, she'd say it was probably

something you ate and you'd feel better soon; and if you said it looked like rain, she'd say it wouldn't last long. Hetty was cheerful to be around.

All the girls worked on slubbing billies. A slubbing billy was really a machine for spinning. But instead of having one little spindle for twisting the wool into yarn, it had eight big ones. It looked like a table without a top—just a frame on legs. The spindles were at one end, about three feet from the other end. The yarn stretched from one end to the other. At the opposite end from the spindles there were two girls, each with a big basket of rolags.[1] We worked just like I did at home in the parlor at the spinning wheel, picking up the rolls of wool, twisting them between our thumb and fingers onto the end of the spinning yarn. You had to watch out for the same things as home—bunching, or stretching too much so the connection broke. Only we didn't march back and forth by the

---

[1] **rolags:** rolls of wool that is ready to be spun

Young women operate looms at a Massachusetts factory.

walking wheel[2]; we just stood in one place all day; and that was much more tiresome than all that walking.

There were some other differences too. First off, the noise. You could hear the great wheel creaking as it turned in the water outside, below the slubbing-room window. And you heard the main axle that came from the waterwheel into the mill, turning its gears and making all the belts turn that then turned the axles that went to each machine. And then every machine made its own whirring, or clanking, or banging, or humming. You had to speak up real loud to be heard.

The other big difference was the speed the spindles turned at without stopping. There would be no time out for tea, I could see that. Hetty told me that each of our machines could turn out three or four times as much yarn in a day as the fastest spinner could on a wheel. And the machine yarn was stronger and smoother than the homespun, she said. Pa was right about one thing; the wages I earned would buy a lot more yarn than I could spin in the same time at home. Except, of course, that's not what Pa was going to spend my wages on.

They rang the mill bell at four-thirty in the morning to wake everybody up. But if the wind was wrong we couldn't hear it out on the farm, so George[3] would wake me up. George slept in the back of the house and when the animals started moving around in the morning they'd wake him up. He'd climb up the loft ladder, put his head over the top, and call my name. I'd jump up and dress in two minutes, come down the loft ladder, and grab a piece of johnnycake[4] to eat on the way to the mill. It didn't take me more than twenty minutes to get to the mill, if I hurried.

---

[2] **walking wheel:** a high wheel used in spinning; the spinner has to walk back and forth
[3] **George:** Annie's brother
[4] **johnnycake:** a kind of bread made with cornmeal

They rang the mill bell again at five o'clock. We were supposed to be ready to start work then. At seven o'clock the bell rang again for breakfast, and again at noon for dinner, and again at five o'clock to let us quit and go home. From where I stood at the slubbing billy in the wool mill, I could see the bell tower, which was on the cotton mill. There was a clock in the bell tower, and I could see that, too, and now I knew what it meant to work by clock time, instead of sun time.

With sun time, the way we always worked before, and our grandpas and grandmas before us, and their grandpas and grandmas before them, you could rest a little when you were tired, and take a drink of something when you were thirsty, or a bite of bread and cheese when you were hungry. But with clock time you weren't allowed to get tired or hungry or thirsty on your own; you had to wait until the clock told you it was time to be thirsty or tired. I wasn't used to it.

Back on the farm Ma and me would spin all the livelong day half the winter, it seemed like. And if it wasn't spinning it was cutting and sewing to make frocks for ourselves and trousers and shirts for Pa and George. But now and again, when we felt like it, we'd stop working and rest. Ma'd make tea and we'd eat a baked apple left over from supper with cream on it, and talk. Ma would tell about Mrs. Reed's school, or how handsome Pa was when he was courting her, and I'd tell about being a teacher when I was grown up, and the eagle I'd seen the day before in the top of the pine trees.

But you couldn't do that on clock time. You had to wait until the bell said you could rest and eat and talk about things. Oh, it didn't take me but two days to come to hate that bell and that clock in the tower. But there wasn't anything to change that. I just had to get used to being hungry when I was told to be hungry.

## Literature Review

1. How did the Industrial Revolution affect Annie Steele's life?
2. Would you rather have worked as a spinner at home or in a factory? Explain your answer.
3. On a large sheet of graph paper, design a model factory of the future. Develop a floor plan for the factory that will increase production. Take into account the workers' health and their interest in their jobs.

Factory workers head for home after a hard day's work at a New England factory in this engraving based on the work of American artist Winslow Homer.

# Lesson 3

# CAPITALISM and CLASSES

## Link to Our World

*How can economic differences cause conflicts between people?*

**Focus on the Main Idea**
*As you read, look for ways that economic differences led to conflicts between social classes in Europe and the United States.*

**Preview Vocabulary**

| | |
|---|---|
| economic system | capitalism |
| traditional economy | laissez-faire |
| command economy | free enterprise |
| | strike |
| market economy | labor union |
| demand | socialism |
| supply | utopian |

This nineteenth-century painting, *Industry of the Tyne*, shows workers in Britain.

The European industrial countries grew rich in the 1800s, but the wealth was not shared equally. Some people became very wealthy, while others stayed very poor. In many countries the gap between rich and poor grew wider, leading to social conflict.

## ADAM SMITH AND CAPITALISM

One of the reasons Britain led the way in the Industrial Revolution was its economic system. An **economic system** is the way a country produces and uses goods and services.

Today there are three main kinds of economic systems. A **traditional economy** is one that does not see much change over time. For example, children do the same jobs that their parents and their parents before them did. If the parents are farmers, the children too will be farmers. For the most part, people with a traditional economy spend most of their time raising food for themselves. They are able to produce little surplus. Without a surplus to sell, the people are not able to buy better tools or improve their ways of farming. They continue to work as they always have.

In a **command economy** the government owns almost all land and natural resources. It has complete control over farms and factories. That is, the government of a country commands the direction the economy takes. Government leaders decide what is to be produced and in what quantity. And the government tells how

In the 1800s countries that practiced free enterprise grew rich and powerful. Shown in this nineteenth-century painting are merchants at the Cloth Hall in Leeds, England.

much workers earn and how much goods will cost.

In a **market economy** the people decide which goods and services they will buy. Every day individual people make choices about how they will spend their money. In addition, they decide how they will earn their living.

A market economy works on the principle of supply and demand. When an individual buys a product or service, he or she is showing a **demand** for that product or service. If there is a great demand, the provider will increase the **supply**, or amount offered for sale. The provider will do this in order to make a greater profit.

During the Middle Ages, Britain had a traditional economy. Under the feudal system, most people worked as their parents did, and they earned just enough to survive. They had little say in their own economic affairs. Peasants were expected to work for nobles, who seldom shared the profits of the peasants' labor.

In the 1700s Britain adopted an economic system that today we would consider to be a market economy system. This system is known as **capitalism**. Entrepreneurs in Britain invested money, or capital, in businesses. They hoped that the businesses would do well and make more money for

them. The key to capitalism was that the individuals had control of how they would earn money.

Around the time the Industrial Revolution began, a Scottish economics professor named Adam Smith wrote a book titled *The Wealth of Nations* (1776). In this book Smith explained how capitalism works.

This system, he said, works because of "the natural effort of every individual to better his own condition." He explained, "It is not from the benevolence [kindness] of the butcher, the brewer, or the baker that we expect our dinner, but from their regard to their own interest."

In other words, business owners do not make and sell goods because they are kind people. They do it because they want to make a profit. Still by acting to help themselves, the business owners help everyone. They give jobs and wages to workers. By having to compete with other businesses, they offer consumers better goods.

Smith felt that in a capitalist system the government did not have to become involved in a country's economy. He encouraged the idea of **laissez-faire** (le•say-FAYR), letting the economy continue without interference. Smith believed that the principles of supply and demand would naturally take place and keep the economy going. Businesses would boom, there would be more jobs, and the country would gain much wealth. Over time everyone would share a portion of these riches.

Smith's ideas, which became known as **free enterprise**, pleased the working class. In fact, these ideas became the "battle plan" for the Industrial Revolution. Just as Smith had predicted, the countries that followed the free enterprise approach grew rich and powerful.

 **According to Adam Smith, how would capitalism benefit both owners and workers?**

## ECONOMIC CLASSES IN EUROPE

As capitalism took hold in Europe, economic classes saw change. As always, the wealthy landowners, the aristocracy, were considered the upper class. With the beginning of the agricultural revolution, the landowners had turned to large-scale farming. Rather than farming the land themselves, they rented it to tenant farmers.

Joining the aristocracy at the top of the economic ladder were those business owners who had grown extremely rich in the Industrial Revolution. Unlike the aristocracy, the business owners were a part of the upper class because of the money they earned, not because of the family into which they were born.

Perhaps the greatest change during this period was the growth of the middle class. The middle class consisted of the bankers, merchants, shopkeepers, and professional people such as doctors and lawyers. Also in the middle class were the business owners who had made money in the Industrial Revolution.

At the bottom of the social ladder were the factory and farm workers. Both of these groups worked from dawn to dusk for very low wages. They are called members of the working class.

For centuries the members of the aristocracy had separated themselves from other people. Now the Industrial Revolution was bringing others into their social circles. At the same time, differences grew between the middle class and the peasant workers. Members of the middle classes lived in different types of neighborhoods than the working class and could afford to send their children to school to train for well-paying jobs and even better futures. The working class had little hope of ever leaving the crowded slums where they lived.

 **How were Europeans divided into social classes as the Industrial Revolution took hold?**

Shopkeepers were among the growing middle class of Europe in the 1800s.

# CONFLICT AMONG THE CLASSES

Disagreements soon arose among the economic classes. Upper-class people had a low opinion of business. Socially, they looked down on the wealthy members of the middle class. In turn, the middle class charged that the upper class did nothing to earn its wealth. The landlords simply waited for the rents to come in. The economist John Stuart Mill agreed. "They grow richer . . . in their sleep," he wrote, "without working, risking, or economizing."

Working people were angry at the middle class. They were unhappy that they were forced to work long hours at low pay in poor working conditions. They believed that business owners treated them like a raw material, such as iron or coal, to be bought at the lowest price possible.

Over time the working people's anger grew. Without their labor, they believed, there would be no wealth. They wanted a share of the riches that they produced. To back up their demands for better wages, some workers went on **strike**—they stopped working. Unfortunately for the workers, many of these strikes were poorly planned. Besides, there were many new workers ready to take their jobs. Some workers thought they could get better results if they formed groups called **labor unions**. At first most people were against these workers' groups. Many European governments passed laws against unions. By the end of the 1800s, however, these laws had been changed. Unions spoke for the workers, organizing major strikes that won them better working conditions and higher wages.

✔ **Why did conflicts arise among the social classes in Europe?**

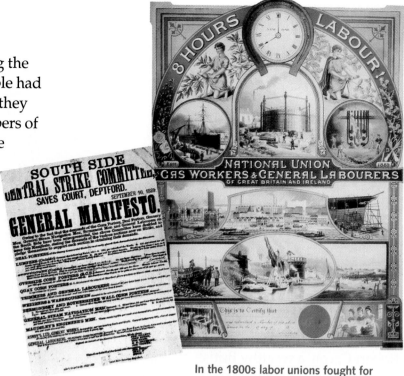

In the 1800s labor unions fought for more pay and better working conditions. This manifesto (left), or written statement of a viewpoint, was printed during the Great London Dock Strike, and this paper (right) was a certificate of membership in a gas-workers' union. Both were typical signs of the times.

# CALLS FOR CHANGE

For some people, strikes and labor unions did not change the economic system enough. They said capitalism should be replaced with a system called socialism. Under **socialism** the government owns all industries and runs them for the benefit of all the people. Socialists said that capitalism made life hard for working people. To have a better life, they said, all people should work together and share equally the results of their labor.

The early socialists believed that socialism would work best in small communities. They set up a number of model towns where all the people jointly owned all houses and factories. The people also shared the money they made from their work. Many of these model communities were in the United States because land there was cheap and easy to get. One such community was New Harmony,

Robert Owen started several cooperative communities. His New Harmony in Indiana (left) was short-lived. In 1832 Owen explained many of his ideas in *The Crisis* (below), which he wrote with his son.

Indiana. It was founded in the 1820s by Robert Owen, a wealthy British business owner. Owen hoped that New Harmony would be a place where "all will be equal in their condition." Owen and people who shared his views were called **utopians**, or believers in a perfect society. For the most part, the utopias failed.

Some socialists thought that a community based on cooperation was not the answer. The leader of this group was a German writer named Karl Marx. He argued that history had moved through many stages. Each stage had been marked by struggles among social classes. In the age of capitalism, the conflict was between the wealthy middle class and the poor working class. Marx believed that this conflict would

Karl Marx urged workers to fight against capitalism.

lead to a revolution, which the working class would win. After this revolution a new social system without classes would develop.

Marx published his ideas in 1848. He called for the workers to revolt against the ruling classes, but workers did not rise to Marx's call. Even so, his words sent chills through the governments and business leaders of Europe during the second half of the 1800s.

✓ **What did utopians call for?**

## LIFE IN THE UNITED STATES

The United States also faced social and economic division during the 1800s. Two different economic systems separated the new nation. The southern United States continued an economic and social system based on agriculture. Plantation owners and their families, like the lords and ladies of Europe during the Middle Ages, made up the upper class. The middle class included owners of smaller farms, merchants, and business people. Next came the workers and poor farmers. Below this class were the people who made it possible for the very small upper class to have its wealth and privileges—enslaved Africans.

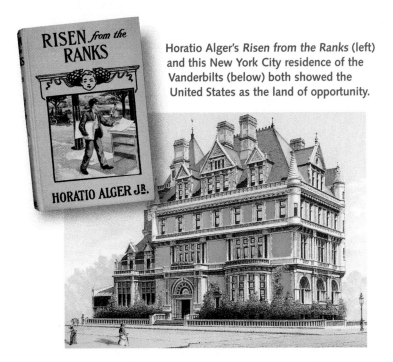

Horatio Alger's *Risen from the Ranks* (left) and this New York City residence of the Vanderbilts (below) both showed the United States as the land of opportunity.

wealth through hard work. This feeling was described in the "rags-to-riches" stories written by Horatio Alger. As one of Alger's characters said, "I don't mean always to be a newsboy or errand boy. I shall work my way upward as fast as I can, and in time I may come to fill a good place in society."

Eventually, American workers did form unions, though. They also used strikes to get better pay, shorter working days, and improved working conditions.

 **Why was there less class conflict in the United States than in European countries?**

In contrast to the South, the North developed a three-class economic and social system as it accepted capitalism and the Industrial Revolution. In the upper class were wealthy land and industry owners who were born in the United States. The upper class also included immigrants or former members of the middle class who had made their fortunes in such industries as railroads, iron and steel, oil, and mining.

The middle class included business owners and merchants. Below them were the working people. The workers of the North faced many of the same problems the workers of Europe faced—low wages, long hours, and poor working conditions.

Even so, American industrialists did not have the same fears of socialist revolution as European industrialists did. In the democratic United States, working people were able to take action to help themselves by voting for political leaders who shared the same concerns that they did. Also, Americans, for the most part, were better off economically than Europeans.

Most Americans looked on the United States as a land of opportunity. Anyone, they felt, could start with nothing and rise to

## LESSON 3 REVIEW

### Check for Understanding

1. **Recall the Facts** What is the difference between capitalism and socialism?
2. **Focus on the Main Idea** How did economic differences affect social classes in Europe and in the United States?

### Think Critically

3. **Past to Present** Do economic differences cause conflict in the United States today? Explain your answer.
4. **Explore Viewpoints** Why did many workers believe they needed to form labor unions? Why were many business owners against such unions?

### Show What You Know

 **Letter-Writing Activity** Work with a partner. One of you is a European business owner in the second half of the 1800s. The other is an unhappy industrial worker. The business owner should write a letter to the editor of the local newspaper, expressing an opinion about the activities of workers. Then the worker should write a reply to the opinion presented in the first letter.

# REVIEW

## CONNECT MAIN IDEAS

Use this organizer to show that you understand how the chapter's main ideas are connected. Copy the organizer onto a separate sheet of paper. Then complete it by writing three details to support each main idea.

### The Beginning of the Industrial Age

**The Industrial Revolution**
The new technology of the Industrial Revolution changed life in Britain and elsewhere.

1. _____
2. _____
3. _____

**Capitalism and Classes**
Economic differences led to conflicts between social classes in Europe and the United States.

1. _____
2. _____
3. _____

## WRITE MORE ABOUT IT

1. **Write a Report**   Research an occupation of the 1700s, and write a report on how the Industrial Revolution changed the way that job was done. Conclude your report by comparing the way technology might change a similar job today.

2. **Write a Diary Entry**   Write a diary entry about your first day at a job in a factory in England around 1750. What was your life like before you started your job? What did you do at the factory? How did you feel when you got home? Explain why you liked or disliked this change in your life.

3. **Write a Story**   Write your own "rags-to-riches" story about someone living in the United States in the nineteenth century.

## USE VOCABULARY

For each group of terms, write a sentence or two that explains how the terms are related.

1. capitalism, free enterprise

2. Industrial Revolution, cottage industry, textile

3. patent, entrepreneur

4. socialism, utopian

5. strike, labor union

## CHECK UNDERSTANDING

1. What is crop rotation?

2. What did James Hargreaves invent, and what industry did it help?

3. Why did textile making stop as a cottage industry?

4. How did the Industrial Revolution affect children?

5. Why was Britain called "the workshop of the world"?

6. How are a command economy and a market economy different?

7. Who was Adam Smith, and what ideas did he write about that became known as "free enterprise"?

8. What did early socialists believe?

9. Why did most people think of the United States as a land of opportunity?

## THINK CRITICALLY

1. **Cause and Effect** How did the Industrial Revolution affect living conditions in cities?

2. **Think More About It** What would have happened if the government of Britain had discouraged the development of new technology?

3. **Past to Present** In the 1700s the Industrial Revolution affected the lives of many people. Today the technological revolution is doing the same. How has this revolution affected your life?

4. **Explore Viewpoints** Why do you think the ideas of socialism were popular with the middle and lower classes in Europe?

5. **Personally Speaking** Do you think Robert Owen had a good idea in starting New Harmony? Why or why not?

## APPLY SKILLS

**How to Read and Compare Population Maps** Use the maps on pages 492 and 493 to answer these questions.

1. What were the largest cities in Europe in 1715? in 1815? How do you know this?

2. Which city had more people in 1815, Constantinople or St. Petersburg? How do you know this?

3. Based on the information shown on the maps, what generalization can you make about cities from 1715 to 1815?

## READ MORE ABOUT IT

*The Industrial Revolution,* edited by John D. Clare. Harcourt Brace. This book describes the many different changes brought about by the Industrial Revolution in Europe and the United States.

*Lyddie* by Katherine Paterson. Lodestar. Lyddie Worthen of Vermont plans to earn some money and gain her independence by becoming a factory worker in Lowell, Massachusetts, in the 1840s.

*The Tenement Writer: An Immigrant's Story* by Ben Sonder. Steck-Vaughn. A young Jewish immigrant from Poland works to build a new life in the United States and make her dream of becoming a writer come true.

# GROWTH OF NATIONALISM *and* IMPERIALISM

> ❝ We, the undersigned chiefs of _____, with a view of bettering the condition of our country and people, do this day [give] to the . . . Company, for ever, the whole of our territory. ❞
>
> from a treaty prepared by a British company seeking to gain land in Africa

Queen Victoria, ruler of the United Kingdom of Great Britain and Ireland throughout much of the nineteenth century

# RISE of NATIONALISM

## Link to Our World

*What are some reasons why people today feel proud of their country?*

**Focus on the Main Idea**
*As you read, think about how people in the 1800s began to develop a sense of belonging to a country.*

**Preview Vocabulary**
nationalism
kaiser

Today most people feel that they are a part of the country in which they live. Through much of recorded history, however, many people felt a part of only a town, city, or region. For most people a sense of belonging to a country did not exist.

## NATIONALISM GROWS

All through history, people have felt a sense of belonging to their family and to the place where they were born. Some people also felt loyalty to a monarch. Yet for a long time, a person usually did not feel a link with other people who lived under the same government.

This attitude began to change at the end of the eighteenth century. The Americans felt pride in their new country. The French, too, were proud that they had fought together to gain a greater voice in government during the French Revolution. Because of this united action, they began to think of one another as members of the same large group who shared the same beliefs, hopes, and fears. They felt a sense of **nationalism**, or loyalty to a nation.

Working together as the French people did can promote nationalism. The geography of a region can also add to the growth of national feeling. A map of France shows that the country has natural boundaries—oceans, mountains, and rivers—on almost all sides. These boundaries helped give the French people a sense of identity. In addition, a language, religion, or race can unite a people as a nation.

In some countries people have come together as a nation, even though they seem to share very little. The people of the United States have a variety of heritages, follow different religions, and are of different races. Still, they have a strong sense of belonging to a nation. Their shared love of freedom defines the United States and gives its people their national identity.

In the 1800s strong nationalist feelings spread across the European nations and the rest of the world. Throughout the world, nationalism affected people and their dealings with others.

> ✓ **What conditions encourage the rise of national feelings?**

## ITALIAN NATIONALISM

Italy experienced the rise of nationalism early. In the 1830s Italy was a collection of

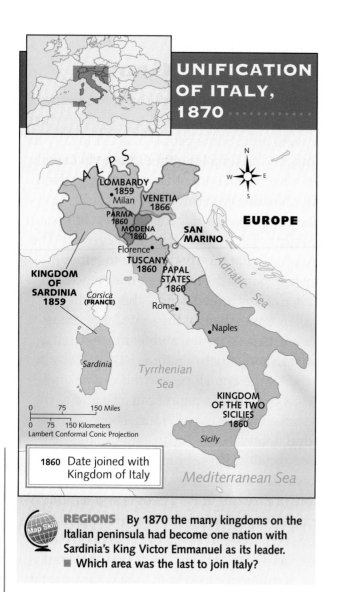

**UNIFICATION OF ITALY, 1870**

ALPS

LOMBARDY
1859
Milan

VENETIA
1866

PARMA
1860

MODENA
1860

SAN MARINO

EUROPE

Florence
TUSCANY
1860

PAPAL STATES
1860

KINGDOM OF SARDINIA
1859

Corsica (FRANCE)

Rome

Adriatic Sea

Naples

Sardinia

Tyrrhenian Sea

KINGDOM OF THE TWO SICILIES
1860

0    75    150 Miles
0    75    150 Kilometers
Lambert Conformal Conic Projection

Sicily

Mediterranean Sea

**1860** Date joined with Kingdom of Italy

**REGIONS** By 1870 the many kingdoms on the Italian peninsula had become one nation with Sardinia's King Victor Emmanuel as its leader.
■ Which area was the last to join Italy?

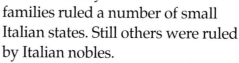

Giuseppe Garibaldi devoted his life to fighting for Italian unity. In his autobiography he tells of his life as adventurer, sailor, and nation builder.

separate states and kingdoms. The Catholic Church ruled Rome and the states around it. Members of the Austrian and French royal families ruled a number of small Italian states. Still others were ruled by Italian nobles.

Many people believed that these separate states and kingdoms should unite to form a single nation. A leader of these people was the lawyer and writer Giuseppe Mazzini (joo•SEP•ay maht•SEE•nee). He pointed out that the mountains and coast formed Italy's natural boundaries. The land within those boundaries should be one country, he said. In 1831 Mazzini founded Young Italy, a nationalist group. Its goal was to unite Italy into one democratic republic governed by and for the Italian people.

Mazzini spread his ideas with great passion. He urged Italians to think of themselves as one people. "Do not say *I*," he wrote, "say *we*." He also called on the Italians to free the country from foreign rulers.

Mazzini may have been the voice of Italian freedom, but Giuseppe Garibaldi was its heart. An adventurer and a sailor, Garibaldi joined Young Italy in 1834. His work for Italy's freedom earned him a death sentence, which he escaped by fleeing to South America. Returning to Italy in 1848, he took part in a short revolution that failed. This time he escaped to the United States. Before

This painting shows Garibaldi's volunteer army—known as the Red Shirts—in action during the battle of Calatafimi, near Naples, in southern Italy.

### Garibaldi's Red Shirts

Garibaldi made his soldiers wear red shirts for a reason. Years earlier he had met some members of a utopian society who wore unusual clothing. When he asked them why they dressed that way, they said it gave them a sense of belonging to the group. When Garibaldi formed his army, he wanted a uniform that would do the same thing for his soldiers. The choice of a red shirt came about by chance, however. Red shirts were the cheapest ones that the clothing merchant had for sale!

he left, he called on his soldiers with these words:

> 66 This is what I have to offer: hunger, cold, the heat of the sun; no wages, no barracks, no ammunition. . . . Those of you who love your country and love glory, *follow me.* 99

In 1860 Garibaldi returned. He and a thousand followers, all wearing red-shirted uniforms, captured the island of Sicily. Garibaldi and his Red Shirts then sailed to the mainland, taking Naples. Soon they had freed much of southern Italy.

Meanwhile, Count Camillo di Cavour (kah•VUR), chief minister of the Kingdom of Piedmont-Sardinia, had united much of the north. Cavour convinced Garibaldi to set up a kingdom of Italy. King Victor Emmanuel of Sardinia became the first ruler of this new nation. Italy became fully united in 1870, when Victor Emmanuel's soldiers finally captured Rome.

✓ **How did Mazzini, Garibaldi, and Cavour help unite Italy?**

## GERMAN UNIFICATION

In the early 1800s Germany, like Italy, was a collection of separate states. Since 1815 these states had been united in a confederation, or loose alliance, which had little authority. One of the main goals of the alliance was to stop any nationalist feelings and keep the German states independent.

Not everyone agreed that the states should stay separate. King Wilhelm, who in 1861 had become the ruler of Prussia, one of the most powerful states, believed that Germany was meant to be united under Prussian rule. "All that remains to be determined," he said, "is when and how." The when and the how were largely decided by Otto von Bismarck, who became the chancellor, or prime minister, of Prussia in 1862.

Bismarck immediately made it clear that he thought the world was run "not by speeches and decisions" but by "iron and blood." He took violent action to unite Germany. In 1864 Bismarck declared war on Denmark, claiming

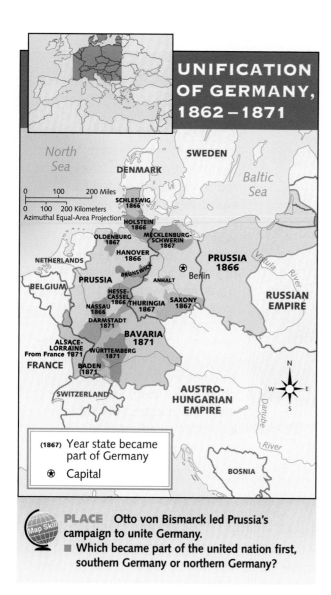

## UNIFICATION OF GERMANY, 1862–1871

North Sea

SWEDEN

DENMARK

Baltic Sea

0      100      200 Miles

0   100   200 Kilometers
Azimuthal Equal-Area Projection

SCHLESWIG 1866

HOLSTEIN 1866

OLDENBURG 1867

MECKLENBURG-SCHWERIN 1867

HANOVER 1866

NETHERLANDS

PRUSSIA 1866

BRUNSWICK

Berlin

ANHALT

PRUSSIA

Vistula River

RUSSIAN EMPIRE

BELGIUM

HESSE-CASSEL 1866

NASSAU 1866

THURINGIA 1867

SAXONY 1867

DARMSTADT 1871

BAVARIA 1871

ALSACE-LORRAINE From France 1871

WÜRTTEMBERG 1871

FRANCE

BADEN 1871

SWITZERLAND

AUSTRO-HUNGARIAN EMPIRE

Danube River

N
W      E
S

BOSNIA

(1867) Year state became part of Germany

⊛ Capital

**PLACE** Otto von Bismarck led Prussia's campaign to unite Germany.

■ Which became part of the united nation first, southern Germany or northern Germany?

an area where many German people lived. He next attacked and defeated Austria, Prussia's rival for control of the confederation.

In 1871 all the German states, except for Austria, had joined with Prussia and its "Iron Chancellor" to form a new German Empire. They named King Wilhelm I of Prussia **kaiser** (KY•zer), or emperor, and they then named Bismarck chancellor of the empire.

Bismarck worked hard to make Germany strong. He sponsored laws that gave help to industry and took steps to build up the army and navy. In time Germany became the leading power in Europe.

✓ *How did Bismarck unite Germany?*

## NATIONAL FEELING GROWS IN JAPAN

Japanese national pride took a different form. It did not grow out of a wish to unite many different states but out of concern over threats from other countries. In 1853 two American warships sailed into the harbor of Edo (present-day Tokyo). The Japanese feared the ships' huge guns could be used against their nation. The commander of the ships, Matthew Perry, told the Japanese that he wanted peace. At the same time he insisted that they open their ports to American traders.

Since the arrival of the first Europeans in Japan, the Japanese had argued among themselves about how they should deal with foreigners. Some wanted to allow Western traders into the country. Others believed that opening the country to outside influences would destroy the Japanese way of life. Perry's visit worried the Japanese government. The shogun knew that Japan's army would have difficulty keeping the United States out of Japan.

Perry returned the following year with seven heavily armed ships. Knowing they had no choice, the Japanese signed a treaty,

King Wilhelm (right) and Otto von Bismarck (left) discuss battle plans during an 1870 war with France.

This Japanese woodblock print shows United States Commodore Matthew Perry's arrival in Japan in 1853.

or agreement, with the United States. This opened two ports to American merchants. Soon after that, Japan signed treaties with the European powers.

Many Japanese people hated the treaties. One samurai wrote of his shame: "Now the Japanese sword is tarnished, and the warrior's spirit is broken." With the cry "Honor the emperor; expel the barbarians," samurai attacked and killed many foreigners. Then, in 1868, these samurai overthrew the shogun and restored the emperor to power. The emperor called his reign *Meiji* (MAY•jee), or "enlightened rule." This time in Japanese history is called the Meiji Restoration.

The emperor and his advisers took advantage of the new nationalist feeling and challenged the West. To compete with the new industrial nations, Japan had to become more modern. Meiji officials looked to the West for the technology that would make this change possible. However, they did not want to change the "spirit of old Japan." By the early 1900s the Meiji government's program of "Eastern ways, Western science" had made Japan a world power.

 **What caused the rise of nationalism in Japan?**

## LESSON 1 REVIEW

### Check Understanding

1. **Recall the Facts**   What is nationalism? In what ways do people develop a feeling of nationalism?
2. **Focus on the Main Idea**   What factors helped unite people in Italy, in Germany, and in Japan?

### Think Critically

3. **Past to Present**   What are the main causes of nationalist feelings today?
4. **Think More About It**   What do you think is the strongest cause of nationalism? Support your choice with information from the lesson.
5. **Personally Speaking**   How does clothing sometimes give people today a feeling of belonging to a group?

### Show What You Know

**Simulation Activity**   Imagine that you and your classmates are students in Italy, Germany, or Japan during the time when nationalism first came to be in one of those countries. Act out a scene in which group members discuss their growing sense of belonging to a country.

# Evaluate Information and Sources

## Why Is This Skill Important?

You can get information from many sources, such as television, radio, newspapers, the Internet, and reference books. Before you use this information, however, you need to evaluate it. To **evaluate** information is to decide whether or not you can trust it.

## Information and Sources

One kind of information is facts. A **fact** is a statement that can be proved to be true. Suppose you are reading a story about Japan. In the story you read the statement "Japan is about the same size as the state of California." You can check whether the statement is true by finding the areas of both Japan and California in an almanac or another source.

Some kinds of information cannot be proved so easily. Archaeologists study ancient cultures about which little may be known. Instead of using written sources of information, archaeologists find and study ancient buildings, tools, and other artifacts. Based on their studies, they form opinions. An **opinion** is a statement of someone's belief or judgment. Although some opinions can be supported by fact, opinions are not trusted as much as facts.

For historians, written or picture records are important sources of information. They describe or show facts and help to explain their meaning. These records may be firsthand accounts, or **primary sources**, that tell the authors' own ideas. Others are secondhand accounts, or **secondary sources**, that tell about other people's ideas.

Picture A

Picture B

## Understand the Process

To evaluate information and its sources, you can follow these steps:

- Study the material carefully. What kind of material is it? Is it in the form of words or pictures? Is it based on firsthand information or on the accounts of others?
- Think about the audience. For whom was this message meant? Whether it was meant for the general public or for a certain audience may have affected what was written and the way it was written.
- Check for bias. Some messages may display **bias**, or a leaning toward or against someone or something. Watch for words or phrases that show a one-sided view of a person or event.
- When possible, compare sources. Study more than one source on a topic if you can. Comparing sources gives you balanced information.

Now that you know more about evaluating information and sources, study the pictures on these pages and answer the questions. Picture A is a drawing made by a Japanese artist after seeing an American steamship arrive in his country in 1853. Picture B is a drawing another artist made of the American fleet after it returned from Japan in 1854.

1. Is Picture A based on firsthand information or on the accounts of others? Explain how you know.
2. For whom do you think Picture A was meant? Explain how you know.
3. Does Picture A show bias? What details in the picture show the Japanese artist's feelings about Americans? Explain how you know.
4. In what ways is Picture A like Picture B? How is it different?
5. Which of the pictures is a better source for what the American steamships really looked like? Why is it better?

## Think and Apply

With a partner, preview the illustrations in the next lesson. Identify them as primary or secondary sources. Then follow the steps in Understand the Process to study the pictures more closely. Discuss the advantages and disadvantages of using these illustrations as sources of information.

BUILDING CITIZENSHIP

# AGE of IMPERIALISM

## Link to Our World

**Why do some nations try to control the governments and economies of other nations?**

**Focus on the Main Idea**
*As you read, think about why the Western industrial nations wanted colonies in Africa and Asia.*

**Preview Vocabulary**

imperialism          sepoy
indirect rule        Great Mutiny
direct rule          Open Door policy
cash crop

Life changed greatly for the people living in the interior of Africa during the 1800s. In this scene an enslaved African works under the watchful eye of a European colonist.

To keep their factories humming, the industrialized countries needed many kinds of raw materials. They also needed markets for their manufactured goods. In the 1800s they found both in Africa and Asia.

## THE SCRAMBLE FOR AFRICA

Europeans had been increasing their contact with the Africans since the 1400s. That contact, for the most part, was limited to the African coasts. Europeans knew little about Africa's interior. It was not until the 1800s that Europeans began to explore these central parts.

Perhaps the most famous of the explorers was the Scottish doctor and missionary David Livingstone. Livingstone arrived in Africa in 1841 and spent more than 30 years exploring its interior. Livingstone kept a journal in which he described the land and people he met. When the journal was published in Europe, it quickly became a best-seller. Reading the journal, European business leaders realized that they could get rich in Africa.

Traders soon followed the explorers. To feed the machines of the Industrial Revolution, Europeans wanted timber, rubber, and other raw materials from Africa. They also wanted Africans to buy their goods. European trade in Africa quickly became big business, and European traders formed large companies. These companies then tried to get their governments to conquer the lands where they did business.

During the 1870s many European governments did just that. They established colonies and took control of

African lands to protect their trade. The Europeans believed that they acted not only from a legal right but also from a duty. They saw it as their responsibility to bring their way of life to the "less-fortunate" Africans. In time the European countries began to compete with one another to add more lands to their colonial empires. Such empire building is called **imperialism**.

The European scramble to control parts of Africa went on until 1884. In that year representatives from 14 European nations met in Berlin, Germany, to divide Africa among themselves. Each country got the regions where it had the most settlements and trading posts. No African representatives were invited to the meeting. The Europeans did not think it necessary to let the Africans say how they felt about the European takeovers. Because of this, the division did not take into account the physical geography of the continent or the similarities and differences in religions, languages, and ways of life in Africa.

By 1900 the Europeans had colonies almost everywhere in Africa. Different countries ruled their colonies in different ways. Many of the British colonies were governed by **indirect rule**. African officials were allowed to run their own communities, but British officials handled important matters that affected the colony as a whole. In contrast, most French and German colonies were governed by **direct rule**. This means that European officials handled all colonial affairs.

Whatever the form of government that was set up, European officials ran the economy of each colony. To get the resources they wanted, the Europeans built mines, factories, and plantations. Often the Europeans treated the African workers like slaves.

The Europeans made African farmers grow **cash crops**—crops raised to sell rather than to use at home. These crops were then exported to markets in Europe, where they were sold for European profit. Up to now, African farmers had always grown what they needed to feed their families. Now they had less land and less time to grow their own food. They became dependent on European traders for the things they needed.

 **Why did the European countries build colonial empires in Africa?**

## AFRICAN REACTION

The European colonial powers changed life in Africa enormously. Some Africans accepted these changes, but others fought to keep their lands and their ways of life. The people of East Africa fiercely resisted German

The African colonies provided raw materials to the industrialized Western nations. Below is a nineteenth-century East African coffee estate.

515

rule. "If it should be friendship that you desire, then I am ready for it, today and always," one leader told the Germans. "If it should be war you desire, then I am ready, but never to be your subject." The Germans answered with a war that took the lives of more than 100,000 East Africans.

In West Africa, Samori Touré, ruler of a Muslim empire, declared that he would never surrender to the French. His 30,000 well-trained soldiers held off the French armies for more than 15 years. In 1898, however, the French took Samori prisoner in a surprise attack. Soon after that, his empire fell.

Samori Touré, ruler of a Muslim West African empire, tried to resist European imperialism.

The British also faced stiff opposition. For years Muslims kept them out of what is today Sudan, in northeastern Africa. The peoples of southern Africa, too, made the British fight for every inch of land they took. In West Africa the Ashanti (uh•SHAHN•tee) waged a number of wars before they finally gave in to the British.

✓ **How did African leaders respond when European countries came to take control?**

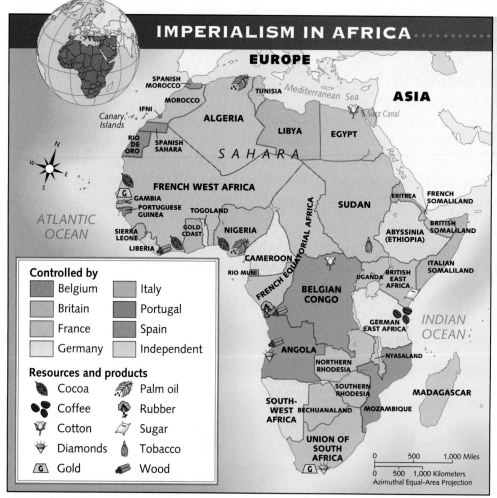

## IMPERIALISM IN AFRICA

**Controlled by**

- Belgium
- Britain
- France
- Germany
- Italy
- Portugal
- Spain
- Independent

**Resources and products**

- 🌰 Cocoa
- ☕ Coffee
- 🌼 Cotton
- ◈ Diamonds
- Ⓖ Gold
- 🍃 Palm oil
- Rubber
- Sugar
- Tobacco
- Wood

**REGIONS** By 1884 most of Africa had been claimed by Europe.
■ Why do you think European countries wanted colonies in different parts of Africa?

⬆ Queen Victoria ruled over the United Kingdom of Great Britain and Ireland during its time of greatest expansion. The time of her reign, from 1837 to 1901, is often called the Victorian Age.

# EGYPT AND THE SUEZ CANAL

By 1900 Britain controlled African lands from the Mediterranean coast to the southern tip of the continent. One of the most important of these lands was Egypt. Egypt was formally a part of the Ottoman Empire, but it had acted independently for many years. Several Egyptian rulers had requested that Europeans help them make their country more modern. As a result, European countries such as Britain and France had much influence in Egypt. Still, until the mid-1800s, they did not try to take full control of the country.

Between 1859 and 1869, French engineers dug a canal through the Isthmus of Suez. The Isthmus of Suez connects northeastern Africa and Asia. The Suez Canal allowed direct water travel between the Mediterranean and Red seas, shortening the sea route from Europe to Asia. Instead of going all the way around Africa, ships could now go through the Suez Canal, saving several months of travel. Suddenly the European trading nations showed much more interest in Egypt.

In 1875, money problems forced Egypt to sell its shares in the Suez Canal. Britain quickly bought the shares and took control of this important waterway. In the early 1880s Egyptian nationalists rebelled, hoping to drive out the Europeans. The British government sent soldiers to Egypt to stop the rebellion. The British explained this action by stating that they had to protect the canal. For many years the British remained in control of the canal and of Egypt.

✔ **Why did European nations show interest in Egypt after the building of the Suez Canal?**

# BRITISH INDIA

Control of the Suez Canal gave the British a fast route to India, their most prized colony.

The official opening of the Suez Canal, in 1869, is shown on this lithograph.

Lord Curzon, a high official, said, "As long as we rule India we are the greatest power in the world. If we lose it we shall drop straight away to a third-rate power."

In 1600 Queen Elizabeth I had given the East India Company the right to control trade between India and England. This group of merchants built trading posts at large Indian ports, such as Bombay, Calcutta, and Madras. The company grew rich in trade goods.

In the 1700s, however, things began to go badly for the East India Company's business. The Mogul Empire, which had ruled India for more than 200 years, started to collapse, and princes of the individual Indian states fought for control of Mogul lands. Also, merchants from other European countries tried to take away some of the Indian trade. To protect their business, company leaders made agreements with the Indian princes. They also formed their own army of **sepoys** (SEE•poyz), Indian soldiers led by British officers. Through treaties and war the company improved its position in India. By the mid-1800s the company controlled much of the Indian subcontinent.

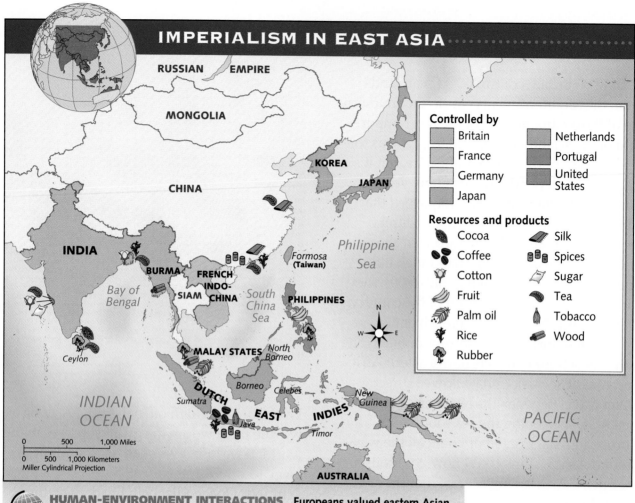

# IMPERIALISM IN EAST ASIA

RUSSIAN EMPIRE

MONGOLIA

KOREA

JAPAN

CHINA

INDIA

Formosa
(Taiwan)

BURMA

FRENCH
INDO-
CHINA

SIAM

Bay of
Bengal

South
China
Sea

Philippine
Sea

PHILIPPINES

Ceylon

MALAY STATES

North
Borneo

INDIAN
OCEAN

Sumatra

DUTCH

Borneo

Celebes

EAST

Java

INDIES

Timor

New
Guinea

PACIFIC
OCEAN

AUSTRALIA

**Controlled by**
- Britain
- France
- Germany
- Japan
- Netherlands
- Portugal
- United States

**Resources and products**
- Cocoa
- Coffee
- Cotton
- Fruit
- Palm oil
- Rice
- Rubber
- Silk
- Spices
- Sugar
- Tea
- Tobacco
- Wood

0   500   1,000 Miles
0   500   1,000 Kilometers
Miller Cylindrical Projection

**HUMAN-ENVIRONMENT INTERACTIONS** Europeans valued eastern Asian land for its many natural resources. In the 1700s and 1800s, Europe claimed much of this region.
■ Which country claimed the Philippines? What resources did it find there?

The East India Company brought British government and British ways to the lands it controlled. Spreading British culture was not the company's main purpose, though. The company was in business to take India's raw materials for British industry and sell British industrial goods in India. It also tried to prevent Indians from starting their own businesses and put many Indian industries out of business.

Many Indians became angry about the East India Company's rule. More than anything else, they disliked having to adopt British ways. In 1857 anger flared into rebellion. Thousands of sepoys, backed by the Indian people, mutinied, or turned against, the company. Fighting went on for more than a year.

When British soldiers were sent to India, the **Great Mutiny** finally ended.

After the mutiny the East India Company gave control of its Indian lands to the British government. Britain's Queen Victoria became empress of India. A viceroy was appointed to govern "British India" through regional governors and councils. Some Indian leaders were on these councils, but they had little say in making decisions.

Some order now returned to India, but Britain was mainly concerned about its interests, not those of the Indians. Many Indians wanted freedom from the British.

 **How did the East India Company gain authority in India? How did it lose that authority?**

## CARVING UP CHINA

Trade brought the Western countries to China, just as it had brought Europeans to India and Africa. In the early 1800s it seemed as if all the industrialized nations wanted China's goods. The Chinese, on the other hand, seemed quite happy to live without anything made in the West. The small amount of trade the Chinese carried on with the outsiders came through one port, Guangzhou. Chinese leaders wanted to keep the foreigners on the coast, away from most of their large cities. This would keep the Chinese people from learning Western ways.

Western traders wanted China to open up more ports for trade. To do this, they knew they had to offer something the Chinese wanted. The East India Company found just such a product—opium. Opium is a dangerous, habit-forming drug made from the poppy plant. Poppies grew well on company lands in India. Company traders began smuggling opium from India into China. More and more Chinese became addicted to opium.

In 1839 the Chinese tried to stop the drug trade by destroying British supplies of opium stored at Guangzhou. This led to the Opium War between Britain and China. Using gunboats, the British were able to defeat the Chinese. In a treaty, signed in 1842, China gave Britain special trading rights. Soon all the imperialistic nations of Europe wanted the same rights as the British. In 1894 the Japanese, who felt that some Chinese lands belonged to them, declared war on China. They seized the Chinese island of Formosa (present-day Taiwan). By this time Britain, France, Germany, Russia, and the United States also controlled parts of China.

The Chinese reacted angrily to this control by outsiders. In 1900 the Boxers, a secret Chinese society, began attacking missionaries and foreign officials. The leaders of a number of nations sent soldiers, who quickly put down the Boxer Rebellion. The leaders then agreed to follow an Open Door policy. An **Open Door policy** means that all countries have an equal opportunity to trade freely in a certain place. This policy allowed Westerners to keep control of China.

This Chinese porcelain bowl shows the factories of foreign traders.

✓ *How did foreign powers come to control much of China?*

## *LESSON 2 REVIEW*

### Check Understanding

1. **Recall the Facts**   What is imperialism?
2. **Focus on the Main Idea**   Why did the Western industrial nations want colonies in Africa and Asia?

### Think Critically

3. **Think More About It**   How do you think Africa, India, and China might have developed without Western control?
4. **Cause and Effect**   How did Western influence change farming in Africa? What were the effects of these changes?

### Show What You Know

**Map Activity**   Use an outline map of the world to show the empires of the European nations at the beginning of the 1900s. Color-code the different colonial empires. Give your map a title and a key. Write a caption for your map to explain why the European countries built large empires. You may need to use library resources to do this activity.

# WERE EUROPEAN *I*MPERIALISTS HELPFUL OR HARMFUL?

**D**uring the 1800s the industrial nations in Europe competed with one another in a race to build global empires. Britain was so successful in gaining colonies throughout the world that the British people boasted, "The sun never sets on the British Empire."

The main reason for European imperialism was to gain control of trade. But most Europeans also believed that the people they conquered were in need of their help and guidance. Read the following points of view from people in China, Central Africa, and India to learn how each person viewed the European imperialists. Did these conquered people consider the Europeans helpful or harmful?

## Lin Zexu, a government official in China

"Of all that China exports to foreign countries there is not a single thing which is not beneficial . . . the things that must be had by foreign countries are innumerable . . . foreign countries cannot get along for a single day without them. If China cuts off these benefits . . . then what can the barbarians rely upon to keep themselves alive? . . . On the other hand, articles coming from the outside to China can only be used as toys. We can take them or get along without them. They are not needed by China."

## A Mangbetu leader in Africa

"Foreigners have always deceived us. . . . We have been the prey in succession [one after another] to the Zandes [a Central African people], the Turks, and the Arabs. Are the whites worth more? No, beyond doubt. But whatever they may be, our territory is today freed from the presence of any foreigners, and to introduce another would be an act of cowardice. I do not wish to be a slave to anyone, and I will fight the whites."

### Girischandra Ghose, a writer from India

❝The final cause of the advent [arrival] of the English in India is to forward the progress of mankind toward perfection. They are the destined instrument in the hand of Providence [God] for this great work. . . . The march of civilization throughout the world is forward. . . . Progress is a necessary condition of creation. . . . The course of nature is perpetual [unending] development.❞

⬆ Under British control, India saw a contrast in the treatment of Indians and British subjects.

The Great Indian Peninsula Revolving Terminus in Bombay was one of the many structures built during the time of British imperialism in India. ⬇

## COMPARE
### VIEWPOINTS

1. How does Lin Zexu view the European imperialists? How do you know?

2. How does the Mangbetu leader view the coming of Europeans to Central Africa? How do you know?

3. How is the viewpoint of Girischandra Ghose different from the viewpoints of Lin Zexu and the Mangbetu leader? Do you think that most people in India held the same view as Ghose? Tell why you think as you do.

## THINK
### –AND–
## APPLY

People who live in different places often have different views on the actions of a nation or group of nations. You have read that people from three different places in the world had different views on European imperialism. At what other times in history have people of different places disagreed about the actions of a nation or group of nations?

# REVIEW

## CONNECT MAIN IDEAS

Use this organizer to show that you understand how the chapter's main ideas are connected. Copy the organizer onto a separate sheet of paper. Then complete it by writing three details for each main idea.

**Rise of Nationalism**

People in the 1800s developed more of a sense of belonging to a country.

1. _____

2. _____

3. _____

**Growth of Nationalism and Imperialism**

**Age of Imperialism**

The Western industrial nations claimed colonies in Africa and Asia.

1. _____

2. _____

3. _____

## WRITE MORE ABOUT IT

1. **Write an Explanation** Write down what comes to mind when you think of the term *nationalism*. Then write an explanation of the term as it might appear as an article in an encyclopedia.

2. **Write a Speech** Imagine that you are living in Africa at the time of European imperialism. Write a speech that tells people of the effects that imperialism has had on you and your community.

## USE VOCABULARY

Write a term from this list to complete each of the sentences that follow.

**direct rule**
**imperialism**
**nationalism**
**Open Door policy**
**sepoy**

1. _____ means that a country continues to add lands to its colonial empires.

2. An _____ means that all countries have an equal opportunity to trade freely in a certain place.

3. _____ is a feeling of loyalty to a country.

4. Under _____ European officials handled all the affairs of African colonies.

5. In colonial India, a _____ was an Indian soldier led by a British officer.

## CHECK UNDERSTANDING

1. What are three things that can give people a shared sense of identity?

2. How did Giuseppe Garibaldi affect the history of Italy?

3. What method did Otto von Bismarck use to unite Germany?

4. What made Japanese nationalism during the 1800s different from nationalism in many European nations at the same time?

5. Why did European countries try to control lands in Africa?

6. What was the importance to Britain of the Suez Canal?

7. What was the result of the Great Mutiny in India?

8. What was the Boxer Rebellion?

## THINK CRITICALLY

1. **Think More About It**   How can nationalism make a country stronger? How can nationalism make a country weaker?

2. **Explore Viewpoints**   Why did outsiders want to enter Japan in the mid-1800s? Why did the Japanese want to keep outsiders from their country?

3. **Cause and Effect**   What effect do you think the Suez Canal had on trade in Egypt?

4. **Past to Present**   What factors make people today unite for a common purpose? How are these factors like or unlike the ones that united Europeans in the 1800s?

## APPLY SKILLS

**How to Evaluate Information and Sources**
Imagine that you have been asked to write a report on how European imperialism affected ways of life in Africa.

• Would you use primary sources, secondary sources, or both? Why?
• Do you think you might find bias in primary sources on this topic? Why or why not?
• Do you think you might find bias in secondary sources on this subject? Why or why not?

## READ MORE ABOUT IT

*Commodore Perry in the Land of the Shogun* by Rhoda Blumberg. Lothrop, Lee & Shepard. This book explains Commodore Matthew Perry's role in opening Japan to the rest of the world in the 1850s.

*The Eagle and the Dragon: The History of U.S.–China Relations*  by Don Lawson. Crowell. This book is about the history of the relationship between the United States and China, from trading in the 1700s to the reopening of official communication and trade.

# RELEVANT

# THE NATION OF TEXAS

The rise of nationalism in the 1700s and 1800s created many of the nations we have today. Among these are the United States, Haiti, Argentina, Venezuela, Chile, Brazil, Germany, and Italy. However, some nations that were set up during that period are no longer countries. Among these is Texas.

In 1836, before it became part of the United States, Texas won its independence from Mexico. For nearly ten years after that, Texas was an independent republic. It had its own president, its own constitution, and its own flag—the Lone Star flag. Then, in 1845, Texas joined the United States, and the Lone Star flag became the Texas state flag.

National flags are important symbols of pride and loyalty for people everywhere. The Pledge of Allegiance, which people make to the United States flag, says that its citizens promise to stand up for their flag as well as for their country and the freedoms it promises.

*I pledge allegiance to the Flag*
*of the United States of America,*
*and to the Republic for which it stands,*
*one Nation under God, indivisible,*
*with liberty and justice for all.*

Because it was once a nation, Texas is the only state to have a pledge to its state flag.

*Honor the Texas Flag.*
*I pledge allegiance to thee,*
*Texas, one and indivisible.*

Think of times when you have felt proud to live in your state or country. Imagine that you want to tell your feelings to a pen pal in another country, with whom you communicate by letter or computer. Describe what makes you feel proud of your state or country.

BUILDING CITIZENSHIP

545

# STORY CLOTH

Study the pictures shown in this story cloth to help you review the events you read about in Unit 8.

## Summarize the Main Ideas

1. The actions of leaders such as George Washington in what would become the United States, King George III in Britain, and King Louis XVI and Napoleon in France caused great change.

2. The spirit of revolution spread to Latin America. The peoples of Latin America wanted to change their ways of life and their governments.

3. The new technology of the Industrial Revolution changed life in Britain and in other parts of the world.

4. Economic differences among social classes in Europe led to conflicts.

5. In the latter part of the 1800s, more and more people began to develop a sense of nationalism, or loyalty to a nation.

6. During the Age of Imperialism, industrialized nations in the West took control of the governments and economies of nations in Africa and Asia.

**Dramatize the Story**   Choose one scene in this story cloth. With a group, write a short one-act play based on the main idea of the scene. Perform your play for classmates.

**Write Creatively**   Imagine that you are one of the people shown in this story cloth. Quickly write down your thoughts and feelings. Are you happy? sad? afraid? proud? Explain why.

## COOPERATIVE LEARNING WORKSHOP

### Remember
- Share your ideas.
- Cooperate with others to plan your work.
- Take responsibility for your work.
- Show your group's work to the class.
- Discuss what you learned by working together.

### Activity 1
## Create a Time Line

Work in a group to create a time line of the events in one place between 1750 and 1850. First, choose one of the following places where a fight for rights occurred: the United States, France, or Latin America. Then, make a list of important events and dates for the place you have selected. Next, create a time line for display on a wall or a bulletin board. Use a long strip of paper for a title. You can then form your time line with another long strip of paper or with several individual sheets. Use a sheet of paper to describe each event and to show its date. Add illustrations as appropriate. Make sure each event is shown in the correct place on the time line. Display the time line for all to see.

### Activity 2
## Hold a Class Fair

The Industrial Revolution caused great change in the way people lived and worked in the nineteenth century. In your classroom, hold a fair about "revolutionary" ideas for the twenty-first century. With a group of six or seven classmates, make an exhibit of photographs, drawings, or three-dimensional models that show changes affecting how people will live and work in the new century. Once each group has completed an exhibit, hold the fair. Group members should explain each exhibit while other students view it.

### Activity 3
## Present an Oral Report

In Chapter 18 you learned about the colonies in Africa and Asia that were controlled by the Western industrialized nations. In a group, select one such colony. Then find out more about that colony. Next, prepare and present an oral report that communicates the information you have found. Be sure to tell about how colonization affected the people of Africa or Asia.

# USE VOCABULARY

Write each term in a sentence that will help explain its meaning.

1. Constitution of the United States of America

2. Bill of Rights

3. Declaration of the Rights of Man and of the Citizen

4. hacienda

5. junta

6. traditional economy

7. imperialism

8. Open Door policy

# CHECK UNDERSTANDING

1. Who were Jean-Jacques Rousseau and Voltaire? To what eighteenth-century movement did they contribute ideas?

2. What was the relationship between King Louis XVI and the French Revolution?

3. What caused the Creoles of Latin America to try to change their government?

4. What effect did the spinning jenny and other new machinery have on the textile industry?

5. How were the ideas of Adam Smith and Karl Marx different?

6. What was Germany's political structure like before unification in 1871?

7. How did completion of the Suez Canal affect ships traveling between Europe and Asia?

# THINK CRITICALLY

1. **Think More About It** In what ways did the Enlightenment affect politics in the eighteenth century?

2. **Explore Viewpoints** Why did employers allow children to work during the Industrial Revolution? Why did parents allow so many children to risk injury or even death to work in a factory?

3. **Past to Present** Which of these topics— the struggle for individual freedom, nationalism, technological advances—are still important today? Explain.

# APPLY GEOGRAPHY SKILLS

**How to Use a Population Map** Look closely at the two maps shown below. Then answer the questions.

1. About how much larger is the population of London today than it was in 1815?

2. What patterns do you notice in the populations of the large cities in Britain?

## POPULATION MAPS: GREAT BRITAIN

- More than 5 million people
- 1 million to 5 million people
- 500 thousand to 1 million
- Fewer than 500 thousand

0    75    150 Miles
0   75   150 Kilometers
Lambert Conformal Conic Projection

# UNIT 9

# *The* WORLD *at* WAR

**1910**

**1920**

**1930**

**1940**

**1950**

**1914**
World War I
begins

**1917**
Russian
Revolution

**1918**
Central
Powers are
defeated,
ending
World War I

**1929**
Great
Depression
begins

**1933**
Franklin
Roosevelt
declares
New Deal

**1939**
World War II
begins

**1945**
Germany and
Japan surrender

United Nations
is established

**1950**
Korean
War
begins

I WANT YOU
FOR U.S. ARMY
NEAREST RECRUITING STATION

NORFOLK LEDGER-DISPATCH
WAR OVER
Japan Surrenders Unconditionally
Army To Cut
5,000,000
Within Year
MacArthur
To Accept
Capitulation

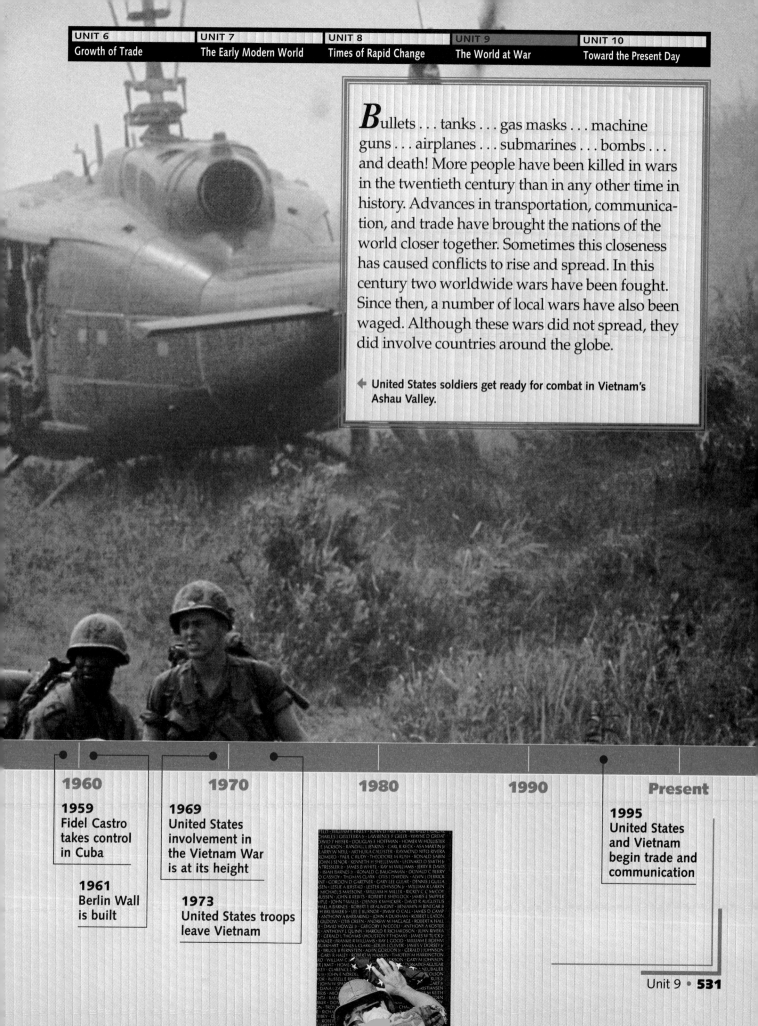

*B*ullets . . . tanks . . . gas masks . . . machine guns . . . airplanes . . . submarines . . . bombs . . . and death! More people have been killed in wars in the twentieth century than in any other time in history. Advances in transportation, communication, and trade have brought the nations of the world closer together. Sometimes this closeness has caused conflicts to rise and spread. In this century two worldwide wars have been fought. Since then, a number of local wars have also been waged. Although these wars did not spread, they did involve countries around the globe.

← United States soldiers get ready for combat in Vietnam's Ashau Valley.

1960

**1959**
Fidel Castro takes control in Cuba

**1961**
Berlin Wall is built

1970

**1969**
United States involvement in the Vietnam War is at its height

**1973**
United States troops leave Vietnam

1980

1990

Present

**1995**
United States and Vietnam begin trade and communication

# Scene of War

## by Mildred Aldrich

War affects everyone, not just the soldiers who fight in it. It becomes part of the way of life of all men, women, and children in a battle-torn country. Read now as Mildred Aldrich, an American living in France, describes the coming of war to the French countryside in 1914.

This painting by Claude Monet (moh•NAY) shows haystacks at the end of summer in the French countryside. The painting represents the artist's first impressions of an outdoor scene.

Artist Jules Brenton captures on canvas a scene of French women gathering leftover grain from a field.

A dozen times during the afternoon I went into the study and tried to read. Little groups of old men, women, and children were in the road, mounted on the barricade that the English had left. I could hear the murmur of their voices. In vain I tried to stay indoors. The thing was stronger than I, and in spite of myself, I would go out on the lawn and, field glass in hand, watch the smoke. To my imagination every shot meant awful slaughter, and between me and the terrible thing stretched a beautiful country, as calm in the sunshine as if horrors were not. In the field below me the wheat was being cut. I remembered vividly afterward that a white horse was drawing the reaper, and women and children were stacking and gleaning.[1] Now and then the horse would stop, and a woman, with her red handkerchief on her head, would stand, shading her eyes a moment, and look off. Then the white horse would turn and go plodding on. The grain had to be got in if the Germans were coming, and these fields were to be trampled as they were in 1870.

It was just about six o'clock when the first bomb that we could really see came over the hill. The sun was setting. For two hours we saw them rise, descend,[2] explode. Then a little smoke would rise from one hamlet, then from another; then a tiny flame—hardly more than a spark—would be visible; and by dark the whole plain was on fire, lighting up Mareuil[3] in the foreground, silent and untouched. There were long lines of grain stacks and mills stretching along the plain. One by one they took fire, until, by ten o'clock, they stood like a procession of huge torches across my beloved panorama.[4]

*As you read this unit, you will find out how wars touched the lives of millions of people.*

[1] **gleaning:** gathering grain left scattered in a field

[2] **descend:** fall
[3] **Mareuil:** (muh•ROY) a town in France
[4] **panorama:** complete view in all directions

# THE EARLY TWENTIETH CENTURY

> "There's just one thing that I know, mister
> Our hungry babies must be fed. . . ."
>
> Jim Garland, American songwriter

This photograph captures the emotions of the Great Depression.

# WORLD WAR I

## Link to Our World

**How can cooperation lead to conflict?**

**Focus on the Main Idea**
*As you read, think about how alliances of nations led to World War I.*

**Preview Vocabulary**
militarism
conscription
arms race
armistice

Napoleon's plan to conquer all of Europe in the early 1800s placed much of the continent into war. After Napoleon's defeat in 1815, European leaders avoided war by not letting any one country get too strong. This balance of power kept the peace among nations for much of the nineteenth century. Then, in the late 1800s, this balance broke down as rivalries, or competition, among the European nations grew stronger. These rivalries would send Europe and the rest of the world into war.

## UNSETTLED CONFLICTS

The spirit of nationalism, or strong feelings of pride in a nation, which arose in Europe in the late 1800s, created many conflicts. Often strong national pride drove countries to take actions that helped their own people but not others. Many times this competition led to disputes. Although war was usually avoided by making agreements, nobody was really happy with the results. Angry feelings continued.

Conflicts also arose in regions where people who wanted to rule themselves were not allowed to do so. Throughout the Balkan Peninsula such nationalist feelings were especially strong. Many different peoples lived in this region, including Hungarians, Greeks, Albanians, Turks, and German-speaking Austrians. Slavic peoples such as Serbs, Croats, Bulgarians, and Slovenes also made the Balkans their home. Some of these ethnic groups—ruled by Austria-Hungary—wanted to build independent nations. Other groups, such as the Bulgarians and the Serbs, already had independence. They wanted others who shared their

In the early 1900s many world leaders built up their armies and navies. Here German emperor Wilhelm II speaks to a ship's crew.

culture to gain their freedom from Austria-Hungary or from the Ottoman Empire and join them.

 **How did nationalism create conflicts in Europe at the end of the nineteenth century?**

## PREPARING FOR WAR

The growing tensions among European nations led to a spirit of **militarism**, or interest in armed power. Many leaders believed that if they used force, they would soon get what they wanted. Therefore, they began to build up their nations' military power.

A number of European countries formed huge armies. They kept their armies large through **conscription**, the drafting of young men to serve in the armed forces for a set number of years. These nations also spent a lot of money on weapons and built their own large naval forces. All of Europe became involved in an **arms race**, or competition to have the most weapons.

As the number of weapons grew, so did people's fear of war. European leaders began to form alliances, or agreements, with other nations. These alliances included the promise to help one another against enemies in case of war.

In 1882 Austria-Hungary, Germany, and Italy formed the Triple Alliance. Fearing the strength of this alliance, France allied itself with Russia in 1893. As the arms race sped up, the British joined the French and the Russians. This alliance became known as the Triple Entente (ahn•TAHNT).

The system of alliances created a balance of power among the major nations. Yet it also divided Europe into two sides. Even a minor event might start a war. Such an event soon came to be in the Balkans.

 **Why did the European nations build up their military power?**

## THE WORLD AT WAR

In 1908 Austria-Hungary seized the Balkan provinces of Bosnia (BAHZ•nee•uh) and Herzegovina (hairt•suh•goh•VEE•nuh). This angered the Serbs who lived there. They thought that these provinces should be part of Serbia. By 1914 tempers could no longer be controlled.

On June 28, 1914, Archduke Francis Ferdinand, who was to be the future ruler of Austria-Hungary, arrived in the Bosnian capital, Sarajevo (sair•uh•YAY•voh). As he and the archduchess rode through the streets in an open car, a young Serbian nationalist shot and killed them. The leaders of Austria-Hungary thought that the Serbian government had something to do with the assassination. A month later Austria-Hungary declared war on Serbia.

The system of alliances quickly went into operation. The Russians supported their fellow Slavs, the Serbs. Austria-Hungary's main ally, Germany, declared war on Russia. Russia's allies—France and Britain—declared war on Germany. By early August 1914 most of Europe was at war. Britain, France, Russia, and their allies soon became

This 1914 photograph shows Archduke Ferdinand and the archduchess just one hour before their assassination.

known as the Allied Powers, or Allies. Germany, Austria-Hungary, and their allies were called the Central Powers.

In time, the conflict reached beyond Europe. Japan had made agreements with the Allies, so it declared war on Germany and attacked German territory in the Pacific Ocean and in China. The war spread to Southwest Asia when the Ottoman Empire entered on the side of the Central Powers. Fighting also broke out in East Africa, where British and French troops attacked German colonies. Around the globe British colonists in Australia, Canada, India, and New Zealand also joined the fight. As Australia's prime minister said, "Remember that when the [British] Empire is at war so is Australia at war."

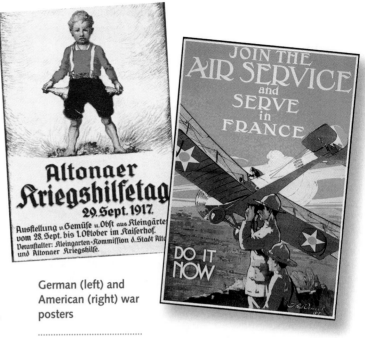

German (left) and American (right) war posters

## Where?

### The Balkans

Both the beginning and the end of the twentieth century have seen a growth of national feeling in the Balkan Peninsula. This map shows the countries that make up the Balkan Peninsula today.

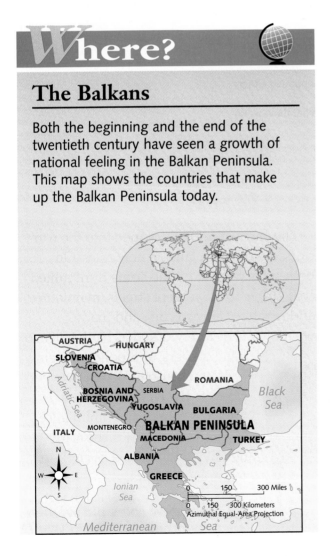

The United States tried to stay out of the war. Many Americans felt the war was a European problem and none of their business. Those against having the United States in the war were called isolationists. For the most part, President Woodrow Wilson agreed with the idea of isolation. He said he hoped that Americans would remain "impartial in thought as well as in action." Then in 1917 German submarines attacked United States ships that were trading with Germany's enemies. Also, the British found out about a German plan to draw Mexico into the war by helping the Mexicans regain land that had been lost to the United States.

The United States citizens were outraged. President Wilson realized there was only one thing to do. On April 2, 1917, he asked Congress to declare war to "bring peace and safety to all nations and make the world itself at last free." Four days later the United States entered the war on the side of the Allies. American soldiers would travel overseas to fight in World War I—the Great War, as it was called at the time.

 **How did the assassinations of Archduke Francis Ferdinand and his wife lead to war?**

## EUROPE IN 1918

NORWAY

SWEDEN

Jutland

DENMARK

Riga

Moscow ✪

RUSSIA

UNITED
KINGDOM

IRELAND

North
Sea

Baltic Sea

ATLANTIC
OCEAN

GREAT
BRITAIN

London ✪

NETHERLANDS

Ypres

Somme

Meuse-Argonne

BELGIUM

Paris ✪

Seine River

Marne

FRANCE

LUXEMBOURG

Verdun

Elbe R.

Rhine R.

Berlin ✪

GERMANY

Danube R.

Tannenberg

Warsaw

Vistula R.

Lodz

Lemberg

Vienna ✪

SWITZERLAND

AUSTRIA-HUNGARY

Rhone River

Po River

Isonzo

ITALY

Sarajevo

SERBIA

Rome ✪

Corsica

MONTENEGRO

Sardinia

ALBANIA

Bucharest ✪

ROMANIA

Black Sea

Sarikamish

Sofia ✪

BULGARIA

Constantinople ✪

Gallipoli

OTTOMAN EMPIRE

PERSIA

PORTUGAL

Madrid ✪

Lisbon ✪

SPAIN

Mediterranean Sea

Sicily

GREECE

SPANISH
MOROCCO

MOROCCO
(FRANCE)

ALGERIA
(FRANCE)

TUNISIA
(FRANCE)

Crete

Cyprus
(U.K.)

**Legend:**
- Allied Power
- Central Power
- Neutral nation
- Triple Alliance
- Triple Entente
- — Western Front trench
- ✪ Capital
- Battle site

0     250     500 Miles
0   250   500 Kilometers
Azimuthal Equal-Area Projection

**REGIONS** In the early 1900s, most countries in Europe supported either the Triple Entente or the Triple Alliance.
- What three world powers made up the Triple Entente? What three world powers made up the Triple Alliance?

# ROLE OF WOMEN IN THE WAR

The entry of millions of men into the war caused women to take on new roles. On both sides women on the home front mined coal, drove trucks, swept streets, maintained and repaired railroad cars, and made weapons. They also worked as bank tellers, mail carriers, and police officers.

Women also took part in events closer to the war itself. Some served as nurses and ambulance drivers. Others joined the army and navy and worked as clerks or telegraph operators.

Working in factories and serving as nurses were just two of the roles women took on during World War I.

✓ *What new roles did women take on during World War I?*

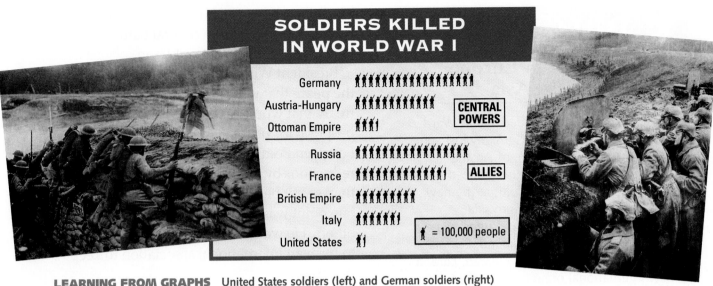

## SOLDIERS KILLED IN WORLD WAR I

| | | |
|---|---|---|
| Germany | 𝍫𝍫𝍫𝍫𝍫𝍫𝍫𝍫𝍫𝍫𝍫𝍫𝍫𝍫𝍫𝍫𝍫 | |
| Austria-Hungary | 𝍫𝍫𝍫𝍫𝍫𝍫𝍫𝍫𝍫𝍫𝍫 | CENTRAL POWERS |
| Ottoman Empire | 𝍫𝍫𝍫𝍫 | |
| Russia | 𝍫𝍫𝍫𝍫𝍫𝍫𝍫𝍫𝍫𝍫𝍫𝍫𝍫𝍫𝍫𝍫𝍫 | |
| France | 𝍫𝍫𝍫𝍫𝍫𝍫𝍫𝍫𝍫𝍫𝍫𝍫𝍫𝍫 | ALLIES |
| British Empire | 𝍫𝍫𝍫𝍫𝍫𝍫𝍫𝍫𝍫 | |
| Italy | 𝍫𝍫𝍫𝍫𝍫𝍫𝍫 | |
| United States | 𝍫𝍫 | 𝍫 = 100,000 people |

**LEARNING FROM GRAPHS** United States soldiers (left) and German soldiers (right) were among the many troops who fought in World War I. Millions of soldiers lost their lives. ■ Which side lost more soldiers, the Allied Powers or the Central Powers?

## WAR IN AN INDUSTRIAL AGE

When the war began, people thought it would not last long. However, the war kept on without a winner. For more than three years, neither side gained much territory.

Enemy soldiers faced each other across a long line of deep trenches, or ditches. The trenches protected them from machine-gun fire. The trenches, though, were horrible places. Soldiers were forced to eat, sleep, and fight in the same spot for weeks at a time. Sickness was everywhere. Rain and mud added to the soldiers' misery.

Troops could only defend their territory from the trenches. To gain territory, soldiers had to leave their trenches and attack the enemy head-on. Soldiers dreaded the command "over the top," which forced them out of the trenches. Outside the trenches lay a "no-man's land" of barbed wire and exploding mines. At best, trips over the top meant tiny gains of territory. They always brought death for some soldiers.

By the end of the war, more than 8 million soldiers would be killed. An additional 20 million would be wounded. Many others would suffer from a nervous condition called shell shock.

The high numbers of injuries and deaths during the war resulted partly from new technology. Inventors had produced many deadly new weapons, such as machine guns, tanks, and a poisonous spray called mustard gas. The new guns could fire shells at targets that were miles away. A direct hit by one of these shells killed many soldiers and scattered bodies everywhere. "Death roars around one," a German soldier said, "a hail of machine-gun and rifle bullets; every moment one expects to be hit."

 **How did new technology add to the destruction during World War I?**

## A FRAGILE PEACE

By the summer of 1918, the war seemed to be coming to an end. A revolution had overthrown the Russian government in 1917. Soon the new government signed a peace treaty with the Central Powers. With the war against Russia over, the Central Powers sent all their forces to western Europe. They thought this would bring them victory.

# What?

## New Nations in Europe and Southwest Asia

The peace treaty that ended World War I brought many changes. Germany lost some of its land. The old empire of Austria-Hungary was broken up and reduced to two small countries. In addition, the new nations of Poland, Czechoslovakia (che•kuh•sloh•VAH•kee•uh), Yugoslavia (yoo•goh•SLAH•vee•uh), Finland, Estonia, Latvia, and Lithuania were created. Later a new international organization called the League of Nations reduced the Ottoman Empire to the independent state of Turkey. New borders were drawn in the lands once part of the Ottoman Empire, creating Iraq, Syria, Lebanon, Palestine, and Trans-Jordan, all under French or British control.

The Allies, however, had fresh American troops. They soon won several battles. It now looked as if the Allies would win.

President Wilson turned his attention to the peace that would follow. He wanted a treaty that would create a lasting peace. His proposal for peace became known as the Fourteen Points. The points included arms reductions by all nations and open rather than secret peace agreements. For Wilson one point was more important than all the others. He wanted the nations of the world to form an international association to keep the peace.

By late October the Germans were ready to end the war's killing and destruction. On November 11, 1918, Germany asked for an **armistice** (AR•muh•stuhs), or agreement to stop fighting. Two months later a meeting took place in Paris to decide peace terms.

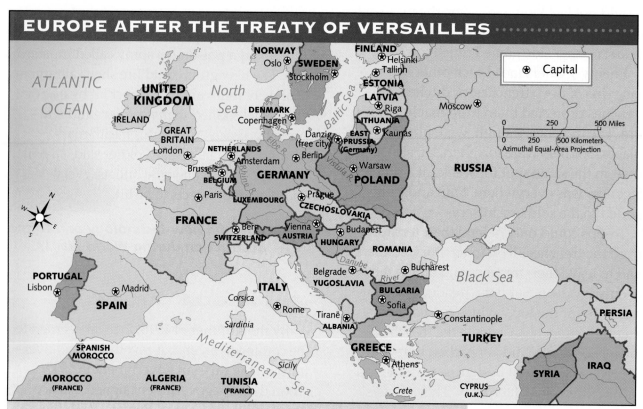

**EUROPE AFTER THE TREATY OF VERSAILLES**

⊛ Capital

0    250    500 Miles
0    250    500 Kilometers
Azimuthal Equal-Area Projection

**REGIONS** The Treaty of Versailles caused borders in Europe to change. Compare this map with the map on page 538.
■ What new countries were formed in Europe because of the treaty?

As World War I drew to a close, United States President Woodrow Wilson (far right) wrote a peace proposal that became known as the Fourteen Points (near right).

## • FOURTEEN POINTS •

*Listed below is one of the Fourteen Points proposed by United States President Woodrow Wilson at the end of World War I.*

**14.** A GENERAL ASSOCIATION OF NATIONS MUST BE FORMED UNDER SPECIFIC COVENANTS FOR THE PURPOSE OF AFFORDING MUTUAL GUARANTEES OF POLITICAL INDEPENDENCE AND TERRITORIAL INTEGRITY [RIGHTS] TO GREAT AND SMALL STATES ALIKE.

The delegates signed a document called the Treaty of Versailles on June 28, 1919. The delegates agreed to some of Wilson's points, including the creation of a new international organization called the League of Nations. For the most part, however, the treaty was very different from the document of peace Wilson wanted.

For one thing, the treaty dealt very harshly with Germany. The Germans had to take full responsibility for the war. They also had to pay huge sums of money to the Allied nations to repair damages caused by the war. The German army and its supply of weapons were to be cut back. Germany also had to give up territory in Europe, Africa, and the Pacific.

The treaty left many people bitter. The Germans were angry about the harsh treatment they received. The Italians had wanted to gain more land as a reward for their role on the side of the Allies. Also, the United States did not join the League of Nations because many Americans wanted to return to a policy of isolation. The uneasy peace that followed the war would last no more than 20 years.

✓ **How did the Treaty of Versailles punish Germany?**

## *L*ESSON 1 REVIEW

### Check Understanding

1. **Recall the Facts**   What were the two major alliances in Europe in the years leading up to World War I? What nations were in each?
2. **Focus on the Main Idea**   How did the system of alliances among European nations lead to World War I?

### Think Critically

3. **Cause and Effect**   How did nationalism create tensions in Europe in the early 1900s?

4. **Past to Present**   How have nationalist feelings affected recent international conflicts?

### Show What You Know

**List Activity**   President Wilson's Fourteen Points were designed to help the nations of the world work out their differences peacefully. Think about ways in which your classmates could work out their differences without fighting. Then make a poster titled *Points for Keeping Peace at School* that lists your ideas. Discuss them with classmates.

# S·K·I·L·L·S
# HOW TO
## Use a Time Zone Map

### Why Is This Skill Important?

The measurement of time is important to many people's daily activities. Trains, buses, and airplanes must keep to time schedules. Television and radio programs must start at certain times. Imagine the problems people would face if every community had its own way of measuring time! In the 1880s most of the countries of the world agreed to follow a system of standard time zones to end confusion about times. Modern travel and communication make understanding time zones even more important for people today than it was for people living in the 1800s.

### Time Zones

Time on Earth is measured by meridians. You have learned the word *meridian* as another name for a line of longitude. The prime meridian, or line of 0° (degrees) longitude, passes through Greenwich (GREH•nich), which is a suburb of

London, England. Many years ago an observatory was built there. It had very accurate tools that scientists used to tell the exact time of day. Because of this the meridian that passes through Greenwich was chosen as the prime meridian, or the starting point for the world's time zones.

All the time zones lie east or west of the prime meridian. There are 24 standard time zones, 12 of them to the east of Greenwich and 12 to the west. Each time zone covers 15 degrees of longitude. Every 15 degrees east or west, the standard time changes by one hour.

All the time zones to the east of the prime meridian are ahead of Greenwich time. All zones to the west are behind Greenwich time. The meridian where the east and west time zones meet is known as the International Date Line. It is 12 time zones from the prime meridian, so when it is noon in Greenwich, it is midnight at the International Date Line, the time when the date changes.

**CLOCKS AROUND THE WORLD**

**NEW YORK**
7:00 A.M.

**BUENOS AIRES**
9:00 A.M.

**LONDON**
NOON

**CAIRO**
2:00 P.M.

**DELHI**
5:30 P.M.

**TOKYO**
9:00 P.M.

## Understand the Process

The map on this page shows all 24 standard time zones. It tells what time it is in each zone when it is noon at the prime meridian. By international agreement, all places within the same time zone have the same time. When it is 7:00 A.M. in Montreal, Canada, it is also 7:00 A.M. in Lima, Peru, and in New York City.

Look at the times at the top of the map. The time in each time zone is one hour ahead or one hour behind the times in the neighboring zones. If you go east from Greenwich, the time in each zone you come to is one hour later than the last. When it is noon in Greenwich, it is 1:00 P.M. in Vienna, Austria. Vienna is in the first time zone to the east of Greenwich. Meanwhile, it is 9:00 P.M. in Tokyo, Japan, which is in the ninth time zone to the east. As you go west from Greenwich, the time in each zone is one hour earlier. When it is noon in Greenwich, it is 6:00 A.M. in Mexico City, which is in the sixth time zone to the west.

You can also see on the time zone map that the boundary between two time zones does not always follow the meridian exactly. The boundary may zigzag in places so that neighboring cities and towns can keep the same time. In some places the people in a time zone have chosen not to use the time of their zone. Notice on the time zone map that all of India uses a time that is 30 minutes ahead of the time in Pakistan. Also notice that Australia's central time zone is 90 minutes ahead of its western time zone. Such places are shown on the map as having nonstandard time zones.

## Think and Apply

Write five word problems about time zones, and give them to a partner to solve. Here is an example: "At 9:00 P.M. Maria telephones from Mexico City, Mexico, to her sister in Buenos Aires, Argentina. What time is it in Buenos Aires?"

# LESSON 2

# THE RUSSIAN REVOLUTION

## Link to Our World

**How can a country change political systems and yet remain much the same?**

### Focus on the Main Idea
*As you read, think about how the government of Russia changed and yet stayed much the same after the revolution of 1917.*

### Preview Vocabulary
autocrat          collective
czar              purge
communism         totalitarian
soviet

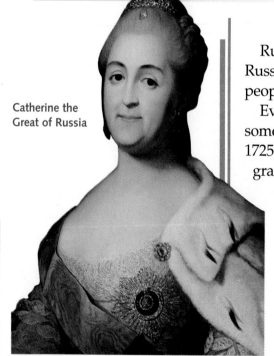

Catherine the Great of Russia

Since the late 1400s, **autocrats**, or leaders with unlimited authority, had ruled Russia. These autocrats often treated their people badly. By the early 1900s the Russian people wanted change. They overthrew their rulers and set up a new form of government.

## CZARIST RUSSIA

In the 1400s, after 200 years of Mongol rule, the Russian provinces were able to gain their freedom. Moscow, a province that had gained great strength, managed to drive out the Mongols. Most of the Russian lands became united under a leader known as Ivan III. Later, the leader of Russia would be known as the **czar** (ZAR), meaning "caesar," or ruler.

Russia's czars extended the country's borders and built Russia into a rich nation. However, most czars treated the people very harshly.

Even czars who brought positive changes to Russia were sometimes cruel. Peter the Great, who ruled from 1682 to 1725, helped Russia become more modern and built the grand city of St. Petersburg as his capital. To complete the project, however, he forced people to work on building the city and collected high taxes from everyone in Russia. Catherine the Great, who came to power in 1762, supported learning and the arts. But she did little to improve the lives of the Russian people.

By the late 1800s the czar and nobles held all the wealth and authority. Peasants and factory workers owned almost nothing. Czar Nicholas II, who came to the throne in 1894, wanted to keep things as they were.

In January 1905 thousands of workers and their families marched peacefully to the czar's palace in St. Petersburg to ask for reforms, or improvements. Their requests were met by bullets from the czar's troops. The people answered by going on strike, which brought the country to a stop. Reluctantly Nicholas II agreed to make reforms, but little changed.

When Russia became involved in World War I, Nicholas II insisted on taking charge of the war effort himself. Russia suffered defeat after defeat. The people blamed their czar for their losses.

While Nicholas led the war effort, Czarina (zah•REE•nuh) Alexandra took over the everyday running of the government. A peasant from Siberia named Rasputin (ra•SPYOOT•uhn), who claimed to be a holy man with special powers, influenced her greatly. Seeing their country being run by a priest—who might be a fake—made the Russian people even angrier than they had been before. In 1916 a group of nobles killed Rasputin. By this time the czar had completely lost the loyalty of the people.

**Why were the Russian people unhappy with their leaders?**

## REVOLUTION!

The angry Russian people formed many groups that worked for political change. Some groups wanted democracy. Others were made up of revolutionaries who followed the ideas of Karl Marx. Of special interest to them was Marx's idea that socialism would lead to communism. **Communism** is a system in which all property and all means of production, such as factories and farms, belong to the people as a group. The revolutionaries who supported that system came to be known as communists.

By early 1917 food had become hard to find in the Russian capital. Late in the winter, Russian workers marched through the streets, demanding bread. "End the war!" and "Down with the czar!" they shouted. The rebellion quickly spread across the country. Finally, the soldiers themselves even refused to obey government orders to put down the revolt.

Czarina Alexandra and Czar Nicholas II seemed to care little that their subjects faced hard lives.

Russian men and women wait in line for food during the early 1900s. What types of emotions do you think these people felt?

On March 15 Czar Nicholas II gave up his throne. At the same time, leaders in the Duma (DOO•muh), or parliament, set up a temporary government. The czar had been overthrown by a revolution of the workers. Marx believed that a worker revolution was one step toward a new way of life based on communism. However, the leaders of the temporary government wanted democracy, not communism. The communists would not have control of the revolution until later—under a leader who went by the name of Lenin (LEH•nuhn).

The poster (above left) asks, "Have you volunteered for the Red Army?" In the painting (above right) the Red Army marches through Moscow.

**How did Czar Nicholas II fall from power?**

This painting shows the second All-Russian Congress of Soviets. The members of the congress appointed Lenin (center) to head the newly formed Soviet Union.

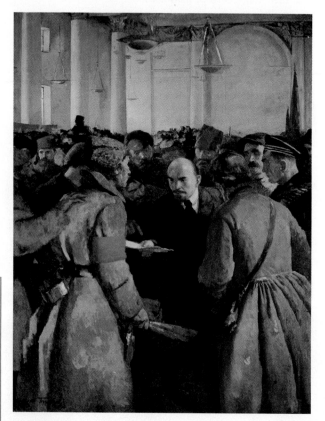

## THE COMMUNISTS COME TO POWER

As a young man, Lenin became a follower of Karl Marx. He helped found a Marxist group that later became known as the Russian Social Democratic Labor Party. Lenin strongly believed that only active revolutionaries should be allowed to become party members. This idea split the party in two. Those who followed Lenin became known as Bolsheviks (BOHL•shuh•viks).

After the fall of the czar, Lenin called for an end to the new democratic government. He believed that a communist government should lead Russia. Lenin and the Bolsheviks won many followers by promising, "Peace, Land, and Bread." These were the things the peasants and workers wanted most.

In early November 1917 Lenin and the Bolsheviks took control of the government. First, they signed peace treaties with the Central Powers and withdrew from World War I. Then, they made the Communist party the only legal political party in Russia. They also formed a secret police force, called the Cheka (CHAY•kuh). Saying "He who is not with us is against us," Lenin ordered the

# RUSSIAN EXPANSION, 1500–1922

ARCTIC OCEAN

0    500    1,000 Miles
0    500    1000 Kilometers
Two-Point Equidistant Projection

Baltic Sea
Barents Sea
Warsaw
Riga
Tallinn
St. Petersburg
Novgorod
Archangel'sk
Kiev
Moscow
Odessa
Black Sea
Volga River
Mediterranean Sea
Tiflis (Tbilisi)
Caspian Sea
Aral Sea
Omsk
Irkutsk
Bukhara
Gulf of Oman
Kamchatka Peninsula
Okhotsk
Sea of Okhotsk
Amur River
Vladivostok
Sea of Japan

Border of the Soviet Union, 1922

**Growth of Russia under:**

Ivan III, around 1500

Peter the Great, around 1725

Catherine the Great, around 1796

Nicholas I, around 1855

**HUMAN-ENVIRONMENT INTERACTIONS** Over the centuries Russia grew to include much of northern Asia.
■ Under whose rule did Russia grow most in size?

Cheka to track down anyone against his government. The Cheka killed or put into prison tens of thousands of men and women. The government of the czars had been replaced by one that was just as cruel.

Not all Russians were happy to see the Bolsheviks in control. Some who opposed them put together a fighting force called the White Army. The Bolsheviks then formed the Red Army. A civil war between Red and White followed. By 1921 the Red Army had defeated the White. The Bolsheviks were in control, but Russia was in ruins and many Russians were dead. Among the civil war's victims were Czar Nicholas II and his family, who had been executed by the Bolsheviks.

 **What did the Bolsheviks promise the Russian people?**

# STALIN AND TOTALITARIANISM

In 1922 Russia was renamed the Union of Soviet Socialist Republics. The word **soviet** refers to the workers' groups that planned and carried out the revolution. Lenin started rebuilding the country. After Lenin died in 1924, Joseph Stalin (STAH•luhn) took over the job of running the Union of Soviet Socialist Republics, or Soviet Union.

Stalin believed that his most important task was to make the Soviet Union one of the world's strongest nations. To produce more food, he ordered that farms be grouped together into **collectives**. These were large farms on which people worked together as a group. Stalin's secret police killed or put into prison peasants who were against the

Millions of people were sent to slave labor camps during Stalin's purges. Shown here are the barracks, or sleeping quarters, of one such labor camp.

collectives. He then had hundreds of huge factories built and forced people to work in them.

Stalin placed all parts of the economy under government control. In doing so he created a command economy. He then laid out a path for economic growth in five-year plans. The plans set up production schedules for farms and factories. By the late 1930s Stalin had met his goal of making the Soviet Union a leading industrial nation. But his success came at a high cost.

Most Soviet people now had jobs and enough food, but not much more. They had no voice in the government. In fact, when citizens protested and called for change, Stalin

ordered **purges**. All those who opposed him were killed or put into prison. Millions of his purge victims were sent to slave labor camps in Siberia.

Under Stalin the Soviet Union became a world power. It also became a **totalitarian** (toh•ta•luh•TAIR•ee•uhn) state—a state in which the government has complete control over people's lives. Even with all the changes, however, Soviet citizens had no more freedom or political power than they had had under the czars.

 **How did Stalin build a totalitarian state?**

# LESSON 2 REVIEW

## Check Understanding

1. **Recall the Facts** Who led the Bolsheviks to power?
2. **Focus on the Main Idea** In what ways was the government and the economy of Lenin and Stalin different from that of the czars? How was it similar?

## Think Critically

3. **Explore Viewpoints** Lenin and Stalin seemed to believe that any action to help the revolution was all right. Do you think the

leader of a democratic nation would have shared such a view? Explain your answer.
4. **Personally Speaking** If you had been a Russian peasant or worker in 1917, would you have supported Lenin? Why or why not?

## Show What You Know

 **Writing Activity** Russian revolutionaries often discussed the ideal society. Describe in writing your ideal society. Tell how it would be created.

# THE GREAT DEPRESSION

## Link to Our World

**How can events in one nation affect life in other nations?**

**Focus on the Main Idea**
*As you read, find out how an economic crisis in the United States added to problems in other countries.*

**Preview Vocabulary**
*Great Depression*
*inflation*
*propaganda*

In 1929 United States President Herbert Hoover said, "We have reached a higher degree of comfort and security than has ever existed before in the history of the world." For a while it looked as if he was right. After World War I, the United States and many other nations made economic progress. Unfortunately, the good times that followed the war did not last. The United States looked prosperous, but it had hidden economic problems.

## A DEPRESSION IN THE MAKING

The United States has always had a market economy. That is, the people decide which goods and services to buy and sell. They make choices about how to earn their living and spend their money.

Just after World War I, Americans made decisions to buy huge amounts of goods. Factories increased production to meet the demand of buyers. Over time, however, demand fell. People could not afford to keep buying more goods. Warehouses and stores soon overflowed with unsold goods. Even so, industries made more and more products, thinking that someone would buy them.

Government policies made the problem worse. To protect American farms and industries, the government put high taxes on goods imported into the United States. This made it harder for other countries to sell their goods in the United States. If they could not sell their own goods, they could not afford to buy American goods. The American economy suffered because of this.

Hard times during the Great Depression forced many people to wait in long lines at food kitchens.

As doubts about the strength of the economy grew, many people in the United States began to invest in the stock market. They bought and sold shares of stock in the hope of making a quick profit. Many people did make huge profits. But stockbrokers, or people who bought and sold stock for others, allowed buying on credit. The buyer paid the stockbroker only a small part of the actual price of the stock at the time of the sale. The broker expected the buyer to pay the rest of the price at a later date.

In October 1929 some major stock market investors, worried about the economy, began selling their stock. Panic set in. Soon nearly everyone wanted to sell stock, but few people wanted to buy. Stock prices went way down, or crashed. Brokers demanded the money that was owed them. Most investors, however, did not have the money to pay back what they owed. Many investors and brokers lost all their money.

Economic problems grew rapidly. Few people had money for goods and services. Factories already had full warehouses, so they cut back production and laid off workers. More and more people lost their jobs and worried about paying rent or making house payments. Many tried to withdraw their savings from banks. Most banks could not pay back so many people so quickly, though. Hundreds of banks closed.

As sources of money became scarce, more businesses closed. The failure of businesses left even more people without jobs. As the 1930s began, the United States began the worst economic decline in the world's history—the **Great Depression**.

 **What economic problems were hidden by the prosperity of the 1920s?**

## DEPRESSION SPREADS

The stock market "crash" ruined the economies of nations around the world. Many Americans had invested large amounts of money in Europe after World War I. After the crash they could not afford to keep their money invested abroad. The European

The Great Depression was the time of the worst economic trouble in the history of the world. This Oklahoma family travels in search of a better life. Oklahoma was part of the United States region that became known as the Dust Bowl. A series of dust storms and droughts ruined many farms in this region.

economy, already weak, suffered even more from the loss of American dollars. Banks closed, and people who had deposited money could not get it back. Factories shut down, putting millions out of work. In Asia, Africa, and South America, demand for raw materials dropped. Many people there suffered poverty and hunger. By the early 1930s the world economy was in a mess. World trade and production were down, and unemployment was the highest it had ever been.

As the depression dragged on, people who were out of work felt that their governments did not care about them. With unrest growing daily, people everywhere looked for political leaders who might offer them hope.

> **How did the Great Depression affect the world economy?**

**LEARNING FROM GRAPHS** The stock market crash brought about a time of high unemployment.
■ In what year did the United States face the highest unemployment?

**UNITED STATES UNEMPLOYMENT RATE**

President Roosevelt's "fireside chats" over the radio offered hopeful news about the economy of the United States.

## ROOSEVELT AND THE NEW DEAL

In 1933 most Americans felt they had found a leader who could help them. The new President, Franklin D. Roosevelt, had bold ideas to save the economy and was not afraid to try them out. "The only thing we have to fear is fear itself," he said.

Roosevelt proposed new laws and programs to help people quickly. He also urged Congress to pass laws to reform the economic system. Roosevelt called the new laws and programs the New Deal. The New Deal provided money to allow farmers to keep their land and to help people who were out of work. It created millions of new jobs by paying for many public works. An important New Deal law was the Social Security Act of 1935. This gave money to people who were retired, disabled, or unable to work for other reasons.

The New Deal changed the way the United States government operated. Never before had the government taken such a direct role in people's lives. Even so, the American democratic system remained basically unchanged. In some other countries, however, the search for solutions to the Great Depression meant an end to democracy.

> **What steps did President Roosevelt take to bring the United States out of the Great Depression?**

Ein Volk, ein Reich, ein Führer!

"One People, one Empire, one Leader!" reads this 1938 poster of Adolf Hitler.

## HITLER AND THE RISE OF THE NAZIS

After World War I, Germany became a federal republic. During the 1920s and 1930s, the German republic had terrible problems. Jobs were hard to find. Also, high **inflation**—a continuing increase in prices—made German money almost worthless.

Most German people had lost faith in their government. Many complained bitterly against the government for signing the Treaty of Versailles. They felt the treaty had turned Germany into a poor, weak country. They wanted a strong leader who would make Germany powerful again. Some thought that leader was Adolf Hitler.

Hitler had fought in World War I and felt the shame of Germany's loss. Shortly after the war, he began to look for a way to make up for the defeat. In 1920 he helped form a highly nationalistic, anticommunist group called the National Socialist, or Nazi (NAHT•see), party.

At first the party had little influence, and few people joined. However, when the Great Depression started, more and more people began listening to Hitler's emotional speeches. Many Germans liked his idea that the Germans were a "superrace," a group of people better than all others. Business people liked his promises to rebuild Germany's ruined economy.

By 1933 the Nazis had more elected representatives in the Reichstag (RYKS•tahk)—the German legislature—than any other party. Hitler forced Germany's president to make him chancellor, and he forced the Reichstag to give him control of the government. He then took the title of führer, leader of the German people.

German money had so little value that people often chose to burn it as fuel rather than use it to buy firewood.

# What?

## The Nazis and German Youth

The Nazis were successful partly because of support from young people. By 1930 a Nazi youth organization controlled student government at many German universities. By 1933 more than 40 percent of Nazi party members were under 30 years old. Once in power, Hitler set up the Hitler Youth for younger students. Many thousands joined. Some were so loyal that they turned in their own parents as traitors to the government.

As führer, Hitler banned all political parties except the Nazi party and put an end to elections. He also formed a strong secret police force called the Gestapo. The Gestapo arrested anyone who disagreed with Hitler's government. At the same time, Hitler began to rebuild Germany's army.

To get the people to accept all these actions, Hitler used propaganda. **Propaganda** is the spreading of information or rumors to help or hurt a cause. To spread his propaganda, Hitler took control of newspapers, radio stations, and schools. He also screamed speeches filled with hate to huge crowds.

A key part of Hitler's message was that Germany's political and economic troubles were the fault of the Jewish people. Hitler argued that the Jews had to lose their economic power and their place in society for Germany to become strong again. The Nazi party propaganda convinced many Germans that Hitler was right. Most did not complain when he passed laws that took away Jewish citizens' rights and property.

✓ **How did Hitler and the Nazis take control in Germany?**

# LESSON 3 REVIEW

## Check Understanding

1. **Recall the Facts** What event marked the beginning of the Great Depression in the United States?
2. **Focus on the Main Idea** How did economic problems in the United States lead to problems in other countries?

## Think Critically

3. **Think More About It** How were the political reactions to the Great Depression in Germany different from those in the United States?
4. **Past to Present** Do totalitarian forms of government still exist? If so, in what countries are they found?

## Show What You Know

**Chart Activity** Prepare a chart that shows how the economic problems of the Great Depression created a "vicious circle" in the United States.

# REVIEW

## CONNECT MAIN IDEAS

Use this organizer to show that you understand how the chapter's main ideas are connected. Copy the organizer onto a separate sheet of paper. Then complete it by writing three details to support each main idea.

**World War I**
Alliances of nations led to World War I.

1. _____
2. _____
3. _____

**The Russian Revolution**
The Russian government changed yet stayed much the same after the Russian Revolution of 1917.

1. _____
2. _____
3. _____

**The Early Twentieth Century**

**The Great Depression**
An economic crisis led to the Great Depression and affected countries around the world.

1. _____
2. _____
3. _____

## WRITE MORE ABOUT IT

1. **Write a News Story** Imagine that you are a news reporter in the early 1900s. Write a news story to tell the people of the United States about life in Europe in the months before the Great War. Describe how events in Europe affect the United States.

2. **Write a Letter** Imagine that you are a young man or woman whose life has changed because of the United States' entry into the Great War. Write a letter to a relative, telling how the war has affected your life.

3. **Write a Diary Entry** Imagine that you are a student during the Great Depression. Write a diary entry describing your thoughts about a cousin's family that has no money and so has moved in with you.

4. **Write a Song** Imagine that you are a songwriter during the Great Depression. Write one or more verses of a song that describes the hardships people are facing. Once you have written your song, you may want to perform it for your family or your class.

# USE VOCABULARY

For each pair of terms, write a sentence or two that explains how the terms are related.

1. armistice, arms race
2. autocrat, czar
3. communism, collectives
4. conscription, militarism
5. purge, totalitarian

# CHECK UNDERSTANDING

1. How did nationalism contribute to war in Europe?

2. Which countries formed the Triple Alliance? Which countries formed the Triple Entente?

3. Why did Austria-Hungary declare war on Serbia in 1914?

4. How did the role of women change during World War I?

5. How did new technology affect the number of deaths and injuries during World War I?

6. Why was the peace that followed the Treaty of Versailles an "uneasy peace"?

7. How did the Bolsheviks encourage the peasants and workers of Russia to support them?

8. Under which leader did the Soviet Union become a world power?

9. Who was affected by the United States' stock market crash of 1929?

10. What problems in Germany helped Hitler rise to power?

# THINK CRITICALLY

1. **Past to Present**   In what ways do alliances between people today help them? In what ways can alliances hurt people?

2. **Cause and Effect**   What effect do you think the new roles of women during World War I had on everyday life after the war?

3. **Think More About It**   Why did the democratic system in the United States stay unchanged after World War I? Why did democracy end in some other parts of the world?

4. **Personally Speaking**   What do you think made President Roosevelt a strong leader during the Great Depression?

5. **Explore Viewpoints**   Why do you think the German people listened to Hitler?

# APPLY SKILLS

 **How to Use a Time Zone Map**   Use the time zone map on page 543 to answer these questions.

1. Raju lives in Delhi, India. At 8:00 P.M. his time, he telephones his uncle in Montreal, Canada. What time is it in Montreal?

2. Sarah is traveling by automobile west from New York City. Her trip will cross two time zones. Should she set her watch back or forward for each time zone she crosses?

3. Justin lives in Chicago. He wants to communicate by computer to a pen pal in Cairo. Justin sends his message at 9 A.M. What time is it in Cairo, Egypt, when Justin sends his message?

# READ MORE ABOUT IT

*The Night the Bells Rang* by Natalie Kinsey-Warnock. Cobblehill. During the last year of World War I, a Vermont farm boy helps with chores and feels the effects of the war overseas.

*No Hero for the Kaiser* by Rudolf Frank. Lothrop, Lee & Shepard. A Polish boy whose town is invaded in World War I joins the German army and sees for himself the horrors of battle.

# CHAPTER 20

# THE LATER TWENTIETH CENTURY

> ❝ From Stettin in the Baltic to Trieste in the Adriatic, an iron curtain has descended across the Continent. ❞
>
> Sir Winston Churchill, former British prime minister, 1946

A United States marine in Vietnam

# WORLD WAR II

## Link to Our World

**How can the desire of some people to control others lead to war?**

**Focus on the Main Idea**
As you read, find out how some people's attempts to control others led to a second war that involved the whole world.

**Preview Vocabulary**
fascism
appeasement
concentration camp
genocide
Holocaust
refugee

Benito Mussolini with his highest-ranking officers

By 1939 Hitler had turned his slogan "One People, One Empire, One Leader" into reality. His Nazi party ruled Germany's government, army, and press. Through his propaganda and fiery speeches, Hitler had gained control over the minds and emotions of the German people. In time Germany would join forces with Italy and Japan to try to control much of the world.

## SEEDS OF WAR

Hitler's Nazi party followed a set of political ideas known as **fascism** (FA•shih•zuhm). Fascists valued strong government control, military strength, and intense nationalism. They admired strong leaders and cared little for the freedoms and rights that are important to democracy.

Many Italians were unhappy with the small gains of land they received under the Treaty of Versailles. They also disliked the way their government had handled the country's economic problems. Many wanted change.

Led by Benito Mussolini (moo•suh•LEE•nee), the Fascist party quickly gained support among the Italian people. The Fascists soon took steps to take power. "Either they will give us the government or we shall seize it," Mussolini said boldly. The Italian king gave in to pressure and named Mussolini prime minister in 1922. Mussolini banned all political parties except the Fascist party. He then set up a secret police force and limited the freedom of the press.

Around this time Japan also had a change in government. There, however, the army, rather than a political party, took charge. A group of army officers gained control of the country and promised to build a great empire.

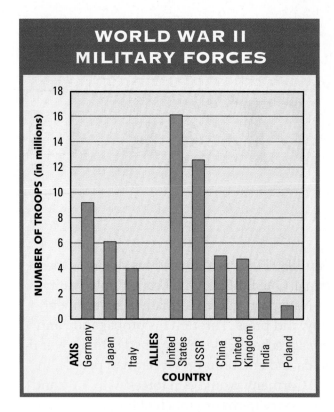

## WORLD WAR II MILITARY FORCES

**NUMBER OF TROOPS (in millions)** (vertical axis: 0, 2, 4, 6, 8, 10, 12, 14, 16, 18)

**AXIS:** Germany, Japan, Italy
**ALLIES:** United States, USSR, China, United Kingdom, India, Poland

**COUNTRY**

**LEARNING FROM GRAPHS** Troops from around the world took part in World War II.
■ Which nation supplied more troops, Italy or China?

By the mid-1930s Japan, Italy, and Germany were making their dreams of empire a reality. In 1935 Italy conquered the African country of Ethiopia. In 1937 the Japanese military swept into the middle of China. In 1938 the Germans took control of Austria and parts of Czechoslovakia.

European leaders did very little to stop the German and Italian takeovers. They did not want to risk another world war. Also, many of them thought that the Fascists' desire for glory and power would soon be met. This policy of not opposing the fascists became known as **appeasement**.

In 1939 the Germans showed that they would not be satisfied. They seized the rest of Czechoslovakia and attacked Poland. Britain and France felt that Hitler had gone too far. They declared war on Germany.

 **What were some of the reasons for the start of war in 1939?**

## WORLDWIDE CONFLICT

Hitler's soldiers had been training for war for years. Once their tanks and dive-bombers went into action, German forces seemed unstoppable. By 1940 Germany had taken over Poland, Denmark, Norway, Belgium, the Netherlands, and France.

Britain remained undefeated. The British leader, Winston Churchill, inspired his people to resist. Even in the worst times, Churchill encouraged his people with words like these:

66We shall fight on the beaches, we shall fight on the landing grounds, we shall fight in the fields and in the streets, we shall fight in the hills; we shall never surrender. 99

Failing to take Britain in 1940, Hitler turned his attention elsewhere. With Mussolini he planned to conquer the Mediterranean region. And even though Hitler had made a peace agreement with Stalin, he attacked the Soviet Union in mid-1941. After the attack, the Soviet Union joined the Allies.

Meanwhile, the Japanese rapidly added to their Asian empire. They captured other areas of China and much of Indochina, the eastern part of a peninsula just south of

Bombs dropped during air raids by Germany caused much destruction in Britain. In this 1940 photograph Winston Churchill inspects bomb damage.

Some of the many faces of war: (left to right) African American artillery troops, American troops in Tunisia, a wartime poster for recruiting women.

China. They also began to move across the Pacific, capturing island after island.

Then, in 1941, Germany, Italy, and Japan—the Axis Powers—faced a number of setbacks. In December 1941 the Japanese bombed the United States naval base at Pearl Harbor in Hawaii. Immediately the United States joined Britain and the Soviet Union in the war against the Axis Powers. Also, the Germans were caught up in a long and bitter struggle against Soviet military forces and Soviet winters. The advantage the Axis Powers had once held over the Allies began to slip away.

In late 1942 and in 1943, the Allies won victories against the Germans and Italians in North Africa and Sicily. Early in 1943 the German army was forced to pull back from the Soviet Union. Soviet troops then began to move into eastern Europe on their way to Germany. The Italians surrendered in September 1943. Meanwhile, the Allies were winning naval battles in the Pacific.

 **Which events in 1941 proved to be turning points in the war? Why?**

## THE WAR ENDS

In mid-1944 the Allies felt ready to take on Hitler's forces in northern Europe. Their plan involved landing large numbers of Allied soldiers on the beaches of Normandy in northern France. The June 6 invasion—code-named D day—did not go smoothly. Some troops landed on the beach only to find steep cliffs ahead. German soldiers immediately began shooting.

But the Allies held the beaches. Within a month they had moved far inland. By late August they had taken Paris from the Germans and had destroyed German cities in bombing raids. On May 7, 1945, the Germans surrendered, ending the war in Europe.

In the Pacific the Allies were slowly driving the Japanese back. First they began taking Japanese-held islands. Then in the spring of 1945, the Allies bombed Japanese cities. They destroyed Japan's war industries and left most of its cities in ruins. The Japanese, however, showed no signs of surrender.

On August 6, 1945, the United States dropped a terrible new weapon, the atomic

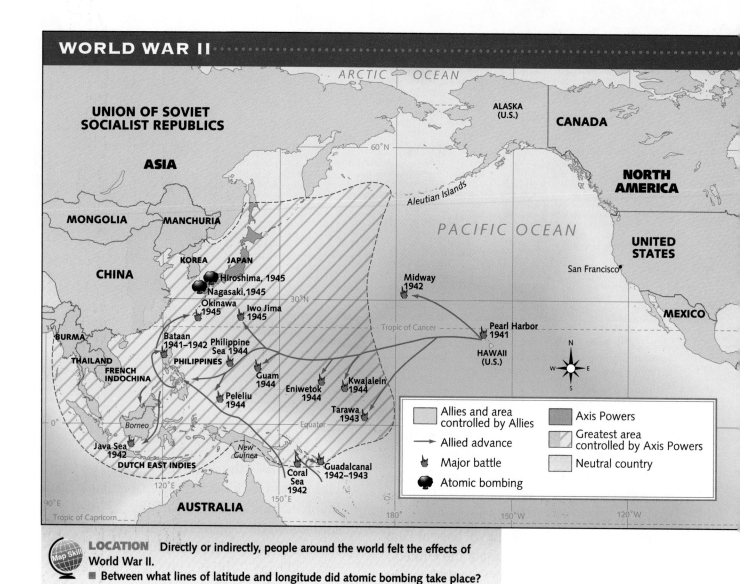

ARCTIC OCEAN

UNION OF SOVIET
SOCIALIST REPUBLICS

ALASKA
(U.S.)

CANADA

ASIA

60°N

NORTH
AMERICA

MONGOLIA    MANCHURIA

Aleutian Islands

PACIFIC OCEAN

UNITED
STATES

KOREA    JAPAN

San Francisco

CHINA

Hiroshima, 1945
Nagasaki,1945

Midway
1942

Okinawa
1945    Iwo Jima
1945

30°N

MEXICO

BURMA

Bataan
1941–1942   Philippine
Sea 1944

Tropic of Cancer

Pearl Harbor
1941

THAILAND
FRENCH
INDOCHINA

PHILIPPINES

HAWAII
(U.S.)

N

Guam
1944

Kwajalein
1944

W        E

Peleliu
1944

Eniwetok
1944

S

0°

Tarawa
1943

Borneo

Equator

Allies and area
controlled by Allies

Axis Powers

Java Sea
1942

New
Guinea

Allied advance

Greatest area
controlled by Axis Powers

DUTCH EAST INDIES

Guadalcanal
1942–1943

Major battle

Neutral country

Coral
Sea
1942

Atomic bombing

120°E

150°E

AUSTRALIA

90°E

180°

150°W

120°W

Tropic of Capricorn

**LOCATION**  Directly or indirectly, people around the world felt the effects of
World War II.

■ Between what lines of latitude and longitude did atomic bombing take place?

bomb, on the Japanese city of Hiroshima
(hir•uh•SHEE•muh). The explosion of the
atomic bomb sent shock waves that knocked
down buildings miles away. Its heat melted
stone and steel and turned human bodies
into gases. This "rain of ruin from the air"
killed more than 70,000 people and destroyed
much of Hiroshima. Three days later a
second atomic bomb exploded over the city
of Nagasaki. Once again, the explosion
caused terrible damage. Finally the Japanese
offered to surrender.

✓ **How did the Allies gain victory in
Europe and in the Pacific during
World War II?**

## THE HOLOCAUST

As the Allies marched through Europe,
they began to realize the full horror of what
the Nazis had done. Hitler believed that to
rebuild after World War I, Germany had to
rid itself of "undesirable" people. In this way
the pure German Aryan race, as he called it,
could become a master race and conquer the
world. Hitler put into action his plan to get
rid of all those he thought were inferior—
especially the Jews. Gypsies, persons with
disabilities, and opponents of Nazism were
also targets of Hitler's hate.

The first arrests of Jews began in the early
1940s. Those who were arrested were sent to

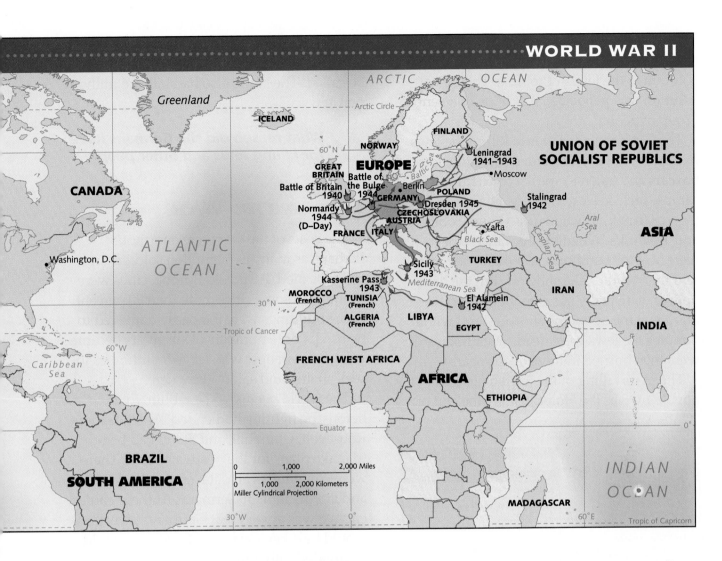

a type of prison called a **concentration camp**. Many of the prisoners in the camps served as slave labor for the German war effort. Others were killed.

To avoid capture many Jews were forced to go into hiding. The Frank family of Amsterdam, a city in the Netherlands, will long be remembered for how they lived in secret. The Franks had earlier fled Germany because Jews there were being terrorized. When Jews in Amsterdam started being sent to concentration camps, the Franks hid above their family business. Anne, the younger daughter, kept a diary about her family's life in hiding. Her diary gives us a touching description of the pain that many suffered during this time. Tragically, Anne was discovered by the Nazis and sent to a concentration camp, where she died.

The Nazis purposely made camp conditions terrible. In most camps guards beat inmates for no reason. In some, such as Auschwitz (OWSH•vits), Nazi doctors used prisoners for strange and cruel medical experiments.

⬆ Young prisoners at Auschwitz

Anne Frank ➡

During the winter of 1941–1942, Germany's leaders developed what they called the Final Solution to the Jewish Problem. Their Final Solution was **genocide**, the killing of an entire group of people.

The Germans' plan was to kill all the Jews in Europe. Jews were herded like cattle into boxcars and taken to special concentration camps, such as Auschwitz, Majdanek (my•DAH•nek), Dachau (DAH•kow), Sobibór, and Treblinka. When they got there, they were sent to "bathhouses," where they were told they would take showers. But the bath-houses were really gas chambers. A poison-ous gas came out of the showers, and within minutes the Jews were dead. Their bodies were then burned in huge ovens nearby.

The mass killing of the Jewish people is now known as the **Holocaust**. By the end of the war, 6 million Jews had died in the death camps, as the concentration camps came to be called. The Nazis also had killed 6 million non-Jews.

 **What reason did the Germans have for killing Jews and other people?**

## AFTER THE WAR

The costs of the war were enormous. Perhaps as many as 50 million soldiers and civilians died. All across Europe, cities were in ruins. In some cities more than 90 percent of the buildings were too badly damaged to be used. Large numbers of survivors became **refugees**—people who leave their homes to seek shelter and safety elsewhere.

The world needed to be rebuilt. Even before the fighting had ended, Allied leaders Roosevelt, Churchill, and Stalin had begun to make plans for the postwar world. There were conferences at Yalta, on the Black Sea, and at Potsdam, in Germany. At these confer-ences it was agreed that Germany's weapons would be taken away and Germany would be divided into four zones. Britain, the United States, the Soviet Union, and France would govern these zones. Berlin, the German capital, located in the eastern Soviet zone, would be divided in a similar way. A new international organization, the United Nations, would replace the old League of Nations and help prevent new wars.

The future of eastern Europe was not decided. The Soviet Union had set up com-munist governments in several eastern European nations. Stalin wanted these gov-ernments to remain. The United States and Britain did not. It soon became clear that the alliance that had won the war was already starting to come apart.

 **What were the results of the Yalta and Potsdam conferences?**

**BERLIN, 1945**

Berlin • POLAND
EAST GERMANY
CZECHOSLOVAKIA
WEST FRANCE GERMANY
AUSTRIA

- American sector
- British sector
- French sector
- Soviet sector
- Canal
- Road

EAST GERMANY

West Berlin

East Berlin

Charlottenburg Palace
Brandenburg Gate
Checkpoint Charlie
West Berlin
Tempelhof Airport

Havel River
Spree R.

Potsdam

0   3   6 Miles
0   3   6 Kilometers
Transverse Mercator Projection

**REGIONS** After the war the city of Berlin was divided into four sectors, or parts.
■ In which part was Charlottenburg Palace?

# THE UNITED NATIONS

## INTERNATIONAL COURT OF JUSTICE

Hears and decides legal disputes between nations

Interprets the UN Charter and international law

Made up of 15 elected judges

## SECURITY COUNCIL

Deals with disputes between nations

Recommends settlements for disputes

May send troops to settle disputes

Made up of 5 permanent members (France, Britain, China, Russia, and the United States) and 10 elected members

## TRUSTEESHIP COUNCIL

Deals with territories that are not self-governing

Made up of representatives from the governments overseeing the non self-governing nations as well as permanent members of the Security Council

## GENERAL ASSEMBLY

Discusses and makes recommendations about world problems

Controls UN finances

Made up of one representative from each member nation

## SECRETARIAT

Manages day-to-day business of the UN

Made up of an elected Secretary-General and a staff of interpreters, guides, writers, and clerks

## ECONOMIC AND SOCIAL COUNCIL

Studies and makes recommendations about economic and social problems

Promotes human rights

Works with specialized agencies and commissions

Made up of 54 representatives

**LEARNING FROM CHARTS**   The chart above shows the six main agencies of the United Nations. Each agency has its own duties and responsibilities.
- Which agency decides whether the UN will send peace-keeping troops to a war-torn nation?

# LESSON 1 REVIEW

## Check Understanding

1. **Recall the Facts**   What were the three major Axis Powers?
2. **Focus on the Main Idea**   How did the desires of some people to control others lead to a world war?

## Think Critically

3. **Cause and Effect**   What factors led to the rise of fascism in Europe?
4. **Explore Viewpoints**   What arguments might people in the United States have made against getting into the war?

5. **Past to Present**   Do people today still try to gain control over other people? Explain your answer, using present-day examples.

## Show What You Know

**News-Reporting Activity**
Imagine that you are a radio news reporter at the start of World War II. Write a brief report explaining the rise of fascism. Be sure to answer the questions Who? What? Where? When? Why? and How? about your subject. If you have a tape recorder, you might tape your report and "broadcast" it to the class.

# HOW TO

# Use a Double-Bar Graph

## Why Is This Skill Important?

A good way to compare statistics is by making a graph. **Statistics** are facts shown with numbers. **Double-bar graphs**, such as those in this lesson, make it easy to compare two sets of statistics.

## Statistics of World War II

World War II was the most destructive war in world history. More people were killed or wounded in World War II than in any other war. No one knows how many civilians died. Millions of people in war-torn areas died from hunger or disease when food production and health services stopped. Bombing raids often destroyed the records that showed

how many people were killed. In all, as many as 20 million Soviet civilians and 10 million Chinese civilians may have died.

More is known, however, about the casualties —people killed or wounded—in the military. Of the more than 70 million people who served in the armed forces of the Allies and the Axis Powers, about 17 million were killed and another 17 million were wounded.

A United States Army nurse feeds a wounded soldier in this 1943 photograph taken during World War II.

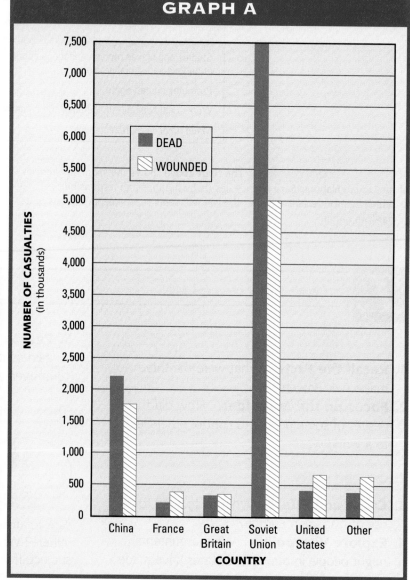

## Understand the Process

The double-bar graphs on these two pages show by country the numbers of those who were killed and those who were wounded. Graph A shows the Allies' casualties, and Graph B shows the Axis Powers' casualties. Use these steps as a guide to study the graphs.

1. Look at the words and numbers along the bottom and left-hand side of each graph. Countries are listed along the bottom, and the numbers of people are listed along the left-hand side.

2. Notice that there are two different kinds of bars for each country. The solid-colored bar shows the number who died. The striped bar shows the number who were wounded.

3. Read each graph by running your finger up to the top of each bar and then left to the number. If the top of the bar is between two numbers, the correct number is between those two.

4. Compare the heights of the solid-colored bars for any two countries. Which country had more people killed?

5. Compare the heights of the striped bars for any two countries. Which country had more people wounded?

6. Compare the heights of the solid-colored bar and the striped bar for any one country. Which bar is higher? How much higher is one bar than the other?

7. Now compare the heights of all the bars to compare casualties among all the countries. How do the double-bar graphs help you understand the human cost of World War II?

## Think and Apply

Make a double-bar graph of your test scores in social studies and in your other subjects. List the subjects along the bottom of your graph. Along the left-hand side, list possible test scores by tens from 0 percent on the bottom to 100 percent at the top. For each subject, make two bars to show your next two test scores. Remember to use different colors or solids and stripes for the first and second tests. Study your completed graph. What does it tell you?

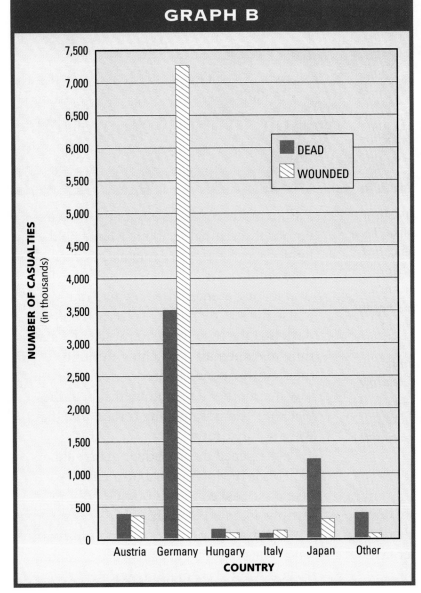

GRAPH B

NUMBER OF CASUALTIES (in thousands)

DEAD
WOUNDED

Austria   Germany   Hungary   Italy   Japan   Other
COUNTRY

# Number the STARS

## by Lois Lowry   illustrated by Tony Meers

*As the Nazis marched across Europe, they subjected Jewish people to special abuse. They forced Jews to live in segregated areas called ghettos. They also made Jews wear yellow Stars of David, six-pointed stars that are a symbol of Judaism. Later, as the Nazis began their Final Solution, they sent millions of Jewish people to concentration camps.*

*Now read about how a Danish couple protected a Jewish child, Ellen, by pretending she was their oldest daughter, who had actually died. As you read, consider how responsible people should be for protecting the rights of others.*

**A**nnemarie eased the bedroom door open quietly, only a crack, and peeked out. Behind her, Ellen was sitting up, her eyes wide.

She could see Mama and Papa in their nightclothes, moving about. Mama held a lighted candle, but as Annemarie watched, she went to a lamp and switched it on. It was so long a time since they had dared to use the strictly rationed electricity after dark that the light in the room seemed startling to Annemarie, watching through the slightly opened bedroom door. She saw her mother look automatically to the blackout curtains, making certain that they were tightly drawn.

Papa opened the front door to the soldiers.

"This is the Johansen apartment?" A deep voice asked the question loudly, in terribly accented Danish.

"Our name is on the door, and I see you have a flashlight," Papa answered. "What do you want? Is something wrong?"

"I understand you are a friend of your neighbors the Rosens, Mrs. Johansen," the soldier said angrily.

"Sophy Rosen is my friend, that is true," Mama said quietly. "Please, could you speak more softly? My children are asleep."

"Then you will be so kind as to tell me where the Rosens are." He made no effort to lower his voice.

"I assume they are at home, sleeping. It is four in the morning, after all," Mama said.

Annemarie heard the soldier stalk across the living room toward the kitchen. From her hiding place in the narrow sliver of open doorway, she could see the heavy uniformed man, a holstered pistol at his waist, in the entrance to the kitchen, peering in toward the sink.

Another German voice said, "The Rosens' apartment is empty. We are wondering if they might be visiting their good friends the Johansens."

"Well," said Papa, moving slightly so that he was standing in front of Annemarie's bedroom door, and she could see nothing except the dark blur of his back, "as you see, you are mistaken. There is no one here but my family."

"You will not object if we look around." The voice was harsh, and it was not a question.

"It seems we have no choice," Papa replied.

"Please don't wake my children," Mama requested again. "There is no need to frighten little ones."

The heavy, booted feet moved across the floor again and into the other bedroom. A closet door opened and closed with a bang.

Annemarie eased her bedroom door closed silently. She stumbled through the darkness to the bed.

"Ellen," she whispered urgently, "take your necklace[1] off!"

Ellen's hands flew to her neck. Desperately she began trying to unhook the tiny clasp. Outside the bedroom door, the harsh voices and heavy footsteps continued.

"I can't get it open!" Ellen said frantically. "I never take it off—I can't even remember how to open it!"

Annemarie heard a voice just outside the door. "What is here?"

"Shhh," her mother replied. "My daughters' bedroom. They are sound asleep."

"Hold still," Annemarie commanded. "This will hurt." She grabbed the little gold chain, yanked with all her strength, and broke it. As the door opened and light flooded into the bedroom, she crumpled it into her hand and closed her fingers tightly.

Terrified, both girls looked up at the three Nazi officers who entered the room.

One of the men aimed a flashlight around the bedroom. He went to the closet and looked inside. Then with a sweep of his gloved hand he pushed to the floor several coats and a bathrobe that hung from pegs on the wall.

There was nothing else in the room except a chest of drawers, the blue decorated trunk in the corner, and a heap of Kirsti's dolls piled in a small rocking chair. The flashlight beam touched each thing in turn. Angrily the officer turned toward the bed.

"Get up!" he ordered. "Come out here!"

Trembling, the two girls rose from the bed and followed him, brushing past the two remaining officers in the doorway, to the living room.

---

[1] **necklace:** The necklace was a gold chain with a Star of David attached to it.

Annemarie looked around. These three uniformed men were different from the ones on the street corners. The street soldiers were often young, sometimes ill at ease, and Annemarie remembered how [one] had, for a moment, let his harsh pose slip and had smiled at Kirsti.

But these men were older and their faces were set with anger.

Her parents were standing beside each other, their faces tense, but Kirsti was nowhere in sight. Thank goodness that Kirsti slept through almost everything. If they had wakened her, she would be wailing—or worse, she would be angry, and her fists would fly.

"Your names?" the officer barked.

"Annemarie Johansen. And this is my sister—"

"Quiet! Let her speak for herself. Your name?" He was glaring at Ellen.

Ellen swallowed. "Lise," she said, and cleared her throat. "Lise Johansen."

The officer stared at them grimly.

"Now," Mama said in a strong voice, "you have seen that we are not hiding anything. May my children go back to bed?"

The officer ignored her. Suddenly he grabbed a handful of Ellen's hair. Ellen winced.

He laughed scornfully. "You have a blond child sleeping in the other room. And you have this blond daughter—" He gestured toward Annemarie with his head. "Where did you get the dark-haired one?" He twisted the lock of Ellen's hair. "From a different father? From the milkman?"

Papa stepped forward. "Don't speak to my wife in such a way. Let go of my daughter or I will report you for such treatment."

"Or maybe you got her someplace else?" the officer continued with a sneer. "From the Rosens?"

For a moment no one spoke. Then Annemarie, watching in panic, saw her father move swiftly to the small bookcase and take out a book. She saw that he was holding the family photograph album. Very quickly he searched through its pages, found what he was looking for, and tore out three pictures from three separate pages.

He handed them to the German officer, who released Ellen's hair.

"You will see each of my daughters, each with her name written on the photograph," Papa said.

Annemarie knew instantly which photographs he had chosen. The album had many snapshots—all the poorly focused pictures of school events and birthday parties. But it also contained a portrait, taken by a photographer, of each girl as a tiny infant. Mama had written, in her delicate handwriting, the name of each baby daughter across the bottom of those photographs.

She realized too, with an icy feeling, why Papa had torn them from the book. At the bottom of each page, below the photograph itself, was written the date. And the real Lise Johansen had been born twenty-one years earlier.

"Kirsten Elisabeth," the officer read, looking at Kirsti's baby picture. He let the photograph fall to the floor.

"Annemarie," he read next, glanced at her, and dropped the second photograph.

"Lise Margrete," he read finally, and stared at Ellen for a long unwavering moment. In her mind, Annemarie pictured the photograph that he held: the baby, wide-eyed, propped against a pillow, her tiny hand holding a silver teething ring, her bare feet visible below the hem of an embroidered dress. The wispy curls. Dark.

The officer tore the photograph in half and dropped the pieces on the floor. Then he turned, the heels of his shiny boots grinding into the pictures, and left the apartment. Without a word, the other two officers followed. Papa stepped forward and closed the door behind him.

Annemarie relaxed the clenched fingers of her right hand, which still clutched Ellen's necklace. She looked down, and saw that she had imprinted the Star of David into her palm.

## Literature Review

1. What made Annemarie think the men were not ordinary soldiers?
2. How did Annemarie and her parents show courage and cleverness in protecting Ellen from the Nazis?
3. Write a diary entry that Ellen Rosen might have written the day following the events described in the story. Be sure to include how Ellen felt about the actions of the Johansens.

# LESSON 3

# COLD WAR TENSIONS

## Link to Our World

**How can differing ideas about economics and government lead to conflict today?**

*Focus on the Main Idea*
*As you read, think about how differing ideas about economics and government led to tensions and fighting in the years after World War II.*

*Preview Vocabulary*
superpower      limited war
Cold War         détente
containment

After World War II the United States and the Soviet Union became the world's most powerful nations. Tensions between these two **superpowers** soon arose. Americans and Europeans feared that the Soviets wanted to make other nations communist and would use force to meet this goal. Such fears led to a new kind of conflict, the **Cold War**. During this time the two superpowers did not fight face to face. They did, however, prepare for war with all kinds of weapons. Both sides wanted to have not only the most weapons but also the most powerful weapons.

## THE SUPERPOWERS COMPETE IN EUROPE

In 1946 Winston Churchill said that an "iron curtain" had "descended across the Continent" of Europe. He noted that all the nations to the east of this curtain were under Soviet control. Churchill had good reason to say this. The Soviet Union had promised free elections in the eastern European nations it had freed from Nazi control. But the Soviets had not kept their promise. Instead, they banned all opposition to the communist governments they had set up in those nations.

Many Americans urged their government to adopt a policy of **containment**. That is, they wanted to develop ways to keep the Soviets from gaining control of other countries. In 1947 President Harry S. Truman said that the United States would give money and supplies to help any nation that wanted to keep out the Soviets. Truman also suggested that the United States was prepared to give

The European Recovery Program (ERP), or Marshall Plan, helped European countries rebuild their economies.

E·R·P

You hold the Key

# EUROPEAN ALLIANCES IN 1955

**Legend:**
- NATO country
- Noncommunist country not in NATO
- Warsaw Pact country
- Communist country not in Warsaw Pact

Canada and the United States are also NATO members.

**REGIONS** By 1955 most European nations had joined an alliance.
■ In what part of Europe were most of the Warsaw Pact members located? In what part of Europe were most of the NATO members located?

military help to any such nation. This new policy became known as the Truman Doctrine.

Truman also saw to it that the European Recovery Act, or the Marshall Plan, passed Congress in 1948. This plan provided $12 billion to help the European countries rebuild their economies. Truman believed that an economically healthy Europe would have little interest in communism.

To speed up the work of the Marshall Plan, Britain, France, and the United States decided to unite their zones in Germany and create a new German government. The Soviet Union saw this action as a threat to its control of eastern Germany. Immediately the Soviets blocked all land and water routes between the western part of Germany and the western zone of Berlin. Britain and the United States

then began sending supplies by air to Berlin. In May 1949, after 11 months, the Soviets ended the blockade.

The Western countries continued with their plans to form the democratic Federal Republic of Germany. The Soviets created the communist German Democratic Republic, or East Germany, in their zone. The city of Berlin was also divided into two parts.

In 1949 the Western powers formed a military alliance called the North Atlantic Treaty Organization (NATO) to help defend themselves against Soviet attack. In 1955 Soviet leaders organized the eastern European nations into an opposing alliance called the Warsaw Pact.

 **What was the Western response to the threat of Soviet expansion?**

# THE SPREAD OF COMMUNISM IN ASIA

The Cold War soon spread beyond Europe to Asia. In 1945, communists fought to take over the Chinese government. In October 1949 they set up a communist state called the People's Republic of China. Beijing, then known as Peking, became its capital.

The conflict between communism and democracy next spread to Korea. After World War II Korea had been divided into two parts, with Soviet forces in the north and American troops in the south. With the Soviets' help, a communist government took control of North Korea. In June 1950, North Korean soldiers crossed the border into South Korea in an attempt to reunite the country under communism. The United States and the United Nations quickly sent troops to help the South Koreans. The Soviet Union and newly communist China gave aid to the North Koreans. Tensions between the communist and noncommunist nations reached an all-time high level. Many people felt that these tensions might explode into another world war.

Refugee women and children pass American soldiers marching into the Naktong River area of Korea.

President Truman wanted to keep the conflict from spreading. Still, he decided that the conflict would be a **limited war**. This meant that the United States would not insist on total victory. This decision made it less likely that atomic, or nuclear, weapons would be

## THE KOREAN WAR

CHINA

SOVIET UNION

NORTH KOREA
- Chosan
- Iwon
- Hungnam
- Wonsan
P'yongyang

38th Parallel (pre-war boundary line)
Panmunjom
Inchon
Seoul

Yellow Sea

Sea of Japan

SOUTH KOREA
- Taejon
- Taegu
- Pusan

0    50    100 Miles
0    50    100 Kilometers
Conic Projection

42°N
40°N
38°N
36°N

124°E    126°E    128°E    130°E

→ North Korean troops, beginning June 1950
→ UN troops, beginning September 1950
→ Chinese troops, beginning October 1950
→ UN troops, beginning January 1951
— Boundary line, formed July 1953
⊛ Capital

**LOCATION** North Korea hoped to unite all of Korea under one communist government.
■ Why would you expect heavy fighting on the land around 38°N?

used. This was a fear because the Soviet Union had tested its first nuclear bomb in 1949.

In 1953 both sides agreed to end the war. Their truce set a new border between North Korea and South Korea, near the 38th parallel. Although the fighting in Korea stopped, the Cold War continued.

 **Why were Cold War tensions at their worst in the early 1950s?**

## KHRUSHCHEV AND KENNEDY

In 1958 Nikita Khrushchev (nuh•KEE•tuh KRUSH•chawf) became leader of the Soviet Union. As the Soviet leader, Khrushchev used harsh methods to control the eastern European communist countries. At the same time, he led Western nations to believe there could be peace. "Peaceful coexistence among different systems of government is possible," Khrushchev said. As a step in improving Soviet–American relations, he visited the United States.

This thaw in the Cold War did not last long. In the 1960s the United States and the Soviet Union came very near to war. In May 1961 Khrushchev demanded that United States President John F. Kennedy remove all American troops from West Berlin. The Soviets said the troops were a threat to East Germany. President Kennedy refused. Khrushchev threatened to use nuclear weapons if the Americans did not leave. Kennedy still stood firm.

In August, East German troops set up a fence of bricks and barbed wire between East and West Berlin. They wanted to stop East Germans from running to freedom in West Berlin. Kennedy answered by sending more troops to the city. Khrushchev also sent more troops. The danger of war seemed very real. Then the Soviet troops left.

Tensions eased after this, but the fence stayed. In time the East Germans replaced

U.S. President Kennedy and Soviet leader Khrushchev shake hands in Vienna in 1961 (above). Berliners look over the wall that divided their city (right). How do you think the division of Berlin affected those who lived there?

the barbed wire with the concrete Berlin Wall. The wall soon became a symbol of the Cold War and the division between the free world and the communists.

Shortly after the Berlin crisis, another conflict came about. This time the location was Cuba, a small island nation south of Florida. In 1959, revolutionaries led by Fidel Castro had taken control of the island. The Castro government quickly formed close ties with the Soviet Union.

The strength of those ties became clear in 1962. Americans learned that the Soviet

Union had built launching sites for nuclear missiles in Cuba, less than 100 miles (161 km) from the coast of Florida. President Kennedy ordered a blockade of ships around Cuba to stop the Soviets from shipping military supplies to the island. When Soviet cargo ships began sailing toward the blockade, war seemed certain.

Suddenly the Soviet ships turned around. "We're eyeball to eyeball," United States Secretary of State Dean Rusk said, "and I think the other fellow just blinked." Within a week the Soviets agreed to take away the missiles. In return, Kennedy agreed not to invade Cuba. In 1963 the two superpowers signed a treaty ending the testing of nuclear bombs above ground.

✓ **What became the symbol of the Cold War?**

## VIETNAM

Vietnam, a country in Indochina, became the focus of the next Cold War conflict. At the end of World War II, Vietnamese leaders had declared independence from their colonial ruler, France. The French, however, wanted to take back control of the country. The United States supported France because the Vietnamese leader, Ho Chi Minh

**THE VIETNAM WAR**

0    100    200 Miles
0    100    200 Kilometers
Mercator Projection

CHINA

NORTH VIETNAM
Dien Bien Phu
Hon Gai
Xam Nua
Hanoi
Haiphong
Luang Prabang
Gulf of Tonkin
Hainan
Muang Ngat
Vientiane
Vinh
LAOS
Quang Khe
Dong Hoi
Quang Tri, 1968, 1972
Khe Sanh, 1968
Hue, 1968, 1972
Da Nang, 1968
THAILAND
Dak To
Chu Lai
My Lai
Kontum, 1968, 1972
Qui Nhon
Bangkok
Pleiku, 1965, 1968
SOUTH VIETNAM
Nha Trang, 1968
CAMBODIA
An Loc, 1972
Phnom Penh
An Loc
Da Lat, 1968
Bien-hoa, 1968
Saigon, 1968, 1975
Gulf of Thailand
Can Tho, 1968
Mekong Delta
South China Sea

✹ Capital city    🔥 Major fighting
——— Line of division    ——→ Trail of Vietcong

🌐 **LOCATION** The present-day country of Vietnam was once divided into warring parts.
■ In which part of Vietnam did most of the fighting take place?

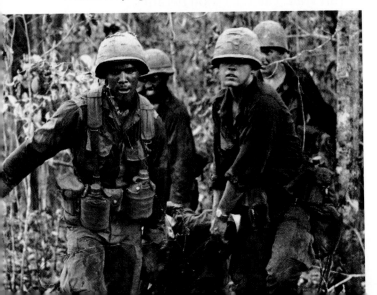

American soldiers carry the wounded out of a South Vietnamese jungle in 1967.

(HOH CHEE MIN), had communist ties. By 1954, after years of fighting, the French were defeated. An agreement was reached to divide Vietnam into northern and southern parts.

With the help of China and the Soviet Union, Ho Chi Minh built a communist state in the north. He also gained a strong following among people in the south. These Vietcong, or "Vietnamese Communists," began a campaign to overthrow the government of South Vietnam. War then broke out between North and South Vietnam. In the

A helicopter brings fresh troops into battle (above). A young Vietnamese girl cuddles a baby in the middle of a war zone (right).

early 1960s the United States began helping South Vietnam in its fight against the Communists.

By 1969 there were 550,000 American troops in Vietnam. Yet victory seemed no nearer, and Americans were dying every day. Millions of Vietnamese in the north and south also were killed. Fighting spread to other countries in the region as well.

America's role in the war caused conflict in the United States. Some Americans believed that the United States had a duty to fight communism. Others believed that the United States should not be involved in another country's battle. Those who opposed the war held protests and marches.

More and more Americans began to question their government's reasons for fighting in Vietnam. Therefore, United States leaders tried to end their country's role in the war. In 1973 North Vietnamese and American leaders reached a cease-fire agreement. Soon after that, United States troops withdrew.

About 58,000 Americans had died in the war, and 360,000 had been wounded. In 1974 North Vietnam again attacked South Vietnam. By April 1975 the Communists had gained control of all of Vietnam. Not until 1995 did the United States again begin trade and communication with the Vietnamese.

After its withdrawal from Vietnam, the United States government began a new policy toward communist nations. Called **détente** (day•TAHNT), the policy was meant to relax tensions between the communists and the free world. In the spirit of détente, American leaders

This button reflects the mood of Americans opposed to the war.

**SICK OF THE WAR IN VIETNAM**

began talks with China. They also signed an agreement with the Soviet Union to limit the making of nuclear weapons.

In 1979 tensions flared once again. In that year leaders of the Soviet Union sent troops to its neighbor Afghanistan to keep that country's failing communist government in power. President Jimmy Carter responded by stopping grain sales to the Soviet Union. President Carter also refused to allow U.S. teams to play in the 1980 Summer Olympics, which were held in the Soviet Union. In addition, he threatened to send American troops to Afghanistan, if needed. The spirit of détente had temporarily disappeared.

 **Why did United States leaders decide to end their country's role in Vietnam?**

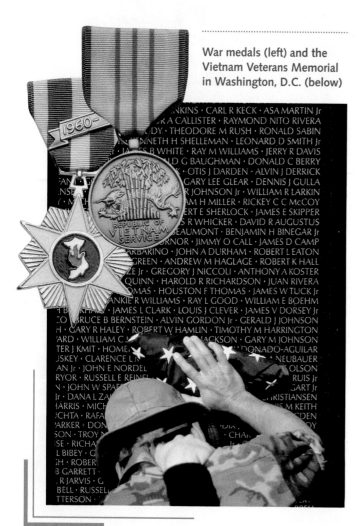

War medals (left) and the Vietnam Veterans Memorial in Washington, D.C. (below)

## UNITED STATES FORCES IN TWENTIETH-CENTURY WARS

**LEARNING FROM GRAPHS** This graph shows the number of soldiers who fought for the United States in each of four wars.

■ About how many more U.S. soldiers fought in World War II than in the Vietnam War?

# LESSON 3 REVIEW

## Check Understanding

1. **Recall the Facts** What was détente?
2. **Focus on the Main Idea** How did differing ideas about government and economics lead to tensions and armed conflict in the years after World War II?

## Think Critically

3. **Think More About It** How do you think the division of a country into two parts might affect that country's people?
4. **Cause and Effect** What events caused tensions to ease between the superpowers?

## Show What You Know

**Political Cartoon Activity**
Create a political cartoon that illustrates the idea of a cold war. Write a caption to explain your cartoon, if needed.

# Make a Thoughtful Decision

## Why Is This Skill Important?

Every action you take has a consequence, or result. Some consequences are short-term—they happen right away and last a short time. Other consequences are long-term—they happen in the future and last a long time. An action can also have either positive or negative consequences—or both. To make thoughtful decisions, you need to think about all the possible consequences before you take action.

## Remember What You Have Read

You have read that the leaders of the superpowers during the Cold War had to make many difficult decisions. In the Cuban Missile Crisis of 1962, United States President John F. Kennedy and Soviet leader Nikita Khrushchev both had to make important decisions and then take action.

President Kennedy had to decide what to do to stop the Soviets from shipping military supplies to Cuba, the island nation 90 miles (145 km) south of Florida. No matter what action he decided to take, he risked the consequence of going to war with the Soviet Union. He could have ordered a military attack on Cuba. Instead, he ordered a shipping blockade to stop Soviet cargo ships from landing in Cuba. He hoped this would have a less serious consequence.

In turn, Khrushchev had to decide what to do in response to the United States' blockade. He knew that the consequence of some actions could be going to war with the United States. He could have ordered his ships to try to sail through the blockade. Instead, Khrushchev ordered the ships to return to the Soviet Union.

## Understand the Process

To make a difficult decision, you can use a set of steps that many people use. Following these steps can help you make your decision more thoughtfully.

- Identify your goal.
- Think about the problem that is keeping you from reaching your goal.
- List the actions you could take. Begin with those you think would have the most positive consequences, and end with those you think would have negative consequences.
- Make the choice that seems best.
- Put your choice into action.
- Think about whether your choice helped you reach your goal.

## Think and Apply

Think about a decision you made at school. What steps did you follow? What choice did you make? What were the consequences? Do you think you made a thoughtful decision? Explain.

Nikita Khrushchev

John F. Kennedy

## CONNECT MAIN IDEAS

Use this organizer to show that you understand how the chapter's main ideas are connected. Copy the organizer onto a separate sheet of paper. Then write several sentences to describe each of the following topics.

**The Later Twentieth Century**

**World War II**
_____
_____
_____

**Cold War Tensions**
_____
_____
_____

**The Holocaust**
_____
_____
_____

## WRITE MORE ABOUT IT

1. **Write a Report**  Write a short report that explains how the United States became involved in World War II.

2. **Write an Interview**  Many people lost their lives in concentration camps, but some managed to survive. Write five questions that you might ask a survivor of a concentration camp.

3. **Write a Magazine Article**  Write a short magazine article about how the Vietnam War affected people differently. Talk with two or three people who lived during the time of the Vietnam War. Ask them to describe their experiences. Then write your magazine article from this information.

4. **Write a Tribute**  Write a paragraph honoring the men and women who lost their lives as civilians or soldiers in a twentieth-century conflict.

# USE VOCABULARY

Use each term in a complete sentence that helps explain its meaning.

appeasement          genocide
concentration camp   limited war
containment          superpower
détente

# CHECK UNDERSTANDING

1. What event caused Britain and France to declare war on Germany?

2. What countries made up the Axis Powers? What countries made up the Allies?

3. What events led to the surrender of Germany and Japan in World War II?

4. What was the Nazis' Final Solution?

5. What organization replaced the League of Nations, and what is its main purpose?

6. What happened to Germany after World War II?

7. Why did President Truman want the Korean conflict to be a limited war?

8. Why did the United States take part in the Vietnam War?

# THINK CRITICALLY

1. **Past to Present**   Could an event like the Holocaust happen today? Explain why or why not.

2. **Personally Speaking**   Do you think the United States should give military support to countries involved in war? Explain your answer.

3. **Explore Viewpoints**   Some people believe it was necessary for the United States to use atomic bombs on Japanese cities during World War II. Others disagree. What reasons might each group give to support its view?

4. **Think More About It**   Would the United States have become involved in World War II even if the Japanese had not bombed Pearl Harbor? Explain your answer.

# APPLY SKILLS

**How to Use a Double-Bar Graph**   Use the double-bar graphs on pages 564 and 565 to answer these questions:

1. According to the bar graphs, were there more deaths among the Axis Powers or among the Allies?

2. Which country had more casualties, China or Japan?

**How to Make a Thoughtful Decision**
Answer these questions about making a thoughtful decision:

1. What is the first thing you should do when making a decision?

2. Why would you want to think about possible negative consequences?

3. Why is it important to think about whether you made the right decision, after you have already put your choice into action?

# READ MORE ABOUT IT

*Rescue: The Story of How Gentiles Saved Jews in the Holocaust* by Milton Meltzer. HarperCollins. The author tells how non-Jews throughout Europe risked their lives to help Jewish people survive the Holocaust. Quotations from diaries, letters, and interviews make the many true stories told come to terrifying life.

*The Upstairs Room* by Johanna Reiss. Bantam. This story follows the days of two Jewish sisters who are hiding in the home of a Christian family in Nazi-held Holland during World War II.

# RELEVANT

## YOUNG SOLDIERS

In 1974, when Arn Chorn of Cambodia was 8 years old, he was taken from his home by an invading army called the Khmer Rouge (kuh·MAIR ROOZH). With other children, he was forced to work all day in rice fields. Then one day, when Arn was 12 years old, the Khmer Rouge handed him a gun and told him he had to fight the Vietnamese, who were invading Cambodia.

Arn had never fired a gun before, and he did not know how to load one. Finally he asked one of his captors, "Where do you put the bullets?" "Figure it out for yourself," the man said before sending Arn off to battle.

Young people have always been at risk in wartime. In some early societies, fighting in battles was a part of becoming an adult. In the 1800s, drummer boys marched into battle in both the United States and Europe. In World Wars I and II, as well as in the Korean War and Vietnam War, children fought and died for their countries.

Today international law forbids the use of children under age 15 as soldiers. Still, throughout the world, young people fight in battles, whether they choose to or not.

Young soldier in Afghanistan

BUILDING CITIZENSHIP

At different times throughout the years, young men in the United States have had to register for the draft at age 18. Tell why you think this is a good or a bad policy.

Boy soldiers in Uganda

# STORY CLOTH

Study the pictures shown in this story cloth to help you review the events you read about in Unit 9.

## Summarize the Main Ideas

1. The assassination of the Serbian archduke Francis Ferdinand launched rival European nations into war. This war is now known as World War I.

2. The Russian people rebelled against their czar, forcing him to give up the throne. In time, the Communist party came to power, yet the citizens of what became the Soviet Union still had little freedom or political authority.

3. An economic crisis in the United States developed into the Great Depression and affected people around the world.

4. The actions of countries that became known as the Axis Powers led to a second war that involved the whole world—World War II.

5. Jews and other people suffered greatly during the Holocaust. Millions were put into concentration camps and killed.

6. Differing ideas about government and economics led to tensions and fighting in the years after World War II. The Korean War and the Vietnam War were major conflicts during this time.

**Write About the Story**   Select one scene in the story cloth. Think about the events shown in the scene. Then write about how you think these events have affected the world of today.

# UNIT 9
# REVIEW

## COOPERATIVE LEARNING WORKSHOP

### Remember

- Share your ideas.
- Cooperate with others to plan your work.
- Take responsibility for your work.
- Show your group's work to the class.
- Discuss what you learned by working together.

**Activity 1**

### Develop a Peace Plan

With three or four classmates, develop your own Fourteen Points for Peace. Include all the ways you think countries can avoid future wars. Show your Fourteen Points on a poster for display in your classroom.

**Activity 2**

### Draw a Map

Work with a partner to draw a large map of the world as it was during World War II. Use different colors on the map to identify the Allied nations, the Axis nations, and the nations that were neutral. Label each country, title your map, and add a key.

**Activity 3**

### Create a Remembrance

Brainstorm with a group of three or four students to think of ways to encourage young people to remember the Holocaust. You might suggest creating artwork, a song, or a poem, or you might have other ideas. Once you have considered different ideas, select one, make a plan, and act on your plan.

**Activity 4**

### Hold a Class Debate

Imagine that the year is 1967. The people of the United States are divided because of the Vietnam War. Hold a class debate about United States involvement in the Vietnam War. Form two debate teams. One team should argue for involvement. The other should argue for withdrawal.

Write the term that correctly matches each definition.

| Cold War | inflation | refugee |
|----------|-----------|---------|
| Holocaust | propaganda | totalitarian |

**1.** a continuing increase in prices

**2.** the spreading of information or rumors to help or hurt a cause

**3.** the mass killing of the Jewish people

**4.** having complete control over people's lives

**5.** a person who is forced to leave his or her home to seek safety and shelter elsewhere

**6.** a conflict that led to an arms buildup by the world's superpowers

## CHECK UNDERSTANDING

**1.** What caused European nations to develop a spirit of militarism in the years before World War I?

**2.** What was the spark that started World War I?

**3.** Why were the Germans angry about the terms of the Treaty of Versailles?

**4.** Why did the Germans arrest Jews and other groups of people in the 1940s?

**5.** Where was World War II fought?

**6.** What world superpower supported South Vietnam? Why? What superpower supported North Vietnam? Why?

## THINK CRITICALLY

**1. Think More About It** How was World War I different from wars that had been fought in the past?

**2. Cause and Effect** How did Hitler's belief in a "master race" lead to the Holocaust?

**3. Explore Viewpoints** Woodrow Wilson wanted a lasting peace to follow World War I. What seemed most important to those who signed the Treaty of Versailles?

## APPLY GEOGRAPHY SKILLS

**How to Use a Time Zone Map**
World War II was fought around the world and crossed many time zones. On December 7, 1941, at 7:55 A.M., the Japanese bombed Pearl Harbor in Hawaii. Use the time zone map below to answer these questions about the bombing of Pearl Harbor.

**1.** When the Japanese bombed Pearl Harbor, what time was it in Washington D.C.?

**2.** What time was it and what date was it in Tokyo, Japan?

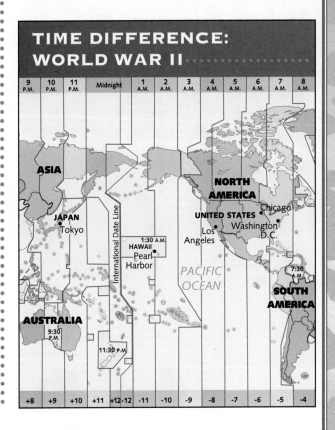

TIME DIFFERENCE: WORLD WAR II

## UNIT 10

# *T*OWARD *the* *P*RESENT *D*AY

1975

1980

1985

**1978**
Camp David Accords
between Israel and Egypt

**1986**
Mikhail
Gorbachev
introduces
policies of
perestroika and
glasnost in the
Soviet Union

*M*ajor changes took place around the world during the second half of the twentieth century. Countries in Africa and Asia, long held as colonies by European countries, won their independence. Long-time enemies signed peace agreements in Southwest Asia. Communism in Europe failed, allowing eastern Europe to emerge from behind the Iron Curtain. Even countries that were still ruled by communist leaders, such as China, tried out free enterprise economic ideas. This time of change allowed nations to work together in new ways. It also created problems that world leaders had to face.

← The 1989 peaceful protest by Chinese students in Tiananmen Square was followed by violent government action.

**1990**

**1989**
Fall of the Berlin Wall

Students massacred in China's Tiananmen Square

**1991**
Soviet Union breaks up

Persian Gulf War fought in Southwest Asia

**1993**
Israel and PLO agree to peace

**1995**

**1994**
Nelson Mandela wins election in South Africa

**Present**

**1995**
U.S. shuttle *Atlantis* and Russia's space station *Mir* link up in space

Serb, Croat, and Muslim leaders sign Bosnian peace agreement

# THE BERLIN WALL

*by Doris M. Epler*

*Late in 1989 communism began to fall apart in eastern Europe. On November 9 the East German government stunned the world by announcing that it planned to begin opening its borders—including the Berlin Wall—at midnight. Read now about the excitement of East Berliners as they heard this news. As you read, think about why the opening of the Berlin Wall interested not only those in Berlin but also people around the world.*

In East Berlin, people began to go to the Wall to see if what they had heard was true. It was. Within two hours of the announcement, the trickle[1] of people had turned into jubilant[2] crowds. By midnight, thousands of East Berliners were walking, biking, or driving to crossing points in the Wall and entering the western half of the city—something that, just a few hours earlier, they could only dream of.

At Checkpoint Charlie, the place where U.S. and Soviet tanks had faced off while the infamous[3] Wall was being erected,[4] long lines of cars and people moved into West Berlin unimpeded.[5] Berliners were shouting, "Gates open! Gates open!" and "The Wall is gone!" Some exuberant[6] Germans even scampered to the top of the Wall, now that all fear of being shot was gone.

As East Berliners drove their cars down the splendid Kurfürstendamm, West Berlin's equivalent of New York's Fifth Avenue, their enthusiasm grew. They had dreamed of entering the western zone for years, and now they were seeing their dreams come true. It was an emotional time—many had difficulty describing how they felt. One woman exclaimed, as she viewed the shop windows of West Berlin, "There is so much color, so much light." "It's incredible," "The eighth wonder of the world!" "I never believed I would be able to do this!" were other

[1] **trickle:** movement of just a few at a time
[2] **jubilant:** joyful
[3] **infamous:** evil
[4] **erected:** built
[5] **unimpeded:** not blocked
[6] **exuberant:** high-spirited

remarks. Of the West Berliners, one East German student said, "It's amazing how warmly we were greeted. We were applauded. They cried. They were just as happy as we were."[7] A blind man, guided by a seeing-eye dog, remarked, "I just wanted to smell the air of a free Berlin."[8]

East German guards, who hours before would have shot anyone trying to escape, now posed happily as people snapped pictures of the scene. "The East German soldiers don't know what to do now," said one West Berliner. "They behave a bit crazy tonight, so calm and so quiet."[9] One man rushed across the border carrying a copy of a newspaper that proclaimed, in an enormous headline, "Berlin is Berlin Again!" The guards, who previously would have confiscated[10] such material, merely reached out eagerly to see the newspaper.

The celebrations continued all through the night and into the morning. People began to dance on top of the Wall. Others blew trumpets, embraced, and laughed while tears streamed down their faces. The ringing of chisels and hammers could be heard as people began to chip away at the once-impregnable[11] barrier.

The next day more crossings were opened, including the Glienicke Bridge, the site of many East-West spy exchanges. A hundred thousand East Berliners inundated[12] the western zone. Among them was an East Berlin man who had borrowed three books from the American Memorial Library in West Berlin the day before the Wall went up. Now, twenty-eight years later, he returned the books—in excellent condition. (Presumably, no late-book fines were imposed.)

*In this unit you will read more about the opening of the Berlin Wall and other events of the late twentieth century that have had far-reaching effects on world affairs.*

---

[7] Quotation from *Newsweek,* "The Fall of the Wall," November 20, 1989
[8] Quotation from *Maclean's,* "Free at Last!" November 20, 1989
[9] Quotation from *Newsweek,* "The Fall of the Wall," November 20, 1989
[10] **confiscated:** taken by authority

---

[11] **impregnable:** not possible to overcome
[12] **inundated:** flooded

On November 9, 1989, the gates of the Berlin Wall opened (photo on page 590). Excited Berliners (below) climbed the Berlin Wall to celebrate the fact that the "Wall of Shame" would no longer separate Berlin and its people. Germans of all ages (inset) soon began to chip pieces from the much-hated wall.

# ECONOMIC CHALLENGES

> 66 All the big questions confronting the world in the century ahead are basically economic. 99
>
> Bruce W. Nelan,
> American journalist, 1992

Woman of Peru, South America,
wearing traditional clothing

# LESSON 1

# CHINA *in the* MODERN WORLD

## *L*ink to Our World

*How is a country's economy affected by the ideas and actions of its leaders?*

**Focus on the Main Idea**
*As you read, find out how China's industry, agriculture, and trade changed as the country's leaders changed.*

**Preview Vocabulary**
warlord
Long March
commune
Cultural Revolution
Red Guard
quota

Sun Yat-sen (center) visits the site of an ancient Chinese tomb in 1912.

At the beginning of the twentieth century, China was mainly a rural, agricultural country with a traditional economy. Economic growth was slow because foreign powers controlled many of China's resources. Later, the introduction of communism did not help economic conditions.

## CHINESE NATIONALISM

By the early 1900s parts of China were controlled by other countries. The Qing emperors seemed unable to stop this, but many young Chinese demanded change. "The foreigners must leave," they said. At the same time, they wanted China to learn foreign ways and become a modern country.

A new political party, the Guomindang (GWOH•min•dahng), or People's Nationalist party, grew out of the calls for change. Its leader, Sun Yat-sen (SUN YAHT•SEN), wanted to create a republic based on the "Three Principles of the People"—nationalism, democracy, and a strong economy. Sun Yat-sen thought that China needed to get rid of foreign control, form a democratic government, and become an industrial power.

By 1911 the Nationalists had forced the last Qing emperor to step down. Sun Yat-sen became the president of a new Chinese republic. The new government, though, was not able to unite China. **Warlords**, individuals with their own small armies, had taken over many parts of the country. The warlords refused to follow the orders of the Nationalist government. The Nationalists seemed to have little chance of success in bringing the Chinese people together.

The situation changed in 1925, when Sun Yat-sen died. Chiang Kai-shek (jee•AHNG KY•SHEK) became leader of the Nationalists. Chiang soon built up the Nationalist army and began defeating the warlords.

At the same time, the Nationalist party split. The newly formed Communist party wanted the peasants to have more say in government. Chiang, supported by wealthy landowners, disagreed with this and took action against the Communists.

By 1934 the Nationalist armies had forced the Communists into a small area in south-eastern China. About 100,000 Communists began a walk of 6,000 miles (9,656 km) across China to safety in the northwest. This hard journey, now known as the **Long March**, took more than a year. Nationalists attacked all along the way. Fewer than 20,000 people survived the march. Yet on the way they found a leader—Mao Zedong (MOW ZUH•DUNG).

✓ **Why were the Nationalists unable to unite China?**

## COMMUNISM IN CHINA

In the northwest, which was now under Communist rule, Mao Zedong lowered taxes and gave the peasants control of the land.

In the rest of China, Chiang Kai-shek was unable to bring about much economic change. More and more peasants joined the Communists, hoping for a better life.

Years before the Long March, Mao had made this prediction:

> 66Several hundred million peasants . . . will rise like a tornado or tempest— a force so extraordinarily swift and violent that no power, however great, will be able to suppress it.99

As Mao had hoped, an army of peasants rose up. After a long and violent war, this peasant army drove out the Nationalists. In 1949 Mao set up a communist state, the People's Republic of China. Chiang and his followers escaped to the island of Taiwan (TY•WAHN). There they set up their own government, which they called the Republic of China.

Mao began to change every area of Chinese life to fit his ideas. He appointed Communists to all leadership positions. He then divided the country into many small districts. In each district the people ran the factories and farms where they worked. Still, the real authority belonged with the central government, which was controlled by Mao and other Communist leaders. Together they created five-year plans to set economic goals for the country.

Mao Zedong (left) led Chinese Communist forces. Followers of Mao are shown (far right) after the completion of the Long March in 1934. During that 6,000-mile journey, marchers crossed 24 rivers and 18 mountain ranges.

## SPREAD OF COMMUNISM IN CHINA

SOVIET UNION

MONGOLIA

MANCHURIA

Sea of Japan

NORTH KOREA

SOUTH KOREA

JAPAN

Beijing ⊛

Yellow Sea

Huang He

TIBET (occupied by China)

CHINA

Xian

Shanghai

East China Sea

Chang Jiang

NEPAL

SIKKIM

BHUTAN

INDIA

EAST PAKISTAN

TAIWAN

Guangzhou

BURMA

FRENCH INDOCHINA

Macao (PORTUGAL)

Hong Kong (U.K.)

Hainan

South China Sea

THAILAND

0   300   600 Miles
0   300   600 Kilometers
Two-Point Equidistant Projection

→ Route of Long March
⊛ National Capital (after Communist takeover)

**Areas occupied by communists, 1934–1949**
- 1934–1945
- 1945–June 1946
- July 1946–June 1947
- July 1947–June 1948
- July 1948–June 1949
- July–September 1949
- After October 1949

**MOVEMENT** In 1934 the Long March took the Chinese Communists to safety in the northwest. Just 15 years later the Communists controlled all of China.
■ Why do you think the Long March did not follow a more direct route?

Mao's first five-year plan in 1953 called for rapid growth of industry. It also forced most peasants to live in **communes**. These were government-run farming communities in which the people shared housing, food, and work. For the most part, Mao's plan worked. Leaders were pleased to see an increase in farm production. Industry grew as well.

Mao's second five-year plan, the Great Leap Forward, tried to do much more. It created hundreds of large communes, where as many as 25,000 people lived and worked. The goal was to bring China's production levels up to those of Western nations. Poor planning brought industry almost to a stop. Also, bad harvests from 1959 to 1961 left millions of people starving. China had failed to take the Great Leap Forward.

Some members of the Communist party criticized Mao's plans. They believed production would increase only through rewards to workers. Mao accused them of "walking the capitalist road." Their goal, Mao said, was to return to the days of the emperors.

**What steps did Mao Zedong take to change the Chinese economy?**

## THE CULTURAL REVOLUTION

In 1966 Mao decided that too many people were refusing to accept his ways. What China needed, he said, was a **Cultural Revolution** to cut people's ties to the past. Mao felt that high school and college students would

Members of the Red Guard wave copies of a book by their leader, Mao Zedong. Mao urged the youth of China to abandon the past and accept his changes.

be the best people to lead this revolution. Having grown up under communism, they had little respect for China's past.

The **Red Guard**, as these young people came to be known, destroyed anything that showed the past or the ways of the West—books, works of art, buildings. They even changed the traffic signals, making red the color for "go" and green the color for "stop."

The Red Guard made life hard for those who they felt were not good Communists. The people they questioned lost their jobs and their membership in the Communist party. Many were thrown into jails or sent to work camps. Some were killed.

In time even Mao thought the Red Guard had gone too far. In 1968 he called an end to the Cultural Revolution.

The Cultural Revolution had destroyed the Chinese economy. Large numbers of managers, factory workers, and peasant farmers had been put out of work by the Red Guard. Because of this, farm and factory production dropped. China needed many years to recover from this economic disaster.

✓ **How did the Cultural Revolution affect life in China?**

## NEW FREEDOMS, NEW CHALLENGES

After Mao died in 1976, two groups of Communist party leaders fought for control. The moderates—the group that won—believed that the country's economy would be improved by forming closer ties with Western nations. The leaders of the losing group, which was headed by Mao's widow, Jiang Qing, were put in jail.

In 1977 Deng Xiaoping (DUHNG SHOW•PING) became the leader of the moderates. Deng soon announced a new economic program based on the Four Modernizations. The leader's plan aimed at improvements in four areas: farming, manufacturing, armed forces, and technology. Under this plan the government gave managers more control over farms and factories. The government still set **quotas**, or required amounts of particular goods to be produced. But farmers and factory managers could sell any extra goods they produced and keep the profits. The program also introduced the idea of free enterprise. Some Chinese were allowed to start their own businesses. Free enterprise has gained the interest of many Chinese, particularly the young.

The taste of economic success made the Chinese people want even more changes. During the late 1980s thousands called for political changes as well as economic ones. In early 1989, students protested peacefully day after day in Tiananmen (TYAHN•AHN•MEN) Square in Beijing. The students demanded political freedom. As the weeks went by, their cry for democracy grew stronger.

On June 3, 1989, soldiers fired on the students in Tiananmen Square. "Tell the world our government has gone mad!" an angry young woman said to Western journalists. By the next day the army had moved into the Square and thousands of students lay dead or wounded.

# Where?

## Tiananmen Square

Tiananmen Square lies just outside Beijing's Forbidden City, a group of buildings once used by China's emperors. At one time no one but the emperor and his court could enter the city. Tiananmen Square—the world's largest square—has been the center for political events since the Communists took power. Mao Zedong announced the creation of the People's Republic of China there. Some of the biggest meetings of the Cultural Revolution were held there, too. It was not by chance that Beijing students chose the Square for their 1989 political demonstrations. Ever since the massacre, the government has kept tight control over who may enter the square.

**CHINA**

Great Wall

Beijing

Bo Gulf

Inner City

Imperial City

0   1 Mile
0   1 Kilometer

Palace Museum

**Forbidden City**

historic city wall

Gate of Heavenly Peace

Tiananmen Square

Outer City

N W E S

The Tiananmen Square killings shocked people around the world. Some governments cut trade ties with China. Chinese leaders responded by saying that other governments had no right to criticize their actions. The Chinese government then made all traces of the massacre disappear—as though the killings had never taken place!

In the early 1990s Chinese leaders gave back some freedoms to the people and began to rebuild economic ties with Western countries. Whether the Chinese people will gain political freedom as well as economic freedom remains to be seen.

More than 1 billion people live in China. With China's large population comes a large problem: How can so many people be fed? Since the late 1970s China has tried to keep its population from growing. One way it has done this is by requiring families to have just one child. Only time can tell how China's actions will affect the country's economy and society.

 **How did Deng Xiaoping change China's economy?**

# LESSON 1 REVIEW

## Check Understanding

1. **Recall the Facts**   What was the Great Leap Forward? What was the Four Modernizations program?
2. **Focus on the Main Idea**   How did China's economy change as new leaders took control after Mao?

## Think Critically

3. **Explore Viewpoints**   Compare the economic ideas of Mao Zedong and Deng Xiaoping. Which of the two leaders helped China's economy more? Explain.
4. **Personally Speaking**   How would you feel if you were free to make decisions about earning your living but not about choosing your leaders? Do you think the two freedoms belong together? Do you think one can exist without the other? Explain.

## Show What You Know

**Time-Line Activity**   Use library resources to create a time line showing important events relating to the Chinese economy from 1911 to the present.

# Read a Cartogram

## Why Is This Skill Important?

As you know, population is not evenly spread around the world. Some areas are nearly empty, while other areas are very crowded. Some small countries and continents have larger populations than large countries and continents. Many different factors—such as available resources, elevation, climate, historical events, and people's ways of life—affect an area's population.

One interesting way to show population is to use a kind of map called a cartogram. A **cartogram** is a map that gives information about places by the size shown for each place. Knowing how to read a population cartogram can help you find out in which countries of the world many or few people live.

## Population Cartograms

A cartogram is not like most maps. On most maps, the size of each country or continent is based on its land area. On a cartogram, the size of the country or continent is based on a geographical statistic. On the cartogram on page 599, size is based on population.

A population cartogram shows the countries of the world as the sizes they would be if everyone had the same amount of land. A country with many people would be much bigger than a country with few people. When countries are shown this way, you can quickly compare populations around the world. A population cartogram does not, however, show the number of people in an area.

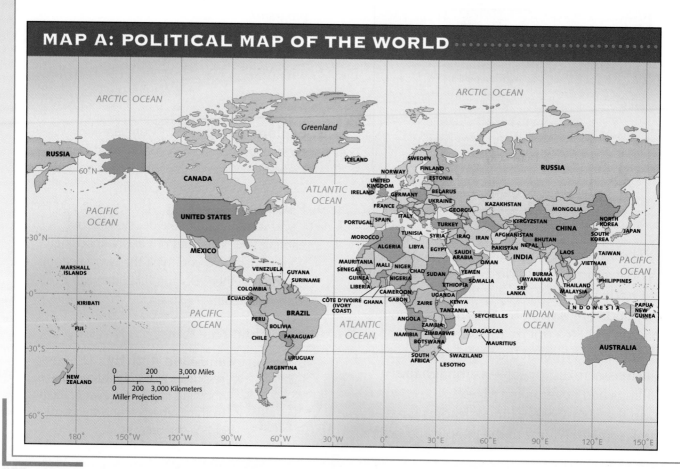

MAP A: POLITICAL MAP OF THE WORLD

## Understand the Process

Map A is a political map of the world. The size of each country is based on its land area. Compare the size of Russia with the size of China. Which is larger? Map B is a population cartogram. The size of each country is based on its population. Compare the sizes of Russia and China again. Although China has a smaller land area than Russia, it is shown larger than Russia on the cartogram because it has more people.

Locate Australia and Japan on Map A. You can see that Australia has a much larger land area than Japan. Now find Australia and Japan on the cartogram. Which of these countries has the larger population?

Continue to compare land area and population by answering these questions.

1. Which country in Africa has the largest population?
2. Which country in Africa has the greatest land area?
3. Which country in North America has the second-largest population?
4. Which country in North America has the second-largest land area?
5. Which continent has the largest population? Tell how you know.
6. Which continent has the fewest people? Tell how you know.

## Think and Apply

 With a partner, brainstorm other uses for cartograms. What other statistics could be shown this way to help people compare and contrast countries of the world? If these types of statistics are available in your local library, locate them and make your own cartogram. Then prepare a list of questions that could be answered by looking at your cartogram. Ask several classmates to take your cartogram quiz. Accept a classmate's challenge to take his or her cartogram quiz as well.

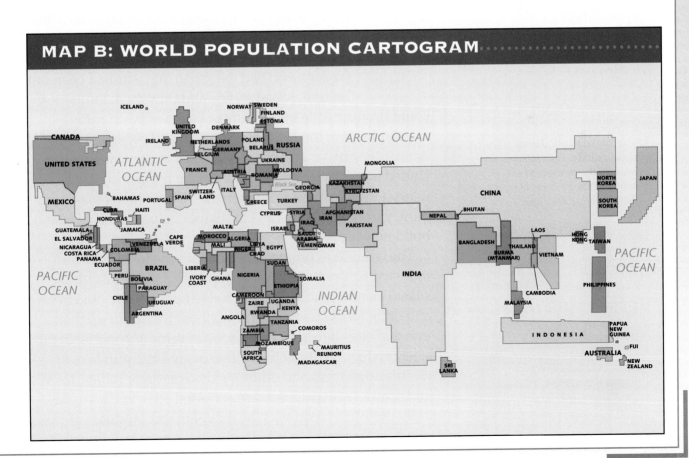

MAP B: WORLD POPULATION CARTOGRAM

# JAPAN BECOMES A WORLD POWER

## Link to Our World

**How does a country grow rich and powerful?**

**Focus on the Main Idea**
As you read, look for things Japan did to gain importance in the industrial world.

**Preview Vocabulary**
gross domestic product
balance of trade
standard of living
megalopolis
trade surplus
protectionism
free port

Japan became an industrial nation in the late 1800s, many years after countries in Europe had industrialized, but long before China had. By the 1930s Japan had become the major industrial power in Asia. In the 1940s, however, World War II destroyed Japan's economy.

## JAPAN REBUILDS

After World War II, it seemed that Japan's economy might never recover. United States Army troops led by General Douglas MacArthur occupied the country. Japanese emperor Hirohito (hir•oh•HEE•toh) had lost his authority. Military leaders who had led Japan into war had been put on trial, found guilty, and punished. Industries could produce little because most factories lay in ruins.

After the war the Japanese immediately began to rebuild. At first they had a great deal of help from the United States. United States leaders thought it was in the world's best interest to assist their former enemy. Government loans and money from United States companies helped the Japanese build new factories.

The rebuilding program began with the textile, or cloth, industry. Before World War II, Japan had made beautiful silks. The new textile factories made not only silk but cotton and other fabrics as well. The Japanese then built up their iron and steel industry. Japan soon became a world leader in steel production. Its factories also made large numbers of electric appliances and other goods. Transistor radios, toys, and a variety of gadgets were exported all over the world.

By the 1970s Japan was the third-highest producer of goods in the world. It led all other nations in building ships,

After World War II, Japan rebuilt quickly. Now Japan is a leader in the production of high-technology items like the bullet train pictured here.

and it was second only to the United States in making cars. What Japan did was remarkable because it has so few natural resources. It has to import almost everything that it needs for its industries.

Surprisingly, the war that destroyed most of Japan's industry also helped the country succeed in starting over. When the Japanese rebuilt their factories, they used the latest technology. This put Japan ahead of most other industrial nations, whose factories had older equipment.

Even so, the people of Japan were the main reason the country did so well. The goal of rebuilding their country united the Japanese. They realized that they would have to co-operate to reach this goal. The Japanese people were willing to put the good of their country first. They worked long hours and saved much of their money.

Using the money that was deposited in savings accounts, banks made loans to help rebuild Japanese industries. Japanese companies rewarded their workers by giving them free social activities, vacations, and health care. The Japanese government helped by lowering taxes for businesses. It also set up high tariffs to keep out goods from other countries, forcing the Japanese people to buy Japanese goods.

✔️ **What made Japan's growth possible?**

Computers and other electronic goods are produced in factories throughout Japan.

## PROBLEMS BELOW THE SURFACE

Today Japan is one of the world's industrial leaders, second only to the United States. Its **gross domestic product** (GDP), the total value of a country's goods and services produced within the country's borders each year, is more than four trillion dollars. Japan also has a favorable **balance of trade**. This means that it exports, or sells to other countries, more than it imports, or buys from other countries.

The Japanese people are also doing well. Most industrial workers earn a good salary and can be sure of keeping their jobs. Their **standard of living**—a measure of how well people live—is one of the highest in the world.

**LEARNING FROM GRAPHS** The bar graph compares Japan's gross domestic product to that of other countries.
■ How much higher is Japan's GDP than China's GDP?

GDP FOR SELECTED COUNTRIES

Highly industrialized nations often must deal with environmental problems such as smog. This air pollution threatens people's health and well-being. Smog often covers the thriving city of Tokyo, Japan (above).

## JAPAN'S MAJOR INDUSTRIES

CHINA
RUSSIA
Hokkaido
Sapporo
NORTH KOREA
Sea of Japan
40° N
130° E
Electronics, Textiles
SOUTH KOREA
PACIFIC OCEAN
Iron and Steel, Ships and Cars, Textiles
Honshu
Tokyo
Iron and Steel, Ships and Cars, Electronics
Electronics
Nagoya
Hiroshima
Kobe
Kyoto
Osaka
Kitakyushu
Iron and Steel, Ships and Cars, Textiles
Shikoku
Kyushu
East China Sea
30° N
Iron and Steel, Ships and Cars
0          150          300 Miles
0    150    300 Kilometers
Two-Point Equidistant Projection

Farmland | Industrial region
Forest | ○ Center for industry
Fishing | Cars Products exported

**PLACE** Japan produces a wide variety of goods and services.
■ Where in Japan are textiles produced?

Japan does have some problems, though. Its industries must buy raw materials from other countries to operate. Oil is a very important example. Since oil is needed for energy and for making plastics, a break in the flow of oil to Japan would hurt the country's economy.

Japan also faces the problem of rapid growth and limited space. After World War II, Japan's industries grew quickly. As more land was used for industry, less could be used for houses. The cost of homes became very high. Nearby cities seemed to grow to meet one another, forming a **megalopolis**. In the large cities many middle-class Japanese could afford only tiny, two-room apartments in high-rise buildings. Today most large cities are overcrowded and have a shortage of houses and apartments. In these cities pollution also threatens people's health.

Another problem for Japan is its location. Japan is on a part of the Earth's crust that is not stable. Because of this, both earthquakes and volcanoes are common in Japan. In 1995 an earthquake lasting only 20 seconds destroyed much of the city of Kobe (KOH•bee).

 **What problems do the Japanese face as the twentieth century ends?**

## JAPAN AND TRADE

Japan has a favorable balance of trade with nearly every one of its trading partners. It has a **trade surplus** with the United States. This means that it exports to the United States more goods than it imports from our country.

Some Americans have claimed that Japan built this trade surplus in unfair ways. In the 1970s and 1980s, more and more Japanese cars were shipped to the United States. Because of the cars' high quality and low prices, many people bought them instead of American cars. United States automobile makers closed factories and laid off workers partly as a result of Japan's stiff competition. Some people blame Japan for causing unemployment in the United States.

American feelings about this issue grew stronger in the 1990s. Some politicians urged the government to use a policy of **protectionism** in dealing with Japan. Such a policy calls for actions, such as raising tariffs, to protect a market from imports.

In 1994 the United States government said it would take such actions if Japan did not end "procedures that lock American or other foreign products out of the Japanese market."

In July 1995 the United States and Japan agreed on a plan to open up the American automobile market to Japanese consumers. Many people believe that this is a good first step toward a more balanced trade.

 **How did Japan respond to United States concerns about Japanese trade practices?**

## JAPAN'S COMPETITORS

Japan is no longer the only industrial power in Asia. South Korea, Taiwan, Hong Kong, and Singapore are catching up. Their economies are among the fastest-growing in the world.

South Korea borrowed money from Japan and used Japanese ideas to build its manufacturing industry. Today South Korea is a leader in building ships and making textiles. Its low-priced goods compete with those of Japan in the electronics and automobile markets. Taiwan, too, exports electronic goods, textiles, and machinery.

Hong Kong's most important industries include textiles, electronics, plastics, and toys. Many foreign companies have built factories in Hong Kong because people there work for low pay. Foreign companies also like Hong Kong's status as a **free port**. This means that the government does not charge tariffs on

imports or exports. No one knows if this situation will continue. For more than 150 years, Hong Kong has been under British control. The year 1997 marks the date of Hong Kong's becoming part of China. Even experts admit that they cannot predict how this political change will affect Hong Kong's economy.

The nation of Singapore lies at the tip of the Malay Peninsula, on the Strait of Malacca (muh•LA•kuh). Its location makes Singapore an ideal stop for ships from all over the world and has helped it grow strong economically.

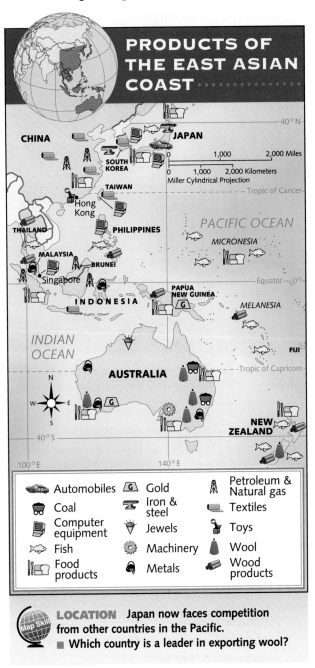

**PRODUCTS OF THE EAST ASIAN COAST**

| Legend | | |
|---|---|---|
| Automobiles | Gold | Petroleum & Natural gas |
| Coal | Iron & steel | Textiles |
| Computer equipment | Jewels | Toys |
| Fish | Machinery | Wool |
| Food products | Metals | Wood products |

**LOCATION** Japan now faces competition from other countries in the Pacific.
■ Which country is a leader in exporting wool?

### Hong Kong

Located off the southern coast of China, Hong Kong includes Kowloon, which is on the mainland, and about 200 islands. Kowloon and one of the largest of these islands—the island of Hong Kong—form a fine natural harbor. British ships began using the harbor to trade with China around 1700. Britain took control of the area in 1842, after the Opium War. The colony, however, did not begin its rise to economic power until after World War II. Many people wonder if Hong Kong's economy will keep growing under Chinese control.

Hong Kong at night

Some non-Asian countries along the Pacific Rim are also challenging Japan in economic growth. Among these are Australia and New Zealand. Mines in Australia supply precious metals, iron ore, coal, and petroleum. Australia also exports wool and cereals. New Zealand produces a variety of foods for export. It is also a source of cork, wood, wool, and machinery.

 **Which industrial powers are now sharing economic leadership of Asia with Japan?**

## LESSON 2 REVIEW

### Check Understanding

1. **Recall the Facts**   What problems did Japan face at the end of World War II?
2. **Focus on the Main Idea**   How did Japan gain importance in the industrial world?

### Think Critically

3. **Think More About It**   What do you think is Japan's greatest economic problem today? Explain.
4. **Explore Viewpoints**   What have American leaders said about the ways in which Japanese companies conduct business? What might the Japanese say in response?

### Show What You Know

**Simulation Activity**   With a group of classmates, create your own country. Give it a name, a location, and a population. Create a flag and perhaps a national anthem. Next list the country's resources. Then draw up a plan for how your country can become a leading industrial power in the world.

# HowTo

# Read a Climograph

## Why Is This Skill Important?

Climate affects the foods people can grow in a place and the kinds of shelter and clothing they need to live there. One way to learn more about the climate of a place is to study a climograph. A **climograph** shows the average monthly temperature and the average monthly precipitation for a place. Knowing about the climate can help you understand more about a place and its people.

## Understand the Process

A climograph shows both temperature and precipitation information. It is a line graph and a bar graph in one. Temperatures are shown as a line graph. Amounts of precipitation are shown as a bar graph. Along the bottom of a climograph are the months of the year.

Along the left-hand side of a climograph is a Fahrenheit scale to measure temperature. A dot is placed to show the average temperature for each month. These dots are connected with a line. By studying the line, you can see which months are hotter and which are colder.

Along the right-hand side of a climograph is a scale to measure precipitation in inches. A bar is drawn up to the average amount for each month. By studying the heights of the bars, you can see which months are drier and which are wetter.

The climograph shown here gives weather averages for the Japanese city of Tokyo. Japan's climate is much like that of the eastern United States. It is colder in the north and warmer in the south. Tokyo is located in Japan's warmer southern region. Study the climograph and answer the questions about the temperature and precipitation of the city.

1. Which are the warmest and coldest months in Tokyo?
2. Which are the wettest and driest months in Tokyo?
3. What is the average temperature for Tokyo in January? in May? in October?
4. What relationship is there between the temperature and amount of precipitation in Tokyo?
5. What generalizations can you make about the climate of Tokyo?

## Think and Apply

Use an almanac to create a climograph for your town or city. Compare your climograph with that for Tokyo. Share your findings with a friend or a family member. What does the information tell you about the place where you live?

## CLIMOGRAPH
## TOKYO, JAPAN

# SOUTH AMERICA

LESSON 3

## Link to Our World

### What happens when nations grow and change?

#### Focus on the Main Idea
*Look for problems the South American nations have faced while growing and changing in the twentieth century.*

#### Preview Vocabulary
*hydroelectric power*
*developing nation*
*subsistence farming*
*nationalize*
*favela*
*deforestation*

Angel Falls, the world's highest waterfall, is on Auyán-Tepuí mountain in eastern Venezuela.

Although Japan is a small island nation with few natural resources, it has become a leading industrial power. Compared to Japan, the countries of South America have many more natural resources. Even so, most of those countries have had a hard time building strong economies.

## THE GEOGRAPHY OF SOUTH AMERICA

South America has a variety of physical features. Among these are the Andes, the world's longest mountain range. These mountains curve about 4,500 miles (7,242 km) down the Pacific coast of South America from Venezuela to Tierra del Fuego (TEE•air•ah del FWAY•goh) at the tip of Argentina. The mighty Amazon River in northern South America is second only to the Nile River in length, but it has a much greater volume of water. Angel Falls in Venezuela, at 3,212 feet (979 m), is the world's highest waterfall.

South America also has many climates and types of plants. The huge tropical rain forest of the Amazon River basin occupies much of the continent. Amazonia, as the rain-forest region is called, covers about 2.5 million square miles (6.58 million sq km). One-third of the world's plant and animal species live in this hot, wet region.

South America has desert lands, too. The Atacama (a•tuh•KAH•muh) Desert in northern Chile gets almost no rain. Few plants or animals can live in such a dry climate.

As much as 80 percent of the land in South America is good for farming. Beneath the soil lie many minerals—oil, iron ore, copper, tin, silver, lead, zinc, gold, and precious stones. Many rivers can be used for making hydroelectric power. **Hydroelectric power** is electricity produced by water power.

 **What are the main features of the geography of South America?**

## THE SOUTH AMERICAN ECONOMY

Even with their rich resources, most South American countries are considered to be **developing nations**. Such nations usually have fast-growing populations, use few resources, and base their economies on agriculture. Since the end of World War II, the population of South America has more than doubled. Such fast growth can cause problems for a nation's economy.

South America does not lack resources, but the resources often are not used as well as they could be. Much land that could be farmed is not being used. It is held by the rich, who think of the land only as wealth, not as a resource for producing food. Despite this, nearly half of South America's workers are farmers. Most carry on **subsistence farming**, raising only enough food for their families.

South American countries are trying to use their resources in better ways. In some plains areas farmers now raise cattle to take advantage of good land for grazing. Many countries have begun to look for better ways to use their mineral resources as well. Chile, for example, has about 25 percent of the world's copper, and this metal has become Chile's most important source of income.

These changes have brought problems as well as benefits. For example, some South American countries have gone into debt trying to improve their mining industries. South American countries still face economic challenges.

 **How have the countries of South America tried to change their economies?**

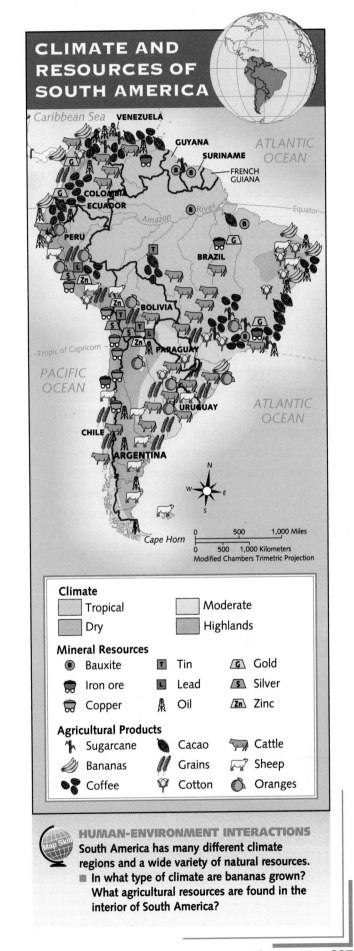

### CLIMATE AND RESOURCES OF SOUTH AMERICA

**Climate**

☐ Tropical ☐ Moderate
☐ Dry ☐ Highlands

**Mineral Resources**

| | | |
|---|---|---|
| Ⓑ Bauxite | Ⓣ Tin | Ⓖ Gold |
| 🛒 Iron ore | Ⓛ Lead | Ⓢ Silver |
| 🛒 Copper | Ⓐ Oil | Ⓩ Zinc |

**Agricultural Products**

| | | |
|---|---|---|
| Sugarcane | Cacao | Cattle |
| Bananas | Grains | Sheep |
| Coffee | Cotton | Oranges |

**HUMAN-ENVIRONMENT INTERACTIONS**
South America has many different climate regions and a wide variety of natural resources.
■ In what type of climate are bananas grown? What agricultural resources are found in the interior of South America?

# VENEZUELA AND COLOMBIA

Venezuela and Colombia are located in northwestern South America. In many ways their economies are similar.

A series of military dictators had control of Venezuela during much of the first half of the twentieth century. For the most part they let foreign companies control the country's greatest resource—oil. In 1958 a group of military leaders who wanted to set up a democracy seized control of the country. A freely elected government took office the following year and began working to improve education, health care, and other social services.

In the 1970s the government of Venezuela **nationalized** the oil industry. That is, it took control of the industry on behalf of the nation's people. Oil soon became the most important part of the country's economy. High prices for oil in the 1970s and 1980s helped make Venezuela a rich country. However, not all people shared in the wealth. Many people remained poor, especially those living in the countryside.

In the late 1980s oil prices fell, and so did the Venezuelan economy. As oil prices rose

Oil production has helped make Venezuela one of the richest countries in South America.

again in the early 1990s, the economy improved. Unfortunately, as long as Venezuela depends on a single product, its economy will slide up and down. Recent finds of iron ore may help the economy become more stable.

Colombia's economy also depends on a single product. Coffee makes up about half of Colombia's exports. In the 1970s coffee prices were fairly low. So peasant farmers turned to an illegal crop that was in high demand— coca leaves. The addictive drug cocaine is made from these leaves. This drug is smuggled from Colombia to the United States and other countries.

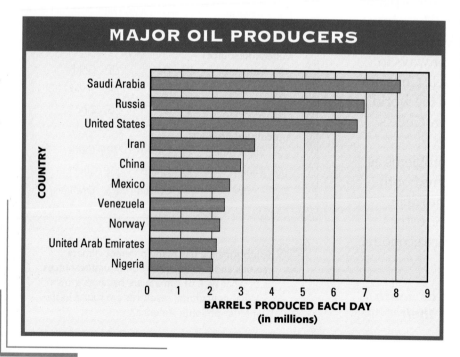

**MAJOR OIL PRODUCERS**

BARRELS PRODUCED EACH DAY (in millions)

**LEARNING FROM GRAPHS**
Countries from around the globe make up the list of the world's top oil producers.
■ About how many millions of barrels of oil does Venezuela produce in a day?

By demanding basic human rights, protesters helped bring an end to Augusto Pinochet's dictatorship in Chile.

Soon gangs began to fight for control of the drug trade. Violence became part of everyday life. At the same time, guerrilla bands, or small groups of fighters, began trying to overthrow the government. By the early 1990s the violence had decreased. Still, drug-related crimes and political unrest continue in Colombia today.

 **What do the economies of Venezuela and Colombia have in common?**

## CHILE

Political changes have greatly affected Chile's economy. In 1970 the people of Chile elected Salvador Allende (ah•YEN•day) as president. Allende immediately began to change the economy from free enterprise to socialist. He put most industries under the control of the national government. Then he gave the workers a say in how those industries would be run. He also ordered that the industries pay their workers more and set limits on how high the prices of goods could rise.

At first these actions seemed to work, and business boomed. Then prices for copper,

Chile's main export, fell. Inflation soared and the economy failed. Many Chileans in the middle and upper classes demanded change.

In September 1973 General Augusto Pinochet (pee•noh•CHET) seized power and became dictator. Allende and many of his supporters were killed. Pinochet declared that the constitution was no longer in effect. He got rid of all political parties. He sold industries owned by the government to private businesses and removed the tariffs on imports. He also stopped pay raises for workers and put strong control on the activities of labor unions.

After ten years of Pinochet's rule, inflation was lower and the economy had improved. However, most workers were suffering. By the early 1980s more people than ever were out of work. Without the tariffs many of Chile's industries found it hard to compete with cheap imports, and they went out of business. Chile depended on copper even more than before.

By the late 1980s the people of Chile had grown tired of Pinochet's dictatorship. In March 1989 they removed him from office through free elections. The new government allowed other countries to invest in Chile and brought about a more open economy. The country is now learning how to produce more of its own food by irrigating its desert lands. Chile's exports are also rising dramatically.

 **How did General Augusto Pinochet change the Chilean economy?**

## BRAZIL

In the first half of the twentieth century, Brazil's economy was based almost entirely on coffee. Today, however, Brazil is the most heavily industrialized of all the South American countries, and it exports a variety of products.

The drive to build new industries for Brazil began under President Getúlio Vargas (zheh•TOO•lyoo VAR•guhs), who held office from 1930 to 1945. Brazilian industry got another boost in the 1950s under President Juscelino Kubitschek (zhoo•seh•LEE•noh KOO•buh•chek). President Kubitschek promised "50 years of progress in 5." A new capital, Brasília (bruh•ZIL•yuh), and

11,000 miles (17,702 km) of new highways were built.

Today such goods as automobiles, ships, and steel make up more than half of Brazil's exports. Brazil also exports farm products, such as bananas, oranges, beef, coffee, and cacao—the beans used to make cocoa. These activities have made Brazil's economy the strongest in all of South America.

Not all Brazilians share in the economic success. The rich are very rich and live in fine homes in the cities. Yet in the **favelas** (fuh•VEH•luhz), or slums outside the cities, poor families live in one-room shacks.

Careless development of Brazil's resources has caused a huge problem for Amazonia— and for the whole Earth. Farmers and timber companies have been clearing huge sections of rain forest. The Brazilian government has passed environmental laws to try to stop such **deforestation**, or clearing of forests. Unfortunately, the laws are being ignored. At least 4,000 square miles (10,359 sq km) of Brazilian rain forest are still being destroyed each year.

Destroying the rain forest harms the whole world. Workers usually clear the land to

Many places in Brazil, such as the Monumental Axis (below), offer positive signs of a growing economy. At the same time, this favela (right) in Rio de Janeiro is an example of the poverty that many of Brazil's people face.

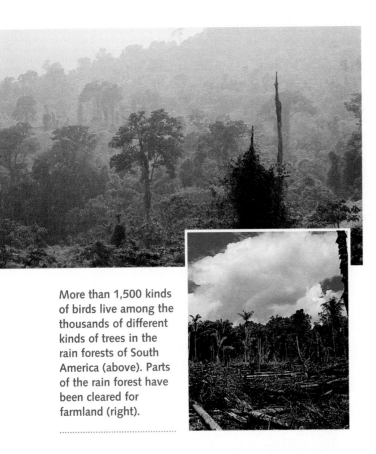

More than 1,500 kinds of birds live among the thousands of different kinds of trees in the rain forests of South America (above). Parts of the rain forest have been cleared for farmland (right).

make room for farms by burning many trees. These huge fires cause pollution and leave the soil bare. The rain forest's soil has few natural nutrients. When heavy rains fall on the bare soil, the few nutrients present are washed away. This means that the farmers can grow crops there only for about two or three years after clearing. Once the soil loses its nutrients, people must clear new land if they want to continue farming.

The loss of rain forest trees also changes the world's air and climate. All trees produce oxygen, which we need to breathe. Trees also take in carbon dioxide. With fewer trees, there is more carbon dioxide in the air. The burning of the trees adds even more carbon dioxide. This increased carbon dioxide may be causing a warming of the Earth's atmosphere. Rising temperatures and drier conditions could hurt farming around the globe. Global warming also might cause polar ice to melt, raising the levels of ocean water and flooding coastal lands.

Clearing the rain forest hurts people in other ways as well. Many native peoples have to find new places to live because they have lost their forest homes. As they come into contact with workers and other people they have never met before, they catch diseases. Also, away from their homes, they may lose touch with their own culture. The loss of the rain forest also means the loss of thousands of plants that cannot grow anywhere else. We will never know if these plants could have been important to science, perhaps even for curing diseases.

✓ **What economic and environmental problems does Brazil face?**

# *L*ESSON 3 REVIEW

## Check Understanding

1. **Recall the Facts** Why are most South American countries called developing nations?
2. **Focus on the Main Idea** What problems have South American nations faced while developing their economies?

## Think Critically

3. **Personally Speaking** Which of their economic problems do you think South American countries need to deal with first? Why do you think so?
4. **Cause and Effect** Why are changes in world prices for copper, coffee, and oil a problem for some South American countries?

## Show What You Know

**Article-Writing Activity**
Choose one South American country, and imagine that you have just become its leader. Write an article titled "The Economy: Today's Problems, Tomorrow's Hopes." Post your article on a class bulletin board for others to read.

# WHAT IS THE BEST WAY TO
# *U*SE *the W*ORLD'S
# *R*ESOURCES?

Just as a person must make spending choices, nations must make economic choices. For some nations, especially developing nations, these choices are difficult. To help their economies grow, developing nations need to decide on the best uses for their resources. To use their resources one way, they give up the possibility of using them in other ways. This is called a **trade-off**. If nations clear parts of their rain forests for other uses, the trade-off is that they will no longer have the forests.

When a nation makes an economic choice, what it gives up is the **opportunity cost** of what it gets. If nations keep their rain forests, it costs them the opportunity to use the land in other ways, such as for farming, mining, or logging. If they clear their rain forests, it costs them the use of the forests and the benefits of the forests to the Earth itself.

People have different viewpoints about the economic choices nations should make about their rain forests. Read the following quotations from a writer, a government worker, and a person who lives in the Amazon region to learn what each person believes is the best use of rain-forest resources.

Writer Jonathan Burton believes in finding more-profitable uses for rain forests:

**"**One proposal is to harvest the forests for useful and renewable resources instead of cutting them down. A 1989 study showed that an acre in the Peruvian Amazon would be worth $148 if used for cattle pasture, $1,000 if cut for timber, and $6,820 if selectively combed for fruits, rubber, and other products. Using this method, known as 'sustainable development,' countries could gain economic benefits and at the same time preserve one of the planet's most biologically diverse areas. **"**

Zoran Bosnic, who works for the Brazilian government, believes that Brazil must use its natural resources, including its rain forests, in order to grow stronger.

66Europe and America [the United States] destroyed their forests to become industrial powers, but when it comes to the Amazon they say, 'Stop!' Brazil has a debt, people to feed and employ. The economy is under terrific pressure. It must industrialize as soon as possible.99

Santos Adam Afsua, a Peruvian Indian, believes that the people who live in the rain forest should be the ones to make decisions about it.

66We live to protect the forest with the best ecological and environmental knowledge that we possess, a knowledge we inherited from our ancestors. We do this with the understanding that we will continue living there, and we have to protect this forest because we have to think of future generations. . . . We have come to meet with the different environmental organizations to tell them, first of all, that the only people that can really conserve the environment are our people.99

People have many different ideas about how to preserve or make use of the world's rain forests. Above is a scene of the undisturbed El Yunque rain forest in Puerto Rico. At right, work continues on the Carajas Mining Project in Brazil on land that was once rain forest.

# COMPARE
## VIEWPOINTS

1. Why does Jonathan Burton believe that sustainable development is the best use of rain forest resources?

2. Why does Zoran Bosnic believe that it is necessary to clear parts of rain forests for industrial use?

3. How is the viewpoint of Santos Adam Afsua different from those of Jonathan Burton and Zoran Bosnic?

# THINK
## –AND–
# APPLY

People often have different viewpoints about the best way to solve a problem. Which of the three ideas given above do you think is the best? Why? What other ideas do you have about using rain-forest resources?

# FREE TRADE

## *Link to Our World*

*How might cooperation among neighboring countries affect the economies of those countries?*

### *Focus on the Main Idea*
*As you read, think about how Canada, Mexico, and the United States are working together economically in the late twentieth century.*

### *Preview Vocabulary*
| | |
|---|---|
| bilingual | Great Society |
| ratify | national debt |
| secede | bloc |

Canada, Mexico, and the United States have all made great economic progress during the twentieth century. Still, as a new century begins, they all face economic challenges.

## A NORTHERN GIANT

The beginning of the twentieth century seemed to promise a bright future for Canada. In the late 1890s gold had been discovered in the Yukon Territory, in Canada's far northwest. Canadians soon found that they had other natural resources that the world wanted. Their nickel, copper, zinc, and other metals turned out to be worth as much as the Yukon gold. Canada's forests became valuable as well, because people needed wood pulp to make paper. Also, the land of southwestern Canada proved to be good for wheat farming and for ranching.

In 1931 Canada gained its independence from Britain. Not long after, Canada, like many other nations, suffered through the Great Depression. People all over Canada lost their jobs. After World War II, Canada began to recover. Canadians built up their iron, steel, and aluminum industries and discovered deposits of oil, natural gas, and minerals.

Today Canada has a strong economy and one of the world's highest standards of living. But Canada, like many other countries, has problems such as inflation and unemployment. In addition, Canada has some problems that are purely Canadian.

Canada, like the United States, has a federal form of government. But the provinces of Canada have more authority than the states that make up the United

In the Canadian gold rush of 1898, people dug for gold in the streets of this Yukon town.

States. The federal government and the provinces cannot agree on which should run Canada's oil industry and have more of the profits.

Canada faces still another problem. In 1763 Britain took over Quebec from the French. Since that time, Canada has been a country with two main cultures and languages. French Canadians are a minority in Canada, but in Quebec they make up more than 80 percent of the population. French is Quebec's official language. For many years the people of Quebec have wanted their language and culture recognized by all of Canada.

In 1969 the Official Languages Act made Canada a **bilingual** country, a nation with two official languages. Then in the late 1980s

Bilingual sign in a Canadian park

the Canadian government planned to recognize the people of Quebec as a "distinct society" within Canada. The other Canadian provinces, however, refused to **ratify**, or approve, this. Many people in Quebec called for the province to **secede**, or separate, from Canada. In October 1995 the people of Quebec narrowly voted to remain part of Canada. Leaders of the movement that fought to separate vowed to continue trying for an independent Quebec.

 **Why does Quebec want to secede from the rest of Canada?**

REGIONS
Canada has a great wealth of resources.
■ For what resources is Quebec known?

The city of Quebec, capital of the Canadian province of Quebec, is a major tourist center.

**CANADA AND ITS RESOURCES**

Copper
Fish and shellfish
Forest products
Gold
Iron ore

N  Nickel
A  Oil or natural gas
S  Silver
Wheat
Zn  Zinc
⊛  National capital
★  Provincial capital

# PROGRESS IN MEXICO

Since World War II, Mexico has faced the same economic problems as its neighbors in Central and South America. Slowly, the Mexican economy has come to depend less on agriculture and more on industry. The most important industry is now oil refining. Instead of exporting the oil in its crude form—as it comes from the ground—the Mexican government refines it first. Refined oil products are worth more than crude oil exports. Refining also provides more jobs for the Mexican people.

To build its industries, Mexico used aid from the United States. Both the United States government and private businesses loaned money to Mexican business people. Companies in the United States also set up *maquiladoras* (mah•kee•lah•DOH•rahs), or border industries, in Mexico. Mexican workers at the *maquiladora* plants make finished goods using parts shipped from the United States.

While the *maquiladora* system has created jobs for many Mexican men and women, it has had some unwelcome effects in Mexico as well. For example, pollution has increased greatly because of the factories.

Over the years Mexico has made much economic progress. Today it is one of the most highly industrialized countries in Latin America. However, because Mexico's economy depends so much on the price of oil, the country has problems when oil prices fall. Mexico also owes a lot of money to other countries.

Perhaps the biggest problem Mexico faces is its fast population growth. Mexico City alone has grown by 3 million people in the past ten years. It may have another 10 million by the year 2025. In Mexico City thousands of

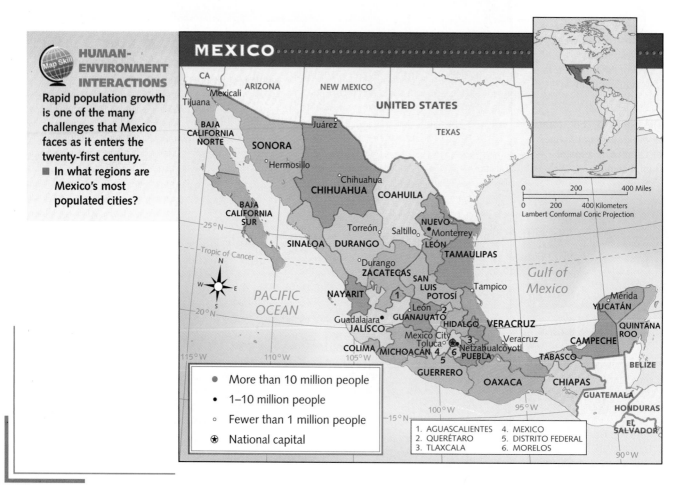

**HUMAN-ENVIRONMENT INTERACTIONS**

Rapid population growth is one of the many challenges that Mexico faces as it enters the twenty-first century.

■ In what regions are Mexico's most populated cities?

**MEXICO**

- ● More than 10 million people
- • 1–10 million people
- ○ Fewer than 1 million people
- ✸ National capital

1. AGUASCALIENTES
2. QUERÉTARO
3. TLAXCALA
4. MEXICO
5. DISTRITO FEDERAL
6. MORELOS

This newly built university in Mexico City (left) and this telephone-repair plant (above) reflect Mexico's rapid growth.

poor people have made their homes next to garbage dumps. They pick through the trash, trying to find something they can sell. Elsewhere in Mexico the poor face equally hard conditions.

People in Chiapas (chee•AH•pahs), Mexico's poorest state, were angry that their living conditions were so bad. Indian tribes in Chiapas rebelled in early 1994, asking for major economic and political changes. Government and rebel leaders worked out an end to the fighting. Many experts, however, think the rebellion in Chiapas may be only the first sign that major political unrest will happen elsewhere in Mexico.

 **How are Mexico's economic problems similar to those of other Latin American countries?**

## A LEADING ECONOMIC POWER

In the United States, industries making goods for use in World War II created new jobs. This put money into the economy and helped pull the United States out of the Great Depression. By the mid-1950s the country was doing well. Labor union leader George Meany told union members, "You've never had it so good!" At the same time, however, many people lived in poverty.

In the mid-1960s President Lyndon Johnson felt that the federal government needed to do something for poor people. He proposed to Congress what he called the **Great Society**. In the Great Society, he said, every American would have the chance for a good life. His Great Society programs covered civil rights, health care, education, and housing.

At the same time, the United States became heavily involved in the Vietnam War. The government borrowed money to pay for the Great Society at home and for the war in Vietnam. Because government spending was so high, the economy weakened.

Both President Richard Nixon, who followed Johnson, and the next two Presidents, Gerald Ford and Jimmy Carter, faced high inflation because of increased government spending. Each tried something new to solve the problem, but all failed.

President Ronald Reagan, who was elected in 1980, also had a plan to help the economy. He believed that the United States had spent too much money helping the poor. Reagan reduced government spending and cut taxes. Inflation decreased. Defense spending rose, however. The government then borrowed more money by selling bonds to individuals and banks. The **national debt**—the amount of money that is owed by the government—increased greatly.

In the early 1990s many Americans questioned why their taxes should pay for social service programs. Also, many people wanted to end the country's role as the world's "police officer." They felt that other countries should settle their own conflicts without help from the United States.

In the years since World War II, both the economy of the United States and the government's role in the economy have changed. In the 1950s the economy was based on manufacturing. Today most Americans work in service industries. Also, in the 1950s, the United States was the world's leading economic power. Today the United States is one of a number of economic powers. Japan and Germany are just two of the countries that compete with the United States for economic leadership of the world.

 **How has the American economy changed since the 1950s?**

## THE NORTH AMERICAN FREE TRADE AGREEMENT

In 1992 Canada, Mexico, and the United States, with the backing of United States President George Bush, proposed the North American Free Trade Agreement. This agreement is more commonly known as NAFTA. Under the agreement the participating countries would, over a 15-year period, end all tariffs and other trade restrictions among them. Some farmers in Mexico disliked the idea of NAFTA. They feared that the agreement would bring farm products from the United States and Canada and hurt their sales. Some labor leaders in Canada and the United States also opposed NAFTA. They believed that large companies would move to Mexico so they could hire people for less money. As a result, many workers in Canada and the United States would lose their jobs.

Business leaders claimed, however, that NAFTA would actually strengthen the economies of Canada and the United States. They said that an improved Mexican economy would increase the Mexican demand for goods from Canada and the

From right to left: U.S. President Bill Clinton with former Presidents George Bush, Jimmy Carter, and Gerald Ford at the signing of a NAFTA side agreement

## FREE-TRADE GROUPS IN THE AMERICAS

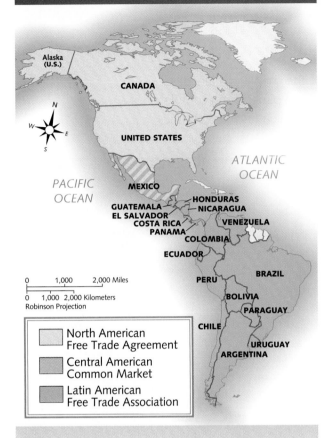

Alaska (U.S.)

CANADA

UNITED STATES

ATLANTIC OCEAN

PACIFIC OCEAN

MEXICO

GUATEMALA
EL SALVADOR
COSTA RICA
PANAMA

HONDURAS
NICARAGUA

VENEZUELA

COLOMBIA

ECUADOR

PERU

BRAZIL

BOLIVIA

PARAGUAY

CHILE

URUGUAY

ARGENTINA

0   1,000   2,000 Miles
0  1,000  2,000 Kilometers
Robinson Projection

☐ North American Free Trade Agreement

☐ Central American Common Market

☐ Latin American Free Trade Association

 **REGIONS** Most countries in the Americas have entered into trade agreements with their Western Hemisphere neighbors.
■ According to the map, of what trade groups is Mexico a member?

United States. A Canadian business leader put it this way:

> 66I'm a very firm believer that for every activity we lose to Mexican . . . competition, we're simply putting dollars into the pockets of people bound to be buying something.99

After much debate United States President George Bush and the leaders of Canada and Mexico signed the agreement in late 1992. NAFTA went into effect in January 1994. Business leaders in the three countries hope NAFTA will lead to a powerful North American free-trade **bloc**, or group of nations

with the same interests. This free-trade bloc, they believe, will help them compete against Asian and European companies.

In 1993 a number of Central American countries signed their own free-trade agreement. Some South American countries have done the same. Business leaders from Canada to Argentina believe that one day all the countries of the Western Hemisphere will be part of one free-trade agreement. No one knows when that day will be, but in 1994 the country of Chile was invited to join NAFTA.

 **What do business leaders in Canada, Mexico, and the United States hope NAFTA will achieve?**

# LESSON 4 REVIEW

## Check Understanding

1. **Recall the Facts**   What does NAFTA stand for?
2. **Focus on the Main Idea**   How are Canada, Mexico, and the United States working together in the late twentieth century?

## Think Critically

3. **Think More About It**   Do you think that moving Canadian and United States companies to Mexico will benefit the people of Canada and the United States? Explain.
4. **Explore Viewpoints**   Why did some people oppose NAFTA? Why did other people support NAFTA?
5. **Cause and Effect**   How can the lowering of tariffs help both consumers and industries that produce consumer goods?

## Show What You Know

 **Letter-Writing Activity**   Write a letter to a local business leader. Ask whether NAFTA has changed his or her business, and if so, what changes has it brought? Report to your classmates on what you learn.

# CHAPTER 21
# REVIEW

## CONNECT MAIN IDEAS

Use this organizer to show that you understand how the chapter's main ideas are connected. Copy the organizer onto a separate sheet of paper. Then complete it by writing several sentences to describe the economic challenges that countries have faced in the twentieth century.

**China**
_____
_____
_____

**Japan**
_____
_____
_____

**Economic Challenges**

**The Countries of South America**
_____
_____
_____

**The Countries of North America**
_____
_____
_____

## WRITE MORE ABOUT IT

1. **Write a Biography**   Research and write a one-page biography on one of the following Chinese leaders or would-be leaders: Sun Yat-sen, Chiang Kai-shek, Mao Zedong, Jiang Qing, Deng Xiaoping, or a present-day leader of China. The first paragraph should provide background information, such as details about the person's birth, early life, education, and death. The second paragraph should explain the leader's rise to power, and the third should explain the leader's ideas about governing. At the end of your report, describe the characteristics you think a good leader should have. Then tell whether the individual you selected had or has the characteristics needed to be a good leader.

2. **Write a Paragraph**   What do you think life is like economically for the people of Japan today? Write a one-page description of a day in the life of a Japanese worker. Be sure to describe living and working conditions.

3. **Write Your Opinion**   Do you think Quebec will try again to secede from the rest of Canada? If so, will it be successful? Explain why you hold the opinion you do.

4. **Write a Pamphlet**   Think about the environmental problems the world faces today. Some of these problems are air pollution, noise pollution, and loss of natural resources. Select one problem, and write a short pamphlet about the problem and ways to solve it.

## USE VOCABULARY

For each pair of terms, write a sentence or two that explains how the terms are related.

1. commune, Cultural Revolution

2. developing nation, subsistence farming

3. Great Society, national debt

4. ratify, secede

5. trade surplus, protectionism

## CHECK UNDERSTANDING

1. What political party grew out of China's demand for change in the early 1900s?

2. What type of change has China recently made—political or economic?

3. How did the United States help Japan rebuild its economy after World War II?

4. Why do foreign companies like Hong Kong's status as a free port?

5. What is a developing nation?

6. How has Brazil's economy changed since the first half of the twentieth century?

7. What makes Canada a bilingual country?

8. What is NAFTA?

## THINK CRITICALLY

1. **Cause and Effect**   What were the effects of Mao's Cultural Revolution in China?

2. **Personally Speaking**   Do you think the United States was right to help Japan rebuild after World War II? Explain.

3. **Think More About It**   The economy of Colombia depends on one product—coffee. What problems can come about when an economy is supported by just one product?

4. **Explore Viewpoints**   What are some reasons why some people want to save the rain forests? What are some reasons why others want to use the resources of the rain forests?

5. **Past to Present**   How might the increasing national debt in the United States affect you and future generations of Americans?

## APPLY SKILLS

**How to Read a Cartogram**   Draw a cartogram that compares the populations of Arizona, Nevada, New Mexico, California, and Texas. To find the population of each state, look in an almanac. Once you have drawn your cartogram, answer these questions.

1. Which state shown in your cartogram has the largest population?

2. Which state shown in your cartogram has the smallest population?

3. Compare each state's population with its physical size. Is there a relationship between population and size among these states? Explain.

**How to Read a Climograph**   Select a large city in the United States. Look in an almanac to find that city's average temperature and precipitation for each month of the year. Make a climograph of that information. Then exchange climographs with a classmate. Write a paragraph that describes the information shown in your classmate's climograph.

## READ MORE ABOUT IT

*The Forty-Third War* by Louise Moeri. Houghton Mifflin. Twelve-year-old Uno is drafted into the revolutionary army of a Central American country.

*Pacific Crossing* by Gary Soto. Harcourt Brace. Lincoln Mendoza, a fourteen-year-old Mexican American, spends a summer with a host family in Japan and has many new experiences.

# CHAPTER 22

# RELIGIOUS INFLUENCES

> 66 Here religion is the strongest feature of civilizations, at the heart of both their present and their past. 99

Historian Fernand Braudel, describing the people of Southwest Asia

Young Muslim woman from North Africa

# LESSON 1

# The INDIAN SUBCONTINENT

## L ink to Our World

**How can religious beliefs shape people's lives?**

*Focus on the Main Idea*
*As you read, look for ways that religion has affected the history of the Indian subcontinent.*

*Preview Vocabulary*
satyagraha
passive resistance
discriminate
harijan
Mahatma
boycott
minority rights

Mohandas Gandhi

At the beginning of the twentieth century, most people in India agreed about one thing—they wanted the British to leave. Yet as they worked toward this goal, religious differences divided them. Religious conflict has continued to affect the Indian subcontinent to the present day.

## GANDHI WORKS FOR INDEPENDENCE

In 1893 Mohandas Gandhi (moh•HAHN•dahs GAHN•dee), a young Indian lawyer who had studied in London, took a job in South Africa. Shortly after he arrived, he went by train to visit some clients. As he had always done in Britain, he bought a first-class ticket. As soon as he got on the train, the conductors threw him out. Nonwhites could not travel first class, they told him. Gandhi realized that much work needed to be done to gain rights for the Indian people who lived in South Africa.

Gandhi remembered what his mother had taught him. A very religious woman, she had instructed him to respect all forms of life and to never hurt anyone or anything. With her teachings in mind, Gandhi came to believe that people must pay back bad actions with good ones, until those doing wrong grow tired of their actions. He called this idea **satyagraha** (suh•TYAH•gruh•huh), or "soul force." People practicing *satyagraha* must use peace instead of violence to bring about change. This approach to handling conflict is also known as **passive resistance**.

The Indians in South Africa used Gandhi's passive resistance with some success. By the time Gandhi left

South Africa, the government had removed the harshest laws that **discriminated**—or treated unfairly because of race or other reason—against Indians.

In 1914 Gandhi returned to India to help it win its independence from Britain. To show his support for the movement to free India, he wore traditional Indian clothing instead of his English suits. He gave away nearly everything he owned and lived very simply. Then he began to teach the idea of passive resistance. He said people should work for independence without violence. All people, whatever their race or religion, should be respected, he said, even India's outcasts, the untouchables. Gandhi began calling the untouchables by another name—**harijans** (har•ih•JAHNZ), or "children of God."

When the people of India heard how he lived and what he taught, many thought Gandhi was a holy man. They began to call him **Mahatma** (muh•HAHT•muh), or "Great Soul."

 **What way of working to gain rights did Gandhi encourage?**

## INDIAN INDEPENDENCE

Indian calls for independence grew louder and louder. The British answered by trying to stop the protests in any way they could. In April 1919, British Brigadier-General Reginald H. Dyer ordered soldiers to fire on peaceful protesters in the city of Amritsar (uhm•RIT•ser). About 400 people were killed and another 1,200 were wounded. Gandhi, feeling that there was no way to cooperate with the British, called for passive resistance across all of India.

This campaign of noncooperation took many forms. Some government leaders quit their jobs. Many workers stayed at home. Sometimes Gandhi and his followers simply sat down in the middle of a street, which,

Prime Minister Nehru reviews a troop of soldiers at an Independence Day ceremony in Bombay, India.

of course, stopped traffic. Gandhi also called on his followers to **boycott**, or refuse to buy, British goods. In all these ways the Indians brought business and government almost to a stop without using violence.

The British did not know how to deal with passive resistance. They tried to keep Gandhi away from his followers. In fact, they put him in jail several times. However, Gandhi was a strong leader even from behind prison walls. He wrote to his followers, urging them to continue their actions. He also prayed and went on long hunger strikes, refusing to eat until his demands were met.

By the end of World War II, the British saw that they were losing India. In 1947 they passed governing power to Jawaharlal Nehru (juh•WAH•her•lahl NAIR•oo). Nehru was a wealthy Brahman who had been working for India's independence since 1916. He seemed the ideal person to lead his country to freedom.

✓ **How did Gandhi help achieve India's freedom from Britain?**

## HINDUS AND MUSLIMS

Gandhi and Nehru wanted an independent India in which people of all religions could live in peace. Hindus and Muslims on the Indian subcontinent had been quarreling for hundreds of years. Their religions and their ways of life were very different.

Because there were fewer Muslims than Hindus in India, Muslims felt unsafe there. They believed they would never be guaranteed minority rights. **Minority rights** are freedoms given to groups of people who make up a small part of a population. Muslim leader Muhammad Ali Jinnah (JIH•nuh) demanded that his people have their own homeland. It should be in the north, he said, where there were more Muslims than Hindus. Reluctantly, Nehru and Gandhi agreed.

As August 15, 1947—the day set for Indian independence—came closer, millions of Muslims rushed north and millions of Hindus streamed south. People from both sides attacked each other. A million or more died, most of them Muslims.

Muslims crowd into railroad cars to travel to the land that is now Pakistan, where they would not be a minority.

# RELIGIONS OF THE INDIAN SUBCONTINENT

0    300    600 Miles
0    300    600 Kilometers
Two-Point Equidistant Projection

AFGHANISTAN
Islamabad • JAMMU AND KASHMIR
Amritsar
CHINA
PAKISTAN
Delhi
New Delhi
NEPAL   BHUTAN
HIMALAYAS
Karachi
Ganges River
Varanasi (Benares)
BANGLADESH
Calcutta
BURMA (MYANMAR)
Narmada River
INDIA
Formerly East Pakistan; split from Pakistan in 1971
Bombay
Arabian Sea
Madras
SRI LANKA
INDIAN OCEAN

**Major religions**
- Hinduism
- Islam
- Buddhism
- Sikhism
- Christianity
- Tribal and traditional

**REGIONS** Most of the people who live in India today practice the religion of Hinduism. ■ Where in India are other religions practiced?

The Indian independence agreement created not one new country, but two. The northwestern and northeastern corners of British India became Pakistan. The rest became India, led by Nehru. Today most of the people of Pakistan are Muslims, while most of the people of India are Hindus.

During the fighting between the Hindus and the Muslims, Gandhi was killed. In January 1948 he was shot by a Hindu who believed that Gandhi was hurting his people by saying that Hindus and Muslims should work together. When telling the country of Gandhi's death, Nehru said, "The light has gone out of our lives." Around the world, many people agreed.

✓ **Why did Muslims move north while Hindus moved south?**

Indira Gandhi gives a speech (above). At left the leader reviews her troops.

## MAJOR RELIGIONS

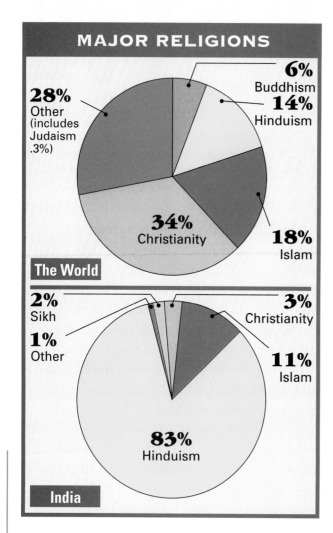

**The World**
- 6% Buddhism
- 14% Hinduism
- 18% Islam
- 34% Christianity
- 28% Other (includes Judaism .3%)

**India**
- 2% Sikh
- 1% Other
- 3% Christianity
- 11% Islam
- 83% Hinduism

**LEARNING FROM GRAPHS** More than three-fourths of the world's Hindus live in India.
■ Of the world's approximately 6 billion people, about how many practice Hinduism?

# MORE RELIGIOUS DIFFERENCES

Religious differences caused many conflicts between the two new nations. The biggest problem was the northern state of Kashmir. Its ruler, a Hindu, chose to join India, not Pakistan. However, most of Kashmir's people were Muslims, so Pakistan felt that it should get the state. This disagreement brought India and Pakistan to war in 1947 and again in 1965. Even today the Kashmir problem is not settled.

In the 1980s another religious problem developed. This one involved a different religious group, the Sikhs (SEEKS). This group, which began in the 1500s, combines ideas from both Hinduism and Islam. From the beginning the Sikhs have struggled with both Hindus and Muslims. In time the Sikhs demanded a land of their own for their safety.

Some Sikhs turned to violence to gain their own homeland. Indian Prime Minister Indira (in•DIR•uh) Gandhi, the daughter of Nehru, was determined to end the trouble. In June 1984 Gandhi ordered the army to attack the Golden Temple in Amritsar, which the Sikhs had turned into a fort. Almost 1,000 Sikhs died in the fighting. Many Sikhs wanted revenge for their losses. In October 1984 two of Gandhi's own bodyguards—both Sikhs—shot and killed her. Riots followed, and angry Hindus attacked any Sikhs they could find.

In the 1990s, Hindu leaders in India kept religious hatred alive. In Pakistan, Muslim leaders did the same. Religious conflict remains a problem on the Indian subcontinent today.

 **Who are the Sikhs?**

## WOMEN LEADERS

In the past, Hindu and Muslim traditions in India limited women's public roles. In the later part of the twentieth century, however, women began to take a more active part in governing. For example, Indira Gandhi was a leader in Indian politics for more than 19 years. Also, in 1988 Benazir Bhutto (BOO•toh) became prime minister of Pakistan. This made her the first woman in modern times to lead a Muslim country. Bangladesh (bahn•gluh•DESH), which gained independence from Pakistan in 1971, also elected a woman leader in the 1990s.

Although many Indian women stay at home, especially in rural areas, things are changing. In the cities more women are going to school, and many work outside the home. Some have become doctors, lawyers, and business leaders.

 **What two women have been important political leaders in India and Pakistan?**

### Benazir Bhutto 1953–

Benazir Bhutto was born in Pakistan to a wealthy Muslim family that was active in politics. At age 16 she left Pakistan to study in the United States and Britain. While she was away, her father, Zulfikar Ali Bhutto, became Pakistan's prime minister. She returned home in 1977, planning to follow her father into government service. Soon after her return, however, the army overthrew her father's government. In 1979, army leaders had him killed. In 1988, Benazir Bhutto struck back by running in the first free elections held since the army took over. She became the leader of her political party, and because it was the largest party, she became prime minister. Voted out of office in 1990, she won elections held in 1993 and once again became the leader of Pakistan.

## LESSON 1 REVIEW

### Check Understanding

1. **Recall the Facts**   Why did the agreement for Indian independence call for the creation of two countries—India and Pakistan?
2. **Focus on the Main Idea**   How did religion shape the history of the Indian subcontinent?

### Think Critically

3. **Think More About It**   What do you think Gandhi meant by the term *satyagraha*, or "soul force"?
4. **Cause and Effect**   How has India's history reflected conflict between Hindus and Muslims?

### Show What You Know

**Speaking Activity**   Search newspapers, magazines, and books to find an event in which nonviolent resistance proved to be the best way to handle a social or political problem. Describe what you learn to a family member or classmate.

# How To

# Use Different Types of Population Maps

## Why Is This Skill Important?

Like most geographic information, population can be shown on maps in many different ways. In Chapter 21 of Unit 10, you learned that cartograms use size to show population. Other ways to show population on maps are with dots and with color. Knowing how to read different kinds of population maps can make it easier for you to find out where few or many people live in the world and how many people live in each place.

## Understand the Process

The population of the world is not spread evenly across the seven continents. Map A uses dots to show the **population distribution** of India, or where people live on the subcontinent. Each dot on the map stands for 100,000 people. In some places on the map, the dots are so close that they run together. In these places, many people live close together. In other places on the map, there are no dots. Such places either have fewer than 100,000 people or have no people.

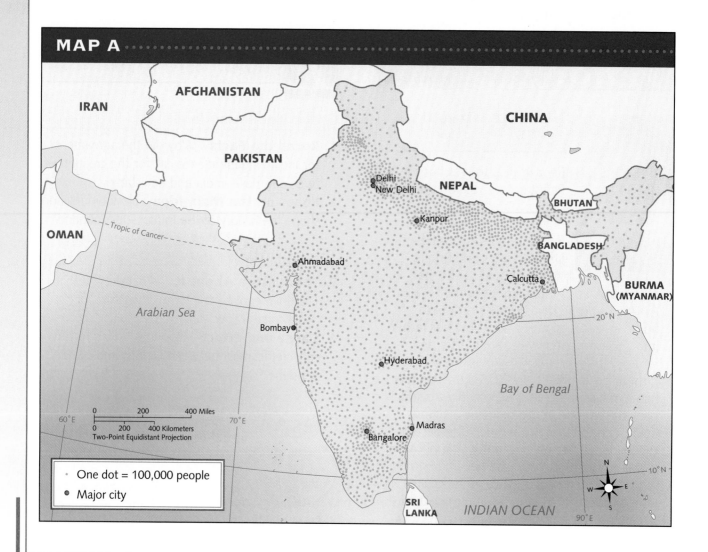

MAP A

One dot = 100,000 people

Major city

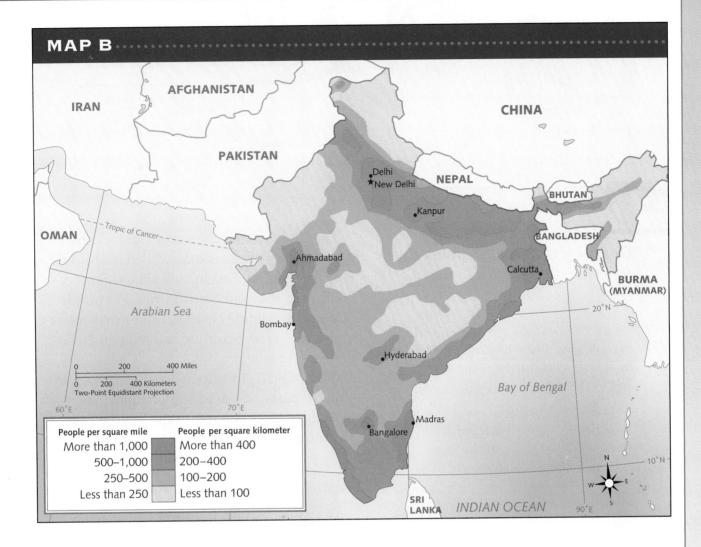

## MAP B

AFGHANISTAN
IRAN
CHINA
PAKISTAN
Delhi
★New Delhi
NEPAL
Kanpur
BHUTAN
OMAN
Tropic of Cancer
BANGLADESH
Ahmadabad
Calcutta
BURMA (MYANMAR)
20°N
Arabian Sea
Bombay
Hyderabad
Bay of Bengal
0   200   400 Miles
0   200   400 Kilometers
Two-Point Equidistant Projection
60°E                70°E
Madras
Bangalore

**People per square mile**
More than 1,000
500–1,000
250–500
Less than 250

**People  per square kilometer**
More than 400
200–400
100–200
Less than 100

SRI LANKA   INDIAN OCEAN
10°N
90°E

Where there are a great many people living close together, the population is *dense.* Where there are only a few people living far apart, the population is *sparse.* Both these terms describe population density. **Population density** is the average number of people living on a square unit of land. You can find this figure by dividing the number of people living on a given amount of land by the area of that land.

Dense populations are usually found in areas where the climate allows a long growing season. In India, good farming areas have very dense populations. Nearness of natural resources can also affect population density. But population density depends most of all on how easy communication and trade are. This explains why the coasts of India have dense populations.

Map B uses color to show the population density of India. Yellow stands for areas with populations of fewer than 250 people per square mile. Green stands for areas with populations of between 250 and 500 people per square mile. Brown stands for areas with populations of between 500 and 1,000 people per square mile. Red stands for areas with dense populations of more than 1,000 people per square mile.

### Think and Apply

With a partner, study the population maps of India on these pages. Together, prepare a list of five questions you might have your classmates answer to better understand how to use these population maps.

# LESSON 2

# THE MIDDLE EAST

## *Link to Our World*

**How can different peoples live together in peace?**

**Focus on the Main Idea**
*As you read, look for ideas and beliefs that have unified or divided people in Southwest Asia and North Africa.*

**Preview Vocabulary**
Zionism
Balfour
  Declaration
terrorism
partition
intifada
autonomy
hostage

The lands around the eastern and southern Mediterranean Sea are often called the Middle East. The Middle East includes the regions of Southwest Asia and North Africa. For hundreds of years the Middle East has been a crossroads for trade, warfare, culture, and religion. In fact, three world religions—Judaism, Christianity, and Islam—all grew up in Southwest Asia. In both the past and the present, religion has played an important role in the Middle East. The future promises more of the same.

## ARABS AND JEWS

The Arabs and the Jews have roots in the Middle East going back thousands of years. They both claim the same ancestor—Abraham. Yet these two peoples have been fighting each other for much of the twentieth century. The reasons for this conflict lie partly in the ancient past and partly in the recent past.

The early Jews and Arabs settled in Southwest Asia thousands of years ago. In A.D. 70, however, the Romans destroyed the Jewish capital of Jerusalem. Not long after that they forced many Jews from the region, which the Jews had called Judah. The Romans gave the area a new name, Palestine, to remove the Jewish people's connection with the land they had once controlled.

Over the centuries Jews settled in nearly every part

Jewish (left) and Arab (right) merchants share market space to sell their fruit in Jerusalem.

of the world. Those who left never forgot their homeland, however. Jews around the world end their Passover Seder (SAY•der)—the religious ceremony reminding them of their ancestors' departure from Egypt—with these words: "next year in Jerusalem."

As time passed, much changed in the land that had become known as Palestine. After the rise of Islam in the seventh century A.D., most Arabs became Muslims. Like the Jews and Christians, they considered Jerusalem a holy city. The Arab Muslims built an empire that governed most of the land in the Middle East. The Muslim Empire is remembered for its many achievements in science, medicine, and art.

In time, however, the Arabs lost control of much of their empire, including Palestine. For 400 years, beginning in the early 1500s, the land fell under the rule of another Muslim group, the Ottoman Turks. The Arabs longed to be free of Ottoman control.

During the late nineteenth and early twentieth centuries, more and more Jews began to come to the Middle East. Anti-Semitic, or anti-Jewish, activities in eastern Europe caused many Jews to leave that region and settle in Palestine. As more and more Jews settled there, some Jewish leaders decided to build a modern Jewish state in their homeland. This idea grew into a movement called **Zionism**.

Arab nationalism also began to grow around this time. Arabs throughout the Middle East looked forward to a time when they would have their own independent states.

During World War I, the British wanted the Jewish people to support the Allied war effort. In 1917 the British government issued the **Balfour Declaration**. This document stated that the British favored "the establishment in Palestine of a national home for the Jewish people." At the same time, the declaration stated that "nothing shall be done which may

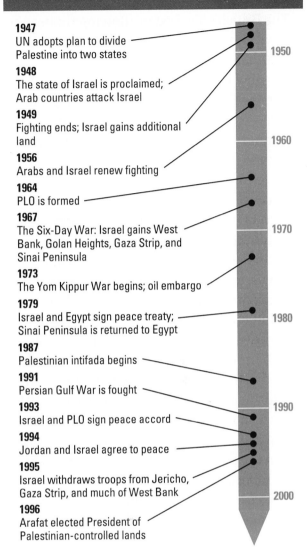

## THE ARAB-ISRAELI CONFLICT

**1947**
UN adopts plan to divide Palestine into two states

**1948**
The state of Israel is proclaimed; Arab countries attack Israel

**1949**
Fighting ends; Israel gains additional land

**1956**
Arabs and Israel renew fighting

**1964**
PLO is formed

**1967**
The Six-Day War: Israel gains West Bank, Golan Heights, Gaza Strip, and Sinai Peninsula

**1973**
The Yom Kippur War begins; oil embargo

**1979**
Israel and Egypt sign peace treaty; Sinai Peninsula is returned to Egypt

**1987**
Palestinian intifada begins

**1991**
Persian Gulf War is fought

**1993**
Israel and PLO sign peace accord

**1994**
Jordan and Israel agree to peace

**1995**
Israel withdraws troops from Jericho, Gaza Strip, and much of West Bank

**1996**
Arafat elected President of Palestinian-controlled lands

1950
1960
1970
1980
1990
2000

**LEARNING FROM TIME LINES** The years since Israel's independence have brought both war and the promise of peace.
■ Do you think other events belong on this time line? If so, which ones?

prejudice the civil and religious rights of existing non-Jewish communities." The British hoped that the wording of the Balfour Declaration would please the Jews, yet not anger the Arabs.

After World War I, control of Palestine went from the Ottomans to the British. According to the new League of Nations, Britain was to get Palestine ready for independence. Both the Jews and the Arabs believed that they would soon be given the right to their own homelands.

The British soon began allowing thousands of Jews to immigrate to Palestine. The Palestinian Arabs were alarmed to see so many new people in the area. To stop Arab anger, the British limited Jewish immigration and settlement. This action, in turn, made the Jews angry. Clashes between Arabs and Jews took place regularly. Both sides sometimes used **terrorism**, or acts of violence, to further their causes.

Adolf Hitler's rise to power in Germany in 1933 caused many Jews to flee Europe and settle in Palestine. Hitler's campaign against the Jews, the Zionists argued, proved that they needed their own land, where they could live in peace. When reports of the Holocaust were made public, British limits on Jewish immigration seemed cruel.

By this time war-weary Britain saw that it was losing control in the Middle East. In 1947 the British withdrew from the region without taking action. They placed the Palestine question in the hands of the United Nations. On November 29, 1947, the UN decided to **partition**, or divide, Palestine into two separate states—one Jewish and one Arab.

Having escaped death in the Nazi camps, these Jewish refugees hope to find peace in Palestine.

 **Why did Jews and Arabs both feel that Palestine was their homeland?**

## ARAB-ISRAELI CONFLICT

Jews around the world joyously welcomed the creation of their own state, Israel, in 1948. Arabs, however, did not accept the decision of the United Nations. Five Arab nations declared war on Israel and invaded the new country. The Arabs began making great advances. Within a few months, however, Israeli troops drove back the Arab armies. When both sides agreed to a cease-fire in January 1949, Israel had already taken much

of the Arab part of Palestine. The rest of the Arab land became part of the country of Jordan.

During and after the war, more than 700,000 Arabs left Israel for neighboring Arab states. Many of them lived and suffered in refugee camps there. Meanwhile, thousands of other Arabs remained in Israel and became citizens. Most Arabs, however, refused to accept Israel's existence as a nation.

Over the years Israel and the Arab nations clashed again and again. The superpowers of the time—the United States and the Soviet Union—soon became involved in the Middle Eastern conflict. The United States became Israel's most important ally. The Soviet Union backed some of the Arab countries.

In the 1950s most Arab countries united under the leadership of Egyptian president Gamal Abdel Nasser. The Israelis, surrounded by Arab neighbors who did not want them, began to build a strong army. The Israeli army, with the help of British and French forces, weakened Arab military strength in a 1956 war.

In 1967 Egypt, Syria, and Jordan prepared to attack Israel again. However, the Israelis acted first and drove back the Arab forces. During what is now called the Six-Day War, Israel captured large areas of land from Egypt, Syria, and Jordan. Israel gained control of the Sinai Peninsula, the Golan Heights, the Gaza Strip, and the West Bank. It also united the city of Jerusalem, which had been divided since 1948.

When Nasser died in 1970, Anwar as-Sadat (suh•DAT) became president of Egypt. In 1973, on Yom Kippur—the holiest day of the year for the Jewish people—Sadat launched a surprise attack on Israel. The Arabs made early gains, but later the Israelis took back most of those gains.

The Arabs then turned to economic weapons. The Arab countries supplied more than one-third of the oil used by non-communist countries. For a few months Arab

**ISRAEL: 1947 TO PRESENT**

Security zones

Land gained after Six-Day War, 1967, and still occupied

Land gained after Six-Day War, 1967, some Palestinian self-rule

Land gained after Six-Day War, 1967

Land gained after 1948 War

Israeli troops have withdrawn from area

Jewish state under 1947 partition plan

Land gained after Six-Day War, 1967, and returned to Egypt

Under Palestinian control

LEBANON
SYRIA
GOLAN HEIGHTS
Acre
Haifa
Nazareth
Lake Tiberias (Sea of Galilee)
Mediterranean Sea
Tel Aviv
WEST BANK
Jordan River
Amman
Jericho
Jerusalem
Bethlehem
Hebron
Dead Sea
GAZA STRIP
Gaza
Beersheba
ISRAEL
JORDAN
EGYPT
NEGEV
SINAI PENINSULA

**PLACE** The shape of the land controlled by Israel has changed since 1947.
■ Why do you think Israelis and Palestinians disagree about control of Jerusalem?

Palestinian refugees in the Gaza Strip in 1954

Sunni Muslim majority

Shiite Muslim majority

Jewish majority

KURDS Ethnic group

☩ Christian minority area

**PLACE** The majority of the peoples of the Middle East are Arabs, but other peoples live in the region as well. The names printed in red on the map show some of the major ethnic groups in the Middle East.

■ In what Middle Eastern country are most people Persian? How else are the people different from others in the Middle East?

members of the Organization of Petroleum Exporting Countries (OPEC) refused to sell oil to countries they felt supported Israel. Many countries had to search for other sources of oil. The Arab OPEC members lifted the oil embargo in 1974. However, the idea that OPEC might do this again worried Japan, the United States, and other countries that depended on imported oil.

Palestinian Arabs also took another type of action against Israel. In 1964, at a meeting of Arab leaders, a group called the Palestine Liberation Organization (PLO) was formed. The group's purpose was to organize the Palestinians in their struggle for a homeland. PLO members often used terrorist tactics in Israel and then in the lands taken over by the Israelis in the Six-Day War.

In 1969 Yasir Arafat (AH•ruh•faht) became chairperson of the PLO. Throughout the

1970s Arafat and the PLO became known and widely feared for their sudden attacks on civilian and military targets.

In the late 1980s a change in the Palestinian struggle took place. Many young Palestinians who had spent their lives under Israeli occupation in the territories of the West Bank and the Gaza Strip began to take part in the struggle. The Palestinians started an **intifada** (in•tee•FAH•duh), or people's uprising, in areas occupied by Israel. The Israelis tried to crush the intifada, but the outside world criticized their actions. The young Palestinians became more determined than ever. "Palestine is ours, and we shall shed our blood for it," they chanted.

***What role did oil play in the conflict between Israel and the Arab nations?***

# WORKING FOR PEACE

The Israelis and the Arabs have fought one another for many years. Some leaders on both sides, though, have tried to bring peace to their region. An important step forward came in 1977, when Anwar as-Sadat agreed to visit Israel. He flew to Jerusalem, where he met with Israeli prime minister Menachem Begin (muh•NAH•kuhm BAY•gin).

Later in 1977 American President Jimmy Carter invited Sadat and Begin to the United States. Carter hoped that if the two talked openly, they might overcome their differences. This did happen, in 1978, and the three leaders signed an agreement called the Camp David Accords. The agreement laid out a plan for a peace treaty, which Israel and Egypt signed in 1979. In 1980 Egypt became the first Arab country to recognize Israel as a nation. Two years later Israel gave back much of the Egyptian land it had taken in the Six-Day War. The PLO was not included in the peace talks and therefore did not feel that the agreement applied to them.

In the 1990s Israel and the PLO held secret peace talks. After months of negotiations, often stopped because of continuing violence against both sides, an agreement was reached in late 1993. The agreement, signed by Israeli prime minister Yitzhak Rabin (rah•BEEN) and Yasir Arafat, called for Israel to give limited **autonomy**, or the right of a state to rule itself, to Palestinian areas.

In mid-1994 Rabin and Arafat established limited self-rule for Palestinians in the Gaza Strip and in the city of Jericho and its surrounding areas. Shortly afterward, Israel began to withdraw its troops from Jericho and the Gaza Strip.

For their work toward peace, Rabin, Arafat, and Israeli foreign minister Shimon Peres (shee•MOHN PAIR•EZ) were awarded the Nobel Peace Prize in late 1994. In 1995 the Israelis began to pull troops out of the West Bank, allowing the Palestinians more control there as well. However, other Palestinian–Israeli issues, such as who should have control of Jerusalem, remain unsettled. Both the Palestinians and the Israelis claim the city as their capital.

The Israelis and the Palestinians were not the only ones to work toward peace in the Middle East in the 1990s. In 1994 Jordan signed a peace treaty with Israel. Also Syria and Israel have held peace talks.

However, the end of 1995 brought tragedy to the Middle East. At a rally for peace, Yitzhak Rabin was assassinated by an Israeli who was angry that Israel had turned over control of lands to the Palestinians. Israeli leaders and Yasir Arafat promised that the search for peace will continue. By early 1996 it seemed clear that Arafat would remain the voice of the Palestinian people. The Palestinians elected a ruling council with Arafat as their president.

 **What major peace agreements did the Arabs and Israelis sign between 1979 and 1994?**

United States President Bill Clinton (center), Israeli prime minister Rabin (left), and PLO chairman Arafat (right) after the signing of a peace accord between Israel and the PLO

# ISLAMIC RENEWAL

While Jews and Arabs moved toward peace, another important development was taking place in the Middle East. Since the nineteenth century, Muslims in countries across the region were concerned that Western ideas had begun to replace the Islamic way of life. During the 1960s and 1970s, many Muslims returned to a more traditional practice of Islam. They attended prayer regularly and wore Muslim dress. They also wanted to make Islamic law, or *Shari'a*, the basis for governing Muslim nations.

Perhaps the most dramatic example of this Islamic renewal came in Iran in the late 1970s. Iran differs from most other Islamic nations in the region. Most of its people are Persians rather than Arabs. Also, most Iranians have long disagreed with other Muslim groups about religious issues.

Starting in the 1950s Mohammad Reza Pahlavi (rih•ZAH PA•luh•vee), the shah, or ruler of Iran, tried to modernize the country and turn it into an industrial power. Many Iranians objected to the Western ways introduced by the shah. They felt that Iran should become a truly Islamic state. Some of the

strongest attacks on the shah's programs came from a religious leader, Ayatollah Khomeini (eye•uh•TOH•luh koh•MAY•nee). In January 1979 a revolt by Khomeini's supporters and other groups forced the shah to leave Iran.

Khomeini then took over the government. He quickly made it clear that Western powers were no longer welcome in Iran. The United States soon learned *how* unwelcome its citizens were. In November 1979, Iranian students took over the United States Embassy in the city of Tehran, taking more than 50 Americans hostage. A **hostage** is a prisoner who is held until certain demands are met. The students wanted the United States government to return the shah—who was being treated for cancer at an American hospital— to face trial. The shah died in July 1980, but the hostages were not freed until January 1981.

The Iranians planned to spread their Islamic revolution to other Muslim countries. Saddam Hussein (suh•DAHM hoo•SAYN), the leader of Iraq, wanted to keep this from happening. He also wanted to capture a part of Iran's land. In 1980 war broke out between the two countries. As fighting raged, Khomeini urged the Shiites in Iraq to overthrow their Sunni leader. The war dragged on for eight years. Neither side gained a clear victory.

Ayatollah Khomeini died in 1989. New Iranian leaders have spent less time spreading revolution and more time building the economy. Still, the renewal of traditional Islamic beliefs and practices has continued.

 **What is meant by Islamic renewal?**

# THE PERSIAN GULF WAR

Not all conflicts in the Middle East relate to religion. One such conflict gained worldwide attention in the early 1990s. That event was the Persian Gulf War.

Saddam Hussein, the president of Iraq, ordered his army to invade the oil-rich country of Kuwait so that he would not have

The U.S. hostages appear happy after finally being released from captivity in Iran (below). The Ayatollah Khomeini (inset) granted their release in 1981.

WELCOME BACK TO FREEDOM

The Persian Gulf War was different from past wars. Women soldiers played greater roles than ever before (above). Advanced technology allowed live television reports (upper right) and the use of U.S. stealth bombers (lower right).

Cleared by Iraqi Censors
Peter Arnett
Baghdad, Iraq
CNN LIVE

to pay a debt owed. Almost immediately the United Nations stated that the attack was wrong and took steps to make Iraq suffer economically. It set January 15, 1991, as the deadline for Iraq to pull out of Kuwait. But Iraq stayed.

When Iraq would not cooperate with the United Nations, countries such as the United States, Saudi Arabia, Egypt, and France joined forces to free Kuwait. After all, they did not want Iraq to control Kuwait's oil. The United States and its allies began Operation Desert Storm—a series of air- and ground-bombing attacks. The Iraqis were quickly forced to leave Kuwait.

This war was different from any other war in the history of the world. People around the world watched and listened to their televisions to hear up-to-the-minute reports on the events of the war. Also, the war was fought almost completely with high-technology weapons that had never been used in battle. In addition, American women soldiers played an important role in the war.

**Why did the Iraqis invade Kuwait?**

# LESSON 2 REVIEW

## Check Understanding

1. **Recall the Facts**   What links do Jews and Arabs have to the Middle East?
2. **Focus on the Main Idea**   How have ideas and beliefs both united and divided people in the Middle East?

## Think Critically

3. **Cause and Effect**   How do you think the creation of the state of Israel affected events in the Middle East?
4. **Personally Speaking**   What do you think gives people the right to live where they do?

## Show What You Know

**Current Events Activity**   Look in newspapers and magazines to find articles about conflicts and peace efforts in the Middle East. Using these articles, make a class bulletin board display. Update the display as new events occur.

# CONNECT MAIN IDEAS

Use this organizer to show that you understand how the chapter's main ideas are connected. Copy the organizer onto a separate sheet of paper. Then complete it by writing three details to support each main idea.

**Religious Influences**

**The Indian Subcontinent**
Religion has greatly affected the history of the Indian subcontinent.

1. _____

2. _____

3. _____

**The Middle East**
Ideas and beliefs have both united and divided people in Southwest Asia and North Africa.

1. _____

2. _____

3. _____

# WRITE MORE ABOUT IT

1. **Write a Biographical Sketch** Find out more about Mohandas Gandhi. Then prepare a one-page biographical sketch on the life of this Indian leader. Describe his background and his beliefs. Also, explain how his idea of passive resistance led not to conflict but to cooperation and finally to independence for India.

2. **Write a History** In your own words, tell the background of the Arab-Israeli conflict. Be sure that your report is fair to both sides. Use illustrations, time lines, and maps.

3. **Write Questions** Write five questions you might ask someone who fought in the Persian Gulf War.

# USE VOCABULARY

Write the term that correctly matches each meaning.

boycott          Mahatma
discriminate     terrorism
hostage          Zionism

1. a prisoner who is held until certain demands are met

2. "Great Soul"

3. to refuse to buy goods

4. acts of violence

5. the movement that called for a modern Jewish state in the homeland of the Jewish people

6. to treat unfairly because of race or other reasons

# CHECK UNDERSTANDING

1. What event made Gandhi realize that much work was needed to gain rights for Indian people in South Africa?

2. What important lesson did Gandhi learn from his mother? How did this affect Gandhi?

3. What forms of noncooperation did Gandhi and his followers use in India?

4. How did Gandhi die?

5. Why was Benazir Bhutto's election as prime minister of Pakistan so important?

6. To which three religions is the Middle East an important region?

7. What was the Balfour Declaration?

8. What was the result of the Six-Day War?

9. What is the Palestine Liberation Organization, or PLO? What is its goal?

10. Why was the Persian Gulf War fought?

# THINK CRITICALLY

1. **Cause and Effect**   What effects did passive resistance have on the British and their control of India?

2. **Personally Speaking**   Why do you think Mohandas Gandhi began to dress in traditional clothing?

3. **Explore Viewpoints**   The Israelis want to keep control over all of Jerusalem. The Palestinians believe that part of Jerusalem should be under their control. Why do you think the two peoples cannot agree about the future of Jerusalem?

4. **Past to Present**   In 1995, terrorists bombed a United States federal building in Oklahoma City. How do acts of terrorism, in this country and throughout the world, affect everyone?

# APPLY SKILLS

**Use Different Types of Population Maps**   Use the maps on pages 628 and 629 to answer these questions.

1. How would you describe India's population? Support your answer with the information the maps give you.

2. Which parts of India have the most people?

3. Which of the two maps do you find is easier to use? Why?

# READ MORE ABOUT IT

*Mahatma Gandhi: The Man Who Freed India and Led the World in Nonviolent Change* by Michael Nicholson. Gareth Stevens. This book follows Gandhi's role in India's fight for independence.

*Middle East: A Background to the Conflicts* by John Pimlott. Gloucester. This book examines the Arab-Israeli conflicts as well as the Persian Gulf War.

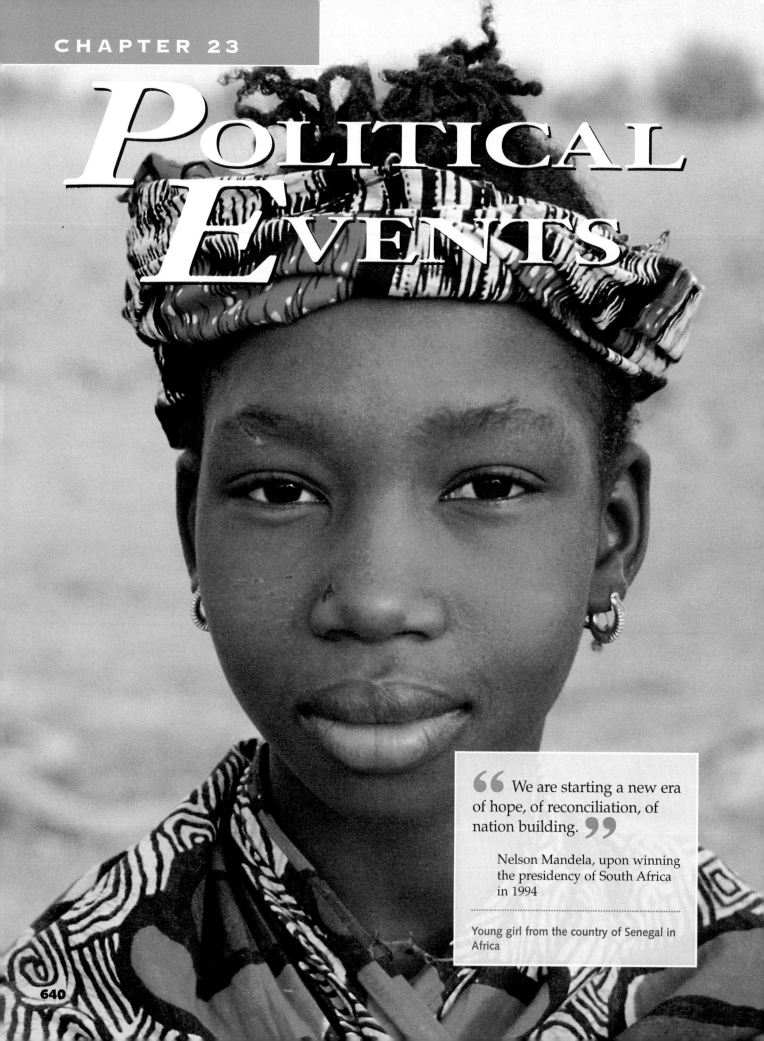

# POLITICAL EVENTS

" We are starting a new era of hope, of reconciliation, of nation building. "

Nelson Mandela, upon winning the presidency of South Africa in 1994

Young girl from the country of Senegal in Africa

# AFRICA
## SOUTH of the
## SAHARA

## Link to Our World

**What challenges do newly independent nations face?**

**Focus on the Main Idea**
*As you read, think about some of the problems African nations have faced after winning independence.*

**Preview Vocabulary**
*Afrikaans*
*apartheid*
*Bantustan*

At the beginning of the twentieth century, only two African countries—Ethiopia and Liberia—had their independence. The others were under European control. By mid-century, however, nearly all the countries south of the Sahara had won freedom.

## WINNING INDEPENDENCE

Africans had resisted European rule from the beginning. Yet it was not until after World War II that a group of young leaders began to push for independence. They had one demand—freedom now! In the end the European powers had to free their African colonies.

Some former colonies gained their freedom peacefully. In the Gold Coast a young African named Kwame Nkrumah (KWAH•mee en•KROO•muh) formed the Convention People's Party (CPP) with this aim of "self-government now." The CPP organized strikes, boycotts, and demonstrations against British rule. In 1951 the British agreed to hold national elections. The CPP won easily, and the British asked Nkrumah to form a government under their direction. In 1957 the British gave full independence to the Gold Coast. The new African nation took the name Ghana, after the West African empire of earlier times.

The former British colony of Kenya, in East Africa, did not win freedom so peacefully. Most whites in Kenya had settled in the central highlands, a very good area for farming. They then passed laws to keep Africans from owning land there. These laws angered Kenya's largest ethnic group, the Kikuyus (kee•KOO•yooz). After all, their ancestors had held the central highlands for hundreds of years. The

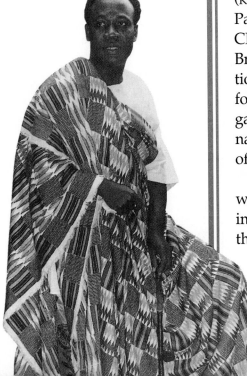

Prime Minister Kwame Nkrumah of Ghana in 1958

Chapter 23 • **641**

Kikuyu leader Jomo Kenyatta (JOH•moh ken•YAHT•uh) wanted a fair share of these lands for his people.

In the early 1950s some Kikuyus formed the Mau Mau. The goal of this political group was to drive the whites from Kenya, by violence if necessary. The British met Mau Mau attacks with more violence. During the five-year Mau Mau rebellion, about 18,000 black Africans died.

In time the British realized that holding on to Kenya was impossible. They began to prepare the country for independence. Elections were held in 1963. The Kenya African National Union (KANU) won, and Jomo Kenyatta, KANU's leader, became the first prime minister of independent Kenya.

 **How was Kenya's path to independence different from Ghana's?**

## THE COLONIAL LEGACY

Whether or not they won their independence peacefully, the new nations in Africa faced problems left over from colonial days. When the European powers carved the continent into colonies, they drew boundaries to suit themselves. In some cases the borders separated people of the same ethnic group. In other cases they grouped together people of very different backgrounds. The West African nation of Nigeria, for example, became home to more than 250 ethnic groups.

Nigeria won independence from Britain peacefully in 1960. From the start, however, the government struggled with the country's ethnic differences. In 1967 one of the largest groups, the Igbos (EEG•bohz), seceded from Nigeria and started their own country, called Biafra (bee•AH•fruh). This set off a civil war that lasted more than two years. A million people died—many from hunger—before the Biafrans gave up.

In some cases European rulers encouraged fighting among groups within their colonies. They believed that if Africans fought one another, they would never be able to unite against colonial rule. For example, colonial rulers tried to divide the peoples of the Belgian Congo, now known as Zaire. To the Belgians' surprise, the people set aside their differences to work for independence. The

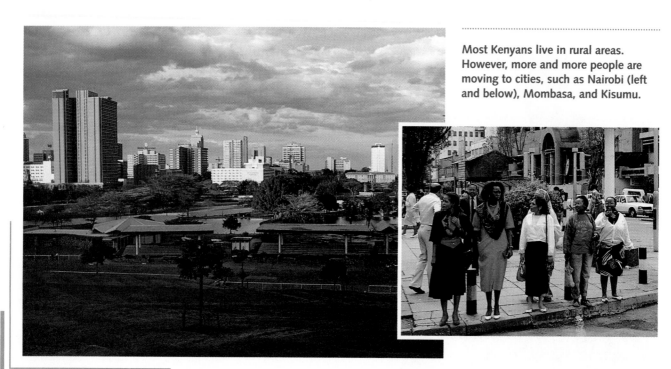

Most Kenyans live in rural areas. However, more and more people are moving to cities, such as Nairobi (left and below), Mombasa, and Kisumu.

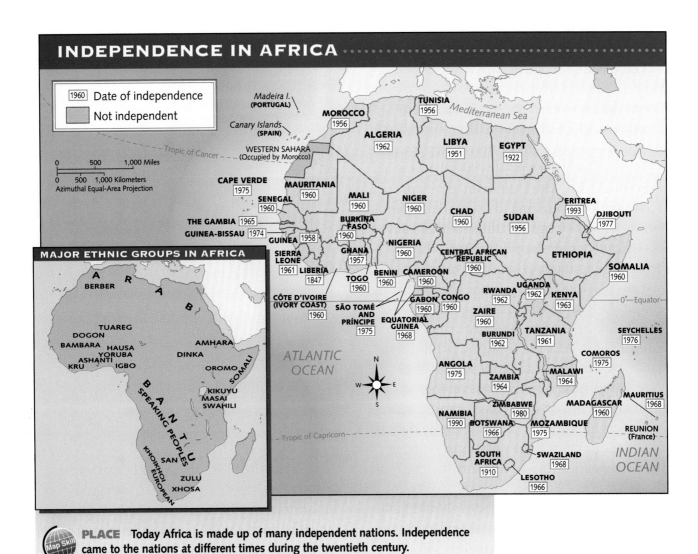

# INDEPENDENCE IN AFRICA

1960 Date of independence

Not independent

0   500   1,000 Miles
0   500   1,000 Kilometers
Azimuthal Equal-Area Projection

Madeira I. (PORTUGAL)
Canary Islands (SPAIN)
Tropic of Cancer
Mediterranean Sea
Red Sea

TUNISIA 1956
MOROCCO 1956
ALGERIA 1962
LIBYA 1951
EGYPT 1922
WESTERN SAHARA (Occupied by Morocco)
CAPE VERDE 1975
MAURITANIA 1960
MALI 1960
NIGER 1960
CHAD 1960
SUDAN 1956
ERITREA 1993
DJIBOUTI 1977
SENEGAL 1960
THE GAMBIA 1965
GUINEA-BISSAU 1974
GUINEA 1958
BURKINA FASO 1960
NIGERIA 1960
CENTRAL AFRICAN REPUBLIC 1960
ETHIOPIA
SIERRA LEONE 1961
GHANA 1957
LIBERIA 1847
TOGO 1960
BENIN 1960
CAMEROON 1960
SOMALIA 1960
CÔTE D'IVOIRE (IVORY COAST) 1960
SÃO TOMÉ AND PRÍNCIPE 1975
GABON 1960
CONGO 1960
EQUATORIAL GUINEA 1968
RWANDA 1962
UGANDA 1962
KENYA 1963
ZAIRE 1960
BURUNDI 1962
TANZANIA 1961
SEYCHELLES 1976
Equator
ATLANTIC OCEAN
ANGOLA 1975
ZAMBIA 1964
MALAWI 1964
COMOROS 1975
NAMIBIA 1990
ZIMBABWE 1980
MADAGASCAR 1960
MAURITIUS 1968
BOTSWANA 1966
MOZAMBIQUE 1975
REUNION (France)
Tropic of Capricorn
SOUTH AFRICA 1910
SWAZILAND 1968
LESOTHO 1966
INDIAN OCEAN

## MAJOR ETHNIC GROUPS IN AFRICA

ARAB
BERBER
TUAREG
DOGON
BAMBARA  HAUSA
YORUBA
ASHANTI
KRU  IGBO
AMHARA
DINKA
OROMO
SOMALI
BANTU SPEAKING PEOPLES
KIKUYU
MASAI
SWAHILI
KHOIKHOI
SAN
ZULU
XHOSA
EUROPEAN

**PLACE** Today Africa is made up of many independent nations. Independence came to the nations at different times during the twentieth century.
■ What places became independent countries in the 1990s?

---

colony gained its freedom from Belgium in 1960 and changed its name simply to Congo.

This cooperation did not last long. The regional conflicts that the Belgians had encouraged soon surfaced once again. After Congo's independence, the province of Katanga, which is rich in resources, seceded. In the political unrest that followed, Congo's first prime minister, Patrice Lumumba (luh•MUHM•buh), was assassinated.

The United Nations sent troops to stop the violence in Congo. Yet after they left, fighting began again. Then, in 1965, General Mobutu Sese Seko (muh•BOO•too SAY•say SAY•koh) took control. He united Congo by setting up a government that allowed only one political party. He would hear no arguments against government policies.

The newly independent African nations also often faced serious economic problems. In most cases the colonial powers had not allowed the colonies to develop more than one resource or cash crop. After gaining independence, many countries stayed too dependent on this single source of income. Ghana, for example, exported little besides cacao, the beans used to make cocoa. When world prices for cacao fell in the mid-1960s, Ghana's economy also fell.

**What types of problems did the new African nations face?**

# SOUTH AFRICA

The country of South Africa developed very differently from the rest of the continent. South Africa won its independence from Britain in 1910, but white settlers—not black Africans—controlled the new government.

Two different groups of whites had settled in South Africa. The Dutch came first, in 1652. These settlers were first known as the Boers (BOHRZ). As they came to think of themselves as Africans rather than Europeans, they began calling themselves Afrikaners (a•frih•KAH•nerz). They spoke their own language, Afrikaans, which is based on Dutch. The British arrived in South Africa in 1795. From 1899 to 1902 the two groups fought for control of South Africa in the Anglo-Boer War. The British won the war, yet the Afrikaner point of view ruled South Africa.

Almost all white South Africans held racist views about black South Africans. However, the Afrikaners' attitude was much more rigid than that of the English settlers. Afrikaners believed that blacks and whites should have as little contact with one another as possible. When Afrikaner leaders won the 1948 elections, this idea became government policy. The Afrikaners called the policy apartheid (uh•PAR•tayt), which means "apartness."

Life under apartheid was hard for black South Africans. Although they made up more than two-thirds of South Africa's population, black South Africans had few rights. They could own land and govern themselves only within certain areas of the country. These were known as Bantustans (ban•too•STANZ), or "homelands." Black South Africans had to have permits to live outside the Bantustans. Even then they could not live in the same neighborhoods as white South Africans, and they did not have the right to vote.

Protests against South African racism had begun long before apartheid. The African National Congress (ANC) was founded in 1912 to fight for the rights of black South

This photo shows a bus bearing a "non-whites only" sign, a typical example of the policy of apartheid, or separation of the races, in South Africa.

Africans. After 1948 the ANC began using passive resistance to demonstrate against apartheid. In 1960 the South African government banned the ANC and jailed many of its leaders.

Shocked by the actions of the South African government, other countries limited or ended trade with South Africa. The South African government stuck to its policy of apartheid. At last things changed after Frederik Willem de Klerk became president of South Africa in 1989.

De Klerk was an Afrikaner and a supporter of apartheid. Still, he believed that apartheid had "landed us in a dead-end street." He, like many other white South Africans, knew that sooner or later the black majority in South Africa would gain control of the country. De Klerk removed the ban on the ANC and ended many apartheid laws. He also freed ANC leader Nelson Mandela, who had been in prison for more than 25 years. De Klerk then met with black leaders to work out a way to share power.

By November 1993 the leaders agreed to open South African elections to all races. On April 27, 1994, black and white South Africans waited in line together to vote. "My heart tells me it's the best day of my life," said one new voter. "I don't have to carry a pass. I can work anywhere in the country I want. I am free."

The election resulted in victory for Mandela and his party. In one of his first speeches as president, Mandela told of a new South Africa, "in which all South Africans, both black and white, will be able to walk tall, without any fear in their hearts."

✓ **What is apartheid? How did it end in South Africa?**

## PRESENT-DAY CONCERNS

In the past few years, democracy has begun to spread across Africa. In 1989, thirty-five African nations were governed as single-party states. By 1994 most of these nations had given up this political system and held multiparty elections. In addition, more nations are trying forms of free enterprise.

Today African nations face problems other than politics and economics. Lack of rain has ruined many harvests and has led to famine. In Somalia, drought and famine led to civil war in the early 1990s. Clans of Somalis fought over the little water and food they had. Some clans even stole food and supplies sent from around the world. The clans used

A changing South Africa: people support Nelson Mandela in his bid for the South African presidency (below); Mandela votes (below right); a woman shows off her new voting card (below left).

the goods to make money and gain power. Meanwhile, millions of people died from starvation. Eventually, the United Nations sent more food and supplies as well as troops to make sure that help got to those who needed it. Somalia is still struggling with drought, famine, and conflicts.

The countries of Rwanda and Burundi were also divided by civil war in the early 1990s. Both countries consist of two different cultures: the Hutus and the Tutsis. Each group wanted to control the government at the expense of the other. In Rwanda, this meant that, by August 1993, hundreds of thousands of Rwandans had been killed. Millions more were forced to flee for safety.

Population growth is another concern for Africa. More people live on the continent than ever before. Countries must find ways to make sure all these people have enough to eat. Also, lack of food in rural areas has brought many people to Africa's few large cities, causing overcrowding there.

Some countries in Africa have been particularly hard hit by AIDS, or acquired immunodeficiency syndrome. AIDS is caused by a virus that does not allow the body to fight disease. The spread of AIDS is a worldwide health problem.

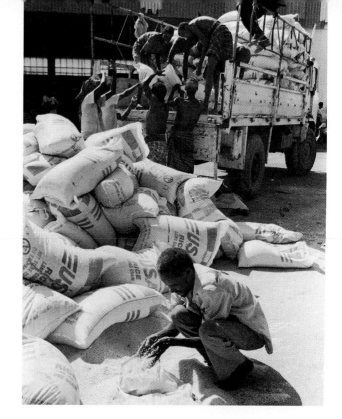

A worker in Mogadishu, Somalia, scoops up rice donated by the United States. Food shortages in Somalia were just one effect of civil war there.

The African people know that solving their problems will not be easy. Their determination is their strength, though. It should lead them to a stronger, more democratic, and more prosperous tomorrow.

 **What problems do African nations still face?**

# LESSON 1 REVIEW

## Check Understanding

1. **Recall the Facts** When did most African countries south of the Sahara gain their independence?
2. **Focus on the Main Idea** What problems have African nations faced since winning independence?

## Think Critically

3. **Cause and Effect** How did the policies of colonial powers later cause problems for newly independent African nations?

4. **Past to Present** What lessons might other nations learn from South Africa's recent history?

## Show What You Know

**Map Activity** Using atlases, almanacs, and encyclopedias as resources, create two maps. One map should show the European colonies in Africa around the beginning of the twentieth century. The other should show the independent African nations and the year each nation won its freedom.

**LEARN with LITERATURE**

Focus on Apartheid

# Journey to Jo'burg

### by Beverley Naidoo

### illustrated by Beatrice Lebreton

For more than 40 years, apartheid ruled the lives of black South Africans. Read now about Naledi, Tiro, and their baby sister, Dineo, who live with their grandmother in a black homeland. To support the family their mother has taken a job with a white family in Parktown, a suburb of Johannesburg. When young Dineo becomes very ill, Naledi and Tiro travel to Johannesburg to find their mother and bring her home. On their journey they learn what it really means to live under apartheid. As you read, think about how you might have felt if you were forced to live under this system.

## A New Friend

As they turned toward the road, there was a bus with the word "PARKTOWN" in big letters on the front. It was slowing down a little way up the road and the doors were opening. Through the front windscreen they could see the driver was black.

"Come on, Tiro!" called Naledi, pulling him by the arm. They were just about to jump aboard, when someone shouted at them in English, "What's wrong with you? Are you stupid?"

Startled, they looked up at the angry face of the bus driver and then at the bus again. White faces stared at them from inside as the bus moved off.

Naledi and Tiro stood on the side of the road, shaken, holding hands tightly, when a voice behind them said, "Don't let it bother you. That's what they're like. You'd better come out of the road."

A young woman put out her hand to bring them onto the pavement.

"You must be strangers here if you don't know about the buses. This stop has a white sign, but we have to wait by the black one over there."

She pointed to a small black metal signpost.

"You must also look at the front of the bus for the small notice saying 'Non-whites only.'"

"I'm sorry. We forgot to look," Naledi explained.

"It's not you who should be sorry!" said the young woman forcefully. "They should be sorry, those stupid people! Why shouldn't we use any bus? When our buses are full, their buses are half empty. Don't you be sorry!"

The children glanced at each other. This person was different from their mother. Mma never spoke out like that.

## SOUTH AFRICA

ZAIRE

TANZANIA

ANGOLA

MALAWI

ZAMBIA

MOZAMBIQUE

ZIMBABWE

MADAGASCAR

NAMIBIA

INDIAN OCEAN

BOTSWANA

ATLANTIC OCEAN

Pretoria

Johannesburg

SWAZILAND

Area of inset

SOUTH AFRICA

LESOTHO

Cape Town

Cape of Good Hope

0    250    500 Miles
0    250    500 Kilometers
Azimuthal Equal-Area Projection

| Feet | | Meters |
|---|---|---|
| Above 13,120 | | Above 4,000 |
| 6,560 | | 2,000 |
| 1,640 | | 500 |
| 655 | | 200 |
| 0 | | 0 |
| Below sea level | | |

**ROUTE TO JOHANNESBURG**

The Children's Village

Pretoria

Parktown

Soweto    Johannesburg

0    50    100 Miles
0    50    100 Kilometers

**MOVEMENT**    The story takes place in the country of South Africa at the southern tip of the continent of Africa. The inset shows the route the children followed.

■ About how many miles did they travel?

The young woman asked where they were going. Naledi took out the letter, and when the young woman looked at the address, she exclaimed, "But this is near where my mother works. I'm on my way to visit her today, so I can show you the place."

"Thank you, Mma." The children smiled. Lucky again.

"By the way, I'm Grace Mbatha. Now who are you both, and where are you from? You speak Tswana the way my mother does. Maybe you live near my mother's people."

So, once again, the children began their story.

Luckily the bus wasn't full when it arrived. Grace had warned them that in the rush hour you were almost squeezed to death. As the bus trundled along, stopping and starting with the traffic, there was a chance to stare out the windows. Tiro thought the cyclists were very brave, riding in between all the cars. Naledi kept trying to see the tops of the tall buildings, twisting her neck around until it began to hurt!

The bus now heaved its way up a steep hill and soon they were leaving the city buildings, seeing the sky again, as well as trees, grass lawns and flowers either side of the road. Behind the trees were big houses, such as they had never seen before. Grace smiled at the way the children were staring, amazed.

"Don't you know the people in this place have a lot of money? My mother looks after two children in a very big house, and there is another person just to cook, and another person to look after the garden."

Naledi and Tiro listened with interest. Mma never liked to talk much to them about her work when she was at home, although once they had overheard Mma talking to Nono about the child whom she looked after. Mma had said, "The little girl is very rude. She thinks I belong to her mother. You should hear how she can shout at me."

Naledi wanted to ask Grace to tell them some more, but she was still a little shy, and soon they had reached their stop.

They stepped off the bus onto a wide pavement along a street lined with great leafy trees.

"That's the road where your mother works at number twenty-five. My mma works at number seventeen in the next road down there. Can you manage now?"

The children nodded, and then Grace added, "If you need somewhere to stay tonight, you can come back with me to Soweto. I'm going home at six o'clock, O.K.?"

Tiro and Naledi thanked Grace, although they were a little puzzled about needing somewhere to stay. After all, they would be with their mother now and they would be going home with her as quickly as possible, back to Dineo.

As they turned to go down the road, they suddenly felt very excited—and anxious too. So much had been happening that they hadn't been thinking all along of their little sister.

*Please let her be all right* now pounded in Naledi's brain.

Half walking, half running, they made for number 25.

# Mma

There it stood, a great pink house with its own grass lawn and trees in front, even its own road leading up to the front door! The two children stopped at the wide iron gates, looking up to it. The gates were closed, with a notice on them: "BEWARE OF THE DOG."

"Are we allowed in?" Tiro whispered.

"We must go in," Naledi replied, opening the gate a little.

Nervously they slipped in and slowly walked up the drive to the large front door.

Before they dared to knock, they heard a fierce barking from inside, which made them grip each other's hands, ready to run back to the street. Then they heard a sharp voice inside call out, in English, "Joyce, see who it is!"

The door opened.

As Mma gasped, the children flung themselves at her and she clasped them in her arms, hugging them. Tears welled up in her eyes as the children sobbed against her.

"What is wrong? What is wrong?" Mma cried softly.

"Who is it, Joyce?" came a brisk voice from behind. The dog was still barking.

"Be quiet, Tiger!" ordered the brisk voice, and the barking stopped.

Mma stifled her sobs.

"Madam, these are my children."

"What are they doing here?" asked the white lady.

"Madam, I don't know. They haven't told me yet."

"Dineo is very ill, Mma." Naledi spoke between sobs. "Her fever won't go away. Nono and Mmangwane don't want to trouble you, but I told Tiro we must come and bring you home."

Mma gasped again and held her children more tightly.

"Madam, my little girl is very sick. Can I go home to see her?"

The Madam raised her eyebrows.

"Well, Joyce, I can't possibly let you go today. I need you tonight to stay in with Belinda. The Master and I are going to a very important dinner party."

She paused.

"But I suppose you can go tomorrow."

"Thank you, Madam."

"I hope you realize how inconvenient this will be for me. If you are not back in a week, I shall just have to look for another maid, you understand?"

"Yes, Madam."

The children couldn't follow everything the Madam was saying in English, but her voice sounded annoyed, while Mma spoke so softly. Why does the white lady seem cross with Mma? It's not Mma's fault that Dineo is sick, Naledi thought.

The children huddled close to Mma's starched white apron. They hadn't seen her in this strange servant's uniform before.

As Mma led the children through to the kitchen, they glanced across at open doors leading into other large rooms. A wide staircase also led upward. Never had they imagined a house could be this size!

In the kitchen Mma gave them a drink of water and some porridge she had cooked earlier. The kitchen seemed like a picture out of a magazine Mma had once brought home from the Madam. Their mother must have been busy cleaning that afternoon, because glistening plates of different sizes, cups and saucers, and delicate glasses were neatly stacked close to a large empty cupboard.

Naledi noticed that Mma took the tin plates and mugs for them from a separate little cupboard. While they ate, Mma quickly got on with her work.

When she had finished, she took the children to her room at the back of the yard. The children looked around the little room with interest. On the big iron bed was a white cover which Mma had neatly embroidered. It must be strange sleeping all on your own, thought Tiro. At home they all shared a room.

When the children noticed the electric light, Mma said they could try it. But after Tiro had flicked it on and off about ten times, Mma told him to stop.

Bringing the children close to her now, Mma sat down at last and asked them to tell her fully what had happened.

The Madam had made it clear to Mma that the police wouldn't like it if the children spent the night in Parktown. So when Naledi spoke about Grace and her offer to take them to Soweto, Mma seemed of two minds. She knew Grace's mother well, but Soweto was also dangerous.

After getting the Madam's permission to go out for a little, Mma took her children by the hand and they walked to number 17 in the next road. They went around to the back of the house and found Grace still there.

"These two will be just fine with me," Grace assured Mma.

It was arranged that Grace and the children would meet Mma at Johannesburg station at seven the next morning. Mma gave Grace some money for the fares and, close to tears again, she hugged the children goodbye.

"Cheer up, you two," said Grace. "You can come and meet my brothers."

## Literature Review

1. What features of the apartheid system did Naledi and Tiro learn about on their journey and in Parktown?

2. What does the Madam think of Mma? How does her treatment of Mma show her attitude?

3. Compare the ways that Grace and Mma act when they are treated badly. Write about how you would feel and act if you were treated that way.

# LESSON 3

# EASTERN EUROPE and RUSSIA

## Link to Our World

*How can greater freedom change the way of life in a country?*

### Focus on the Main Idea
As you read, discover how new freedoms in the former Soviet Union changed life all over Europe.

### Preview Vocabulary
perestroika
glasnost
dissident
ethnic cleansing
common market

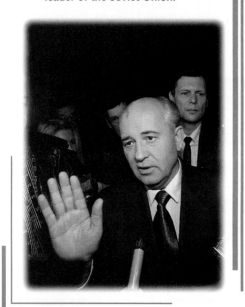

Mikhail Gorbachev was the last leader of the Soviet Union.

The 1990s have brought many changes to both Europe and Asia. After World War II eastern Europe and large parts of northern and central Asia were controlled by the Soviet Union and closed to the outside world. All that has changed in recent years.

## GORBACHEV'S REFORMS

In the early 1980s the Soviet Union was without question a world superpower. Yet beneath its military strength lay troubling economic and social problems. Years of poor planning by its leaders had destroyed the economy. There was never enough food or goods. Also, factories built in Stalin's time dumped chemicals into the water and the air. These chemicals polluted the environment, causing sickness and death. In addition, the people of the Soviet Union had few freedoms.

In early 1985 Mikhail Gorbachev (mee•kah•EEL gawr•buh•CHAWF) came to power in the Soviet Union. Gorbachev had new ideas about governing the country. In 1986 he announced a plan for a "moral revolution." Two keys to this plan were the policies of **perestroika** (pair•uh•STROY•kuh) and **glasnost** (GLAZ•nohst).

*Perestroika*, or "restructuring," meant a rebuilding of the Soviet political and economic systems. Under this policy Gorbachev reduced the authority of the Communist party and formed a new legislative body. He also called for open elections. When these elections took place, many longtime members of the Communist party were voted out of office.

Gorbachev's economic reforms took most of the authority for production decisions away from central planners and gave it to local farm and factory managers. Gorbachev also started a reward system to boost productivity.

*Glasnost*, or "openness," gave Soviet citizens new freedom to speak out without fear of being punished. The news media gained the freedom to report information that once had been hidden. Gorbachev also changed the Soviet policy toward religion so that people could now practice their beliefs openly. In addition, he set free from prison many **dissidents**—people who had spoken out against the government.

With the introduction of *glasnost*, some people began to speak out very strongly. In fact, people living in the Soviet Baltic republics—Lithuania, Latvia, and Estonia—called for total independence.

**What new ideas did Gorbachev have about governing?**

## THE COLLAPSE OF COMMUNISM

Citizens of eastern European Communist countries that were not actually a part of the Soviet Union but under its control also wanted more freedom. In the past the Soviet Union had stepped in and even used its army when any communist government faced demands for more freedom from its citizens. But by 1989 Gorbachev realized that it was no longer possible to stem the tide of change. He decided to keep the Soviet Union out of political developments in eastern Europe.

Poland's system changed first. During the 1980s a workers' group called Solidarity led a campaign for a more democratic government. Lead by Lech Walesa (vah•LEHN•sah), Solidarity called for strikes across Poland. After years of struggle, Communist leaders agreed to hold free elections. In August 1989 Communist rule in Poland ended, and Solidarity took control of the government.

Poland soon became a democracy. Its command economy was transformed into a market economy.

Widespread peaceful demonstrations in 1989 brought new freedoms to people in Bulgaria, Hungary, and Czechoslovakia, too. Their communist governments promised reforms and free elections.

In Romania the move toward democracy proved more violent. For years President Nicolae Ceauşescu (chow•SHES•koo) had ruled the country with threats and force. When Romanians took to the streets to demand change, Ceauşescu ordered the army to stop the revolt. Instead, many soldiers sided with the people. By the end of 1989, Ceauşescu had been removed from office. The new leaders promised to put the country on the path toward democracy.

Perhaps the greatest changes came in East Germany. Huge protests in 1989 had little effect on the East German government. It rejected all calls for reform. More and more unhappy East Germans found ways to leave the country. Many got permission to visit other communist countries and then fled to West Germany. On November 9, 1989, East German leaders said that they would open their borders. In Berlin joyous demonstrators gathered at the hated Berlin Wall, which had divided the city. They climbed on top of it, breaking off chunks of concrete with whatever they had at hand. The wall that had separated East and West Berlin for twenty-eight years finally crumbled. In October 1990 the two Germanys united to form the Federal Republic of Germany.

Elections in other eastern European countries also created new democratic governments. People who had been against the communists now found that they were the ones in control. They quickly cut themselves off from the Soviet Union, because they felt that their future lay with the West. They also withdrew from the Warsaw Pact, the

In 1986 an explosion at the Chernobyl nuclear power plant near Kiev, in what was then the Soviet Union, caused concern for the environment.

economic and political alliance led by the Soviet Union. By mid-1991 this organization no longer existed.

People in the Soviet Union watched carefully what was happening in eastern Europe. Some watched with hope. Others, including many communist leaders, watched with fear. In August 1991 some longtime Communist Party leaders tried to overthrow Gorbachev and take back the freedoms Gorbachev had given the

This photograph shows Boris Yeltsin campaigning in 1991 for the presidency of the Russian Republic, which was then part of the Soviet Union. Later that year the breakup of the Soviet Union made Russia an independent country. Yeltsin continued as its president.

people. Even though they failed, Gorbachev's authority was weakened.

More and more people in the Soviet Union began to want full democracy, not just a change in the Communist ways. "You can't ride two horses at once," said Boris Yeltsin (YELT•suhn), the president of the Russian Republic, the largest state in the Soviet Union.

In December 1991 Yeltsin and the presidents of the other Soviet republics declared that the Soviet Union no longer existed. In its place they set up a loose association, or group, called the Commonwealth of Independent States (CIS). Gorbachev stepped down and handed over authority to Yeltsin. The CIS was created to build a new market economy for the former Soviet republics and to keep the new nations at peace. By 1995, 12 republics had joined the CIS. These republics are Armenia, Azerbaijan (a•zer•by•JAHN), Belarus, Georgia, Kazakhstan (ka•zak•STAN), Kyrgyzstan (kir•gi•STAN), Moldova, Russia, Tajikistan (tah•jih•kih•STAN), Turkmenistan (terk•meh•nuh•STAN), Ukraine (yoo•KRAYN),

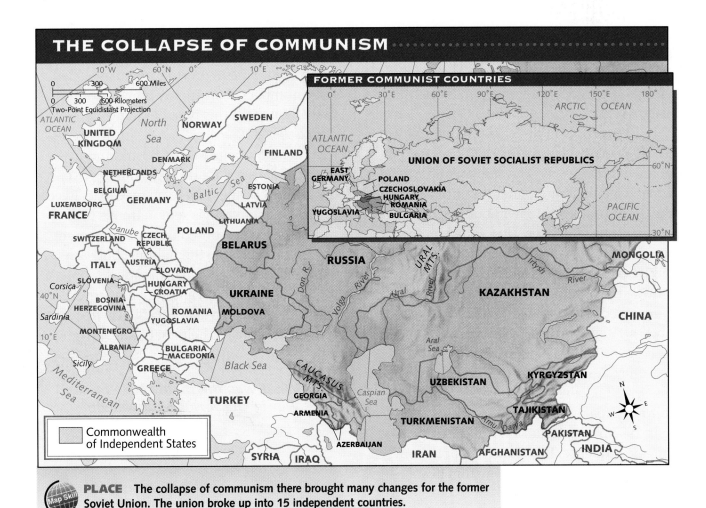

# THE COLLAPSE OF COMMUNISM

**FORMER COMMUNIST COUNTRIES**

UNION OF SOVIET SOCIALIST REPUBLICS

EAST GERMANY
POLAND
CZECHOSLOVAKIA
HUNGARY
ROMANIA
YUGOSLAVIA
BULGARIA

Commonwealth of Independent States

**PLACE** The collapse of communism there brought many changes for the former Soviet Union. The union broke up into 15 independent countries.
■ What new nations were formed from the former Soviet Union?

and Uzbekistan (uz•beh•kih•STAN). Of the 15 former Soviet Republics, only the Baltic States—Estonia, Lithuania, and Latvia—have not joined the CIS.

The fall of communism completely changed international relations. The breakup of the Soviet Union brought the Cold War to an end. The former communist countries now wanted to cooperate with the countries of the West. In 1991, for example, during the Persian Gulf War, some joined with the West to drive Iraq out of Kuwait. In the mid-1990s, however, communists made new gains in Europe. As a result the new democracies of Europe may suffer setbacks.

 **What led to the fall of communism in eastern Europe and the Soviet Union?**

## NATIONALISM IN THE BALKANS

Not every change that happened in Europe after the fall of communism was positive. People in the Balkans turned back to their old religious, ethnic, and national rivalries. After World War I the different peoples of that region had been forced to become citizens of a newly created nation called Yugoslavia. Their union had always been an uneasy one because of differences among the nation's three main ethnic groups: Muslims, Serbs, and Croats.

After World War II a strong communist leader, Marshal Tito (TEE•toh), took control of Yugoslavia. Tito would not let religious, ethnic, and nationalist feelings among the different Yugoslavian groups break up the country. However, when Tito died in 1980, nationalist feelings began to rise. With the fall of communism in 1989, a number of ethnic groups demanded their independence from Yugoslavia.

In 1991 people in the Yugoslav republics of Slovenia (sloh•VEE•nee•uh) and Croatia voted to break away. The Serbian minority in Croatia feared living under the authority of the Croats (KROH•ahtz) without the protection of a communist leader. They called on the republic of Serbia for help. In the summer of 1991, Serbian soldiers attacked Croatia. During the fighting, about 10,000 people were killed. Thousands more left their homes, fleeing to other countries as refugees. In 1992 the United Nations worked out a cease-fire agreement. By that time, however, the Serbs had already taken over about one-third of Croatia's territory.

In 1992 the republic of Bosnia also declared its independence. Right away, people from each of the different groups within Bosnia—

Muslims, Serbs, and Croats—began using violence to drive other groups from their areas. Sometimes a group's members killed large numbers of an enemy ethnic group. They thought of this type of killing as **ethnic cleansing**. At the same time the Serbs tried to take a large part of Bosnia and make it part of Serbia. Croatia began taking over the areas of Bosnia where many Croats lived.

The United Nations sent in troops to restore peace. It worked out one agreement after another to stop the fighting, but each was quickly broken. Finally, leaders representing Serbs, Croats, and Muslims agreed to peace for Bosnia. In late 1995 NATO troops arrived in Bosnia to help make sure no new fighting broke out.

 **What was the main cause of civil war in the former Yugoslavia?**

Adults and children alike (below left and right) are forced to leave their homes and flee to other countries. Peace-keeping troops (above right) patrol an area of Sarajevo, Bosnia, a city hard hit by the war.

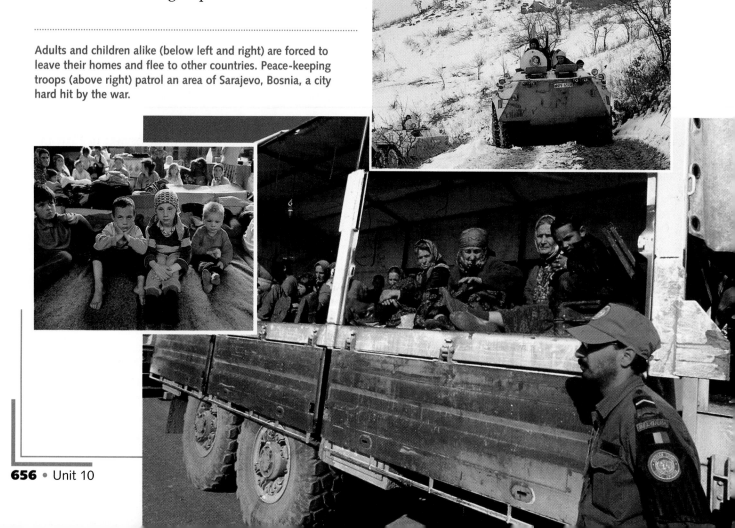

## CARTOGRAM: GROSS DOMESTIC PRODUCT

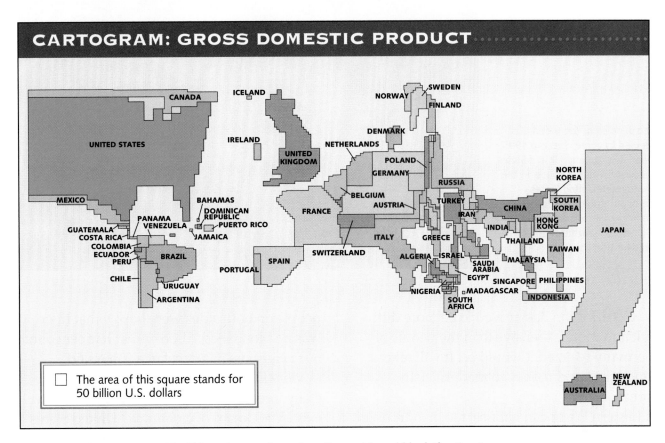

The area of this square stands for 50 billion U.S. dollars

**LEARNING FROM GRAPHS** This cartogram shows how the world would look if nations' sizes were based on GDP.
■ What country has the highest GDP in Europe?

## THE UNITED STATES OF EUROPE?

When meeting with western European leaders, Mikhail Gorbachev often spoke of the "common house of Europe." He meant that all Europeans shared a heritage. After the fall of communism, many people felt that this heritage would help bring eastern and western Europe closer together. Perhaps a "United States of Europe" would develop.

Many years before, in 1957, several western European nations had formed an economic union, or **common market**. The purpose of this European Economic Community (EEC) was to make sure the economic policies of its member nations did not conflict. The EEC set as its goal the creation of the European Union (EU). The EU would be a single economic market with no tariffs on

goods and no rules on crossing national borders. The EU would also have its own money.

The EU began in 1993—but it was not like its planners had imagined. Many member nations felt that the original plans gave too much control to the EU's governing body. Also, members could not agree on what to do about the former Yugoslavia.

While many dreamed of all Europeans coming closer together, some countries, such as Germany, found it difficult to keep their own people together. Most Germans were happy when the eastern and western parts of their country were united in 1990. But their joy did not last long. People in the former East Germany felt that the new government was not doing enough to help them make the change from communism to capitalism. People in the former West Germany felt that the government was doing too much.

The peoples of the world seemed to come closer in 1995 when Russian and United States spacecrafts met in space. In this photograph United States astronaut Robert L. Gibson (right) and Russian cosmonaut Vladimir N. Dezhurov shake hands.

Reunification has proved to be more difficult and more expensive than the people of Germany realized it would be. It will take much time and money to modernize the former East Germany.

Eastern European nations, too, had trouble bringing their people together. Then Czechoslovakia broke into two separate nations—the Czech Republic and Slovakia. This division caused some problems, but the people on both sides were happy that there was no bloodshed. "Look what happened to our neighbors in Yugoslavia," one said.

More Europeans than ever before now enjoy freedom. However, many divisions still exist. The dream of creating a "United States of Europe" seems to have been forgotten.

 **What problems made it hard for European nations to unite in the late twentieth century?**

# LESSON 3 REVIEW

## Check Understanding

1. **Recall the Facts** What were the goals of *perestroika* and *glasnost*?
2. **Focus on the Main Idea** How did new freedoms in the former Soviet Union change life all over Europe in the late 1980s?

## Think Critically

3. **Explore Viewpoints** Some people blamed Mikhail Gorbachev for not going far enough or fast enough with his reform programs. Others praised him for beginning a new Europe. How could people have such widely differing viewpoints about the same man?
4. **Past to Present** What part, if any, should the United States take in creating a new Europe? What can the United States learn from past experiences, such as the civil war in the Balkans? Explain your answer.
5. **Think More About It** There are many ethnic groups in the United States. Regional differences also separate many Americans. Why do you think the individual states do not want to be totally free and independent from one another?

## Show What You Know

 **Journalism Activity** Imagine that you are a journalist working for a European newspaper. Write a news story showing how the changes made by Mikhail Gorbachev in the Soviet Union led to the Europe of today.

# Resolve Conflicts

## Why Is This Skill Important?

Disagreements are a part of everyday life. There are many ways to handle disagreements with other people. You can walk away and let strong feelings fade over time. You can try to show the other person your way of thinking. You can also **compromise**, or give up some of what you want in order to reach an agreement. Knowing how to compromise gives you another way to handle, or resolve, disagreements.

## Remember What You Have Read

Many people believe that without compromise many of the world's problems will never be solved. Through compromise, leaders of nations or groups within a nation are sometimes able to resolve conflicts.

You have read about conflicts in the former Yugoslavia during the 1990s. Beginning in 1991, Serbs, Croats, and other groups disagreed over leadership and control of land. These disagreements go far back in history. Longtime religious, ethnic, and national rivalries have made compromising to resolve conflicts almost impossible in the former Yugoslavia. Yet unless conflicts are resolved, there will always be war among these peoples.

## Understand the Process

To be able to compromise is as important for you as it is for world leaders. To compromise, you can follow steps like those used when world leaders meet.

- Before you begin to talk with the person you disagree with, be prepared to give up some things you would like, in order to solve the disagreement.
- Tell the other person clearly what you want.
- Decide which of the things that you want are most important to you.

Peace talks held in the United States in 1995 brought about an agreement to end the fighting in Bosnia. From left to right are Serbian President Slobodan Milosevic, Bosnian President Alija Izetbegovic, Croatian President Franjo Tudjman, and United States Secretary of State Warren Christopher.

- Present a plan for compromise. Let the other person present his or her plan.
- Talk about any differences in the two plans.
- Present another plan for a compromise, giving up something else. Continue talking until the two of you agree on a compromise.
- If either of you becomes angry, take a break and calm down before you go on talking.
- If there are many people on each side of the disagreement, each side should choose one or two people to do most of the talking.

## Think and Apply

Think of a disagreement that you or your class might be facing in school. Form groups to discuss it, using the steps in Understand the Process. Vote on which plan for compromise should be chosen.

BUILDING CITIZENSHIP

## CONNECT MAIN IDEAS

Use this organizer to show that you understand how the chapter's main ideas are connected. Copy the organizer onto a separate sheet of paper. Then write the main idea for each topic.

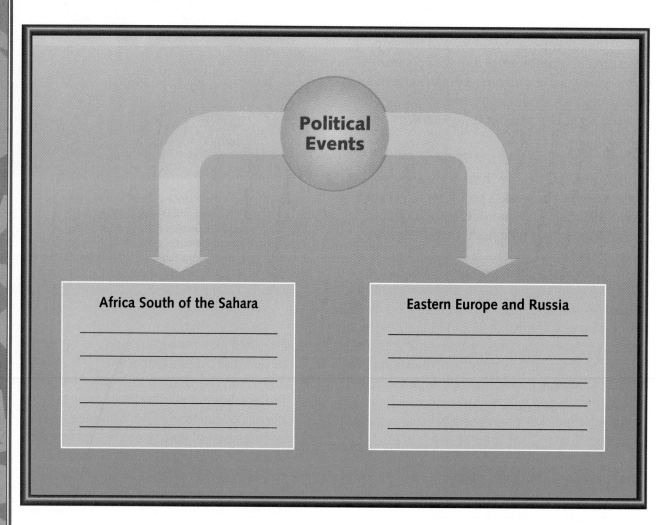

**Political Events**

**Africa South of the Sahara**

_____
_____
_____
_____
_____

**Eastern Europe and Russia**

_____
_____
_____
_____
_____

## WRITE MORE ABOUT IT

**1. Write a Letter** Imagine that you are an eleven- or twelve-year-old living in South Africa. Write a letter to a pen pal in the United States explaining recent changes in South Africa. As background, tell what life was like before the changes.

**2. Write an Article** From newspapers, magazines, and television news programs, find out about the latest developments in Bosnia. Then write your own article that might appear in a current-events magazine for eleven- and twelve-year-olds.

Write a term from this list to complete each of the sentences that follow.

Afrikaans      common market
apartheid      dissident
Bantustans      ethnic cleansing

1. Dutch settlers in South Africa spoke their own language, known as _____.

2. The EEC is an economic union, or _____, of European nations.

3. _____ was the name given to the homelands of black South Africans.

4. A _____ is a person who speaks out against a government.

5. The various groups within Bosnia have tried to carry out a policy of _____ to drive other groups from certain areas.

6. For many years South Africans lived under a political system known as _____, which separated people of different skin color.

## HECK UNDERSTANDING

1. Who was Kwame Nkrumah? What was his goal?

2. After the British gave freedom to the African colony known as the Gold Coast, what African name did the nation choose? Why was this name chosen?

3. Who became the first prime minister of an independent Kenya?

4. What actions did President de Klerk take toward ending apartheid in South Africa?

5. Who became the first president of the new South Africa? What role had this leader played in the country in the past?

6. What was *perestroika*? How did it affect leadership in the Soviet Union?

7. What was the Solidarity movement?

8. The breakup of which country led to a war in the Balkans?

 HINK CRITICALLY

1. **Cause and Effect** What were some of the effects of colonial rule on African nations?

2. **Personally Speaking** If you were the leader of South Africa, how would you help bring together the different peoples of your country?

3. **Past to Present** Make a prediction about the way of governing one year from today in each of these countries: Russia, Poland, Bosnia, South Africa, the United States.

4. **Explore Viewpoints** How do you think people your age who live in the former Soviet Union feel about the changes there? How do you think people there who are the age of your grandparents feel about the changes?

 PPLY SKILLS

**How to Resolve Conflicts** Think about a conflict between you and a friend or family member. Then write several paragraphs about ways you can solve this conflict. Answer these questions in your writing: What compromises are you willing to make? What compromises are you unwilling to make?

 EAD MORE ABOUT IT

*African Journey* by John Chiasson. Bradbury. Find out how nature affects the ways of life of people in the different regions of Africa.

*Gorbachev/Yeltsin: The Fall of Communism* by Stuart A. Kallen. Abdo & Daughters. Events leading up to the break up of the Soviet Union are examined.

## MAKING SOCIAL STUDIES
# RELEVANT

# FORCES FOR UNITY AND DIVISION

As the world enters the twenty-first century, it seems that people are as divided as ever. Serbs, Bosnians, and Croats have fought a terrible war. Palestinian Arabs and Israelis do not have lasting peace. Some Muslims and Hindus are fighting one another on the Indian subcontinent. There are many national, regional, and ethnic rivalries in Africa, Asia, Europe, and the Americas in which groups fight one another over civil rights and land.

In spite of these conflicts, some groups and leaders are helping to bring people together. Many international organizations have been formed to promote economic, social, and cultural cooperation. In addition to the United Nations, the main organizations are the Association of Southeast Asian Nations, the Caribbean Community and Common Market, the League of Arab States, the Commonwealth of Independent States from the former Soviet Union, the Organization of African Unity, and the Organization of American States. These groups work for unity in their regions of the world.

Find out more about one of the international organizations. Write a letter asking for information, and do library research. Based on the information you gather, write an article summarizing the group's recent achievements.

World leaders at a World Summit for Social Development, in Copenhagen, Denmark

Leaders from Europe and the United States gather to discuss world issues.

The PLO's Yasir Arafat meets with President Hosni Mubarak of Egypt and United States Secretary of State Warren Christopher.

# STORY CLOTH

Study the pictures shown in this story cloth to help you review the events you read about in Unit 10.

## Summarize the Main Ideas

1. China's industry, agriculture, and trade changed as Mao Zedong introduced communism to the country. In recent years the Chinese people have gained some economic freedoms but no political freedoms.

2. Following its defeat in World War II, Japan rebuilt and became a leader in industry.

3. The countries of South America have faced many economic and environmental challenges while growing and changing in the twentieth century.

4. Religious beliefs have played a part in the shaping of the present-day countries in the Indian subcontinent.

5. Ideas and beliefs both unite and divide the peoples of the Middle East.

6. After winning independence African nations faced a number of challenges. Only recently have all the people in South Africa begun to have equal rights.

7. The decline of communism in eastern Europe has brought many changes.

**Predicting Events**  In the future, world events may be very different from the way they are shown in this story cloth. What do you think the future will hold for cultures around the world? On a separate sheet of paper, draw scenes that you think might show the world in the year 2010. Then write a brief summary for each scene.

# UNIT 10
# REVIEW

## COOPERATIVE LEARNING WORKSHOP

### Remember

- Share your ideas.
- Cooperate with others to plan your work.
- Take responsibility for your work.
- Show your group's work to the class.
- Discuss what you learned by working together.

### Activity 1
## Conduct an Interview

Mohandas Gandhi was a leader in India's independence movement. What would it have been like to talk with him about his life and his ideas? Work with a classmate to make a list of ten questions you would have asked the Indian leader. The questions could focus on any of these topics: his early life, his views on conflict and cooperation, his religious beliefs. Once you have completed your questions, work with your partner to think of answers that Gandhi might have given. Then, with one of you playing the part of the interviewer and the other playing the part of Gandhi, present your interview to the class.

### Activity 2
## Present a Report

Work in a group to learn more about one of the African countries that became independent during the twentieth century. Find out about the nation's languages, peoples, colonial history, present-day ways of governing, and other topics of interest.

Then, with your group, make an oral presentation about the country you have researched.

### Activity 3
## Make a Scrapbook

Important world events happen daily. Look through recent newspapers and magazines for articles and pictures about the latest political events in eastern Europe and in the member countries of the CIS. Then, with several classmates, make a scrapbook that contains the most important articles and pictures. For each article, write a brief description.

### Activity 4
## Hold a World Summit

Each student in your class should find out more about one country in the world. The class should then hold a world summit, a meeting of the highest level of leaders, with each student representing his or her selected country. The topic of the summit should be Concerns for the Twenty-first Century.

# USE VOCABULARY

Write each term in a sentence that will help explain its meaning.

1. quota
2. gross domestic product
3. standard of living
4. deforestation
5. terrorism
6. partition
7. autonomy
8. apartheid

# CHECK UNDERSTANDING

1. What important event occurred on June 3, 1989, in China's Tiananmen Square?

2. Why does Japan have a favorable balance of trade?

3. Why are many of the South American countries known as developing nations?

4. Why was NAFTA created?

5. What is "passive resistance"?

6. Which United States President played an important role in getting Egypt and Israel to sign a peace treaty?

7. Who is Nelson Mandela?

# THINK CRITICALLY

1. **Cause and Effect**   What effect have the conflicts in the Middle East and in Bosnia had on the United States?

2. **Think More About It**   Why is autonomy so important to the Palestinian people? Why are the Israelis cautious about granting autonomy to the Palestinians?

3. **Past to Present**   How is your life affected by each of the following: the end of apartheid, the collapse of communism in eastern Europe and the former Soviet Union, war and peace in the former Yugoslavia, the Arab-Israeli conflict, and NAFTA?

# APPLY GEOGRAPHY SKILLS

**Reading a Population Density Map**
In Unit 10 you have read about problems in present-day Japan caused by the growth of industry and the increasing population. Use the map below to answer the questions.

1. Which colors cover most of the country? What does this show about Japan and its population?

2. Where has most of Japan's population settled? Why do you think this is so?

3. Are there areas in Japan with fewer than 100 people per square mile? If so, where are these areas? Why do you think this is so?

4. What do you think will happen if Japan's population continues to grow? What are some possible solutions to Japan's problem of overpopulation? Which solutions are best? Why?

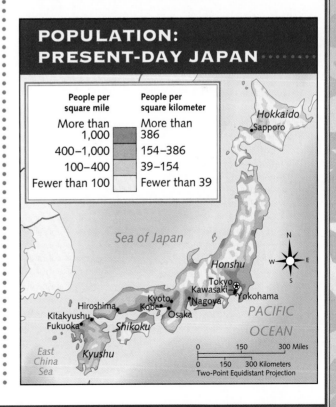

**POPULATION: PRESENT-DAY JAPAN**

| People per square mile | People per square kilometer |
|---|---|
| More than 1,000 | More than 386 |
| 400–1,000 | 154–386 |
| 100–400 | 39–154 |
| Fewer than 100 | Fewer than 39 |

# FOR YOUR REFERENCE

## CONTENTS

# HOW TO GATHER AND REPORT INFORMATION

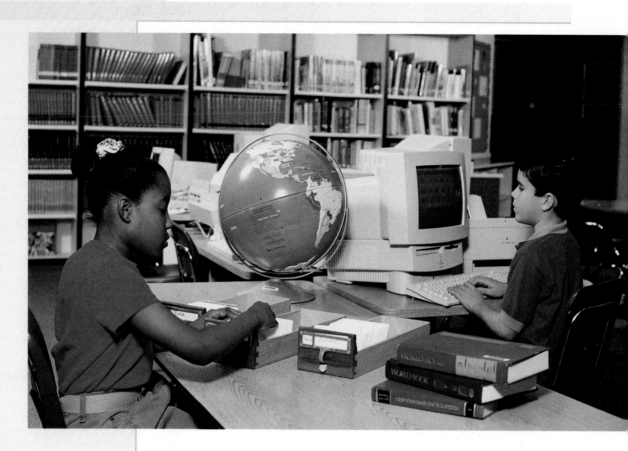

To write a report, make a poster, or do many other social studies projects, you may need information that is not in your textbook. You would need to gather this information from reference books, electronic references, or community resources. The following guide can help you in gathering information from many sources and in reporting what you find.

## HOW TO USE REFERENCE TOOLS

Reference works are collections of facts. They include books and electronic resources, such as almanacs, atlases, dictionaries, and encyclopedias. In a library a reference book has an *R* or *REF* for *reference* on its spine along with the call number. Most reference books may not be taken home. They are for use only in the library. Many libraries also have electronic references on CD-ROM and the Internet.

### WHEN TO USE AN ENCYCLOPEDIA

An encyclopedia is a good place to begin to look for information. An encyclopedia has articles on nearly every subject. The articles are in alphabetical order. Each gives basic facts about people, places, and events. Some electronic encyclopedias allow you to hear music and speeches and see short movies.

### WHEN TO USE A DICTIONARY

A dictionary can give you information about words. Dictionaries explain word meanings and show the pronunciations of words. A dictionary is a good place to check the spelling of a word. Some dictionaries also include the origins of words and lists of foreign words, abbreviations, well-known people, and place names.

### WHEN TO USE AN ATLAS

You can find information about places in an atlas. An atlas is a book of maps. Some atlases have road maps. Others have maps of countries around the world. There are atlases with maps that show crops, population, products, and many other things. Ask a librarian to help you find the kind of atlas you need.

### WHEN TO USE AN ALMANAC

An almanac is a book or electronic resource of facts and figures. It shows information in tables and charts. However, the subjects are not in alphabetical order. You would need to use the index, which lists the subjects in alphabetical order. Most almanacs are brought up to date every year. So an almanac can give you the latest information.

# How to Find Nonfiction Books

Nonfiction books give facts about real people and things. In a library all nonfiction books are numbered and placed in order on the shelves. To find the nonfiction book you want, you need to know its call number. You can find the call number by using a card file or a computer catalog, but you will need to know the book's title, author, or subject. Here are some sample entries for a book on the early Mayas, a Native American people.

**Subject Card**

```
          INDIANS OF CENTRAL AMERICA.

REF       Meyer, Carolyn.
972.81        The mystery of the ancient Maya / Carolyn
MEYE      Meyer and Charles Gallenkamp. -- New York :
          Atheneum, 1985.

              ix, 159 p. : ill. ; 24 cm.

          ISBN 0-689-50319-9
```

**Author Card**

```
REF       Meyer, Carolyn.
972.81        The mystery of the ancient Maya / Carolyn
MEYE      Meyer and Charles Gallenkamp. -- New York :
          Atheneum, 1985.

              ix, 159 p. : ill. ; 24 cm.

          "A Margaret K. McElderry book."
          Includes index.
          SUMMARY: Explores the advanced civilization
          and unsolved mysteries of the Mayas, who
          reigned for six centuries and then
          disappeared.
              ISBN 0-689-50319-9
```

**Title Card**

```
          The mystery of the ancient Maya

REF       Meyer, Carolyn.
972.81        The mystery of the ancient Maya / Carolyn
MEYE      Meyer and Charles Gallenkamp. -- New York :
          Atheneum, 1985.

              ix, 159 p. : ill. ; 24 cm.

          ISBN 0-689-50319-9



          F1435.M56 1985     ●        REF 972.81
                                      84-24209 /AC/r90
```

**Computer Catalog**

## HOW TO FIND PERIODICALS

Libraries have special sections for periodicals—newspapers and magazines. Periodicals are good sources for the latest information and for topics not covered in books. New issues are usually displayed on a rack. Older issues are stored away, sometimes on film. Most libraries have an index that lists magazine articles by subject. The most widely used are the *Children's Magazine Guide* and the *Readers' Guide to Periodical Literature.*

The entries in these guides are in alphabetical order by subject and author and sometimes by title. Abbreviations are used for many parts of an entry, such as the name of the magazine and the date of the issue. Here is a sample entry for an article on the Korean War.

**Heading:**
The general topic you are researching

**Title:**
The title of the article

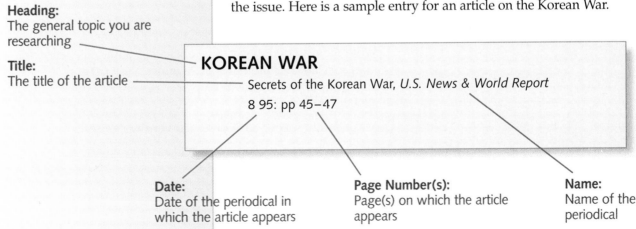

**KOREAN WAR**

Secrets of the Korean War, *U.S. News & World Report*
8 95: pp 45–47

**Date:**
Date of the periodical in which the article appears

**Page Number(s):**
Page(s) on which the article appears

**Name:**
Name of the periodical

# How to Conduct an Interview

Conducting interviews, or talking with people, is a good way to get facts and points of view.

## Planning an Interview

1. Make a list of people to interview.

2. Call or write to each person to request an interview. Identify yourself, and let the person know what you want to talk about.

3. Ask the person you will interview to set a time and place to meet.

## Before the Interview

1. Read more about your topic, and, if possible, about the person. That way, you will be better able to talk with the person about your topic.

2. Make a list of questions to ask.

## During the Interview

1. Listen carefully. Do not interrupt or argue with the person.

2. Take notes, and write down the person's exact words.

3. If you want to use a tape recorder, first ask the person if you may do so.

## After the Interview

1. Before you leave, thank the person you interviewed.

2. Follow up by writing a thank-you note.

# How to Conduct a Survey

A good way to get information about the views of people in your community is to conduct a survey.

1. Identify your topic, and make a list of questions. Write them so that they can be answered with "yes" or "no" or with "for" or "against." You may also want to give a "no opinion" or "not sure" choice.

2. Make a tally sheet to use to record your responses.

3. Decide how many people you will ask and where you will conduct your survey.

4. During the survey, record the responses carefully.

5. When you have finished your survey, count the responses and write a summary statement or conclusion that your survey supports.

## HOW TO WRITE FOR INFORMATION

People in places far away can also give you information. You can write a letter to ask for it. When you write, be sure to do these things:

- Write neatly by hand or use a word processor.
- Say who you are and why you are writing.
- Make your request specific and reasonable.
- Provide a self-addressed, stamped envelope for the answer.

You may or may not get a reply, but if you do, you may find that it was worth your time to write.

## HOW TO WRITE A REPORT

You may be asked to write a report on the information you have gathered. Most reports are 300 to 500 words long.

### GATHER AND ORGANIZE YOUR INFORMATION

Gather information about your topic from reference books, electronic references, or community resources. Then organize the information you have gathered.

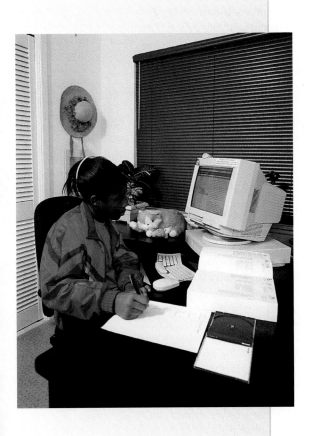

- Take notes as you find information that you need for your report.
- Review your notes to make sure that you have all the information you want to include.
- Outline your information.
- Make sure the information is in the order in which you want to present it.

### DRAFT YOUR REPORT

- Review your information. Decide whether you need more.
- Remember that the purpose of your report is to share information about your topic.
- Write a draft of your report. Put all your ideas on paper.

### REVISE

- Check that you have followed the order of your outline. Move sentences that seem out of place.
- Add any information that seems needed.
- Add quotations that show people's exact words if you can.
- Reword sentences if too many follow the same pattern.

### PROOFREAD AND PUBLISH

- Check for errors.
- Make sure nothing has been left out.
- Write a clean copy of your report by hand, or use a word processor.

# ALMANAC

## FACTS ABOUT THE WORLD

| Country | Capital | Population* | Area (sq. mi.) | Economy |
|---|---|---|---|---|
| **Africa** | | | | |
| Algeria | Algiers | 27,895,000 | 919,595 | oil, light industry, food processing |
| Angola | Luanda | 9,804,000 | 481,354 | textiles, coffee, bananas, iron, diamonds |
| Benin | Porto-Novo | 5,342,000 | 43,500 | palm products, peanuts, cotton, coffee, oil |
| Botswana | Gaborone | 1,359,000 | 224,607 | livestock processing, corn, coal, big game |
| Burkina Faso | Ouagadougou | 10,135,000 | 105,946 | grain, manganese, gold |
| Burundi | Bujumbura | 6,125,000 | 10,740 | coffee, cotton, tea |
| Cameroon | Yaoundé | 13,132,000 | 183,569 | aluminum, oil products, palm products, cocoa, coffee, timber |
| Cape Verde | Praia | 423,000 | 1,557 | bananas, coffee, beets, salt |
| Central African Republic | Bangui | 3,142,000 | 240,324 | textiles, cotton, coffee, diamonds |
| Chad | N'Djamena | 5,467,000 | 495,755 | cotton, uranium, fish |
| Comoro Islands | Moroni | 530,000 | 719 | perfume, vanilla, copra, plants, fruits |
| Congo | Brazzaville | 2,447,000 | 132,047 | palm oil, cocoa, coffee, tobacco, gold |
| Djibouti | Djibouti | 413,000 | 8,950 | salt |
| Egypt | Cairo | 59,325,000 | 385,229 | textiles, chemicals, cotton, rice, beans, oil |
| Equatorial Guinea | Malabo | 410,000 | 10,831 | cocoa, coffee, bananas, sweet potatoes, timber |
| Eritrea | Asmara | 3,200,000 | 45,300 | cotton, coffee, tobacco |
| Ethiopia | Addis Ababa | 58,710,000 | 437,794 | cement, textiles, coffee, grain, platinum, gold |
| Gabon | Libreville | 1,139,000 | 103,347 | cocoa, coffee, manganese, uranium, oil |
| Gambia | Banjul | 959,000 | 4,127 | tourism, peanuts, rice, fish |
| Ghana | Accra | 17,225,000 | 92,098 | aluminum, cocoa, gold, manganese |
| Guinea | Conakry | 6,392,000 | 94,926 | bananas, pineapples, iron, diamonds |
| Guinea-Bissau | Bissau | 1,098,000 | 13,948 | peanuts, cotton, rice, bauxite |
| Ivory Coast (Côte d'Ivoire) | Yamoussoukro | 14,296,000 | 124,504 | coffee, cocoa, diamonds, timber, rubber |
| Kenya | Nairobi | 28,241,000 | 224,961 | tourism, coffee, corn, gold |
| Lesotho | Maseru | 1,944,000 | 11,716 | corn, grain, peas, beans, diamonds |
| Liberia | Monrovia | 2,973,000 | 38,250 | mining, rice, cassava, coffee, iron, diamonds, gold, rubber, timber |
| Libya | Tripoli | 5,057,000 | 679,359 | carpets, textiles, petroleum, dates, olives, gypsum, oil, gas |
| Madagascar | Antananarivo | 13,428,000 | 226,658 | textiles, coffee, cloves, vanilla, chromium, graphite |
| Malawi | Lilongwe | 9,732,000 | 45,747 | textiles, sugar, cement, tea, tobacco, coffee, rubber |
| Mali | Bamako | 9,113,000 | 482,077 | millet, rice, peanuts, cotton, bauxite, iron, gold |
| Mauritania | Nouakchott | 2,193,000 | 398,000 | dates, grain, iron ore, gypsum |
| Mauritius | Port Louis | 1,117,000 | 788 | tourism, sugarcane, tea |
| Morocco | Rabat | 28,559,000 | 177,117 | carpets, clothing, leather goods, grain, fruits, copper, cobalt |

| Country | Capital | Population* | Area (sq. mi.) | Economy |
|---|---|---|---|---|
| Mozambique | Maputo | 17,346,000 | 313,661 | cement, alcohol, textiles, cashews, cotton, sugar, coal, titanium |
| Namibia | Windhoek | 1,596,000 | 318,146 | diamonds, sheep, cattle, fish |
| Niger | Niamey | 8,635,000 | 497,000 | peanuts, cotton, uranium, coal, iron |
| Nigeria | Abuja | 98,091,000 | 356,669 | textiles, cocoa, tobacco, oil, gas |
| Rwanda | Kigali | 8,374,000 | 10,169 | coffee, tea, tin |
| São Tomé and Príncipe | São Tomé | 137,000 | 386 | cocoa, coconut |
| Senegal | Dakar | 8,731,000 | 75,951 | food processing, fishing, peanuts, phosphates |
| Seychelles | Victoria | 72,000 | 176 | food processing, coconut products, cinnamon, vanilla |
| Sierra Leone | Freetown | 4,630,000 | 27,699 | mining, tourism, cocoa, coffee, diamonds |
| Somalia | Mogadishu | 6,667,000 | 246,300 | incense, sugar, bananas, iron, tin |
| South Africa | Cape Town | 43,931,000 | 473,290 | steel, tires, corn, wool, gold, diamonds |
| Sudan | Khartoum | 29,420,000 | 966,757 | gum arabic, cotton, sesame, peanuts, chrome, mahogany |
| Swaziland | Mbabane | 936,000 | 6,704 | wood pulp, sugar, corn, cotton, asbestos |
| Tanzania | Dar es Salaam | 27,986,000 | 364,017 | food processing, clothing, cotton, diamonds, hides |
| Togo | Lomé | 4,255,000 | 21,925 | textiles, shoes, coffee, cocoa, yams, phosphates |
| Tunisia | Tunis | 8,727,000 | 63,378 | textiles, oil products, grain, olives, citrus fruits, figs, phosphates |
| Uganda | Kampala | 19,859,000 | 93,070 | coffee, cotton, tea, copper, cobalt |
| Zaire | Kinshasa | 42,684,000 | 905,446 | coffee, rice, sugar cane, cobalt, copper |
| Zambia | Lusaka | 9,188,000 | 290,586 | corn, tobacco, peanuts, cobalt, rubber, ivory |
| Zimbabwe | Harare | 10,975,000 | 150,872 | clothing, chemicals, tobacco, sugar, cotton, chromium, gold |

## Asia

| Country | Capital | Population* | Area (sq. mi.) | Economy |
|---|---|---|---|---|
| Afghanistan | Kabul | 16,903,000 | 251,825 | textiles, furniture, fruits, copper, coal, wool |
| Armenia | Yerevan | 3,522,000 | 11,500 | mining, cotton, figs, copper |
| Azerbaijan | Baku | 7,684,000 | 33,400 | oil, grain, cotton, iron, cattle |
| Bahrain | Manama | 586,000 | 268 | oil products, aluminum |
| Bangladesh | Dhaka | 125,149,000 | 57,295 | jute, textiles, fertilizers, rice, tea |
| Bhutan | Thimphu | 1,739,000 | 18,147 | handicrafts, rice, corn, timber |
| Brunei | Bandar Seri Begawan | 285,000 | 2,226 | petroleum, rice, bananas, cassava |
| Burma (Myanmar) | Rangoon (Yangôn) | 44,277,000 | 261,228 | textiles, petroleum, rice, sugar cane, lead, silver, precious stones |
| Cambodia | Phnom Penh | 10,265,000 | 70,238 | rice, wood, rubber, corn |
| China | Beijing | 1,190,431,000 | 3,696,100 | iron, steel, textiles, grain, rice, cotton, tea |
| Cyprus | Nicosia | 730,000 | 3,572 | grains, carobs, citrus fruits, olives, copper |
| Georgia | Tbilisi | 5,681,000 | 26,900 | manganese, citrus fruits, wheat, grapes |
| India | New Delhi | 919,903,000 | 1,222,559 | textiles, steel, rice, grain, coffee, spices, coal |

*These population figures are from the most recent available statistics.

Almanac • **R9**

| Country | Capital | Population* | Area (sq. mi.) | Economy |
|---------|---------|-------------|----------------|---------|
| Indonesia | Jakarta | 200,410,000 | 741,052 | textiles, rice, coffee, sugar, nickel, tin, rubber |
| Iran | Tehran | 65,612,000 | 632,457 | cement, sugar refining, carpets, grain, rice, oil, gas |
| Iraq | Baghdad | 19,890,000 | 167,975 | textiles, cement, dates, oil |
| Israel | Jerusalem | 5,051,000 | 7,992 | diamond cutting, textiles, electronics, citrus fruit, potash |
| Japan | Tokyo | 125,107,000 | 145,850 | electronics, autos, rice, grain |
| Jordan | Amman | 3,961,000 | 34,342 | textiles, cement, grain, olives, phosphate |
| Kazakhstan | Almaty | 17,268,000 | 1,049,200 | steel, cement, footwear, grain, cotton |
| Kuwait | Kuwait City | 1,819,000 | 6,880 | oil, oil products, gas |
| Kyrgyzstan | Bishkek | 4,698,000 | 76,642 | tobacco, textiles, mining, wheat, sugar beets |
| Laos | Vientiane | 4,702,000 | 91,429 | wood products, mining, rice, corn, tobacco, |
| Lebanon | Beirut | 3,620,000 | 3,950 | textiles, oil products, fruits, olives, vegetables |
| Malaysia | Kuala Lumpur | 19,283,000 | 127,584 | rubber goods, steel, electronics, palm oil, copra, tin, iron |
| Maldives | Male | 252,000 | 115 | fish processing, tourism, coconuts, fruit, millet, shells |
| Mongolia | Ulaanbaatar | 2,430,000 | 604,800 | textiles, chemicals, grain, coal, copper |
| Nepal | Kathmandu | 21,042,000 | 56,827 | sugar, jute, tourism, rice, grain |
| North Korea | P'yongyang | 23,067,000 | 47,399 | textiles, corn, potatoes |
| Oman | Muscat | 1,701,000 | 118,150 | fruits, quartz, vegetables, wheat, oil |
| Pakistan | Islamabad | 121,856,000 | 339,697 | textiles, chemicals, petroleum products, rice, wheat, natural gas, iron ore, wool |
| Philippines | Manila | 69,809,000 | 115,860 | textiles, clothing, wood products, sugar, cobalt, copper |
| Qatar | Doha | 513,000 | 4,412 | oil, petroleum products |
| Saudi Arabia | Riyadh | 18,197,000 | 865,000 | oil products, dates, wheat, oil, gas |
| Singapore | Singapore | 2,859,000 | 247 | shipbuilding, oil refining, electronics, banking, tourism |
| South Korea | Seoul | 45,083,000 | 38,330 | electronics, textiles, clothing, motor vehicles, rice, barley |
| Sri Lanka | Colombo | 18,033,000 | 25,332 | plywood, paper, tea, coconuts, rice, graphite, gems |
| Syria | Damascus | 14,887,000 | 71,498 | oil products, textiles, cotton, grain, olives |
| Taiwan | Taipei | 21,299,000 | 13,969 | textiles, clothing, electronics, rice, bananas, coal, marble |
| Tajikistan | Dushanbe | 5,995,000 | 55,300 | cement, barley, coal, lead |
| Thailand | Bangkok | 59,510,000 | 198,115 | tourism, rice, corn, tapioca, sugar cane |
| Turkey | Ankara | 62,154,000 | 300,948 | iron, steel, tobacco, grain, mercury |
| Turkmenistan | Ashgabat | 3,995,000 | 188,417 | mining, textiles, grain, cotton, coal, sulfur, salt |
| United Arab Emirates | Abu Dhabi | 2,791,000 | 30,000 | vegetables, dates, limes, oil |
| Uzbekistan | Tashkent | 22,609,000 | 172,700 | steel, tractors, cotton, coal |
| Vietnam | Hanoi | 73,104,000 | 127,246 | food processing, textiles, rice, rubber, phosphates |
| Yemen | Sanaa | 11,105,000 | 205,356 | mining, petroleum refining, wheat, sorghum, salt |

| Country | Capital | Population* | Area (sq. mi.) | Economy |
|---|---|---|---|---|
| **Australia and Oceania** | | | | |
| Australia | Canberra | 18,077,000 | 2,966,200 | iron, textiles, electrical equipment, wheat, coal |
| Fiji | Suva | 764,000 | 7,056 | tourism, sugar, bananas, gold |
| Kiribati | Tarawa | 78,000 | 313 | copra, coconuts, breadfruit, bananas, fish |
| Marshall Islands | Majuro | 54,000 | 70 | agriculture, tourism |
| Micronesia | Palikir | 120,000 | 271 | tropical fruits, vegetables, coconuts |
| Nauru | Yaren | 10,000 | 8 | phosphate mining, coconuts |
| New Zealand | Wellington | 3,389,000 | 104,454 | textiles, machinery, fish, forest products, grain, fruits, oil, gas |
| Papua New Guinea | Port Moresby | 4,197,000 | 178,704 | coffee, coconuts, cocoa, gold, copper, silver |
| Solomon Islands | Honiara | 386,000 | 10,954 | fish canning, coconuts, rice |
| Tonga | Nuku'alofa | 105,000 | 301 | tourism, coconut products, bananas |
| Tuvalu | Funafuti | 10,000 | 9 | copra, coconuts |
| Vanuatu | Portvila | 170,000 | 4,707 | fish freezing, meat canneries, tourism, copra |
| Western Samoa | Apia | 204,000 | 1,093 | cocoa, copra, bananas, hardwoods, fish |
| **Europe** | | | | |
| Albania | Tiranë | 3,374,000 | 11,100 | cement, textiles, food processing, corn, wheat |
| Andorra | Andorra la Vella | 64,000 | 181 | tourism, tobacco products, commerce, services |
| Austria | Vienna | 7,955,000 | 32,378 | steel, machinery, autos, grain, iron ore |
| Belarus | Minsk | 10,405,000 | 80,134 | food processing, chemicals, grain, potatoes, sugar beets |
| Belgium | Brussels | 10,063,000 | 11,787 | steel, diamond cutting, wheat, coal |
| Bosnia and Herzegovina | Sarajevo | 4,651,000 | 19,741 | textiles, carpets, timber, corn, bauxite |
| Bulgaria | Sofia | 8,800,000 | 42,855 | chemicals, machinery, metals, textiles |
| Croatia | Zagreb | 4,698,000 | 21,829 | textiles, chemicals, olives, bauxite |
| Czech Republic | Prague | 10,408,000 | 30,449 | machinery, oil products, chemicals, wheat, sugar beets |
| Denmark | Copenhagen | 5,188,000 | 16,639 | machinery, textiles, furniture, dairy products |
| Estonia | Tallinn | 1,617,000 | 17,413 | agricultural machinery, grain, vegetables |
| Finland | Helsinki | 5,069,000 | 130,559 | machinery, metal, shipbuilding, grain, potatoes, copper |
| France | Paris | 57,840,000 | 210,026 | steel, textiles, wine, perfume, grain, fruits, vegetables |
| Germany | Berlin | 81,088,000 | 137,735 | steel, ships, motor vehicles, grain, potatoes, coal |
| Greece | Athens | 10,565,000 | 50,949 | textiles, chemicals, wine, grain, olives, citrus fruits, bauxite |
| Hungary | Budapest | 10,319,000 | 35,919 | iron, steel, pharmaceuticals, grain, bauxite, coal |
| Iceland | Reykjavik | 264,000 | 36,699 | fish products, aluminum, potatoes |

*These population figures are from the most recent available statistics.

| Country | Capital | Population* | Area (sq. mi.) | Economy |
|---|---|---|---|---|
| Ireland | Dublin | 3,539,000 | 27,137 | textiles, chemicals, brewing, tourism, potatoes, grain, zinc |
| Italy | Rome | 58,138,000 | 116,333 | steel, machinery, autos, textiles, shoes, grapes, olives |
| Latvia | Riga | 2,749,000 | 24,900 | railway cars, paper, oats, barley, potatoes |
| Liechtenstein | Vaduz | 30,000 | 62 | machines, instruments, chemicals, furniture, ceramics |
| Lithuania | Vilnius | 3,848,000 | 25,213 | shipbuilding, grain, potatoes, vegetables |
| Luxembourg | Luxembourg | 402,000 | 999 | steel, chemicals, beer, corn, wine, iron |
| Macedonia | Skopje | 2,214,000 | 9,928 | steel, cement, wheat, cotton, tobacco |
| Malta | Valletta | 367,000 | 122 | textiles, tourism, potatoes, tomatoes |
| Moldova | Chisinau | 4,473,000 | 13,012 | wine, textiles, grain, lignite, gypsum |
| Monaco | Monaco | 31,000 | 0.75 | tourism, chemicals, plastics |
| Netherlands | Amsterdam | 15,368,000 | 16,033 | metals, machinery, chemicals, grain, potatoes, flowers, natural gas, oil |
| Norway | Oslo | 4,315,000 | 125,050 | paper, shipbuilding, grain, potatoes, oil, copper |
| Poland | Warsaw | 38,655,000 | 120,727 | shipbuilding, chemicals, grain, potatoes, sugar beets, coal |
| Portugal | Lisbon | 10,524,000 | 35,672 | textiles, footwear, cork, grain, potatoes |
| Romania | Bucharest | 23,181,000 | 91,699 | steel, metals, textiles, grain, oil |
| Russia** | Moscow | 149,609,000 | 6,592,800 | steel, machinery, motor vehicles, chemicals, cement, grain, sugar beets |
| San Marino | San Marino | 24,000 | 24 | postage stamps, tourism, woolen goods |
| Slovakia | Bratislava | 5,404,000 | 18,933 | iron, steel, glass, wheat, potatoes |
| Slovenia | Ljubljana | 1,972,000 | 7,821 | steel, textiles, coal, mercury, wheat, potatoes |
| Spain | Madrid | 39,303,000 | 194,898 | machinery, grain, olives, lignite, uranium, cork |
| Sweden | Stockholm | 8,778,000 | 173,732 | steel, machinery, automobiles, grain, potatoes, zinc, iron |
| Switzerland | Bern and Lausanne | 7,040,000 | 15,943 | instruments, watches, food, banking, tourism |
| Ukraine | Kiev | 51,847,000 | 233,100 | steel, chemicals, grain, sugar beets, potatoes, iron, manganese |
| United Kingdom | London | 58,135,000 | 94,251 | steel, motor vehicles, shipbuilding, banking, grain, sugar beets, coal, tin |
| Vatican City | none | 811 | .17 | tourism, postage stamps |
| Yugoslavia | Belgrade | 10,760,000 | 39,449 | steel, wood products, corn, grain |

## North and Central America

| Country | Capital | Population* | Area (sq. mi.) | Economy |
|---|---|---|---|---|
| Antigua and Barbuda | St. John's | 65,000 | 171 | manufacturing, tourism |
| Bahamas | Nassau | 273,000 | 5,382 | tourism, rum, banking |
| Barbados | Bridgetown | 256,000 | 166 | sugar, tourism |
| Belize | Belmopan | 209,000 | 8,867 | sugar |
| Canada | Ottawa | 28,114,000 | 3,849,674 | nickel, zinc, copper, gold, livestock, fish |
| Costa Rica | San José | 3,342,000 | 19,730 | furniture, aluminum, textiles, fertilizers, coffee, gold |

**in both Asia and Europe

| Country | Capital | Population* | Area (sq. mi.) | Economy |
|---|---|---|---|---|
| Cuba | Havana | 11,064,000 | 42,804 | cement, sugar, tobacco, rice, coffee |
| Dominica | Roseau | 88,000 | 290 | tourism, bananas, pumice |
| Dominican Republic | Santo Domingo | 7,826,000 | 18,704 | sugar, cement, cocoa, coffee |
| El Salvador | San Salvador | 5,753,000 | 8,124 | food products, textiles, petroleum, coffee |
| Grenada | St. George's | 94,000 | 133 | rum, nutmeg, bananas, cocoa |
| Guatemala | Guatemala City | 10,721,000 | 42,042 | tires, textiles, coffee, sugar, bananas, oil |
| Haiti | Port-au-Prince | 6,491,000 | 10,695 | textiles, coffee, sugar, bananas, bauxite, timber |
| Honduras | Tegucigalpa | 5,315,000 | 43,277 | textiles, wood products, bananas, coffee, gold, silver |
| Jamaica | Kingston | 2,555,000 | 4,244 | rum, molasses, tourism, sugar cane, coffee, bananas, bauxite |
| Mexico | Mexico City | 92,202,000 | 756,066 | steel, chemicals, textiles, rubber, petroleum, tourism, cotton, coffee, silver, lead, natural gas |
| Nicaragua | Managua | 4,097,000 | 50,880 | chemicals, textiles, cotton, fruit, yucca, coffee, gold, silver |
| Panama | Panama City | 2,630,000 | 29,157 | oil refining, international banking, bananas, copper, mahogany |
| Saint Kitts and Nevis | Basseterre | 41,000 | 104 | sugar |
| Trinidad and Tobago | Port-of-Spain | 1,328,000 | 1,980 | oil products, rum, cement, tourism, sugar, cocoa, asphalt |
| United States of America | Washington, D.C. | 260,714,000 | 3,787,318 | coal, electronics, machinery, computers, wheat |

## South America

| Country | Capital | Population* | Area (sq. mi.) | Economy |
|---|---|---|---|---|
| Argentina | Buenos Aires | 33,913,000 | 1,073,518 | food processing, chemicals, grain, oil |
| Bolivia | La Paz/Sucre | 7,719,000 | 424,164 | textiles, mining, potatoes, sugar, coffee, tin |
| Brazil | Brasília | 158,739,000 | 3,286,470 | steel, automobiles, ships, coffee |
| Chile | Santiago | 13,951,000 | 292,135 | fish, wood, grain, copper |
| Colombia | Bogota | 35,578,000 | 440,831 | textiles, chemicals, coffee, emeralds |
| Ecuador | Quito | 10,677,000 | 105,037 | wood, textiles, bananas, coffee, rice, oil |
| Guyana | Georgetown | 729,000 | 83,044 | mining, textiles, sugar, bauxite, diamonds |
| Netherlands Antilles | Willemstad | 184,000 | 385 | oil, tourism, shipbuilding |
| Paraguay | Asunción | 5,214,000 | 157,048 | wood products, textiles, cement, corn, cotton, iron |
| Peru | Lima | 23,651,000 | 496,225 | fish meal, textiles, cotton, copper, wool |
| Saint Vincent and the Grenadines | Kingstown | 115,000 | 150 | tourism, bananas, arrowroot, coconuts |
| Suriname | Paramaribo | 423,000 | 63,251 | rice, sugar, fruits, bauxite |
| Uruguay | Montevideo | 3,199,000 | 68,037 | meatpacking, textiles, wine, oil products, corn, wheat |
| Venezuela | Caracas | 20,562,000 | 352,144 | textiles, paper, coffee, rice, oil, iron |

*These population figures are from the most recent available statistics.

# BIOGRAPHICAL DICTIONARY

*This Biographical Dictionary lists many of the important people introduced in this book. The page number tells where the main discussion of each person starts. See the Index for other page references.*

# A

**Abraham** *c. 2000s B.C.* The earliest ancestor of the Israelites, according to the Bible. p. 72

**Akbar** (AK•ber) *1542–1605* Considered the greatest of Mogul emperors, he united nearly all of India and was responsible for many reforms. p. 453

**Akhenaton** (ahk•NAH•tuhn) *c. 1300s B.C.* Egyptian ruler who changed his name from Amenhotep IV. He and Nefertiti, his wife, urged the Egyptians to worship only one god, Aton. p. 104

**Alaric** (AL•uh•rik) *c. 370–410* King of the Visigoths, he crossed the Alps and attacked the city of Rome in 410. p. 258

**Alexander the Great** *356 B.C.–323 B.C.* Son of Philip II. He was tutored by Aristotle and became king of Macedonia in 336 B.C. As ruler, Alexander built a huge empire. p. 229

**Alexandra** *1872–1918* Czarina of Russia and wife of Czar Nicholas II. She controlled the Russian government while Nicholas II led the World War I effort. p. 545

**Alger, Horatio** *1832–1899* American author of more than 100 popular books. p. 503

**Allende, Salvador** (ah•YEN•day) *1908–1973* Chilean politician; president from 1970 until 1973. p. 609

**Amenemhet** *1991 B.C.–1962 B.C.* Vizier who made Egypt an empire. Started the period called the Middle Kingdom, which lasted for 200 years. p. 102

**Antony, Mark** *c. 82 B.C.–30 B.C.* Roman orator and general. He lost control of Roman lands when he was defeated by Octavian in 31 B.C. p. 243

**Arafat, Yasir** (AH•ruh•faht) *1929–* Palestinian political leader, chairperson of the Palestine Liberation Organization, and President representing the Palestinian people. He was awarded the Nobel Peace Prize in 1994. p. 634

**Archimedes** (ar•kuh•MEE•deez) *c. 287 B.C.–212 B.C.* Greek teacher and inventor who used mathematics to build many useful machines. p. 233

**Aristarchus** (air•uh•STAHR•kuhs) *c. 200s B.C.* Greek teacher who used mathematics to discover that the Earth and the other planets move around the sun. p. 233

**Aristophanes** (air•uh•STAH•fuh•neez) *c. 450 B.C.–c. 388 B.C.* Ancient Greek writer of humorous plays, or comedies. p. 225

**Aristotle** (AIR•uh•stah•tuhl) *384 B.C.–322 B.C.* Greek philosopher and tutor of Alexander the Great. He is considered one of the greatest thinkers of all time. p. 227

**Asoka** (uh•SHOH•kuh) *c. 232 B.C.* Mauryan emperor, remembered as "the greatest and noblest ruler India has known." p. 188

**Atahuallpa** (ah•tah•WAHL•pah) *c. 1502?–1533* Last Inca king to rule what is now Peru. He was killed in the Spanish conquest of the Incas. p. 430

# B

**Babur** (BAH•ber) *1483–1530* A descendant of Genghis Khan, he was emperor of India, and founder of the Mogul dynasty. p. 453

**Bakri, al-** (BAHK•ree al) *c. 1000s* Muslim geographer. p. 344

**Bar Sauma, Rabban** *c. 1220–1294* A Christian born in China, he traveled to Europe and brought back goods and tales of the West. p. 312

**Batu** *c. 1200s* Grandson of Genghis Khan and conqueror of what is now Russia, Poland, and Hungary in Europe and parts of Asia. p. 311

**Begin, Menachem** (BAY•gin, muh•NAH•kuhm) *1913–1992* Prime minister of Israel. He and Anwar as-Sadat signed the Camp David peace agreement. p. 635

**Belisarius** (beh•luh•SAR•ee•uhs) *c. 505–c. 565* Byzantine general during the reign of Justinian I. He reclaimed much of the old Roman Empire. p. 278

**Bhutto, Benazir** (BOO•toh) *1953–* A prime minister of Pakistan. She is the first woman in modern times to lead a Muslim nation. p. 627

**Bismarck, Otto von** *1815–1898* Prussian statesperson and first chancellor of the German Empire. p. 509

**Bolívar, Simón** (boh•LEE•var, see•MOHN) *1783–1830* South American soldier, statesperson, and revolutionary leader. He freed Colombia, Venezuela, Ecuador, and Peru from Spanish rule. p. 482

**Bonaparte, Joseph** (BOH•nuh•part) *1768–1844* Napoleon Bonaparte's brother; ruled Spain from 1808 to 1814, after Napoleon conquered that country. p. 482

**Bonaparte, Napoleon** (BOH•nuh•part, nuh•POH•lee•uhn) *1769–1821* French military leader and emperor of France. He was defeated at the Battle of Waterloo. p. 476

**Bush, George** *1924–* Forty-first President of the United States. p. 618

# C

**Cabot, John** *c. 1450–c. 1499* Italian navigator and explorer. While seeking a western route to Asia, he reached North America and claimed it for England. p. 418

**Cabral, Pedro** (kah•BRAHL) *c. 1467–1520* Portuguese navigator who claimed Brazil for Portugal. p. 430

**Caesar, Julius** *100 B.C.–44 B.C.* Roman general and statesperson. He was dictator of Rome until he was murdered by a group of nobles. p. 242

**Carter, Jimmy** *1924–* Thirty-ninth President of the United States. He brought about a peace agreement between Israel and Egypt. p. 578

**Cartier, Jacques** (kar•TYAY, ZHAHK) *1491–1557* French sailor and explorer. His explorations gave France its claim to Canada. p. 431

**Castro, Fidel** *1926–* Cuban revolutionary leader, prime minister, and president. p. 575

**Catherine the Great** *1729–1796* Russian empress who supported learning and the arts but neglected the Russian peasant class. p. 544

**Cavour, Camillo di** (kah•VUR) *1810–1861* Italian statesperson who united much of northern Italy and encouraged Garibaldi to set up a kingdom of Italy. p. 509

**Ceauşescu, Nicolae** (chow•SHES•koo) *1918–1989* Romanian dictator from 1974 to 1989. He was overthrown and executed by the Romanian people during their revolt. p. 653

**Chandragupta I** (chuhn•druh•GUP•tuh) *c. 300s* Mauryan emperor in fourth-century India. He gave up his throne to his son Samudra Gupta. p. 189

**Chandragupta II** *c. 400s* Grandson of Chandragupta I of India's Maurya dynasty. He encouraged learning during his reign, which lasted from about 380 to 415. p. 189

**Chandragupta Maurya** (chuhn•druh•GUP•tuh MOW•ree•uh) *?–c. 297 B.C.* Emperor who united India. He gave up the throne to his son in 297 B.C. p. 187

**Charlemagne** (SHAR•luh•mayn) *742–814* King of the Franks and emperor of the Romans. He strengthened Christianity, resulting in the start of the Holy Roman Empire. p. 287

**Charles Martel** *c. 688–741* Charlemagne's grandfather and the ruler who united Frankish lands. p. 288

**Chiang Kai-shek** (jee•AHNG KY•SHEK) *1887–1975* Chinese general and politician. He followed Sun Yat-sen as president of the Chinese Nationalist government. p. 594

**Churchill, Winston** *1874–1965* British statesperson, author, and prime minister of Britain from 1940 to 1945. p. 558

**Cicero** (SIH•suh•roh) *106 B.C.–43 B.C.* Roman orator, statesperson, and philosopher. He served as a consul of Rome. p. 242

**Cleisthenes** (KLYS•thuh•neez) *c. 570 B.C.–508 B.C.* Athenian leader who is regarded as the founder of democracy. p. 219

**Cleopatra** *69 B.C.–30 B.C.* Egyptian queen who, with Mark Antony, planned to set up an independent empire until the Roman leader Octavian defeated them. p. 243

**Clinton, William** *1946–* Forty-second President of the United States. p. 635

**Columbus, Christopher** *1451–1506* Italian explorer and the first European to reach the Americas and return. He landed on San Salvador Island in 1492, believing it was Asia. p. 417

**Confucius** *551 B.C.–479 B.C.* Philosopher considered to be the most revered person in Chinese history. His philosophy, known as Confucianism, became a guide for the way people lived. p. 158

**Constantine** (KAHN•stuhn•teen) *c. 280–337* Roman general and emperor. The Edict of Milan, which was issued in 313 (during his reign), made Christianity an accepted religion within the Roman Empire. p. 257

**Copernicus, Nicolaus** (koh•PER•nih•kuhs, nik•uh•LAY•uhs) *1473–1543* Polish astronomer and philosopher. Against popular belief, he formed the theory that the Earth rotates on its axis and revolves around the sun. p. 408

**Cortés, Hernando** (kawr•TEZ, er•NAHN•doh) *1485–1547* Spanish explorer and conqueror of Mexico. p. 429

**Cyrus the Great** *c. 585 B.C.–529 B.C.* Leader who built the Persian Empire and conquered Babylon. p. 192

# D

**Darius** (duh•RY•uhs) *550 B.C.–486 B.C.* Persian ruler who brought order to the Persian Empire. He also built roads; established a postal system; and standardized weights, measures, and coinage. p. 193

**David** *c. 1010 B.C.–962 B.C.* Second king of Israel; led the defeat of the Philistines. p. 74

**de Klerk, Frederik Willem** *1936–* President of South Africa. Although an Afrikaner, he lifted the bans on the African National Congress and freed Nelson Mandela and other political prisoners. p. 644

**Deng Xiaoping** (DUHNG SHOW•PING) *1904–* Deputy premier and leader of the Chinese Communist party during the 1970s. His economic changes helped make China an industrial power. p. 596

**Dias, Bartholomeu** (DEE•ahsh, bar•too•loo•MAY•oo) *1450–1500* Portuguese navigator who sailed around the tip of Africa and into the Indian Ocean. p. 416

**Drake, Francis** *c. 1540–1596* Admiral who was the first English navigator to circumnavigate the globe. p. 418

**Dyer, Reginald H.** *1864–1927* British general who ordered his troops to fire on the Indian protesters at Amritsar, India, in April, 1919. p. 624

# E

**Elizabeth I** *1533–1603* Daughter of Henry VIII and Anne Boleyn. Known as Good Queen Bess, she made England a world power during her 45-year reign; gave the East India Company the right to control trade between India and England. p. 407

**Equiano, Olaudah** (ek•wee•AHN•oh, oh•LOW•duh) *c. 1750–1797* Nigerian who wrote of his life as a slave and helped in the movement to end slavery. p. 426

**Euclid** (YOO•kluhd) *c. 300s B.C.* Greek teacher who began the study of geometry. p. 233

# F

**Fatima** *c. 616–633* Daughter of Muhammad and Khadija p. 286

**Fa-xien** (FAH•SHYUHN) *c. 400s* Buddhist missionary from China who traveled in India and wrote about the scenes he observed. p. 190

**Ferdinand** *1452–1516* Spanish king who, with Queen Isabella, drove the Moors from Spain. He and Isabella paid for Columbus's expeditions to the Americas. p. 409

**Ford, Gerald** *1913–* Thirty-eighth President of the United States. p. 617

**Francis Ferdinand** *1863–1914* Archduke of Austria whose assassination in 1914 is considered the direct cause of World War I. p. 536

**Frank, Anne** *1929–1945* Young Jewish girl who hid with her family in order to escape the Nazi terror during the Holocaust. She is remembered for the diary she kept while in hiding. She met her death in a German concentration camp. p. 561

# G

**Galilei, Galileo** (ga•luh•LAY•ee, ga•luh•LAY•oh) *1564–1642* Italian mathematician, astronomer, and physicist. He improved the telescope and used it to prove Nicolaus Copernicus's theory that the Earth revolves around the sun. p. 408

**Gama, Vasco da** *c. 1460–1524* Portuguese navigator who completed the first voyage from western Europe around Africa to the East. p. 416

**Gandhi, Indira** (GAHN•dee, in•DIR•uh) *1917–1984* Prime minister of India in the 1980s. p. 626

**Gandhi, Mohandas** (GAHN•dee, moh•HAHN•dahs) *1869–1948* Indian nationalist and spiritual leader. He was called Mahatma, or "Great Soul," by his followers and was considered the founder of independent India. p. 623

**Gao Zu** (GOW ZOO) *256 B.C.–195 B.C.* Ruler during the Han dynasty of China. He was a respected leader who combined ideas from both Legalism and Confucianism. p. 166

**Garibaldi, Giuseppe** (joo•SEP•ay) *1807–1882* Italian military and nationalist leader who fought for freedom in southern Italy. p. 508

**Genghis Khan [Temujin]** (TEM•yug•juhn) *c. 1162–1227* Mongol leader who was the first outsider to conquer China. He was known for his boldness, cruelty, and military genius. p. 310

**Gilgamesh** *c. 2700s B.C.* King of the ancient Sumerian city-state of Uruk. He is the subject of one of the world's oldest stories. p. 64

**Gorbachev, Mikhail** (gawr•buh•CHAWF, mee•kah•EEL) *1931–* Secretary general of the Communist party of the Soviet Union from 1985 to 1991. He supported new ideas that included restructuring the government and making it more open to Soviet citizens. p. 652

**Gouges, Olympe de** (GOOZH, oh•LAMP duh) *1748–1793* Author of *The Rights of Woman*, which helped identify the roles of women in the French Revolution. p. 475

**Gracchus, Gaius** *153 B.C.–121 B.C.* Ancient Roman who died, like his brother, Tiberius, because he was trying to change Roman law to help the plebeian class. p. 241

**Gracchus, Tiberius** *163 B.C.–133 B.C.* Ancient Roman who was killed for trying to change Roman law to help the plebeian class. p. 241

**Gregory IX** *1170?–1241* Pope who set up the first Inquisition, in the 1230s. p. 412

**Gutenberg, Johannes** (GOO•tuhn•berg, yoh•HAHN•uhs) *c. 1400–1468* German who brought the idea of movable type to Europe. He printed Europe's first book, a 1,200-page Bible. p. 407

# H

**Hammurabi** King of the city-state of Babylon *c. 1792 B.C.–1750 B.C.* He wrote the set of laws known as the Code of Hammurabi. p. 69

**Hannibal** *247 B.C.–183 B.C.* Carthaginian general who attacked Rome during the Second Punic War. p. 240

**Hargreaves, James** *1720?–1778* English weaver who invented the spinning jenny. p. 488

**Hatshepsut** (hat•SHEP•soot) Female Egyptian pharaoh who expanded Egyptian trade routes *c. 1503 B.C.–1482 B.C.* p. 103

**Hawkins, John** *1532–1595* English naval commander who led expeditions to the West Indies. p. 418

**Henry VIII** *1491–1547* King who began the English Reformation by separating from the Roman Catholic Church and becoming supreme head of the Church of England. p. 418

**Henry the Navigator** *1394–1460* Founder of a school of navigation, he made Portugal a world sea power. p. 416

**Herod** *21 B.C.–1 B.C.?* He was King of Judaea when Jesus was born. p. 254

**Herodotus** (hih•RAH•duh•tuhs) *c. 484 B.C.–c. 430 B.C.* Greek historian who traveled through most of the world known to the Greeks during his time. p. 194

**Heyerdahl, Thor** (HAY•er•dahl, THAWR) *1914–* Norwegian explorer who sailed a balsa-wood raft from Peru to Polynesia to prove that Native Americans could have made such a trip. p. 385

**Hidalgo, Miguel** (ee•DAHL•goh) *1753–1811* Mexican priest and revolutionary leader who campaigned for Mexican independence. p. 483

**Hippocrates** (hip•AHK•ruh•teez) *c. 460 B.C.–c. 377 B.C.* Greek physician known as the "Father of Medicine." p. 225

**Hirohito** (hir•oh•HEE•toh) *1901–1989* Emperor of Japan. In 1947 the divine monarchy of Emperor Hirohito was transformed into a democratic government. p. 600

**Hitler, Adolf** *1889–1945* German politician and führer. As Nazi dictator of Germany, he planned to conquer the world, believing that the German race was superior to others. During his time of power he ordered 12 million people killed. p. 552

**Ho Chi Minh** (HOH CHEE MIN) *1890–1969* Vietnamese political leader and president of North Vietnam during the Vietnam War. p. 576

**Homer** *c. 700s B.C.* Greek poet and author of the *Iliad* and the *Odyssey*. Much of what we know of the Mycenaeans comes from his stories. p. 214

**Hong Wu** *1328–1398* Ruler who founded the Ming dynasty. He drove out the Mongols, ending the Yuan dynasty. Although he unified all of China, he proved to be a cruel leader. p. 445

**Hoover, Herbert** *1874–1964* Thirty-first President of the United States. p. 549

**Horace** *65 B.C.–8 B.C.* Roman poet. p. 247

**Hussein, Saddam** (hoo•SAYN, suh•DAHM) *1937–* Military ruler of Iraq since 1979. His invasion of Kuwait in 1990 led to the defeat of Iraq in the Persian Gulf War. p. 636

## I

**Ibn Battuta** *c. 1304–c. 1377* Muslim geographer and traveler. p. 370

**Ibn Rustah** *c. 900s* Muslim geographer. p. 380

**Idris Aloma** (EE•drees AL•oh•muh) *c. 1500s* Ruler of Kanem-Bornu in Africa in the late 1500s, during its time of greatest growth. p. 423

**Imhotep** *c. 2600s B.C.* Royal architect of Egypt who built Pharaoh Zoser's step pyramid around 2650 B.C. p. 100

**Irene** *c. 700s* Byzantine empress who ruled the empire from 780 to 802. p. 279

**Isaac** *c. 2000s B.C.* Son of Abraham. p. 73

**Isabella** *1451–1504* Spanish queen who, along with King Ferdinand, drove the Moors from Spain. She and King Ferdinand paid for Columbus's expeditions to the Americas. p. 409

**Ishmael** *c. 2000s B.C.* Son of Abraham. p. 73

## J

**Jacob** *c. 2000s B.C.* Early leader of the descendants of the Israelites. Also called Israel, he was the son of Isaac and grandson of Abraham. p. 73

**Jefferson, Thomas** *1743–1826* Third President of the United States and the main writer of the Declaration of Independence. p. 471

**Jesus** *c. 6 B.C.–c. A.D. 30* The person whose teachings are the basis of Christianity. His disciples proclaimed him the Messiah and savior of humankind. p. 254

**Jiang Qing** *1913–1991* Mao Zedong's widow, who attempted to gain control of China after Mao's death. p. 596

**Jinnah, Muhammad Ali** (JIH•nuh) *1876–1948* Indian politician and first governor general of Pakistan. He opposed Gandhi's methods and fought for separate Muslim statehood. p. 625

**John** *1167–1216* King of England who was made to sign the Magna Carta. p. 293

**Johnson, Lyndon** *1908–1973* Thirty-sixth President of the United States. p. 617

**Jonson, Ben** *1572–1637* English playwright and poet. p. 407

**Justinian I** *483–565* Byzantine emperor. His set of laws, known as the Justinian Code, is the basis of law in Europe today. p. 275

## K

**Kalidasa** (kah•lih•DAH•suh) *c. 400s* An author during India's Golden Age, he is considered to be among India's greatest writers. p. 190

**Kashta** (KAHSH•tuh) *700s B.C.* King of Kush who led an army of invasion into Egypt and seized control of Upper Egypt. p. 113

**Kennedy, John F.** *1917–1963* Thirty-fifth President of the United States. p. 575

**Kenyatta, Jomo** (ken•YAH•tuh, JOH•moh) *1894–1978* First prime minister of independent Kenya. As leader of the Mau Mau terrorists, he freed Kenya from British rule. p. 642

**Khadija** (kah•DEE•juh) *c. 555–619* Wife of the prophet Muhammad. She provided encouragement to him and support for his mission. p. 282

**Khomeini, Ayatollah** (koh•MAY•nee, eye•uh•TOH•luh) *1900–1989* A religious leader of Iran. He was the leader of Shiite Muslims in Iran and supported the taking of American hostages. p. 636

**Khrushchev, Nikita** (KRUSH•chawf, nuh•KEE•tuh) *1894–1971* Soviet politician and premier. p. 575

**Khufu** *c. 2500s B.C.* Egyptian king who built the Great Pyramid at Giza, the most famous of Egypt's pyramids. p. 101

**Khwarizmi, al-** (kwar•UHZ•mee al) *c. 780–c. 850* Arab mathematician. He was considered one of the greatest scientific minds of the Muslim Empire. p. 353

**Kubitschek, Juscelino** (KOO•buh•chek, zhoo•seh•LEE•noh) *1902–1976* President of Brazil during the 1950s. p. 610

**Kublai Khan** (KOO•bluh KAHN) *1215–1294* Grandson of Genghis Khan and founder of the Mongol dynasty in China. p. 311

## L

**Lenin** (LEH•nuhn) *1870–1924* Russian leader of the Communist revolution of 1917 and first premier of the Soviet Union. p. 546

**Leo** *c. 680–741* Byzantine emperor who ordered all icons in the empire to be destroyed. p. 279

**Leo Africanus** (LEE•oh af•rih•KAY•nuhs) *c. 1485–c. 1554* Arab traveler and geographer. For a long time his writings were the only source of information about the geography of Sudan. p. 346

**Leo X** *1475–1521* Pope from 1513 to 1521. He was a patron of the arts but drained the papal treasury by his rich living; he excommunicated Martin Luther. p. 411

**Leonardo da Vinci** (lee•uh•NAR•doh duh VIN•chee) *1452–1519* Italian Renaissance painter, sculptor, architect, engineer, and scientist. The Mona Lisa is one of his best-known works. p. 405

**Li Bo** (LEE BOH) *c. 705–c. 762* Chinese poet and writer. His work describes China's progress during its Golden Age. p. 307

**Livingstone, David** *1813–1873* Scottish missionary and explorer who spent nearly 30 years exploring Africa. His writings influenced traders to become interested in Africa. p. 514

**Louis XI** (LOO•ee) *1423–1483* King of France from 1461 to 1483. p. 409

**Louis XVI** *1754–1793* King of France. His efforts to raise taxes led to the French Revolution. p. 474

**Lumumba, Patrice** (luh•MUHM•buh) *1925–1961* First prime minister of Congo now the country of Zaire. He was murdered because of political unrest. p. 643

**Luther, Martin** *1483–1546* German religious reformer whose ideas led to the Protestant Reformation. p. 412

# M

**MacArthur, Douglas** *1880–1964* General of the United States Army and Commander-in-Chief of the Allied forces in the Pacific during World War II. p. 600

**Magellan, Ferdinand** (mah•JEH•lahn) *c. 1480–1521* Portuguese navigator who sailed through what is now known as the Strait of Magellan. One of his ships completed a circumnavigation of the globe. p. 418

**Malintzin** [Doña Marina] (mah•LINT•chin) *c. 1500s* Aztec princess who was Cortés's interpreter and adviser. p. 431

**Mandela, Nelson** *1918–* South African leader of the African National Congress. He was imprisoned for 25 years for conspiracy to overthrow the South African government. In 1994 he became President of South Africa. p. 644

**Mansa Musa** *?–c. 1332* Emperor of Mali who is remembered for his pilgrimage to Mecca. During his rule Mali became known as a wealthy state and a center of learning. p. 345

**Mao Zedong** (MOW ZUH•DUNG) *1893–1976* Chinese soldier and statesperson. He was chairman of the Communist party and of the People's Republic of China. p. 594

**Marie Antoinette** (an•twuh•NET) *1755–1793* Wife of Louis XVI. Disliked for her extravagance and her influence on the king, she was tried for treason and executed. p. 475

**Marquette, Jacques** *1637–1675* French Jesuit missionary and explorer in North America. p. 432

**Marx, Karl** *1818–1883* German political philosopher. With Friedrich Engels, he wrote *The Communist Manifesto* and *Das Kapital*—books on social and political reform. p. 502

**Mary** *? B.C.–c. A.D. 63* Mother of Jesus. p. 254

**Matsuo Basho** (maht•SOO•oh BAH•shoh) *1644–1694* Japanese poet and master of haiku. p. 449

**Mazzini, Giuseppe** (maht•SEE•nee, joo•SEP•ay) *1805–1872* Italian patriot and founder of Young Italy, a group that worked to unite Italy under a republican form of government. p. 508

**Meany, George** *1894–1980* American labor leader. p. 617

**Mehmed II** (meh•MET) *1432–1481* Sultan of the Ottoman Empire who organized a well-run government and encouraged education. p. 450

**Michelangelo Buonarroti** (my•kuh•LAN•juh•loh bwaw•naw•RAW•tee) *1475–1564* Italian Renaissance sculptor, painter, architect, and poet. He is perhaps best remembered for his Sistine Chapel frescoes. p. 406

**Mill, John Stuart** *1806–1873* English philosopher and economist. He studied the conflict among social classes in Europe. p. 501

**Minamoto Yoritomo** (MEE•nah•MOH•toh YOH•rih•TOH•moh) *1147–1199* As shogun he created a system that ended in Japan's being divided by civil war. p. 319

**Minos** (MY•nuhs) *c. 2000s B.C.* According to legend, the ruler of ancient Crete during the years of its greatest success. p. 213

**Mobutu Sese Seko** (muh•BOO•too SAY•say SAY•koh) *1930–* President of the Republic of Zaire. He united Congo by allowing only one political party. p. 643

**Mohammad Reza Pahlavi** (rih•ZAH PA•luh•vee) *1919–1980* Shah, or emperor, of Iran from 1941 to 1979. p. 636

**Moses** *c. 1200s B.C.* Prophet and lawgiver who, according to the Bible, led the Israelites out of Egyptian captivity and received the Ten Commandments. p. 73

**Motecuhzoma** [Montezuma] (maw•tay•kwah•SOH•mah) *1466–1520* King of the Aztecs when they were conquered by the Spanish. p. 429

**Muhammad** *c. 570–632* Prophet who brought the message of Islam to the world's people. His family and friends became the first Muslims, or believers in Islam. p. 282

**Murasaki Shikibu, Lady** (MUR•ah•SAHK•ee SHEE•KEE•boo) *c. 978–1026* Japanese writer of *The Tale of Genji*. Her work is considered the first real novel in the world and is a classic of Japanese literature. p. 318

**Mussolini, Benito** (moo•suh•LEE•nee) *1883–1945* Italian dictator and Fascist prime minister of Italy. p. 557

# N

**Narmer** *c. 2900s B.C.* Ruler who united the Two Lands of Egypt and founded the capital city of Memphis. p. 97

**Nasser, Gamal Abdel** *1918–1970* Egyptian soldier, politician, and president of Egypt during the 1950s. p. 633

**Nefertiti** (nef•er•TEET•ee) *c. 1300s B.C.* Wife of Akhenaton. p. 103

**Nehru, Jawaharlal** (NAIR•oo, juh•WAH•her•lahl) *1889–1964* Indian political leader and first prime minister of independent India. His work with Mohandas Gandhi helped bring about India's freedom. p. 624

**Newton, Isaac** *1642–1727* British physicist and mathematician who explained the theory of gravity and used the scientific method. p. 408

**Nicholas II** *1868–1918* Russian czar when the Russian Revolution began. p. 544

**Nixon, Richard** *1913–1994* Thirty-seventh President of the United States. p. 617

**Nkrumah, Kwame** (en•KROO•muh, KWAH•mee) *1909–1972* First president of the Ghana republic. He was the leader in liberating the Gold Coast in Africa from British rule. p. 641

**Nur Jahan** (NOOR juh•HAHN) *?–c. 1645* Empress during the rule of Jahangir, she ruled the Mogul Empire on her husband's behalf. p. 454

# O

**Octavian** (ahk•TAY•vee•uhn) *63 B.C.–A.D. 14* Julius Caesar's grandnephew, later known as Augustus. By defeating Mark Antony, he gained rule of all Roman lands. He was Rome's first true emperor. p. 243

**Olympias** *c. 375 B.C.–316 B.C.* Macedonian queen who was mother of Alexander the Great. p. 230

**Omar ibn Abi Rabi'a** *644–c. 712* Muslim whose poetry is considered the greatest of early Arabic literature. p. 284

**Owen, Robert** *1771–1858* Welsh founder of a utopian community in Indiana during the late 1820s. p. 502

# P

**Pachacuti** (pah•chah•KOO•tee) *?–1471* Inca ruler whose empire extended from Peru to Ecuador. p. 323

**Paul** *c. 5 B.C.–c. A.D. 62* Born a Jew, he converted to Christianity and became an apostle. He founded new churches and wrote many epistles, or letters, about Jesus to church members. p. 255

**Pedro** *1798–1834* Portuguese prince and emperor of Brazil who peacefully gained independence for Brazil from Portugal in 1825. p. 483

**Peres, Shimon** (PAIR•ez, shee•MOHN) *1923–* Israeli prime minister; he was awarded the Nobel Peace Prize in 1994 while foreign minister of Israel. p. 635

**Pericles** (PAIR•uh•kleez) *c. 495 B.C.–429 B.C.* Leader who ruled Athens during its Golden Age. p. 223

**Perry, Matthew** *1794–1858* American naval officer who persuaded Japan to open its ports for trade with the United States and other countries. p. 510

**Peter the Great** *1672–1725* Russian czar from 1682 to 1725 who helped place Russia among the great European powers. p. 544

**Philip II** *382 B.C.–336 B.C.* King of Macedonia and father of Alexander the Great. A military genius, he controlled most of the Greek peninsula by 338 B.C. p. 229

**Piankhi** (PYANG•kee) King of Kush *c. 751 B.C.–719 B.C.* and son of Kashta. He conquered Lower Egypt. p. 113

**Pilate, Pontius** *? B.C.–c. A.D. 36* Roman governor of Judaea. He tried Jesus and condemned him to death by crucifixion. p. 254

**Pinochet, Augusto** (pee•noh•CHET) *1915–* Chilean general and dictator. He seized control of the Chilean government from Allende and held control until 1990, when a freely elected government took charge. p. 609

**Pizarro, Francisco** (pee•ZAR•oh, fran•SIS•koh) *c. 1475–1541* Spanish conqueror of Peru. p. 430

**Plato** *c. 428 B.C.–c. 348 B.C.* Greek philosopher, student of Socrates and teacher of Aristotle. p. 227

**Pliny the Younger** (PLIH•nee) *c. 61–c. 113* Roman government official in Asia Minor known both for his treatment of Christians and for his account of the volcanic eruption of Vesuvius. p. 255

**Polo, Marco** *1254–1324* Venetian traveler who was among the first European traders to visit China and record his experiences. p. 312

**Pompey** *106 B.C.–48 B.C.* Roman general and statesperson who became consul after Sulla. p. 242

# R

**Rabin, Yitzhak** (rah•BEEN) *1922–1995* Prime minister of Israel who was assassinated in 1995. He signed a peace agreement with Palestinian leader Yasir Arafat. p. 635

**Raleigh, Walter** *1554–1618* English navigator, historian, and poet. In the service of Elizabeth I, he led many voyages of exploration. p. 418

**Rasputin, Grigori** (ras•PYOOT•uhn) *1872–1916* Russian peasant monk who greatly influenced the Czarina Alexandra. He was killed in 1916 by Russian nobles. p. 545

**Reagan, Ronald** *1911–* Fortieth President of the United States. p. 617

**Richard III** *1452–1485* Defeated by Henry Tudor, who then became king. His niece married Henry Tudor, thereby strengthening Henry's claim to the throne. p. 410

**Roosevelt, Franklin D.** *1882–1945* Thirty-second President of the United States. p. 551

**Rousseau, Jean-Jacques** (roo•SOH, ZHAHN•ZHAK) *1712–1778* French author and philosopher who was an important thinker during the time of the Enlightenment. p. 472

**Roxelana** (rahk•suh•LAHN•uh) *c. 1500s* Wife and adviser of Süleyman, who led the Ottoman Empire. p. 452

# S

**Sadat, Anwar as-** (suh•DAT) *1918–1981* Egyptian soldier, statesperson, and president of Egypt after Nasser's death; signer of the Camp David peace agreement. p. 633

**Samori Touré** *c. 1830–1900* West African ruler who held off French invasion of his Muslim empire for 15 years before being captured. He died in exile. p. 516

**Samudra Gupta** (suh•MUH•druh) *c. 300* Son of Chandragupta I of India's Maurya dynasty. He extended the empire and for the next 200 years, India enjoyed peace and growth. p. 189

**San Martín, José de** (sahn mar•TEEN) *1778–1850* Argentinian soldier and statesperson; led the fight for independence from Spanish rule in southern South America. p. 482

**Sarah** *c. 2000s B.C.* Abraham's wife. p. 72

**Sargon** Warrior who founded the Akkadian Empire and was the first ruler of an empire in the Fertile Crescent *c. 2334 B.C.–2279 B.C.* p. 68

**Saul** *c. 1000s B.C.* First king of Israel. p. 74

**Scipio** (SIH•pee•oh) *c. 237 B.C.–183 B.C.* Roman general who defeated Hannibal of Carthage. p. 240

**Sennacherib** (suh•NA•kuh•ruhb) *c. 700s B.C.–681 B.C.* King of Assyria from 704 to 681 B.C. p. 70

**Shabaka** (SHA•buh•kuh) *?–695 B.C.* Piankhi's brother and the pharaoh who established the Kushite dynasty in Egypt. He revived the practice of pyramid burials. p. 113

**Shah Jahan** (SHAH juh•HAHN) *1592–1666* During his reign Mogul power reached its highest point. He constructed the Taj Mahal, a beautiful tomb built in memory of his wife. p. 454

**Shakespeare, William** *1564–1616* British dramatist and poet. Considered among the greatest writers of all time. p. 407

**Shi Huangdi** (SHEE HWAHNG•DEE) *c. 259 B.C.–210 B.C.* Ruler of the Qin dynasty and unifier of China. The Great Wall of China was built during his reign. p. 161

**Siddhartha Gautama** (sih•DAHR•tuh GOW•tuh•muh) *563 B.C.–c. 483 B.C.* Known as Buddha, or "Enlightened One," he gave up worldly goods to search for enlightenment and truth. He founded the religion of Buddhism in India. p. 178

**Sima Qian** (SOO•MAH CHEN) *c. 100s B.C.* Scholar who recorded China's history during the Han dynasty. p. 168

**Sinan** (suh•NAHN) *1489–1588* Considered the greatest Ottoman architect. His ideas influenced nearly all later Turkish architecture. p. 452

**Smith, Adam** *1723–1790* Scottish economist and author. p. 499

**Socrates** (SAH•kruh•teez) *c. 470 B.C.–c. 399 B.C.* Greek philosopher who taught by asking questions. p. 226

**Solomon** *c. 900s B.C.* David's son and king of Israel under whose rule Israel rose to the height of its greatness. He was known for his wisdom. p. 74

**Solon** *c. 630 B.C.–c. 560 B.C.* Poet and statesperson who helped bring democracy to Athens, Greece. p. 219

**Sophocles** (SAHF•uh•kleez) *c. 496 B.C.–c. 406 B.C.* Ancient Greek writer of serious plays, or tragedies. p. 225

**Stalin, Joseph** (STAH•luhn) *1879–1953* Soviet dictator after Lenin's death. During his rule the Soviet Union became a totalitarian state and a world power. p. 547

**Süleyman I** (SOO•lay•mahn) *c. 1494–1566* Sultan whose reign was considered a high point of the Ottoman Empire. He made Istanbul into a great capital and encouraged arts and sciences. p. 451

**Sulla, Lucius** *138 B.C.–78 B.C.* Roman general, politician, and dictator of Rome for three years. p. 241

**Sun Yat-sen** (SUN YAHT•SEN) *1866–1925* Chinese statesperson and revolutionary leader of the Guomindang, or People's Nationalist party. p. 593

**Sundiata** (sun•JAHT•ah) *?–1255* Founder and ruler of the ancient Mali Empire. p. 345

# T

**Theodora** *c. 500–548* Empress and wife of Justinian I of the Byzantine Empire. Her influence helped women gain rights. p. 277

**Thucydides** (thoo•SIH•duh•deez) *471 B.C.–c. 400 B.C.* Greek teacher who is considered the greatest historian of ancient times. p. 219

**Thutmose I** *c. 1500s B.C.* Pharaoh whose armies retook Egypt after 100 years of Hyksos rule. p. 103

**Thutmose II** *c. 1500s B.C.* Son of Thutmose I. He continued to regain Egyptian lands from the Hyksos. p. 103

**Thutmose III** *c. 1500s B.C.* Son of Thutmose II. He continued Egypt's conquests after Pharaoh Hatshepsut. During his rule the Egyptian Empire grew to its largest size and was at its wealthiest. p. 103

**Tito, Josip Broz** (TEE•toh) *1892–1980* Yugoslav political leader. He established Yugoslavia as a communist state after World War II and became the first president of the republic in 1953. p. 655

**Tokugawa Ieyasu** (toh•ku•GAH•wah ee•uh•YAH•soo) *1543–1616* Japanese ruler who discouraged the Japanese from having contact with the West. p. 448

**Tomyris** (tuh•MY•ruhs) *c. 600s B.C.* Queen whose land was invaded by Cyrus the Great of Persia. Cyrus was killed during the battle with her armies. p. 192

**Toussaint-Louverture** (TOO•san LOO•vair•tyoor) *c. 1743–1803* Haitian general and liberator who established a free and independent country of Haiti. p. 481

**Trajan** *53–117* Roman emperor. p. 256

**Truman, Harry S.** *1884–1972* Thirty-third President of the United States. p. 572

**Tudor, Henry** *1457–1509* Defeated Richard III at the Battle of Bosworth. He became King Henry VII and the first of the house of Tudor. p. 410

**Tull, Jethro** *1674–1741* English farmer who invented a machine drill for sowing seeds. p. 487

**Tupac Amarú** (too•PAHK ahm•ar•OO) *c. 1742–1781* Descendant of the last Inca ruler, he led an uprising in Peru to try to gain rights for the Inca people. p. 481

**Tutankhamen** (too•tahng•KAH•muhn) *c. 1370 B.C.–1352 B.C.* During his brief reign as pharaoh, his ministers restored the old religion of Egypt. He was buried in a solid-gold coffin. p. 104

# V

**Vargas, Getúlio** (VAR•guhs, zheh•TOO•lyoo) *1883–1954* Brazilian politician and dictator. He encouraged Brazilians to expand into other industries besides coffee. p. 610

**Vespucci, Amerigo** (veh•SPOO•chee, uh•MAIR•ih•goh) *1454–1512* Italian navigator who explored the coast of what is now Brazil. The Americas are named after him. p. 418

**Victor Emmanuel** *1820–1878* King of Piedmont-Sardinia and first king of Italy. p. 509

**Victoria** *1819–1901* Queen of England who became empress of India after the Great Mutiny. p. 516

**Virgil** (VER•juhl) *70 B.C.–19 B.C.* The greatest of Rome's poets, he wrote the epic *Aeneid*, which is about the founding of Rome. p. 247

**Voltaire** (vohl•TAIR) *1694–1778* French writer who was an important thinker during the Enlightenment. p. 472

# W

**Walesa, Lech** (vah•LEHN•sah) *1943–* Leader of a workers' group called Solidarity, in Poland during the 1980s. He was elected president in Poland's first free election, in 1990. p. 653

**Washington, George** *1732–1799* Commander in chief of the Continental Army during the Revolutionary War and first President of the United States. p. 472

**Watt, James** *1736–1819* Scottish engineer and inventor who made many improvements to the steam engine. p. 488

**Wilhelm I** *1797–1888* King of Prussia and German emperor. p. 509

**Wilson, Woodrow** *1856–1924* Twenty-eighth President of the United States. p. 537

**Wu** *c. 1100s B.C.* Founder of the Zhou dynasty in China, he claimed the Mandate of Heaven in 1122 B.C. p. 155

**Wu Di** (WOO DEE) *156 B.C.–87 B.C.* Han ruler who established a civil administration to run the daily business of government in China. p. 168

# X

**Xerxes** (ZERK•seez) *c. 519 B.C.–c. 465 B.C.* King of Persia and son of Darius I. p. 222

**Xilingshi** (SEE•LING•SHEE) *c. 2700s B.C.* Chinese ruler's wife who, according to a legend, discovered silk in 2700 B.C. p. 130

# Y

**Yeltsin, Boris** (YELT•suhn) *1931–* Russian political leader and first popularly elected president in Russia. p. 654

**Yong Le** (YUHNG LEH) *1360–1424* Hong Wu's son. The power of China's Ming dynasty reached its highest point during his reign. p. 445

**Yoo** (YOO) *c. 1100s B.C.* Zhou dynasty king who reigned during the Warring States Period. p. 157

**Yu the Great** *c. 2000s B.C.* King of the Huang He Valley in about 2000 B.C. His family started the Xia dynasty. p. 126

# Z

**Zarathustra** (zar•uh•THOOS•trah) *c. 628 B.C.–c. 551 B.C.* Persian religious leader who founded a religion now known as Zoroastrianism. Its basic belief is that there are two gods—one good and one evil. p. 195

**Zheng He** (JUHNG HUH) *c. 1371–?* Chinese admiral and diplomat. During his travels he visited many ports and encouraged trade with China. p. 368

**Zoser** *c. 2600s B.C.* King of Egypt in the twenty-seventh century B.C. p. 100

**Zuhri, al-** (al•ZUKH•ree) *c. 1000s* Muslim scholar who wrote about Ghana's rise to power. p. 343

# GAZETTEER

*The Gazetteer is a geographical dictionary that will help you locate places discussed in this book. The page number tells where each place appears on a map.*

# A

**Aachen** (AHK•uhn) A city near the western border of central Germany; former capital and cultural center of Charlemagne's empire. (51°N/6°E) p. 288

**Acre** An old crusader capital and harbor; present-day city located on the west coast of Israel. (33°N/35°E) p. 354

**Adirondack Mountains** A mountain group in northeastern New York. p. 433

**Adriatic Sea** An extension of the Mediterranean Sea; located east of Italy and west of the Balkan Peninsula. p. 212

**Aegean Sea** (ih•JEE•uhn) An arm of the Mediterranean Sea between Asia Minor and Greece. p. 77

**Aegina** (ih•JY•nuh) A Greek island in the southwestern Aegean Sea. p. 217

**Afghanistan** A country in Asia; located between Pakistan and Iran. p. 122

**Africa** One of the world's seven continents. p. 41

**Agra** The capital of the historic Mogul Empire; located in northern central India on the Yamuna River. (27°N/78°E) p. 453

**Akhetaton** [also called El-Amarna] The ancient Egyptian capital built by Akhenaton; located on the Nile River in central Egypt. (28°N/31°E) p. 103

**Al-Ubaid** (oo•BAYD) An ancient settlement in what is now southeastern Iraq. (31°N/46°E) p. 46

**Albania** A European country on the Balkan Peninsula on the Adriatic Sea. p. 537

**Alberta** A province of Canada; located between British Columbia and Saskatchewan. p. 615

**Aleppo** A large city in northwestern Syria. (36°N/37°E) p. 311

**Aleutian Islands** A chain of volcanic islands extending southwest from the Alaska Peninsula; they separate the Bering Sea from the Pacific Ocean. (52°N/175°W) p. 560

**Alexandria** (a•lig•ZAN•dree•uh) A port on the Mediterranean Sea; located on the northern coast of Egypt on the Nile delta; also the name of many cities founded by Alexander the Great. (31°N/30°E) p. 231

**Algeria** A country in North Africa on the coast of the Mediterranean Sea. p. 516

**Algiers** The capital of Algeria; located in northern central Algeria on the Bay of Algiers. (36°N/2°E) p. 452

**Allegheny River** A river in the northeastern United States; joins with the Monongahela at Pittsburgh, Pennsylvania. p. 433

**Alps** The largest group of mountains in Europe; located in France, Switzerland, Italy, Austria, Slovenia, and Croatia. p. 212

**Alsace-Lorraine** An historic region in northeastern France. (48°N/7°E) p. 510

**Altai Mountains** A mountain system in Asia where Russia, China, and Mongolia meet. p. 127

**Amalfi** A town on the western coast of southern Italy on the Gulf of Salerno, an inlet of the Tyrrhenian Sea. (41°N/14°E) p. 374

**Amazon River** The largest river in the world; flows across northern Brazil in South America and into the Atlantic Ocean. p. 434

**Amman** The capital of Jordan; located northeast of the Dead Sea. (32°N/36°E) p. 633

**Amritsar** (uhm•RIT•ser) A manufacturing city located in northern India. (32°N/75°E) p. 625

**Amsterdam** The capital and the largest city of the Netherlands; located on the IJ River in the western central Netherlands. (52°N/5°E) p. 476

**Amur River** A river in northeastern Asia; forms part of the border between Russia and China. p. 311

**An Loc** A city in southern Vietnam. (11°N/106°E) p. 576

**Andaman Sea** A body of water in Southeast Asia; forms the eastern part of the Bay of Bengal. p. 133

**Andes Mountains** A great mountain system in South America extending along the western coast from Panama to Tierra del Fuego. p. 430

**Angola** A former part of the historic African kingdom of Kongo and a colony of Portugal; present-day country in southern Africa on the Atlantic coast. (12°S/18°E) p. 516

**Antarctica** One of the world's seven continents. p. 41

**Antioch** A center of early Christianity; located in western Asia Minor located near the town of Yalvac, Turkey. (36°N/36°E) p. 231

**Antwerp** An agricultural and manufacturing province; located in northern Belgium. (51°N/4°E) p. 492

**Anyang** (AHN•yahng) The last capital of the Shang dynasty of ancient China; located in what is today central China. (36°N/114°E) p. 128

**Apennine Mountains** (AP•uh•nyn) A mountain range; runs north and south through the center of Italy. p. 212

**Arabia** The historic name for the lands now known as the Arabian Peninsula, the Sinai Peninsula, Syria, and Mesopotamia. p. 77

**Arabian Peninsula** A peninsula bordered by the Red Sea, the Persian Gulf, and the Arabian Sea in Southwest Asia; location of the present-day countries of Saudi Arabia, Yemen, Oman, the United Arab Emirates, Qatar, and Kuwait. p. 77

**Arabian Sea** The sea located west of India and east of the Arabian Peninsula; forms the southern border of Southwest Asia. p. 62

**Aragon** (AIR•ah•gohn) An historic region and kingdom in northeastern Spain. (41°N/1°W) p. 410

**Aral Sea** A large inland body of water, flowing through the countries of Kazakhstan and Uzbekistan in central Asia. p. 176

**Archangel'sk** A Russian port city in Europe. (65°N/41°E) p. 547

**Arctic Ocean** One of the four oceans of the world. p. 41

**Argentina** A South American country on the Atlantic Coast. p. 481

**Argos** An ancient Greek city-state; present-day town in the northeastern Peloponnesus. (38°N/23°E) p. 217

**Arkansas River** A tributary of the Mississippi River; begins in central Colorado and ends in Mississippi. p. 271

**Armenia** An ancient kingdom in western Asia; a present-day country in southeastern Europe. p. 354

**Asia** One of the world's seven continents. p. 41

**Asia Minor** A peninsula at the western end of Asia between the Black Sea and the Mediterranean Sea; now occupied by Turkey. p. 103

**Assisi** A town in central Italy; home of St. Francis of Assisi during the Middle Ages. (43°N/13°E) p. 404

**Assur** An ancient Mesopotamian city on the Tigris River; included lands from the Mediterranean coast to Iraq; also called Assyria. (35°N/43°E) p. 62

**Assyria** An ancient empire in Southwest Asia. p. 78

**Asti** An ancient and present-day city; located in north-western Italy. (45°N/8°E) p. 404

**Asturias** (uh•STOOR•ee•uhs) An historic region and former kingdom in northwestern Spain. p. 410

**Aswan** Ancient trade center; present-day city located on the Nile River near Lake Nasser in southeastern Egypt; near the site of the Aswan Dam. (24°N/33°E) p. 94

**Athens** A city-state of ancient Greece; capital of present-day Greece; located near the southeastern coast of Greece. (38°N/24°E) p. 217

**Atlantic Ocean** One of the world's four oceans. p. 41

**Atlas Mountains** A mountain system in North Africa. p. 212

**Attica** (AT•ih•kuh) An ancient region in the southeastern part of the Greek mainland; home of the ancient Greek city-state of Athens. p. 226

**Australia** One of world's seven continents; a present-day country filling the continent of Australia. (23°S/135°E) p. 41

**Austria** A country in central Europe. p. 413

**Azerbaijan** (a•zer•by•JAHN) A country in southeastern Europe; located west of the Caspian Sea; formerly part of the Soviet Union. p. 655

# B

**Babylon** The capital of ancient Babylonia; located on the Euphrates River in central Iraq. (34°N/45°E) p. 62

**Babylonia** An ancient kingdom in the lower Tigris-Euphrates River Valley in Southwest Asia. p. 193

**Bactria** An ancient country of southwestern Asia; at location of parts of present-day northern Afghanistan and southern Tajikistan. p. 193

**Baden** A former German state; now part of the state of Baden-Württemberg in western Germany. p. 510

**Baghdad** The capital of Iraq; located on both sides of the Tigris River in the eastern part of the country. (33°N/44°E) p. 283

**Baja California Norte** The northern part of a peninsula extending between the Pacific Ocean and the Gulf of California. p. 616

**Baja California Sur** The southern part of a peninsula extending between the Pacific Ocean and the Gulf of California. p. 616

**Balearic Islands** (bal•ee•AIR•ik) An island group in the western Mediterranean Sea, off the eastern coast of Spain; forms the Spanish province of Baleares. (39°N/3°E) p. 288

**Balkan Peninsula** A peninsula extending from mainland Europe into the Mediterranean Sea; occupied by Greece, Albania, Slovenia, Croatia, Bosnia and Herzegovina, Serbia, Montenegro, Romania, Bulgaria, and Turkey. p. 212

**Baltic Sea** The sea located on the southern side of the Scandinavian Peninsula. p. 276

**Bangalore** The capital city of Karnataka; located in southern India. p. 628

**Bangkok** The capital of Thailand; located on the southern end of the Chao Phraya River on the Gulf of Thailand. (14°N/101°E) p. 133

**Bangladesh** (bahn•gluh•DESH) A country in South Asia on the coast of the Bay of Bengal. p. 122

**Barcelona** A province and city of Spain; located northeast of Madrid. p. 492

**Barents Sea** A sea comprising the part of the Arctic Ocean between Spitsbergen and Novaya Zemlya. p. 547

**Basra** A port city in southeastern Iraq, near the Persian Gulf. (31°N/48°E) p. 360

**Bataan** A peninsula located in the Philippines on Manila Bay. p. 560

**Bavaria** An historic and modern state in southeastern Germany. p. 379

**Bay of Bengal** An inlet of the Indian Ocean between India and the Malay Peninsula. p. 122

**Beersheba** A city in southern Israel; a part of the Negev region; the ancient town in which Abraham settled. (31°N/35°E) p. 74

**Beijing** (BAY•JING) The capital of China; located in north-eastern China; present-day name for Kublai Khan's historic capital of Khanbalik. (40°N/116°E) p. 311

**Belarus** A country located north of Ukraine, west of Russia, and east of Poland; formerly part of the Soviet Union. p. 655

**Belgium** A country in Europe, on the coast of the North Sea. p. 510

**Belgrade** The capital of Serbia; located at the junction of the Sava and Danube rivers. (45°N/21°E) p. 493

**Belize** A country in Central America, near the Caribbean Sea. p. 137

**Benin** (buh•NIN) A former kingdom of West Africa; present-day country in West Africa. (10°N/2°E) p. 424

**Berlin** The capital of Germany; located in the northeastern part of Germany. (53°N/12°E) p. 492

**Bern** The capital of Switzerland. (47°N/7°E) p. 540

**Bethlehem** A city in Southwest Asia's West Bank; birthplace of Jesus. (31°N/35°E) p. 633

**Bhutan** (boo•TAN) A country in Asia, south of China and north of India. p. 122

**Bien-hoa** (bee•en•WAH) A town in southern Vietnam; located northeast of Ho Chi Minh City. (11°N/107°E) p. 576

**Birmingham** A city located northwest of London. (52°N/2°W) p. 493

**Black Sea** A sea between Europe and Asia; surrounded by Bulgaria, Romania, Moldova, Ukraine, Russia, Georgia, and Turkey. p. 46

**Bohemia** An historic region and kingdom in central Europe; located in present-day Czech Republic. p. 413

**Bolan Pass** A mountain pass located in Pakistan. (30°N/67°E) p. 176

**Bolivia** A country in central South America. p. 481

**Bologna** An historic and present-day city in northern central Italy. (45°N/11°E) p. 404

**Bombay** A city on the western coast of central India, also known as Mumbai. (19°N/73°E) p. 453

**Bordeaux** (bawr•DOH) A city in southwestern France on the Garonne River. (45°N/1°W) p. 379

**Borneo** An island in the Malay Archipelago. (1°N/115°E) p. 354

**Borodino** A Russian village; located southwest of Moscow. (56°N/36°E) p. 476

**Bosnia and Herzegovina** (BAHZ•nee•uh hairt•suh•goh•VEE•nuh) A country in Europe; part of the former Yugoslavia. p. 537

**Botswana** A country in southern Africa. p. 643

**Brahmaputra River** A river in southern Asia; flows through China, India, and Bangladesh into the Bay of Bengal. p. 453

**Brazil** A country in eastern South America. p. 481

**Bremen** (BREE•muhn) A port on the banks of the Weser River in northwestern Germany. (53°N/9°E) p. 381

**Bristol** A city on the Avon River, in southwestern England. (51°N/3°W) p. 492

**British Honduras** The colonial name of Belize, a Central American country on the Caribbean Sea coast. p. 481

**British Isles** The islands of Ireland and Great Britain; located off the northwestern coast of mainland Europe. (54°N/4°W) p. 276

**British Somaliland** The now independent country of Somalia in northeastern Africa; once controlled by Italy and the British Empire. p. 516

**Brittany** A region in northwestern France. p. 379

**Bruges** (BROOZH) An historic city near the North Sea, in northwestern Belgium. (51°N/3°E) p. 381

**Brunei** A country in northwestern Borneo. (5°N/115°E) p. 603

**Brunswick** A former German province; part of the German state of Lower Saxony. p. 510

**Brussels** The capital city of Belgium in Europe. (51°N/4°E) p. 492

**Bucharest** A city in Romania. (44°N/26°E) p. 493

**Budapest** A city in Hungary; includes the former towns of Buda and Pest. (47°N/19°E) p. 493

**Buenos Aires** (BWAY•nahs IRE•ees) A port city in Argentina, South America, on the Río de la Plata. (34°S/58°W) p. 543

**Bukhara** (boo•KAR•uh) An historic Muslim city; located in southwestern Uzbekistan in central Asia. (40°N/64°E) p. 354

**Bulgaria** A country in southeastern Europe; located on the Balkan Peninsula along the Black Sea. p. 537

**Burkina Faso** A country in West Africa. p. 643

**Burma** (Myanmar) A country on the Indochina peninsula in Southeast Asia. p. 122

**Burundi** A country in Central Africa. p. 643

**Byzantium** (buh•ZAN•tee•uhm) See Constantinople.

**Cádiz** (KAYD•iz) A port in southwestern Spain on the Gulf of Cádiz, an inlet of the Atlantic Ocean. (37°N/6°W) p. 410

**Cahokia** (kuh•HOH•kee•uh) An ancient settlement of the Mound Builders of the Mississippian culture; located near present-day East St. Louis, Illinois. p. 271

**Cairo** The capital of Egypt; located in northeastern Egypt on the Nile River. (30°N/31°E) p. 101

**Cajamarca** A city in northwestern Peru. (7°S/78°W) p. 430

**Calcutta** A port in northeastern India, near the Bay of Bengal. (23°N/88°E) p. 453

**Calicut** A city in southwestern India, on the coast of the Arabian Sea. (11°N/76°E) p. 453

**Cambodia** A country in Southeast Asia, in the southern part of Indochina. p. 133

**Cameroon** (ka•muh•ROON) A former French and British colony; now an independent country in western Africa. p. 516

**Campeche** A state and a city; located in southeastern Mexico. (20°N/91°W) p. 616

**Can Tho** A town in southern Vietnam; located on the Mekong delta. (10°N/106°E) p. 576

**Canaan** The ancient name of a region of Southwest Asia that is located between the Jordan River and the Mediterranean Sea. p. 78

**Canada** A country in the northern part of North America. p. 560

**Canary Islands** An island group in the Atlantic Ocean, off the northwestern coast of Africa. (29°N/16°W) p. 516

**Cape Horn** The southernmost point of South America. p. 607

**Cape of Good Hope** The southernmost point of Africa. p. 648

**Cape Town** A seaport city of Cape Province and the capital of the country of South Africa. (34°S/18°E) p. 648

**Cape Verde** An island country in the Atlantic Ocean, located off the coast of West Africa. (17°N/25°W) p. 643

**Caracas** (kah•RAH•kahs) The capital city of Venezuela, South America; located near the coast of the Caribbean Sea. (10°N/67°W) p. 543

**Caribbean Sea** The sea bordered by Central America, South America, and the West Indies. p. 137

**Caroline Islands** Islands located in the western Pacific Ocean; part of the United States Trust Territory of the Pacific Islands. (8°N/150°E) p. 386

**Cartagena** (kar•tah•HEN•nah) A city and port in southeastern Spain. (38°N/1°W) p. 241

**Carthage** An ancient Phoenician city-state, on the Mediterranean Sea, located on the northern coast of what is present-day Tunisia. (37°N/10°E) p. 238

**Caspian Sea** A salt lake between Europe and Asia, east of the Black Sea. p. 46

**Castile** (ka•STEEL) A region and ancient kingdom of central Spain. p. 410

**Çatal Hüyük** One of the earliest human agricultural settlements discovered; dating from c. 7000 B.C. to c. 5600 B.C.; located in central Turkey. (38°N/33°E) p. 46

**Caucasus Mountains** (KAW•kuh•suhs) A mountain range between the Black and Caspian seas; borders Russia, Georgia, and Azerbaijan. p. 77

**Celebes** (SEL•uh•beez) An Indonesian island; located in Southeast Asia in the Malay Archipelago. (2°S/120°E) p. 518

**Central African Republic** A country in Central Africa. p. 643

**Ceylon** See Sri Lanka.

**Chad** A country in North Africa. p. 643

**Chalco** A dry lake and a municipality; located in central Mexico, southeast of Mexico City. (19°N/99°W) p. 327

**Chang Jiang** A river in East Asia; flows from the Plateau of Tibet in southwestern China to the East China Sea. p. 127

**Chang'an** An ancient capital of the Han and the Tang dynasties of China; now known as Xian/Sian; located in central China on the Wei River. (34°N/109°E) p. 167

**Chao Phraya** (CHOW PRY•uh) A river in Thailand. p. 133

**Chapultepec** A Mexican fort; located southwest of Mexico City. (19°N/99°W) p. 327

**Chatham Islands** An island group; located in the southern Pacific Ocean, east of New Zealand. (44°S/177°W) p. 386

**Chattahoochee River** A United States river that begins in northeastern Georgia; flows southwest and south along the Alabama-Georgia border into Lake Seminole. p. 271

**Chiapas** (chee•AH•pahs) A Mexican state; located in southeastern Mexico. p. 616

**Chihuahua** (chee•WAH•wah) A city and a state of northern Mexico. (29°N/106°W) p. 616

**Chile** A country on the southwestern coast of South America. p. 481

**China** A country in East Asia; it has the world's largest population. p. 122

**Coahuila** (koh•ah•WEE•lah) A Mexican state; located in northeastern Mexico. p. 616

**Colima** A Mexican state; located in western Mexico. p. 616

**Cologne** A city in northwestern Germany on the Rhine River. p. 379

**Colombia** A country in northwestern South America. p. 607

**Constantinople** (Istanbul) (kahn•stan•tuhn•OH•puhl) Formerly the ancient city of Byzantium; rebuilt, renamed, and made capital of the Byzantine Empire by Constantine I in A.D. 330; now known as Istanbul, Turkey. (41°N/29°E) p. 256

**Copenhagen** The capital city and a port of Denmark. (56°N/13°E) p. 492

**Coral Sea** A sea located north of Queensland, Australia, and south of Papua New Guinea. p. 560

**Córdoba** The historic capital of Andalusia; located in southern Spain on the Guadalquivir River. (38°N/5°W) p. 283

**Corinth** An ancient city-state in Greece and a present-day city; located on the isthmus between the Peloponnesus and the Greek mainland. (38°N/23°E) p. 217

**Corsica** A French island in the Mediterranean Sea, near the western coast of Italy. (42°N/9°E) p. 212

**Costa Rica** A Central American country; located west of Panama, bordered by the Caribbean Sea and Pacific Ocean. p. 619

**Côte d'Ivoire** (koht dee•VWAHR) A country in West Africa; also known as the Ivory Coast. p. 643

**Crete** A large Greek island; located southeast of the Balkan Peninsula; separates the Mediterranean and Aegean seas. (35°N/25°E) p. 212

**Croatia** A country in southeastern Europe; part of the former Yugoslavia. p. 537

**Cuba** An island country, south of the United States in the Greater Antilles of the West Indies. (22°N/79°W) p. 481

**Cuzco** (KOO•skoh) The capital of the ancient Inca Empire and a present-day city in southern Peru. (14°S/72°W) p. 324

**Cyprus** An island country in the eastern Mediterranean Sea. (35°N/33°E) p. 62

**Cyrene** (sy•REE•nee) An ancient city in North Africa, on the Mediterranean Sea in Libya. (33°N/22°E) p. 241

**Czech Republic** A country in central Europe; formerly part of Czechoslovakia. p. 655

**Czechoslovakia** (che•kuh•sloh•VAH•kee•uh) A former country in central Europe; where the Czech Republic and Slovakia are today. p. 540

# D

**Dahomey** (duh•HOH•mee) The early name for the land that today makes up the country of Benin in Africa. p. 424

**Damascus** The capital of Syria in Southwest Asia. (34°N/36°E) p. 77

**Danube River** A river in central Europe; flows from southwest Germany to the Black Sea. p. 231

**Danzig** A port in central northern Poland, on the Gulf of Gdansk, an inlet of the Baltic Sea; now known as Gdansk. (54°N/19E°) p. 381

**Dead Sea** A salt lake in Israel and Jordan; the lowest place in the world, at 1,302 feet (397 m) below sea level. p. 77

**Deccan Plateau** A triangle-shaped plateau in central India between the Western and Eastern Ghats. p. 176

**Delhi** A city in northern India. (29°N/77°E) p. 453

**Delphi** A sacred place to the ancient Greeks; located in central Greece, near the Gulf of Corinth. (38°N/23°E) p. 217

**Denmark** A country in northern Europe; occupies the northern part of the Jutland Peninsula. p. 379

**Dien Bien Phu** (DYEN BYEN FOO) A village located in northwestern Vietnam. (21°N/103°E) p. 576

**Djibouti** (juh•BOO•tee) A country in East Africa. p. 643

**Dnieper River** (NEE•per) A river in western Asia; flows from west of Moscow, Russia, to the Black Sea. p. 379

**Dresden** A German industrial city and the capital of Dresden district; located southeast of Leipzig. (51°N/14°E) p. 493

**Dublin** The capital of the Republic of Ireland; located on the River Liffey, near Dublin Bay. (53°N/6°W) p. 492

**Duero River** (DWAIR•oh) A river on the Iberian Peninsula; begins in Spain, flows across Portugal and into the Atlantic Ocean. p. 410

**Dunhuang** A city in eastern Asia; located in western China. (40°N/95°E) p. 360

**Dutch East Indies** A Southeast Asian republic; an archipelago extending from 95°E to 141°E. p. 560

# E

**East China Sea** The part of the China Sea north of Taiwan. p. 127

**Easter Island** An island off the western coast of South America, in the Pacific Ocean. (27°S/109°W) p. 386

**Eastern Ghats** A chain of mountains in southeast India. p. 122

**Ecuador** A country in northwestern South America, on the Pacific coast. p. 481

**Edessa** (ih•DES•uh) The ancient capital of Macedonia and present-day city in central Greece. (41°N/22°E) p. 256

**Edinburgh** The capital of Scotland; located in southeast Scotland, on the North Sea coast. (56°N/3°W) p. 490

**Edo** The historic name for Tokyo, the capital of Japan; located on the coast of the island of Honshu, on Tokyo Bay. (36°N/140°E) p. 448

**Egypt** An ancient land and present-day country in northern Africa, on the coast of the Mediterranean and Red seas. p. 62

**El Salvador** A Central American republic; located south of Guatemala, on the Pacific Ocean. p. 616

**Elba** An Italian island in the Tyrrhenian Sea off the northern coast of Italy. (43°N/10°E) p. 404

**Elbe River** A river in northern Europe; flows from the Czech Republic, across Germany, and into the North Sea. p. 381

**England** One of the four divisions of the United Kingdom; occupies most of the southern part of Great Britain. (53°N/2°W) p. 379

**English Channel** An extension and connection of the Atlantic Ocean and the North Sea; south of the British Isles and north of France. p. 490

**Ephesus** (EF•uh•suhs) An ancient city on the coast of western Asia Minor; located between the Mediterranean Sea and the Dardanelles. (38°N/27°E) p. 217

**Equatorial Guinea** A country in West Africa. p. 643

**Eridu** (AIR•uh•doo) The earliest known Sumerian city; located in Mesopotamia on the Euphrates River in what is today southeastern Iraq. (31°N/46°E) p. 46

**Eritrea** (air•uh•TREE•uh) A country on the Red Sea in North Africa, north of Ethiopia. p. 516

**Eshnunna** A locality in Iraq; located northeast of Baghdad. (33°N/45°E) p. 87

**Estonia** A country in northeastern Europe; formerly part of the Soviet Union. p. 540

**Ethiopia** A country in North Africa. p. 561

**Etowah** An ancient settlement of the Mound Builders of the Mississippian culture in what is now northwestern Georgia in the United States. (34°N/85°W) p. 271

**Euphrates River** A river that begins in Turkey, flows through Syria and Iraq, and empties into the Persian Gulf. p. 46

**Europe** One of the world's seven continents. p. 41

**Ezion-geber** (ee•zee•uhn•GEE•ber) An ancient town and present-day archaeological site; located near Aqaba, in southwestern Jordan. (29°N/35°E) p. 78

# F

**Ferghana** A city in northwestern China, near the border of Kyrgyzstan. (40°N/70°E) p. 360

**Fez** A sacred Muslim city in northern Morocco, near the Middle Atlas Mountains. (34°N/5°W) p. 346

**Fiji** An island country in Melanesia, Oceania, in the southern Pacific Ocean. (17°S/179°E) p. 386

**Finland** A country in northern Europe located south of Norway and east of the Gulf of Bothnia and Sweden. p. 573

**Florence** A city on the Arno River in central Italy. (44°N/11°E) p. 354

**Formosa** See Taiwan.

**France** A country in western Europe. p. 52

**Frankfurt** A city and district of Germany. p. 493

**French Equatorial Africa** The colonial name of former French territories in North Africa: Chad, Ubangi-Shari, Gabon, and Middle Congo. p. 516

**French Guiana** An overseas department of France, located on the northern Atlantic coast of South America. (4°N/53°W) p. 481

**French Indochina** The colonial name of former French territories in Southeast Asia; located where Cambodia, Laos, and Vietnam are now. p. 518

# G

**Gabon** A country in West Africa. p. 643

**Ganges River** A sacred river in India; flows from the Himalaya Mountains into the Bay of Bengal. p. 122

**Gao** (GOW) A trading center of the ancient Songhay Empire of West Africa; located on the Niger River in central Mali. (15°N/4°W) p. 346

**Gaul** An ancient land that included most of the present-day countries of France and Belgium; once part of the Roman Empire. p. 244

**Gaza** A city in southern Palestine, near the Mediterranean Sea. (32°N/34°E) p. 74

**Genoa** An important city-state trading center and present-day seaport on the Ligurian Sea, on the coast of northwestern Italy. (44°N/9°E) p. 354

**Georgia** A country on the Black Sea in southeastern Europe; formerly part of the Soviet Union. p. 655

**Germany** A European country; located in northern central Europe. p. 381

**Ghana** (GAH•nuh) A country on the coast of West Africa; called the Gold Coast by Portuguese and Dutch colonizers. p. 643

**Ghent** Belgian city and capital of East Flanders province; located in northwestern Belgium. (51°N/4°E) p. 492

**Giza** (GEE•zuh) An ancient and present-day city in northeastern Egypt, on the Nile River, across from Cairo. (30°N/31°E) p. 101

**Glasgow** A port near the Atlantic coast of southwestern Scotland. (56°N/4°W) p. 490

**Goa** A state in India; located on the Malabar coast. (16°N/74°E) p. 453

**Gobi** (Desert) A desert in East Asia; located in Mongolia and China. p. 127

**Golan Heights** A region under the control of Israel. (33°N/36°E) p. 633

**Gold Coast** See Ghana.

**Granada** A city in the Sierra Nevada, in southern Spain. (37°N/4°W) p. 256

**Great Britain** A West European kingdom; includes England, Scotland, and Wales. p. 561

**Great Zimbabwe** An ancient African settlement; located in what is present-day Zimbabwe. p. 369

**Greece** An ancient center of civilization and present-day country in Europe; located on the southern end of the Balkan Peninsula. (40°N/23°E) p. 217

**Greenland** The largest island in the world; located in northeastern North America; a territory of Denmark. p. 615

**Guadalajara** (gwah•duh•luh•HAR•uh) The capital of Jalisco state; located in central Mexico. (21°N/103°W) p. 616

**Guadalcanal** An island of the Solomon Islands in the western Pacific Ocean. (10°S/160°E) p. 560

**Guam** An unincorporated United States territory; largest and southernmost of the Mariana Islands; located in the western Pacific Ocean. (13°N/145°E) p. 560

**Guangzhou** (GWAHNG•JOH) A Chinese port once known as Canton; located on the Zhu River in southeastern China. (23°N/113°E) p. 203

**Guatemala** A former part of the Mayan Empire and later a colony of Spain; now an independent country in Central America. p. 137

**Guinea** A country in West Africa. p. 643

**Guinea-Bissau** (gih•nee•bih•SOW) A former Portuguese province; now an independent country in West Africa. p. 643

**Gulf of Aqaba** An inlet of the Red Sea, between Saudi Arabia and the Sinai Peninsula. p. 78

**Gulf of Bothnia** An inlet of the Baltic Sea, between Sweden and Finland. p. 381

**Gulf of Guinea** A gulf located on the western coast of Africa. p. 339

**Gulf of Mexico** A gulf located south of the United States, east of Mexico, and west of Cuba. p. 137

**Gulf of Oman** An arm of the Arabian Sea; located between northern Oman and the southeastern coast of Iran. p. 547

**Gulf of Suez** An inlet of the Red Sea, between Egypt and the Sinai Peninsula. p. 78

**Gulf of Thailand** An inlet of the South China Sea, between Malaysia and Thailand. p. 133

**Gulf of Tonkin** An inlet of the South China Sea, between Vietnam and China. p. 133

**Guyana** A country in the northern part of South America. p. 607

# H

**Haifa** A district and city located in northwestern Israel. (33°N/35°E) p. 633

**Hainan** An island in the South China Sea; located in southeastern China. (19°N/110°E) p. 576

**Haiphong** (HY•FAWNG) A Vietnamese seaport, near the Gulf of Tonkin, east of Hanoi. (21°N/107°E) p. 576

**Haiti** A country in the Caribbean, southeast of Cuba. p. 481

**Hamburg** A city in northern Germany; located near the Elbe River and the North Sea. (54°N/10°E) p. 379

**Hangzhou** (HAHNG•JOH) A former capital of the Song Dynasty and present-day city; located on the eastern coast of central China. (30°N/120°E) p. 306

**Hanoi** The capital of Vietnam; located on the Red River. (21°N/106°E) p. 133

**Hanover** A former German state; now part of the German state of Lower Saxony; also spelled Hannover. p. 510

**Harappa** (huh•RA•puh) An ancient center of Indus civilization, in the Indus River Valley, in what is present-day Pakistan. (31°N/71°E) p. 123

**Harbin** The capital of Heilungkiang province; located in northeastern China. p. 203

**Hawaii** A state of the United States; the Hawaiian Islands are a chain of volcanic and coral islands in the northern central Pacific Ocean. (21°N/156°W) p. 386

**Hebron** An ancient city of Judaea; located southwest of Jerusalem in the West Bank; long controlled by Israel. (32°N/35°E) p. 74

**Helsinki** The capital city and port of Finland in Europe. (60°N/25°E) p. 540

**Heracleopolis Magna** (hair•uh•klee•AHP•uh•luhs) The capital of the ninth and tenth dynasties of ancient Egypt; located on the Nile River, in central Egypt. (41°N/31°E) p. 103

**Herat** The present-day name of an ancient city located in what is today northwestern Afghanistan. (34°N/62°E) p. 360

**Hesse-Cassel** A region located in southwestern Germany. p. 510

**Hidalgo** A state of central Mexico. p. 616

**Himalaya Mountains** (hih•muh•LAY•uh) A mountain system on the northern edge of South Asia; runs through Nepal, Bhutan, southern Tibet, and northern India. p. 122

**Hindu Kush Mountains** A mountain system that extends southwest from the Pamir Knot in eastern Tajikistan through northwestern Afghanistan. p. 122

**Hiroshima** (hir•uh•SHEE•muh) An industrial city in Japan; located on the island of Honshu, Japan. (34°N/133°E) p. 560

**Hispaniola** An island in the Greater Antilles of the West Indies in the Caribbean; occupied by the countries of Haiti and the Dominican Republic. (19°N/71°W) p. 430

**Hokkaido** (hah•KYD•oh) The northernmost of the four main islands of Japan. (44°N/143°E) p. 448

**Holstein** (HOHL•styn) A former German state; now part of the German state of Schleswig-Holstein. p. 510

**Honduras** A country in Central America; located west of the Caribbean Sea, north of Nicaragua, and east of Guatemala. p. 616

**Hong Kong** Long a British crown colony set to become part of China; located in southeastern China, south of Guangzhou. (22°N/114°E) p. 595

**Honshu** The largest of the four main islands of Japan. (36°N/138°E) p. 448

**Huang He** (HWAHNG HUH) A river in China that flows east from the Plateau of Tibet. p. 127

**Hudson Bay** A bay located in northern Canada; borders the Northwest Territories, Manitoba, Ontario, and Quebec; reaches the Atlantic Ocean through the Hudson Strait. p. 615

**Hudson River** A river in the northeastern United States; begins in upper New York and flows into the Atlantic Ocean. p. 433

**Hungary** A country in central Europe. p. 413

**Hyderabad** A former Indian state; land absorbed by the states of Andhra Pradesh, Mysore, and Maharashtra; located in central India. p. 629

# I

**Iberian Peninsula** A peninsula forming southwestern Europe; extends into the Atlantic Ocean and the Mediterranean Sea; occupied by the countries of Portugal and Spain. p. 212

**Iceland** A European island country in the northern Atlantic Ocean; located southeast of Greenland. (65°N/19°W) p. 379

**Illinois River** Located in Arkansas and Oklahoma; flows west, joins the Arkansas River in Oklahoma. p. 271

**Inchon** A South Korean seaport; located southwest of Seoul. (37°N/127°E) p. 574

**India** A country in South Asia; occupies much of a large peninsula extending from central Asia into the Indian Ocean. p. 122

**Indian Ocean** One of the world's four oceans. p. 41

**Indonesia** A country in Southeast Asia. p. 386

**Indus River** A river in South Asia; flows from Tibet, through northern India and Pakistan, and into the Arabian Sea. p. 122

**Ionian Sea** The sea located east of Italy and west of Greece. p. 212

**Iran** A country in Southwest Asia; formerly known as Persia; located on the Persian Gulf. p. 62

**Iraq** A country in Southwest Asia; includes former lands of the Mesopotamians, Babylonians, Sumerians, and Assyrians. p. 62

**Ireland** A country of Europe, located on the British Isles. p. 379

**Irkutsk** (ir•KOOTSK) A city located in Irkutsk Oblast, Russia, on the Angara River. (58°N/104°E) p. 547

**Irrawaddy River** A river in southern central Burma (Myanmar). p. 133

**Islamabad** The capital of Pakistan. (34°N/73°E) p. 180

**Isonzo River** A river in Slovenia and northeast Italy; area of heavy fighting during World War I. p. 538

**Israel** An ancient kingdom and present-day country; a holy land for Jews, Christians, and Muslims; located on the eastern coast of the Mediterranean Sea. p. 62

**Isthmus of Panama** (IHS•muhs) A narrow land bridge containing the country of Panama; located between the Caribbean Sea and the Pacific Ocean; connects Central and South America. p. 481

**Italian Peninsula** A boot-shaped peninsula extending from southern central Europe into the Mediterranean Sea; occupied by Italy. p. 212

**Italy** An ancient center of civilization and present-day European country; located on the Italian Peninsula. p. 276

**Ithotwe** A city located in Egypt on the Nile River. (31°N/30°E) p. 103

**Iwo Jima** (EE•woh JEE•muh) Center island of the Volcano Islands; located south of Tokyo, Japan. p. 560

# J

**Jamaica** An island country in the Greater Antilles of the West Indies. (18°N/78°W) p. 430

**Jammu and Kashmir** A former princely state; now divided into Indian states and Pakistan territory. p. 625

**Japan** An island country in East Asia, off the Pacific coasts of China and Russia. (36°N/136°E) p. 127

**Jarmo** Site of the ancient Kurdish village of Qallat Jarmo; located in northern Iraq. (36°N/45°E) p. 46

**Java** The most important island of Indonesia; located in southern Indonesia. (7°S/110°E) p. 384

**Java Sea** Part of the Pacific Ocean north of Java, south of Borneo, and east of Sumatra. p. 560

**Jenné** (jeh•NAY) A city of the ancient Songhay Empire of West Africa; located on the Niger River in central Mali. (14°N/4°W) p. 339

**Jericho** The oldest known city in the world; located north of the Dead Sea, in Jordan. (32°N/35°E) p. 46

**Jerusalem** The capital of Israel; a holy city for Jews, Christians, and Muslims. (32°N/35°E) p. 74

**Johannesburg** A city located in the country of South Africa. (26°S/28°E) p. 648

**Joppa** An ancient city in Israel, now known as Jaffa; located northwest of Jerusalem. (32°N/35°E) p. 74

**Jordan** A country in Southwest Asia. p. 62

**Jordan River** A river that flows from the mountains of Syria in Southwest Asia into the Dead Sea. p. 74

**Jutland** A peninsula occupied by the mainland of Denmark. p. 538

# K

**Kalahari Desert** A desert in southern Africa; located in Botswana, Namibia, and South Africa. p. 343

**Kamchatka Peninsula** A peninsula in northeastern Russia; surrounded by the Sea of Okhotsk and the Bering Sea. (57°N/160°E) p. 547

**Kanem-Bornu** (KAHN•em BAWR•noo) An ancient African kingdom, later part of French Equatorial Africa, northeast of Lake Chad. p. 424

**Kanpur** A city in northern India; located on the Ganges River, southeast of Delhi. (26°N/80°E) p. 628

**Karachi** A city and seaport, former capital of Pakistan; located northwest of the Indus River mouth. (25°N/67°E) p. 625

**Karakorum** (kar•uh•KOHR•uhm) The capital of Mongolia under Genghis Khan; located in the Gobi on the southern end of the Orhon River. (47°N/103°E) p. 311

**Kashgar** A city in the Takla Makan Desert in northwestern China near the border with Kyrgyzstan. (39°N/76°E) p. 360

**Kathmandu** The capital of Nepal on the Indian subcontinent; located in a valley of the Himalayas. (27°N/85°E) p. 180

**Kazakhstan** (ka•zak•STAN) A country in Central Asia; formerly part of the Soviet Union. p. 127

**Kenya** A country in East Africa. p. 643

**Kerma** A capital of the ancient kingdom of Kush; located on the Nile River in Sudan. (20°N/30°E) p. 113

**Khanbalik** (kahn•buh•LEEK) See Beijing. p. 311

**Khyber Pass** A narrow pass through the Hindu Kush Mountains on the border between Afghanistan and Pakistan in Asia. p. 176

**Kiev** (KEE•ef) The capital of Ukraine; located on the Dnieper River, in central Ukraine. (50°N/31°E) p. 311

**Kilwa** (KIL•wah) An ancient Swahili trading city on a small island near what is today the country of Tanzania in eastern Africa. (9°S/40°E) p. 369

**King's Lynn** An English town; located in Norfolk on the Ouse. (53°N/0°) p. 381

**Kish** An ancient Sumerian city-state on the Euphrates River, in present-day Iraq in Southwest Asia. (33°N/45°E) p. 62

**Kitakyushu** (kee•tah•kee•OO•shoo) A Japanese city located in the northern part of the island of Kyushu in southwestern Japan. p. 602

**Knossos** (NAHS•uhs) The capital of the ancient Minoan civilization; located on central Crete off the Greek Peninsula. (35°N/25°E) p. 212

**Kobe** (KOH•bee) A Japanese seaport and commercial city; located on the southern coast of Honshu. (35°N/135°E) p. 602

**Kongo** (Congo) An historic kingdom in southern Africa; located within the present-day countries of Angola and Zaire. p. 424

**Königsberg** (KAY•nigz•berg) A port city in western Russia and former capital of East Prussia, also known as Kaliningrad. (55°N/21°E) p. 492

**Korea** An East Asian country now divided into North and South Korea; occupies a peninsula on the eastern coast of China. p. 574

**Kowloon** A town on western Kowloon Peninsula; located in southeastern China. (22°N/114°E) p. 604

**Kowloon Peninsula** A peninsula opposite Hong Kong Island. p. 604

**Kumbi-Saleh** (KOOM•bee SAH•lay) The ancient capital of the empire of Ghana in West Africa; located in the southwestern corner of what is today Mauritania. (16°N/15°W) p. 346

**Kunlun Shan** (KOON•LOON SHAN) A mountain range in western China. p. 127

**Kush** An ancient Nubian kingdom; located in the Nile Valley in northern Sudan in Africa. (20°N/30°E) p. 113

**Kuwait** An independent state on the northwestern Persian Gulf; located between Iraq and Saudi Arabia. (30°N/48°E) p. 634

**Kyoto** (kee•OH•toh) Formerly Heian-Yo, the imperial capital of Japan for more than a thousand years; now a leading cultural center of Japan; located in south-central Honshu. (35°N/136°E) p. 318

**Kyrgyzstan** (kir•gih•STAN) A country in Central Asia; formerly part of the Soviet Union. p. 127

**Kyushu** (kee•OO•shoo) The southernmost of the four main islands of Japan. (33°N/131°E) p. 448

# L

**Lagash** (LAY•gash) A city of ancient Sumer and a city-state in ancient Babylonia; located near the coast of the Persian Gulf, in the southeast part of Iraq in Southwest Asia. (32°N/47°E) p. 62

**Lake Chad** A lake in northern Africa on the border of Chad, Cameroon, Nigeria, and Niger. p. 346

**Lake Erie** The fourth-largest of the Great Lakes; borders Canada and the United States. p. 473

**Lake Huron** The second-largest of the Great Lakes; borders Canada and the United States. p. 473

**Lake Malawi** A large lake along the eastern border of Malawi in southern Africa; also called Lake Nyasa. p. 369

**Lake Michigan** The third-largest of the Great Lakes, the only one entirely within the United States. p. 473

**Lake Ontario** The smallest of the Great Lakes; borders Canada and the United States. p. 473

**Lake Superior** The largest of the Great Lakes; borders Canada and the United States. p. 473

**Lake Tanganyika** (tang•uhn•YEE•kuh) A lake in Tanzania and Zaire, in the Great Rift Valley of southern Africa. p. 369

**Lake Texcoco** A dry lake near Mexico City; an island in the lake was the site of the Aztec capital Tenochtitlán. p. 324

**Lake Tiberias** See Sea of Galilee.

**Lake Victoria** A lake in Tanzania, Kenya, and Uganda in southeastern Africa. p. 343

**Lake Xaltocan** (hahl•tuh•KAHN) A lake in the Valley of Mexico; located northeast of Mexico City. p. 327

**Lake Xochimilco** (soh•chih•MEEL•koh) A lake in central Mexico in North America; located southeast of Mexico City. p. 324

**Lamu** (LAHM•oo) A port on the Indian Ocean; located in eastern Kenya in Africa. (2°S/41°E) p. 370

**Laos** A country located on the Indochina Peninsula in Southeast Asia; once part of former French Indochina. p. 127

**Larsa** A city in ancient Babylonia, near the Euphrates River, in what is today southeastern Iraq in Southwest Asia. (31°N/46°E) p. 62

**Latvia** A country in eastern Europe; formerly part of the Soviet Union. p. 540

**Lebanon** The land of the ancient Phoenicians and present-day country on the eastern shore of the Mediterranean Sea in Southwest Asia. p. 62

**Leeds** An inland port in central England, on the River Aire. (54°N/2°W) p. 490

**Leningrad** See St. Petersburg.

**León (Spain)** An historic region and former kingdom in northwestern Spain. (43°N/6°W) p. 410

**León (Mexico)** A city in central Mexico; located northwest of Guanajuato. (21°N/102°W) p. 616

**Lepanto** An ancient Greek seaport, also known as Návpaktos. (38°N/22°E) p. 452

**Lesotho** An independent country located within the borders of the country of South Africa in Africa. (30°S/28°E) p. 643

**Liberia** A country in West Africa; originally a republic for freed slaves from the United States; located on the Atlantic coast of West Africa. p. 516

**Libya** A country in northern Africa; located on the Mediterranean Sea. p. 516

**Libyan Desert** A desert in northern Africa; located in Libya, Egypt, and Sudan. p. 94

**Liège** (lee•EZH) A province in eastern Belgium. p. 492

**Lisbon** The capital of Portugal; located on the Atlantic coast of Europe. (39°N/9°W) p. 379

**Lithuania** A country in eastern Europe; formerly part of the Soviet Union. p. 540

**Liverpool** A port on the English coast of the northwestern British Isles. (53°N/3°W) p. 490

**Lodz** A province of central Poland. (52°N/19°E) p. 538

**Loire River** (luh•WAR) The longest river in France; located in southeast France. p. 379

**Lombardy** A region in northern Italy. (46°N/10°E) p. 508

**London** The capital of the United Kingdom; located on the Thames River, in southeast England. (51°N/0°) p. 291

**Lothal** An ancient settlement in northern India. (22°N/72°E) p. 123

**Lübeck** (LOO•bek) A port in northern Germany, near the Baltic Sea. (54°N/11°E) p. 381

**Luoyang** (luh•WOH•yahng) Former capital of the Zhou dynasty in ancient China; located in what is present-day central China, on the Huang He River. (35°N/113°E) p. 167

**Luxembourg** A medieval county and duchy; now largely in the Grand Duchy of Luxembourg and the Belgian province of Luxembourg. p. 538

**Lydia** A region and ancient kingdom in Asia Minor, on the Aegean Sea. (39°N/28°E) p. 193

**Lyons** A manufacturing and commercial city, capital of Rhône department; located in central France. (46°N/5°E) p. 492

# M

**Macao** (muh•KOW) A Portuguese colony in southern China, on the South China Sea. (22°N/114°E) p. 447

**Macedonia** An ancient kingdom on the Aegean Sea; located on lands that are part of present-day Greece and Turkey. p. 193

**Machu Picchu** (mah•choo PEE•choo) The ruins of an ancient Inca city; located in the Andes mountains in what is today central Peru in South America. (13°S/73°W) p. 324

**Madagascar** An island country in the Indian Ocean, off the eastern coast of southern Africa. (20°S/47°E) p. 343

**Madras** The capital of Tamil Nadu state, India. (13°N/80°E) p. 625

**Madrid** A city located in central Spain, in Europe, on the Manzanares River. (40°N/4°W) p. 410

**Majorca** (mah•YOR•kah) The largest island of the Balearic group, in Spain. (40°N/3°E) p. 374

**Malawi** A country in southeastern Africa. p. 643

**Malay Peninsula** A peninsula in Southeast Asia, divided between Thailand and Malaysia. p. 354

**Malaysia** An independent federation; located in southeastern Asia. (5°N/110°E) p. 386

**Mali** A former West African empire and present-day country. p. 339

**Manchester** A manufacturing port city on the Irwell River in England. (54°N/2°W) p. 490

**Manchuria** A large region on the northeastern end of China. p. 447

**Manitoba** A province in central Canada. p. 615

**Mantua** A town on the Mincio River in northern Italy. (45°N/11°E) p. 404

**Marathon** An ancient Greek town in eastern Attica; the site of an ancient Greek victory during the Persian Wars. (38°N/24°E) p. 223

**Mari** An ancient city-state near the Euphrates River in east central Syria; its ruins are called Tell Hariri; located near present-day Abu Kemal, Syria. (34°N/41°E) p. 62

**Mariana Islands** An island group in Micronesia, Oceania; includes the unincorporated United States territory of Guam. (13°N/145°E) p. 386

**Marne** A river in northeastern France: flows west into the Seine River. p. 538

**Marquesas Islands** (mar•KAY•zuhz) A group of ten islands of French Polynesia; located in the southern Pacific Ocean. (10°S/140°W) p. 386

**Marrakesh** A city near the Grand Atlas Mountains, in Morocco. (32°N/8°W) p. 346

**Marseilles** (mar•SAY) The capital of Bouches-du-Rhône department, seaport; located in southeast France; on the Gulf of Lions. (43°N/5°E) p. 492

**Marshall Islands** A group of 32 islands and more than 867 reefs; located in the western Pacific Ocean. (9°N/171°E) p. 386

**Mauritania** (maw•ruh•TAY•nee•uh) A country in West Africa. p. 643

**Mauritius** (maw•RIH•shuhs) An island of the Mascarene Islands; located in the Indian Ocean. (20°S/57°E) p. 643

**Mecca** (MEH•kuh) A city in Saudi Arabia near the Red Sea; a holy city for Muslims. (22°N/40°E) p. 283

**Mecklenburg-Schwerin** (MEK•luhn•berg shfay•REEN) A former German duchy. p. 510

**Media** The ancient country of the Medes; located in what is today northwestern Iran. p. 193

**Medina** A city in western Saudi Arabia. (25°N/40°E) p. 283

**Mediterranean Sea** The sea south of Europe, north of Africa, and west of Asia; connects to the Atlantic Ocean, the Red Sea, and the Black Sea. p. 46

**Mekong Delta** The fertile region across which flow the several mouths of the Mekong River; near Ho Chi Minh City. p. 576

**Mekong River** A river in Southeast Asia; flows from the mountains of Tibet into the South China Sea. p. 360

**Melanesia** (meh•luh•NEE•zhuh) The name given to a group of the southwestern Pacific Islands; located northeast of Australia and south of the equator. (4°S/155°E) p. 386

**Memphis** An ancient Egyptian capital built by King Narmer; located along the Nile River in northern Egypt. (30°N/31°E) p. 78

**Meroë** A capital of the ancient Kingdom of Kush; located on the eastern bank of the Nile River in northern Sudan. (17°N/34°E) p. 113

**Mesopotamia** An ancient land in Southwest Asia; located between the Tigris and Euphrates rivers. p. 62

**Messina** An ancient seaport and modern province of Sicily, Italy. (38°N/16°E) p. 492

**Mexicali** The capital of Baja California Norte; located in northwestern Mexico. (33°N/116°W) p. 616

**Mexico** A country in southern North America; located between the United States and Central America. p. 137

**Mexico City** The capital of Mexico and of the Federal District; located in central Mexico. (19°N/99°W) p. 616

**Micronesia** (my•kruh•NEE•zhuh) The name of a group of western Pacific Islands, east of the Philippines and north of the equator. (9°N/150°E) p. 386

**Middle America** A world region; includes Mexico, the countries of Central America, and sometimes the islands of the Caribbean Sea. p. 137

**Midway** Comprised of Eastern and Sand islands, parts of a coral atoll; located in the central Pacific Ocean. (28°N/177°W) p. 560

**Milan** A city in northern Italy. (45°N/9°E) p. 374

**Mississippi River** The largest river in the United States; flows from Minnesota to the Gulf of Mexico. p. 271

**Missouri River** A tributary of the Mississippi River; flows from Montana to St. Louis, Missouri. p. 434

**Modena** A city in northern Italy. (45°N/11°E) p. 476

**Mogadishu** (mah•guh•DIH•shoo) A port on the Indian Ocean in southern Somalia in Africa. (2°N/45°E) p. 369

**Mohenjo-Daro** (moh•HEN•joh•DAR•oh) An important center of the ancient Indus civilization, on the western bank of the Indus River, in what is present-day southeastern Pakistan. (27°N/68°E) p. 123

**Moldova** A country in eastern Europe; formerly part of the Soviet Union. (47°N/27°E) p. 655

**Mombasa** An island port on the coast of the Indian Ocean, in southern Kenya in Africa. (4°S/40°E) p. 369

**Mongolia** Known as the Mongolian People's Republic; located in East Asia, south of Russia and north of China. p. 127

**Montenegro** A remaining part of Yugoslavia. (43°N/19°E) p. 476

**Monterrey** The capital of Nuevo León state; located in northeastern Mexico. (26°N/100°W) p. 616

**Montferrat** A former Italian duchy; located south of the Po River. p. 404

**Montreal** Canada's largest city and chief port of entry. (46°N/74°W) p. 615

**Morocco** A country in North Africa; bordered by the Mediterranean Sea and the Atlantic Ocean. p. 516

**Moscow** The capital of Russia; located on the Moscow River. (56°N/38°E) p. 311

**Moundville** An ancient settlement of the Mound Builders of the Mississippian culture; located in central Alabama. (33°N/87°W) p. 271

**Mount Olympus** Believed to be the home of the gods and goddesses of ancient Greek mythology; located on the eastern coast of the northern end of the Greek Peninsula. (40°N/23°E) p. 212

**Mount Sinai** A mountain peak located on the Sinai Peninsula. p. 78

**Mozambique** (moh•zuhm•BEEK) A country in southern Africa; formerly Portuguese East Africa. p. 424

**Mureybit** A village in ancient Mesopotamia. (37°N/38°E) p. 46

**My Lai** A Vietnamese village located south of Chu Lai. (15°N/109°E) p. 576

**Mycenae** (my•SEE•nee) An ancient city-state and empire in ancient Greece; ruins located on the eastern side of the Peloponnesus. (38°N/23°E) p. 212

# N

**Nagasaki** (nah•guh•SAH•kee) A Japanese city on the coast of Kyushu in southern Japan; the United States dropped an atomic bomb on the city during World War II. (33°N/130°E) p. 448

**Nagoya** (nuh•GOY•uh) A Japanese city on the coast of Honshu. (35°N/137°E) p. 602

**Namibia** A country in southwestern Africa; a territory governed by South Africa until 1990. (22°S/18°E) p. 643

**Napata** A capital of the ancient kingdom of Kush in ancient Nubia; located on the Nile River, in northern Sudan in Africa. (19°N/32°E) p. 113

**Naples** An Italian port on the Tyrrhenian Sea; located on the western coast of southern Italy. (41°N/14°E) p. 238

**Nara** A former capital of Japan; a Buddhist center located in southwestern Honshu. (35°N/136°E) p. 318

**Narmada River** A sacred Hindu river; begins in eastern India, and empties into the Gulf of Cambay. p. 123

**Nassau** A former duchy and region in Germany. p. 510

**Nazareth** A city in northern Israel. (33°N/35°E) p. 74

**Negev** A desert located in southern Israel. (31°N/35°E) p. 633

**Nepal** A country located in South Asia, on the Indian subcontinent. p. 122

**Netherlands** A country on the northern coast of central Europe, on the North Sea. p. 476

**Netzahualcóyotl** (nayt•sah•wahl•KOH•yoht•uhl) A suburb of Mexico City, Mexico. (19°N/99°W) p. 616

**New Carthage** See Cartagena.

**New Delhi** The capital of India; located in northern India. (29°N/77°E) p. 180

**New Guinea** An island in the Malay Archipelago; located north of eastern Australia; occupied by Papua New Guinea and part of Indonesia. (4°S/136°E) p. 386

**New Zealand** An island-group country in the southwestern Pacific Ocean, southeast of Australia. (40°S/176°E) p. 386

**Newcastle upon Tyne** A city in northern England on the Tyne River. (55°N/2°W) p. 490

**Newfoundland** An island in the Atlantic Ocean; located east of Canada. (49°N/56°W) p. 615

**Niani** An ancient Songhay trading center and present-day city; located in the country of Mali on the Niger River. (12°N/8°W) p. 339

**Nicaragua** A country in Central America. p. 619

**Niger** A country in West Africa. p. 643

**Niger River** A river in West Africa; flows from Guinea through Mali, Niger, and Nigeria into the Gulf of Guinea. p. 339

**Nigeria** (ny•JIR•ee•uh) A former territory of the Portuguese; country on the Gulf of Guinea, in West Africa. p. 516

**Nile River** A river in northeastern Africa; flows from Lake Victoria to the Mediterranean Sea at the northeastern coast of Egypt. p. 46

**Nineveh** The capital of the ancient Assyrian Empire; ruins located on the Tigris River, in northern Iraq. (36°N/43°E) p. 46

**Nippur** An ancient Sumerian and Babylonian city in what is today called Southwest Asia; located between the Tigris and Euphrates rivers, in present-day central Iraq. (32°N/45°E) p. 62

**Normandy** An historical region of northwestern France; site of Allied D Day invasion during World War II. (49°N/1°E) p. 561

**North America** One of the world's seven continents. p. 41

**North Borneo** The British colonial name of Sabah; a state of Malaysia; located in northeastern Borneo. p. 518

**North Korea** See Korea. p. 127

**North Sea** The sea located in Europe east of Great Britain and west of Denmark. p. 52

**North Vietnam** A former country located in Southeast Asia; now part of Vietnam. p. 576

**Norway** A European country; located on the northwestern Scandinavian Peninsula. p. 379

**Nova Scotia** A province of Canada; located on the eastern coast of Canada. p. 615

**Novgorod** (NAHV•guh•rahd) A medieval principality in eastern Europe in what is present-day Russia. (58°N/31°E) p. 379

**Nubia** An ancient land in Africa that extended along the Nile River from Egypt's southern border almost to where the city of Khartoum, Sudan, stands today. (22°N/34°E) p. 94

**Nubian Desert** A desert region in Sudan, Africa; east of the Nile River. (22°N/34°E) p. 94

# O

**Ocmulgee** An ancient settlement of the Mound Builders of the Mississippian culture in what is today the United States; located in present-day central Georgia. (33°N/83°W) p. 271

**Oder River** A large river in central Europe; flows from northeastern Czech Republic to the Baltic Sea. p. 381

**Ohio River** A tributary of the Mississippi River; begins in Pittsburgh, Pennsylvania, and ends in Cairo, Illinois. p. 271

**Okinawa** An island group; center of Ryukyu Islands between the East China Sea and the Pacific Ocean. (27°N/128°E) p. 560

**Olympia** A plain in the northwestern Peloponnesus; an ancient Greek religious center and site of early Olympic Games. (40°N/22°E) p. 217

**Oman** A country located on the Arabian Peninsula on the Gulf of Oman in Southwest Asia. p. 122

**Ontario** A Canadian province; located between the provinces of Quebec and Manitoba. p. 615

**Oporto** A port city located in northwestern Portugal, on the Douro River. (41°N/9°W) p. 493

**Orkney Islands** A Scottish archipelago; located off the northeastern coast of Scotland. (59°N/3°W) p. 52

**Osaka** A Japanese port in southern Honshu where the Yodo River meets Osaka Bay. (35°N/136°E) p. 448

**Oslo** The capital of Norway; located in southeastern Norway at the northern end of the Oslo Fjord. (60°N/11°E) p. 540

**Ottawa** The capital of Canada; located in the province of Ontario. (45°N/76°W) p. 615

**Oxus River** A river in Asia flowing from Pamir Plateau into the Aral Sea; also known as Amu Darya. p. 360

**Oyo** (oh•YOH) A town and state in southwestern Nigeria. (8°N/4°E) p. 424

# P

**Pacific Ocean** The largest of the world's four oceans. p. 41

**Pagan** The ruins and capital of a powerful dynasty; located in central Burma (Myanmar). (21°N/95°E) p. 354

**Pakistan** A country in South Asia. p. 122

**Palermo** The capital of Sicily, Italy; located on the Bay of Palermo, southeast of Rome. (38°N/13°E) p. 492

**Pamirs** A mountainous region in Central Asia in Tajikistan. p. 360

**Pamplona** (pam•PLOH•nah) A city in northern Spain. (43°N/2°W) p. 410

**Panama** A country in Central America. p. 430

**Papal States** The home and kingdom of the Roman Catholic Church from 754–1870; located in central Italy. p. 404

**Paraguay** A country in central South America; former colony of Spain. p. 481

**Paris** The capital of France; located on the Seine River. (49°N/2°E) p. 288

**Parthia** A land that was part of the ancient Assyrian and Persian empires; located in what is today northeastern Iran. p. 193

**Pearl Harbor** An inlet on the southern coast of Oahu island, Hawaii; site of the Japanese bombing attack that brought the United States into World War II. p. 560

**Peloponnesus** (pehl•uh•puh•NEE•suhs) A wide peninsula on the southern end of Greece; home of the ancient city-states of Sparta and Corinth. p. 212

**Persepolis** (per•SEH•puh•luhs) The capital of the ancient Persian Empire; located near Shiraz in what is present-day Iran. (30°N/53°E) p. 193

**Persia** An ancient empire that included the ancient lands of Persia, Egypt, Syria, Assyria, Mesopotamia, and Babylonia. p. 193

**Persian Gulf** A gulf in Southwest Asia; connected to the Gulf of Oman and the Arabian Sea. p. 62

**Peru** A country on the Pacific coast of South America; former center of the Inca Empire. p. 481

**Perugia** A city in central Italy on the Tiber River. (43°N/12°E) p. 238

**Philippine Sea** The part of the western Pacific Ocean east of the Philippines. p. 560

**Philippines** An archipelago of Southeast Asia; located east of the Indochina Peninsula. (12°N/123E°) p. 384

**Philistia** An ancient land in Southwest Asia. p. 74

**Phnom Penh** (NAHM PEN) The capital of Cambodia. (12°N/105°E) p. 133

**Phocaea** (foh•SEE•uh) An ancient Ionian city, now known as Foca, Turkey; located on the western coast of Asia Minor, on the Aegean Sea. (39°N/27°E) p. 217

**Phoenicia** (fih•NIH•shuh) An ancient land; located in what is present-day Syria and Lebanon. p. 74

**Pisa** (PEE•zuh) A city on the Arno River in northern Italy. (44°N/10°E) p. 374

**Plataea** (pluh•TEE•uh) The site of an ancient Greek land victory that led to the end of the Persian Wars; located in what is today southeastern Greece, near Thebes. (38°N/23°E) p. 223

**Po River** A river in northern Italy; flows from Mount Viso, across northern Italy, into the northern Adriatic Sea. p. 241

**Polynesia** (pah•luh•NEE•zhuh) The name of a group of central Pacific Islands; includes New Zealand, Samoa, Tahiti, and the Hawaiian Islands. (10°S/162°W) p. 386

**Portsmouth** An English port on the island of Portsea in the English Channel. (51°N/1°W) p. 490

**Portugal** A country in Europe. (40°N/8°W) p. 410

**Portuguese Guinea** A colony on the West African coast; formerly controlled by Portugal; the present-day country of Guinea-Bissau. p. 516

**Potsdam** A German industrial city; located southwest of Berlin. (52°N/13°E) p. 562

**Prague** The capital of the Czech Republic; located on both sides of the Vltava River. (50°N/14°E) p. 492

**Pretoria** The administrative capital of the Republic of South Africa. (26°S/28°E) p. 648

**Prince Edward Island** A Canadian province; located in the Gulf of St. Lawrence. p. 615

**Prussia** A former kingdom in northern Europe; located in what is present-day Germany. (51°N/10°E) p. 510

**Puerto Rico** An island and a self-governing commonwealth of the United States; located in the Greater Antilles of the West Indies. (18°N/67°W) p. 481

**P'yongyang** (pee•AWNG•yahng) The capital of North Korea; located on the Taedong River. (39°N/126°E) p. 317

**Pyrenees Mountains** The mountain range that separates the Iberian Peninsula from the rest of Europe; forms the border between Spain and France. p. 212

## Q

**Quebec** A province in eastern Canada. p. 615

## R

**Ramses** An ancient Egyptian city; located in Goshen, near Tanis. p. 78

**Rangoon** The capital of Burma (Myanmar). Also known as Yangon. (17°N/96°E) p. 133

**Red Sea** The long, narrow sea between northeastern Africa and the Arabian Peninsula; connected to the Mediterranean Sea by the Suez Canal and to the Arabian Sea by the Gulf of Aden. p. 46

**Reunion** One of the Mascarene Islands; located in the Indian Ocean. (21°S/56°E) p. 643

**Reval** The capital of the country of Estonia; now known as Tallinn. (60°N/25°E) p. 381

**Rhine River** A river in western Europe; flows across Switzerland, western Germany, and the Netherlands to the North Sea. p. 241

**Rhodes** A Greek island in the southeast Aegean Sea. (36°N/28°E) p. 452

**Rhone River** A river in Switzerland and France, rising in the Alps and flowing into the Gulf of Lions. p. 538

**Riga** The capital of the country of Latvia in eastern Europe. (57°N/24°E) p. 379

**Romania** A country in southeast Europe, bordering the Black Sea. p. 538

**Rome** The capital of the ancient Roman Empire and of present-day Italy; located on the Tiber River. (42°N/13°E) p. 238

**Russia** An historic empire and the largest republic of the former Soviet Union; a country in northeastern Europe and northern Asia. p. 127

**Rwanda** A country in East Africa. p. 643

## S

**Sahara** A desert covering the northern third of Africa. p. 94

**Saigon** The city that was the capital of South Vietnam; located on the Saigon River; renamed Ho Chi Minh City; now part of Vietnam. (11°N/107°E) p. 576

**Sakata** A Japanese port; located on the western coast of northern Honshu. (39°N/140°E) p. 448

**Salamis** (SAL•uh•muhs) A Greek island in the Aegean Sea; the site of an ancient Greek sea victory leading to the end of the Persian Wars. (38°N/24°W) p. 223

**Samaria** An ancient area of what is today called Southwest Asia, between Judaea and Galilee. (32°N/35°E) p. 74

**Samarkand** A city in eastern Uzbekistan. (40°N/67°E) p. 311

**Samoa** A group of Pacific islands in southwestern Polynesia. (14°S/171°W) p. 386

**San Luis Potosí** A Mexican city and state; located in central Mexico. (22°N/101°W) p. 616

**San Marino** A small country on Mount Titano within northern Italy. (44°N/12°E) p. 508

**San Salvador** One of the Bahama Islands; where Christopher Columbus first landed in the Americas on October 12, 1492. (24°N/75°W) p. 417

**São Tomé and Príncipe** (SOW tuh•MAY PRIN•suh•puh) Equatorial islands; located off West Africa, in the Gulf of Guinea. (0°/7°E) p. 643

**Sapporo** A Japanese city. (43°N/141°E) p. 602

**Saragossa** A Spanish province; located in western Aragon. p. 493

**Sarajevo** (sair•uh•YAY•voh) A city in central Bosnia and Herzegovina. (44°N/18°E) p. 538

**Sardinia** An Italian island in the Mediterranean Sea; located west of the Italian peninsula. (40°N/9°E) p. 212

**Sardis** The capital of ancient Lydia, in the Hermus Valley, in western central Turkey. (38°N/28°E) p. 77

**Saskatchewan** A Canadian province; located in western Canada. p. 615

**Saudi Arabia** A country that occupies most of the Arabian Peninsula in Southwest Asia. p. 62

**Savannah River** A river forming the boundary between Georgia and South Carolina in the United States; flows into the Atlantic Ocean. p. 271

**Saxony** An historic region of Germany; now part of the German state of Lower Saxony. p. 379

**Scotland** One of four kingdoms in the United Kingdom; occupies the northern part of the isle of Great Britain. p. 379

**Sea of Galilee** A freshwater lake in northern Israel. p. 74

**Sea of Japan** The sea located west of Japan and east of Russia, North Korea, and South Korea. p. 127

**Sea of Marmara** A small sea in northwestern Turkey; connects the Black and Aegean seas. p. 212

**Sea of Okhotsk** (oh•KAHTSK) A sea off the eastern coast of Russia. p. 547

**Seine River** (SAYN) A river in northern France; flows northwest into the Bay of Seine. p. 538

**Senegal** A country in West Africa p. 643

**Senegal River** A river in West Africa; flows from the highlands of Guinea into the Atlantic Ocean at Senegal. p. 346

**Seoul** The capital of South Korea; located on the Han River. (38°N/127°E) p. 317

**Serbia** Part of the former Yugoslavia. (44°N/21°E) p. 537

**Seville** A city on the Guadalquivir River in southwestern Spain. (37°N/6°W) p. 379

**Seychelles** An island group and republic; located in the Indian Ocean. (5°S/56°E) p. 643

**Shanghai** (shang•HY) A port on the East China Sea; located near the mouth of the Chang Jiang. (31°N/121°E) p. 595

**Shechem** (SHEEK•uhm) An ancient town; located north of Jerusalem, Israel. (32°N/35°E) p. 78

**Shikoku** The smallest of the four main islands of Japan; located south of Honshu. (34°N/134°E) p. 448

**Siam** See Thailand.

**Sicily** An Italian island off the southwestern tip of the Italian Peninsula. (38°N/15°E) p. 212

**Siena** A city in central Italy, near the Arno River. (43°N/11E°) p. 354

**Sierra Leone** A country on the Atlantic coast of West Africa; a former slave colony. p. 516

**Sierra Madre del Sur** A mountain range in southern Mexico, along the Pacific coast. p. 137

**Sierra Madre Occidental** A mountain range in north-western Mexico, along the Pacific coast. p. 137

**Sierra Madre Oriental** A mountain range in eastern Mexico, along the coast of the Gulf of Mexico. p. 137

**Sikkim** A state in northeastern India. p. 595

**Sinai Peninsula** The peninsula between northeastern Africa and Southwest Asia; part of the country of Egypt. (30°N/34°E) p. 77

**Singapore** A small island country off the southern tip of the Malay Peninsula, in Southeast Asia. (1°N/104°E) p. 354

**Skara Brae** A Neolithic settlement located on the western coast of Mainland Island in the Orkneys. p. 52

**Slovenia** (sloh•VEE•nee•uh) A country in eastern Europe. (46°N/15°E) p. 537

**Sofala** (soh•FAHL•uh) A province on the eastern coast of Mozambique in Africa. (20°N/35°E) p. 369

**Sofia** A city in western Bulgaria. (43°N/23°E) p. 538

**Somalia** A country in East Africa; formerly British Somaliland and Italian Somaliland. p. 643

**South Africa** A country located on the southern tip of Africa, between the Atlantic and Indian oceans. p. 643

**South America** One of the world's seven continents. p. 41

**South China Sea** The part of the western Pacific Ocean south of Taiwan. p. 127

**South Korea** See Korea. p. 127

**South Vietnam** A former independent country; located east of the South China Sea; now part of Vietnam. p. 576

**Soweto** An area west of Johannesburg, South Africa. (26°S/28°E) p. 648

**Spain** A country in southwestern Europe, on the Iberian Peninsula. p. 52

**Sparta** An ancient Greek city-state and rival of Athens; located on the southern end of the Peloponnesus. (37°N/22°E) p. 217

**Sri Lanka** An island country in South Asia, once known as Ceylon; located in the Indian Ocean west of India. (8°N/81°E) p. 122

**St. John's** The capital of Newfoundland, Canada. (48°N/53°W) p. 615

**St. Lawrence River** A river located in northeastern North America; forms part of the border between the United States and Canada. p. 433

**St. Petersburg** A city formerly known as Leningrad when it served as the capital of the Russian empire; located on the Neva River on the Gulf of Finland. (60°N/30°E) p. 547

**Stalingrad** The former name of Volgograd; located on the Volga River. (49°N/44°E) p. 561

**Stockholm** The largest city in Sweden; located on the Baltic Sea. (59°N/18°E) p. 381

**Strasbourg** A city located in northeastern France. (48°N/8°E) p. 492

**Sudan** A country on the eastern coast of North Africa. p. 516

**Suez Canal** A canal linking the Mediterranean Sea and the Gulf of Suez; located in northeastern Egypt. p. 516

**Sumatra** (su•MAH•truh) The westernmost island of Indonesia; located off the Malay Peninsula in Southeast Asia. (2°S/101°E) p. 354

**Sumer** An ancient region in southern Mesopotamia; located near the Persian Gulf, in what is today southeastern Iraq. p. 62

**Suriname** A country in South America. p. 435

**Swaziland** A country in southern Africa. p. 643

**Sweden** A European country on the southeastern part of the Scandinavian Peninsula. p. 379

**Switzerland** A country in central Europe. p. 476

**Syracuse** A seaport city in Sicily, Italy; located on the Ionian Sea. (37°N/15°E) p. 374

**Syria** A country located on the eastern end of the Mediterranean Sea. p. 62

**Syrian Desert** A desert covering southern Syria, northeast Jordan, western Iraq, and northern Saudi Arabia in Southwest Asia. p. 46

# T

**Tabasco** A Mexican state; located in southeastern Mexico. p. 616

**Tabriz** (tuh•BREEZ) A city in northwestern Iran, on a small river near Lake Urmia. (38°N/46°E) p. 311

**Taejon** (ta•JAWN) A city in South Korea; located northwest of Taegu. (36°N/127°E) p. 574

**Tagus River** (TAY•gahs) A river running through the center of the Iberian Peninsula; flows from Spain through Portugal. p. 241

**Taiwan** (TY•WAHN) An island country; located off the southeastern coast of China. p. 127

**Tajikistan** (tah•jihk•ih•STAN) A country in western Asia; formerly part of the Soviet Union. p. 655

**Takla Makan** A desert in northwestern China. p. 127

**Tanzania** A country in East Africa. p. 643

**Tashkent**  The capital of Uzbekistan; located in western Asia.  (41°N/69°E)  p. 360

**Taurus Mountains**  A mountain range in southern Turkey; runs parallel to the southern Mediterranean coast and the border between Turkey and Syria.  p. 46

**Tel Aviv**  A city in and former capital of Israel.  (32°N/35°E)  p. 633

**Tennessee River**  A tributary of the Ohio River; begins in eastern Tennessee and flows into the Ohio River.  p. 271

**Tenochtitlán** (tay•nohch•teet•LAHN)  The capital of the ancient Aztec Empire; located in central Mexico near Mexico City.  (19°N/99°W)  p. 324

**Teotihuacán** (tay•oh•tee•wah•KAHN)  A city in central Mexico.  (20°N/99°W)  p. 327

**Tepotzotlan**  An ancient Aztec city located near Lake Texcoco.  (19°N/99°W)  p. 327

**Texcoco** (tes•KOH•koh)  A city in central Mexico, east of Lake Texcoco.  (19°N/99°W)  p. 327

**Thailand**  A country formerly known as Siam; located in Southeast Asia on the Indochina and Malay peninsulas.  p. 122

**Thar Desert**  Also called the Great Indian Desert; located in India and Pakistan.  p. 123

**Thebes**  The capital of ancient Egypt during the Middle Kingdom; located in southern Egypt.  (26°N/33°E)  p. 94

**Thermopylae** (ther•MAHP•uh•lee)  The site of an ancient Greek defeat during the Persian Wars; a mountain pass in southern Greece.  (39°N/23°E)  p. 223

**Thessaly** (THES•uh•lee)  An ancient and present-day region in Greece; located on the eastern Greek Peninsula.  p. 223

**Thimphu**  A city in central Bhutan; located north of western India.  (28°N/90°E)  p. 180

**Thrace**  An ancient land; included in what are today the countries of Bulgaria, Macedonia, and much of northwestern Greece.  p. 193

**Thuringia**  German state located in eastern Germany.  p. 510

**Tian Shan**  A mountain system in central Asia; extends northeast from the Pamirs into Xinjiang Uygur.  p. 127

**Tiber River**  A river in central Italy; flows from the Apennine Mountains, through Rome, and into the Tyrrhenian Sea.  p. 238

**Tibet**  A region covering most of southwestern China.  p. 354

**Tigris River**  A river in Southwest Asia; begins in eastern Turkey and joins the Euphrates River.  p. 46

**Tijuana** (tee•WAH•nah)  A town in Baja California Norte in Mexico.  (33°N/117°W)  p. 616

**Timbuktu** (tim•buhk•TOO)  An ancient Songhay trading center and present-day city; located in Mali in the Sahara, north of the Niger River.  (17°N/3°W)  p. 339

**Timor**  An island in Indonesia; formerly belonged to Portugal.  (9°S/125°E)  p. 518

**Tiranë**  A city located in Albania, east of Durrës.  (41°N/20°E)  p. 540

**Tlacopan**  An ancient Aztec city.  (19°N/99°W)  p. 327

**Tokyo**  The capital of Japan.  (36°N/140°E)  p. 602

**Toledo**  A Moorish capital during the Middle Ages and a present-day city; located in central Spain, on the Tagus River.  (40°N/4°W)  p. 410

**Toronto**  The capital of Ontario, Canada.  (44°N/79°W)  p. 615

**Toulouse** (tu•LOOZ)  The capital of Haute-Garonne department; located in southern France.  (44°N/1°E)  p. 492

**Tours**  A French city; located southwest of Paris.  (47°N/1°E)  p. 288

**Transoxiana**  A region in western Asia.  p. 360

**Transylvania**  A former region in southeastern Europe; now part of Romania; located in northwestern Romania.  p. 413

**Tres Zapotes** (trays suh•POHT•uhs)  A village located in eastern Mexico.  (18°N/96°W)  p. 327

**Tripoli**  The ancient Phoenician city of Oea and present-day capital of Libya.  (33°N/13°E)  p. 346

**Trondheim**  A port on the central Atlantic coast of Norway.  (64°N/10°E)  p. 379

**Troy**  An ancient city in northwestern Asia Minor.  (40°N/26°E)  p. 212

**Tunis**  Capital of Tunisia.  (37°N/10°E)  p. 346

**Tunisia**  A country in North Africa.  p. 516

**Turin**  An ancient and modern city; located in northwestern Italy.  (45°N/8°E)  p. 241

**Turkey**  A country formerly known as Thrace; located mostly in northern Southwest Asia.  p. 62

**Turkmenistan** (terk•mehn•uh•STAN)  A country in western Asia; formerly part of the Soviet Union.  p. 655

**Tuscany**  A region on the western coast of Italy.  (42°N/12°E)  p. 476

**Tyre**  The capital of ancient Phoenicia and present-day town in southern Lebanon.  (33°N/35°E)  p. 77

**Tyrrhenian Sea** (tuh•REE•nee•uhn)  The sea located west of the Italian Peninsula, north of Sicily, and east of Sardinia and Corsica.  p. 212

# U

**Uganda**  A country in East Africa; formerly part of British East Africa.  p. 516

**Ukraine** (yoo•KRAYN)  A country in eastern Europe; formerly part of the Soviet Union.  p. 655

**Union of South Africa**  The country now called South Africa; created from former British and Portuguese territories.  p. 516

**Union of Soviet Socialist Republics**  Another name for the Soviet Union, which ended in 1991.  p. 561

**United Arab Emirates**  A country on the eastern Arabian Peninsula.  p. 634

**United Kingdom**  A European country made up of four kingdoms in the British Isles:  England, Scotland, Wales, and Northern Ireland.  p. 52

**United States**  A country in North America; a federal republic of fifty states.  p. 481

**Ur** A city in ancient Sumer; located on the Euphrates River, near the coast of what is present-day southeastern Iraq. (31°N/46°E) p. 62

**Ural Mountains** A mountain range in Russia and Kazakhstan; extends from the coast of the Arctic Ocean and borders part of Europe and Asia. p. 311

**Ural River** A river in Russia and Kazakhstan. p. 655

**Uruguay** A country on the Atlantic coast of southern South America. p. 481

**Uruk** An ancient Sumerian city in what is today known as Southwest Asia; located near the eastern bank of the Euphrates River, in present-day southeastern Iraq. (31°N/46°E) p. 62

**Utrecht** (YOO•trekt) A city on the Oude Rijn River, in the central Netherlands. (52°N/5°E) p. 379

**Uzbekistan** (uz•behk•ih•STAN) A country in western Asia; formerly part of the Soviet Union. p. 655

# V

**Valencia** A city on the Turia River, near the eastern coast of Spain. (39°N/0°) p. 410

**Valley of Mexico** A large valley in central Mexico; site of the ancient Aztec Empire capital, Tenochtitlán; location of present-day Mexico City. p. 137

**Vancouver** A city in southwestern Canada; located in British Columbia. (50°N/125°W) p. 543

**Venezuela** A country in northern South America; former territory of Spain. (8°N/66°W) p. 481

**Venice** A city of 118 islands in northeastern Italy on the Adriatic Sea. (45°N/12°E) p. 354

**Veracruz** A seaport in eastern Mexico, on the Gulf of Mexico. (19°N/96°W) p. 430

**Verdun** A city in northeastern France, on the Meuse River. (49°N/5°E) p. 538

**Verona** A town in northern Italy, on the Adige River. (45°N/11°E) p. 404

**Victoria** A port city of Hong Kong. (22°N/114°E) p. 604

**Victoria Falls** The Zambezi River waterfall; located between Zimbabwe and Zambia, in Central Africa. (18°S/26°E) p. 343

**Vienna** The capital city of Austria in Europe; located in northeastern Austria, on the Danube River. (48°N/16°E) p. 476

**Vientiane** An administrative capital of Laos. (18°N/103°E) p. 133

**Vietnam** A country in Southeast Asia; located on the Indochina Peninsula. p. 127

**Vindhya Range** (VIN•dyuh) A mountain range in central India; forms part of the northern border of the Deccan Plateau. p. 122

**Vistula River** A river in Poland in eastern Europe; flows from the Carpathian Mountains into the Baltic Sea. p. 510

**Volga River** The longest river in Europe; runs from Russia to the Caspian Sea. p. 311

# W

**Wabash River** Located in Indiana and Illinois; empties into the Ohio River in southwestern Indiana. p. 271

**Warsaw** The capital of Poland. (52°N/21°E) p. 538

**Waterloo** A small city; located in central Belgium, near Brussels. (51°N/4°E) p. 476

**West Indies** A group of islands between North and South America in the Caribbean Sea. (15°N/65°W) p. 427

**Western Ghats** A chain of mountains in southwestern India. p. 122

**Western Sahara** A former Spanish province; located in northwestern Africa. p. 643

**Württemberg** (WUHR•tuhm•berg) A former German monarchy and state; now part of the German state of Baden-Württemberg. (49°N/9°E) p. 510

# X

**Xian** (SHEE•AHN) A city in eastern China; also known as Sian; formerly Chang'an. (34°N/109°E) p. 595

# Y

**Yalta** A city in Ukraine. (45°N/34°E) p. 561

**Yellow Sea** The sea west of the Korean Peninsula and east of China. p. 127

**Yellowknife** The capital of the Northwest Territories in Canada. (63°N/114°W) p. 615

**Yucatán** A state in southeastern Mexico; located on the northern Yucatán Peninsula. p. 616

**Yucatán Peninsula** A peninsula extending from the eastern coast of Central America; occupied by the countries of Mexico, Belize, and Guatemala. p. 137

**Yugoslavia** (yoo•goh•SLAH•vee•uh) The former country in eastern Europe, which broke up into several independent republics. p. 573

**Yukon Territory** A territory in northwestern Canada. p. 615

# Z

**Zagros Mountains** A mountain range; located in western and southern Iran. p. 46

**Zaire** A country in Central Africa. p. 643

**Zaire River** River in Central Africa. p. 343

**Zama** The site of Hannibal and Carthage's final defeat in the Second Punic War; located in northern Tunisia. (35°N/9°E) p. 241

**Zambezi River** A river in southern Africa; flows from northwestern Zambia to the Indian Ocean. p. 343

**Zambia** A country in southern Africa. p. 643

**Zaragoza** (za•ruh•GOH•zuh) A city along the Ebro River in northeastern Spain. (42°N/1°W) p. 410

**Zimbabwe** A country in southern Africa. p. 643

# GLOSSARY

The Glossary contains important social studies terms and their definitions. Each word is respelled as it would be in a dictionary. When you see this mark ´ after a syllable, pronounce that syllable with more force than the other syllables. The page number at the end of the definition tells where to find the term in your book.

add, āce, câre, pälm; end, ēqual; it, īce; odd, ōpen, ôrder; tŏŏk, pōōl; up, bûrn; yōō as u in *fuse;* oil; pout; ə as a in *above,* e in *sicken,* i in *possible,* o in *melon,* u in *circus;* **ch**eck; ri**ng**; **th**in; **th**is; zh as in *vision*

## A

**A.D.** (ā•dē) Stands for *anno Domini,* a Latin phrase meaning "in the year of the Lord." This abbreviation identifies how many years have passed since the approximate birth of Jesus Christ. p. 48

**absolute location** (ab´sə•lōōt lō•kā´shən) Exact location on Earth. p. 26

**acid rain** (as´id rān) Water in the form of rain that is mixed with harmful gases. p. 246

**acropolis** (ə•kro´pə•ləs) A walled fortress built on a hill. p. 216

**Afrikaans** (a•fri•känz´) The language spoken by the Boers in South Africa. p. 644

**agora** (a´gə•rə) An open-air market and gathering place in many ancient Greek city-states. p. 216

**agriculture** (a´gri•kul•chər) The raising of domesticated plants and animals; farming. p. 45

**alliance** (ə•lī´əns) An agreement to cooperate. p. 229

**ambassador** (am•ba´sə•dər) A representative of a government. p. 168

**analyzing** (a´nəl•īz•ing) A thinking process in which something is broken down into its parts and looked at closely to see how those parts connect with each other. p. 24

**ancestor** (an´ses•tər) A deceased relative who lived longer ago than a grandparent. p. 129

**annex** (ə•neks´) To take over. p. 112

**apartheid** (ə•pär´tāt) The government policy of South Africa that stressed the separation, or "apartness," of races. p. 644

**apostle** (ə•pä´səl) A person sent on a mission. p. 254

**appeasement** (ə•pēz´mənt) The policy of not opposing fascism. p. 558

**aqueduct** (a´kwə•dəkt) A network of bridges and canals that carries water from place to place. p. 246

**Arabic numerals** (ar´ə•bik nüm´rəlz) The base-ten number system: 1 through 9 and the zero; used in India as early as A.D. 595. p. 191

**archipelago** (är•kə•pe´lə•gō) A chain of islands. p. 387

**aristocracy** (ar´ə•stä•krə•sē) A wealthy ruling class. p. 216

**Armada** (är•mä´də) A fleet of warships. p. 419

**armistice** (är´mə•stəs) An agreement to stop fighting. p. 540

**arms race** (ärmz rās) A competition among nations to have the most weapons. p. 536

**artifact** (är´tə•fakt) A humanmade object representing a specific culture or group especially from long ago. p. 42

**Aryans** (ar´ē•ənz) Warriors and herders who came from central Asia to India, beginning about 3,000 years ago. p. 175

**assassination** (ə•sas•ən•ā´shən) Murder for a political reason. p. 187

**assembly** (ə•sem´blē) A lawmaking group. p. 216

**astrolabe** (as´trə•lāb) An instrument that helped sailors navigate using the positions of the stars. p. 285

**atoll** (a´tôl) An island formed from a coral reef. p. 383

**authority** (ə•thôr´ə•tē) The right to command or influence. p. 64

**autocrat** (ô´tə•krat) A leader with unlimited authority. p. 544

**autonomy** (o•tä´nə•mē) The right of a state to rule itself. p. 635

## B

**B.C.** (bē•sē) Stands for "before Christ." p. 48

**B.C.E.** (bē•sē•ē) Stands for "before the Common Era." p. 49

**balance of trade** (ba´ləns uv trād) The comparison of a country's exports with its imports. p. 601

**Balfour Declaration** (bal´fər de•klə•rā´shən) A British letter that called for a national home for the Jewish people. p. 631

**Bantustan** (ban•tōō•stan´) An all-black neighborhood in South Africa. p. 644

**bar graph** (bär graf) A graph that uses horizontal or vertical bars to show and compare information. p. 376

**barter** (bär´tər) The exchange of one good or service for another. p. 76

**basilica** (bə•si´li•kə) A huge marble government building in ancient Rome. p. 245

**bias** (bī´əs) A leaning toward or against someone or something. p. 513

**bilingual** (bī•ling´gwəl) Having two official languages, as Canada has. p. 615

**Bill of Rights** (bil uv rīts) The first ten amendments that were added to the Constitution of the United States of America to protect the rights of individuals. p. 473

**bloc** (blok) A group of nations with the same interests. p. 619

**boycott** (boi´kot) To refuse to buy or use goods. p. 624

**bubonic plague** (byo͞o•bä´nik plāg) A deadly sickness spread throughout Europe in the 1340s by fleas on rats; also called the Black Death. p. 292

**Buddhism** (bo͞o´diz•əm) An Asian religion based on the teachings of Siddhartha Gautama, who became Buddha. p. 179

**bureaucracy** (byo͝o•rok´rə•sē) A network of appointed government officials. p. 164

**Bushido** (bo͝o´shi•dō) The Japanese samurai code. p. 448

# C

**C.E.** (sē•ē) Stands for "Common Era." p. 49

**caliph** (kā´ləf) A "successor" to Muhammad. p. 283

**calligraphy** (kə•li´grə•fē) The art of beautiful handwriting. p. 446

**capitalism** (kap´ə•təl•iz•əm) An economic system in which individuals invest money, or capital, in businesses. p. 499

**caravan** (kar´ə•van) A group of traders. p. 170

**caravansary** (kar•ə•van´sə•rē) An inn where desert travelers could find food and shelter. p. 352

**caravel** (kar´ə•vəl) A type of ship that used either square or lateen sails to travel long distances swiftly. p. 416

**cartogram** (kär´tə•gram) A map that gives information about places by the size shown for each place. p. 598

**cartographer** (kär•tä´grə•fər) A mapmaker. p. 353

**cash crop** (kash krop) A crop that is raised to sell to others rather than to use at home. p. 515

**caste** (kast) An unchanging class or group in India's society. p. 177

**cataract** (ka´tə•rakt) A waterfall or a place where water runs fast over rocks. p. 96

**catholic** (kath´lik) All-embracing. p. 279

**cavalry** (ka´vəl•rē) Soldiers who ride horses or other animals to make swift attacks. p. 192

**census** (sen´səs) A count of a country's people. p. 244

**chinampa** (chē•näm´pä) An island made from platforms of woven reeds. Aztec farmers grew vegetables on these "floating gardens." p. 321

**Christendom** (kri´sən•dəm) The community of Christians from all kingdoms and nations. p. 290

**Christianity** (kris•chē•an´ə•tē) The religion based on the life and teachings of Jesus Christ. p. 255

**chronology** (krə•nä´lə•jē) A record of events in the order in which they happened. p. 23

**circle graph** (sûr´kəl graf) A graph that shows information by means of a circle divided into parts; also called a pie chart. p. 376

**circumnavigation** (sər•kəm•nav•ə•gā´shən) A journey around the world by ship. p. 418

**citizen** (sit´ə•zən) A member of a town, state, or country. p. 19

**city-state** (sit´ē•stāt) A city or village and its surrounding farmlands with its own leaders and government. p. 63

**civil service** (siv´əl sûr´vəs) The part of a bureaucracy that oversees the day-to-day business of running a government. p. 168

**civil war** (siv´əl wôr) A war in which groups of people from the same place or country fight one another. p. 166

**civilization** (siv•ə•lə•zā´shən) A complex society. p. 61

**clan** (klan) A group of related families brought together for a common purpose. p. 39

**classified** (kla´sə•fīd) Sorted. p. 171

**clergy** (klûr´jē) Ordained church officers. p. 411

**climograph** (klī´mə•graf) A graph that shows both the average monthly temperature and the average monthly precipitation for a place. p. 605

**Code of Hammurabi** (kōd uv ha•mə•rä´bē) The collection of laws that Hammurabi wrote for the people of Babylon to follow. p. 69

**cold war** (kōld wôr) A conflict of words and ideas between nations rather than armies. p. 572

**collective** (kə•lek´tiv) A large farm on which people work together as a group. p. 547

**colony** (kol´ə•nē) A settlement separated from, but under the control of, a home country. p. 75

**Columbian exchange** (kə•lum´bē•an iks•chānj´) The movement of people, animals, plants, diseases, and ideas between Europe and the Americas in the 1400s and 1500s. p. 431

**comedy** (kom´ə•dē) A humorous play. p. 225

**command economy** (kə•mand´ i•kon´ə•mē) An economy in which the government owns almost all the land and natural resources. p. 498

**common market** (kom´ən mär´kit) A union formed to improve trade and encourage the economic growth of member nations. p. 657

**commune** (kom´yo͞on) In China, a government-run farming community in which people share housing, food, and work. p. 595

**communism** (kom´yə•niz•əm) A system in which all property and all means of production belong to the people as a group. p. 545

**compass rose** (kum´pəs rōz) A direction marker on a map. p. 29

**compromise** (kom´prə•mīz) To give up some of what you want in order to reach an agreement. p. 659

**concentration camp** (kon•sən•trā´shən kamp) A type of prison. p. 561

**confederation** (kən•fed•ə•rā´shən) A loose group of governments. p. 473

**conformal projection** (kən•fôr´məl prə•jek´shən) A map projection that shows directions correctly but distorts sizes, especially of places near the poles. p. 349

**Confucianism** (kən•fyo͞o´shə•ni•zəm) The ideas of the Chinese philosopher Confucius, which became a guide for the way people live. p. 159

**conquer** (käŋ´kər) To take over. p. 67

**conquistador** (kon•kēs´tä•dôr) A Spanish adventurer who came to the Americas in search of gold. p. 429

**conscription** (kən•skrip´shən) The drafting of citizens to serve in the armed forces for a set number of years. p. 536

**consequence** (kän´sə•kwens) An effect. p. 39

**Constitution of the United States of America**
(kon•stə•tōō´shən uv the yōō•nī´təd stāts uv
ə•mer´ə•kə) The document describing the plan for
governing the United States. It was accepted in 1787
and is still the supreme law of the United States. p. 473

**consul** (kon´səl) One of the officials from the Roman
Senate who ran the daily affairs and acted on behalf of
the citizens of Rome. p. 239

**containment** (kən•tān´mənt) The policy of preventing a
country from gaining control of another country. p. 572

**contour line** (kän´tûr līn) On an elevation map, a line that
connects all points of equal elevation. p. 132

**contract** (kän´trakt) A written agreement. p. 290

**cottage industry** (kä´tij in´dəs•trē) A business in which
family members work in their homes to prepare products for a merchant. p. 488

**coureurs de bois** (kōō•rûr´ də bwä´) A term that means
"runners of the woods," referring to French trappers
who traded with Native Americans. p. 432

**courier** (kŏŏr´ē•ər) A person who delivers messages.
p. 194

**covenant** (kəv´ə•nənt) A special agreement. p. 73

**Creole** (krē´ōl) A person of Spanish or Portuguese descent
who was born in the Americas. Creoles belonged to the
middle class of people in colonial Latin America. p. 479

**crop rotation** (krop rō•tā´shən) A farming method in
which the kinds of crops planted in a field are alter-
nated every year to help the soil remain fertile. p. 487

**crucifixion** (krōō•sə•fik´shən) The type of execution in
which a person is nailed to a cross and left to die.
p. 254

**crusader** (krōō•sā´dər) A Christian soldier who fought to
free the Holy Land from Muslim Turks in the Middle
Ages. p. 291

**cultural borrowing** (kəlch´rəl bär´ə•wing ) Adapting customs from one culture for use in another. p. 213

**cultural diffusion** (kəlch´rəl di•fyōō´zhən) The spreading
of new ideas to other places. p. 76

**cultural identity** (kəlch´rəl ī•den´tə•tē) A connection
people feel with one another. p. 220

**Cultural Revolution** (kəlch´rəl rev•ə•lōō´shən) Mao
Zedong's unsuccessful attempt from 1966 to 1968 to cut
the Chinese people's ties to the past. p. 595

**culture** (kəl´chər) A unique way of life that sets a group of
people apart from others. p. 42

**currency** (kər´ən•sē) Money. p. 307

**czar** (zär) A Russian title meaning "caesar," or ruler.
p. 544

# D

**daimyo** (dī´mē•ō) A local noble in feudal Japan. p. 318

**Daoism** (dou´i•zəm) A religion and philosophy that
teaches that the key to long life and happiness is to
accept life as it is. p. 169

**Declaration of Independence** (dek•lə•rā´shən uv
in•di•pen´dəns) The document that proclaimed the
American colonies' freedom from Britain. p. 471

**Declaration of the Rights of Man and of the Citizen**
(dek•lə•rā´shən uv the rīts uv man ənd uv the
si´tə•zən) A document, issued during the French
Revolution, that guaranteed certain human rights and
other freedoms. p. 475

**deforestation** (dē•fôr•ə•stā´shən) The clearing of forests.
p. 610

**delta** (del´tə) A triangle-shaped area of islands and
marshes at the mouth of a river. p. 93

**demagogue** (de´mə•gog) A bad leader. p. 226

**demand** (di•mand´) In economics, the amount of a good
or service that people want to buy. p. 499

**democracy** (di•mok´rə•sē) Rule by the people. p. 219

**desertification** (di•zər•tə•fə•kā´shən) Any change of
fertile land into desert. p. 93

**détente** (dā•tänt´) An easing of tensions. p. 577

**developing nation** (di•ve´lə•ping nā´shən) A country
with a fast-growing population, few resources, and an
economy based on agriculture. p. 607

**dhow** (dou) An Arab ship. p. 367

**dictator** (dik´tā•tər) A ruler with absolute authority.
p. 239

**diplomat** (di´plə•mat) A person skilled in developing
treaties between nations. p. 369

**direct rule** (di•rekt´ rōōl) A type of colonial government
in which Europeans chose all government officials.
p. 515

**discriminate** (dis•kri´mə•nāt) To treat unfairly because of
race or for other reasons. p. 624

**dissident** (di´sə•dənt) A person who speaks out against
his or her government. p. 653

**distortion** (di•stôr´shən) An area that is not accurate on a
map projection. p. 348

**division of labor** (də•vi´zhən uv lā´bər) A system in
which different members of a group do different tasks
according to their abilities and the group's needs. p. 42

**doge** (dōj) A leader in the Italian city-states. p. 375

**domesticate** (də•mes´tə•kāt) To control plants and animals for people's use. p. 44

**double-bar graph** (də´bəl bär graf) A bar graph that
shows two sets of statistics, or facts shown with
numbers. p. 564

**draft** (draft) A system for choosing citizens to serve in an
army. p. 306

**dynasty** (dī´nəs•tē) A series of rulers from the same
family. p. 98

# E

**economic system** (ek•ə•nom´ik sis´təm) The way a country produces and uses goods and services. p. 498

**economy** (i•kon´ə•mē) The way people use resources to
meet their needs. p. 44

**edict** (ē´dikt) A command. p. 98

**elevation** (el•ə•vā´shən) The height of land. p. 132

**embargo** (im•bär´gō) A ban on trade. p. 381

**emperor** (em´pər•ər) The ruler of an empire. p. 68

**empire** (em´pīr) A conquered land of many people and places governed by one ruler. p. 68

**encomienda** (en•kō•mē•en´dä) A system in which Native Americans had to work for European colonists and accept their religion. p. 431

**English Bill of Rights** (in´glish bil uv rītz) A British document, written in 1689, that granted individual rights. p. 471

**Enlightenment** (in•līt´ən•mənt) A movement that began in France in the 1700s and focused on ways to create a government for protecting the rights of individuals. p. 472

**entrepreneur** (än•trə•prə•nûr´) A person who takes a financial risk by providing money to start a business venture. p. 489

**environment** (en•vī´rən•mənt) Surroundings. p. 46

**epic** (e´pik) A long story-poem. p. 214

**equal justice** (ē´kwəl jus´təs) Fair treatment under the law. p. 69

**equal-area projection** (ē´kwəl âr´ē•ə prə•jek´shən) A map projection that shows the sizes of regions in correct relation to one another but distorts shapes. p. 348

**equidistant projection** (ē•kwə•dis´tənt prə•jek´shən) A map projection that shows accurate distances from a central point. p. 349

**ethnic cleansing** (eth´nik klenz´ing) Using threats or violence to drive certain groups out of an area. p. 656

**evaluate** (i•val´yə•wāt) To decide whether information can be trusted. p. 512

**evidence** (e´və•dəns) Proof. p. 49

**export** (ek•spōrt´) To send out goods for sale to other places. p. 170

# F

**fact** (fakt) A statement that can be proved to be true. p. 512

**factory** (fak´tə•rē) A large building where goods are made. p. 488

**fascism** (fa´shi•zəm) Political ideas that stress strong government control, military strength, and intense nationalism. p. 557

**favela** (fə•ve´lə) A slum outside a city in Brazil. p. 610

**feudal system** (fyōōd´əl sis´təm) A system of trading loyalties for protection in the Middle Ages. p. 290

**forum** (fōr´əm) A public square in ancient Rome. p. 243

**free enterprise** (frē en´tər•prīz) A system in which people choose how they make and spend their money. p. 500

**free port** (frē pôrt) A place that does not charge tariffs on imports or exports. p. 603

# G

**generalization** (je´nə•rəl•ī•zā´shən) A general statement made about people, events, or relationships. p. 57

**genocide** (je´nə•sīd) The killing of an entire group of people. p. 562

**gladiator** (glad´ē•ā•tər) A slave or prisoner forced to fight, often to the death. p. 246

**glasnost** (glaz´nōst) The "openness," or new freedom, that allowed Soviet citizens to speak out without fear of punishment. p. 652

**Gospels** (gäs´pəlz) The first four books of the New Testament that describe Jesus Christ's life and actions. p. 255

**government** (guv´ərn•mənt) An organized system that groups use to make laws and decisions. p. 63

**grand vizier** (grand və•zir´) The chief minister in the Ottoman Empire. p. 452

**graph** (graf) A diagram for showing relations between numbers. p. 376

**gravity** (gra´və•tē) The force that holds objects to the Earth and keeps the planets circling around the sun. p. 408

**great circle** (grāt sûr´kəl) Any imaginary circle that divides the Earth into equal parts. p. 350

**Great Depression** (grāt di•pre´shən) The economic decline during the 1930s that was the worst in the world's history. p. 550

**Great Mutiny** (grāt myōō´tən•ē or myōōt´nē) The rebellion in which Indians and sepoys mutinied against the East India Company's rule. p. 518

**Great Society** (grāt sə•sī´ə•tē) A goal proposed by United States President Lyndon Johnson according to which every American would have the chance for a good life. p. 617

**Greek fire** (grēk fīr) A chemical mixture, used by the Byzantine navy, that caught fire when water hit it. p. 372

**grid** (grid) The north-south and east-west lines on a map that cross each other to form a pattern of squares. p. 29

**gross domestic product** (grōs də•mes´tik prä´dəkt) (GDP) The total value of a country's goods and services produced in that country. p. 601

# H

**hacienda** (ä•sē•en´dä) A huge farm or plantation in colonial Latin America. p. 479

**haiku** (hī´kōō) A 17-syllable Japanese poem that is often about nature. p. 449

**Hansa** (han´sə or hän´zä) A group of Northern European merchants who worked together to protect themselves. p. 381

**harijan** (här•i•jän´) The name that Mohandas Gandhi gave to the untouchables of India. It means "child of God." p. 624

**Hellenistic** (he•lə•nis´tik) "Greek-like." p. 231

**heraldry** (her´əl•drē) The system of colors, patterns, and picture symbols that knights used during the Middle Ages in Europe. p. 294

**heresy** (her´ə•sē) The denial of the beliefs of a church. p. 412

**heritage** (her´ə•tij) A set of ideas that have been passed down from one generation to another. p. 155

**hieroglyphics** (hī•rə•gli´fiks) A writing system in which pictures or symbols stand for ideas, objects, or sounds. p. 99

**Hinduism** (hin´dōō•iz•əm) A religion native to India, featuring a belief in many gods and in reincarnation. p. 176

**historical empathy** (hi•stôr•i•kəl em´pə•thē) Understanding the actions and feelings of people from other times and other places. p. 24

**historical map** (hi•stôr•i•kəl map) A map that provides information about the past. Historical maps may show where events took place or how the world looked at a certain time in the past. p. 248

**Holocaust** (hōl´ə•kôst) The mass killing of millions of Jewish people during World War II. p. 562

**hostage** (hos´tij) Someone who is taken prisoner and held until demands are met. p. 636

**human features** (hyōō´mən fē´chərz) Buildings, bridges, farms, roads, and people themselves. p. 27

**hydroelectric power** (hī•drō•i•lek´trik pou´ər) Electricity produced by water power. p. 607

# I

**Ice Age** (īs āj) A long cold-weather period when huge sheets of ice covered part of the Earth's surface. p. 41

**icon** (ī´kän) A holy picture of Jesus Christ or the saints. p. 278

**immunity** (i•myōō´nə•tē) Resistance to disease. p. 431

**imperialism** (im•pir´ē•əl•iz•əm) The practice by a country of adding more lands, establishing colonies, and controlling the colonies. p. 515

**import** (im´pôrt) To bring in goods for sale from other places. p. 169

**independence** (in•di•pen´dəns) Complete freedom. p. 112

**indirect rule** (in•də•rekt´ rōōl) A type of colonial government that allowed some participation by local officials. p. 515

**indulgence** (in•dul´jəns) A pardon for sins. p. 412

**Industrial Revolution** (in•dus´trē•əl rev•ə•lōō´shən) The period of technological advances, beginning in the 1700s, that forever changed the way people live and work. p. 487

**inflation** (in•flā´shən) A continuing increase in the price of goods and services. p. 552

**innovation** (i•nə•vā´shən) A new way of doing things. p. 66

**inoculation** (i•nä•kyə•lā´shən) Giving a person a mild form of a disease so that he or she will not get sick with a more serious form. p. 191

**inscription** (in•skrip´shən) A written message etched into a long-lasting surface. p. 124

**inset map** (in•set´ map) A small map within a larger map. p. 29

**intercropping** (in•tər•krä´ping) Planting different crops together. p. 134

**intifada** (in•tē•fä´də) The Palestinian uprising against Israeli occupation of the West Bank and the Gaza Strip. p. 634

**Islam** (is•läm´) The religion of Muslims, based on belief in one God, or Allah. p. 282

**isolation** (ī•sə•lā´shən) Separation from others. p. 446

**isthmus** (is´məs) A small strip of land, with water on both sides, that connects two larger areas of land. p. 211

# J

**Janissary** (ja´nə•sâr•ē) A member of a well-trained group of soldiers who served in the Ottoman army. p. 451

**Judaism** (jōō´dē•iz•əm) The religion of the Jewish people. p. 74

**junk** (jungk) A Chinese wooden boat with four-sided sails. p. 368

**junta** (hōōn´ta) In Latin America, an independent governing council. p. 482

**Justinian Code** (jus•tin´ē•ən kōd) A set of laws, written by the Byzantine emperor Justinian, that served the Byzantine Empire for hundreds of years. p. 276

# K

**kaiser** (kī´zər) The German word for emperor. p. 510

**kami** (kä´mē) In the Shinto religion, spirits that live in all natural things. p. 316

**khan** (kän) The title given to strong Mongol leaders who sometimes brought rival clans together and created almost unstoppable fighting forces. p. 310

# L

**labor union** (lā´bər yōōn´yən) An organized workers' group whose goal is to ensure good working conditions and fair treatment by employers. p. 501

**lagoon** (lə•gōōn´) A small body of water found in the center of an atoll. p. 383

**laissez-faire** (le•sā•fâr´) A government policy of letting an economy continue without interference. p. 499

**lateen sail** (lə•tēn´ sāl´) A triangle-shaped sail that allows a ship to travel into the wind. p. 367

**league** (lēg) A group of allies. p. 223

**Legalism** (lē´gə•li•zəm) Chinese teachings that say people obey their rulers out of fear, rather than respect. p. 161

**legend** (le´jənd) A story handed down from earlier times to explain the past. p. 126

**legion** (lē´jən) A unit of soldiers. p. 245

**limited war** (li´mət•əd wôr) A war in which total victory is not the goal. Such limitations make it less likely that nuclear weapons are used. p. 574

**line graph** (līn graf) A graph that shows change over time by using one or more lines. The lines connect dots that stand for specific information. p. 376

**livestock** (līv´stok) Domesticated animals such as cattle, sheep, and pigs. p. 45

**logical conclusion** (läˊji•kəl kən•klooˊzhən) A decision or idea reached by thoughtful study of all the known facts. p. 382

**Long March** (lông märch) Mao Zedong and his followers' 6,000-mile (9,656 km) journey across China to escape Nationalist forces. p. 594

**Magna Carta** (magˊnə kärˊtə) The document that English nobles forced King John to sign in 1215, limiting the king's power and protecting the rights of the people. p. 293

**Mahatma** (mə•hätˊmə) A word meaning "Great Soul." Indians called Mohandas Gandhi *Mahatma* because they considered him a holy man. p. 624

**maize** (māz) Corn. p. 47

**majority rule** (mə•jôrˊə•tē rool) A system in which the ideas and decisions supported by the most people are followed. p. 219

**mandate** (manˊdāt) An order. p. 128

**Mandate of Heaven** (manˊdāt uv hevˊən) An order to rule; the Chinese believed it was given from heaven to their emperors. When an emperor was weak or disasters occurred, the emperor was thought to have lost the Mandate of Heaven. p. 128

**manor** (maˊnər) A large block of land made up of forests, meadows, farmland, a village, a church, and the house or castle of the noble who owned it all. p. 289

**mansa** (mänˊsə) The title for an emperor in West Africa. p. 345

**map key** (map kē) On a map, the part that explains what the symbols on the map stand for; sometimes called a map legend. p. 28

**map scale** (map skāl) The part of a map that gives a comparison of distance on the map itself with distance in the real world. p. 29

**map title** (map tīˊtəl) The words on a map that describe the subject of the map. p. 28

**market economy** (märˊkit i•konˊə•mē) An economy in which people not the government decide which goods and services they will buy. p. 499

**martyr** (märˊtər) A person who suffers or dies for his or her beliefs. p. 256

**megalopolis** (meg•ə•lopˊə•lis) A large, heavily populated area where cities have grown together. p. 602

**merchant** (mûrˊchənt) A person who buys and sells goods for a living. p. 64

**mesa** (māˊsä) A flat-topped hill with steep slopes. p. 325

**messiah** (mə•sīˊə) A wise leader who would establish the kingdom of God on Earth, according to Judaism. p. 254

**mestizo** (me•stēˊzō) A person of European and American Indian descent, living in the Spanish colonies. p. 480

**Middle Ages** (miˊdəl āˊjəz) The period of European history that lasted from about A.D. 500 to 1500. p. 287

**Middle America** (miˊdəl ə•merˊə•kə) The region between North and South America where southern Mexico, Belize, Guatemala, Honduras, El Salvador, Nicaragua, Costa Rica, and Panama are located. p. 134

**Middle Passage** (miˊdəl paˊsij) In the triangle trade system, the part in which enslaved peoples were shipped across the Atlantic from Africa to the Americas. p. 426

**migration** (mī•grāˊshən) Movement of groups of people from one place to another. p. 40

**militarism** (miˊlə•tə•ri•zəm) A nation's interest in armed power. p. 536

**militia** (mə•lishˊə) Volunteer soldiers. p. 155

**minaret** (min•ə•retˊ) A tower on top of a mosque, from which the faithful are called to prayer. p. 284

**minority rights** (mə•norˊə•tē rīts) Freedoms that are given to groups of people who make up a small part of a population. p. 625

**missionary** (miˊshə•ner•ē) A person sent out to teach about his or her religion. p. 189

**monarchy** (monˊər•kē) The system of government in which a king or a queen rules. p. 63

**money economy** (muˊnē i•konˊə•mē) An economic system based on money rather than on barter. p. 76

**monopoly** (mə•näˊpə•lē) Complete control or ownership. p. 276

**monotheism** (mäˊnə•thē•i•zəm) A belief in one supreme being. p. 72

**monsoon** (mon•soonˊ) Strong seasonal winds in the Indian Ocean. p. 367

**mosaic** (mō•zāˊik) A picture made from bits of colored stone or glass. p. 276

**mosque** (mosk) An Islamic house of worship. p. 284

**Mound Builders** (mound bilˊdərz) People who lived in the Eastern Woodlands region of North America. They got their name from the mounds of earth they used to bury their dead and to build temples on. p. 325

**movable type** (mooˊvə•bəl tīp) Letters and numbers made from individual pieces of metal that can be positioned to form rows of words. p. 407

**mulatto** (moo•läˊtō) A person of African and European background living in Portuguese America. p. 480

**multicultural** (məl•tē•kəlchˊrəl) Relating to many cultures. p. 231

**mummy** (mumˊē) A preserved body. p. 100

**Muslim** (moosˊləm) A follower of Islam. p. 282

**myth** (mith) A story that is passed down from generation to generation and usually tells about an ancient god or hero. p. 220

**Napoleonic Code** (nə•pō•lē•on´ik kōd) A set of laws made in 1804 that guaranteed certain freedoms for the people of France. French law is still based on this code. p. 477

**national debt** (nashˊnəl *or* naˊshə•nəl det) The amount of money a government owes. p. 618

**nationalism** (nashˊnə•li•zəm *or* naˊshə•nəl•i•zəm) A strong feeling of loyalty to one's nation, or country. p. 507

**nationalize** (nashˊnə•līz *or* naˊshə•nəl•īz) To put under government control. p. 608

**nation-state** (nā´shən•stāt) A country with a strong central government and a single ruler and usually a common history and culture. p. 292

**New Testament** (nōō tes´tə•mənt) The second part of the Christian Bible. It tells about the life and teachings of Jesus Christ and his followers. p. 255

**nomad** (nō´mad) A person who moves from place to place. p. 45

**oasis** (ō•ā´səs) A water hole in the desert. p. 352

**obelisk** (ō´bə•lisk) An ancient stone monument. p. 111

**Old Testament** (ōld tes´tə•mənt) The Christian Bible's first part, which contains the same books as the Jewish Bible. p. 255

**oligarchy** (ä´lə•gär•kē) A system in which a small group controls the government. p. 218

**Open Door policy** (ō´pən dōr pä´lə•sē) A policy whereby all countries have an equal opportunity to trade freely in a certain place. p. 519

**opinion** (ō•pin´yən) A statement of belief or judgment. p. 512

**opportunity cost** (ä•pər•tü´nə•tē kôst) The cost of giving up something when choosing something else instead. p. 612

**oracle** (ôr´ə•kəl) A person who gives wise advice. p. 129

**orthodox** (or´thə•däks) In religion, supported and accepted by tradition. p. 278

**outrigger** (out´ri•gər) A wooden frame placed on the side of a boat or canoe to keep the craft steady in rough seas. p. 386

## P

**papyrus** (pə•pī´rəs) A paperlike material used by Egyptians for writing; made from reeds that grow in the Nile River. p. 99

**parallel time line** (par´ə•lel tīm līn) A grouping of time lines that display different types of information for the same period of time. p. 48

**partition** (pär•ti´shən) To divide. p. 632

**passive resistance** (pa´siv ri•zis´təns) The use of peaceful means instead of violence to bring about change. p. 623

**patent** (pa´tənt) A document giving the inventor of a new idea or product the exclusive right to make or sell it for a limited period of time. p. 489

**patriarch** (pā´trē•ärk) A church leader. p. 279

**patrician** (pə•tri´shən) A descendant of Rome's earliest settlers. p. 239

**patron** (pā´trən) A wealthy person who pays artists and writers to produce their work. p. 404

**peasant** (pe´zənt) A poor person who lives on and farms the land. p. 102

**peninsular** (pe•nin´sû•lär) A person born in Spain or Portugal and belonging to the highest social class of people in colonial Latin America. p. 479

**perestroika** (pâr•ə•stroi´kə) A "restructuring," or rebuilding, of the Soviet political and economic systems. p. 652

**perspective** (pər•spek´tiv) A painting technique that shows the differences between things that are close and things that are far away. p. 405

**pharaoh** (fer´ō) A ruler of ancient Egypt. p. 98

**philosopher** (fi•los´ə•fər) A person who studies the meaning of life. p. 158

**physical features** (fiz´i•kəl fē´chərz) Landforms, bodies of water, climate, soil, plant and animal life, and other natural resources. p. 27

**pictograph** (pik´tə•graf) A drawing or symbol used to represent a word in the Chinese language. p. 130

**plantation** (plan•tā´shən) A huge farm. p. 425

**plateau** (pla•tō) A high, flat area of land. p. 192

**plebeian** (pli•bē´ən) A farmer, worker, merchant, or craftworker whose family came to ancient Rome later than the families of patricians. p. 239

**plunder** (plun´dər) To take goods by force. p. 311

**polar projection** (po´lər prə•jek´shən) An equidistant map projection that has one of the poles as its central point. p. 350

**policy** (pä´lə•sē) A plan. p. 243

**polis** (pä´ləs) In ancient Greece, a city-state consisting of a town and the farms and villages around it. p. 216

**political cartoon** (pə•li•ti•kəl kär´tün) A cartoon that presents the artist's point of view about people and current events in politics and government. p. 478

**pope** (pōp) The leader of the Roman Catholic Church. p. 288

**population density** (pop•yə•lā´shən den´sə•tē) The average number of people living on a square unit of land. p. 629

**population distribution** (pop•yə•lā´shən dis•trib•yōō´shən) The number of people who live in different places in a given part of the world. p. 628

**population pyramid** (pop•yə•lā´shən pir´ə•mid) A graph that shows how a country's population is divided by age. p. 455

**porcelain** (pôr´sə•lin) A kind of clay pottery so thin it looks almost clear. p. 307

**predict** (pri•dikt´) To tell what will happen ahead of time. p. 95

**primary source** (prī´mär•ē sôrs) A record made by people who saw or took part in an event. p. 512

**profit** (prä´fət) Money gained. p. 170

**projection** (prə•jek´shən) A representation of the Earth on a map; a view of the round Earth on a flat surface. p. 348

**propaganda** (prä•pə•gan´də) The spreading of information, ideas, or rumors to help or hurt a cause. p. 553

**prophet** (prä´fət) A person who others believe speaks or writes a divine message. p. 195

**protectionism** (prə•tek´shə•ni•zəm) A government policy that calls for some type of action, such as raising tariffs, to protect a market from imports. p. 603

**protein** (prō´tēn) A substance in food that helps build the body and keeps it healthy. p. 134

**Protestant** (prä´təs•tənt) Name of the churches that were formed as a result of protests against the Roman Catholic Church. p. 413

**province** (prä´vins) A self-governing region.  p. 241

**public works** (pu´blik wûrks) Structures built by the government for use by everyone.  p. 156

**pueblo** (pwe´blō) An apartment-like shelter built on a cliff ledge or on a mesa in what is now the southwestern part of the United States.  p. 325

**purge** (pərj) A government order to kill or imprison citizens who oppose the government.  p. 548

**pyramid** (pir´ə•mid) A tomb for the dead, often for a dead ruler.  p. 100

# Q

**quota** (kwō´tə) A required amount of particular goods to be produced.  p. 596

**Qur'an** (kə•ran´ *or* kə•rän) The holy book of Islam.  p. 282

# R

**racism** (rā´siz•əm) The belief that one person is better than another because of color or race.  p. 428

**rajah** (rä´jə) An Indian prince.  p. 187

**ratify** (rat´ə•fī) To approve an agreement.  p. 615

**raw material** (rô mə•tir´ē•əl) A natural resource, such as cotton, lumber, or wool, that can be made into a useful product.  p. 489

**reclaimed** (ri•klām´d) In archaeology, taken back by the surrounding environment, as humanmade structures can be.  p. 137

**Reconquista** (rā•kôn•kēs´tä) A plan to make Spain all Catholic; also called the Reconquest.  p. 409

**Red Guard** (red gärd) Young people who supported Mao Zedong and tried to carry out the Cultural Revolution.  p. 596

**Reformation** (re•fər•mā´shən) A religious movement that began in sixteenth-century Europe as an attempt to reform the Roman Catholic Church; resulted in the founding of Protestantism.  p. 413

**refugee** (re´fyo͞o•jē) A person who leaves his or her home to find shelter and safety elsewhere.  p. 562

**regent** (rē´jənt) A person who governs in place of a ruler.  p. 318

**region** (rē´jən) An area on Earth whose features make it different from other areas.  p. 27

**Reign of Terror** (rān uv ter´ər) A period of rule by fear during the French Revolution; thousands of people were executed.  p. 475

**reincarnation** (rē•in•kär•nā´shən) The belief that the soul lives on after death and returns to life in a new body.  p. 176

**relative location** (re´lə•tiv lō•kā´shən) What a place is near or what is around it.  p. 26

**Renaissance** (re´nə•säns) The time from about 1400 to 1600 in which Europeans entered an age of thought, learning, art, and science; a French word meaning "rebirth."  p. 403

**republic** (ri•pu´blik) A form of government in which the citizens elect representatives to make all government decisions.  p. 238

**responsibility** (ri•spän•sə•bi´lə•tē) A duty.  p. 158

**role** (rōl) The part a person plays in society.  p. 42

# S

**saga** (sä´gə) An adventure story about the brave deeds of people.  p. 378

**samurai** (sa´mə•rī) A Japanese warrior.  p. 318

**Sanskrit** (san´skrit) A language of India, first spoken by the ancient Aryans.  p. 176

**satyagraha** (sə•tyä´grə•hə) A term that Mohandas Gandhi used, meaning "soul force." It refers to a way for people to gain rights through peaceful methods.  p. 623

**savanna** (sə•va´nə) A grassy plain.  p. 341

**scientific method** (sī•ən•ti´fik me´thəd) A system of observing and experimenting to determine whether an idea should be accepted as true.  p. 408

**scribe** (skrīb) A person who writes.  p. 65

**secede** (si•sēd) To separate from.  p. 615

**secondary source** (sek´ən•dâr•ē sôrs) A record of an event, written by someone not there at the time.  p. 512

**Senate** (se´nət) A council of representatives.  p. 239

**sepoy** (sē´poi) An Indian soldier led by British officers.  p. 517

**serf** (sûrf) A peasant who worked on a manor.  p. 289

**Shiite** (shē´īt) A group of Muslims who stayed loyal to the descendants of the fourth caliph, Ali, during the eighth century.  p. 286

**Shinto** (shin´tō) A religion of Japan. The word means "the way of the gods."  p. 316

**shogun** (shō´gən) In Japan, a "leading general" who held all the authority.  p. 319

**Silk Road** (silk rōd) A trade route that stretched 5,000 miles (8,047 km) from China to the Mediterranean Sea.  p. 170

**silt** (silt) Fine bits of rock and soil carried or deposited by water.  p. 94

**social class** (sō´shəl klas) A group that has a particular amount of power in a society.  p. 65

**socialism** (sō´shə•li•zəm) An economic system in which a government owns and runs all industries.  p. 501

**society** (sə•sī´ə•tē) An organized group of people living and working under an established set of rules and traditions.  p. 42

**soviet** (sō´vē•et) A workers' group that formed in Russia to plan and carry out the revolution.  p. 547

**standard of living** (stan´dərd uv liv´ing) A measure of how well people in a country live.  p. 601

**standardization** (stan•dər•də•zā´shən) The practice of making all things of a certain type alike.  p. 164

**star path** (stär path) The way stars seem to move because of the Earth's rotation.  p. 386

**statistics** (stə•tis´tiks) Facts shown with numbers.  p. 564

**steppe** (step) Semi-dry plain that produces some grasses and thorny plants.  p. 281

**strike** (strīk) The action of refusing to work until certain requirements are met.  p. 501

**subcontinent** (sub•kon´tə•nənt) A large land area isolated from the rest of a continent. p. 121

**subsist** (səb•sist´) To survive. p. 47

**subsistence farming** (səb•sis´təns färm´ing) Farming in which people raise only enough food for their families. p. 607

**sultan** (sul´tən) A Muslim ruler in India. p. 453

**Sunni** (soo´nē) A group of Muslims who accepted the changing dynasties of the Muslim Empire during the eighth century. p. 286

**superpower** (soo´pər•pou´ər) A nation that is one of the world's most powerful. p. 572

**supply** (sə•plī) The amount of a product or service offered for sale. p. 499

**surplus** (sûr´plus) An extra supply. p. 64

**Swahili** (swä•hē´lē) A people and a language of East Africa. p. 369

## T

**table** (tā´bəl) A chart that lists information in categories. p. 171

**tariff** (tar´if) A tax on goods or services. p. 344

**taxation** (tak•sā´shən) The practice of requiring people to pay taxes to support a government. p. 69

**technology** (tek•nol´ə•jē) The use of tools and skills to make a product or achieve a goal. p. 62

**telescope** (tel´ə•skōp) An instrument that can make faraway objects look close. p. 408

**telescoping time line** (tel´ə•skōp•ing tīm līn) A time line that includes a second time line in order to give a closer view of one time period. p. 259

**Ten Commandments** (ten kə•mand´mənts) A set of laws for responsible behavior, which, according to the Bible, were given to Moses by God. p. 73

**tenant** (te´nənt) Someone who pays rent to a landowner. p. 289

**territorial expansion** (ter•ə•tôr´ē•əl ik•span´shən) The adding of new lands. p. 379

**terrorism** (ter´ər•i•zəm) The use of violent acts to further a cause. p. 632

**textile** (teks´tīl) Cloth. p. 488

**time zone** (tīm zōn) A division of the Earth in which all places have the same time; the time is different from that in other zones. p. 542

**Torah** (tôr´ə) Jewish scriptures; the first five books of the Bible. p. 74

**totalitarian** (tō•ta•lə•târ´ē•ən) Having complete control over people's lives. p. 548

**trade surplus** (trād sûr´plus) A balance of trade in which a country exports more goods than it imports. p. 602

**trade-off** (trād•of) Giving up the use of resources in one way in order to use them in another way. p. 612

**trading network** (trād´ing net´wərk) A group of buyers and sellers. p. 114

**traditional economy** (trə•dish´ən•əl i•kon´ə•mē) An economy that does not change much over time. p. 498

**tragedy** (traj´ə•dē) A serious play in which the main character comes to an unhappy end. p. 225

**trend** (trend) The way something changes over time. p. 376

**triangle trade** (trī´ang•əl trād) A system in which traders exchanged goods for slaves, sold the slaves for products from plantations, and then sold the products in Europe. p. 426

**tribune** (tri´byoon) A plebeian official who could attend meetings of the Senate in ancient Rome. p. 239

**tributary** (tri´byə•ter•ē) A smaller river that feeds into a larger river. p. 121

**tribute** (tri´byoot) Yearly payments. p. 193

**tropical rain forest** (trä´pi•kəl rān fôr´əst) A hot, wet land with tall trees that block the sunlight. p. 341

**tundra** (tun´drə) A cold, treeless plain whose subsoil is permanently frozen. p. 41

**turning point** (tərn´ing point) A time of important change. p. 188

**typhoon** (tī•foon´) A type of fierce storm. p. 316

**tyrant** (tī´rənt) Someone who takes control of a government illegally and rules alone. p. 216

## U

**untouchables** (un•tuch´ə•bəlz) In India, people below all castes. The name came from the idea that others would be made dirty and impure from their touch. p. 177

**utopian** (yoo•tō´pē•ən) A person who believes in and wants to create a perfect society. p. 502

## V

**vassal** (va´səl) In the Middle Ages, a noble who agreed to perform services for the king in return for being given the use of land. p. 289

**Vedas** (vā´dəz) Books of ancient Hindu sacred writings. p. 176

**veto** (vē´tō) To stop passage of a law; from a Latin word meaning "I forbid." p. 239

**virtue** (vər´choo) A good quality. p. 155

## W

**warlord** (wôr´lôrd) In China, a person who commanded his own small army. p. 593

## Z

**ziggurat** (zi´gə•rat) A huge mud-brick temple built by the ancient Sumerians. p. 62

**Zionism** (zī´ə•ni•zəm) The movement to build a modern Jewish state. p. 631

**Zoroastrianism** (zōr•ə•was´trē•ə•ni•zəm) A religion started by Zarathustra that teaches the belief in two gods—one good and one evil. p. 195

# INDEX

*Page references for illustrations are set in italic type. An italic **m** indicates a map.
Page references set in boldface type indicate the pages on which vocabulary terms are defined.*

**Abbasid family**                                                    *arms race*

Centrale al I'piano, Roma/Scala/Art Resource, NY; 255 (tr) Scala/Art Resource, NY; 255 (b) Vatican Museum/C M Dixon; 257 (t) Robert Harding Picture Library; 257 (b) Peter Scholey/Robert Harding Picture Library; 262-263 (t) James Blank/The Stock Market; 262-263 (b) Duomo Photography; 262-263 (bg) Cowgirl Stock Photography; 263 Catherine Ursillo/Photo Researchers.

## Unit 5
Pages 268-269 (t) Robert Frerck/Odyssey Productions, Chicago; 268 (bl) Erich Lessing/Art Resource, NY; 268 (bc) Superstock; 268 (br) Victoria and Albert Museum/Michael Holford Photographs; 269 (bl) The Granger Collection; 269 (br) Robert Frerck/Odyssey Productions; 271 (t) Cahokia Mounds, Illinois State Historic Site; 271 (b) Cahokia Mounds, Illinois State Historic Site; 273 Illinois Transportation Archaeological Research Program, University of Illinois, Urbana; 274 Scala/Art Resource, NY; 275 Werner Forman Archive/Thessalonicki Archaeological Museum/Art Resource, NY; 277 (t) Scala/Art Resource, NY; 277 (b) Robert Frerck/Odyssey Productions, Chicago; 277 (inset) Roland & Sabrina Michaud/Woodfin Camp & Associates; 278 Erich Lessing/Art Resource, NY; 279 E.T. Archive; 280 Hungarian National Museum, Budapest, Hungary/Scala/Art Resource, NY; 281 Robert Azzi/Woodfin Camp & Associates; 282 (l) The British Museum/Michael Holford Photographs; 282 (r) E.T. Archive; 284 (r) Superstock; 284 (l) Robert Frerck/Woodfin Camp & Associates; 285 Michael Pasdzior/The Image Bank; 286 C M Dixon; 287 E.T. Archive; 288 Scala/Art Resource, NY; 289 (tl) Scala/Art Resource, NY; 289 (tr) Scala/Art Resource, NY; 290 (t) Mike Howell/Superstock; 290 (b) Sonia Halliday Photographs; 290 (inset) The British Museum/E. T. Archive; 293 The Granger Collection; 295 The World Almanac and Book of Facts 1996. Copyright 1995 Funk & Wagnalls Corporation. All rights reserved; 296 The Granger Collection; 301 (t) Museum del'Armee/Robert Harding Picture Library; 301 (b) Robert Harding Picture Library; 304 Ancient Art & Architecture Collection; 305 E.T. Archive; 306 Wang Lu/ChinaStock Photo Library; 307 (tl) Wolfgang Kaehler Photography; 307 (tr) Art Resource, NY; 308 National Palace Museum, Taiwan/E.T. Archive; 309 Robb Kendrick; 310 Werner Forman Archive/Imperial Library, Teheran/Art Resource, NY; 312 (l) E.T. Archive; 312 (r) Giraudon/Art Resource, NY; 313 Ancient Art & Architecture Collection; 314 E.T. Archive; 315 E.T. Archive; 316 Ancient Art & Architecture Collection; 318 (r) Victoria and Albert Museum/Michael Holford Photographs; 319 Michael Holford Photographs; 320 National Museum of Anthropology, Mexico City, Mexico/Michel Zabe/Art Resource, NY; 321 (l) Robert Frerck/Woodfin Camp & Associates; 321 (r) Lenars, Explorer/Mary Evans Picture Library; 322 National Geographic painting

by Felipe Davalos/National Geographic Society; 323 (t) Martin Rogers/Woodfin Camp & Associates; 323 (c) Michael Holford Photographs; 323 (b) Robert Frerck/Odyssey Productions, Chicago; 325 David Muench; 330-331 (bg) "Our Peaceful World" by Natalie Szymanski, age 11, USA, courtesy of the International Children's Art Museum/Paintbrush Diplomacy; 330-331 (fg) John Chaisson/Gamma Liaison; 330 (inset) "World Peace" by Samrat Chatterjee, age 12, India, courtesy of the International Children's Art Museum/Paintbrush Diplomacy.

## Unit 6
Pages 336-337(t) ChinaStock Photo Library; 336(bl) Historical Museum, Stockholm, Giraudon/Art Resource, NY; 336(br) C M Dixon; 337(bl) Collection Musée de l'Homme, Paris; 337(bc) Giraudon/Art Resource, NY; 337(br) ChinaStock Photo Library; 338 Bibliotheque Nationale, Paris (detail); 340 Richard Nowitz; 341 Museum of Mankind (British Museum)/Michael Holford Photographs; 342 (l) Geoff Renner/Robert Harding Picture Library; 342 (c) Michael Fogden/DRK; 342 (r) T.A. Wiewandt/DRK; 344 (l) Collection Musée de l'Homme, Paris; 344 (r) Collection Musée de l'Homme, Paris; 345 Bibliotheque Nationale, Paris; 346 Photograph copyright The Detroit Institute of Arts, 1995 Founders Society Purchase, Eleanor Clay Ford Fund for African Art; 347 (l) Ronald Sheridan/Ancient Art & Architecture Collection; 347 (r) Werner Forman Archive/Art Resource, NY; 351 Michael Holford Photographs; 353 (tl) Jean-Loup CHARMET; 353 (tr) Arabic ms. of De Materia Medica, Baghdad/The Granger Collection; 353 (b) The Granger Collection; 355 (l) Ancient Art & Architecture Collection; 355 (r) Ancient Art & Architecture Collection; 356 (l) Sonia Halliday Photographs; 356 (r) Ronald Sheridan/Ancient Art & Architecture Collection; 366 Oslo, Historical Museum/Knudsens-Giraudon/Art Resource, NY; 367 Sonia Halliday Photographs; 368 (t) Wendy Stone/Odyssey, Chicago; 368 (b) Ronald Sheridan/Ancient Art & Architecture Collection; 368 (r)(inset) ChinaStock Photo Library; 369 ChinaStock Photo Library; 370 Philadelphia Museum of Art: Given by John T. Dorrance; 371 (inset) Naomi Peck/Robert Harding Picture Library; 371 M.P. Kahl/DRK; 372 (l) British Museum/Werner Forman Archive/Art Resource, NY; 372 (r) Diozescanmuseum Trier/E. T. Archive; 374 (l) Museo degli Argenti, Palazzo Pitti, Florence, Italy/Art Resource, NY; 374 (r) Correr Museum, Venice/E.T. Archive; 378 Historical Museum, Stockholm/Giraudon/Art Resource, NY; 379 (l) Richard Nowitz; 379 (r) C M Dixon; 380 The Granger Collection; 382 (t) Helge Ingstad; 382 (b) Helge Ingstad; 383 Guido Alberto Rossi/The Image Bank; 384 ChinaStock Photo Library; 385 Tom Till/DRK; 387 (l) Ron Testa/The Field Museum, Chicago, Neg. #A107959C; 387 (r) Wolfgang Kaehler Photography; 390-391 (t) Robert Frerck/Woodfin Camp & Associates; 391 Bob Daemmrich/Stock, Boston.

## Unit 7
Page 396 (bl) E.T. Archive; 396 (br) The Granger Collection; 396-397 (t) Scala/Art Resource, NY; 397 (bl) Boltin Picture Library; 397 (br) C M Dixon; 398 Scala/Art Resource, NY; 399 Copyright, 1989, Malcolm Varon, NYC/The Metropolitan Museum of Art, Fletcher Fund, and Bequest of Miss Adelaide Milton de Groot (1867-1967), by exchange, supplemented by gifts from friends of the Muse; 400 Prado, Madrid/E.T. Archive; 401 Museo del Prado, Madrid, Spain/Erich Lessing/Art Resource, NY; 402 Scala/Art Resource, NY; 403 Musee Rheinisches Landesmuseum/Giraudon/Art Resource, NY; 404 Basel Museum of Fine Arts/SEF/Art Resource, NY; 405 Vatican Museum & Galleries, Rome/Scala/Superstock; 406 (tl) Scala/Art Resource, NY; 406 (tr) Giraudon/Art Resource, NY; 406 (b) Scala/Art Resource, NY; 407 (l) The Granger Collection; 407 (r) Jean-Loup CHARMET; 408 (t) Erich Lessing/Art Resource, NY; 408 (b) E.T. Archive; 409 E.T. Archive; 410 The Granger Collection; 411 Bridgeman/Art Resource, NY; 412 (t) Alinari/Art Resource, NY; 412 (b) Foto Marburg/Art Resource, NY; 414 The Bettmann Archive; 415 Sonia Halliday Photographs; 416 (l) Jean-Loup CHARMET; 416 (r) Michael Holford Photographs; 417 The Granger Collection; 418 (t) Museo Navale di Pegli Genova/Scala/Art Resource, NY; 418 (b) The Granger Collection; 419 (l) Michael Holford Photographs; 419 (r) C M Dixon; 422 Musee des Arts Africains et Oceaniens, Paris; 423 Boltin Picture Library; 424 (t) The British Museum/Michael Holford Photographs; 424 (b) Boltin Picture Library; 425 (t) The British Museum/J.R. Freeman/Robert Harding Picture Library; 425 (b) The Granger Collection; 426 The Granger Collection; 429 Werner Forman Archive/Art Resource, NY; 430 Boltin Picture Library; 431 E.T. Archive; 434 Robert Frerck/Odyssey Productions, Chicago; 435 Jeff Greenberg/MRP/Photo Researchers; 440 (t) Antonio Mercado/Art Resource, NY; 440 (b) National Collection of Fine Arts, Smithsonian Institution/Robert Harding Picture Library; 444 The Granger Collection; 445 British Museum/C M Dixon; 446 (l) E.T. Archive; 446 (r) Musée Guimet, Paris/G. Dagli Orti; 448 Ueno, Ninja Museum/Werner Forman/Art Resource, NY; 449 Paris Collection, Paris/G. Dagli Orti; 450 Topkapi Palace Museum, Istanbul/Sonia Halliday Photographs; 451 (l) G. Dagli Orti; 451 (r) Giraudon/Art Resource, NY; 453 (t) Michael Holford Photographs; 453 (b) Boltin Picture Library; 454 Chris Haigh/Tony Stone Images; 458 (tl) Steven Needham/Envision; 458 (tr) Pictures of London/Envision; 458-459 (bg) Steve Needham/Envision; 459 (tl) Steven Needham/Envision; 459 (tr) Steven Needham/Envision.

## Unit 8
Pages 464-465 (t) The Granger Collection; 464 (b) The Granger Collection; 465 (bl) Mus. Nat. de la Legion d'Honneur/Lauros-Giraudon/Art Resource, NY; 465 (br) The

Granger Collection; 467 Clich'e Museum, Paris/Jean-Loup CHARMET.; 469 Musée de Louvre, Paris/AKG, Berlin/Superstock; 470 Museum of National History, Buenos Aires, Argentina/G. Dagli Orti; 471 The Granger Collection; 472 Giraudon/Art Resource, NY; 473 The Granger Collection; 474 Musée de Carnavalet, Paris/G. Dagli Orti; 475 G. Dagli Orti; 477 (l) E.T. Archive; 477 (r) Musée Malmaison/E.T. Archive; 478 (t) Courtesy, Museum of Fine Arts, Boston, Babcock Bequest; 478 (b) The Granger Collection; 479 The Granger Collection; 480 (t) Museo de America, Madrid/E.T. Archive; 480 (b) Robert Freck/Odyssey Productions, Chicago; 480 (b)(inset) Robert Frerck/Odyssey Productions, Chicago; 481 E.T. Archive; 482 (l)(inset) E.T. Archive; 482 (r) Museu Nacional de Historia, Peru/E.T. Archive; 483 The Granger Collection; 486 Hulton Duetsch Collection/Woodfin Camp & Associates; 487 Mary Evans Picture Library; 488 (l) The Granger Collection; 488 (r)(inset) The Mansell Collection Limited; 489 Jean-Loup CHARMET; 491 (l) Mary Evans Picture Library; 491 (r)(inset) Hulton Deutsch Collection Limited/Woodfin Camp & Associates; 494 (l) The Granger Collection; 494-495 The Granger Collection; 496-497 The Granger Collection; 498 British Museum/Michael Holford Photographs; 499 Mary Evans Picture Library; 500 Victoria & Albert Museum, London/Art Resource, NY; 501 (l) The Granger Collection; 501 (r) The Granger Collection; 502 (b) The Mansell Collection Limited; 502 (tl) The Granger Collection; 502 (tr) The Bettmann Archive; 503 (l) The Granger Collection; 503 (r) Archive Photos; 506 The Granger Collection; 508 Jean-Loup CHARMET; 509 Risorgimento Museum, Milan/Scala/Art Resource, NY; 510 Mary Evans Picture Library; 511 The British Museum/E.T. Archive; 512 Courtesy of The Mariner's Museum, Newport News, Virginia; 513 Franklin D. Roosevelt Library; 514 City Museum, Copenhagen/E. T. Archive; 515 E.T. Archive; 516 (t) The Granger Collection; 516 (b) The Granger Collection; 517 Jean-Loup CHARMET; 519 E.T. Archive; 521 (t) E.T. Archive; 521 (b) The Granger Collection; 524-525 (bg) Kaiser/Stock Imagery; 524-525 (b)(fg) Bob Daemmrich Photo, Dobie Middle School; 524 (l)(bg) Bob Daemmrich Photography; 525 (t) Bob Daemmrich/Bob Daemmrich Photography.

### Unit 9
Pages 530-531 (t) P.J. Griffiths/Magnum Photos; 530 (bl) The Granger Collection; 530 (br) The Granger Collection; 531 (b) Peter Marlow/Magnum Photos; 532 Musée d'Orsay, Paris, France/Erich Lessing/Art Resource, NY; 533 Musée d'Orsay, Paris, France/Erich Lessing/Art Resource, NY; 534 Detail, photo by Dorothea Lange, The Bettman Archive.; 535 Erich Lessing/Art Resource, NY; 536 The Bettmann Archive; 537 (l) Scala/Art Resource, NY; 537 (r) The Granger Collection; 538 (l) The Bettmann Archive; 538 (r)(inset) Culver Pictures; 539 (l) The Bettmann Archive; 539 (r) The

Bettmann Archive; 541 The Bettmann Archive; 544 Christies, London/Superstock; 545 (tl) Giraudon/Art Resource, NY; 545 (tr) Giraudon/Art Resource, NY; 545 (b) Itar-Tass/Sovfoto; 546 (tl) The Granger Collection; 546 (tr) Scala/Art Resource, NY; 546 (b) Museo Statale Russo/Scala/Art Resource, NY; 548 Ria Novosti/Sovfoto; 549 The Bettmann Archive; 550 The Bettmann Archive; 551 The Bettmann Archive; 552 (t) The Granger Collection; 552 (b) The Bettmann Archive; 553 The Bettmann Archive; 556 detail, photo by Phillip Jones Griffiths/Magnum Photos; 557 The Bettmann Archive; 558 Hulton Deutsch/Woodfin Camp & Associates; 559 (l) Reuters/The Bettmann Archive; 559 (c) Robert Capa/Magnum Photos; 559 (r) The Granger Collection; 561 (t) The Bettmann Archive; 561 (b) The Bettmann Archive; 564 The Bettmann Archive; 572 Library of Congress; 574 Ed Hoffman, Acme, UPI/Bettmann; 575 (t) Keystone/Hulton Deutsch/Woodfin Camp & Associates; 575 (b) Dan Budnik/Woodfin Camp & Associates; 576 Kyoicki Sawada/UPI/The Bettmann Archive; 577 (t) Kyoicki Sawada, UPI/The Bettmann Archive; 577 (c) P. Jones Griffith/Magnum Photos; 577 (b) Sara Matthews/Swathmore College Peace Collection; 578 Peter Marlow/Magnum Photos; 578 (inset) Tommy Thompson/Black Star; 579 (l) Yousuf Karsh/Woodfin Camp & Associates; 579 (r) Erich Lessing/Magnum Photos; 582 (fg) Steve McCurry/Magnum Photos; 582-583 (b)(fg) Mike Goldwater-Network-Matrix.

### Unit 10
Pages 588-589 (t) Ed Nachtrieb/The Bettmann Archive; 588 (bl) Susan Mcelhinney/Woodfin Camp & Associates; 588 (br) A. Nogues/Sygma; 589 (bl) J. Langevin/Sygma Photo News; 589 (br) Wide World Photos; 590 (t) Alexandra Avakian/Woodfin Camp & Associates; 590 (b) Patrick Piel/Gamma Liaison; 591 (inset) Chip Hires/Gamma Liaison; 591 Eric Bouvet/Gamma Liaison; 592 Mireille Vautier/Woodfin Camp & Associates; 593 Bettmann/Hulton/Woodfin Camp & Associates; 594 (l) Sovfoto; 594 (r) New China Pictures/Eastfoto; 596 Sovfoto/Eastfoto; 600 Tony Stone Images; 601 Tom Wagner/Odyssey Productions, Chicago; 602 Kim Newton/Woodfin Camp & Associates; 604 Peter Menzel Photography; 606 D. Donne Bryant; 608 Alain Keler/Sygma; 609 Susan Meiselas/Magnum Photos; 610 (l) Luiz C. Marigo/Peter Arnold, Inc.; 610 (r) David R. Frazier/Tony Stone Images; 611 (t) Mireille Vautier/Woodfin Camp & Associates; 611 (b) Will & Deni McIntyre/Photo Researchers; 613 (l) Wolfgang Kaehler Photography; 613 (r) Mireille Vautier/Woodfin Camp & Associates; 614 The Bettmann Archive; 615 (t) Robert Mackinlay/Peter Arnold, Inc.; 615 (b) Tibor Bognar/The Stock Market; 617 (l) Robert Frerck/Odyssey/The Stock Market; 617 (r) Bob Daemmrich/Uniphoto; 618 Al Stephens/Woodfin Camp & Associates; 622 Francios Perri/Cosmos/Woodfin Camp & Associates; 623 Brown

Brothers; 624 The Bettmann Archive; 625 Wide World Photos; 626 (l) Baldev/Sygma; 626 (r) Jehangir Gazdar/Woodfin Camp & Associates; 627 Victoria Brynner/Gamma Liaison; 630 Jeff Dunn/Stock, Boston; 632 (ACME)/The Bettmann Achive; 633 The Bettmann Archive; 635 Ron Edmonds/Wide World Photos; 636 (l) M. Philippot/Sygma; 636 (r)(inset) Olivier Rebbot/Woodfin Camp & Associates; 637 (tl) Eric Bouvet/Gamma Liaison; 637 (b)(inset) B. Markel/Gamma Liaison; 637 (t)(inset) CNN International/Gamma Liaison; 640 Jeremy Hartley/Panos Pictures; 641 Hulton Deutsch Collection/Woodfin Camp & Associates; 642 (l) Betty Press/Woodfin Camp & Associates; 642 (r) Betty Press/Woodfin Camp & Associates; 644 Alon Reininger/Woodfin Camp & Associates; 645 (t) Brooks Kraft/Sygma; 645 (bl) Broods Kraft/Sygma; 645 (br) Jon Jones/Sygma; 646 Charles Platiau Reuter/The Bettmann Archive; 652 Chuck Nacke/Woodfin Camp & Associates; 654 (t) Michael Springer/Gamma Liaison; 654 (b) Klaus Reisinger/Black Star; 656 (l) S. Morgan-Spooner/Gamma Liaison; 656 (t) Enrico Dagino/Woodfin Camp & Associates; 656 (b) Art Zamur/Gamma Liaison; 658 NASA Electronic Image/Wide World Photos; 659 Wide World Photos; 662-663 (bg) Douglas Struthers/Tony Stone Images; 663 (t) AP/Wide World Photos; 663 (c) Harry Downing/Sygma Photo News; 663 (b) Frederic Neema/Sygma Photo News.

### Reference
Page Facing R1 Michael Holford Photographs; R1 (t) Science Museum, London/Michael Holford Photographs; R1 (bl) John M. Roberts/The Stock Market; R1 (br) Pierre Boulat/COS/Woodfin Camp & Associates; R6 Bob Daemmrich Photography.